Stamp Taxes 2020/21

Stamp Taxes 2020/21

Ken Wright BA, CA, CTA, Senior SDLT and LBTT specialist

Andrew MA Evans CTA

Bloomsbury Professional

LONDON • DUBLIN • EDINBURGH • NEW YORK • NEW DELHI • SYDNEY

Bloomsbury Professional
Bloomsbury Publishing Plc
41–43 Boltro Road, Haywards Heath, RH16 1BJ, UK

Reprinted 2020

British Library Cataloguing-in-Publication Data

A catalogue record for this book is available from the British Library.

ISBN: 978 1 52651 482 0

Typeset by Compuscript Ltd, Shannon
Printed and bound by CPI Group (UK) Ltd, Croydon, CR0 4YY

Preface

This book provides comprehensive coverage for the non-specialist of what are commonly referred to as the 'stamp taxes', comprising stamp duty land tax (SDLT), stamp duty and stamp duty reserve tax (SDRT). The complexity and volume of legislation, particularly in relation to SDLT, has increased over the years. Fundamental changes were made to the structure of SDLT during 2016. Transactions over commercial and mixed-use property ceased to be taxed under the so called 'slab' tax structure and, with effect from 17 March 2016, moved to a progressive tax structure (like income tax) with new tax rates. With effect from 1 April 2016 a 3% surcharge was levied on the acquisition of most residential properties unless an individual is replacing his or her only or main residence or the individual does not own any other property at the time of the acquisition. In 2017 a relief was introduced for first-time buyers who are individuals and who are acquiring a property costing £500,000 or less. With effect from 1 April 2018, and subject to certain transitional provisions, SDLT ceased to apply to transactions over land situated in Wales, being replaced by the land transaction tax (LTT). For transactions with an effective date on or after 1 March 2019, the window for notifying and paying SDLT was reduced from 30 days to 14 days. At the 2020 Budget, the government confirmed that an SDLT surcharge of 2% on top of the existing SDLT rates would apply to the acquisition of residential property by non-UK residents with effect from 1 April 2021. This will be the first time that a purchaser's residence status will have an impact on the quantum of their SDLT liability.

At the same time the government's tax take from stamp taxes is substantial, with SDLT receipts in 2017/18 amounting to £12.9 billion, before falling back to £11.9 billion in 2018/19 and an expected £11.8 billion in 2019/20. However, the Office for Budget Responsibility (OBR) is forecasting in its 'Economic and fiscal outlook' report dated March 2020 that SDLT receipts will increase from the expected outturn for 2019/20 of £11.8 billion to £17.2 billion by 2024/25. The impact of the coronavirus pandemic on that forecast could, however, be substantial, dependent upon how quickly the housing market recovers from the current 'lock-down', and the depth of the recession which is likely to follow the easing of the lock-down. Indeed, the OBR acknowledges in its report that its forecasts were made before the spread of coronavirus was expected to have a significant effect on economic activity outside of China. This means that the forecast tax take from SDLT going forward is even more uncertain than normal but, in the short term at least, may be significantly below forecast.

The receipts from stamp duty are significantly less than SDLT, amounting to £3.5 billion in 2017/18 followed by a small increase to £3.6 billion for 2018/19.

On 10 July 2017 the Office of Tax Simplification (OTS) published its report in relation to stamp duty on paper documents, recommending the reform, simplification and digitalisation of stamp duty. The Chancellor of the Exchequer responded to the OTS's report on 14 August 2017 agreeing to consider the recommendations carefully, weighing up the benefits of the proposed reforms in the context of the ongoing reforms to the tax system.

However, the only changes made to date are to introduce a market value charge for both stamp duty and SDRT where either (a) listed securities are transferred to a company with which the transferor is connected, or (b) unlisted securities are transferred to a company with which the transferor is connected, and some or all of the consideration comprises an issue of shares. Neither of these changes were recommended by the OTS.

It therefore seems that the government has opted to enact targeted anti-avoidance provisions against certain transactions which it saw as avoidance of stamp duty (and SDRT), rather than implement the fundamental reform of stamp duty which is required.

All of the above means that for those dealing with stamp taxes, in whatever capacity, the need to have an understanding of those taxes has never been greater. Non-specialists sometimes find their minds go blank when faced with a stamp tax question. It is true that stamp taxes are different from other taxes, and indeed from each other. However, once the fundamentals have been understood, they are like other taxes in that they comprise a mixture of the relatively simple, the tediously lengthy and the horribly complicated.

The aims of this, the eleventh edition of this book, remain to help the tax-literate non-specialist:

- understand the basic ideas and concepts;
- deal confidently with straightforward matters; and
- recognise when specialist input is needed.

To this end, examples, checklists and tables have been included, together with cross-references to legislation, tax cases and HMRC guidance wherever they are expected to be helpful. HMRC material is generally available on their website, and web addresses are given where possible.

As with other taxes, law and practice are fluid. The government has in the past made it clear that the law will be changed with immediate or even retrospective effect to close perceived loopholes. Therefore, it will always be important to maintain an awareness of recent developments and pronouncements.

Whatever the reader's purpose in consulting this volume, it is suggested that he or she read Chapter 1 first – it is mercifully brief – as a kind of orientation exercise before using the contents, index or table of statutes to research particular points.

Chapter 2 provides an outline of land and buildings transaction tax (LBTT), which applies to most transactions over land in Scotland from 1 April 2015, sets out the principal differences between SDLT and LBTT, and considers the transitional provisions governing the move between the taxes. However, anyone dealing with LBTT on a regular basis may need to consult a more detailed exposition which can be found in *Land and Buildings Transaction Tax* also published online by Bloomsbury as part of its Scottish Tax Series.

Chapter 3 provides an outline of LTT which applies to most transactions over land in Wales from 1 April 2018, sets out the principal differences between SDLT and LTT, and considers the transitional provisions governing the move between the taxes.

As ever I am grateful to all at Bloomsbury Professional for their help as I updated the book, and to Andrew Evans (tax partner at Geldards LLP) for his work on Chapter 3. I have attempted to translate the legislation and practice into words which are concise, accurate and user-friendly. I hope I have had at least partial success. Any errors or omissions are entirely down to me.

Ken Wright
May 2020

Contents

Table of Statutes

[References are to paragraph number and appendices]

H

I

L

M

Table of Statutory Instruments etc

[References are to paragraph number]

T

Table of EC Materials

[*References are to paragraph number*]

Table of Cases

[References are to paragraph number]

List of Abbreviations

ARTL	Automated Registration of Title to Land
ATED	annual tax on enveloped dwellings
CFD	contract for differences
CTA 2010	Corporation Tax Act 2010
DOTAS	disclosure of tax avoidance schemes
FA [year]	Finance Act [year]
GAAR	general anti-abuse rule
HMRC	Her Majesty's Revenue and Customs
ICTA 1988	Income and Corporation Taxes Act 1988
LBTT	Land and buildings transactions tax
LBTT(S)A 2013	Land and Buildings Transaction Tax (Scotland) Act 2013
LLP	limited liability partnership
LTR	land transaction return
LTT	Land transaction tax
MiFID	Markets in Financial Instruments Directive
NPV	net present value
OEIC	open ended investment company
PIK	payment in kind
PIP	property investment partnership
PFI	private finance initiative
RI	recognised intermediary
RSL	registered social landlord
RSTPA 2014	Revenue Scotland Taxation and Powers Act 2014
SA 1891	Stamp Act 1891
SDLT	Stamp duty land tax
SDLTM	Stamp Duty Land Tax Manual
SDRT	Stamp duty reserve tax
SP	Statement of Practice
SPV	special purpose vehicle/company
SRN	scheme reference number
STM	Stamp Taxes Manual
TNPV	total net present value
UTRN	unique transaction reference number

Stop Press

Temporary Reduction of SDLT, LTT and LBTT Rates

TEMPORARY REDUCTION OF SDLT RATES ON THE ACQUISITION OF RESIDENTIAL PROPERTY DURING THE PERIOD 8 JULY 2020 UNTIL 31 MARCH 2021 INCLUSIVE

On 8 July 2020, the Chancellor of the Exchequer announced a temporary increase in the SDLT zero rate threshold from £125,000 to £500,000, for both the acquisition of, and the grant of a new lease over, residential property (see **4.38** et seq). The increase in the zero rate threshold applies to transactions which are completed (see **4.91**) or substantially performed (see **4.91**) during the period 8 July 2020 to 31 March 2021. This change does not apply where the transaction was substantially performed before 8 July 2020.

If a transaction is substantially performed (see **4.91**) during the period 8 July 2020 to 31 March 2021, but the contract concerned is then completed after 31 March 2021, no additional SDLT is payable in relation to the completion of the contract, and there is no need to notify the completion of the contract, provided that the sole reason that additional SDLT would have been payable on the completion transaction was that the increase in the SDLT zero rate threshold does not apply to that transaction as the effective date of the transaction was after 31 March 2021.

The temporary increase in the SDLT zero rate threshold was the subject of a resolution under the *Provisional Collection of Taxes Act 1968*. This was followed by the publication of the *Stamp Duty Land Tax (Temporary Relief) Bill 2019–21*, which became the *Stamp Duty Land Tax (Temporary Relief) Act 2020*, having received Royal Assent on 22 July 2020.

The temporary rates and bands are as follows:

Standard rates of SDLT for purchases and lease premiums

Consideration (£)	Residential property – with an 'effective date' on or after 8 July 2020 but on or before 31 March 2021 – additional 3% rate does not apply (see 4.56 et seq)
Not exceeding £500,000	0%
£500,001 to £925,000	5%
£925,001 to £1,500,000	10%
Exceeding £1,500,000	12%

Note: For acquisitions of residential property during the period 8 July 2020 to 31 March 2021 the first-time buyers' relief (see **5.47** et seq) is replaced by the reduced rates set out above.

Higher rates of SDLT for additional dwellings and dwellings purchased by companies and other non-individual purchasers (see 4.56 et seq)

The 3% higher rate of SDLT on purchases of additional dwellings and dwellings purchased by companies and other non-individual purchasers continues to apply on top of the revised standard rates set out above during the period 8 July 2020 to 31 March 2021.

Consideration (£)	Residential property – with an 'effective date' on or after 8 July 2020 but on or before 31 March 2021 – additional 3% rate applies (see 4.56 et seq)
Not exceeding £500,000	3%
£500,001 to £925,000	8%
£925,001 to £1,500,000	13%
Exceeding £1,500,000	15%

Grant of new leases over residential property during the period 8 July 2020 to 31 March 2021

The zero-rate threshold which applies to the 'net present value' of the rent payable under a new lease of residential property is also increased to £500,000 for transactions with an 'effective date' on or after 8 July 2020 but on or before 31 March 2021. The following rates and bands apply:

Net present value of any rent (£)	Residential property – with an 'effective date' on or after 8 July 2020 but on or before 31 March 2021
Not exceeding £500,000	0%
Over £500,000	1%

From 1 April 2021 the SDLT rates and bands shown in the above tables will cease to apply and the rates and bands will revert to those shown at **4.37** (standard rates of SDLT), **4.56** (higher rates of SDLT) and **6.3** (grant of a new lease).

The following points should be noted:

(1) Companies and other non-individual purchasers (as well as individual purchasers) will benefit from the SDLT rates and bands shown in the above tables when acquiring, or leasing, residential property unless the 15% slab rate of SDLT applies to an acquisition for a consideration of more than £500,000 (see **4.87**).

(2) At **4.39** it is stated that:

> 'The distinction between residential and non-residential property is important given the higher rates of tax that apply to residential property. As set out in **4.37** the highest rate of SDLT for a residential property transaction is 12% (15% if the additional 3% rate applies: see **4.56** et seq), whereas for a non-residential property transaction it is 5%.'

As a result of the increase in the zero-rate threshold to £500,000 during the period 8 July 2020 to 31 March 2021, the SDLT liability on the acquisition of residential property (assuming that the higher rate 3% does not apply) will only be greater than that on the acquisition of non-residential property if the chargeable consideration exceeds £1,215,000. Under the SDLT rates and bands which applied before 8 July 2020, and which will apply after 31 March 2021, the SDLT liability on the acquisition of residential property (assuming that the higher rate 3% does not apply) is greater than that on the acquisition of non-residential property if the chargeable consideration exceeds £125,000, although the difference is only £500 (assuming the chargeable consideration is more than £150,000) until the chargeable consideration exceeds £925,000.

TEMPORARY REDUCTION OF LTT RATES ON THE ACQUISITION OF RESIDENTIAL PROPERTY DURING THE PERIOD 27 JULY 2020 UNTIL 31 MARCH 2021 INCLUSIVE

On 14 July 2020 the Minister for Finance and Trefnydd announced that the zero-rate threshold for LTT on residential property will temporarily be increased from £180,000 to £250,000. The change to the threshold will come into force for transactions with an 'effective date' on or after 27 July 2020 and remain in place until 31 March 2021. From 1 April 2021 the standard LTT rates and bands shown in the table below will cease to apply and the rates and bands will revert to those shown at **3.8**. The increase in the zero-rate threshold should mean that approximately 80% of home purchasers will pay no LTT and purchasers buying a home for more than £180,000 can save LTT of up to £2,450. Unlike the changes which have been made to the SDLT and LBTT zero-rate thresholds applying to residential property, the Welsh Government has decided to make no changes to the rates and thresholds that apply to the higher rates of LTT on additional dwellings (see **3.10**), and therefore those rates and thresholds remain unchanged.

Standard rates of LTT for purchases of residential property

Consideration (£)	Residential property – with an 'effective date' on or after 27 July 2020 but on or before 31 March 2021 – higher rate of LTT of 3% does not apply
Not exceeding £250,000	0%
£250,001 to £400,000	5%
£400,001 to £750,000	7.5%
£750,001 to £1,500,000	10%
Exceeding £1,500,000	12%

Higher rate of LTT which applies to additional dwellings and dwellings purchased by companies and other non-individual purchasers (see 3.10)

As indicated above, the rates and thresholds for higher rate residential property transactions remain unchanged. Therefore the 3% higher rate of LTT on purchases of additional dwellings and dwellings purchased by companies and other non-individual purchasers continues to apply on top of the existing standard rates of LTT.

Consideration (£)	Residential property – with an 'effective date' on or after 27 July 2020 but on or before 31 March 2021 – higher rate of LTT of 3% applies (see 3.10)
Not exceeding £180,000	3%
£180,001 to £250,000	6.5%
£250,001 to £400,000	8%
£400,001 to £750,000	10.5%
£750,001 to £1,500,000	13%
Exceeding £1,500,000	15%

TEMPORARY REDUCTION OF LBTT RATES ON THE ACQUISITION OF RESIDENTIAL PROPERTY DURING THE PERIOD 15 JULY 2020 UNTIL 31 MARCH 2021 INCLUSIVE

On 9 July 2020 the Cabinet Secretary for Finance announced in her statement to the Scottish Parliament that the zero-rate threshold for LBTT on residential property transactions would temporarily be increased from £145,000 to £250,000. The change to the threshold will come into force for transactions with an 'effective date' on or after 15 July 2020 and remain in place until 31 March 2021. From 1 April 2021 the LBTT rates and bands shown in the tables below will cease to apply and the rates and bands will revert to those shown at **2.3** (both standard rates of LBTT and the rates of LBTT when the 'additional dwelling supplement' is chargeable). Excluding the additional dwelling supplement, the increase in the threshold should mean that approximately 80% of home purchasers will pay no LBTT and that purchasers buying a home for more than £145,000 can save LBTT of up to £2,100.

The temporary increase in the zero-rate threshold was effected by the *Land and Buildings Transaction Tax (Tax Rates and Tax Bands) (Scotland) Amendment (No 2) (Coronavirus) Order 2020 (SSI 2020/215)* which was approved by the Scottish Parliament on 15 July 2020 and came into effect from that date.

The temporary rates and bands are as follows:

Standard rates of LBTT for purchases of residential property

Consideration (£)	**Residential property – with an 'effective date' on or after 15 July 2020 but on or before 31 March 2021 – additional dwelling supplement of 4% does not apply**
Not exceeding £250,000	0%
£250,001 to £325,000	5%
£325,001 to £750,000	10%
Exceeding £750,000	12%

Additional dwelling supplement which applies to additional dwellings and dwellings purchased by companies and other non-individual purchasers (see 2.3)

The 4% 'additional dwelling supplement' on purchases of additional dwellings and dwellings purchased by companies and other non-individual purchasers continues to apply on top of the revised standard rates set out in the table above.

Consideration (£)	**Residential property – with an 'effective date' on or after 15 July 2020 but on or before 31 March 2021 – additional dwelling supplement of 4% applies (see 2.3)**
Not exceeding £250,000	4%
£250,001 to £325,000	9%
£325,001 to £750,000	14%
Exceeding £750,000	16%

Chapter 1

Introduction to Stamp Taxes

THREE TAXES

1.1 This book deals with stamp duty land tax (SDLT), stamp duty and stamp duty reserve tax (SDRT), which together are often referred to as 'stamp taxes'. However, almost all tax which people call 'stamp duty' is really one of the two more modern of these taxes, being SDLT and SDRT. The tax on enveloped dwellings (ATED), which is an annual tax on residential properties with a value of more than £500,000 held by a company, partnership with at least one corporate partner or collective investment scheme, is also briefly considered.

With effect from 1 April 2015 SDLT ceased to apply to transactions over land situated in Scotland being replaced, from that date, by land and buildings transaction tax (LBTT). **Chapter 2** of this book briefly considers the key differences between SDLT and LBTT and sets out the transitional provisions which applied on the transition from SDLT to LBTT. For those who require more detail regarding LBTT, the tax is comprehensively covered in *Land and Buildings Transaction Tax* also published by Bloomsbury as one of its Scottish Tax Series.

With effect from 1 April 2018, SDLT ceased to apply to transactions over land situated in Wales being replaced, from that date, by land transaction tax (LTT). **Chapter 3** of this book covers the main provisions within the LTT regime and briefly considers the key differences between SDLT and LTT.

Consequently, with effect from 1 April 2018 there were three land taxes in the UK, with SDLT applying to land in England and Northern Ireland, LBTT applying to land in Scotland and LTT applying to land in Wales.

SDLT accounts for the overwhelming majority of revenue raised by the stamp taxes. In 2018/19 total stamp tax receipts were £15.5 billion of which £11.9 billion (76.8%) related to SDLT. Together with its counterparts in Scotland (LBTT) and Wales (LTT), it is also the tax most likely to impact ordinary commercial and private transactions. Its application to most ordinary house purchases is fairly straightforward. In relation to commercial transactions, and even some house purchases, it can be an inordinately complex tax. Therefore, the greater part of this book is devoted to SDLT.

SDRT is mostly administered and paid by professionals in the financial services industry, often operating on the basis of rules and arrangements negotiated directly with HMRC. These rules and arrangements are beyond the scope of this book, which contains only a fairly brief outline of SDRT, concentrating on the impact of the tax on transactions in unquoted securities.

1.2 Each of the stamp taxes has its own legislative code, with relatively little interaction between SDLT and the other taxes. There is more interaction between stamp duty and SDRT because, for many transactions, they are alternatives. The following table indicates where to find the main legislation governing each tax. The principal charging provisions are in bold, while other important provisions are shown in normal type. Especially in the case of stamp duty, there are numerous other provisions in various *Finance Acts* and other legislation. These are referred to in the text of this book where appropriate. For SDRT and SDLT, most changes since original enactment of the main provisions have proceeded by amendment; if an up-to-date copy of the main law is available, it is not often necessary to consult subsequent *Finance Acts*, unless investigating the effective date of a change, dealing with a transaction governed by transitional provisions or concerned about the application of general anti-avoidance provisions such as the general anti-abuse rule or GAAR.

Tax	Legislation
Stamp duty	***FA 1999, Sch 13*** *FA 1999, ss 109–123, Schs 12, 14–19* *FA 1986, ss 64–85* *Stamp Act 1891; FA 1930, s 42; FA 1967, s 27* *FA 2003, s 125* *FA 2019, s 47 and 47A*
SDRT	***FA 1986, ss 86–99*** *Stamp Duty Reserve Tax Regulations 1986, SI 1986/1711* *FA 1999, ss 116–122, Sch 19* *FA 2019, s 48 and 48A*
SDLT	***FA 2003, ss 42–124, Schs 3–19*** *Stamp Duty Land Tax (Administration) Regulations 2003, SI 2003/2837* *Stamp Duty Land Tax (Electronic Communications) Regulations 2005, SI 2005/844* *FA 2004, ss 306–319; SI 2004/1864; SI 2004/1865; SI 2005/1868* *FA 2013, Pt 5*

1.3 There are three reasons why practitioners and taxpayers need some knowledge of the rules relating to stamp duty itself:

(1) because non-stock market share transactions are still generally dealt with under stamp duty, failure to deal with this tax may leave unrecognised SDRT liabilities outstanding (see **12.12**);

(2) some other transactions finalised on or after 1 December 2003 may still give rise to stamp duty charges because of actions taken before that date (see **4.93** and **13.29**); and

(3) many of the principles and ideas in the other two taxes are derived from equivalent provisions under stamp duty and are most easily understood in that context.

It is therefore suggested that at least a brief study of the chapters on stamp duty would be worthwhile, even if the reader is dealing exclusively with transactions which may be subject only to one of the other taxes.

1.4 The names given to SDLT and SDRT are potentially misleading. They have 'stamp' in their name only because they collect tax which used to be collected through stamp duty. Unlike stamp duty, SDLT and SDRT are chargeable on transactions or agreements no matter how, where or even whether documented; no stamps are involved. They are compulsory, self-assessment taxes, with enforcement provisions similar to those which apply to corporation tax and income tax. SDLT, in particular, has draconian anti-avoidance rules and is within the scope of the General Anti-Abuse Rule introduced in 2013.

1.5 In contrast, stamp duty is often referred to as a voluntary tax because, with few exceptions (such as the charge on issue of bearer instruments, **10.56**), there is no direct obligation to pay. The only payment enforcement mechanism comes from the fact that a document which should be stamped cannot be used for UK official purposes, such as registration of title, evidence in a civil court, or for cancelling an SDRT charge, until it has been stamped. Stamping after the due date will generally lead to charging of interest and penalties, so if a document is to be stamped, it is best to deal with this promptly. However, where a document, despite being within the charge to stamp duty, is unlikely to be needed for any relevant UK purpose, the decision may validly be taken not to pay the stamp duty and to leave the document unstamped. Under current rules, this is only likely for some transfers of interests in partnerships which hold stock or marketable securities, or where the transfer relates to non-UK securities – it is highly unlikely that a stampable transfer of UK registered securities may safely be left unstamped. Historically, many other documents were left unstamped, as explained at **13.29**.

1.6 All three taxes are administered by HMRC, who publish two manuals on their website, setting out their views and practices on the taxes:

- The Stamp Taxes on Shares Manual, which is available at www.hmrc.gov.uk/so/manuals/stsmanual/index.htm, deals with stamp duty and SDRT. In this book, references to this manual are in the form 'STSM123456'. This interactive manual was published on 23 July 2014, replacing the old Stamp Duty Manual which had been available only as a downloadable PDF file with limited interactive functionality. However, the old Stamp Duty Manual remains an essential reference when dealing with the current completion or unwinding of 'old' transactions, dealt with in **Chapter 13**.
- The second manual is the Stamp Duty Land Tax Manual, available at www.hmrc.gov.uk/manuals/sdltmanual/index.htm. This is also published as an online interactive document. It is widely referred to in this book, references being in the form 'SDLTM12345'.

1.7 HMRC provide online tools for calculation of SDLT, especially useful in relation to leases, and a facility for online completion and submission of SDLT returns. Further details of these are set out below in the chapters on SDLT. Use of the online submission facility is not yet compulsory, but it may become so in due course. HMRC also provide a wide array of other useful information and guidance in the stamp tax section of their website (www.hmrc.gov.uk/so). The volume is so great that it is not always easy to find specific items, but references are given in this book where appropriate.

A BRIEF HISTORY OF STAMP DUTY

1.8 Stamp duty was introduced over 325 years ago, copying a Dutch tax. Like income tax, it was intended to be a temporary measure to finance a war. Unlike income tax, it did not require annual renewal. A hundred years later, Pitt the Younger described stamp duty as a tax 'easily raised, widely diffused, pressing little on any particular class'. In other words, the thought was that those who paid the tax would scarcely notice – so it may, perhaps, be thought of as the original stealth tax. Unfortunately, the American colonists had noticed a few years previously – the 'Boston Tea Party', an event widely regarded as marking the start of the American War of Independence, was in fact a protest against the imposition of UK stamp duty on documents in the American Colonies. Pitt also commented that stamp duty was 'safely and expeditiously collected at a small expense'. Government statistics show that stamp duty is by far the cheapest tax to collect, although this may be because the taxpayer and his advisers have to do most of the work in calculating and administering the tax.

1.9 Stamp duty has always been a tax on documents. As the name indicates, payment is evidenced by fixing or embossing stamps on the relevant document; in general, if no document is created, there is no stamp duty. Its range has varied enormously over three centuries. Those whose memories stretch back to the mid-twentieth century may remember the practice of signing receipts across a 2d (0.8p) stamp in order to ensure their legal validity – an example of a postage stamp being used for fiscal purposes. Until 1971, bank cheques were also subject to a 2d stamp duty, and the issue of a new chequebook by the bank led to an immediate deduction from one's bank account.

During the latter half of the twentieth century, the scope of stamp duty was steadily reduced until it applied only to transactions in shares and securities, land and buildings, and intangible assets such as partnership interests, intellectual property and goodwill. In 1986, SDRT was introduced in response to market developments which allowed transfer of beneficial ownership of securities without a document. As explained at **12.1**, it was at one stage proposed to abolish stamp taxes on shares and securities. However, that proposal was abandoned and the new government of 1997 began to increase stamp duty rates on assets other than shares and securities. The yield to the Exchequer did not increase as expected, because avoidance of the tax on larger transactions became the norm. To counter this, stamp duty on property transactions was replaced by SDLT from 1 December 2003.

1.10 The original intention seems to have been for documents to be stamped no later than the time they were finally executed and, to this end, the government sold stamps and pre-stamped paper to 'authorised dealers' such as law firms, who would then use them on documents or sell them on to the end user. The government sold the stamps at a discount to face value, allowing the dealer to make a profit upon onward sale. This was, therefore, an early example of the privatised collection of tax. William Wordsworth was perhaps the most famous individual involved in this process – he was Distributor of Stamps for the county of Westmoreland. It used to be possible to buy blank stock transfer forms pre-stamped with a £5 stamp (the rate then applicable to many transfers otherwise than on sale), although sadly no discount was given!

Adhesive stamps were open to abuse (*Stamp Act 1891, s 9* still imposes penalties for fraudulent removal of adhesive stamps from a document with intent to re-use), and eventually the predecessors of HMRC became directly responsible for all stamping of documents at a number of Stamp Offices situated in major cities. The section of HMRC responsible for stamp taxes is still generally referred to as 'the Stamp Office'. Stamp Offices had stamping presses, allowing them to emboss appropriate value stamps on documents whilst keeping track of the value embossed, for audit purposes. The Stamp Offices provided an 'over the counter' service for routine stamping and even, by arrangement, for 'adjudication' (see **10.48**). Stamp Office public counters have now been closed and most of the machines decommissioned. Documents requiring physical stamping are sent to the Birmingham Stamp Office, and specific arrangements have to be agreed in advance for those transactions where, for commercial or perhaps overseas tax or regulatory reasons, stamping of documents on the day of execution is required.

1.11 Stamp duty is generally chargeable on the document which formally transfers the asset in question – the conveyance. In relation to shares and securities, a mere contract to transfer will not normally be liable, as this will not itself transfer the assets. When stamp duty was chargeable on other assets such as goodwill, the contract was usually the document liable to stamp duty, because no separate transfer document is needed to complete the transaction. This led to a practice of completing transactions without a written contract (for example, a written offer to sell, completed by the purchaser paying the consideration). In the absence of a written contract, there was no document on which stamp duty could be charged (see **13.30**).

1.12 As mentioned above, in most cases there is no direct obligation to pay stamp duty or have a document stamped, but an unstamped document cannot be used for certain purposes. Where documents were executed outside the UK, it was the case for a long time that no interest and penalties accrued, provided the document was stamped within 30 days of first being brought into the UK. In the case of large transactions, if there was no current need for the document to be stamped, it became standard practice to execute and retain it offshore (often in the Channel Islands or the Isle of Man) and many such unstamped documents remain there to this day. In an attempt to reduce the attractiveness of this practice, the rules were changed in 1999 to charge interest from 30 days after execution, no matter where this took place. Another common mitigation technique was simply to avoid executing a conveyance (generally referred to as resting on, or in, contract). For example, legal title to the asset might be held by a special purpose vehicle/company (SPV) for the benefit of the beneficial owner. The current beneficial owner would contract to sell to a purchaser. The purchaser would make payment, thus gaining beneficial ownership, and the owner would transfer the SPV to the purchaser. In the absence of a conveyance, no stamp duty arose. There were many disputes between taxpayers and the Stamp Office over whether other documents created in this process could be treated as conveyances. To discourage the practice, the rules were changed in 2002 to treat contracts for transfer of land for more than £10 million as conveyances.

1.13 Numerous other ingenious methods were devised to mitigate stamp duty, and the government began consultations on modernising the tax, concentrating on property transactions. However, it quickly became clear that it would be very difficult to create a tax which was relatively simple and certain yet dealt fairly with the wide range of modern property transactions. Consultations ended abruptly, and SDLT was introduced in *Finance Act 2003*, replacing stamp duty on transactions in UK land and buildings with effect from 1 December 2003. At the same time, the scope of stamp duty itself was restricted to transactions in stock and marketable securities and interests in certain partnerships which hold stock or marketable securities. The inadequacy of the consultation process is reflected in the complexity of SDLT, the uncertainty over its application to many transactions, and the amendments made to the legislation, by regulations even before the tax came into effect and then in several subsequent *Finance Acts*.

1.14 The new rules had the desired effect, raising the stamp tax take on property transactions from £5 billion in 2003/04 to £10 billion in 2007/08. However, economic factors (the 2008 financial crisis) then intervened and by 2009/10 the total tax take had fallen below its 2003/04 level, largely as a result of the reduced numbers and values of domestic transactions. It then recovered to £10.9 billion in 2015/16, £11.7 billion in 2016/17, £12.9 billion in 2017/18 before falling back to £11.9 billion in 2018/19. A number of factors will have contributed to the £1 billion reduction in the tax take for 2018/19 compared to 2017/18 including:

(a) the devolution of land transaction tax to the Welsh Government with effect from 1 April 2018 (see **Chapter 3**);

(b) the introduction of first-time buyer's relief from 22 November 2017 (see **5.47** et seq) with the amount of SDLT relieved in 2018/19 being £0.5 billion; and

(c) uncertainties over Brexit.

The increase in tax receipts which arose from 2016/17 will, in part, have been caused by the introduction of the higher rates of SDLT on additional properties (see **4.56** et seq) which came into effect on 1 April 2016.

The Office for Budget Responsibility (OBR) is forecasting in its 'Economic and Fiscal Outlook' report dated March 2020 that SDLT receipts will increase from the estimated outturn for 2019/20 of £11.8 billion to £17.2 billion by 2024/25. In that report the OBR state that, compared to their March 2019 forecast, they have increased the forecast SDLT receipts by around £0.4 billion a year on average to reflect:

(a) an increase in forecast house price inflation partly offset by lower commercial property transactions;

(b) the proposed introduction of a 2% SDLT surcharge for non-UK residents buying UK residential property to be introduced with effect from 1 April 2021 (see **1.18**); and

(c) the indirect effect of the 2020 budget measures on house prices.

However, the OBR acknowledges in its report that its forecasts were made before the spread of Covid-19 was expected to have a significant effect on economic activity outside of China. They state that: 'As discussed in the document, the outlook is therefore likely to be significantly less favourable than this central forecast suggests – especially in the short term – but to a degree that remains highly uncertain even now.' Given that at the time of writing the Covid-19 has all but closed the UK property market there is likely, in the short term at least, to be a significant reduction in SDLT receipts.

The total estimated SDLT receipts in 2019/20 of £11.8 billion comprises £8.6 billion (72.9% of total receipts) in relation to residential properties and £3.2 billion (27.1% of total receipts) in relation to non-residential properties, emphasising the importance of the residential property market to the amount of the tax raised.

Receipts from the additional 3% SDLT charge on higher rate transactions (see **4.56** et seq) were £1.7 billion in 2016/17, £1.9 billion in 2017/18, £1.7 billion in 2018/19 and £1.6 billion in 2019/20, accounting for around 19% of total receipts from residential property transactions in 2019/20 (2018/19 – 20%). The level of tax being repaid in relation to higher rate transactions was £0.1 billion in 2016/17, £0.3 billion in 2017/18, £0.4 billion in 2018/19 and an estimated £0.4 billion in 2019/20. Individuals have three years from acquiring their new main residence to dispose of their old main residence and claim a refund of the 3% tax charge (see **4.84**).

From the introduction of the first-time buyer's relief (see **5.47** et seq) in November 2017 through to the end of the financial year on 31 March 2018 the relief was claimed on 69,100 transactions (19% of all residential property transactions during that period) with the amount of SDLT relieved being estimated at £159 million. The amount of SDLT relieved in 2018/19 was £521 million and the estimated amount relieved in 2019/20 was £542 million.

1.15 Over the five years to 2012/13 there was a slow decline in the total raised by stamp taxes on shares, falling to £2.2 billion by 2012/13. Given that share prices had recovered significantly from their low point of 2009, this probably reflected a reduction in volumes, possibly because of a shift toward trading derivatives, which are not subject to stamp taxes. Since then the tax raised by stamp taxes on shares has begun to increase again with £3.3 billion collected for 2015/16, £3.7 billion for 2016/17, £3.5 billion for 2017/18 and £3.6 billion for 2018/19.

1.16 The annual tax on enveloped dwellings (see **4.94** et seq) raised £100 million in 2013/14, £116 million in 2014/15, £178 million in 2015/16, £175 million in 2016/17 before falling by around 18% to £143 million in 2017/18, with a further fall to £139 million in 2018/19. The fairly minor fall in receipts in 2018/19 compared to 2017/18 applied across all price bands except the £2 million to £10 million range which remained the same as the previous year.

In 2018/19 the number of ATED-liable declarations fell by 690 from 7,020 to 6,330, representing a decrease of 10%. (NB: There was a similar decrease of 10% in ATED-liable declarations between 2016/17 and 2017/18 with a fall of 820 from 7,840 to 7,020.) The decrease in ATED-liable declarations occurred in every price band with the 'more than £20 million' band having the largest percentage fall (25%). No analysis has been carried out to determine the reason for the falls in 2017/18 and 2018/19; however, HMRC state in 'Annual Tax on Enveloped Dwellings (ATED) – Commentary and Tables 2018–19' that the reason for the fall in '... liable declarations may be due to an anticipated increase in the tax burden on envelopers, including the new valuation point for properties that started in April 2018 (see **4.97**). Other changes (eg CGT and Inheritance Tax) may also have led to de-enveloping of property or re-arranging the use of the property to fall within the scope of reliefs (eg leading to the liable claims being liable for shorter periods of time). However, these impacts have not been evaluated.'

The potential SDLT cost of extracting properties from a company, etc (where for example there is debt due to a third party – see **4.103**) to avoid a charge to ATED should be considered before undertaking such a de-enveloping transaction. However, it remains the case that properties are held in companies, etc for a variety of reasons other than avoidance of a future charge to SDLT, and the annual ATED charge may still be a price worth paying for those other benefits.

Properties known to be located in London accounted for 86% of total ATED receipts in 2018/19, an increase of 2% from 2017/18. The London boroughs of Westminster and Kensington and Chelsea, still dominate the receipts by location for ATED.

REFORM OF STAMP DUTY?

1.17 On 10 July 2017 the Office of Tax Simplification (OTS) issued its report in relation to stamp duty on paper documents and recommended its reform, digitalisation and simplification. In particular it highlighted two aspects of the stamp duty regime which are out of date and in urgent need of reform.

First, the time-consuming process which requires that a paper document chargeable to stamp duty must be posted to the stamp office in Birmingham, together with a cheque or bank transfer for the duty, in order that a physical stamp can be impressed on the document which is then sent to the relevant company registrar (see **10.43** et seq). The OTS's recommendation is that the stamp duty process be digitalised, providing the transferee with a unique transaction reference confirming that the transaction has been notified to HMRC. This would eliminate the need for a physical stamp to be impressed on paper documents. It is also suggested that the legal obligations of company registrars could be changed, allowing them to write up the company's books on receipt of the unique transaction reference or confirmation of notification to HMRC.

Secondly, the current scope of stamp duty is significantly broader than is actually applied in practice as, for example, duty is chargeable on paper documents executed in the UK even if those documents give effect to the transfer of non-UK shares. This results in documents transferring non-UK shares being executed and retained outside of the UK to try to avoid the document being chargeable to stamp duty or to avoid a penalty for late stamping being payable should the document actually have to be stamped because, for example, it is required as evidence in a UK civil court. The OTS states in its report that 'This is confusing and inefficient' – sentiments with which the author wholeheartedly agrees! The recommendations from the OTS are that stamp duty be aligned with SDRT so that broadly it does not apply to paper documents transferring non-UK shares unless those shares are registered in a register kept in the UK. They also suggest making the tax assessable and therefore ending the 'voluntary' nature of the tax (see **1.5**).

The core recommendations of the OTS set out in the report are, in more detail, as follows:

(1) Digitise the stamp duty process thereby eliminating the need for stamping machines.

(2) Introduce an online system providing taxpayers with a unique transaction reference confirming that the transaction has been notified to HMRC.

(3) Introduce the group relief and reconstruction reliefs (see **11.7** et seq) directly into SDRT.

(4) Following digitisation, no longer round up stamp duty to the nearest £5 (see **10.23**).

(5) Amend company registrars' legal obligations so that they can write up a company's books on sight of a transaction reference or confirmation of notification.

(6) Make stamp duty an assessable tax, ending the sense in which it is 'voluntary' at present (see **1.5**).

(7) Replace compulsory adjudication of relief claims with a short form notification (see **10.48**).

(8) Narrow the territorial scope of stamp duty to exclude non-UK shares.

(9) Consider, as a policy matter, whether or not stamp duty should apply to instruments granting options for consideration.

(10) Consider, as a policy matter, the extent to which stamp duty should be payable on instruments transferring partnership interests (see **10.2**).

(11) Consider, as a policy matter, the approach to documents relating to pre-2003 (when SDLT was introduced) land transactions.

The OTS has also made the following further recommendations as to how stamp duty could be simplified, either at the same time of implementing the core recommendations considered above or 'as part of a future roadmap of change':

(1) Adopt the 'money or money's worth' concept of consideration, coupled with specific rules and exemptions to address certain specific issues.

(2) In relation to the contingency principle (see **10.39**), adopt the SDLT approach.

(3) Where debt forms part of the consideration (see **10.34**), follow SDLT in clarifying that the charge is limited to the market value of the shares (see **4.24**).

(4) Consider the various types of transactions presently franked by stamp duty exemptions and provide exemptions as appropriate.

(5) Consider increasing the £1,000 threshold (see **10.8** et seq) as a policy matter.

(6) Clarify whether assignments of options are chargeable.

(7) Give serious consideration to combining stamp duty and SDRT, at least making this a clear direction of travel (taking into account the need to reframe the charging provisions).

(8) Consider suggestions regarding further useful features of a digital system, to save time for taxpayers and enhance HMRC compliance capability.

On 14 August 2017, the Chancellor of the Exchequer responded by letter to the OTS's report and agreed to consider the recommendations carefully, weighing up the benefits of the four main elements of the proposed reforms in the context of the ongoing reforms to the tax system. The four main elements of the reforms identified in the Chancellor's letter were as follows:

- providing taxpayers with a unique transaction reference number;
- amending company registrar's legal obligations in respect of share transfer registrations;
- making stamp duty assessable; and
- aligning the scope of stamp duty with SDRT.

The letter acknowledges that a consequence of digitalising stamp duty would be the repeal of the current requirement to round up the amount of the stamp duty to the nearest £5.

The Chancellor also stated that he saw value in his officials looking at the introduction of group relief and reconstruction rules directly into the SDRT regime so that it is no longer necessary to create a paper document for no other reason than to claim these reliefs, and at replacing compulsory adjudication for stamp duty relief claims with a short form notification.

Finally, the Chancellor agreed that if stamp duty is digitalised a review should be carried out to determine whether documents relating to the granting of options, the transfer of partnership interests and the completion of land transactions contracted on or before 10 July 2003 should remain within the scope of stamp duty.

To date the only actions which have been taken are the introduction of a market value rule, for the purposes of both stamp duty and SDRT, on the transfer of both listed and unlisted securities to a connected company, which was not a recommendation from the OTS. These reforms are considered in more detail below.

Finance Act 2019, ss 47 and *48* introduced a new market value rule for the transfer of listed securities to a company (or its nominee), where the person transferring the securities is 'connected' with the company. In these circumstances the consideration chargeable to stamp duty will be the higher of (a) the actual consideration given for the listed securities and (b) the market value of the listed securities. The new rule applies in respect of transfer instruments executed on or after 29 October 2018 (see **10.12**). For SDRT purposes, if a person is 'connected' with a company and agrees to transfer listed securities to that connected company (whether or not for consideration), or the person actually transfers listed securities to that company for consideration in money or money's worth, the consideration chargeable to SDRT will be the higher of: (a) the actual consideration given for the transfer of the listed securities; and (b) the market value of the listed securities at the time the agreement is made. For SDRT purposes, the new market value rule applies where: (a) the agreement to transfer the listed securities is conditional and the conditionality of the agreement is settled on or after 29 October 2018; and (b) in any other case, the agreement to transfer the securities is made on or after that date (see **12.9**).

For the purposes of this market value rule 'connected' has the meaning given in *CTA 2010, s 1122*.

On 7 November 2018 HMRC published a consultation document 'Stamp Taxes on Shares Consideration Rules' and the consultation period ended on 30 January 2019. The consultation considered the following:

- The extension of the market value rule, introduced in relation to listed securities (see above), to (a) unlisted securities and (b) connected party transfers other than to companies.

- The alignment of the stamp duty and SDRT definitions of 'consideration' by adopting the SDRT 'money or money's worth' definition.
- The alignment of the stamp duty and SDRT treatment of contingent, uncertain and unascertainable payments.

On 11 July 2019, HMRC published a summary of the responses to the 'Stamp Taxes on Shares Consideration Rules' consultation document. In that document, HMRC summarised the common themes raised by respondents. For example, it was considered that the proposed extension of the market value rule to both unlisted securities and connected party transfers other than to companies was too wide and could have unintended impacts. Respondents considered that a measure specifically targeted at avoidance which HMRC had seen would be more appropriate. Equally, respondents could see no justification for the market value rule being extended to connected parties other than companies. In particular it was considered that transfers to individuals and family members should not be caught. Finally, respondents also considered that changes to the consideration rules in isolation were likely to add complexity, uncertainty and increased costs particularly on insurance, pension, and fund industries, creating a risk for the UK economy and making the UK less attractive for investment.

Having considered the consultation responses the government has included legislation in the *Finance Act 2020* which they consider tackles contrived arrangements which minimise tax on company reorganisations involving the transfer of unlisted securities (see **10.60**). In their view the legislation is narrowly targeted. The proposed legislation does not extend to connected party transfers other than to companies.

Finance Act 2020, s 77 inserts into *Finance Act 2019 a* new *s 47A* which introduces a market value rule, for stamp duty purposes, for the transfer of unlisted securities to a company (or its nominee) for consideration, where the person transferring the securities is 'connected' with the company, and some or all of the consideration consists of the issue of shares. In these circumstances the consideration chargeable to stamp duty will be the higher of (a) the actual consideration given for the unlisted securities, and (b) the market value of the unlisted securities. The new rule applies in respect of transfer instruments executed on or after the date on which the *Finance Act 2020* receives royal assent (see **10.12**).

Finance Act 2020, s 78 inserts into *Finance Act 2019 a* new *s 48A* which introduces a market value rule for SDRT purposes, if a person is 'connected' with a company and agrees to transfer unlisted securities to that connected company for consideration in money or money's worth, or the person actually transfers unlisted securities to that company for consideration in money or money's worth, and some or all of the consideration consists of the issue of shares, the consideration chargeable to SDRT will be the higher of (a) the actual consideration given for the transfer of the unlisted securities, and (b) the market value of the unlisted securities at the time the agreement is made. For SDRT purposes, the new market value rule applies (a) where the agreement to transfer the unlisted securities is conditional and the conditionality of the agreement is settled on or after the date upon which the *Finance Act 2020* receives royal asset, and (b) in any other case, the agreement to transfer the securities is made on or after that date (see **12.9**).

For the purposes of this market value rule, 'connected' has the meaning given in *CTA 2010, s 1122*.

SDLT: NON-UK RESIDENT SURCHARGE CONSULTATION

1.18 On 11 February 2019 HMRC published a consultation document 'Stamp Duty Land Tax: non-UK resident surcharge consultation' outlining the proposed introduction, in a future Finance Bill, of an SDLT surcharge of 1% on top of the existing SDLT rates (including the rates applicable to the rental element of leasehold property) where residential property (both freehold and leasehold) situated in England or Northern Ireland is purchased by non-UK resident individuals, non-UK resident companies, partnerships which have at least one non-UK resident partner, bare trusts if the beneficiary is non-UK resident and certain trusts which are settlements. The consultation ended on 6 May 2019.

The stated aim of introducing the SDLT surcharge is to control house price inflation with the expected impact being that UK residents can then more easily get onto the housing ladder.

The concept of the SDLT liability being dependent upon the residence status of the purchaser is entirely new and therefore, in the consultation document, the government proposed the introduction of residence tests for different categories of buyer. For example, it was proposed that an individual be treated as non-UK resident if they spent fewer than 183 days in the UK in the 12 months prior to the date of the transaction. A company would be treated as non-UK resident if it was incorporated outside of the UK and, at the time the residential property was acquired, the company's 'central management and control' was not exercised in the UK. In such circumstances the company would not be resident in the UK for corporation tax purposes.

It was also proposed that a UK resident company which was a 'close company' (*Corporation Taxes Act 2010, s 439*) under the direct or indirect control of one or more non-UK residents would be liable for the 1% surcharge.

Where an individual, who had been subject to the 1% surcharge, spent 183 days in the UK in the 12 months following the day of the transaction it was proposed that they would be entitled to a refund of the surcharge.

At Budget 2020, the government announced that it will introduce an SDLT surcharge at a rate of 2% (rather than the 1% proposed in the consultation document) for purchases of residential property in England and Northern Ireland by non-UK residents with effect from 1 April 2021. The 2% surcharge will be added to the existing residential rates including the higher rate for additional dwellings (see **4.56** et seq), the 15% rate for enveloped residential properties (see **4.88** et seq) and the SDLT rates which apply where first-time buyer's relief is available (see **5.47**).

The government have indicated that they will consult on the draft legislation over the summer of 2020 and include the proposed legislation in *Finance Bill 2021*. They have also stated that the money raised from the surcharge will be used to help address rough sleeping.

Where contracts for the purchase of the residential property situated in England or Northern Ireland, by the non-UK resident, were exchanged before 11 March 2020, but are not completed (see **4.10**) or substantially performed (see **4.9**) until after 1 April 2021, transitional rules, subject to satisfying certain conditions, may apply so that the 2% SDLT surcharge is not charged on the transaction.

It is expected that the government will shortly publish a summary of the responses to the 11 February 2019 consultation document.

Chapter 2

Scotland – Land and Buildings Transaction Tax

REPLACEMENT FOR SDLT

2.1 From 1 April 2015, land and buildings transaction tax (LBTT) replaced SDLT in relation to transactions over land and buildings situated in Scotland. However, there are transitional provisions (see **2.19** et seq) covering the move from SDLT to LBTT. Under these transitional provisions some transactions which commenced before 1 April 2015 remained within the ambit of SDLT or potentially fell within both regimes. For example, consider a situation where missives are concluded after 1 May 2012 (the date the *Scotland Act 2012*, which devolved the tax over land transactions in Scotland to the Scottish Parliament, received Royal Assent). The contract was 'substantially performed' (see **4.9**) before 1 April 2015 but settlement (completion) took place after 31 March 2015. In these circumstances the substantial performance of the contract would have been chargeable to SDLT whereas the settlement of the contract was chargeable to LBTT. Under the transitional provisions, credit is given for any SDLT paid on substantial performance in assessing what, if any, LBTT is payable on settlement. Given that LBTT has now been in place for more than five years the number of transactions to which the transitional provisions apply are likely to be greatly reduced. There are however a number of scenarios to which the transitional provisions could still apply including lease transactions, options, targeted anti-avoidance provisions, etc (see **2.19** et seq).

LBTT was introduced by the *Land and Buildings Transaction Tax (Scotland) Act 2013* (*LBTT(S)A 2013*) and references in this chapter are to that Act unless otherwise stated. The Act received Royal Assent on 31 July 2013. The administration, management and compliance aspects of the taxes devolved to the Scottish Parliament, including LBTT, are governed by the *Revenue Scotland and Tax Powers Act 2014* (*RSTPA 2014*), which received Royal Assent on 24 September 2014.

What follows is merely an outline of LBTT; for those who want to know more, the tax is comprehensively covered in *Land and Buildings Transaction Tax*, published by Bloomsbury Professional as part of its Scottish Tax Series.

LBTT is similar to SDLT in many respects and some of the legislation borrows heavily from the corresponding SDLT law. In particular LBTT is a self-assessment tax charged on the consideration given for transactions over land in Scotland. It is payable by the buyer (purchaser), generally within 30 days of the 'effective date' of the transaction. The rules to determine the occasions of charge and the amount of consideration closely parallel those for SDLT. As with SDLT, any VAT payable will be included in the measure of consideration, thus increasing the effective rate of tax for a business which is able to recover VAT as input tax (see **4.23**). Most SDLT reliefs are imported into the new tax, generally with similar rules and conditions.

From 1 April 2015, if a single transaction involves land on both sides of the Scotland/England border it will be necessary to complete separate returns under the two taxes for the respective parcels of land, the overall consideration being apportioned on a just and reasonable basis. The rate of SDLT for the part situated in England should then be determined by reference to the consideration apportioned to that part, not by reference to the overall consideration, because the two parts will not be regarded as linked with each other.

HMRC, in conjunction with Revenue Scotland (the tax authority with responsibility for the collection and management of the taxes devolved to the Scottish Parliament, including LBTT) have published detailed guidance on the transitional provisions at www.hmrc.gov.uk/government/publications/transitional-land-and-building-transaction-tax-guidance.

KEY DIFFERENCES BETWEEN LBTT AND SDLT

There are some significant differences between LBTT and SDLT and these are covered below.

Higher nil tax rate threshold for residential property

2.2 The nil rate tax band for transactions in relation to residential property, at or below which no tax will be charged, is £20,000 higher under LBTT (£145,000) than under SDLT (£125,000).

DIFFERENTIAL TAX CHARGES UNDER LBTT COMPARED TO SDLT

2.3 It is understood that the Scottish Government's plan was to collect broadly the same amount of tax under LBTT as the UK Government would have collected, in Scotland, under SDLT. However, the proposed tax rates and bands announced by the Scottish Government on 9 October 2014 were set at such a level that there would be winners and losers with purchasers at the lower end of the market paying less tax, and those at the higher end of the market paying more tax, compared to SDLT. Subsequent to the release of the proposed LBTT tax rates and bands, the Chancellor of the Exchequer announced that, with effect from 4 December 2014, a progressive tax structure would apply for the purposes of SDLT in relation to the acquisition of residential property. The new SDLT tax rates and bands would have resulted in an SDLT rate of 5% applying to that part of the purchase price above £250,000 compared to an LBTT rate of 10%. In response to the change in the SDLT tax structure and tax rates and bands, the Scottish Government announced on 21 January 2015 that the proposed LBTT tax rates and bands, in relation to residential property, would be revised. The revised tax rates and bands are shown in the table below. The LBTT rates and bands for residential property have applied since the introduction of LBTT and continue to apply for 2020/21.

At the Autumn Statement 2015 the UK Chancellor of the Exchequer announced that on or after 1 April 2016 higher rates of SDLT would apply to purchases of additional residential properties, such as second homes and buy-to-let properties. In fact the legislation is much wider than the policy description and, for example, applies to first purchases of residential properties by companies and other non-individual purchasers. The application of the higher rates of SDLT to the acquisition of additional residential property is considered in detail at **4.56** et seq. In response to the Chancellor's announcement, and ostensibly to avoid distortions in the property market between Scotland and the rest of the UK, the Scottish Government announced that it would also introduce a higher rate of LBTT for purchases of additional residential properties (referred to as the 'Additional Dwelling Supplement' (ADS)). Like its SDLT equivalent, it is also much wider than the policy description and it applies to first purchases of residential properties by companies and other non-individual purchasers. There are however some important differences between the two regimes. In relation to transactions with an 'effective date' on or after 25 January 2019, the ADS was increased from 3% to 4%, subject to a transitional provision. The transitional provision is that the increase in the ADS to 4% does not apply to transactions with an 'effective date' on or after 25 January 2019 if the contract for the land transaction was entered into prior to 12 December 2018. Under SDLT the higher rate does not apply to the acquisition of mixed use properties whereas under LBTT, the ADS would apply, with a just and reasonable apportionment of the consideration being made between the residential and non-residential elements of the property. Under SDLT an individual has 36 months to sell their previous main residence and claim a refund of the additional rate of SDLT paid, whereas under LBTT the period is 18 months. However, a new *s 77*, amending *FA 2003, Sch 4ZA, para 3(7)* was introduced at the Report Stage of the *Finance Act 2020* to extend the three-year time period which applies under SDLT where there are 'exceptional circumstances that could not reasonably have been foreseen' which prevented the sale of the previous main residence within the prescribed three-year period. In such circumstances the three-year period is extended to such longer period as HMRC may allow in response to an application made in accordance with new *FA 2003, Sch 4ZA, para 3(7B)*. The Covid-19 pandemic will be 'exceptional circumstances that could not reasonably have been foreseen' for these purposes: see **4.73**. The extension to the three-year time limit only applies if the new main residence was purchased on or after 1 January 2017. Similarly, as a result of the Covid-19 pandemic, the Scottish Government has extended the period which an individual has under the LBTT regime to sell their old main residence from 18 months to 36 months, but only where the new main residence was acquired between 24 September 2018 and 24 March 2020 (the *Coronavirus (Scotland) No 2 Act*). Where the ADS applies, it adds 4% to each of the LBTT rates, including the 0% rate. The ADS, however, does not apply if the chargeable consideration for the transaction is less than £40,000. The LBTT rates, if the ADS applies, are shown in the table below.

Purchase price	LBTT rate	Additional rate (Effective date on or after 25 January 2019)
Up to £145,000	0%	4%
£145,001–£250,000	2%	6%
£250,001–£325,000	5%	9%
£325,001–£750,000	10%	14%
Above £750,000 The increase in the ADS to 4% (previously 3%) does not apply to transactions with an 'effective date' on or after 25 January 2019 if the contract for the land transaction was entered into prior to 12 December 2018.	12%	16%

Under LBTT, residential property (assuming neither the ADS nor the higher rate of SDLT applies) acquired for a consideration of up to £333,000 will incur a smaller or similar tax liability compared to that under SDLT. However, above those purchase price levels the charge under LBTT will be greater as compared to that under SDLT.

If both the ADS and the higher rate of SDLT apply to the acquisition of a residential property then, following the increase in the ADS to 4% for transactions with an 'effective date' on or after 25 January 2019, the LBTT liability will always be higher than the SDLT liability.

For transactions with an 'effective date' prior to 25 January 2019, or transactions with an 'effective date' on or after 25 January 2019 where the contract for the land transaction was entered into before 12 December 2018, the LBTT non-residential rates and bands are as follows:

Purchase price	LBTT rate
Up to £150,000	0%
£150,001–£350,000	3%
Above £350,000	4.5%

For transactions with an 'effective date' on or after 25 January 2019, provided the contract for the land transaction was entered into on or after 12 December 2018, the LBTT non-residential rates and bands are as follows:

Purchase price	LBTT rate
Up to £150,000	0%
£150,001–£250,000	1%
Above £250,000	5%

As regards non-residential property, under LBTT, an acquisition of a property for a consideration of more than £150,000 will incur a smaller tax liability compared to that under SDLT, with the maximum difference being £1,000.

Set out below are examples comparing the LBTT and SDLT liabilities, for both residential and non-residential property purchases, at different levels of purchase price. These examples demonstrate that at the higher end of the market the LBTT charge in relation to residential property is significantly higher than the equivalent SDLT charge, reflecting the Scottish Government's view that purchases at that level should bear a higher tax burden.

Residential property

House purchase costing £250,000 – assumes that an individual is replacing their main residence so that the additional rate does not apply for either LBTT or SDLT purposes.

LBTT

Purchase Price	Rate	LBTT
£	%	£
145,000	0	NIL
105,000	2	2,100
250,000		2,100

SDLT

Purchase Price	Rate	SDLT
£	%	£
125,000	0	NIL
125,000	2	2,500
250,000		2,500

The LBTT charge is 16% lower compared to the equivalent SDLT charge.

House purchase costing £750,000 – this time the assumption is that both the LBTT and SDLT additional rate for residential property applies, that the effective date of the transaction is on or after 25 January 2019, and that the contract for the transaction was entered into on or after 12 December 2018.

LBTT

Purchase Price	Rate	LBTT
£	%	£
145,000	4	5,800
105,000	6	6,300
75,000	9	6,750
425,000	14	59,500
750,000		78,350

SDLT

Purchase Price	Rate	SDLT
£	%	£
125,000	3	3,750
125,000	5	6,250
500,000	8	40,000
750,000		50,000

The LBTT charge is 57% higher compared to the equivalent SDLT charge.

Non-residential property

Commercial property purchase costing £250,000 on the assumption that the effective date of the transaction is on or after 25 January 2019, and that the contract for the transaction was entered into on or after 12 December 2018.

LBTT

Purchase Price	Rate	LBTT
£	%	£
150,000	0	NIL
100,000	1	1,000
250,000		1,000

SDLT

Purchase Price	Rate	SDLT
£	%	£
150,000	0	NIL
100,000	2	2,000
250,000		2,000

The SDLT charge is £1,000 higher compared to the equivalent LBTT charge.

Commercial property purchase costing £5,000,000 on the assumption that the effective date of the transaction is on or after 25 January 2019, and that the contract for the transaction was entered into on or after 12 December 2018.

LBTT

Purchase Price	Rate	LBTT
£	%	£
150,000	0	NIL
100,000	1	1,000
4,750,000	5	237,500
5,000,000		238,500

SDLT

Purchase Price	Rate	SDLT
£	%	£
150,000	0	NIL
100,000	2	2,000
4,750,000	5	237,500
5,000,000		239,500

The SDLT charge is £1,000 higher compared to the equivalent LBTT charge.

Under SDLT, a rate of 15% applies to the whole of the chargeable consideration where a company or a partnership with one or more corporate members or a collective investment scheme acquires a dwelling for chargeable consideration of more than £500,000 (*FA 2003, Sch 4A*). There are, however, a number of exceptions from that penal rate where, for example, the dwellings are held by property traders and developers or for the purposes of a property development business. There is no similar regime under LBTT.

In the 2020 Budget, the UK Government announced that an SDLT surcharge of 2% on top of the existing SDLT rates would apply for purchases of residential property in England and Northern Ireland by non-UK residents with effect from 1 April 2021 (see **1.18**). The 2% surcharge will be added to the existing residential rates including the higher rate for additional dwellings (see **4.56** et seq), the 15% rate for enveloped residential properties (see **4.88** et seq) and the SDLT rates which apply where first-time buyer's relief is available (see **5.47**). As far as is known, at the time of writing (May 2020), there is no proposal from the Scottish Government that a similar surcharge should be introduced under LBTT.

RELIEF FOR FIRST-TIME BUYERS

2.4 From 22 November 2017, under SDLT, a relief is available where a first-time buyer purchases their first home and the 'chargeable consideration' (see **4.19**) is not more than £500,000 (see **5.47** et seq). If the relief is available, the rate of SDLT on the first £300,000 of consideration is 0% and on any balance of the consideration up to £500,000 the rate of SDLT is 5%. If the consideration for the transaction (or a series of 'linked transactions' (see **4.89**)) exceeds £500,000 no relief is available, and the normal rates of SDLT apply (see **4.37** et seq). The legislation dealing with the relief can be found in *FA 2003, s 57B* and *Sch 6ZA* (introduced by *FA 2018, s 41*). The relief must be claimed in a land transaction return or in an amendment to a land transaction return (see **5.54**).

For transactions with an 'effective date' on or after 30 June 2018, provided the contract was entered into on or after 9 February 2018, the Scottish Government introduced a first-time buyer's relief. Where the conditions for the relief to apply are satisfied the zero rate threshold for LBTT is effectively increased from £145,000 to £175,000 for first-time buyers irrespective of age. First-time buyers acquiring a property for more than £175,000 also benefit from the zero rate up to £175,000. This means that all first-time buyers who satisfy the qualifying conditions will benefit from LBTT relief of up to £600. The legislation dealing with the relief can be found in *LBTT(S)A 2013, Sch 4A* (introduced by *Land and Buildings Transaction Tax (First-Time Buyer Relief (Scotland) Order 2018*) *(SSI 2018/221)*. The relief must be claimed in a land transaction return or in an amendment to a land transaction return.

REGISTRATION OF LAND TRANSACTIONS AND NOTIFICATION AND PAYMENT OF LBTT

2.5 Whilst the collection and administration of LBTT is the responsibility of Revenue Scotland, the Keeper of the Registers of Scotland need not register title in relation to a notifiable transaction until the tax obligations (ie the land transaction return has been filed and any LBTT payable has been paid) have been dealt with by the buyer (*LBTT(S)A 2013, s 43(1)* and the *Land and Buildings Transaction Tax (Ancillary Provision) (Scotland) Order 2014 (SSI 2014/376)*). Differences in land law and practice between Scotland and the rest of the UK have historically meant that there was usually an impetus to register a change of owner of land in Scotland as soon as possible, frequently on the same day as the transaction. This is now less of an issue following the *Land Registration etc (Scotland) Act 2012* coming into force on 8 December 2014, which, *inter alia*, introduced the concept of an 'advance notice' to provide protection, for a period of 35 days, for a deed that is intended to be registered in the Land Register. Despite this protection it is still normal practice for the land transaction return to be filed and LBTT to be paid immediately after, or very soon after, the 'effective date' of a transaction (even though the return need only be filed, and the tax need only be paid, within 30 days of the 'effective date' of the transaction) although in relation to payment this only requires that 'arrangements satisfactory' to Revenue Scotland are in place at that date. The term 'arrangements satisfactory' broadly means that where an electronic return is being filed, arrangements have been made to make payment by direct debit, BACS, CHAPS, or Faster Payment at the time of filing the electronic return, or payment is made by cheque which should reach Revenue Scotland by the third working day after the date on which the electronic return was filed. If a paper return is being filed the only method of payment is by cheque.

Under SDLT the normal deadline for notification and payment for transactions with an 'effective date' (see **4.91**) on or before 28 February 2019, and which became notifiable on or before 28 February 2019 was, like LBTT, 30 days from the 'effective date' of the transaction. However, the UK Government confirmed in the 22 November 2017 Budget that the time limit for filing an SDLT return and paying the tax would be reduced from 30 days to 14 days where the 'effective date' of the transaction was on or after 1 March 2019, or where the 'effective date' of the transaction was prior to 1 March 2019 but the transaction first became notifiable on or after 1 March 2019. Therefore, from that date, SDLT filing and payment obligations generally arise 14 days, rather than 30 days, after the 'effective date' of the transaction', with interest and penalties chargeable if the deadline is missed. The necessary changes to *FA 2003* were made by *FA 2019, s 46*. With the aim of making compliance with the new time limit easier new forms SDLT3 and SDLT4 have been introduced (*The Stamp Duty Land Tax (Administration) (Amendment) Regulations 2018* which were laid before the House of Commons on 10 December 2018 and came into force on 1 March 2019).

In general under SDLT, if the transaction is notifiable the purchaser must file a land transaction return and obtain an SDLT5 certificate from HMRC, before the effect of the transaction can be registered in the Land Registry. However, there is no requirement to pay the tax at the time the land transaction return is filed, as the tax need only be paid within the 14-day period from the 'effective date' of the transaction.

NO GENERAL SUB-SALE RELIEF BUT THERE IS A 'SUB-SALE DEVELOPMENT RELIEF'

2.6 Although most of the reliefs available under SDLT have been imported into LBTT, the one major omission is the relief which was probably most widely used for unacceptable tax mitigation – so called 'sub-sale relief' under *FA 2003, s 45* and *Sch 2A*. By omitting the relief from the LBTT rules, the Scottish Government and Revenue Scotland have doubtless saved themselves a lot of trouble. However, sub-sale relief is not only relied upon for unacceptable tax mitigation. Under SDLT it has also been an important factor in arrangements to finance speculative development, which includes most private residential building, and in so-called forward funding transactions where a developer identifies a site but then sells it on to an institutional investor or owner-occupier prior to development. The omission of a general sub-sale relief may have a detrimental effect on this part of the Scottish economy over the longer term.

Whilst there is no general sub-sale relief within LBTT the Scottish Government has introduced a much narrower relief known as 'sub-sale development relief'. The relief is only available where, at the time of the filing of the land transaction return in relation to the substantial performance or completion of the first contract, the first buyer has entered into a 'qualifying sub-sale' and a 'significant development' is to take place on the land within five years of the date of the 'qualifying-sub-sale' transaction. The relief will be withdrawn, or partially withdrawn, if the significant development is not actually completed, or only part of the significant development is actually completed, within the requisite five-year period.

Assignment of a contract before substantial performance/completion

2.7 It should however be noted that there is a form of more general sub-sale relief within the LBTT legislation due to the fact that the assignation of a contract (which is to be completed by a conveyance), before its substantial performance and completion, triggers 'substantial performance' of that contract (*LBTT(S)A 2013, s 14(1)(c)*). As a consequence, the contract is treated as if it were the transaction provided for in the contract, and the 'effective date' of the deemed land transaction is the date of substantial performance (*LBTT(S)A 2013, s 10(1)* and *(2)*). Any LBTT payable in relation to the deemed land transaction will be payable by the original buyer within 30 days of the 'effective date' of the deemed land transaction (*LBTT(S)A 2013, ss 29(3)* and *40(2)*). Following the assignation, it will be the assignee who will complete the contract, and completion of the contract will also be a notifiable transaction. However, LBTT will only be payable by the assignee to the extent (if any) that the LBTT payable on completion is greater than that which was paid by the original buyer on substantial performance of the contract (*LBTT(S)A 2013, s 10(3)*). Therefore, if the consideration payable on completion is the same as that payable under the contract at the time of its assignation, and no LBTT reliefs applied at substantial performance but not at completion, and assuming no change in LBTT bands and rates, no further LBTT should be payable by the assignee. In such circumstances only one charge to LBTT will have arisen, although it will have been paid by the assignor (ie the original buyer) rather than the assignee. This is similar to the position had sub-sale relief been available, but here it is the assignee which has not incurred an LBTT liability, whereas under sub-sale relief it would have been the original buyer who would have been relieved from paying LBTT.

Whilst it may not always be commercially possible or acceptable to assign a contract, consideration could be given to such a strategy if a person other than the original buyer may look to get the benefit of the contract. In these circumstances it would be necessary to ensure that under the terms of the contract it is possible for the original buyer to assign the contract. If the prospective assignee is unhappy with some of the terms of the existing contract it may be possible to vary the terms of the contract, without giving rise to an LBTT liability, either before or after the assignment.

LEASES

2.8 The special rules for leases are contained in *LBTT(S)A 2013, Sch 19*. In principle, the manner of charging LBTT on the grant of a new lease will be similar to that under SDLT. Tax will be calculated separately on the rent and on any premium, and the two amounts added to give the initial tax bill for the lease. The rules relating to leases of indefinite term, leases for a fixed period that continue beyond that period, and renewals are similar to those under SDLT (see **6.64** et seq).

2.9 However, under SDLT the tax liability on rents payable under a lease is finally determined by reference to the rent payable during the first five years of the term of the lease. Even if it is known that rents will increase after year five, this is not taken into account. There is no such rule in relation to

LBTT – any *known* increases throughout the life of the lease will have to be taken into account in the initial assessment of tax, apart from increases in line with the retail price index, consumer price index or similar index of inflation. But even then, the position will not be finally determined. In addition, assuming the grant of the lease was notifiable or becomes notifiable, the tenant will be required to review the position every three years during the period of the lease, and again when either the lease is assigned or the lease comes to an end, to determine whether further tax is due. The requirement for submission of new returns every three years (whether or not there is any further tax to pay) will be onerous for some lessees, especially those businesses that have numerous leased premises.

The intention under the LBTT legislation is to adjust the tax payable at these three yearly intervals to take account of increases in rent or other changes in the lease. However, this is not entirely clear from the legislation. *LBTT(S)A 2013, Sch 19, para 10(2)* requires a further return to be made at each third anniversary of the effective date of the grant of the lease, if the grant of the lease was notifiable, or at each third anniversary of the event triggering notification of the lease assuming the lease has not been assigned or terminated. The further return must be made irrespective of whether there have been any changes affecting the amount of the tax payable. *Paragraph 10(4)* states that the return must include an assessment of the tax due on the basis of the information in the return. However, it is not stated in the legislation that such information should include any changes such as rent increases. It is assumed that the intention is to rely on the power of the tax authority to specify what information is to be included in returns (*LBTT(S)A 2013, s 35(1)(b)*) for this purpose.

LEASES OF RESIDENTIAL PROPERTY

2.10 Generally in Scotland it is now not possible to grant a lease over residential property for more than 20 years (*Land Tenure Reform (Scotland) Act 1974, ss 8–9*), although it should be noted that there are now exceptions to this general rule following the *Housing (Scotland) Act 2010, ss 138* and *139* and the *Private Rented Housing (Scotland) Act 2011, ss 36* and *37*. Also, unlike in England, it is not common for leases of residential property to be granted for long periods. The Scottish Government therefore took the view that it was unlikely that the rent payable on such leases would be sufficient to breach the nil rate tax band for the NPV of the rent (£150,000) such that an LBTT liability arose on the grant of the lease. As a consequence the grant, assignation, or renunciation of a lease of residential property is exempt from LBTT unless it is an 'ultra-long lease'. An 'ultra-long lease' is broadly a lease which is registered, was granted for a period of more than 175 years, and which on 28 November 2015 had more than 100 years to run. Such 'ultra-long leases' were converted into ownership on 28 November 2015, hence their exclusion from the exemption from LBTT on leases over residential property.

There is no such exemption under SDLT. Currently a 20-year residential lease at a fixed rent greater than about £8,700 per annum would give rise to an SDLT liability, and at lower levels of annual rent there may be an obligation to submit an SDLT return even if no tax is due.

ANTI-AVOIDANCE PROVISIONS

SDLT specific anti-avoidance rule

2.11 The SDLT legislation contains a specific anti-avoidance rule (*FA 2003, s 75A*), which is extremely wide in its scope (see **9.4**). Whilst its objective is clearly to counteract SDLT avoidance, there is no requirement that an SDLT avoidance motive exists to fall within the rule. As a result, wholly commercial transactions, perhaps structured in an SDLT-efficient manner, potentially fall within the rule, which can lead to significant uncertainty for taxpayers.

The Scottish Government very sensibly decided not to incorporate a similar type of rule into the LBTT legislation, meaning that taxpayers are spared the uncertainty that can arise under SDLT. Within the LBTT legislation the Scottish Government places reliance on targeted anti-avoidance provisions and the general anti-avoidance rule (see below), which applies to the devolved taxes, including LBTT.

General anti-avoidance rule

2.12 The Scottish Government has introduced a general anti-avoidance rule (the Scottish 'GAAR') (*Revenue Scotland and Tax Powers Act 2014, ss 62–72*) which is specifically designed to be broader in scope than the UK general anti-abuse rule found in *FA 2013, ss 206–215*. The objective of the Scottish GAAR is to counteract 'tax advantages' arising from a 'tax avoidance arrangement' which is 'artificial'. The Scottish GAAR does not contain the safeguards of an advisory review panel, and the so-called double reasonableness test, which apply to the UK general anti-abuse rule.

Residential property holding companies

2.13 The Scottish Ministers can, by regulation, provide that 'qualifying transfers' of interests in 'residential property holding companies' be treated as land transactions chargeable to LBTT (*LBTT(S)A 2013, s 47*). A 'residential property holding company' is a company whose shares are not listed on a recognised stock exchange, whose sole or main activity is holding interests in land (including interests in land located outside of Scotland) and whose assets include interests in residential property. A 'qualifying transfer' is a transfer of an interest in a 'residential property holding company' that results in the transferee (ie the buyer) acquiring the right to occupy some or all of the company's residential property. The Scottish ministers have not yet made any such regulations and therefore this provision is not currently in force.

There is no similar provision under SDLT for transfers of shares in 'land-rich' companies to be treated as land transactions chargeable to tax.

MULTIPLE DWELLINGS RELIEF

2.14 Under SDLT a claim to multiple dwellings relief cannot reduce the SDLT charge to less than 1% of the 'total dwellings consideration' (*FA 2003, Sch 6B, para 5(2)*). However, following the introduction of the additional rate of SDLT on residential properties with effect from 1 April 2016, it would seem that the 1% minimum charge provision is now effectively redundant, as the additional rate will impose a 3% charge on the first £125,000 of consideration. If a claim for multiple dwellings relief is made the additional rate of SDLT will apply and it is not possible to apply the normal rates of SDLT to the acquisition of, say, one property on the basis it is a replacement of a main residence, and the higher rates to the other properties acquired. This is possible under LBTT.

Multiple dwellings relief in relation to LBTT is similar in most respects; however, it does not specify a lower rate of charge, but states that where the relief is available the tax payable cannot be less than a proportion (25%) of that due had the relief not been available. This is stated by the Scottish Government to be a consequence of LBTT being a progressive tax (see **2.3**) however, following the change to a progressive structure for SDLT on residential property from 4 December 2014, the UK Government has retained the minimum 1% charge on the total chargeable consideration given for dwellings. The higher rate of LBTT on the acquisition of additional residential property, and residential property acquired by non-individual purchasers, will apply when a claim is made for multiple dwellings relief if the relevant conditions for the additional rate to apply are satisfied. However, under LBTT, it is possible for some of the properties to be charged at the additional rate whilst one of the properties is charged at the standard rates, if for example, one of the residential properties being acquired is a replacement of an individual purchaser's main residence. This means that if a claim for multiple dwellings relief is made, and the additional rate of LBTT applies to the purchase of any of the properties, the tax chargeable on each property must be calculated, applying either the normal or additional rate LBTT rates as applicable. The LBTT chargeable on each property is then aggregated to give the total amount of LBTT payable.

ACQUISITION RELIEF

2.15 Under SDLT a successful claim to acquisition relief reduces the rate of SDLT chargeable to 0.5% of the chargeable consideration for the transaction (*FA 2003 Sch 7, para 8(1)*).

A successful claim to acquisition relief in relation to LBTT reduces the tax payable to a proportion (12.5%) of that due had the relief not been available. Again the fact that there is no single reduced rate of LBTT applied to the chargeable consideration is stated by the Scottish Government to be a consequence of LBTT being a progressive tax (see **2.3**).

CROFTING COMMUNITY RIGHT TO BUY RELIEF

2.16 Under SDLT, relief (*FA 2003, s 75*) for a transaction entered into under the crofting community right to buy was provided by dividing the total chargeable consideration being given for the acquisition of the crofts by the number of crofts being acquired, calculating the SDLT chargeable on the amount so determined, and multiplying the amount of the SDLT charge by the number of crofts being acquired to get the total SDLT payable. If that average consideration fell within the nil rate band no SDLT was payable as there was no minimum rate of tax payable under this relief as there is for multiple dwellings relief (see **2.14**).

In contrast, under LBTT (*LBTT(S)A 2013, Sch 9*), the acquisition of two or more crofts under a transaction, which is entered into pursuant to a crofting community right to buy, is wholly exempt from LBTT irrespective of the average consideration paid per croft (the *Land and Buildings Transaction Tax (Addition and Modification of Reliefs) (Scotland) Order 2015, art 2(4) (SSI 2015/93)*).

LICENCES TO OCCUPY PROPERTY

2.17 Under LBTT the grant, assignation or renunciation of a licence to use or occupy property is exempt from charge unless it is a 'prescribed non-residential licence', which is a licence of a description prescribed under regulations made by the Scottish Ministers (*LBTT(S)A 2013, Sch 1, paras 3(1)(b), 3(4)* and s *53(1)*). Currently no such licences have been prescribed by the Scottish ministers, meaning that the grant, assignation or renunciation of a licence to use or occupy non-residential property, irrespective of the use to which the property is to be put, will be an exempt transaction for the purposes of LBTT.

In relation to SDLT, a licence to use or occupy land is an exempt interest (*FA 2003, s 48(2)(b)*), so that any transaction in relation to such a licence will not be chargeable to SDLT.

The only practical impact of this difference in treatment should be that under LBTT the variation of a licence to use or occupy property may give rise to LBTT obligations to file a land transaction return and pay tax (*LBTT(S)A 2013, s 6(1)(c), 3(c)* and *(4)(c)*) if the chargeable consideration given for the variation exceeds the £150,000 nil rate tax band (*LBTT(S)A 2013, s 30(1)(c)*). In contrast, under SDLT, the variation of a licence to use or occupy land would be exempt.

OTHER SDLT RELIEFS NOT AVAILABLE UNDER LBTT

2.18 The following SDLT reliefs are not available under LBTT:

- relief for acquisition by an employer in a case of relocation of employment of an employee (*FA 2003, Sch 6A, para 5*);
- relief for acquisition by a property trader from the personal representatives of a deceased person (*FA 2003, Sch 6A, para 3*); and
- General seeding relief for property authorised investment funds (PAIFs) and co-ownership authorised contractual schemes (CoACSs) (*FA 2016, Sch 16, para 3*). However, on 3 May 2018 the Scottish Government issued a consultation document called 'A Consultation on Land and Buildings Transaction Tax – Property Investment Funds' in which it set out proposals to introduce an LBTT relief for seeding PAIFs and CoACs from sources other than an authorised unit trust whilst also considering providing LBTT parity between PAIFs and CoACs. In this context 'seeding relief' means the initial transfer of property or an existing property portfolio into a new or empty fund. The consultation closed on 2 August 2018. The Scottish Government subsequently confirmed in the 2019/20 Scottish Budget that it would introduce LBTT reliefs for the 'seeding' of properties into a PAIF or CoACS, and a relief for when units in CoACS are exchanged. Draft legislation governing the reliefs will be published for consultation once there is sufficient clarity on the terms of the UK's withdrawal from the EU.

TRANSITIONAL PROVISIONS

Disapplication of SDLT

2.19 The *Scotland Act 2012* contains provisions at s *29* and *Sch 3* for the disapplication of SDLT, in relation to transactions in land situated in Scotland from 1 April 2015.

Scotland Act 2012, s *29(2)* provides that a chargeable interest, for the purposes of SDLT (*FA 2003, s 48*) comprises an interest in land in England and Wales or Northern Ireland, but not in Scotland. Consequently, subject to the transitional provisions described below, a transaction in relation to an interest in land situated in Scotland, with an effective date (*FA 2003, s 119*) which is on or after 1 April 2015, will not be a land transaction for SDLT purposes but will, instead, potentially be within the charge to LBTT (*Scotland Act 2012, s 29(4)*).

Linked transactions

2.20 Based on the *Scotland Act 2012, s 29(2)* and *(4)*, and on the technical guidance issued by HMRC on 15 February 2015 (see **2.1**) transactions in land situated in Scotland with an effective date (*FA 2003, s 119*) on or after 1 April 2015, which would be linked (see *FA 2003, s 108*) for SDLT purposes, will no longer be linked for SDLT purposes with either:

- a transaction in land which is situated in England and Wales or Northern Ireland; or
- a transaction in land which is situated in Scotland but which is subject to SDLT.

Example 2.1—A transaction chargeable to SDLT is not linked to a transaction chargeable to LBTT

An Cala Ltd, as part of a single deal, agrees to acquire two commercial buildings, one located in Inverness and the other in Derby, from the same company. The seller is based in Inverness and the effective date of the acquisition of both buildings is 28 April 2015.

The acquisition of the building located in Derby is chargeable to SDLT, whereas the acquisition of the building in Inverness is chargeable to LBTT. Neither of the transactions is linked for the purposes of SDLT or LBTT.

As a separate deal An Cala Ltd also agrees to acquire two office blocks from a company based in London, with one of the office blocks being situated in Glasgow and one in Dundee. The effective date of the acquisition of the Glasgow property was 31 March 2005 whereas the property in Dundee is not acquired until later, the transaction having an effective date of 10 July 2015.

The acquisition of the Glasgow property is chargeable to SDLT whereas the acquisition of the Dundee property is chargeable to LBTT. Neither transaction is linked for the purposes of SDLT or LBTT.

Acquisition of land located in both Scotland and the rest of the UK

2.21 Where a transaction in land with an effective date on or after 1 April 2015 includes both land in Scotland and land in England and Wales (prior to 1 April 2018 from which date LTT applies in Wales) or Northern Ireland, the acquisition of the land in Scotland is within the charge to LBTT, whereas the acquisition of the land in England and Wales (prior to 1 April 2018 from which date LTT applies in Wales) or Northern Ireland is within the charge to SDLT, and the consideration given for the acquisitions should be apportioned on a just and reasonable basis (*LBTT(S)A 2013, Sch 2, para 4* and *FA 2003, Sch 4, para 4*).

Example 2.2—Apportionment of consideration – acquisition of properties in Scotland and in the rest of the UK

Super Retailer Ltd acquires a number of shops from Discount Retailer Ltd as a single transaction. Some of the shops are situated in England and some in Scotland. The effective date of the transaction (the date of settlement) is 31 October 2020.

The acquisition of the shops in Scotland is not chargeable to SDLT but will be within the charge to LBTT. The acquisition of the shops in England will be within the charge to SDLT. The consideration given for the respective acquisitions should be apportioned on a just and reasonable basis.

Transitional provisions (Scotland Act 2012, s 29(5) and (6))

Land situated in Scotland – transactions to which SDLT continues to apply

2.22 SDLT continues to apply to any transaction in relation to land situated in Scotland, which has an effective date (*FA 2003, s 119*) on or after 1 April 2015, and which is:

(1) effected under a contract entered into and substantially performed (*FA 2003, s 44(5)*) on or before 1 May 2012 (the date the *Scotland Act 2012* received Royal Assent); or

(2) effected under a contract entered into on or before 1 May 2012 (but not substantially performed on or before 1 May 2012) and not excluded by reason of falling into (a), (b) or (c) below:

    (a) the contract is varied, or there is an assignation of rights under the contract, after 1 May 2012;

(b) the transaction is effected as a result of the exercise after 1 May 2012 of an option, right of pre-emption or similar right; or

(c) after 1 May 2012 there is an assignation, subsale or other transaction relating to the whole or part of the land which is the subject of the contract, as a consequence of which a person other than the purchaser (buyer) under the contract becomes entitled to call for a conveyance.

The technical guidance issued by HMRC on 15 February 2015 (see **2.1**) includes a useful table setting out the effect of the transitional provisions. The table is reproduced below.

Table to demonstrate the effect of the transitional provisions for land transactions in Scotland

On or before 1 May 2012	2 May 2012– 31 March 2015	1 April 2015 and after	Tax charge
Conclusion of Missives		Settlement	SDLT on Settlement
Conclusion of Missives + Substantial Performance		Settlement	SDLT on Substantial Performance + SDLT on Settlement*
Conclusion of Missives + Substantial Performance	Variation	Settlement	SDLT on Substantial Performance + SDLT on Settlement*
Conclusion of Missives	Substantial Performance	Settlement	SDLT on Substantial Performance + SDLT on Settlement*
Conclusion of Missives	Variation	Settlement	LBTT on Settlement
Conclusion of Missives	Substantial Performance + Variation	Settlement	SDLT on Substantial Performance + LBTT on Settlement*
Conclusion of Missives		Substantial Performance + Settlement	SDLT on Substantial Performance + SDLT on Settlement*
Conclusion of Missives		Substantial Performance + Variation + Settlement	SDLT on Substantial Performance + LBTT on Settlement*
	Conclusion of Missives	Settlement	LBTT on Settlement

On or before 1 May 2012	**2 May 2012–31 March 2015**	**1 April 2015 and after**	**Tax charge**
	Conclusion of Missives + Substantial Performance	Settlement	SDLT on Substantial Performance + LBTT on Settlement*
	Conclusion of Missives + Substantial Performance	Variation + Settlement	SDLT on Substantial Performance + LBTT on Settlement*
	Conclusion of Missives	Substantial Performance + Settlement	LBTT on Settlement
	Conclusion of Missives	Substantial Performance + Variation + Settlement	LBTT on Settlement

2.23 HMRC have indicated (see technical guidance issued by HMRC on 15 February 2015 – **2.1**) that they will not regard the following post-1 May 2012 events as excluding a transaction from the SDLT regime under *Scotland Act 2012, s 29(6)* (see point (2) in **2.22**):

- a variation of the completion date specified in the contract; or
- a transfer to the nominee or bare trustee of the purchaser (buyer) under the contract.

2.24 Each of the scenarios set out in **2.22** are now considered in turn.

Contracts entered into on or before 1 May 2012

Scenario 1

The missives (exchange of contracts) are concluded on or before 1 May 2012, substantial performance and settlement (completion) take place at the same time but after 1 April 2015. The settlement transaction is within the SDLT regime (*Scotland Act 2012, s 29(5)(b)* and *(6)*).

Scenario 2

The missives (exchange of contracts) and substantial performance are concluded/takes place on or before 1 May 2012 and settlement (completion) takes place on or after 1 April 2015. The settlement transaction is within the SDLT regime (*Scotland Act 2012, s 29(5)(a)*).

Scenario 3

The missives (exchange of contracts) and substantial performance are concluded/takes place on or before 1 May 2012; however, this time the contract is varied before 1 April 2015. The variation does not bring the settlement (completion) transaction into the LBTT regime, as the contract was substantially performed on or before 1 May 2012 (*Scotland Act 2012, s 29(5)(a)*). The settlement (completion) transaction is therefore within the SDLT regime.

Scenario 4

The missives (exchange of contracts) are concluded on or before 1 May 2012, substantial performance takes place after 1 May 2012 but before 1 April 2015, and settlement (completion) takes place after 1 April 2015. As the contract was entered into on or before 1 May 2012, and has not been varied, the settlement (completion) transaction on or after 1 April 2015 is within the SDLT regime (*Scotland Act 2012, s 29(5)(b)*). As substantial performance took place before 1 April 2015 it will also be within the SDLT regime.

Scenario 5

The missives (exchange of contracts) are concluded on or before 1 May 2012, the contract is varied after 1 May 2012 but before 1 April 2015, and settlement (completion) and substantial performance take place at the same time, but on or after 1 April 2015. As the contract has been varied after 1 May 2012 the settlement (completion) transaction is within the LBTT regime (*Scotland Act 2012, s 29(5)(b) and (6)(a)*).

Scenario 6

The missives (exchange of contracts) are concluded on or before 1 May 2012, the contract is substantially performed after 1 May 2012 but before 1 April 2015, the contract is then varied before 1 April 2015. Settlement (completion) of the contract takes place on or after 1 April 2015. The substantial performance transaction will fall within the SDLT regime, but the settlement (completion) transaction will be within the LBTT regime (*Scotland Act 2012, s 29(5)(b)*). However, LBTT will only be payable on the settlement (completion) transaction if, and to the extent that, the LBTT chargeable on that transaction exceeds the amount of the charge to SDLT, which was paid to HMRC, on the substantial performance of the contract (the *Land and Buildings Transaction Tax (Transitional Provisions) (Scotland) Order 2014, art 3(4) (SSI 2014/377)*).

Scenario 7

The missives (exchange of contracts) are concluded on or before 1 May 2012, there is no variation of the contract, and both substantial performance of the contract and settlement (completion) take place on or after 1 April 2015. Both the substantial performance transaction and the settlement (completion) transaction are within the SDLT regime (*Scotland Act 2012, s 29(5)(b)*).

Scenario 8

The missives (exchange of contracts) are concluded on or before 1 May 2012, the contract is substantially performed on or after 1 April 2015, but is subsequently varied, after which settlement (completion) takes place. The substantial performance transaction is within the SDLT regime as the missives were concluded on or before 1 May 2012 and there was no variation prior to substantial performance taking place (*Scotland Act 2012, s 29(5)(b)*). As the contract is then varied, the subsequent settlement (completion) transaction is within the LBTT regime. However, LBTT will only be payable on the settlement (completion) transaction if, and to the extent that, the LBTT chargeable on that transaction exceeds the amount of the charge to SDLT, which was paid to HMRC, on the substantial performance of the contract (the *Land and Buildings Transaction Tax (Transitional Provisions) (Scotland) Order 2014, art 3(4) (SSI 2014/377)*).

2.25

Contracts entered into after 1 May 2012

Scenario 9

The missives (exchange of contracts) are concluded after 1 May 2012 but before 1 April 2015, and settlement (completion) and substantial performance take place at the same time after 1 April 2015. The settlement (completion) transaction is within the LBTT regime (*Scotland Act 2012, s 29(2)* and *(4)*).

Scenario 10

The missives (exchange of contracts) are concluded after 1 May 2012 but before 1 April 2015, the contract is then substantially performed before 1 April 2015, but settlement (completion) takes place after 1 April 2015. As substantial performance takes place before 1 April 2015 it is within the SDLT regime (*Scotland Act 2012, s 28(2)*). However, as the missives were concluded after 1 May 2012 the post-31 March 2015 settlement (completion) transaction is within the LBTT regime (*Scotland Act 2012, s 29(2) and (4)*). In these circumstances, LBTT is only payable to the extent that the amount of the LBTT chargeable on the settlement (completion) transaction exceeds the amount of the SDLT chargeable, and paid to HMRC, on substantial performance of the contract (the *Land and Buildings Transaction Tax (Transitional Provisions) (Scotland) Order 2014, art 4(4) (SSI 2014/377)*).

Scenario 11

The missives (exchange of contracts) are concluded after 1 May 2012 but before 1 April 2015, the contract is then substantially performed before 1 April 2015, however on or after 1 April 2015 the contract is varied. Some time after the variation settlement (completion) of the contract takes place. As substantial performance takes place before 1 April 2015, and prior to the variation of the contract, it is within the SDLT regime (*Scotland Act 2012, s 28(2)*). As the contract was entered into after 1 May 2012, the variation of the contract has no impact, since the settlement (completion) is in any event within the LBTT regime (*Scotland Act 2012, s 29(2)* and *(4)*). However, LBTT is only payable to the extent that the amount of the LBTT chargeable on the settlement (completion) transaction exceeds the amount of the SDLT chargeable, and paid to HMRC, on substantial performance of the contract (the *Land and Buildings Transaction Tax (Transitional Provisions) (Scotland) Order 2014, art 4(4) (SSI 2014/377)*).

2.26

Scenario 12

The missives (exchange of contracts) are concluded after 1 May 2012 but before 1 April 2015, and the contract is then substantially performed on or after 1 April 2015, after which settlement (completion) takes place.

It seems that in these circumstances the substantial performance of the contract will not give rise to either SDLT or LBTT obligations. The technical analysis appears to be that the substantial performance of the contract does not fall within the SDLT regime as the contract was entered into after 1 May 2012, and therefore on or after 1 April 2015 an interest in land in Scotland is no longer a 'chargeable interest' for the purposes of SDLT (*Scotland Act 2012, s 29(2)*). Equally, from an LBTT perspective, *LBTT(S)A 2013, s 10* (Substantial performance without completion) only applies on the substantial performance of a contract for a 'land transaction' which is to be completed by a conveyance. As the contract was entered into prior to 1 April 2015 it cannot be a contract for a 'land transaction' for LBTT purposes, because when it was entered into the land in Scotland, which is the subject of the contract, was still a 'chargeable interest' for the purposes of SDLT, and had not become a 'chargeable interest' for LBTT purposes (*Scotland Act 2012, s 28(2)*). The subsequent completion of the contract would however give rise to LBTT obligations, and clearly there would be 'no credit' for any SDLT or LBTT arising from the earlier substantial performance of the contract, as no tax would have been paid.

Scenario 13

This scenario is the same as Scenario (12) except that following the substantial performance of the contract a variation of the contract takes place, after which settlement (completion) occurs. As the contract was entered into after 1 May 2012, the variation has no impact, since the settlement (completion) is in any event within the LBTT regime (*Scotland Act 2012, s 29(2)* and *(4)*). The substantial performance of the contract should not give rise to any SDLT or LBTT obligations as discussed above in relation to Scenario 12.

2.27 It should be noted that, in relation to the scenarios set out in **2.24–2.26**, a 'variation' means a disqualifying event prescribed by *Scotland Act 2012, s 29(6)* (see **2.22**) and includes *inter alia* an assignation of rights under the contract or the exercise of an option.

Example 2.3—Contract entered into post-1 May 2012 but before 1 April 2015 and completed post-31 March 2015

Caroline concludes missives for the purchase of a house in Prestwick on 21 March 2015. The agreement is not substantially performed before the date of settlement and the effective date of the transaction (the settlement date) is on 30 May 2015.

The purchase of the house is within the LBTT regime, and is not chargeable to SDLT, despite the fact that the missives were concluded prior to 1 April 2015. The transitional rules in the *Scotland Act 2012, s 29(5)* and *(6)* do not apply, as the missives were not concluded on or before 1 May 2012.

Example 2.4—Contract entered into before 1 May 2012 but completed post-31 March 2015

On 1 April 2012 Pamela concludes missives for the purchase of a completed office block, located in Scotland, before construction begins on 1 May 2012. Completion of the construction work is delayed and, by agreement between the parties, the date of settlement is changed to 1 May 2015. The agreement is not substantially performed before the date of settlement and the effective date (*FA 2003, s 119*) of the acquisition of the office block (the date of settlement) is 1 May 2015.

The acquisition is subject to SDLT as it falls within the transitional provisions (*Scotland Act 2012, s 29(5)(b)* and *(6)*), as the missives were concluded before 1 May 2012, and none of the exclusions in *Scotland Act 2012, s 29(6)* should apply. In particular the change in the date of settlement is not treated as a variation of the contract within *Scotland Act 2012, s 29(6)* (see HMRC technical guidance issued on 15 February 2015 – **2.1**).

Example 2.5—Substantial performance of a contract before 1 April 2015 with completion post-1 April 2015

Andrew concludes missives for the purchase of a retail unit in Dumfries on 28 February 2015, for a consideration of £300,000 and with the date of settlement agreed for 1 May 2015. The agreement is substantially performed (*FA 2003, s 44(5)(a)*) on 14 March 2015 when Andrew goes into the retail unit to undertake the fit-out.

The substantial performance of the agreement will be within the charge to SDLT as the contract is treated as if it were the transaction governed by the contract and the effective date (*FA 2003, s 119*) of the transaction is when the contract is substantially performed, namely 14 March 2015.

However, as the date of settlement takes place on 1 May 2015, that transaction will have an effective date of 1 May 2015 (*LBTT(S)A 2013, s 63(1)(a)*) which means it will be within the LBTT regime, and will not be chargeable to SDLT. The transitional rules in the *Scotland Act 2012, s 29(5)* and *(6)* do not apply as the missives were concluded after 1 May 2012. However, Andrew is only required to pay LBTT in relation to the settlement transaction if, and to the extent that, the LBTT chargeable on the completion transaction exceeds the amount of the SDLT chargeable, and paid to HMRC, on substantial performance of the contract (the *Land and Buildings Transaction Tax (Transitional Provisions) (Scotland) Order 2014, art 4(4) (SSI 2014/377)*).

However, even if no LBTT is payable, Andrew will have an obligation to file an LBTT land transaction return by 31 May 2015 (*LBTT(S)A 2013, ss 10(3)(a)* and *30(1)* and *6(a)*).

Specific provisions

Contract providing for conveyance to a third party (FA 2003, s 44A and LBTT(S)A 2013, s 11)

2.28 Under SDLT, *FA 2003, s 44A* applies where a contract is entered into pursuant to which a chargeable interest in land is to be conveyed by (A) at the request of (B), either to (B) or (C) in circumstances where only (A) and (B) are party to the contract.

If such a contract is substantially performed (*FA 2003, s 44(5)*) on or before 1 May 2012 (the date on which the *Scotland Act 2012* came into force) and, at the request of (B), (A) becomes obliged to convey the land to (B), or a conveyance is made under a contract between (B) and (C), such transactions will be subject to SDLT even if the effective date (*FA 2003, s 119*) of the transaction is on or after 1 April 2015 (see para 6.2 of the HMRC guidance on the transition from SDLT to LBTT and *Scotland Act 2012, s 29(5)(a)*).

Where such a contract is entered into on or before 1 May 2012, but not substantially performed by that date, a conveyance from (A) to (B), or a conveyance under a contract between (B) and (C) will be subject to SDLT if the effective date (*FA 2003, s 119*) of the transaction is on or after 1 April 2015, and none of the exclusions set out at **2.22** (*Scotland Act 2012, s 29(6)*) applies to the contract. However, if any of the exclusions set out at **2.22** do apply, and the effective date of the transaction is on or after 1 April 2015, a conveyance from (A) to (B), or a conveyance under a contract between (B) and (C), will be subject to LBTT (see para 6.3 of the HMRC guidance on the transition from SDLT to LBTT and *Scotland Act 2012, s 29(5)(b)*). If the contract was substantially performed before 1 April 2015, and tax has been paid to HMRC in respect of that substantial performance, LBTT is only payable on the conveyance to the extent (if any) that the LBTT chargeable is greater than the SDLT chargeable, and paid to HMRC, on the substantial performance transaction (the *Land and Buildings Transaction Tax (Transitional Provisions) (Scotland) Order 2014, article 3(4) (SSI 2014/377)*).

Finally, if such a contract is entered into after 1 May 2012, a conveyance from (A) to (B), or a conveyance under a contract between (B) and (C), will not be subject to SDLT if the effective date (*FA 2003, s 119*) of the transaction is on or after 1 April 2015. Such transactions will be within the LBTT regime (see para 6.4 of the HMRC guidance on the transition from SDLT to LBTT). If the contract was substantially performed before 1 April 2015, and tax has been paid to HMRC in respect of that substantial performance, LBTT is only payable on the conveyance to the extent (if any) that the LBTT chargeable is greater than the SDLT chargeable, and paid to HMRC, on the substantial performance transaction (the *Land and Buildings Transaction Tax (Transitional Provisions) (Scotland) Order 2014, art 4(4) (SSI 2015/377)*).

Pre-completion transactions (FA 2003, s 45 and Sch 2A)

2.29 *FA 2003, Sch 2A* (see **5.11** et seq) applies where a person (the original purchaser) enters into a contract (the original contract) for the acquisition of an interest in UK land under which the acquisition is to be completed by a conveyance and, before that contract is substantially performed (see **4.9**) or completed, there is 'a pre-completion transaction'. For these purposes a 'pre-completion transaction' is a transaction which results in a person other than the original purchaser (the transferee) becoming entitled to call for a conveyance to him of the whole or part of the UK land interest to be acquired under the original contract. A pre-completion transaction can either be an 'assignment of rights' or a 'free-standing transfer'. A pre-completion transaction will be an assignment of rights if the entitlement of the transferee to call for the conveyance to be made to him is an entitlement to exercise rights under the original contract, ie the original contract has been assigned in whole or in part to the transferee. A pre-completion transaction which is not an assignment of rights is a free-standing transfer, and this term would therefore include a subsale or a novation of the original contract.

The transitional rules in relation to such pre-completion transactions then operate as follows. If the assignment or free-standing transfer transaction is completed or substantially performed by the 'transferee' (ie the person other than the original buyer who is now entitled to call for a conveyance) on or after 1 April 2015 neither the completion or the substantial performance of the assignment or free-standing transfer transaction, nor a transaction (subsale) or notional transaction (for the purposes of *FA 2013, Sch 2A* on an assignment of rights) entered into by 'the transferor', will be subject to SDLT. For these purposes the transferor in relation to a pre-completion transaction is the party to the pre-completion transaction who immediately before the pre-completion transaction took place was entitled to call for a conveyance of the interest in UK land which was the subject matter of the pre-completion transaction, ie in most cases the original purchaser (see para 7.2 of the HMRC guidance on the transition from SDLT to LBTT).

Unless the original contract was substantially performed on or before 1 May 2012, the assignment of rights or free-standing transfer transaction will mean that the substantial performance and completion of the original contract on or after 1 April 2015 will be excluded from SDLT by virtue of the *Scotland Act 2012, s 29(6)(c)* (see **2.22**).

Instead, if the assignment of rights or free-standing transfer transaction is entered into on or after 1 April 2015, LBTT will be chargeable both on the original buyer in relation to the substantial performance of the original contract, as that original contract will be treated as having been substantially performed under *LBTT(S)A 2013, s 14(1)(c)*, and on the substantial performance and completion of the further agreement, ie the assignment, subsale or novation. This is subject to the availability of sub-sale development relief.

If the pre-completion transaction (ie the assignment of rights or free-standing transfer transaction) is entered into before 1 April 2015 it is considered that *LBTT(S)A 2013, s 14(1)(c)* should not apply, but the subsequent completion of both the original contract and the assignment or free-standing transfer transaction, on or after 1 April 2015, will be chargeable to LBTT. This is subject to the availability of sub-sale development relief.

Options (FA 2003, s 46 and LBTT(S)A 2013, s 12)

2.30 If an option or pre-emption right over land in Scotland is acquired before 1 April 2015, the exercise of the option or pre-emption right on or after 1 April 2015 will not be within the SDLT regime, regardless of whether or not the grant and exercise of the option would have been linked transactions (*FA 2003, s 108*) for SDLT purposes, but for the fact that land in Scotland is not a chargeable interest for the purposes of SDLT on or after 1 April 2015 (see **2.22**). The exercise of the option will potentially be chargeable to LBTT (see para 8.2 of the HMRC guidance on the transition from SDLT to LBTT).

If the option or pre-emption right is acquired on or after 1 April 2015 both the acquisition of that right, and any subsequent exercise, will be chargeable to LBTT and may be linked transactions.

Exchanges (FA 2003, s 47 and LBTT(S)A 2013, s 57)

2.31 Where, on or after 1 April 2015, land in England and Wales (prior to 1 April 2018 from which date LTT applies in Wales) or Northern Ireland is exchanged for land in Scotland, the acquisition of the land in England and Wales (prior to 1 April 2018 from which date LTT applies in Wales) or Northern Ireland will be within the SDLT regime, whilst the acquisition of the land in Scotland will be within the LBTT regime. As the acquisition of land in Scotland is not a land transaction for SDLT purposes, the SDLT exchange provisions (*FA 2003, s 47* and *Sch 4, para 5*) will not apply, and SDLT will be charged on the consideration given for the land in England and Wales (prior to 1 April 2018 from which date LTT applies in Wales) or Northern Ireland under the normal rules (*FA 2003, Sch 4, paras 1* and *7*) (see para 9.2 of the HMRC guidance on the transition from SDLT to LBTT).

Equally, as the acquisition of the land in England and Wales or Northern Ireland will not be a land transaction for LBTT purposes, the LBTT exchange provisions (*LBTT(S)A 2013, s 13* and *Sch 2, paras 5* and *6*) will not apply. LBTT will be charged on the acquisition of the land in Scotland by reference to the market value of the land in England and Wales or Northern Ireland given as consideration (*LBTT(S)A 2013, Sch 2, para 7*), plus the amount of any equality money or other consideration given by the buyer of the land in Scotland (see para 9.5 of the HMRC guidance on the transition from SDLT to LBTT).

2.32 Where the transfer of land in England and Wales or Northern Ireland takes place before 1 April 2015, and the transfer of the land in Scotland takes place on or after 1 April 2015, neither the SDLT nor the LBTT exchange provisions will apply (see para 9.3 of the HMRC guidance on the transition from SDLT to LBTT).

2.33 In contrast, where the transfer of land in Scotland takes place before 1 April 2015 and the transfer of land in England and Wales (prior to 1 April 2018 from which date LTT applies in Wales) or Northern Ireland takes place on or after 1 April 2015, both transactions will be within the SDLT regime, and the SDLT exchange provisions apply (*FA 2003, s 47* and *Sch 4, para 5*) (see para 9.8 of the HMRC guidance on the transition from SDLT to LBTT).

Example 2.6—Exchange of a property in England for one located in Scotland

A company (A Ltd) decides to relocate its head office from England to larger premises in Scotland, and enters into an agreement on 1 March 2015 with another unrelated company (B Ltd) to exchange its offices in England for an office block in Scotland, and to pay £750,000 equality money. The agreement is not substantially performed (see **4.9**) before the date of settlement, which takes place on 30 June 2015.

A Ltd's acquisition of the premises in Scotland is within the LBTT regime. However, the LBTT exchange provisions do not apply as the sale of the English property is not a land transaction for LBTT purposes, as the right over the English property is not a chargeable interest for the purposes of *LBTT(S)A 2013, s 4(2)*. The consideration chargeable to LBTT will be the market value of the property in England plus £750,000.

B Ltd's acquisition of the offices in England will be within the SDLT regime, but the SDLT exchange provisions will not apply as the sale of the Scottish property is not a land transaction for SDLT purposes (*Scotland Act 2012, s 29(2)* and *(4)*). The consideration chargeable to SDLT will be the market value of the property in Scotland given as consideration (*FA 2003, Sch 4, para 7*).

Contingent, uncertain or unascertained consideration (FA 2003, s 51 and LBTT(S)A 2013, ss 18 and 19)

2.34 If a transaction is within the SDLT regime, the obligation to adjust the chargeable consideration when, on or after 1 April 2015, a contingency ceases or consideration is ascertained (*FA 2003, s 80*) remains in place and is not affected by the introduction of LBTT. Similarly the provisions relating to the deferment of SDLT (*FA 2003, s 90*) remain unchanged. The contingency ceasing or the consideration becoming ascertained, in relation to such a transaction, will not be subject to LBTT (see para 10.1 of the HMRC guidance on the transition from SDLT to LBTT).

Sale and leaseback transaction (FA 2003, s 57A and LBTT(S)A 2013, Sch 3)

2.35 Where the effective date (*FA 2003, s 119*) of a sale (or lease) of land situated in Scotland is before 1 April 2015 but the effective date of the grant back of the lease (or sub-lease) is on or after 1 April 2015, the sale (or lease) transaction will be within the SDLT regime, but the lease (or sub-lease) transaction will be within the LBTT regime. This means that neither the SDLT nor the LBTT exchange provisions will apply (see **2.33**).

For SDLT purposes the chargeable consideration for the sale (or lease) transaction will be the consideration given in money or money's worth for the sale (or lease), including the market value, if any, of the lease (or sub-lease) granted back.

For LBTT purposes the grant of the lease (or sub-lease) back on or after 1 April 2015 will potentially be within the LBTT sale and leaseback relief provisions in *LBTT(S)A 2013, Sch 3* and therefore, as long as all of the requisite conditions are satisfied, the grant of the lease back would be exempt from the charge to LBTT, despite the fact that the sale (or lease) transaction took place before 1 April 2015 (see para 11.2 of the HMRC guidance on the transition from SDLT to LBTT).

Multiple dwellings relief (FA 2003, Sch 6B and LBTT(S)A 2013, Sch 5)

2.36 Where a transaction (or linked transactions) comprises multiple dwellings situated in both Scotland and England and Wales (prior to 1 April 2018 from which date LTT applies in Wales) or Northern Ireland, the rate of SDLT payable on a claim for multiple dwellings relief is calculated according to the number of dwellings the acquisition of which is subject to SDLT (see para 12.1 of the HMRC guidance on the transition from SDLT to LBTT).

Similarly, the LBTT payable on a claim for multiple dwellings relief is calculated based on the number of dwellings the acquisition of which is subject to LBTT.

Example 2.7—Claim for multiple dwellings relief where properties are acquired in both Scotland and in the rest of the UK

Property Investments Ltd acquires eight new houses from the same developer on 30 September 2020. It plans to let the eight houses out to a third party. Four of the houses are in Kendal with two costing £200,000 each and two costing £400,000 each. The other four houses are in Aberdeen with two costing £600,000 each and two costing £500,000 each.

Only the four houses in Kendal are chargeable to SDLT and, if a claim for multiple dwellings relief is made, the SDLT chargeable is determined by dividing the aggregate consideration for the Kendal houses of £1,200,000 by the number of dwellings chargeable to SDLT of four, giving an average price per dwelling of £300,000. As the company is only acquiring four properties chargeable to SDLT (the other four properties are chargeable to LBTT) it is considered that the rule which states that where six or more dwellings are acquired as part of a single transaction the transaction is treated as the acquisition of non-residential property (*FA 2003, s 116(7)*) should not apply. Consequently the SDLT additional rates on residential property will apply such that the SDLT charge per dwelling is calculated as follows:

Purchase Price	Rate	SDLT
£	%	£
125,000	3	3,750
125,000	5	6,250
50,000	8	4,000
300,000		14,000

Based on four dwellings the SDLT payable is therefore £56,000 (4 × £14,000). However, if this amount is less than 1% of the total dwellings consideration then the SDLT payable is that 1% amount.

Total dwellings consideration of £1,200,000 × 1% = £12,000.

Consequently the SDLT payable is £56,000.

Note that as none of the properties are acquired for chargeable consideration of more than £500,000, the 15% rate of SDLT in *FA 2003, Sch 4A* is not in point.

In the absence of a claim for multiple dwellings relief the SDLT liability would have been £99,750.

Similarly, if a claim for multiple dwellings relief is made, the LBTT chargeable on the purchase of the four houses in Aberdeen is determined by dividing the aggregate consideration for the Aberdeen houses of £2,200,000, by the number of dwellings chargeable to LBTT of four, such that the LBTT is determined based on an average consideration of £550,000. As the company is only acquiring four properties chargeable to LBTT (the other four properties are chargeable to SDLT) it is considered that the rule which states that where six or more dwellings are acquired as part of a single transaction the transaction is treated as the acquisition of non-residential property (*LBTT(S)A 2013, s 59(8)*) should not apply. Consequently, the LBTT additional rates on residential property will apply and the LBTT charge per dwelling is therefore calculated as follows:

Purchase Price	Rate	LBTT
£	%	£
145,000	4	5,800
105,000	6	6,300
75,000	9	6,750
225,000	14	31,500
550,000		50,350

Based on four dwellings, the LBTT charge would be £201,400 (4 × £50,350).

This is subject to the 'minimum prescribed amount' being 25% of the LBTT which would have been payable if multiple dwellings relief had not been available (see **2.14**).

If multiple dwellings relief had not been available, the LBTT charge would have been as follows:

Purchase price	Rate	LBTT
£	%	£
145,000	4	5,800
105,000	6	6,300
75,000	9	6,750
425,000	14	59,500
1,450,000	16	232,000
2,200,000		310,350

The minimum prescribed is therefore 25% × £310,350 = £77,587.

In this instance therefore the minimum prescribed amount does not apply and the LBTT payable is £201,400.

2.37 If a claim for SDLT multiple dwellings relief was made in relation to a transaction which included land in Scotland, the 'adjustment for change of circumstances' provisions in *FA 2003, Sch 6B, para 6* continue to apply to the transaction even if the event which triggers the adjustment occurs on or after 1 April 2015 (see para 12.2 of the HMRC guidance on the transition from SDLT to LBTT).

Group relief, reconstruction and acquisition reliefs (FA 2003, s 62 and Sch 7)

2.38 Where group relief, reconstruction relief or acquisition relief have been claimed in relation to a transaction within the SDLT regime, and the transaction included land situated in Scotland, the provisions relating to the withdrawal of the relevant relief will continue to apply even if the event giving rise to the withdrawal takes place on or after 1 April 2015 (see para 13.1 of the HMRC guidance on the transition from SDLT to LBTT).

Charities relief (FA 2003, s 68 and Sch 8)

2.39 Where charities relief has been claimed in relation to a transaction within the SDLT regime, and the transaction included land situated in Scotland, the provisions relating to the withdrawal of the relief will continue to apply even if the event giving rise to the withdrawal takes place on or after 1 April 2015 (see para 14.1 of the HMRC guidance on the transition from SDLT to LBTT).

Shared ownership leases (FA 2003, s 70 and Sch 9)

2.40 Where the grant of a shared ownership lease in relation to a dwelling located in Scotland was subject to SDLT (and a market value election has not been made), any 'staircasing transaction' following which the lessee does not hold a total share of the dwelling which exceeds 80% is exempt from the charge to SDLT (see para 15.1 of the HMRC guidance on the transition from SDLT to LBTT).

Any 'staircasing transaction' in relation to a dwelling situated in Scotland which takes the lessee's total share of the dwelling over 80%, or the acquisition of the ownership of the land, will be exempt from SDLT if the effective date of the transaction is on or after 1 April 2015 (see para 15.2 of the HMRC guidance on the transition from SDLT to LBTT).

Alternative property finance (FA 2003, s 72 and s 72A and LBTT(S)A 2013, Sch 7)

2.41 The *Scotland Act 2012, Sch 3, para 10* omits from the SDLT legislation *FA 2003, s 72* (alternative property finance in Scotland: land sold to financial institution and leased to person) and s *72A* (alternative property finance in Scotland: land sold to financial institution and person in common) with effect from 1 April 2015. As a consequence, if the effective date (*FA 2003, s 119*) of the third transaction (*s 72*) or further transaction (*s 72A*) under arrangements falling within those sections is on or after 1 April 2015, those transactions will be neither chargeable to SDLT nor notifiable for the purposes of SDLT (see para 16.1 of the HMRC guidance on the transition from SDLT to LBTT).

Alternative property finance relief is available under LBTT. The Scottish Government has ensured that a party entering into a land transaction in connection with an alternative property finance arrangement prior to 1 April 2015, in relation to land situated in Scotland, is not disadvantaged by the move from SDLT to LBTT, by making subordinate legislation providing that neither a third transaction under *FA 2003, s 72* nor a further transaction under *FA 2003, s 72A*, with an effective date on or after 1 April 2015, will be chargeable to LBTT, provided that the conditions mentioned respectively in *FA 2003 s 72(4)* and s *72A(4)* have been met (the *Land and Buildings Transaction Tax (Transitional Provisions) (Scotland) Order 2014, art 5 (SSI 2014/377)*).

Alternative finance investment bonds (FA 2009, Sch 61 and FA 2003, s 73C and LBTT(S)A 2013, Sch 8)

2.42 A land transaction in relation to land located in Scotland and which is a 'first transaction' within the meaning of *FA 2009, Sch 61, para 6* will be exempt from SDLT if the effective date (*FA 2003, s 119*) of the transaction is before 1 April 2015 and the conditions for the relief are satisfied. In such circumstances SDLT will become chargeable if the relief is withdrawn on or after 1 April 2015 under *FA 2009, Sch 61, para 7(3)* (see para 17.1 of the HMRC guidance on the transition from SDLT to LBTT).

A transaction which is a 'second transaction' for the purposes of *FA 2009, Sch 61, para 8* will be exempt from SDLT if the 'effective date' of the transaction is before 1 April 2015 and the conditions in para 8 are satisfied (see para 17.2 of the HMRC guidance on the transition from SDLT to LBTT).

In either case the transaction will not be subject to SDLT if the effective date (see **4.96**) is on or after 1 April 2015 (see para 17.3 of the HMRC guidance on the transition from SDLT to LBTT).

Relief for alternative finance investment bonds is also available under LBTT (*LBTT(S)A 2013, Sch 8*). The Scottish Government has ensured that a party entering into a land transaction in connection with an alternative finance investment bond prior to 1 April 2015, in relation to land situated in Scotland, is not disadvantaged by the move from SDLT to LBTT, by making subordinate legislation providing that the second transaction for the purposes of *FA 2009, Sch 61, para 8* with an effective date on or after 1 April 2015 will not be chargeable to LBTT provided that the conditions in *FA 2009, Sch 61, para 8(1)(a)* and *(b)* have been met (the *Land and Buildings Transaction Tax (Transitional Provisions) (Scotland) Order 2014, art 6 (SSI 2014/377)*).

Anti-avoidance (FA 2003, s 75A)

2.43 The general anti-avoidance provision within the SDLT legislation will only apply to a disposal and acquisition of land in Scotland if the effective date of the notional transaction (*FA 2003, s 75A(6)*) is before 1 April 2015 (see para 18.1 of the HMRC guidance on the transition from SDLT to LBTT).

The effective date of the 'notional transaction' is the earlier of:

(a) the last date of completion for the 'scheme transactions' (broadly the transactions which are involved in connection with the disposal and acquisition); and

(b) the last date on which a contract in respect of the 'scheme transactions' is substantially performed.

Later linked transactions (FA 2003, s 81A and s 108)

2.44 Where a land transaction in relation to land situated in Scotland has an effective date (*FA 2003, s 119*) before 1 April 2015 but it is not notifiable for SDLT purposes (*FA 2003, s 77*) and the transaction becomes notifiable on or after 1 April 2015 by reason of a later linked transaction (*FA 2003, s 108*), which does not relate to land in Scotland, the pre-1 April 2015 transaction remains chargeable to SDLT and a land transaction return must be filed in accordance with *FA 2003, s 81A* (see para 19.1 of the HMRC guidance on the transition from SDLT to LBTT). In these circumstances a paper SDLT1 form must be submitted to Birmingham Stamp Taxes notifying the pre-1 April 2015 transaction, with a covering letter (see SDLTM50350, para 3), and the effective date of the transaction is the effective date of the later linked transaction. Code 9998 should be entered in Box 29 of the SDLT1 form, and not a Scottish local authority code (see para 19.2 of the HMRC guidance on the transition from SDLT to LBTT).

If the pre-1 April 2015 transaction in relation to land situated in Scotland has been notified but SDLT, or more SDLT, becomes payable as a result of the post-1 April 2015 linked transaction in relation to land in England and Wales or Northern Ireland, then a further SDLT1 form must be submitted by letter to Birmingham Stamp Taxes in accordance with SDLTM50350, paras 1 and 2 (see para 19.3 of the HMRC guidance on the transition from SDLT to LBTT).

Partnerships (FA 2003, s 104 and Sch 15 and LBTT(S)A 2013, Sch 17)

2.45 *FA 2003, Sch 15, para 17* is an anti-avoidance provision which applies where land in the UK is contributed to a partnership by a partner, or a person who becomes a partner as a consequence of the contribution, or a person connected with a partner or a person who becomes a partner as a consequence of the contribution (which is not a 'property-investment partnership') and there is subsequently a transfer of an interest in that partnership under arrangements which were in place at the time the land was transferred to the partnership. *Paragraph 17* treats the transfer of the interest in the partnership as a land transaction chargeable to SDLT, whereas a transfer of an interest in a partnership, which is not a property-investment partnership, would not normally be chargeable to SDLT.

If, in these circumstances, the land transferred to the partnership includes land situated in Scotland, then to that extent the transfer of the interest in the partnership will not be subject to SDLT if the effective date of the transfer of the interest in the partnership is on or after 1 April 2015, even if the transfer of the land to the partnership took place before 1 April 2015 (see para 20.1 of the HMRC guidance on the transition from SDLT to LBTT).

However, the LBTT legislation includes a similar anti-avoidance provision, and the Scottish Government have made subordinate legislation to ensure that the transfer of the interest in the partnership will be chargeable to LBTT, even if the contribution of the land in Scotland took place prior to 1 April, 2015. Consequently, where the effective date of the land transfer referred to in *FA 2003, Sch 15, para 17(1)(a)* is before 1 April 2015 and the transfer of the interest in the partnership referred to in *FA 2003, Sch 15, para 17(1)(c)* is on or after 1 April 2015, the earlier land transfer will be treated for the purposes of *LBTT(S)A 2013, Sch 17, para 17* as though it were the land transfer referred to in *LBTT(S)A 2013, Sch 17, para 17(1)(a)*, such that the provisions of *LBTT(S)A 2013, Sch 17, para 17* will apply to the transfer of the partnership interest (the *Land and Buildings Transaction Tax (Transitional Provisions) (Scotland) Order 2014, art 7 (SSI 2014/377)*).

2.46 In certain circumstances, where land is transferred by a partner or a person who becomes a partner as a consequence of the contribution, or a person connected with a partner or a person who becomes a partner as a consequence of a contribution, to a partnership, and within three years of the land transfer the transferring partner withdraws money or money's worth from the partnership which does not represent income profit, or the partner (or a person connected with a partner) has made a loan to the partnership and that loan is to any extent repaid, or the partner withdraws money or money's worth which does not represent income profit, then a charge to SDLT can arise (*FA 2003, Sch 15, para 17A*).

Where the 'effective date' (*FA 2003, s 119*) of the later deemed land transaction (ie the date the money or money's worth is withdrawn or the loan is repaid) would be on or after 1 April 2015, the deemed land transaction will not be chargeable to SDLT, even if the transfer of land to the partnership took place before 1 April 2015. However, the Scottish Government has made subordinate legislation to ensure that such a deemed land transaction will be chargeable to LBTT.

The land transfer to the partnership which took place prior to 1 April 2015 will be treated for the purposes of *LBTT(S)A 2013, Sch 17, para 18* as if it were the land transfer mentioned in *LBTT(S)A 2013, Sch 17, para 18(1)* and the withdrawal of money or money's worth which does not represent income profit, or the repayment of the loan on or after 1 April 2015, will be treated as though it were a 'qualifying event' for the purposes of *LBTT(S)A 2013, Sch 17, para 18(2)* (the *Land and Buildings Transaction Tax (Transitional Provisions) (Scotland) Order 2014, art 8 (SSI 2014/377)*). As a consequence the provisions of *LBTT(S)A 2013, Sch 17, para 18* will apply.

LBTT(S)A 2013, Sch 17, paras 25 and *26* determine the partnership share attributable to a partner where an interest in land situated in Scotland is transferred from a partnership. It is provided that *paras 25* and *26* will have effect even though the relevant date for the purposes of *para 26(1)* is prior to 1 April 2015. However, any references to obligations to pay tax under *LBTT(S)A 2013*, shall have no effect (the *Land and Buildings Transaction Tax (Transitional Provisions) (Scotland) Order 2014, art 9 (SSI 2014/377)*).

Leases (FA 2003, s 120 and Sch 17A)

Leases that continue after a fixed term (FA 2003, Sch 17A, para 3 and LBTT(S)A 2013, Sch 19, para 20)

2.47 *FA 2003, Sch 17A, para 3* provides that where a lease continues beyond its fixed term, it is treated as a lease for the original fixed term plus one year longer than the original fixed term and so on. Where, as a consequence of the deemed extension of the lease, SDLT, or more SDLT, becomes payable, an SDLT land transaction return or further return must be filed within 30 days of the last day of the one-year period concerned (*FA 2003, Sch 17A, para 3(4)*).

Where the lease which is treated as continuing beyond its fixed term as described above was granted before 1 April 2015, and is a lease over land situated in Scotland, the lease remains subject to SDLT, even if the period for which the lease is treated as having been extended includes a period on or after 1 April 2015 (see para 21.1 of the HMRC guidance on the transition from SDLT to LBTT).

If the deemed extension of the lease on or after 1 April 2015 causes the lease to become notifiable for the first time, an SDLT1 form must be filed in the normal way (SDLTM12050, para 1), the effective date of the transaction is the last day of the one-year period giving rise to the notification requirement and code 9998, and not a Scottish local authority code, must be entered at Box 29.

If the grant of the lease has already been notified but the deemed extension of the lease causes additional SDLT to become payable, notification should be made by way of a letter to Birmingham Stamp Taxes (see SDLTM12050, para 2ff).

Leases for an indefinite term (FA 2003, Sch 17A, para 4)

2.48 A lease for an indefinite term (for example a lease for life – see SDLTM18715 or a lease the duration of which is subject only to a period of notice) is treated in the first instance as though it were a lease for a fixed term of one year and, if the lease continues beyond that first year it is treated as a lease for a fixed term of two years, and so on.

Where a lease of land in Scotland is for an indefinite term, and is granted before 1 April 2015, it will continue to be liable to SDLT even if its deemed term continues beyond 1 April 2015 (see para 21.2 of the HMRC guidance on the transition from SDLT to LBTT). In these circumstances the deemed extension of the lease will not be subject to LBTT.

Example 2.8—Lease for an indefinite term treated as granted before 1 May 2012

George enters into a verbal contract for a lease of an office in Glasgow at a market rate rent. The verbal contract is 'substantially performed' (see **4.9**) by the first payment of rent on 1 April 2012. *FA 2003, Sch 17A, para 19(3)* treats the verbal contract as the grant of a lease, beginning on the date of substantial performance.

The grant of the lease is within the SDLT regime and it remains within that regime after 1 April 2015 so long as it continues from year to year, and an SDLT land transaction return must be filed, or notification given, if SDLT becomes payable or additional tax becomes due (*FA 2003, Sch 17A, para 4*).

Successive linked leases (FA 2003, Sch 17A, para 5 and LBTT(S)A 2013, Sch 19, para 23)

2.49 Where successive leases are granted of the same premises, and the grants of the leases are linked for SDLT purposes, SDLT applies as though there was a single lease granted at the time the first lease in the series was granted, for a term equal to the aggregate of the terms of all of the leases in the series, and in consideration of the rent payable under all of the leases in the series (*FA 2003, Sch 17A, para 5*).

Any lease over land in Scotland, where the effective date of the grant of the lease is on or after 1 April 2015 cannot be treated as successive to a lease over the same premises granted before 1 April 2015, as the later lease is not a land transaction for SDLT purposes (*Scotland Act 2012, s 29(2) and (4)*). However, the grant of the lease on or after 1 April 2015 will be within the LBTT regime (see para 21.3 of the HMRC guidance on the transition from SDLT to LBTT).

Adjustment where rent ceases to be uncertain (FA 2003, Sch 17A, para 8)

2.50 Where the rent payable under a lease subject to SDLT is contingent, uncertain or unascertained *FA 2003, Sch 17A, para 8* provides for a reassessment of the SDLT chargeable on the lease to be made either:

(a) at the end of the fifth year of the term of the lease; or

(b) when the rent payable in respect of the first five years of the term of the lease ceases to be uncertain at an earlier date.

Where such a lease over land situated in Scotland is granted before 1 April 2015 and under the provision of *para 8*, SDLT, or more SDLT, becomes payable on or after 1 April 2015, the lease remains subject to SDLT. An SDLT1 form or further return, must be filed within 30 days of the end of the fifth year of the term of the lease or, if earlier, the date on which the amount of rent payable in the first five years ceases to be uncertain (see para 21.4 of the HMRC guidance on the transition from SDLT to LBTT).

If as a result the grant of the lease becomes notifiable for the first time, an SDLT1 form must be submitted in the usual way. The effective date of the transaction is the date prescribed by *FA 2003, Sch 17A, para 8(1)* and *(3)* and code 9998, and not a Scottish local authority code, must be entered at Box 29.

If the grant of the lease has already been notified but the effect of the reassessment of the SDLT payable is that additional tax becomes payable, notification should be made by letter to Birmingham Stamp Taxes – see SDLTM18525.

Overlap relief (FA 2003, Sch 17A, para 9 and LBTT(S)A 2013, Sch 19, para 24)

2.51 Both the SDLT and LBTT legislation give overlap relief (see **6.83**) where A surrenders (renounces) an existing lease (the old lease) to B and in consideration of that surrender (renunciation) B grants a lease to A (the new lease) of the same or substantially the same premises.

Where a lease of land in Scotland, which was granted before 1 April 2015, is renounced on or after that date and, as consideration for that renunciation, a new lease of the same or substantially the same premises is granted, the grant of the new lease will be within the LBTT regime, and will not be chargeable to SDLT (see para 21.5 of the HMRC guidance on the transition from SDLT to LBTT). The new lease will, however, be chargeable to LBTT.

To ensure that the party entering into the new lease is not disadvantaged by the move from SDLT to LBTT, the Scottish Government has made subordinate legislation which provides that where the old lease was granted before 1 April 2015, and the new lease is granted on or after 1 April 2015, the rent chargeable to LBTT on the grant of the new lease will be reduced by the rent which was charged to SDLT for the period of the overlap of the two leases (the *Land and Buildings Transaction Tax (Transitional Provisions) (Scotland) Order 2014, art 10 (SSI 2014/377)*).

Backdated leases granted to tenant holding over (FA 2003, Sch 17A, para 9A and LBTT(S)A 2013, Sch 19, para 21)

2.52 For SDLT purposes, where the tenant under a lease continues in occupation beyond the fixed term of the lease, the tenant is granted a new lease of the same premises, and the term of the lease is stated to begin immediately after the contractual termination date of the previous lease, the term of the new lease is treated as beginning on the stated date ie immediately following the termination of the previous lease.

Where the effective date of the grant of a new lease over land in Scotland, in circumstances where an earlier lease has continued beyond the fixed term, is on or after 1 April 2015, but the term of the new lease is stated to begin from the termination date of the previous lease, which date is before 1 April 2015, the new lease will not be subject to SDLT. However, the grant of the new lease over land in Scotland on or after 1 April 2015 will be within the LBTT regime (see para 21.6 of the HMRC guidance on the transition from SDLT to LBTT).

Assignment of a lease on or after 1 April 2015 where the lease was granted before 1 April 2015

2.53 Where a lease of land in Scotland was granted before 1 April 2015 and is assigned on or after 1 April 2015, the assignation is not chargeable to SDLT, but may be subject to LBTT if a premium is actually paid or deemed to be paid for the assignation (see para 21.7 of the HMRC guidance on the transition from SDLT to LBTT).

Assignment of lease treated as the grant of a new lease (FA 2003, Sch 17A, para 11 and LBTT(S)A 2013, Sch 19, para 27)

2.54 Both the SDLT and LBTT legislation provide that where the grant of a lease is exempt from the charge to the respective taxes because one of a number of specified reliefs is claimed, the first assignation of that lease which is not so exempt is taxed as though it were the grant of a new lease (see **6.17** et seq).

Where the lease of land in Scotland is granted before 1 April 2015, an assignation of the lease on or after 1 April 2015 will not be subject to SDLT and the provisions of *FA 2003, Sch 17A, para 11* will not apply to tax the assignation as though it were the grant of a new lease. However, the Scottish Government has made subordinate legislation to provide that where a lease of land in Scotland was granted before 1 April 2015 and it was relieved or exempt from SDLT as one of the reliefs specified in *FA 2003, Sch 17A, para 11* applied, the first assignment of that lease, if it takes place on or after 1 April 2015, which is not exempt from LBTT as none of the reliefs specified in *LBTT(S)A 2013, Sch 19, para 27(3)* apply, will be charged to LBTT as though it were the grant of a new lease (the *Land and Buildings Transaction Tax (Transitional Provisions) (Scotland) Order 2014, art 11 (SSI 2014/377)*).

Increases of rent treated as grant of a new lease (FA 2003, Sch 17A, para 13)

2.55 Under SDLT, where a lease is varied so as to increase the amount of the rent payable as from a date before the end of the fifth year of the lease, the variation is treated for SDLT purposes as if it were the grant of a new lease in consideration of the additional rent now payable (*FA 2003, Sch 17A, para 13*). This rule does not apply to any increase in the rent payable as a consequence of a provision within the lease.

A variation of a lease of land in Scotland falling within the above provision will not be treated as the grant of a new lease for SDLT purposes where the effective date of the grant of the deemed new lease would be on or after 1 April 2015 (see para 21.9 of the HMRC guidance on the transition from SDLT to LBTT).

However, the Scottish Government has made subordinate legislation providing that where the effective date of the grant of the deemed new lease would have been on or after 1 April 2015, had the provisions of *FA 2003, Sch 17A, para 13* continued to apply to the lease, that the increase of rent will be charged to LBTT as though it were the grant of a new lease and the chargeable consideration for LBTT purposes (other than in respect of any premium) will be the additional rent payable (the *Land and Buildings Transaction Tax (Transitional Provisions) (Scotland) Order 2014, art 12 (SSI 2014/377)*).

Missives of let (FA 2003, Sch 17A, para 19(2) and LBTT(S)A 2013, Sch 19, para 26)

2.56 *FA 2003, Sch 17A, para 19(2)* deals with the situation where a lease is initially constituted by concluded missives of let (the first lease) and at some later time a lease is executed (the second lease). The equivalent legislation within the LBTT regime is *LBTT(S)A 2013, Sch 19, para 26.*

Where the first lease is constituted by concluded missives of let before 1 April 2015, and the second lease is executed on or after that date, the provisions of *FA 2003, Sch 17A, para 19(2)* do not apply as the second lease is not subject to SDLT and cannot be linked with the first lease. However, the second lease will be subject to LBTT and *LBTT(S)A 2013, Sch 19, para 26* will apply to the second lease despite the fact that the first lease was constituted by concluded missives of let prior to 1 April 2015 (see para 21.10 of the HMRC guidance on the transition from SDLT to LBTT).

Extension of lease treated as grant of a new lease (FA 2003, s 43(3)(d)(i))

2.57 Where a lease of land in Scotland is granted prior to 1 April 2015, there is a variation of the lease on or after 1 April 2015 so as to increase the term of the lease or to extend the premises let (which under English property law is likely to be treated as the grant of a new lease) and, if that variation had taken place before 1 April 2015, it would have been treated as the grant of a new lease for SDLT purposes, then the variation of the lease is treated as the grant of a new lease for LBTT purposes. The consideration chargeable to LBTT, other than in respect of a premium, is the amount of the additional rent payable over the increased period of the lease or the additional rent payable in relation to the extended premises now let (the *Land and Buildings Transaction Tax (Transitional Provisions) (Scotland) Order 2014, art 13 (SSI 2014/377)*).

General anti-avoidance rule (RSTPA 2014, s 62)

2.58 The general anti-avoidance rule (GAAR – see **2.11**) applies in relation to any tax avoidance arrangement which is 'artificial' entered into on or after

1 April 2015 being the date on which the GAAR provisions came into effect. Currently the GAAR only applies to the devolved taxes being LBTT and Scottish landfill tax. Where the tax avoidance arrangement forms part of any other arrangements entered into before that date, those other arrangements are to be ignored unless taking account of those arrangements would mean that the arrangement would not be 'artificial' (*RSTPA 2014, s72(2)* and *(3)*).

The UK general anti-abuse rule found in *FA 2013, ss 206–215* will continue to apply to any land transaction within the SDLT regime but will not apply to any land transaction within the LBTT regime.

Chapter 3

Wales – Land Transaction Tax

INTRODUCTION

3.1 From 1 April 2018, land transaction tax (LTT) replaced stamp duty land tax (SDLT) in relation to all property transactions involving land in Wales. There are transitional rules to deal with some transactions that exchanged before 1 April 2018 and how holding over of leases charged to SDLT will be treated.

BACKGROUND

3.2 The *Wales Act 2014* provided for the devolution of SDLT and Landfill Tax from the UK Government in Westminster to the Welsh Government with effect from 1 April 2018. The devolution of SDLT meant that SDLT would cease to be collected in relation to land transactions in Wales and the funding provided by SDLT as at 31 March 2018 would be removed from the block grant paid by the UK Government to the Welsh Government. Welsh Government decided to introduce LTT as their own version of SDLT.

The LTT provisions are contained in the *Land Transaction Tax and Anti-avoidance of Devolved Taxes (Wales) Act 2017* (*LTTA 2017*). Welsh Government has established the Welsh Revenue Authority (WRA) to collect and administer LTT. The WRA is a non-ministerial department of Welsh Government. The administrative powers of the WRA are contained in the *Tax Collection and Management (Wales) Act 2016* (*TCM(W)A 2016*). Substantial guidance on the application of LTT is available on the WRA website (https://gov.wales/land-transaction-tax).

LTT – KEY CONCEPTS

3.3 LTT is a tax on transactions in land in Wales. The key objective of the legislation is to maintain tax revenues from SDLT so that there is no shortfall in Welsh Government funding and to prevent tax avoidance. The LTT legislation borrows heavily from the SDLT provisions contained in the *Finance Act 2003* and consequently many of the concepts of LTT are similar to SDLT.

A land transaction is the acquisition of a chargeable interest. It does not matter how the transaction is carried out or documented and the tax residence of the buyer is irrelevant. Therefore, a buyer of land in Wales living outside Wales will still be caught by the LTT legislation. The buyer (which can include the tenant on the grant of a lease and the landlord on a surrender of a lease or the reduction in the term of a lease), will be responsible for filing the LTT return paying LTT. LTT is a self-assessed tax and the buyer has to file the return and pay the LTT within 30 days of completion of the transaction. (*LTTA 2017, s 3*)

3.4 A 'chargeable interest' is an estate interest right or power in or over land in Wales. It also includes the benefit of an obligation, restriction or condition affecting the value of the land. Therefore, LTT will be payable on any payment made for the release of a restrictive covenant over land. (*LTTA 2017, s 47*)

LTT is not charged on exempt interests which include security interests, ie mortgages or charges, a licence to occupy, a tenancy at will and a franchise or manor. A franchise is the right to hold a market or fayre or the right to take tolls. A manor 'is a Lord or Ladyship of the manor'. Consequently, buying the right to call yourself the, say, Lord of Cardiff would not be subject to LTT. For lawyers dealing with property on the coast, land does not include land below the mean low water mark. (*LTTA 2017, s 5*)

3.5 'Transactions in land' includes the creation of the interest, the surrender or release of an interest and any variations of an interest in land. As with SDLT there are special rules involving lease transactions. (*LTTA 2017, s 6*)

A 'major interest in land' is defined as an estate in free simple absolute and a term of years absolute and will therefore cover both freehold and leasehold transactions. Market value imports a definition from *ss 272–274* of the *Taxation of Chargeable Gains Act 1992* and deems the transaction to be between a willing buyer and a willing seller. (*LTTA 2017, ss 68* and *70*)

3.6 The effective date for filing of LTT returns and payment of LTT will be completion, or substantial performance if earlier and the 30-day deadline will run from this date. At present, the Welsh Government have not announced any plans to reduce the filing deadline to 14 days (unlike the reduction of the filing deadline for SDLT to 14 days from 1 March 2019).

3.7 'Residential Property' is defined as any building that is used or is suitable for use as a dwelling, has been constructed or adapted for use as a dwelling and is extended to include land that forms part of a garden of the dwelling and any interest that exists for the benefit of the building or land, for example, the benefit of a restrictive covenant. In common with SDLT, a dwelling does not include a children's home, student halls of residence, care homes, hospitals or hospices, prisons or hotels or similar buildings. It is important to note that the LTT definition of residential property does not include the 'and' or 'or' linking the parts of the definition. This means that the sale of part of a garden will always be treated as residential property for LTT purposes even if it has been fenced off from the house. (*LTTA 2017, s 72*)

Any land that does not meet the definition of residential property is treated as non-residential property. In addition, the purchase of six or more dwellings in a single transaction may be treated as non-residential for LTT purposes. A dwelling is defined as a residential property comprising a single dwelling. This could be relevant for clients purchasing six or more flats or houses from a single developer. (*LTTA 2017, s 72(9)*)

The difference between residential and non-residential land is critically important in terms of the rates of LTT and the amount of tax payable. Any land that includes a mixture of residential and non-residential land is treated as a 'mixed' transaction and subject to the non-residential rates of LTT. In many cases it will be easy to determine what is residential or non-residential land. Difficulties may arise where the property is a large country house with extensive gardens and land. Would an area of woodland managed on a commercial basis turn the purchase into a mixed transaction and qualify for the non-residential rates of LTT? Provided there are existing contracts for the operation of the woodland and a clear intention of the buyer to continue the operation, a case can be made for paying LTT using the non-residential rates and bands.

The WRA published guidance on what would qualify as garden and grounds in LTTA Manual 1053. The use of the land at the time of the purchase is the key factor in reaching any decision; the intended use of the buyer is irrelevant. The WRA consider the following factors when deciding whether land is not gardens and grounds and therefore allows the application of the non-residential rates of LTT to apply to the whole purchase:

- Business activities on the land with the intention of making a profit rather than activities undertaken for pleasure, enjoyment or convenience. For example, a working sheep farm which sells meat and wool indicates business use, compared to a grazing licence so the owner does not have to mow the grass.
- Activities are undertaken on sound business principles including retention of full business/tax records.
- Activities undertaken had a reasonable prospect of profit and generating a reasonable income relative to the land.

- Activities are undertaken on the land with reasonable continuity.
- How the land is viewed by other public authorities. For example, qualification for non-domestic rates.
- Planning permission or other licences for business use of the land.

RATES AND BANDS OF LTT

3.8 The proposed rates and bands of LTT were announced in the Welsh Budget on 3 October 2017 and amended on 9 December 2017 following the introduction of the £300,000 first-time buyer SDLT exemption by the Chancellor in the Westminster Budget. No amendments to the rates or bands were made in the 2019 Autumn Budget by Welsh Government. The rates and bands of LTT are more progressive compared to SDLT so that buyers of higher value properties have a higher tax burden. The Welsh Government estimate that 60% of reportable LTT transactions will not pay LTT. LTT operates the progressive system (similar to how income tax is applied) so that each band of consideration is charged to LTT at the rate applicable to that particular band. The LTT rates and bands are set out in the *Land Transaction Tax (Tax Bands and Tax Rates (Wales) Regulations 2018* (*SI 2018/128*). The regulations refer to 'not more than' and 'more than' the relevant figure. Therefore, consideration of £180,000 will fall within the zero rate band for residential property. However, consideration of £180,001 would result in £1 falling within the 3.5% band.

Residential Property LTT rates	
Price Threshold	*LTT rate*
£0–£180,000	0%
£180,000–£250,000	3.5%
£250,000–£400,000	5%
£400,000–£750,000	7.5%
£750,000–£1.5m	10%
Over £1.5m	12%

Less LTT than SDLT will be payable on purchases up to £250,000 and the same amount on purchases between £250,000 and £400,000. Above £400,000 more LTT will be payable compared to SDLT. LTT does not have a higher first-time buyer threshold like the £300,000 threshold that applies to SDLT. Welsh Government estimate that 80% of first time buyers in Wales will not pay LTT.

3.9 The tables below show the difference between LTT and SDLT at different price points.

House purchase costing £230,000, replacement of existing residence so no additional LTT charge

LTT

Purchase Price	*Rate*	*LTT*
£	%	£
180,000	0	NIL
50,000	3.5	1,750
230,000		1,750

SDLT

Purchase Price	*Rate*	*SDLT*
£	%	£
125,000	0	NIL
105,000	2	2,100
230,000		2,100

House purchase costing £600,000, replacement of existing residence so no additional charge

LTT

Purchase Price	*Rate*	*LTT*
£	%	£
180,000	0	NIL
70,000	3.5	2,450
150,000	5	7,500
200,000	7.5	15,000
600,000		24,950

SDLT

Purchase Price	*Rate*	*SDLT*
£	%	£
125,000	0	NIL
125,000	2	2,500
350,000	5	17,500
600,000		20,000

3.10 *Wales – Land Transaction Tax*

3.10 In relation to the purchase of additional residential properties (and the purchase of residential properties by companies and non-natural persons), an additional 3% LTT charge will apply so the rates and bands are:

Additional Residential Property LTT rates	
Price Threshold	*LTT rate*
£0–£40,000	No return required
£0–£180,000	3%
£180,000–£250,000	6.5%
£250,000–£400,000	8%
£400,000–£750,000	10.5%
£750,000–£1.5m	13%
Over £1.5m	15%

It is important to note that the £0 to £40,000 band is not a zero-rate threshold. Rather, any property purchased for less than £40,000 will not be subject to LTT and an LTT return will not be required to be filed with the WRA.

3.11 There is no separate 'super rate' of LTT in relation to the purchase of residential properties by companies in Wales. Therefore, the 15% rate of SDLT that applies to the purchase of residential properties costing more than £500,000 has not been replicated for LTT. The annual tax on enveloped dwellings can still apply to residential properties in Wales if the relevant conditions are satisfied. Please refer to the commentary at **2.70** et seq regarding the 15% rate of SDLT and **2.77** et seq regarding ATED.

Commercial property (any property that is not residential property) and mixed property purchases will be subject to different LTT bands and rates

Commercial Property LTT rates	
Price Threshold	*LTT rate*
£0–£150,000	0%
£150,000–£250,000	1%
£250,000–£1m	5%
Over £1m	6%

3.12 The differences between LTT and SDLT should be noted. The 1% rate of LTT means that less LTT compared to SDLT will be payable on transactions with a value below £1.1m. Transactions up to £1m in value will save up to £1,000 when paying LTT compared to SDLT. However, high value transactions above £1.1 million will pay more LTT compared to SDLT.

Commercial property purchase costing £5,000,000

LTT

Purchase Price	*Rate*	*LTT*
£	%	£
150,000	0	NIL
100,000	1	1,000
750,000	5	37,500
4,000,000	6	240,000
5,000,000		278,500

SDLT

Purchase Price	*Rate*	*SDLT*
£	%	£
150,000	0	NIL
100,000	2	2,000
4,750,000	5	237,500
5,000,000		239,500

In relation to commercial property leases, the rates of LTT are:

Commercial Property Leases LTT rates	
NPV Threshold	LTT rate
£0–£150,000	0%
£150,000–£2m	1%
Over £2m	2%

The difference from SDLT should be noted as the 2% band applies to the Net Present Value above £5m for SDLT rather than £2m with LTT. The Welsh Government estimated that there would be less than 100 commercial lease transactions attracting the 2% LTT rate in 2018/19. It is important to note that no LTT is charged on any rent payable under residential leases (*LTTA 2017, Sch 6, para 27*: see **3.37**).

EXEMPT TRANSACTIONS

3.13 Exempt transactions are transactions that are not subject to LTT and include:

(1) Gifts, ie transfers for no consideration (subject to the deemed market value rule that applies to transfers to connected companies referred to below).

(2) Transactions involving national governments in the UK including the Welsh Assembly Government.

(3) Transfers of land in connection with a divorce or civil partnership dissolution where the transfer is carried out as a result of a court order or a separation order.

(4) Inheritances whether under a will or intestacy. The exemption would also include transfers carried out within the two years of the date of death under a deed of variation.

(*LTTA 2017, Sch 3*)

In the case of an acquisition under a will or intestacy the exemption does not apply to the extent that a payment is made for the transfer, ie an equalisation payment. However, the assumption of secured debt does not prejudice the exemption provided the debt was secured on the property immediately after the death of the deceased person. This means that payment of equality money on inheriting a property under a will could trigger a payment of LTT. However, inheriting a property subject to a mortgage or loan which is taken on by the beneficiary will not trigger an LTT liability.

DEEMED MARKET VALUE

3.14 A transaction will be treated as occurring at deemed market value (*LLTA 2017, s 22*) where the buyer is a company and:

(1) the seller is connected with the buyer; or

(2) some or all of the consideration for the transaction consists of the issue or transfer of shares in a company with which the seller is connected.

The deemed market value rule disapplies the exemption for transactions where there is no chargeable consideration, ie if the transfer to a connected company is by way of gift, the deemed market value rule will apply.

The deemed market value rules will not apply where:

(1) the buyer holds the land as trustee in the course of the business consisting of the management of trusts;

(2) the buyer holds the land as a trustee and is not connected to the seller except in relation to the trustee position; or

(3) the seller is carrying out the transaction as a result of the distribution of the assets of the company (including a distribution on liquidation) and the seller has not claimed group relief in relation to the land in the three years before the transaction.

The WRA LTT partnership guidance confirms that the partnership provisions in *LTTA 2017, Sch 7, paras 21* and *22 (*transfer of land from a partnership*)* will override the deemed market value rule in *LTTA 2017, s 22* where land is transferred out of a partnership and the partners in that partnership are individuals who are connected with the purchaser which is a company (LTTA/5170).

CONSIDERATION

3.15 The definition of consideration (*LTTA 2017, Sch 4*) is very wide-ranging and includes the following:

(1) Money and money's worth. This will include any fees payable by the seller but which are paid by the buyer as part of the transaction. For example, if a tenant pays the landlord's costs on an extension or variation of a lease, these costs will be treated as chargeable consideration (*LTTA 2017, Sch 4, para 1*).

(2) Any VAT charged on the transaction due to an option to tax or otherwise (perhaps a new commercial building or other automatic standard rated supplies of land in Schedule 9 VAT Act 1994). The making of an option to tax after the effective date of the transaction will not require the filing of an amended LTT return or payment of additional LTT. Any changes in rates of VAT will not count as a contingent event (*LTTA 2017*, Sch 4, para 2).

(3) Any consideration that is postponed or is contingent. Any consideration that is payable in instalments must be included in the consideration for LTT purposes. In the case of a contingent event, it is assumed that the contingency will be satisfied for the purposes of calculating LTT (*LTTA 2017, Sch 4, para 3*).

(4) Exchanges. Each part of an exchange is treated as a separate transaction for LTT purposes with LTT being charged on the market value of the land being acquired plus any equality monies that is being paid (*LTTA 2017, Sch 4, para 5*).

(5) The acceptance or assumption of any debt in relation to the land being acquired (*LTTA 2017, Sch 4, para 8*).

(6) Any consideration given in a foreign currency would be converted into sterling based on the currency exchange rate at the close of business on the day of completion (*LTTA 2017, Sch 4, para 10*).

(7) Carrying out of works on the land will be treated as chargeable consideration based on the open market value of the works carried out. Works will not be treated as chargeable consideration if:

    (a) the works are carried out on land that was the subject matter of the transaction or other land already owned by the buyer;

(b) the works are carried out after the effective date of the transaction; and

(c) it is not a condition of the land transaction that the works are being carried out by the seller or a person connected with the seller.

The carrying out of the works definition will mean that advisers will still have the difficulty of deciding whether or not it is possible to draft documentation for a developer to sell land and complete the building work on the development as wholly separate transactions. The WRA have indicated in their guidance that the WRA will apply the decision in *Prudential Assurance Co Ltd v IRC* [1992] STC863 for the purposes of LTT. This means that where the two contracts (the sale of the land and the construction work) are not commercially interdependent it will be possible to apply a just and reasonable apportionment of the consideration between the two elements. Commentary regarding the approach to the carrying out of works for SDLT is found at **2.26** and Examples 2.6 and 2.7.

If the agreement for the sale of the land is so interlocked with the construction contract so that neither contract is capable of independent completion, then the consideration for the purchase of the land will include the value of the construction works (*LTTA 2017, Sch 4, para 11*).

(8) Provision of services by the buyer to the seller, with the consideration being the open market value of the services (including VAT) (*LTTA 2017, Sch 4, para 12*).

(9) The provision of employment benefits e.g. if an employee lives in employment related accommodation they will be treated as paying rent of an amount equal to the cash equivalent chargeable for the rent (*LTTA 2017, Sch 4, para 13*).

3.16 The following items will not be treated as a consideration:

(1) An indemnity provided to the seller by the buyer (*LTTA 2017, Sch 4, para 14*).

(2) A buyer agreeing to pay tax in relation to inheritance tax and capital gains tax in relation to the land (*LTTA 2017, Sch 4, paras 15* and *16*).

(3) Costs paid by the buyer in relation to enfranchisement, ie the buyer paying the landlord's costs as part of buying the freehold of a residential leasehold (*LTTA 2017, Sch 4, para 17*).

In relation to leases the obligations of a tenant to comply with a covenant of the lease are not treated as chargeable consideration and the same rule applies where a lease is assigned (*LTTA 2017, Sch 6, paras 16* and *18*).

SUB SALES

3.17 Understandably there was a huge concern within the Welsh Government about sub sales being used for tax avoidance purposes. In the consultation exercise during the development of LTT the Welsh Government was made aware of the commercial importance of sub sales and that they can form part of genuine property transactions. The LTT provisions copy the revised approach taken for SDLT in *FA 2003, Sch 2A* (see **3.11** et seq where the SDLT sub-sale legislation is considered) which appear to have stopped the schemes that utilised sub sales as a method of avoiding SDLT. The Welsh Government did not follow the restricted approach to sub sales implemented by the Scottish Government for LBTT (see **1A.6** where LBTT sub-sale development relief is considered).

The sub sale rules apply to transfers to third parties and the transfer of rights. In order to fall within the exemptions for sub sales there must be simultaneous completion of the transactions and no substantial performance by a buyer before a sale on to a subsequent buyer. The final buyer in a chain of sub sales is responsible for payment of LTT.

The LTT sub sale provisions are complicated and extensive. Any advisers with clients undertaking sub sales should read provisions for LTT in relation to sub sales in detail. That said, any 'standard' sub sale where there is no tax avoidance motive should be able to claim the relevant relief from LTT.

Any client or adviser seeking to use the sub sale rules for LTT avoidance purposes should be very wary particularly with the new anti-avoidance rules that apply to LTT.

(*LTTA 2017, ss 11–13* and *Sch 2*)

SUBSTANTIAL PERFORMANCE

3.18 Substantial performance will trigger the 30-day time limit for payment of LTT and the filing of the return where substantial performance occurs before completion of the transaction. Substantial performance will be triggered by either:

(1) possession of the whole or substantially the whole of the land being taken; or

(2) a substantial amount of the consideration being paid.

The WRA Manuals confirm that a similar threshold to the 90% threshold applied by HMRC to the consideration for SDLT will be applied by the WRA.

(*LTTA 2017, s 14* and LTTA Manual 2150)

In relation to LTT it should be noted that the type of possession does not matter, so fit out under a licence will trigger a substantial performance of a lease. The first payment of rent can also be a trigger point for payment of the consideration under a lease.

EXCHANGES

3.19 In an exchange of land, both sides of the transaction are treated as separate transactions for LTT purposes. Both land transactions require an LTT return and payment of LTT to be considered based on the market value of the land and any equality money being paid.

For example, on exchange of The Barn valued at £350,000 in return for the transfer of No 1 High Lane, valued at £250,000 plus £100,000, equality money will result in the buyer of The Barn paying LTT on £350,000 and the buyer of No 1 High Lane paying LTT on £250,000.

If one buyer has paid more than market value for the land, perhaps because it was a special purchase, LTT is payable on the lower market value rather than the actual consideration paid. However, if VAT has been charged on the actual consideration, LTT is paid on the VAT calculated by reference to the actual consideration and not the lower market value (*LTTA 2017, s 16*).

LTT RETURNS

3.20 As has been noted above, LTT is operated by the WRA, which implemented a new computer system, together with new online forms and payment facilities.

The LTT return is the buyer or tenant's responsibility (or landlord in the case of a surrender of a lease or a variation to reduce the term of a lease) and there is a 30-day filing deadline. As has been noted the effective date and therefore the trigger point for the payment of LTT and the filing of the return is completion of the transaction or earlier substantial performance. Online filing and payment is encouraged although paper returns are available from the WRA (*LTTA 2017, s 44*).

Where there are joint buyers, the obligations of the buyers are joint although one buyer can discharge those obligations. The liability to pay LTT is joint and several. A single return is required in relation to a joint purchase, but all buyers must make the declaration regarding the accuracy of the LTT return.

To file a LTT return, the solicitor's firm or conveyancer must be registered with the WRA. Each firm has its own registration with the WRA and each fee earner is able to have an individual login under the firm's registration. At present, any joiners and leavers of an agent's firm must be notified to the WRA which will amend the login credentials.

3.21 Penalties for failing to make a return are set out in *TCM(W)A 2016*. The initial penalty for failing to make a return is £100. Further penalties for late returns apply with a £300 penalty if the return is more than six months beyond the filing date (or 5% of the amount of the LTT if greater). If the LTT return is more than 12 months late and there has been deliberate withholding of information from WRA the penalty is the greater of 100% of the amount of the LTT due and £300. If there has been no deliberate withholding of information, the 12-month penalty is the greater of 5% of the LTT due and £300.

There are also penalties for failing to pay the LTT on time. If the LTT is paid late, ie not within the 30-day period, a penalty of 5% of the LTT is due. If the LTT is paid more than six months late, a further penalty of 5% of the LTT is payable. If the LTT is more than 12 months late an additional penalty of 5% of the LTT is payable.

Interest is also charged on the LTT due and the penalties. The rate of interest is set out in regulations made by Welsh Ministers (*TCM(W)A 2016, s 163(1)*). *Regulation 6* of the *Tax Collection and Management (Administration) (Wales) Regulations 2017* (*SI 2017/1022*) sets the interest rate at 2.5% above the Bank of England base rate.

The first reported LTT case involving the WRA concerned a late filing penalty in Winfield v Welsh Revenue Authority [2020] UKFTT 3(TC). Judge John Brooks found that the appellant was unable to appeal the penalty as she was outside the time limit for filing the appeal. In addition, Brooks J decided that, even if the appeal was within time, he would have found against the appellant. This decision was on the basis that reliance on a third party (the appellant's solicitor in this case) to file the LTT return is not a reasonable excuse as the appellant had not taken reasonable care to avoid the failure (see *TCM(W)A 2016, s126*). The case is specific to its facts although the decision highlights the need to comply with any time limits and that a LTT return can be required even when no LTT is payable.

DECLARATION ON LTT RETURNS

3.22 A LTT return must include a declaration by the buyer that the return is correct and complete to the best of the buyer's knowledge and belief. The buyer is also required to declare that they have read the WRA's privacy policy.

If an agent is filing the electronic return on behalf of their client, the agent is required to have given the buyer a copy of the WRA's privacy notice.

If the buyer has approved the effective date of the transaction, ie completion (or earlier substantial performance), the buyer is required to declare to their agent that the information in the return is correct and complete to the best of their knowledge and belief. The agent has to confirm that they have the authority to deal with all matters relating to the transaction on behalf of their clients and submit the return on behalf of their clients.

If the buyer has not approved the effective date of the transaction, perhaps because completion was unknown when the draft LTT return was approved, the agent must have authority from their client to enter the effective date and submit the return. The buyer still has to approve the return and confirm that the information (other than the completion date) is correct and complete to the best of their knowledge and belief.

From a practical point of view, agents will have to ensure that clients are sent the WRA's Privacy Policy in hard copy or electronic format. The draft LTT return must also be sent to the client for approval and either written approval or a note of any verbal approval retained on the file (written approval is preferable).

NOTIFIABLE TRANSACTIONS

3.23 Transactions that have to be notified to the WRA include:

(1) the acquisition of the major interests in land, ie the freehold or leasehold interest;

(2) the acquisition of a chargeable interest in land, for example, a leasehold interest, provided that the interest is not exempt and that tax would be charged at more than 0% (but for a relief). What this means is that if a transaction would have been subject to LTT except for the availability of a relief, an LTT return is required;

(3) substantial performance of a sub sale; and

(4) certain notional transactions which are linked to the sub sale anti-avoidance rule.

(*LTTA 2017, s 45*)

There are a number of exceptions from the filing requirement which include:

(1) the exempt transactions, for example, gifts, transfers on divorce and death;

(2) freehold transaction where the consideration is under £40,000;

(3) the grant of a lease for a term of under seven years where the consideration was less than the zero-rate threshold;

(4) a lease assignment or surrender where the original term of the lease was for less than seven years and the consideration is less than the zero-rate threshold;

(5) a lease granted for a term of seven years or more where the premium is less than £40,000 and the rent is less than £1,000 per annum; and

(6) a lease assignment or surrender where the original term was for seven years or more and the consideration is less than £40,000.

(*LTTA 2017, s 46*)

It should be noted that a LTT return must be filed if the availability of a relief makes the transaction exempt (by relieving the transaction from LTT). For example, the purchase of a property by a charity, where the consideration is greater than £40,000 and charities relief is available, will require an LTT return to be filed even though no LTT will be due.

CONTINGENT AND UNASCERTAINED CONSIDERATION

3.24 Where consideration is contingent it is therefore subject to a condition being satisfied in the future. For LTT purposes, it is assumed that the contingency will be satisfied, and that the consideration will be payable in full. The LTT return and LTT calculation would be based on the maximum amount of the consideration payable.

Where the consideration is uncertain or unascertained at the time of completion, the buyer is required to make a reasonable estimate of the consideration and file the LTT return accordingly. Advisors may wish to consider obtaining a valuation report from a land agent or surveyor to support any claim for a reasonable estimate (*LTTA 2017, s 47*).

Where the contingency has been satisfied a further LTT return will be required if additional LTT is payable. The return and payment of any additional LTT must be made within 30 days of the contingency having been satisfied. If LTT has been overpaid it is possible to make a claim for repayment of the LTT provided that time limits are complied with. The provisions of *TCM(W)A 2016, s 78* require a claim to be made within four years of the LTT filing date for the transaction (*LTTA 2017, s 48*).

PAYMENT OF LTT

3.25 The general rule is that payment of LTT must be made no later than the filing date for the LTT return. Interest and penalties can be charged on LTT paid late.

In the case of contingent or uncertain consideration it is possible to make an application to the WRA for deferral of payment of the LTT. The application must contain a calculation of the LTT and is only permitted where the contingent or uncertain consideration is payable at least six months in the future. Deferral of payment of LTT is not available for the payment of deferred consideration. Fundamentally, the transaction must not include tax avoidance arrangements. If the request does not conform to the conditions the WRA must refuse a request for deferment; there is no discretion. See guidance in LTTA Manuals 6160 et seq.

For example, the purchase of land for four equal instalments of £1m (paid at six monthly intervals) will require LTT to be paid on the whole £4m consideration within 30 days of completion (or earlier substantial performance). Deferral of LTT will not be possible because the consideration is certain.

However, if £500,000 was payable on completion and three further payments were payable at six monthly intervals based on the number of houses constructed, it would be possible to claim deferral of LTT on the three future payments because the consideration is contingent (and uncertain). LTT would be payable and a further return filed when each instalment became certain (*LTTA 2017, s 58*).

REGISTRATION OF LAND TRANSACTIONS

3.26 The LTT legislation makes it clear that no registration of a land transaction will be possible without a WRA certificate. The WRA will issue a certificate following receipt of a correctly completed LTT return payment of the LTT. The issue of a certificate is not confirmation that the LTT return is correct or that the correct amount of LTT has been paid. However, the certificate requirement does not apply where chargeable interests are not acquired by the buyer (*LTTA 2017, s 65* and LTTA Manual 6240).

LEASES

3.27 The provisions relating to leases follow the SDLT legislation to a large extent but with a couple of differences (see Chapter 4 which deals with leases and SDLT) (*LTTA 2017, s 32* and *Sch 6*).

Fixed term and holding over

3.28 Leases for a fixed term are straightforward in relation to the initial return. If a fixed lease is held over (in other words, the tenant continues in occupation and to pay the rent after the expiry of the term of the original lease, usually while details of a new lease are negotiated with the landlord), then a further LTT return is required after one year of holding over with a return being filed on the basis of the original fixed term plus one year. The same process occurs if the lease is held over for two years and so on. If a new lease is granted and the grant occurs within the first year of holding over, the new lease is deemed to start at the end of the old term. The 30-day time limit for filing the LTT return will start at the end of the first year of holding over where the lease is held over for at least one year. If the lease is terminated during the one-year period (or any subsequent period) a LTT return is required to be filed within 30 days of the date of the termination of the lease with additional LTT being paid for the part year of the held over lease (*LTTA 2017, Sch 6, paras 2, 3* and *4*).

Indefinite term

3.29 Leases with an indefinite term are treated as a lease of one year for LTT purposes. For the exceptions to the filing rules, a lease with an indefinite term is treated as a lease of less than seven years (*LTTA 2017, Sch 6, para 5*).

Successive linked leases

3.30 (See **4.76** which considers SDLT and successive linked leases.)

Successive linked leases are treated as a single lease for the aggregate of the terms of each lease. The lease must involve the same or substantially the same premises. The LTTA Manual 4040 state that where a lease is renewed on arm's length terms, then that lease will not normally be treated as linked for these purposes. The WRA will look at the commercial reality and apply the successive link to the leases legislation where a single, longer lease would have been agreed from the outset of the original lease.

A linked transaction involves a number of land transactions that are either a single scheme, an arrangement or series of transactions and have been made between the same seller and buyer or connected person (*LTTA 2017, Sch 6, para 6*).

Overlap relief

3.31 Overlap relief for LTT is available where there is a surrender and re grant of the same or substantially the same premises. Overlap relief is granted by reducing the rent for the purposes of calculating LTT for the overlapped period although the reduction cannot be greater than zero. Overlap relief is also available when a lease has been held over, LTT paid for the held over period and a new lease is granted with the new lease being back dated to commence within the held over period. For example, a LTT lease is granted on 1 January 2019 for two years. The lease is held over from 1 January 2021. A LTT return is submitted on 20 January 2022 for the first held over year. A new lease is granted on 30 March 2022 and the term is deemed to start on 1 January 2021. Overlap relief will be available for the period 1 January to 31 December 2021. There are special rules for overlap relief involving SDLT leases contained within the transitional rules published on 31 January 2018 and contained in the *Land Transaction Tax (Transitional Provisions) (Wales) Regulations 2018* (*SI 2018/126*) (*LTTA 2017, Sch 6, para 7*).

Rent and variations

3.32 Rent does not include any payment made before the grant of the lease, these payments will be treated as a premium. If there is a variation of the rent in the first five years of the lease, then a new LTT return will be required. Rent reviews are ignored after the first five years and in the final quarter of the fifth year. The rent review rules do not apply if the variation is under the original terms of the lease or by virtue of specified statutory rules primarily relating to agricultural holdings (*LTTA 2017, Sch 6, paras 9–11*).

Reverse premiums

3.33 Reverse premiums do not count as consideration. As a reminder, a reverse premium includes:

(1) on the grant of the lease, a payment from the landlord to the tenant;

(2) on an assignment of a lease, a payment from the old tenant to the new tenant; and

(3) on a surrender of the lease a payment from the tenant to the landlord to accept the surrender of an onerous lease.

(*LTTA 2017, Sch 6, para 15*)

Other lease provisions

3.34 An agreement for lease will not trigger LTT. However, if the lease is substantially performed before completion or formal grant, LTT will be triggered (*LTTA 2017, Sch 6, para 20*).

The tenant's obligations contained in the lease will not count as chargeable consideration nor will the surrender of an existing lease be treated as consideration for grant of a new lease. If a loan or deposit is paid in relation to a grant or assignment of a lease, that payment is not treated as rent and therefore it is treated as a premium payable on the grant of the lease (*LTTA 2017, Sch 6, paras 16* and *19*).

On an assignment of a lease which is not exempt from LTT, and the original lease had been subject to a relief, the assignment will be treated as a grant of a new lease and LTT payable accordingly. For example, if group relief was claimed on the grant of a lease, and the lease is then assigned and no LTT relief is available, the assignment will be treated as the grant of a new lease (*LTTA 2017, Sch 6, para 22*).

Transitional rules for leases

3.35 (See the *Land Transaction Tax (Transitional Provisions) (Wales) Regulations 2018* (*SI 2018/126*)).

Where a SDLT lease is held over after 1 April 2018 no LTT should apply to the held over period. SDLT will be payable as the effective date of the lease is before 1 April 2018. Where a new lease is granted during the held over period, hold over relief may be claimed for the hold over period. The new lease will be subject to LTT.

Where a SDLT lease is subject to a surrender and re-grant after 1 April 2018, the new lease will be subject to LTT but overlap relief can be claimed for the rent subject in the overlapped period that was subject to SDLT.

Calculating Net Present Value

3.36 The Net Present Value (NPV) calculations for LTT are the same as for SDLT with the temporal discount rate at 3.5%. NPV is calculated using the following formula:

$$\sum_{i=1}^{n} \frac{r_i}{(1+T)^i}$$

where:

- r_i is the rent payable in respect of year i;
- i is the first, second, third etc year of the term of the lease;
- n is the term of the lease; and
- T is the temporal discount rate.

In basic terms, the following formula applies:

$$\frac{\text{Rent for the year of the lease}}{[1.035]^i}$$

where i = the year of the lease.

Therefore, for the rent in the third year of the lease, the rent will be divided by 1.035^3 to give part of the net present value. The result of the formula for each year of the lease will be added up to give the total net present value. The appropriate rate of LTT will be applied to the NPV figure (after taking account of the nil rate band) to calculate the amount of LTT.

One anti-avoidance trap for leases to watch out for involves rent and the payment of a premium for non-residential land. If the rent equals or exceeds what is defined as the 'specified amount' no zero-rate band will apply to the premium element of the consideration. Regulations published in January 2018 stated that the 'specified amount' will be £9,000. Therefore, if the rent is at least £9,000 pa, no zero-rate band will apply to any premium payable on the grant of the lease and the next (higher) rates of LTT will apply. The provision is designed to prevent tax avoidance by manipulating the rent and premiums to avoid LTT. For example, a lease over non-residential property is granted for a term of 10 years at a rent of £10,000 per annum and a premium of £100,000. Without the anti-avoidance rule, no LTT will be payable. Due to the anti-avoidance rule, LTT will be charged on the £100,000 premium at 1%.

Residential leases

3.37 In the case of residential leases, no LTT will be charged on the rental element. The Welsh Government has retained the power to amend the legislation if these provisions are abused, for example, charging a very large rent over a short period of time rather than a premium on the assignment of a long lease (*LTTA 2017, s 27*).

Where a lease consists of mixed property ie residential and non-residential property, such as a shop with a flat above, it is necessary to look at the main subject matter of the lease to determine whether the transaction should be residential or non-residential. If the transaction is a true mixed lease it is necessary to apportion the consideration between the two types of property.

RELIEFS

3.38 The schedules to *LTTA 2017* contain a large number of reliefs including:

- group relief (*LTTA 2017, Sch 16*) (**3.23** et seq);
- charities (*LTTA 2017, Sch 18*) (**3.66** et seq);
- sale and lease back (*LTTA 2017, Sch 9*) (**3.40** et seq);
- alternative property finance (*LTTA 2017, Sch 10*) (**3.37** et seq);
- incorporation of LLPs (*LTTA 2017, Sch 12*) (**3.23**);
- multiple dwellings (*LTTA 2017, Sch 13*) (**3.65** et seq);
- public bodies/health bodies (*LTTA 2017, Sch 20*) (**3.17** et seq);
- compulsory purchase/planning obligations (*LTTA 2017, Sch 21*);
- reconstructions and acquisitions (*LTTA 2017, Sch 17*) (**3.26** and **3.27**);
- social housing (*LTTA 2017, Sch 15*).

There are also a number of additional reliefs relating to open-ended investment companies and other specific situations. Set out below are the reliefs that are more likely to arise in practice.

Group relief

3.39 Group relief applies where a land transaction involves companies within a corporate group where there is at least a 75% interest between the two companies involved or they are both owned by the same parent company. The purchaser cannot be planning to leave the group and a three-year claw back applies if the purchaser leaves the group whilst holding the property that had been transferred subject to group relief. The provisions contain detailed anti-avoidance provisions and certain exceptions for when the purchaser leaves a group due to liquidations or other receivership type situations. Group relief has to be claimed on the LTT return and great care should be taken to ensure that the transaction falls within the legislative provisions (*LTTA 2017, Sch 16*).

Charities

3.40 Charities may claim relief from LTT where the property is going to be used for charitable purposes, either direct use of the property by the charity or another charity or the profits from the investment, ie rent from the land, is used by the charity to further its charitable purposes. A three-year claw back period applies if the property ceases to satisfy the charitable use of requirements or if arrangements were made within the three-year period for the charitable use condition to fail.

If a charity is jointly purchasing a property as tenants in common with a buyer which is not a charity, it is possible to claim partial charities relief from LTT by carrying out a just and reasonable apportionment of the consideration (*LTTA 2017, Sch 18*).

Sale and lease back

3.41 The leaseback element of a sale and lease back arrangement will not be subject to LTT provided certain conditions are satisfied. The purchaser of a major interest will be subject to LTT. The transaction must include the sale by A to B of a major interest in land and the grant by B of a lease out of that interest to A. The only consideration (other than the lease back) can be the payment of money or the assumption, satisfaction or release of a debt (or both). If A and B are companies, they cannot be members of the same group as the transaction would then be relieved under group relief (and subject to the three-year claw back rule) (*LTTA 2017, Sch 9*).

Multiple dwellings relief

3.42 Multiple dwellings relief is available where at least two dwellings are being purchased as part of the series of transactions or the same transaction. Multiple dwellings relief allows the averaging of the prices between the various dwellings for the purposes of LTT. The averaging cannot result in an LTT rate of less than 1%. Therefore, this avoids the averaging taking the average price of each dwelling below the zero-rate threshold.

The LTT legislation suggests that when six or more residential properties are purchased in the same transaction between the same seller and buyer, the transaction will be treated as a non-residential transaction for LTT. However, the WRA guidance makes it clear that the buyer has a choice between claiming multiple dwellings relief and non-residential rates of LTT on the basis that *LTTA 2017, Sch 13, para 5(1)* refers to 'If relief … is claimed' (*LTTA 2017, Sch 13*).

Multiple dwellings relief: Example.

A claim for multiple dwellings relief can have a dramatic effect on the amount of LTT charged on a transaction as the following example illustrates:

Purchase of a substantial house with two hectares of land and three cottages run as a holiday lets business. Total consideration of £1,080,000. If the whole transaction was treated as an acquisition of a single residence, the LTT charge would be £69,200.

The existence of the holiday cottages goes not turn the transaction into a mixed use transaction. Holiday cottages are still treated as a dwelling even if there is a planning restriction on the use of the cottages (WRA guidance at LTTA/8050). It would be a different matter if the holiday cottages were commercial units such as workshops or offices. LTT on a mixed use transaction would be £43,300.

Multiple dwellings relief provides a real LTT saving although there is a major trap to avoid. The trap is the 3% surcharge on the acquisition of additional residential dwellings. The 3% surcharge can apply to the purchase of more than one dwelling at the same time even if one of the dwellings will be a replacement of a main residence. There is an exception where a dwelling is subsidiary to the main dwelling (LTTA 2017, Sch 5, para 14, LTTA/8080). A dwelling is subsidiary to the main dwelling if the chargeable consideration for the main dwelling, apportioned on a just and reasonable basis, accounts for at least 2/3rd of the total consideration. The test is applied to each subsidiary dwelling. The subsidiary dwelling exception is designed for "granny annexes" but can equally apply to holiday cottages. In the example, the main house (plus garage, outbuildings and garden) has to have a value in excess of £720,000. The actual value of the holiday cottages on a stand-alone basis is not relevant. As the holiday cottages will be subsidiary to the main house, the 3% additional surcharge will not apply to any of the holiday cottages.

Even with the subsidiary dwelling exception it is still possible to claim multiple dwellings relief. In this example, the total consideration is divided by four to give an average price of £270,000 per dwelling. LTT charged on this consideration is £3,450, which multiplied by four gives a total LTT liability of £13,800. This is greater than a 1% charge on the total consideration (£10,800). As the dwellings are acquired in a single transaction, there is no requirement to consider the linked transaction rules. If the subsidiary dwelling exception did not apply, the 3% surcharge would apply to the whole purchase price. The only solution would be to split the acquisition of the main house from the acquisition of the holiday cottages and pay the 3% surcharge on the holiday cottages (and also apply the linked transaction rules).

The WRA have updated and expanded their guidance on multiple dwellings relief and subsidiary dwellings at LTTA Manual 8080. Particular note should be made of the need for the subsidiary dwelling to be independent of the main dwelling in terms of living space, utilities and entrances.

CROSS-BORDER TRANSACTIONS

3.43 Cross-border transactions involve both properties that straddle the physical border between England and Wales (cross-title properties) and property portfolios where properties are based in Wales and any of England, Scotland and Northern Ireland but do not straddle the border, for example, portfolios of industrial property.

In relation to properties that straddle the border, a map search service is available from the Land Registry in order to identify the relevant properties. Any consideration for the property has to be apportioned on a just and reasonable basis between the various elements of the property. Advisers may wish to seek a surveyor's valuation report to support any just and reasonable apportionment where there could be an element of doubt or contention with the WRA. The WRA guidance makes it clear that a taxpayer cannot make a guess at what might be the correct apportionment. The apportionment should reflect the facts of the transaction including the location and value of any buildings, access to the land, development potential and use of the land. The WRA guidance refers extensively to guidance issued by the Valuation Office Agency (LTTA Manual 2060 et seq).

In relation to property portfolios, again the consideration has to be apportioned between the relevant properties. One would hope that valuations of the individual properties would be available as part of reaching the overall value of a portfolio of properties.

In the cases of both cross-title properties and property portfolios, two returns will be required, an LTT return to the WRA and a SDLT return to HMRC. Perhaps surprisingly, two nil rate bands will be available. However, before clients decide to get too creative with their apportionments it can be expected that both the WRA and HMRC will share information regarding property transactions that straddle the border. Although there are a large number of properties that do straddle the border, the number of transactions involving those properties is estimated to be no more than one per week.

LINKED TRANSACTIONS

3.44 Two or more transactions can be linked for the purposes of LTT. A land transaction is linked if it is one of a number of transactions forming part of a single scheme, arrangement or series of transactions between the same seller and buyer or persons connected with the seller or buyer. Land exchanges are specifically excluded from being linked transactions. 'Connected' uses the definitions set out in *s 1122* of the *Corporation Tax Act 2010*.

The impact of linked transactions is that the tax rate bands have to be apportioned between the relevant transactions. There is no time limit on when a transaction could be linked to an earlier transaction. If a linked transaction arises it will be necessary to submit an amended LTT return at the same time as the LTT return for the second (or subsequent) transaction (*LTTA 2017, ss 8* and *74*).

TAX AVOIDANCE

3.45 Tax avoidance measures in *LTTA 2017* include targeted anti-avoidance provisions in relation to the use of LTT reliefs and a tax avoidance GAAR in relation to devolved taxes. The Welsh Government rejected the use of the SDLT tax avoidance legislation in *Finance Act 2003, ss 75A–C* (see **7.4** et seq which discusses *FA 2003, ss 75A–C*).

Reliefs TAAR

3.46 The reliefs TAAR applies to all taxes and not just LTT and landfill disposals tax. The effect of the TAAR is to remove all LTT relief where the transaction is part of a tax avoidance arrangement or which forms part of arrangements which are tax avoidance arrangements. A tax avoidance arrangement is defined as any arrangement where the main purpose or one of the main purposes was the avoidance of tax and the transaction lacks genuine economic or commercial substance other than the obtaining of a 'tax advantage'. An 'arrangement' includes any transaction, scheme, agreement, grant, understanding, promise or undertaking or series of any of those things whether or not legally enforceable. A tax advantage means any relief or any increased relief from tax, a repayment or increased repayment of tax, the avoidance or reduction of a charge to tax and the deferral of a payment of tax or the advancement of the repayment of tax.

Although the reliefs TAAR is targeted at the avoidance of a number of different taxes (LTT, income tax, capital gains tax, corporation tax, stamp duty land tax, stamp duty reserve tax and stamp duty), inheritance tax is not within the list of specific taxes (*LTTA 2017, s 31*).

Tax avoidance GAAR

3.47 The general anti-avoidance rule (note the difference from the UK general anti-abuse rule (see **7.3** which comments on the general anti-abuse rule)) applies to the avoidance of the devolved taxes only and therefore will apply initially to LTT and landfill disposals tax. The GAAR will apply where obtaining a tax advantage is the main or one of the main purposes of the arrangement. The GAAR applies to arrangements that are artificial where those arrangements are not a reasonable course of action and lack a genuine economic or commercial substance or take advantage of something that was not the intent of the legislation. There is an exception to the artificial transactions rule if the arrangement is in accordance with generally prevailing practice and the WRA have published acceptance of that practice.

The impact of the GAAR is that tax schemes to avoid LTT will be extremely difficult to apply. In addition, as there are relatively few high value transactions in Wales it will be relatively straightforward for the WRA to monitor property transfers at the Land Registry and find out whether an LTT return has been submitted and the amount of LTT paid in relation to that return (*TCM(W)A 2016, ss 81A–81I*).

There is no disclosure of tax avoidance schemes for taxes in Wales and therefore the WRA will not be informed in advance of LTT tax avoidance schemes that would otherwise be reported to HMRC under the DOTAS regime if they were being planned for SDLT. However, it is expected that there could be a reasonable amount of information sharing between HMRC and WRA on tax avoidance.

PARTNERSHIPS

3.48 (See **Chapter 5** which deals with partnership rules for SDLT.)

The rules on partnerships for SDLT have always been tricky and the rules for LTT follow the same pattern (*LTTA 2017, Sch 7*). Anyone advising partnerships on transfers of land needs to take particular care. A partnership will include limited partnerships and LLPs as well as traditional partnerships within the *Partnership Act 1890*. Any chargeable interest in land owned by a partnership will be treated as being owned by or on behalf of the partners despite the ability of the partnership to be treated as a legal person (*LTTA 2017, Sch 7, para 4(2)*).

All partners are responsible for the filing of an LTT return and payment of LTT (and have joint and several liability) although the requirements may be carried out by a representative partner (*LTTA 2017, Sch 7, paras 9* and *10*).

Transactions involving partnerships that do not involve any current, joining or leaving partners are treated in the same way as any other acquisition of a chargeable interest in land. When transferring land to a partnership, no LTT is paid on the share of the land owned by the partner (or persons connected with the partner) as determined by the partnership share. Therefore, if John transfers land to a partnership and obtains a 25% interest in the partnership, the partnership will pay LTT on 75% of the market value of the land. The LTT legislation allows for the calculation of the 'Sum of the Lower Proportions' (see **5.13** et seq which deals with the SDLT provisions) which will be familiar to advisers who have dealt with SDLT and partnerships. Anti-avoidance rules apply if there is a tax avoidance arrangement (using the TAAR definition) where the partner uses the partnership rules to reduce the LTT liability and leaves the partnership or withdraws capital from the partnership (*LTTA 2017, Sch 7, para 18*).

When property is transferred out of a partnership, LTT is charged on the proportion of the ownership interest not owned by the partner (and persons connected to the partner) acquiring the property. This can be used to an advantage on the incorporation of a company where all the partners become shareholders in a company – the company is connected with the partners and as the SLP will be 100% no LTT charge should apply. Transfers from a partnership consisting wholly of companies are subject to special rules. Where the SLP would be 75% or more, the transfer is deemed to take place at market value. The partnerships may, depending on the specific circumstances, be able to claim group relief from LTT.

Finally, special rules apply for transfers of land involving property investment partnerships which are beyond the scope of this chapter (see **5.29** which deals with the SDLT provisions).

TRANSITIONAL RULES

3.49 Regulations have been adopted by the Welsh Government on 31 January 2018 which set out transitional rules to deal with transactions that exchanged before 1 April 2018 (commencement date for LTT) and completed on or after 1 April 2018 (the *Land Transaction Tax (Transitional Provisions) (Wales) Regulations 2018* (*SI 2018/126*)).

In basic terms, a contract that exchanged before 1 April 2018 and completed on or after 1 April 2018 is subject to LTT. There a few limited exceptions as set out below.

Contract exchanged before 17 December 2014

3.50 If the contract exchanged on or before 17 December 2014 (which is the date the *Wales Act 2014* received Royal Assent), then any completion will be subject to SDLT even if completion is after 1 April 2018. However, this rule will not apply if the original contract has been varied, subject to an assignment of rights, there has been the exercise of an option or right of pre-emption or there has been an assignment, sub-sale or other transaction whereby someone other than the original buyer would be entitled to call for a conveyance of the land (Reg 3 of the Transitional Provisions).

Contract exchanged after 17 December 2014, substantially performed before 1 April 2018 and completed after 1 April 2018

3.51 SDLT will be payable on substantial performance. LTT will be payable to the extent that there is a greater amount of tax payable as a result of the completion of the transaction. This will be relevant if more LTT is payable, ie if the transaction involves a residential purchase above £400,000 or a commercial purchase above £1,000,000 (*reg 4* of the *Land Transaction Tax (Transitional Provisions) (Wales) Regulations 2018* (*SI 2018/126*)).

Leases and overlap relief

3.52 Where a lease (the old lease) has been granted before 1 April 2018 and a new lease is granted after 1 April 2018 but before the end of the term of the old lease, overlap relief will still be available even though the old lease was subject to SDLT rather than LTT. The rent payable in the overlap period will be adjusted to provide the relief from LTT (the adjustment cannot create a negative amount of rent) (*reg 9* of the *Land Transaction Tax (Transitional Provisions) (Wales) Regulations 2018* (*SI 2018/126*)).

Assignment of a lease granted subject to a relief

3.53 A lease granted before 1 April 2018 may have benefited from a relief on grant (for example, group relief or charities relief). If the lease is assigned after 1 April 2018, and the transaction does not fall within the terms of certain specified LTT reliefs, the assignment will be treated as the grant of a new lease for the purposes of LTT (*reg 10* of the *Land Transaction Tax (Transitional Provisions) (Wales) Regulations 2018* (*SI 2018/126*)).

Variation of leases due to rent increase

3.54 A lease granted before 1 April 2018 that is varied after 1 April 2018 by an increase in rent will be treated as the grant of a new lease and subject to LTT. The rent for the new lease is taken to be the additional rent payable as a result of the variation (*reg 11* of the *Land Transaction Tax (Transitional Provisions) (Wales) Regulations 2018* (*SI 2018/126*)).

WRA APPROACH

3.55 The WRA have spoken publicly of working with agents in relation to the operation of LTT and in dealing with compliance. The WRA plan to operate a compliance model of 'Cooperate, Check and Challenge'. The 'Cooperate' part will involve maximising voluntary compliance by providing guidance to agents and working to support compliance. 'Check' will involve taking a risk-based, intelligence-led approach to compliance by validating and verifying information quickly. Risk profiling will be applied to target resources and the WRA will support whistle blowing and third-party information. 'Challenge' will involve the WRA tackling tax avoidance and evasion using the GAAR and TAAR provisions contained within the tax legislation.

KEY DIFFERENCES BETWEEN SDLT AND LTT

3.56 The following is a list of key differences between SDLT and LTT:

- different rates of LTT which result in higher charges on more valuable property (both residential and non-residential);
- no specific first-time buyer threshold for LTT;
- no 15% LTT rate for the purchase by companies of residential properties;
- specific TAAR applying to the use of LTT reliefs;
- general anti-avoidance rule applying to Welsh devolved taxes only;
- no DOTAS for Welsh devolved taxes;
- no LTT on the rental element of residential leases;
- slight difference in the definition of 'residential land' which will mean all sales of garden plots will be residential land for LTT; and
- from 1 March 2019, a 14 day deadline to file SDLT returns and pay SDLT compared to 30 days for LTT.

Chapter 4

SDLT – General Rules

INTRODUCTION

4.1 Stamp Duty Land Tax (SDLT) replaced stamp duty on transactions involving UK land and buildings from 1 December 2003, although it ceased to apply to transactions involving land and buildings situated in Scotland with effect from 1 April 2015 (see **Chapter 2**), and to transactions involving land and buildings situated in Wales with effect from 1 April 2018 (see **Chapter 3**). Therefore, with effect from 1 April 2018, and subject to the transitional provisions (HMRC published guidance in relation to the SDLT to LBTT transitional provisions on 13 February 2015 – see www.gov.uk/government/publications/transitional-land-and-building-transaction-tax-guidance and in relation to the SDLT to LTT transitional provisions on 16 March 2018 – see www.gov.uk/government/publications/sdlt-to-land-transaction-tax-transitional-guidance), SDLT only applies to transactions involving land and buildings in England and Northern Ireland referred to below as 'RUK', ie the rest of the UK.

Even though SDLT replaced stamp duty on transactions involving UK land and buildings, it would be a mistake to assume that SDLT is merely an updated version of stamp duty. Many transactions which would not have been within the stamp duty net – including informal arrangements and some unilateral actions which might not conventionally be described as transactions – do give rise to SDLT liabilities and obligations. Even where there is no liability, there may be reporting obligations, with penalties for failure to comply. For this reason, this book often refers to 'SDLT obligations', meaning both a liability to pay tax and an obligation to notify a transaction or make a return. So wide ranging are these obligations, it is essential to consider the possible impact of SDLT on almost any change relating to the occupation of, or ownership of rights over, RUK land and buildings.

4.2 Almost all transactions in UK land and buildings completed from 1 December 2003, even if commenced earlier, are within the scope of SDLT. Some 'old' transactions remain within the ambit of stamp duty, or perhaps potentially fall within both regimes (see **4.63**). In stark contrast with stamp duty, SDLT is a true 'self-assessment' tax. The obligation to report liability and make payment falls on the purchaser. The tax is triggered by entering into or performing 'land transactions' (as defined in the legislation), no matter how or even whether documented. Some, but not all, of the reliefs previously available under stamp duty are available under SDLT. There are enforcement powers and specific anti-avoidance rules similar to those that apply to other taxes, plus far-reaching general anti-avoidance provisions. SDLT is within the *FA 2004* regime for disclosure of tax avoidance schemes, but it has its own set of criteria to determine whether disclosure is required (see **9.26** et seq).

4.3 The initial rates of SDLT for purchase of freeholds and existing leases were the same as they were for stamp duty, so the typical home buyer saw little or no practical change when the tax was introduced. Higher rates have been introduced by subsequent *Finance Acts* – from 6 April 2011, 5% for residential property costing more than £1,000,000 (*FA 2010, s 7*) and from 22 March 2012, 7% for residential property costing more than £2,000,000 (*FA 2012, s 211*). A higher rate of 15% was introduced, with effect from 21 March 2012, for the purchase of a single dwelling for more than £2,000,000 by certain non-natural persons (see **4.56**). The threshold for application of this punitive rate was lowered to cover a purchase for consideration exceeding £500,000 from 20 March 2014.

The structure of SDLT changed with effect from 4 December 2014 when the tax payable on a residential property transaction (see **4.38**) ceased to be calculated using the so-called 'slab system' and instead a 'progressive system' (like personal income tax) was adopted, with a top rate of 12% for chargeable consideration exceeding £1,500,000 (see **4.37**). Further changes were made to the tax with effect from 1 April 2016 in relation to residential properties. From that date a 3% additional rate of SDLT applies to purchases of additional dwellings and dwellings purchased by companies (and other non-individual purchasers) such that, where the additional rate applies, the top rate of tax is increased to 15% for chargeable consideration exceeding £1,500,000 (see **4.56**).

Finally, until 16 March 2016 the tax payable on the acquisition of non-residential or mixed-use property was calculated using the so-called 'slab system' (see **4.37**). However, with effect from 17 March 2016, the charge on such acquisitions is calculated using a 'progressive system' (like personal income tax), with a top rate of 5% for chargeable consideration exceeding £250,000 (see **4.37**). This change substantially increased the SDLT charge on high value commercial property transactions.

The increase in the rates of SDLT, anti-avoidance provisions and the absence of some reliefs mean that many commercial transactions suffer a greater tax burden than they would have incurred under stamp duty. The regime for the grant, variation or surrender of leases is sufficiently complex to warrant a separate chapter in this book (**Chapter 6**). In most cases involving a lease at rent, the SDLT charge is substantially higher than would have arisen under stamp duty.

4.4 Obligations in relation to SDLT may extend beyond the time of the original transaction. In some circumstances, reliefs may be withdrawn or liabilities increased as a result of subsequent events as innocuous as an early rent review or the refinancing of a group company. Constant monitoring of potential liabilities is therefore necessary. The tax applies irrespective of country of establishment or residence of the taxpayer, and it is possible that a non-UK entity, unaware of the rules, may unknowingly trigger an SDLT charge. An example would be where RUK land is transferred in the course of a merger of overseas companies by operation of (overseas) law – normally free of stamp duty under the old regime, but may be subject to SDLT under current rules.

4.5 With the introduction of SDLT, stamp duty was abolished on transfers of all other assets apart from stock and marketable securities and, in some circumstances, interests in partnerships which hold such stock or securities (see **10.1** et seq).

GENERAL SCHEME OF SDLT

Importance of definitions

4.6 The SDLT rules rely on a number of concepts and expressions which are defined in *FA 2003*. It is important to apply these definitions and not to rely on the general meaning of the relevant words. The table below details statutory and HMRC SDLT Manual references for definitions of key terms; there is also a useful list of statutory references in *FA 2003, s 122*. Some of the definitions are interdependent, so it is necessary to see the whole picture before it makes sense; the definitions and the following paragraphs may require several readings! These paragraphs give a general outline of the tax and the defined expressions are shown, in the next few paragraphs only, in **bold**. Subsequent paragraphs and chapters examine the interpretation and application of the expressions in more detail.

Term	***FA 2003 section/Schedule***	**SDLTM para**
Acquisition	*s 43(3)*	00270
Chargeable interest	*s 48*	00280
Consideration	*s 52; Sch 4*	03600 et seq
Conveyance	*s 44(10)(b)*	08100
Effective date	*s 119; s 44(4)*	07600
Exempt interest	*s 48(2)–(3A)*	00320

Term	*FA 2003 section/Schedule*	SDLTM para
Land transaction	*s 43(1)*	00260
Linked transactions	*s 108*	30100
Major interest	*s 117*	04130
Purchaser	*s 43(3)–(4); Sch 17A, para 15A*	07200
Substantial amount/ substantially all	*s 44(7)*	07950
Substantial performance	*s 44(5)–(7)*	07700 et seq

The charge

4.7 SDLT is charged on **land transactions**, whether effected by a document or not. Neither the places of residence of the parties, nor the place where any documents are executed, are relevant to the charge. The tax is under the control of HM Revenue & Customs (HMRC), and that departmental name is used here despite the fact that much of the legislation still refers to the Commissioners of Inland Revenue (*FA 2003, s 42*). A **land transaction** for these purposes means the **acquisition** of a **chargeable interest**. **Acquisition** may include not only a normal land sale and purchase, but also the creation, surrender, release or variation of a **chargeable interest**. The **acquisition** may occur under the terms of a court order, a statutory provision or by operation of law. A complex and indirect definition makes clear the intention that any party whose interest in land benefits under the transaction is to be regarded as the **purchaser**. Poor wording of the legislation originally led to uncertainty when leases were varied, so supplementary rules were introduced to deal specifically with this (see **4.18**). A person will only be treated as a **purchaser** if he has either given **consideration** for, or is a party to, the transaction (*FA 2003, s 43(5)*). It can thus be seen that the new charge catches a wider range of transactions than the old stamp duty regime.

Timing

4.8 In general, SDLT obligations arise 14 days after the **effective date** of the transaction (*FA 2003, ss 76(1), 86(1)*). At the latest, the **effective date** is the date of completion. For these purposes, the word 'completion' is not defined and, therefore, bears its normal legal meaning, broadly summarised as the final action required to give the transaction full legal effect. However, in many cases, the **effective date** is triggered by **substantial performance** of the transaction before completion.

The normal deadline for notification and payment for transactions with an 'effective date' (see **4.91**) on or before 28 February 2019, or which had become notifiable on or before 28 February 2019, was 30 days from the 'effective date' of the transaction. However, the government confirmed in the 22 November 2017 Budget that the time limit for filing an SDLT return and paying the tax would be reduced from 30 days to 14 days where the 'effective date' of the transaction was on or after 1 March 2019, or the 'effective date' of the transaction was before 1 March 2019 but the transaction only became notifiable on or after 1 March 2019. Therefore, from that date, SDLT filing and payment obligations arise 14 days, rather than 30 days, after the 'effective date' of the transaction or the event triggering notification, with interest and penalties chargeable if the deadline is missed. The necessary changes to *FA 2003* were made by *FA 2019, s 46*.

With the aim of making compliance with the revised 14-day time limit easier new forms SDLT3 and SDLT4 have been introduced (*The Stamp Duty Land Tax (Administration) (Amendment) Regulations 2018 (SI 2018/1319)* which were laid before the House of Commons on 10 December 2018 and came into force on 1 March 2019).

Substantial performance

4.9 **Substantial performance** is defined using a combination of terms such as 'possession' and 'occupation', which are themselves not clearly defined, together with measurement of the proportion of any consideration actually paid. In any dispute as to whether an agreement has been **substantially performed**, expert legal advice may be required as to the meaning of terms. However, in general, a contract is **substantially performed** where either the purchaser takes possession of **substantially all** of the property passing under the contract, or **substantially all** of the consideration is paid or provided. HMRC have indicated that they will regard 90% or more as **substantially all**, but SDLTM07950 indicates they will not consider themselves tied to this figure if they detect an attempt to exploit it for avoidance. *Any* payment of rent under the terms of a lease will be regarded as **substantial performance** of the lease, as will the purchaser becoming entitled to receipt of *any* rent etc from a tenant.

This gives rise to a potential issue – Standard Terms & Conditions for land transactions may entitle the purchaser to rent from a tenant or sub-tenant earlier than the time of payment for the property, which may trigger early substantial performance. It is worthwhile to review the terms and conditions carefully, to avoid such problems.

Formal completion

4.10 If a contract for a **land transaction** is entered into and is completed by a formal **conveyance** not later than the time of **substantial performance**, the contract and **conveyance** are treated as a single **land transaction**, taking effect at the date of completion (*FA 2003, s 44(3)*). Submission of a return and payment of the tax will be due 14 days from that date (30 days for land transactions with an 'effective date' (see **4.8**) prior to 1 March 2019 and which became notifiable prior to that date). Where, however, the contract is entered into and **substantially performed** before completion, the contract itself is treated as a **land transaction**, the effective date being that of **substantial performance** (*s 44(4)*). The return and tax payment are due 14 days from that date (30 days for land transactions with an 'effective date' (see **4.91**) prior to 1 March 2019 and which became notifiable prior to that date). If such a transaction is later completed by a formal **conveyance**, that **conveyance** will be a separate **land transaction** (in some circumstances, but not always, requiring submission of a further return), but SDLT will only be payable to the extent that the tax payable on the **conveyance** is greater than the tax paid on **substantial performance** of the contract – there should be no overall 'double charge' (*s 44(8)*). However, care is needed where reduced or zero SDLT is paid at the time of **substantial performance** because of a relief or exemption – in some circumstances, the later completion can trigger further liability because conditions for the relief or exemption are not satisfied at that time. The circumstances in which two or more returns may be required for the same transaction are explored in more detail at **8.15** et seq.

What is chargeable

4.11 The terms **conveyance** and transfer are used interchangeably and include any instrument. Accordingly, they cover the grant of a lease as well as a transfer of land. A transaction is chargeable unless it is specifically covered by an exemption. **Chargeable interests** include estates, interests (including beneficial interests), rights (including for example a right to light) and powers over RUK land, as well as the benefit of any obligation, restriction or other condition that would affect the value of any such estate, interest, right or power. However, licences to occupy, mortgages and similar security interests are excluded. The extension of the definition to include obligations and restrictions will mean, for example, that a payment to the owner of a neighbouring plot of land, for a restrictive covenant or wayleave, may give rise to a charge. For some purposes, it matters whether an interest is a **major interest**. This term covers interests generally referred to as freeholds, leaseholds and other tenancies. However, for the purposes of *FA 2003, Sch 4ZA* (*SDLT: Higher Rates for Additional Dwellings and Dwellings Purchased by Companies*) (see **4.56**), a leasehold interest is not a '**major interest**' if the term of the lease does not exceed seven years on the date of its grant (*FA 2003, Sch 4ZA, para 2(4)*). An undivided share in a '**major interest**' in a dwelling is a '**major interest**' in a dwelling for the purposes of *FA 2003, Sch 4ZA* (*FA 2003, Sch 4ZA, para 2(5)* inserted by *FA 2019, s 44(2)* in relation to any transaction with an 'effective date' (see **4.91**) on or after

29 October 2018). Similarly, for the purposes of the relief for first-time buyers (**5.47** et seq), a leasehold interest is not a '**major interest**' if the lease has less than 21 years to run at the beginning of the day after the 'effective date' (see **4.91**) of the transaction (*FA 2003, Sch 6ZA, para 8*).

4.12 The grant of an option to acquire an interest in land is specifically identified as a **chargeable transaction**. The transfer or exercise of an option is a separate transaction from the grant, but the two may be **linked transactions** for determining the amount of tax due. This is intended to counter attempts to take advantage of lower rates of SDLT by splitting a purchase into two steps. HMRC acknowledge that there will be some circumstances where the exercise of the option will not be linked to its grant, for example where the option has been assigned and is exercised by someone not party to, or connected to someone who was party to, the original grant of the option (SDLT01300).

HMRC's view is that, by virtue of *FA 2003, s 55(1)* and *(4)* and *FA 2003, s 116(1)*, the nature of the option as being residential, mixed-use or non-residential property is determined by the nature of the underlying property over which the option has been granted (SDLTM 01300 – updated on 3 June 2020). Therefore, an option granted over residential property will itself be treated as residential property, and the residential property rates will apply in calculating the SDLT payable on the exercise or transfer of the option.

As the grant of an option is the acquisition of a chargeable interest which is not a **major interest** (*FA 2003, s117)* it is not notifiable unless there is SDLT to pay, or there would be SDLT to pay but for the availability of a relief (*FA 2003, s 77(1)(b)*). However, if the grant of the option is linked with the subsequent exercise of the option, the grant will often become notifiable, or if previously notified the return will often require amendment, when the option is exercised (*FA 2003, s 81A*).

4.13 If interests in land (at least one being a **major interest**) are exchanged, each transfer is separately chargeable; see **4.32**.

OCCASIONS OF CHARGE

Chargeable transactions

4.14 SDLT is chargeable on a chargeable land transaction – that is, any acquisition of a chargeable interest unless the transaction is itself exempt from charge. Any interest in RUK land and buildings is a chargeable interest unless it is specifically identified as exempt (see **4.16**). Examples of chargeable interests include freeholds, leases, sporting rights and the benefits of restrictive covenants – but this list is not exhaustive. The following give rise to the acquisition of a chargeable interest:

- transfer of all or part of a freehold or leasehold interest in RUK property;
- grant of a lease out of a freehold or superior leasehold interest in RUK property;
- surrender of a lease over RUK property to the landlord;
- variation of a lease over RUK property where that variation is treated as a surrender and re-grant in law, or where the variation includes a reduction in rent or a reduction in term; and
- grant, transfer, variation or surrender of an interest in RUK property other than a freehold or lease – for example, sporting or mineral rights, right of light, right of passage, etc.

4.15 In relation to leases (and arrangements treated as leases for SDLT purposes), certain events, which are not in law any of the above, are nonetheless deemed to be one of this list and therefore to give rise to SDLT obligations. These matters are considered in **Chapter 6**.

Exempt interests

4.16 The following limited list of interests is regarded as exempt, so that no SDLT liability or obligation arises on their creation, transfer, variation or surrender (*FA 2003, s 48(2)*). All other interests are chargeable:

- a security interest – that is, an interest or right (other than a rentcharge, feu duty or similar) held for the purpose of securing payment of money or performance of other obligations. This has been expanded to include the interest held by a financial institution as a result of an 'alternative property finance' transaction (see *FA 2003, s 73B*);
- a licence to use or occupy land. HMRC have made clear their view that this only applies to an interest which is a licence in both name and substance. They will resist attempts to 'dress up' as a licence an interest which is in substance greater than that, and care is required in relying on this exemption;
- a tenancy at will. Informal occupation arrangements sometimes begin as a tenancy at will but over time may develop into some other form of tenancy which is not exempt and which therefore may give rise to SDLT obligations, see **6.10**; and
- certain somewhat archaic rights which might otherwise be regarded as including interests in land – an advowson (the right to appoint a clergyman to a benefice), a franchise (a right granted by the Crown such as the right to hold a fair or market, or the right to take tolls) and a manor (a right of certain kinds of jurisdiction over a specified area or estate).

Exempt transactions

4.17 Even if the land interest is not exempt, the transaction may be so – see **5.7** for details.

THE PURCHASER IS CHARGEABLE

4.18 SDLT obligations fall on the purchaser, identified in the legislation as the person who acquires the chargeable interest, or whose existing interest is enlarged or enhanced. The identity of the purchaser is obvious in straightforward transfers and grants of leases, but less obvious in some other cases. In particular:

- if a chargeable interest is transferred or granted to the trustees of a settlement, the trustees are joint purchasers (*FA 2003, Sch 16, para 4*);
- if an existing chargeable interest is transferred to bare trustees or nominees, the beneficial owner is the purchaser (*Sch 16, para 3(1)*);
- if a lease is granted to bare trustees, those trustees are (jointly, if more than one) purchasers of the whole interest (*Sch 16, para 3(3)*);
- if a lease is surrendered or the term shortened, the landlord is the purchaser (*FA 2003, s 43(3)(b), Sch 17A, para 15A(2)*);
- if the rent under a lease is reduced, the tenant is the purchaser (*Sch 17A, para 15A(1)*); and
- if any chargeable interest other than a lease (eg an easement) is varied, whoever benefits is the purchaser (*FA 2003, s 43(3)(c)*). This is an enigmatic definition, since it is normally the essence of a commercial transaction that both parties benefit, but it should probably be read as the person whose interest in land is enhanced.

However, a person cannot be a purchaser unless he gives consideration or is a party to the transaction (*FA 2003, s 43(5)*).

Example 4.1—Identifying the purchaser

Peter owns the freehold of property F, and Rachel owns the freehold of property G which abuts F.

In September 2017 Peter pays the HCA* £100,000 for the removal of a restrictive covenant preventing use of F for carrying on a manufacturing business. This is a land transaction and Peter is the purchaser.

In August 2019 Rachel agrees to pay Peter £500 per annum for the right to bring maintenance vehicles through the car park of Peter's property F to service the rear of Rachel's building on her property G. This is a land transaction and Rachel is the purchaser.

In October 2019 Peter and Rachel agree to exchange small parts of their respective properties to create better shaped plots, allowing construction of better buildings on both. Peter is purchaser in respect of the parcel of land he gains, and Rachel is purchaser in respect of the parcel she gains – that is, there are two chargeable transactions, even though no money changes hands. Furthermore, this is an exchange, see **4.32**.

* The Homes and Communities Agency was a UK government body which inherited the benefit of restrictive covenants originally imposed on land by other, now defunct, agencies, such as the Commission for the New Towns. It was replaced in January 2018 by Homes England and the Regulator of Social Housing.

CONSIDERATION

Measuring consideration – valuation

4.19 The basic definition is 'any consideration in money or money's worth, given directly or indirectly by the purchaser or a person connected with him' (*FA 2003, Sch 4, para 1(1)*). The full face value of consideration must be taken into account – no discount is given for the fact that the consideration may be postponed, payable in instalments etc (*FA 2003, Sch 4, para 3*). However, where payment of consideration is postponed because it is contingent or the amount is uncertain, it is sometimes possible to apply for deferral of the corresponding SDLT (see **8.31**). In some circumstances where instalments are payable over many years, the consideration is taken to be the amount payable over 12 years (see **4.28**). Non-sterling consideration is valued at the London closing exchange rate for the 'effective date' (see **4.91**) of the transaction; consideration which is not in the form of money or debt must be valued at its market value at the effective date. One example of this is where a 'roof-space lease' for the installation of solar panels gives the property owner the right to take electricity generated by the panels at reduced or zero price (see **6.14**). However some forms of consideration are ignored in some transactions (see **4.24**, **4.34** and **5.7**); in some cases, actual consideration is replaced or supplemented by deemed consideration (see **4.29**). When a lease at rent is in point, there are specific computational rules (see **6.43–6.56**).

Contingency and uncertainty

4.20 If payment of any part of the consideration is contingent on some future event, it is assumed that the amount will be payable and SDLT must be paid accordingly (*FA 2003, s 51*).

If the amount of consideration is uncertain or has not been finally ascertained by the time payment and submission of the SDLT return are due, a reasonable estimate must be used.

Once the figures are finally known, if the final SDLT amount is higher than originally entered on the return, an amended return must then be submitted and the further SDLT paid. If the final figures show that too much SDLT has been paid, the surplus SDLT may be reclaimed (*FA 2003, s 80*). The stamp duty concepts of unascertainable and contingent consideration (see **10.37, 10.40**) do not apply to SDLT. There is one exception to the treatment of contingent consideration set out above, and that relates to 'right to buy' transactions (see **5.43**).

Where contingent and/or uncertain consideration may not be payable until some time after the effective date of the transaction, it may be possible to apply to postpone payment of the corresponding SDLT (see **8.31**). However the tight deadlines for applying for this postponement are rigidly enforced, so prompt application is essential.

In general, when SDLT is paid after the normal due date (ie more than 14 days after the 'effective date' (see **4.91**) of the transaction), interest will be charged from the normal due date to the date of payment. This may mean that interest will be charged for a period before the date when the final amount of tax is known (*FA 2003, s 87(3)(c)*). However, if HMRC have agreed to postpone the tax as explained in **8.31**, interest will not be charged provided tax is paid in accordance with the postponement agreement (*FA 2003, s 87(3)(b)*).

Example 4.2—Measuring consideration

Lissa agrees to transfer a plot of land M to Norman. In return, Norman agrees to pay Lissa £150,000 cash, payable in ten annual instalments of £15,000, commencing immediately, and to have his family company Quickbuild Ltd build Lissa a new house on a different plot of land P, which Lissa also owns. Norman is subject to SDLT on the acquisition of M, and the consideration is £150,000 plus the market value of the building work to be undertaken by Quickbuild Ltd. Although Lissa gets a new house out of the arrangement, this is built on land she already owns, so she has no SDLT obligations.

Example 4.3—Contingent consideration

Norman cannot afford to fund the development of the land purchased in the previous example so he sells it to Investor Ltd for £300,000 cash upfront plus 50% of the net profit made on eventual sale of the completed development, up to a further £700,000. As a condition of the sale, Quickbuild Ltd is engaged to carry out the development, being paid on a normal commercial basis by Investor Ltd. Investor Ltd is liable to pay SDLT on the total consideration, consisting of £300,000 cash payable at the outset plus £700,000 contingent cash payable However, provided some part of the contingent amount may fall to be paid more than six months after the effective date of the purchase, Investor Ltd may apply to defer payment of SDLT on the whole £700,000 contingent cash payable. The payments to Quickbuild are being paid for the development works and are not consideration for the transfer of the land. It is however necessary to consider the case of *Prudential Assurance Co Ltd v IRC* [1992] STC 863. HMRC set out their view of the impact of this case at SDLTM04015. HMRC consider that the same principles apply for the purposes of SDLT as those set out in SP 8/93 in relation to the stamp duty in that if the land purchase and development contracts are genuinely independent of each other, SDLT will only be charged on the consideration given for the land. However, if there is, in reality, only one transaction, being the acquisition of the completed development then HMRC are likely to seek SDLT on the consideration paid for the development works. If the amount payable under the development contract is chargeable to SDLT and cannot be finally determined at the effective date of the purchase (eg it is a 'cost plus' contract rather than a fixed price) and again assuming some part may fall to be payable more than six months later, Investor Ltd may also apply to defer SDLT on this amount. However, specific rules apply in relation to works as consideration and Investor Ltd will be required to make SDLT payments on an agreed schedule at not more than six-monthly intervals (see SDLTM50920).

If no application is made to defer payment of SDLT, Investor Ltd must pay tax on the full cash price, including the maximum contingent amount of £700,000, so £1 million in total, plus, if the payments under the development contract are chargeable to SDLT, a justifiable estimate of the amount payable under the development contract, no later than 14 days after the 'effective date' (see **4.91**) of the purchase.

Attribution

4.21 When two or more related transactions are entered into, or there is a composite transaction for acquisition of various assets, the overall consideration must be apportioned between the assets on a just and reasonable basis (*FA 2003, Sch 4, para 4*). Apportionment between chargeable and non-chargeable assets has in the past often given rise to difficulties. Until 4 December 2014 SDLT was charged on the acquisition of residential property under the so-called 'slab system' under which a single rate of SDLT applied determined by the highest band into which the chargeable consideration fell. Consequently, where the amount apportioned to chargeable interests was close to the upper limit for a lower SDLT rate, it was likely that HMRC would have taken a close interest in whether the apportionment was justified. This is much less of an issue now that the SDLT charge in relation to residential property is determined using a 'progressive system' with effect from 4 December 2014 (see **4.37**). In the Tax Tribunal (First-tier) case of *Orsman v CIR* [2012] UKFTT 227 (TC), released on 28 March 2012 (see www.financeandtaxtribunals.gov.uk/judgmentfiles/j6342/TC01921.pdf), the taxpayer attributed £250,000 to the fabric of a house and £8,000 to non-liable chattels. On this basis SDLT was due at 1%, £2,500. However, HMRC investigated and concluded that some of the 'chattels' were, in fact, fixtures forming part of the house. The Tribunal agreed that a further £800 should be attributed to the house. This took the consideration into the 3% SDLT band, increasing the SDLT due to £7,524. The case contains interesting comments on the general basis for attributing consideration between assets and is worth reading where such attribution is required.

Inherent goodwill (ie goodwill which is inherent in the land)

4.22 The purchase and sale of a business often involves consideration attributed to 'goodwill'. Where the assets transferred include interests in land, the question arises as to whether any of that goodwill should be regarded as inherent in or attached to the interests in land, such that it should be subject to SDLT. HMRC set out their view on the point at SDLTM04005, which includes a link to the HMRC Capital Gains manual which gives guidance on the distinction between the different types of goodwill. HMRC also make reference to the joint HMRC and Valuation Office practice note on apportioning the price paid for a business as a going concern and the value of the tangible assets (the property, fixtures, fittings, chattels etc). In general terms, if the 'goodwill' element of consideration can be shown to relate to matters such as contracts with customers and suppliers, the specific customer base or a trade name/reputation, it may be accepted that this is true goodwill, separable from the property. However, if the goodwill arises from the location of the property or the fact that the property is constructed or adapted in a way which particularly suits the business, HMRC are likely to argue that the amount attributed to goodwill should be added to the amount paid for the property. Many disputes arise in this area and specialist expert help may be required, if the amounts at stake warrant it.

VAT

4.23 If the consideration is subject to VAT, this must be included in the amount on which SDLT is charged. If the purchaser is able to recover VAT suffered as input tax, this means that SDLT is charged on a greater amount than the cost. At the current standard VAT rate of 20%, the maximum marginal rate of SDLT on non-residential property is 6% (5% × 120/100). If the land is not subject to VAT at the effective date of the transaction, but may become so through exercise of the 'option to tax', VAT is not taken into account, provided the option to tax is not exercised until after the effective date (*FA 2003, Sch 4, para 2*).

Example 4.4—SDLT on VAT

Big Manufacturer Ltd (B) buys a plot of bare land from Land Trader Ltd (L) for £1,600,000 (plus VAT if chargeable), intending to build a new factory. L has exercised the VAT 'option to tax' the land and charges VAT, but B is able to recover this fully through its own VAT returns. B also negotiates to pay the VAT to L on the same day it recovers it from HMRC. So, commercially, the real cost of the land is simply £1,600,000. SDLT is chargeable at rates of 0%, 2% and 5% on the VAT-inclusive price of £1,920,000. This gives a liability of £85,500, which is 5.3% of £1,600,000.

Debt as consideration

4.24 If property is transferred in satisfaction (or in return for the release) of a debt due to the purchaser or owed by the vendor, or in return for the purchaser assuming responsibility for a debt, the amount of debt (including any interest due but unpaid) counts as consideration. However, if the amount of debt exceeds the market value of the property, the consideration is limited to that market value (*FA 2003, Sch 4, para 8*).

4.25 The position may be less clear where there is a debt secured on the property before the transfer, which remains in place after. In principle, it could be possible for the property to be transferred without the purchaser taking on responsibility for payment of the debt, in which case the debt should not be taken into account as consideration for the transfer.

Example 4.5—Debt as consideration?

Parent has purchased a house with the aid of a loan secured on the house. The house is occupied by Student. Parent transfers the house to Student for no consideration and retains full and sole responsibility for the loan. The amount of the loan should not be taken into account as consideration for SDLT purposes.

With a view to prevention of avoidance, it is provided that the amount of debt secured on the property *will* be taken into account as consideration if the rights or liabilities of any party to the transaction in relation to the debt are changed in connection with the transaction (*FA 2003, Sch 4, para 8(1A)*). In the example above, arrangements between Parent and the lender would require very careful drafting to ensure that Parent's rights and obligations in relation to the loan remain unchanged when the property is transferred – and it may prove difficult to persuade a lender to accept the necessary drafting.

Carrying out works on land

4.26 This is a widely misunderstood and, in practice, very limited exclusion from chargeable consideration. If consideration given for a chargeable transaction includes works of construction, repair or improvement, their value is excluded from chargeable consideration if the following conditions are met (*FA 2003, Sch 4, para 10*):

- the works are carried out after the 'effective date' (see **4.91**) of the transaction;
- the works are carried out on the land being acquired or on other land already held by the purchaser or someone connected with him; and
- it is not a condition that the works are carried out by the vendor or someone connected with him.

Example 4.6—Works which do not count as consideration

Chemical Co Ltd (C) agrees to sell land to Housebuilder Ltd (H). The land is contaminated and C is under an obligation to carry out decontamination works within one year. In consideration for the transfer, H pays £500,000 and agrees to engage an unrelated company to carry out the required decontamination works at an expected cost of £1 million. The works do not commence until after completion of the transfer. The value of the decontamination works does not count as consideration for the transfer of the land, and H pays SDLT only on the £500,000 cash consideration.

Example 4.7—Works which are consideration

Beryl (B) agrees to buy a plot of land from Landbank Ltd (L) for £200,000 (its true market value) and, on the same day, engages Quickbuild Ltd (Q) to construct a house on the plot at a cost of £300,000. L and Q are associated with each other but unconnected with B. The provision relating to carrying out of works has no application in this scenario. The £300,000 is being paid for construction of the house and is not consideration for the transfer of the plot of land. Instead, it is necessary to consider the case of *Prudential Assurance Co Ltd v IRC* [1992] STC 863. HMRC set out their view of the impact of this case at SDLTM04015. HMRC consider that the same principles apply as those set out in SP 8/93 in relation to stamp duty liability in this kind of transaction. Provided the land purchase and building contracts are genuinely independent of each other, SDLT will be charged only on the price paid for the land. However, if there is, in reality, only one transaction – for example, if in truth L will only sell the land if B also agrees to engage Q to build the house – HMRC will seek SDLT based on the overall price for the land and completed building. In the present example, HMRC are likely to be difficult to convince that this is anything other than a single transaction, with SDLT due on £500,000.

Services as consideration

4.27 Where services are provided as consideration, they are valued at the amount which would have been paid in the open market for such services. In general, this is likely to be more than the cost to the purchaser of providing the services, since an open market provider would expect to make a profit (*FA 2003, Sch 4, para 11*).

Payment in instalments

4.28 If consideration is payable in instalments, the 'effective date' (see **4.91**) of the transaction is likely to be triggered by something other than payment of consideration (eg occupying the property or even formal completion). Once the effective date arrives, SDLT is payable on the whole consideration, no matter when that consideration is payable. In certain circumstances, it is possible to apply to defer payment of some of the SDLT, as mentioned at **4.19** (see **8.31** for details).

However, where the consideration comprises or includes an annuity capable of lasting for at least 12 years, the consideration is taken to be 12 years' instalments (*FA 2003, s 52*). For these purposes, any consideration payable periodically (other than rent) is an annuity. If the yearly amounts vary, the highest 12 separate years are taken into account (although increases in line with the Retail Price Index are ignored). If this treatment applies, it is not possible to apply for deferral of any of the SDLT, and there is no adjustment to reflect actual consideration if the total payable proves to be more or less than the 12 years' payments initially assessed.

Example 4.8—Annuities

On 1 July 2020, Pru sells her house to ER plc in return for:

(1) a lump sum of £100,000, plus

(2) a rent-free tenancy of the house for life (valued at £40,000), plus

(3) an annuity for life, initially at £15,000 pa, increasing to £20,000 pa after four years and increasing in line with RPI thereafter.

The consideration on which ER must pay SDLT is the sum of (1) and (2) plus 12 times the £20,000 annuity – £380,000 in total. For these purposes, since the annuity is for life, it is assumed Pru will live at least until 30 June 2036, so that at least 12 instalments at £20,000 will be payable, but the subsequent RPI increases are ignored. The SDLT is due by 15 July 2020 with no facility to defer and no adjustment if Pru dies before or after 30 June 2036.

Substitution of market value

4.29 SDLT is generally chargeable by reference to the value of the actual consideration, but in some circumstances this is substituted by the market value of the property acquired. One example is where property is transferred in payment of a debt exceeding the value of the property (see **4.24**); another is where properties are exchanged (see **4.32**) and actual consideration is less than the market value of the property acquired.

Transfer to connected company

4.30 Perhaps the main relevance of market value is when a property is transferred to a company which is connected with the transferor. When this happens, the consideration is to be taken as not less than the market value of the interest transferred (plus any rent where the transaction is the grant of a lease) (*FA 2003, s 53*). For these purposes, 'connected' is as defined in *Corporation Tax Act 2010 (CTA 2010), s 1122*. If the actual consideration, including any VAT chargeable on the transaction, is greater than market value, SDLT is chargeable by reference to the actual consideration, unless a relief or exemption is available.

The market value rule does not apply in the case of some transfers to trustees. Nor does it apply where the transfer is a distribution out of the assets of a company. However, an anti-avoidance rule re-applies the market value rule if group relief has been claimed on the property (or on a superior interest, if the property is a lease) within the previous three years (*FA 2003, s 54*).

4.31 There are two noteworthy points which often cause confusion. First, there is no general relief available where the transfer to a connected company occurs in the course of incorporation of a business by a sole trader or unincorporated partnership. Other tax reliefs are available to ease the process of incorporation but, where the business has substantial property assets, the SDLT cost may act as a significant disincentive. This was the cause of heated parliamentary debate when SDLT was introduced, but the government of the day was not prepared to introduce a relief.

There is a very specific relief on transfer from an unincorporated partnership to a limited liability partnership; see **5.61**. Additionally, application of the special partnership rules may reduce the SDLT on transfers between partners, partnerships and other connected persons, including companies in some cases. For detail on this see **Chapter 7**.

Secondly, where a lease at rent is granted to a connected company, there is no requirement to substitute a market rent. Rather, if the rent is less than a market rate, the lease itself will have a capital value (ie at arm's length, a lease at that rent would also attract a premium). SDLT is chargeable on the actual rent plus the capital value as if paid as a premium.

Exchanges and partitions

4.32 Where interests in property are exchanged, this is treated as two land transactions. Assuming at least one of the interests transferred is a major interest (see **4.6** and **4.11**), the consideration for each acquisition is the greater of (a) the value of the property acquired and (b) the value of the property given in consideration together with any other consideration given (*FA 2003, s 47, Sch 4 paras 5, 6*). Originally the value given in consideration was irrelevant; SDLT was based only on the value of the property acquired. However this was thought to provide an opportunity for avoidance by artificially depressing the value of the property just before it was transferred. The rules were changed to their current form by *FA 2011 Sch 21 para 4* with effect from 24 March 2011 but subject to transitional rules for transactions agreed before that date. How to determine the chargeable consideration on an exchange is covered by HMRC at SDLTM04020. The change has led to increased uncertainty and administration for some 'innocent' commercial transactions.

Particular issues arise, in relation to both amount and timing of tax liability, when interests in the same property are exchanged – for example when A sells to B and B grants A a lease out of the interest just purchased. See Example 4.23 and **5.40** et seq for further details.

Example 4.9—Exchanges

Erica agrees to transfer a plot of land, X, to Hosta, in exchange for Hosta transferring plot of land Z to Erica. It is agreed that the open market value of X is £200,000 and that of Z is £180,000. The parties agree to ignore the difference in value for commercial purposes. Erica will pay SDLT on the acquisition of Z, based on £200,000, being the greater of the market value of Z, and the value given in consideration. Hosta will pay SDLT on the acquisition of X, based on

£200,000, again being the greater of the market value of X and the value given in consideration. The overall SDLT bill would have been lower if each had sold to the other for cash – but there may have been more pressing commercial reasons for proceeding by way of exchange.

In a subsequent transaction, Hosta transfers plot of land W, valued at £1.2 million, to Erica. In return, Erica transfers plot of land Z back to Hosta, and agrees to make cash payments to Hosta based on a formula which takes account of the eventual sales proceeds of houses which Erica will construct on plot of land W. Erica will have to pay SDLT based on a reasonable estimate of the greater of the market value of plot of land W and the total consideration which will be given. Once that total consideration is finally determined – presumably after all of the houses have been constructed and sold – Erica will have to consider whether a further return and payment of SDLT are due (eg if the total consideration exceeds both the original estimate and the original market value of plot of land W). Prior to the 2011 change, the SDLT position would have been finally settled as soon as the value of plot of land W had been agreed.

4.33 If none of the interests is a major interest (ie the interests are limited to options or matters such as sporting rights, wayleaves, etc), the consideration for each acquisition is simply the amount of any further consideration given apart from the interest in land itself.

Example 4.10—Exchanges, not major interests

Juniper Ltd owns fishing rights over a stretch of Minnow River. Unrelated company Gorse Ltd owns shooting rights over Sparrow Moor. The companies agree to exchange their rights, with Juniper paying Gorse £300,000 cash, being the agreed difference in values. Juniper will pay SDLT based on consideration of £300,000. Gorse will not pay SDLT, as the deemed consideration for its acquisition of the fishing rights will be nil.

4.34 Where two or more persons hold a property jointly, whether as joint tenants or as tenants in common, they are generally treated for SDLT purposes as owning separate and distinct (but undefined) parts of the property. A property held in this way may be partitioned, so that each person takes a specific part. If this happens, the interest which each gives up is not treated as consideration for the part of which he becomes sole owner. The only consideration for SDLT purposes will be any payment or other valuable consideration which one may give to another, perhaps to compensate for differing values of the parts taken by each (*FA 2003, Sch 4, para 6*).

Example 4.11—Partition of jointly held property

Brothers Bill and Ben own a plot of land worth £1 million, divided into two paddocks, as joint tenants. They agree to partition it so that Bill owns paddock A and Ben owns paddock B. They agree that paddock A is worth £100,000 more than paddock B, but Bill is short of cash and they agree he will give Ben only £20,000 in compensation for his loss of value. For SDLT purposes, Bill is treated as giving consideration of £20,000 (and, since this is below the relevant threshold, Bill has no SDLT liability or notification obligations); Ben is treated as giving no consideration. Neither the market value of the overall plot nor the difference in values of the divided plots is relevant.

Market values could be relevant where one of the owners is a company which is connected to other owners (see **4.29**).

PFI transactions

4.35 Transactions in which a private sector company performs services, often including provision of premises, for a public sector organisation, were widely referred to as Private Finance Initiative (PFI) transactions. Such transactions often involved transfers and leases of property. There is a specific provision allowing many forms of consideration to be ignored in qualifying transactions. This is dealt with at **5.17**.

Sundry liabilities not treated as consideration

4.36 The following liabilities and obligations taken on by a purchaser do not count as consideration:

- an indemnity given to the vendor in respect of liability to a third party arising from breach of an obligation relating to the land (*FA 2003, Sch 4, para 16*);
- an agreement to bear any inheritance tax liability arising from the transfer (*para 16A*);
- an agreement to bear any capital gains tax liability arising from the transfer if it is not (or is treated as not being) a bargain at arm's length (*para 16B*); and
- certain specified costs borne by a leaseholder in connection with enfranchisement (*para 16C*).

RATES OF SDLT

4.37 The rate at which SDLT is charged on consideration other than rent depends on the amount of the chargeable consideration, and whether the transaction is a residential property transaction or a non-residential property transaction. Until 4 December 2014 the amount of the tax payable for both a residential property transaction and a non-residential property transaction was calculated using the so-called 'slab system'. Under that system the rates were not progressive; rather, the whole consideration was chargeable at a single rate determined by the highest tax band into which the total chargeable consideration fell. However, the tax payable in relation to a residential property transaction, with an 'effective date' (see **4.91**) on or after 4 December 2014, and in relation to a non-residential or mixed-use property transaction, with an 'effective date' on or after 17 March 2016, is now calculated using a 'progressive system' (like personal income tax). This means that it is only that part of the chargeable consideration falling within each tax band that is taxed at the rate for that tax band.

In relation to residential property transactions there are transitional rules, which provide that where contracts were exchanged to acquire the residential property before 4 December 2014, but the contract was not completed until on or after 4 December 2014, the purchaser can choose to pay SDLT based on the old rules. Similarly, where the contract was exchanged and substantially performed (see **4.9**) but not completed (see **4.8**) before 4 December 2014 then the purchaser can choose to apply the old rules to the completion transaction taking place on or after 4 December 2014. To choose to pay SDLT based on the old rules the purchaser just enters the appropriate amount of SDLT in box 14 of the land transaction return.

Similarly, in relation to non-residential or mixed-use property transactions, there are transitional rules which provide that where contracts were exchanged to acquire the non-residential or mixed-use property before 17 March 2016, but the contract was not completed until on or after 17 March 2016, then provided that there is no event of the kind listed in *FA 2016, s 116(15)* which results in the effect of the contract being different from the effect of the contract when first entered into, the purchaser can elect to pay SDLT based on the old rules (*FA 2016, s 127(13)(b)* and *(15)*). Similarly, where the contract was exchanged and substantially performed (see **4.9**) but not completed (see **4.91**) before 17 March 2016 then the purchaser can elect to apply the old rules to the completion transaction taking place on or after 17 March 2016 (*FA 2016, s 127(13)(a)*). To choose to pay SDLT based on the old rules the purchaser simply enters the appropriate amount of SDLT in box 14 of the land transaction return.

A transaction is a residential property transaction if the chargeable interest(s) acquired under the transaction consists **entirely** of an interest in residential property (see **4.38**) or, if the transaction is one of a number of linked transactions (see **4.72**), the chargeable interests acquired under each linked transaction consists **entirely** of residential property (*FA 2003, s 55(1B), (1C),(3)* and *(4)*).

A transaction is a non-residential property transaction if the chargeable interest acquired under the transaction either consists of, or includes, a chargeable interest which is not residential property. If the transaction is one of a number of linked transactions (see **4.99**), it will be a non-residential property transaction if the chargeable interest acquired under any of the linked transactions consists of, or includes, an interest in non-residential property (*FA 2003, s 55(2),(3)* and *(4)*).

A transaction is a mixed-use property transaction if the chargeable interest(s) acquired under the transaction either consists of, or includes, a chargeable interest(s) which comprises both residential and non-residential property. If the transaction is one of a number of linked transactions (see **4.89**), it will be a mixed-use property transaction if the chargeable interest(s) acquired under any of the linked transactions consists of, or includes, an interest in both residential and non-residential property (*FA 2003, s 55(2), (3)* and *(4)*).

Thus the tax rates for residential property will only be applicable if the transaction(s) consist(s) **entirely** of residential property.

The current rates and tax bands, plus those which applied to residential property transactions with an 'effective date' (see **4.91**) on or before 3 December 2014, and those which applied to non-residential or mixed-use property with an 'effective date' (see **4.91**) on or before 16 March 2016, are listed below (*FA 2003, s 55*).

An additional 3% rate of SDLT applies to purchases of additional dwellings (such as second homes and buy-to-let properties) and first purchases of dwellings by companies and other non-individual purchasers (see **4.54** et seq) with an 'effective date' (see **4.91**) on or after 1 April 2016.

On grant (or deemed grant) of a lease at rent, special rules apply for calculation of the SDLT on the rent (see **6.41** et seq).

At the 2020 Budget, the government announced that it will introduce an SDLT surcharge, at a rate of 2%, for purchases of residential property by non-UK residents with effect from 1 April 2021. The 2% surcharge will be added to the existing residential rates including the higher rate for additional dwellings (see **4.54** et seq), the 15% rate for enveloped residential properties (see **4.88** et seq) and the SDLT rates which apply where first-time buyer's relief is available (see **5.47**).

The government have indicated that they will consult on the draft legislation over the summer of 2020 and include the proposed legislation in *Finance Bill 2021*.

Where contracts for the purchase of the residential property by the non-UK resident, were exchanged before 11 March 2020, but are not completed (see **4.10**) or substantially performed (see **4.9**) until after 1 April 2021, transitional rules, subject to satisfying certain conditions, may apply so that the 2% SDLT surcharge is not charged on the transaction.

Consideration (£)	**Residential property[a] – with an 'effective date' on or before 3 December 2014**	**Non-residential[a] or mixed property – with an 'effective date' on or before 16 March 2016**
Not exceeding £125,000	0%	–
Not exceeding £150,000	0%, only for property in a designated Disadvantaged Area[b] Otherwise 1%	0%[c]
Exceeding £125,000/£150,000 but not exceeding £250,000	1%[d]	1%
£250,001 to £500,000	3%	3%
£500,001 to £1,000,000	4%[e]	4%
£1,000,001 to £2,000,000	5%[e]	4%
Exceeding £2,000,000	7%[e]	4%

(a) See **4.38**.
(b) Disadvantaged Areas Relief was abolished with effect from 6 April 2013 (see **5.69**).
(c) 1% in the case of grant of a lease of non-residential or mixed property with a yearly rent of £1,000 or more attributable to the non-residential part (see **6.46**).
(d) 0% for first-time buyers if effective date was before 25 March 2012.
(e) Or 15% in the case of a purchase of an interest in a single dwelling by certain non-natural persons for chargeable consideration of more than £500,000 (see **4.87**).

Consideration (£)	**Residential property[a] – with an 'effective date' on or after 4 December 2014 – additional 3% rate does not apply (see 4.56 et seq)**
Not exceeding £125,000	0%
£125,001 to £250,000	2%
£250,001 to £925,000	5%[b]
£925,001 to £1,500,000	10%[b]
Exceeding £1,500,000	12%[b]

(a) See **4.38**.
(b) Or 15% in the case of a purchase of an interest in a single dwelling by certain non-natural persons for chargeable consideration of more than £500,000 (see **4.87**).

Also note that for transactions with an 'effective date' (see **4.91**) on or after 22 November 2017, a relief for first-time buyers may be available (see **5.47** et seq) which effectively increases the zero rate threshold to £300,000 with a

5% rate applying to any chargeable consideration exceeding £300,000 up to a maximum of £500,000. If the purchase price of the dwelling exceeds £500,000 no relief is available and the normal rates of SDLT, for a residential property transaction, apply to the full amount of the chargeable consideration.

Consideration (£)	**Non-residential property[a] – with an 'effective date' on or after 17 March 2016**
Not exceeding £150,000	0%
£150,001 to £250,000	2%
Exceeding £250,000	5%

(a) See **4.38**.

Example 4.12—Calculation of SDLT chargeable under the rules which apply for residential property transactions with an effective date on or after 4 December 2014.

On 28 April 2020 John (who does not have a spouse or civil partner) exchanges contracts for the purchase of a residential property situated in England for a cash consideration of £2,500,000. This is the first property purchased by John and therefore the 3% additional rate charge (see **4.56**) does not apply. The relief for first-time buyers (see **5.47**) does not apply as the purchase price of the property exceeds £500,000. Finally, as John acquires the property in his own right, and not through a company, a partnership with a corporate partner or a collective investment scheme, the single 15% rate of SDLT does not apply (see **4.87**). The purchase of the property completes on 30 June 2020 without any prior event having taken place which would have 'substantially performed' (see **4.9**) the contract prior to that date.

The SDLT chargeable on the purchase of the property is calculated as follows:

Purchase Price (£)	**Rate (0%)**	**SDLT (£)**
125,000	0	Nil
125,000	2	2,500
675,000	5	33,750
575,000	10	57,500
1,000,000	12	120,000
2,500,000		213,750

John must therefore file a land transaction return, and pay the SDLT due of £213,750, by 14 July 2020.

Example 4.13—Calculation of SDLT chargeable under the rules which apply for non-residential property transactions with an effective date on or after 17 March 2016.

On 31 May 2020 Reid and Wright Ltd exchange contracts for the purchase of an office block situated in England for a cash consideration of £5,250,000. The purchase of the property completes on 30 June 2020 without any prior event having taken place which would have 'substantially performed' (see **4.9**) the contract prior to that date.

The SDLT chargeable on the purchase of the property is calculated as follows:

Purchase Price (£)	Rate (0%)	SDLT (£)
150,000	0	Nil
100,000	2	2,000
5,000,000	5	250,000
5,250,000		252,000

Reid and Wright Ltd must therefore file a land transaction return, and pay the SDLT due of £252,000, by 14 July 2020.

Residential property

4.38 Residential property is defined in *FA 2003, s 116(1)* as follows:

(a) a building that is used or suitable for use as a dwelling, or a building which is in the process of being built or adapted for use as a dwelling; and

(b) land that is or forms part of the garden or grounds of a building falling within (a) above, including any building or structure on such land; or

(c) an interest in or right over land that subsists for the benefit of a building falling within (a) above or for the benefit of land falling within (b) above – for example, access rights across adjacent property.

Non-residential property means any property that is not residential property (*FA 2003, s 116(1)*).

The definitions of residential property and non-residential property are subject to the rule in *FA 2003, s 116(7)* which provides that where six or more dwellings are acquired as a 'single transaction' then the dwellings are treated as **not** being residential property (see **4.47**).

The status of a house or flat as a dwelling is usually obvious. However, there will be other situations where it is not clear as to whether a building is suitable for use as a dwelling, eg when the building is derelict, or where it is used for purposes other than those of a dwelling etc.

4.39 The distinction between residential and non-residential property is important given the higher rates of tax that apply to residential property. As set out in **4.37** the highest rate of SDLT for a residential property transaction is 12% (15% if the additional 3% rate applies: see **4.56** et seq), whereas for a non-residential property transaction it is 5%.

A transaction is a residential property transaction if the chargeable interest(s) acquired under the transaction consists **entirely** of an interest in residential property or, if the transaction is one of a number of linked transactions (see **4.89**), the chargeable interests acquired under each linked transaction consists **entirely** of residential property (*FA 2003, s 55(1B), (1C), (3)* and *(4)*). In contrast a transaction is a non-residential property transaction if the chargeable interest acquired under the transaction either consists of, or includes, a chargeable interest which is not residential property. If the transaction is one of a number of linked transactions (see **4.89**), it will be a non-residential property transaction if the chargeable interest acquired under any of the linked transactions consists of, or includes, an interest in non-residential property (*FA 2003, s 55(2), (3)* and *(4)*).

This means that there is a clear incentive, in appropriate circumstances, for taxpayers to contend that not all of the property acquired is residential property so that the lower SDLT rates apply, whilst in contrast there is a clear incentive for HMRC to argue the opposite view.

4.40 HMRC guidance on the meaning of residential property was updated on 1 October 2019 and can be found at SDLTM00360 to SDLTM00400. As discussed in **4.38,** a transaction will be a residential property transaction if it comprises the acquisition of a building which is used or suitable for use as a **dwelling,** or the acquisition of a building which is in the process of being built or adapted for use as a dwelling. The term 'dwelling' is not defined in the legislation and must therefore take its everyday meaning, being 'a building, or a part of a building that affords those who use it the facilities required for day-to-day private domestic existence and a significant degree of permanence' (SDLTM00372). It also includes buildings under construction where there is evidence to show that it is being built or adapted for use as a dwelling.

The principal definition of residential property in *FA 2003, s 116(1)(a)* therefore comprises two parts as follows:

- a building that is used or suitable for use as a dwelling; or
- a building that is in the process of being constructed or adapted for use as a dwelling.

We will start by looking at the first part of this definition, being 'a building that is used or suitable for use as a dwelling'.

At SDLTM00380, HMRC confirm that it is not necessary for the sellers or previous occupants of the building to be in residence on the 'effective date' of transaction for the property to be considered 'in use' as a dwelling. Use at the 'effective date' of the transaction is a very important factor, but long-standing past use will also be considered. If a building is not in use at the 'effective date' of the transaction, but it was last used as a dwelling, then HMRC are likely to require strong evidence to support any claim that the building, or part of the building, is not suitable for use as a dwelling. They also confirm that any future intention of the purchaser to use the building for non-residential purposes is irrelevant in determining whether it is residential property as at the 'effective date' of the transaction (SDLTM00380). Equally, if a building is being used for a commercial purpose any future intention to use it as a dwelling, should be irrelevant in determining its status at the 'effective date' of the transaction.

4.41 Other factors which may be relevant in determining whether or not a property is suitable for use as a dwelling would include the following (SDLTM00385):

- If the property has the physical attributes of a dwelling then, in HMRC's view, that would indicate that it is suitable for use as a dwelling regardless of its actual use, eg a property may be used as a doctors surgery at the 'effective date' of the transaction but if it could equally be used as a dwelling, without any significant structural alterations being made to the property, HMRC are likely to argue that it is suitable for use as a dwelling.
- Private/public legal conditions (including planning permission) which restrict the use to which a property can be put may be a factor in determining suitability for use as a dwelling, although, in HMRC's view, they are not necessarily determinative. HMRC give the example of a holiday chalet that is used by visitors for short stays and confirm that whilst the property would not have been used as a dwelling by those visitors, the chalet may still be suitable for use as a dwelling. However, if planning restrictions are in place under which the chalet can only be used for short stays, or cannot be used out of season, that would indicate that the property was not suitable for use as a dwelling (see SDLTM00390 for further commentary).
- If a property is subject to council tax, that would indicate that it is suitable for use as a dwelling whereas if it is subject to non-domestic rates that would indicate it is not suitable for such use.
- A property that is no longer habitable as a dwelling, due to dereliction for example, would not be residential property, on the basis that it is not suitable for use as a dwelling. However, HMRC make a clear distinction

between a derelict property and a dwelling which is essentially habitable, but which is in need of modernisation, renovation or repair, which can be carried out without materially changing the structural nature of the property. HMRC state that the removal of bathroom or kitchen facilities before the 'effective date' of the transaction would not make the property unsuitable for use as a dwelling. These are internal fittings and would not constitute structural changes to the dwelling that would mean that the building was not suitable for use as a dwelling. A new bathroom or kitchen could be fitted relatively quickly and cheaply. Similarly, in HMRC's view, substantial repairs to windows or a roof, a need to switch services back on, or dealing with an infestation of pests would also not make the building unsuitable for use as a dwelling.

In the recent case of *PN Bewley Ltd v HMRC* [2019] UKFTT 0065 (TC) the First-tier Tribunal (FTT) ruled that the purchase of a derelict bungalow by a company was not the acquisition of residential property, and therefore that the lower non-residential property SDLT rates applied to the transaction. The FTT considered that the test to be applied was whether, at the time the SDLT became payable, the property was used, or was suitable for use, as a dwelling. The bungalow had been empty for a long period of time, the central heating system had been removed, and there were holes in the walls, ceilings and floors as a result of a survey carried out on the property. The FTT concluded that the bungalow was not suitable for use as a dwelling and was therefore non-residential property. This also meant that the transaction was not liable for the 3% higher rate of SDLT (see **4.56** et seq).

4.42 HMRC acknowledge that it can be more difficult to decide whether a building is suitable for use as a dwelling when a building is used partly as a dwelling and partly for other purposes (SDLTM00390). However, where one or more rooms within a building are used as a 'home office', the rooms used for work will normally still be suitable for use as a dwelling, and the building overall will remain in use as a dwelling. An alternative scenario might be where part of a building is used as a dwelling and another part as, say, a doctor's surgery. The rooms used as the surgery are clearly not being used as a dwelling. However, the actual use of the rooms does not determine whether they are suitable for use as a dwelling. HMRC state that the degree of conversion that was required to create the surgery and the degree of separation from the residential parts of the building will be key factors. If the rooms used as a surgery can easily be used as a dwelling then, irrespective of their actual use, they will remain suitable for use as a dwelling. Alternatively, if the rooms used as a surgery have been converted in some way so as to make them unsuitable for use as a dwelling, then they would not be suitable for use as a dwelling. HMRC give examples of such conversion as the installation of specialist equipment such as a dentist's chair or an X-ray device. Equally, if planning restrictions prevent all or part of the building from being used for residential purposes then it is more likely that the building will no longer be 'suitable for use' as a dwelling.

4.43 The test as to whether the building is suitable for use as a dwelling is applied at the 'effective date' of the transaction, and the future intentions of the purchaser are irrelevant. Whilst the historical use of the building will be a guide as to whether it is suitable for 'use as a dwelling' in HMRC's view it is not determinative, especially if the property has subsequently been adapted (SDLTM00395).

4.44 If a building, which has an area which is not suitable for use as a dwelling, is acquired as a single building then it 'consists of or includes land that is not residential property' and it will therefore be taxed at non-residential rates. This is the case irrespective of the relative sizes of the residential and non-residential areas (SDLTM00395).

4.45 We will now look at the second part of the definition of residential property in *FA 2003, s 116(1)*, being 'a building that is in the process of being constructed or adapted for use as a dwelling'. In this instance it is necessary to consider future intentions as it is only by doing so that you can determine whether the building will ultimately be 'suitable for use as a dwelling' (SDLTM00400).

The construction or adaptation of the building must be physically underway at the 'effective date' of the transaction. HMRC do not consider obtaining planning on its own to be sufficient, if the physical construction or adaptation work has not yet commenced. However, if the physical construction or adaptation work has commenced at the 'effective date' of the transaction then the nature of the planning permission would be a strong indicator as to whether or not the building was to be used as a dwelling.

HMRC consider that the requisite construction or adaption will only have taken place when '… building works on top of the foundations have begun. This will be more than a hole in the ground. Furthermore, preparatory works, including demolition of previous buildings, site preparation etc, are not considered sufficient to determine that construction of a dwelling has started' (SDLTM00400).

This means that, if a building under construction is to be residential property, the work will have to have reached the stage where the foundations of the building have been laid and work has begun to build on top of those foundations.

4.46 HMRC give guidance on whether, in their view, each of the following are likely to be residential property for SDLT purposes (SDLTM00375):

- mobile homes, caravans and houseboats (SDLTM10023);
- holiday homes (SDLTM00385);

- halls of residence and other student accommodation (SDLTM00377); and
- hotels, inns, bed and breakfast or similar establishments (SDLTM00375).

4.47 Where six or more dwellings are the subject of 'a single transaction', they are treated as wholly non-residential property (*s 116(7)*), which effectively limits the highest SDLT rate to 5% subject to a claim for multiple dwellings relief (see **5.57**). The legislation does not define what is meant by 'a single transaction' but it is the author's view that it means one contract between the same vendor and purchaser (and not including parties connected with the vendor and purchaser) for the acquisition of the agreed number of properties. The term 'a single transaction' would not cover, for example, a situation where there are multiple independent contracts between the same vendor and purchaser, since in such a situation there would be a number of transactions, although they would be 'linked' (see **4.89**) for the purposes of *FA 2003, s 108*. However, the fact that completion of the acquisition of different properties under that single contract may take place at different times should not mean that there is not 'a single transaction' for these purposes. For example, the acquisition of six or more properties under a single contract with completion at different times as construction of each of the properties is completed is 'a single transaction' for the purposes of *s 116(7)*. The treatment of the purchase of six or more dwellings as the acquisition of non-residential property now has even greater importance given the higher rates of SDLT which generally apply to the acquisition of residential property, and the additional 3% rate which may apply to the purchase of dwellings (see **4.56**). Care will therefore need to be taken to ensure that where six or more dwellings are being acquired the deal is structured as a single transaction, and not a number of separate transactions, if non-residential property treatment is to be available.

It will often also be important to understand how many dwellings are being acquired within a property. In any case, where a building is considered to contain more than one dwelling, HMRC make it clear that they will require evidence that each dwelling within the building is sufficiently independent to count as a separate dwelling in its own right (SDLTM00410). Some of the factors which HMRC consider should be taken into account in determining the number of dwellings are the facilities within each dwelling, whether there is independent access to the dwelling and the privacy from other dwellings. These are considered in more detail below.

- *Facilities*

  (a) sleeping area – this area would normally have lighting, power points, a window, be of a reasonable size and be separated from the 'living area'.

(b) living area – an area for day-to-day living, including space for chairs, tables, cupboards, furniture and to have visitors. The room would normally have lighting, power points, heating and a window.

(c) Kitchen area – an area where a meal can be prepared and somewhere suitable to eat it, although not necessarily in the kitchen. In HMRC's view it is not necessary for the kitchen to have a cooker or white goods such as a fridge or dishwasher present at the 'effective date' of the transaction, because these are sometimes removed prior to sale. However, there should be space and infrastructure in place to accommodate such items eg plumbing for a sink, power source for a cooker etc.

HMRC confirm that a 'studio flat' which may combine two or more of the above areas into one room should still be treated as having the facilities necessary to be treated as a separate dwelling. This means, for example, that the separation of the sleeping area from the living area, as referred to above, is not actually necessary for a unit to constitute a separate dwelling.

- *Independent entrances*

  Each dwelling must have an access point which is sufficiently independent. This could be a separate entrance from outside of the building, or from common parts of the building such as for flats. Typically, there will be common parts (such as hallways and staircases) to which each dwelling within the building will have access via a lockable door.

- *Privacy and interconnecting doors*

  To be treated as a separate dwelling, the unit must have a degree of privacy from other dwellings. If there are connecting doors between dwellings it will be relevant whether that connecting door can be locked or is capable of being made secure from both sides. The more interconnecting doors there are, the less likely it is that there are separate dwellings. It will also be important whether the connecting door has adequate fire proofing and sound proofing to be considered suitable to separate dwellings.

Other factors to be taken into account in determining the number of dwellings are as follows (SDLTM00430):

- Control of utilities – electricity, cold water, heating and gas.
- Legal constraints – there may be legal conditions, including planning constraints, preventing use as a separate dwelling.
- Council tax – where a property has been assessed as comprising more than one dwelling, this may indicate it should be treated as more than

one dwelling for SDLT purposes. However, the definition of dwelling for council tax purposes is different from its meaning for SDLT purposes, and therefore HMRC do not consider this a strong indicator on its own.

- Marketing material – HMRC consider estate agents' marketing material useful in considering the number of dwellings being acquired; however, it is by no means determinative.
- Separate post and bills – individual letter boxes, separate utility bills and phone bills will provide some evidence as to whether there are separate dwellings, but again it will not be determinative.

4.48 If it is established that a building falls within the definition in *FA 2003, s116(1)(a)* – 'a building that is used or suitable for use as a dwelling, or is in the process of being constructed or adapted for such use' – so that it is residential property, then any land that is or forms part of the garden or grounds of such a building (including any building or structure on such land) will also be residential property (*FA 2003, s 116(1)(b)*). It is, therefore, important to consider whether any land acquired along with the building is, or is part of, the grounds of the building since, if it is, it will also constitute residential property. In contrast, if the land acquired along with the building is not 'garden or grounds' it will not be residential property, the transaction will, therefore, not consist entirely of the acquisition of residential property, and the lower non-residential property SDLT rates will apply to the transaction.

The HMRC guidance, which was updated on 25 June 2019, as to what, in their view, constitutes the garden or grounds of a building, can be found at SDLTM00440 to SDLTM00480.

4.49 The status of the land in question (ie whether it is garden or grounds of a dwelling) must be assessed at the 'effective date' of the transaction, but that does not mean that only the use to which the land is put on that date will be considered. HMRC consider that the aim of the legislation is to capture the real or true relationship between the land and the building at the 'effective date' of the transaction. In so doing the history of the use of the land will be a factor to be taken into account. HMRC state "We should seek to establish the traditional or habitual use of the land to establish its true relationship to the building". Where a purchaser is looking to rely on historic use to support a view that the land is not part of the grounds or garden of the building, and therefore that it is not residential property, HMRC will expect evidence to support that use to be retained and to be available in the event of an enquiry into the SDLT return (SDLTM00450).

4.50 The purchaser's future intentions as to the use of the land are irrelevant in determining whether, at the 'effective date' of the transaction, the land is, or is part of, the grounds of the building. As a consequence, the same piece of land may constitute garden or grounds of a building in one transaction but not in a subsequent transaction. At SDLTM00450 HMRC give the following example:

> 'For instance, a purchaser (Person A) may acquire the garden of a dwelling (whether or not fenced/walled off at that time from the rest of the vendor's property) separately from the dwelling, with the intention to use it for commercial purposes. If at the time of the purchase the garden was enjoyed as a garden by the residents of the dwelling (ie the vendor) then the purchase will be of residential property regardless of the fact that the land is being purchased and the dwelling is not. However, if the same land is subsequently sold on by Person A then it may be the case that by the time of that subsequent sale it is no longer used as the garden of a dwelling and has therefore become non-residential land.'

4.51 A number of factors may need to be taken into account in coming to a view as to whether land is the garden or grounds of a building and it is unlikely that any one factor will be determinative. At SDLTM00455, HMRC state: 'Where a number of contrasting factors exist, weigh up all the factors in order to come to a balanced judgement of whether the land in question constitutes 'garden or grounds'. This judgement will apply to all the land being considered."

Factors to be considered in determining where land is 'garden or grounds' is as follows:

- *The use to which the land is put is likely to be the most important factor*

  If, at the 'effective date' of the transaction, the land in question is put to a commercial use, then that would be a strong indicator that the land is not garden or grounds of the relevant building. At SDLTM00460, HMRC state that 'It would be expected that the land had been actively and substantively exploited on a regular basis [for the purposes of that commercial use] for this to be the case.' HMRC point out that a large number of activities, such as beekeeping, grazing and equestrian activities could be purely a leisure activity or could be carried out on a commercial basis. Whilst livestock may graze on the land, if that activity is not carried out on a commercial basis, and the land "… primarily provides an appealing setting for a dwelling …" then the land is likely to be 'garden or grounds' of the dwelling. Conversely, if the land is grazed under a genuine commercial arrangement then it should not be 'garden or grounds' of the dwelling.

  Where a lease has been granted to a third party for the exclusive occupation of the land it should not be 'garden or grounds' of the dwelling. In contrast, if there is merely a "gentleman's agreement" to occasionally allow the livestock to graze on the land, it will be more difficult to support an argument that the land is not 'garden or grounds' of the building.

If the commercial activity taking place on the land is recorded as a source of income in a self-assessment tax return, that is likely to be strong evidence that a genuine commercial activity is being carried on.

At SDLTM00460 HMRC state that certain types of land can be expected to be 'garden or grounds', or be expected to be non-residential land, unless there is clear evidence to the contrary. For example, they suggest that paddocks and orchards will usually be 'garden or grounds' unless it can be shown that they are actively exploited on a commercial basis. However, if a field has historically been used for arable farming but is sitting fallow at the 'effective date' of the transaction that does not mean the land has become 'garden or grounds'. HMRC acknowledge that fallow periods are an integral part of commercial management of farmland, and therefore the land is likely to continue to be non-residential.

- *Layout of land and outbuildings (SDLTM00465)*

  The presence of the following may indicate that the land is 'garden or grounds':

  - domestic outbuildings;
  - areas laid out for leisure use or carrying out hobbies;
  - small orchards; or
  - stables and paddocks suitable for leisure use.

  The presence of the following may indicate that the land is non-residential:

  - commercial farming/horticulture;
  - commercial woodland;
  - commercial equestrian use; or
  - some other commercial use.

- *Extent of the land*

  The extent/size of the land in question will also be a factor to be considered. At SDLTM00470, HMRC indicate that a small country cottage is unlikely to have dozens of acres of 'garden or grounds' whereas a stately home may well have 'garden or grounds' which extend to that sort of acreage. Large tracts of fells/moorland are unlikely to be 'garden or grounds'.

- *Proximity to the dwelling*

  If the land is physically close to the dwelling and easily accessible from it or separated by a feature which is easily crossed such as a small road or river, or even land owned by third parties, this would indicate that the land is 'ground or gardens'. Fencing off the land would not, in itself, cause the land to cease to be 'garden or grounds'. However, the more difficult it is to get to the land from the dwelling and the greater the degree of separation between the dwelling and the land, the less likely it is that the land will be 'garden or grounds'.

- *Legal factors and constraints*

  If the land is subject to any legal constraints as to use, for example, there may be planning permission in place which permits the land to be used for commercial purposes, then this may indicate that the land is not 'garden or grounds'. However, in HMRC's view planning law by itself is not determinative and actual use will normally be given greater weight. They give two examples as follows:

  – Where planning regulations prohibit commercial use but these are being breached by longstanding commercial use (particularly if the actual use is unlikely to be challenged by the planning authority), then this would indicate the land is not likely to be 'garden or grounds'; or

  – alternatively, where commercial use is permitted but the land is actually being used for residential purposes, then this would be an indicator that the land is 'garden or grounds'.

  The terms of any contracts, leases, restrictive covenants or easements will be relevant factors. However, whether the land is registered under one land registry title, or more than one land registry title, will rarely be relevant.

  If the owner of the dwelling has no rights to access the land then this is likely to indicate it is not 'garden or grounds', particularly if the land is physically separate from the dwelling. In contrast, if physically separated land can be accessed via an easement, this could mean that it is garden or grounds.

  Rights of way over the land for walkers, or rights of access by utility companies to the land, will not normally prevent the land from being 'garden or grounds'.

4.52 HMRC indicate at SDLTM00475 that the following factors are likely to indicate non-residential land:

- a non-domestic rateable value for the land has been assessed;
- non-domestic rates are collected for the land; or
- the land has been classified as agricultural land and buildings for the purposes of exemption from business rates.

4.53 HMRC make it clear that they will closely scrutinise any arrangements which appear to have been put in place for the purpose of changing the SDLT status of land from residential to non-residential (or perhaps, less likely, from non-residential to residential) (SDLTM00475).

4.54 HMRC have in fact been challenging a number of claims that the non-residential rates of SDLT apply to the purchase of a dwelling with land, where the tax payer was claiming that the land acquired was not part of the 'garden or grounds' of the dwelling. Unfortunately, from the perspective of establishing sound precedent case law, none of the cases had particularly strong fact patterns from the purchaser's perspective, and HMRC has successfully argued that the higher residential rates of SDLT applied in each case.

Doctor David Hyman and another v HMRC [2019] UK FTT 469 (TC)

The facts were that Doctor Hyman and his wife acquired a farmhouse together with approximately 3.5 acres of land. In the first instance they paid SDLT at the higher residential SDLT rates but then made a repayment claim when they received advice that the lower non-residential SDLT rates should have applied. The land acquired included a meadow, bridleway and derelict barn (which had been classified as non-residential by the local council). However, even though the land was physically separated by hedges/fences from the farmhouse, and the public had a right of way over the bridleway, the First-tier Tribunal held that the land was the garden or grounds of the farmhouse and therefore that the higher residential rates of SDLT applied, and no repayment was due.

C Goodfellow and another v HMRC [2019] UK FTT 750 (TC)

The facts were that Mr and Mrs Goodfellow purchased a property with approximately 4.5 acres of land. As well as a dwelling there was a detached garage, which was used as an office, together with a stable yard and a paddock for horses. As in *Hyman*, the taxpayer initially paid SDLT at the higher residential rates of SDLT but then made a repayment claim on receiving advice that the lower non-residential property rates of SDLT should have applied. The arguments for non-residential property treatment were largely that some paddocks were let to a neighbour, to allow them to graze horses, for a nominal rent of £12 per annum, and that the office space in the garage was non-residential property. These arguments were rejected by the First-tier Tribunal. The tribunal took the view that the office in the garage was no different from a 'home office' and was therefore residential property. As regards the paddocks, the tribunal found that the property was sold as an 'equestrian property' and the equestrian facilities were therefore a necessary part of the property and there was no commercial activity taking place on the land. As such the land constituted the 'garden and grounds' of the dwelling, the property was wholly residential property, and therefore no repayment of SDLT was due.

Pensfold v HMRC [2020] UK FTT 0116 (TC)

A Cayman Islands company acquired a farm with 27 acres of land and proposed to develop the site as an eco/agritourism venture. The SDLT land transaction return was filed on the basis that the lower non-residential rates applied to the purchase. The basis for treating the property as non-residential was that the land was subject to a grazing agreement with a third party, who had been grazing the land for some years, every year, from April to October. This third party also maintained the land in the intervening winter. No formal agreement was in place to permit the grazing which took place under a traditional gentleman's agreement. However, at the 'effective date' of the transaction, the land was not being grazed. The marketing brochure advertising the farm for sale made no mention of the sale being subject to grazing rights, and likewise the contract to purchase the property made no mention of the grazing rights. The First-tier Tribunal pointed out that, had the entire 27 acres of land been subject to grazing rights, that would have made the plans to develop an eco/agritourism venture rather difficult to implement. The tribunal therefore concluded that, at the 'effective date' of the transaction, the property was entirely residential and, therefore the higher residential rates of SDLT applied.

Lynda Helen Myles-Till v HMRC [2020] UK FTT 0127 (TC)

The facts were that the taxpayer acquired a property with around three acres of land and the property comprised a three-bedroom house (Shepherds Cottage), a detached double garage, a garden to the rear of the house and a grass-covered field known as the "paddock". The estate agent's marketing literature mentioned the paddock a few times; for example, it stated that: 'The garden looks back on to a paddock enclosed by mature hedging and post and rail fencing.' In 1983, the paddock had been part of a neighbouring farm. For many years the paddock had been covered in grass and therefore potentially usable for grazing animals. This potential use of the paddock for grazing caused an agricultural and rural planning consultant to refer to the paddock, in his report, as agricultural land. The arguments for treating the land as non-residential property were largely that the land had historically been used as agricultural land as part of the neighbouring farm, at the 'effective date' of the transaction the paddock was overgrown agricultural land that had not been adapted for any other use, and the size of the paddock was far larger than would usually come with a dwelling of the size and character of Shepherds Cottage. In coming to its decision, the tribunal stated that:

> 'One must, in addition, look at the use or function of the adjoining land to decide if its character answers to the statutory wording in s 116(1) – in particular, is the land grounds "of" a building whose defining characteristic is its "use" as a dwelling? The emphasised words indicate that the use or function of adjoining land itself must support the use of the building

concerned as a dwelling. For the commonly owned adjoining land to be "grounds", it must be, functionally, an appendage to the dwelling, rather than having a self-standing function.'

In the tribunal's view it came down to whether '... the paddock had a self-standing function as opposed to being a functional appendage of Shepherds Cottage.' The tribunal concluded that as there was no evidence of actual use of the paddock for grazing since it was last part of a farm in 1983, that at the 'effective date' of the transaction the paddock was the 'grounds' of Shepherds Cottage, and therefore the property was wholly residential.

4.55 The legislation provides a list of other categories of building which are specifically treated as residential property (*FA 2003, s 116(2)* – the 'Residential' column in the table below), but then removes many examples from the list (*FA 2003, s 116(3)* – the 'Non-residential column in the table below).

Residential	**Non-residential**
Residential accommodation for school pupils	Home or other institution providing residential accommodation for children
Residential accommodation for students	Hall of residence for students in higher or further education
Residential accommodation for members of the armed forces	–
An institution which is the sole or main residence for at least 90% of its residents	Home or other institution providing residential accommodation with personal care to those in need of such care by reason of age, disablement, drug/alcohol dependence or mental illness
–	Hospital or hospice
–	Prison or similar establishment
–	Hotel or inn or similar establishment

Higher SDLT rates for additional dwellings and dwellings purchased by companies and other non-individual purchasers

4.56 At the Autumn Statement on 25 November 2015 the Chancellor of the Exchequer announced that from 1 April 2016 higher rates of SDLT would apply to purchases of additional residential properties (referred to in the legislation as 'dwellings'), such as second homes and buy-to-let properties. In fact the legislation is much wider than the original policy description and, for example, applies to first purchases of residential properties by companies and other non-individual purchasers. The legislation can be found in *FA 2003, Sch 4ZA* ('Stamp Duty Land Tax: Higher Rates for Additional Dwellings and Dwellings Purchased by Companies') and it imposes an additional 3% SDLT charge on chargeable transactions falling within its provisions.

A transaction which falls within the legislation is referred to as a 'higher rates transaction' (*FA 2003, Sch 4ZA, para 2(1)*).

The higher rates of SDLT are as follows:

Consideration (£)	**Rate of SDLT on additional dwellings – 'effective date' on or after 1 April 2016**
Not exceeding £125,000	3%
£125,001 to £250,000	5%
£250,001 to £925,000	8%
£925,001 to £1,500,000	13%
Exceeding £1,500,000	15%

The legislation which imposes the higher rate of SDLT (*FA 2003, Sch 4ZA*) is complex and therefore reference should also be made to the HMRC guidance which is now included in the SDLT manual at SDLTM09730 et seq. The guidance includes some helpful examples.

A calculator is available at www.tax.service.gov.uk/calculate-stamp-duty-land-tax which will calculate the SDLT chargeable on a 'higher rates transaction'.

Meaning of 'higher rates transaction'

4.57 Where there is only one purchaser a transaction will be a 'higher rates transaction' if it falls within any of the five scenarios detailed below (see **4.70–4.80**) by reference to that single purchaser (*FA 2003, Sch 4ZA, para 2(2)*). Where there are two or more purchasers you must take each of the purchasers in turn and determine whether, by reference to any of those purchasers, the transaction falls within any of the five scenarios detailed below (see **4.70–4.80**). If it does then it is a 'higher rates transaction' (*FA 2003, Sch 4ZA, para 2(3)*).

Which of the five scenarios a transaction falls within is generally determined by three factors as follows:

(a) whether or not the purchaser is an individual;

(b) whether a single 'dwelling' or multiple 'dwellings' are being acquired; and

(c) where multiple 'dwellings' are being acquired whether the 'chargeable consideration' (see **4.19**) for only one of the dwellings, or for more than one of the 'dwellings', amounts to £40,000 or more.

Meaning of 'dwelling'

4.58 For the purposes of the higher rates legislation a dwelling is defined (*FA 2003, Sch 4ZA, para 17(2)*) as a building or part of a building that is:

- used or suitable for use as a single dwelling; or
- in the process of being constructed or adapted for use as a single dwelling.

Land that is to be enjoyed with a dwelling as a garden or grounds of the dwelling, including any building or structure on that land (eg a detached garage), and any land which subsists for the benefit of a dwelling, is treated as being part of the dwelling (*FA 2003, Sch 4ZA, para 17(3)* and *(4)*). This is similar to, but slightly different from, the wording in *FA 2003, s 116(1)(b)*, which includes land that is or forms part of the garden or grounds of a building which is suitable for use as a dwelling within the definition of residential property (see **4.56** et seq).

There is no definition of the term 'dwelling' in the legislation which must therefore take its ordinary meaning, that is a building which provides those who use it with the facilities required for everyday private domestic existence. The term will cover holiday homes, including those which cannot be used all year round, and furnished lettings. Purpose-built student accommodation is not a 'dwelling' for the purposes of the higher rates legislation and therefore the acquisition of such a building will not be a 'higher rates transaction'. However, this is the case only for purpose-built student accommodation and, for example, an ordinary house or flat for students to live in would be a dwelling for the purposes of the legislation (see SDLTM09750).

An 'off-plan purchase' will also count as the acquisition of a 'dwelling' if the following conditions are satisfied (*FA 2003, Sch 4ZA, para 17(5)*):

- a contract has been exchanged for the acquisition of a building which is to be constructed or adapted for use as a single dwelling;
- the contract is substantially performed (see **4.9**); and
- at the time of substantial performance the construction or adaptation of the building has not yet started.

It will be a question of fact as to whether a single dwelling, or more than one dwelling, is being acquired. Generally a self-contained building is likely to be a single dwelling if anyone living in that building can live independently of the residents of the rest of the building. This is likely to include having independent access to the building as well as cooking, toilet and washing facilities.

The acquisition of more than one dwelling will be treated as though a single dwelling had been acquired if the dwellings acquired are subsidiary dwellings. A subsidiary dwelling must be within the same grounds of another dwelling purchased in the same transaction ('the principal dwelling'). The principal dwelling and the garden and grounds attributable to that principal dwelling must be at least two thirds of the total chargeable consideration given for the principal and subsidiary dwellings (see SDLTM09755 and *FA 2003, Sch 4ZA, para 5(5)*).

A building, or part of a building, used for any of the following purposes is not used as a 'dwelling' for the purposes of the higher rates legislation (*FA 2003, Sch 4ZA, para 17(7)*):

- residential accommodation for school pupils;
- residential accommodation for students;
- residential accommodation for members of the armed forces;
- an institution that is the sole or main residence of at least 90% of its residents and does not fall within any of the other types of institution in the remainder of this list;
- a home or institution providing residential accommodation for children;
- a hall of residence for students in further or higher education;
- a home or other institution providing residential accommodation with personal care for persons in need of personal care by reason of old age, disablement, past or present dependence on alcohol or drugs or past or present mental disorder;
- a hospital or hospice;
- a prison or similar establishment; and
- a hotel or inn or similar establishment.

It is likely that a bed and breakfast or guest house which has bathing facilities, telephone lines, etc installed in each bedroom will not be a dwelling for the purposes of the higher rates legislation.

In the recent case of *PN Bewley Ltd v HMRC* [2019] UKFTT 0065TC the First-tier Tribunal (FTT) ruled that the purchase of a derelict bungalow by a company was not the acquisition of a 'dwelling' for the purposes of the higher rates legislation and therefore that the lower non-residential property SDLT rates applied to the transaction. The FTT considered that the test to be applied was whether, at the time the SDLT became payable, the property was used, or was suitable for use, as a dwelling. The bungalow had been empty for a long period of time, the central heating system had been removed, and there were holes in the walls, ceilings and floors as a result of a survey carried out on the property. The FTT concluded that the bungalow was not suitable for use as a dwelling and was therefore non-residential property.

Transactions to which the additional rate of SDLT does not apply

4.59 The SDLT higher rates will not apply to the acquisition of:

- **non-residential or mixed-use properties –** For example if, as a single transaction, an individual is acquiring a house with a garden and grounds together with some agricultural land close by but clearly not part of the garden and grounds of the house, and not required for the proper enjoyment of the house and its gardens and grounds, then that transaction should be treated as the acquisition of mixed-use property (ie both residential and non-residential property is being acquired) and the SDLT higher rates should not apply to any part of the transaction. For obvious reasons the acquisition of mixed-use property is coming under increased scrutiny from HMRC. They seem to be taking the view, on enquiry, that when a dwelling is acquired with land that is not currently being used for a commercial purpose, then that land should be treated as grounds to be enjoyed with the dwelling (even if the 'grounds' consist of, say, extensive grassed fields not currently being grazed) and therefore a part of the dwelling to which the higher rate of SDLT applies. This matter is discussed in more detail at **4.48** et seq;

- **transactions for which the 'chargeable consideration'** (see **4.14**) **for the acquisition of the single dwelling is less than £40,000** - It should, however, be noted that the £40,000 amount is not a 0% band and, if the transaction is chargeable to the SDLT additional rate, it is chargeable on the whole of the consideration and not only the amount in excess of £40,000;

- **caravans, houseboats and mobile homes** – this is on the basis that these items are moveable and payments in relation to such items are not generally chargeable to SDLT. However, if the moveable asset became sufficiently fixed to the land so as to become a fixture (ie in law the item has become part of the land) SDLT may be chargeable and the SDLT higher rates may apply if the relevant conditions described below are satisfied; and

- **Enveloped residential properties –** the higher rates of SDLT will not apply to the acquisition of a single dwelling for more than £500,000 if the single rate of SDLT of 15% applies to that transaction by virtue of *FA 2003, Sch 4A* (see **4.87**). However, where such a transaction includes the acquisition of a chargeable interest to which the 15% rate does not apply, the deemed separate transaction may be subject to the higher rates of SDLT if it meets the conditions set out in any of scenarios 1–5 detailed below (see **4.70–4.80**).

Joint purchasers

4.60 If any of scenarios 1–5 detailed below (see **4.70–4.80**) apply by reference to any purchaser under a 'land transaction' (see **4.7**), the 3% additional rate will apply to the transaction. In circumstances where there are two or more individuals acquiring the dwelling as joint purchasers (either as 'joint tenants' or as 'tenants in common'), and any of scenarios 1–5 below (see **4.70–4.80**) apply to any of those purchasers, the transaction will be charged at the higher rates. It does not matter how small the interest of any purchaser is in the dwelling (*FA 2003, Sch 4ZA, para 2(3)*). This is, however, subject to the exemption for transactions where spouses or civil partners are purchasing the dwelling from one another (see **4.62**). This exemption was only available if the 'effective date' (see **4.91**) of the transaction was on or after 22 November 2017.

A partner in a partnership is treated as a joint purchaser of any 'chargeable interest' (see **4.14**) acquired by or on behalf of the partnership (*FA 2003, Sch 15, para 2(b)*). This means that when a 'chargeable interest' is acquired by or on behalf of a partnership each of scenarios 1–5 detailed below (see **4.70–4.80**) must be tested by reference to each of the partners and if any one partner would be liable to the 3% additional rate then the whole of the acquisition will be liable to the higher rates.

Spouse or civil partner

4.61 If an individual, who is purchasing a dwelling, has a spouse or civil partner who they are living with on the 'effective date' (see **4.91**) of the transaction, and who is not a joint purchaser, the spouse or civil partner will be treated as though they were a joint purchaser in respect of the transaction. Consequently, scenarios 1 and 4 below (see **4.70** and **4.78**) must also be considered in relation to the spouse or civil partner (*FA 2003, Sch 4ZA, para 9 (1)* and *(2)*). Thus, if the conditions in scenario 1 and 4 (see **4.70** and **4.78**) below are met in relation to the spouse or civil partner, the higher rates of SDLT will apply. This treatment does not apply if the married couple are either legally separated (by court order or deed of separation) or they are in fact separated in circumstances in which the separation is likely to be permanent (*FA 2003, Sch 4ZA, para 9(3)* and *Income Tax Act 2007, s 1011*).

Exemption where spouses and civil partners purchase a dwelling from one another

4.62 A 'chargeable transaction' is not a higher rate transaction under either *FA 2003, Sch 4ZA, para 3* or *para 6* if there is only one purchaser and one vendor and on the 'effective date' (see **4.91**) of the transaction the purchaser and the vendor are married to, or civil partners, of each other and are 'living together' (*FA 2003, Sch 4ZA, para 9A(1)*). Individuals who are married or in a civil partnership are treated as 'living together' unless they are legally separated (by court order or deed of separation) or they are in fact separated in circumstances in which the separation is likely to be permanent (*FA 2003, Sch 4ZA, para 9(3)* and *Income Tax Act 2007, s 1011*).

The exemption also applies where a dwelling is held by one spouse or civil partner and is transferred into the joint ownership of both spouses or civil partners (*FA 2003, Sch 4ZA, para 9A(2)*). Similarly, the exemption is also available where a dwelling is held jointly by both spouses or civil partners and is transferred to one or other of the spouses or civil partners (*FA 2003, Sch 4ZA, para 9A(3)*).

This exemption applies if the 'effective date' (see **4.91**) of the transaction was on or after 22 November 2017.

Individuals – Interests in dwellings treated as owned by an individual

4.63 It will be seen that for either scenarios 1 or 4 below (see **4.70** and **4.78**) to apply one of the conditions is that the individual purchaser owns a 'major interest' (see **4.11**) in another dwelling at the end of the day that is the 'effective day' of the acquisition of the new dwelling.

If an individual is the legal and beneficial owner of a 'major interest' (see **4.11**) in a dwelling they will own that interest for the purposes of the higher rate legislation. Equally, where an individual only has the beneficial ownership of a 'major interest' (see **4.11**) in a dwelling, with legal ownership held within a bare trust or by a nominee, the individual with the beneficial ownership is treated as owning the interest in the dwelling (*FA 2003, Sch 16, para 3* and *Sch 4ZA, para 11(2)* and *(3)*). Similarly, if the bare trustee or nominee disposes of the interest in the dwelling it is the beneficiary who is treated as making the disposal for the purposes of the higher rates legislation (*FA 2003, Sch 4ZA, para 11(3)(b)*).

4.64 An individual ('A') is treated as not having an interest in a dwelling in circumstances where he or she has a 'major interest' (see **4.11**) in a dwelling, but a 'property adjustment order' has been made by a court in proceedings for divorce, separation or nullity in respect of that interest and for the benefit of another person ('B') and the dwelling is B's only or main residence and is not A's only or main residence (*FA 2003, Sch 4ZA, para 9B*). The term 'property adjustment order' is defined in *FA 2003, Sch 4ZA, para 9B(3)*. Such orders would include the transfer of an interest in a dwelling from one spouse to another, selling the home and splitting the proceeds, settling property for the benefit of the other spouse or children, varying marriage settlements etc.

This provision applies to transactions with an 'effective date' (see **4.91**) on or after 22 November 2017.

Dwellings held by trusts

4.65 Where a 'major interest' (see **4.11**) in a dwelling is held in a 'settlement' (ie a trust which is not a bare trust: *FA 2003, Sch 16, para 1(1))*, and under the terms of the trust the beneficiary is entitled to (a) occupy the dwelling for life, or (b) the income earned in respect of the dwelling, the beneficiary of the trust is treated as holding the interest in the dwelling for the purposes of the higher rates legislation (*FA 2003, Sch 4ZA, para 11(1)* and *(3)(a)*). Equally, if the trustees of such a trust dispose of the interest in the dwelling it is the beneficiary who is treated as making the disposal for the purposes of the higher rates legislation (*FA 2003, Sch 4ZA, para 11(3)(b)*).

If the 'major interest' (see **4.11**) in the dwelling is held by the trustees of a trust and the beneficiaries are not entitled as described above in this **4.65**, and it is not a bare trust (*FA 2003, Sch 16, para 1(1)*), then the trustees are treated as holding the dwelling for the purposes of the higher rates legislation.

Dwellings held by a partnership

4.66 The general rule is that in deciding, for the purposes of the higher rates legislation, whether an individual purchaser, who is a partner in a partnership, holds a 'major interest' (see **4.11**) in another dwelling, that individual will be treated as owning any 'major interest' held by or on behalf of the partnership (*FA 2003, Sch 4ZA, para 14(3)* and *Sch 15, para 2(1)(a)*). However, a 'major interest' in a dwelling held by a partnership can be ignored for the purposes of the higher rates legislation if the individual purchaser is not acquiring the new 'major interest' for the purposes of the partnership, the partnership is carrying on a trade and the existing dwelling is being used for the purposes of the partnership's trade (*FA 2003, Sch 4ZA, para 14(1)* and *(2)*). A property letting business carried on by a partnership is not a trade, and therefore, for the purposes of the higher rates legislation, an individual who is a partner in a partnership carrying on such a business, will be treated as holding all of the 'major interests' (see **4.11**) in dwellings held by the partnership.

Dwellings situated outside of England and Northern Ireland

4.67 In determining whether an individual purchaser holds a 'major interest' (see **4.11**) in another dwelling for the purposes of the higher rates legislation, an interest in a dwelling situated outside of England and Northern Ireland is to be taken into account (*FA 2003, Sch 4ZA, para16(1)*). Other countries may have different land law concepts and it will be a question of fact whether an interest owned by an individual is equivalent to a 'major interest' (ie a freehold interest or a lease granted for a term of more than seven years – see **4.11**), and whether it was originally granted for a term of more than seven years and is not subject to a lease with more than 21 years to run (*FA 2003, Sch 4ZA, para 16(2)(a)*).

Dwellings acquired by inheritance

4.68 Where an individual becomes jointly entitled to a 'major interest' (see **4.11**) in a dwelling in the three-year period before the 'effective date' (see **4.91**) of the acquisition of a new dwelling that interest can be ignored, for the purposes of scenarios 1 and 4 below (see **4.70** and **4.78**), provided the following conditions are satisfied (*FA 2003, Sch 4ZA, para 15(1)* and *(2)*):

- the individual became the joint owner of the interest in the dwelling by inheritance; and
- the individual and any spouse or civil partner's combined interest in the dwelling has not exceeded 50% in the three-year period before the 'effective date' (see **4.91**) of the acquisition of the new dwelling. Where the interest in the dwelling is held as a tenant in common, the declared interest held by the individual and any spouse or civil partner must be 50% or less of the whole interest. Alternatively, if the interest in the dwelling is held as joint tenants, the individual and any spouse or civil partner must make up exactly half, or a minority of the joint tenants.

However, if the interest in the dwelling was inherited more than three years before the acquisition of the new dwelling the individual will be treated as holding an interest in that inherited dwelling at the end of the day which is the 'effective date' (see **4.91**) of the acquisition of the new dwelling.

The date of inheritance is the date the individual becomes entitled to the 'major interest' (see **4.11**) which will normally be the date it is transferred to them. In countries where property passes directly to heirs the date of inheritance will be the date of death.

Determining what is a higher rates transaction

4.69 There are five scenarios which need to be considered in determining whether a transaction is liable to the additional rate of SDLT as follows:

- *Scenario 1* (see **4.70**) – the transaction is the acquisition of a single dwelling and the purchaser is an individual (*FA 2003, Sch 4ZA, para 3*).
- *Scenario 2* (see **4.76**) – the transaction is the acquisition of a single dwelling and the purchaser is not an individual (*FA 2003, Sch 4ZA, para 4*).

- *Scenario 3* (see **4.77**) – the transaction is the acquisition of more than one dwelling, at least two of the dwellings are acquired for £40,000 or more and the purchaser is an individual (*FA 2003, Sch 4ZA, para 5*).
- *Scenario 4* (see **4.78**) – the transaction is the acquisition of more than one dwelling, but only one of the dwellings is acquired for £40,000 or more and the purchaser is an individual (*FA 2003, Sch 4ZA, para 6*).
- *Scenario 5* (see **4.80**) – the transaction is the acquisition of more than one dwelling, at least one of the dwellings is acquired for £40,000 or more and the purchaser is not an individual (*FA 2003, Sch 4ZA, para 7*).

Each of these scenarios is now considered in detail.

Scenario 1 – individual – single dwelling transaction (FA 2003, Sch 4ZA, para 3)

4.70 A 'chargeable transaction' (see **4.14**) is a 'higher rates transaction' if each of the following conditions are satisfied:

- the purchaser is an individual;
- the 'chargeable interest' (see **4.11**) acquired consists of a 'major interest' (see **4.11**) in a single dwelling, referred to as 'the purchased dwelling' (for these purposes a 'major interest' does not include a lease originally granted for a term not exceeding seven years);
- the 'chargeable consideration' (see **4.19**) given for the transaction is £40,000 or more;
- on the 'effective date' (see **4.91**) of the transaction, 'the purchased dwelling' is not subject to a lease which at that date has an unexpired term of more than 21 years (eg where a freehold interest is being acquired that interest is not subject to a lease which has more than 21 years to run at the 'effective date' (see **4.91**) of the transaction);
- at the end of the day which is the 'effective date' (see **4.91**) of the transaction the purchaser (or any of the joint purchasers if there is more than one purchaser) has, or is treated as having (see **4.61–4.68**), a 'major interest' (see **4.11**) in a dwelling, which has a market value of £40,000 or more (any loans related to the other dwelling are ignored in determining its market value), *other* than the 'purchased dwelling', and the interest which the individual holds in that other dwelling is not subject to a lease with an unexpired term of more than 21 years (note that this condition will be satisfied if the individual is a joint owner of another dwelling and the interest which the individual holds has a market value of £40,000 or more). The 'major interest' held at the end of the day must normally be an interest in another dwelling (see **4.71**); and

- the 'purchased dwelling' is not a replacement for the purchaser's only or main residence (see **4.71** as to what is meant by a purchaser replacing their only or main residence).

If any of the above conditions are not satisfied, then the transaction will not be a 'higher rates transaction'.

In summary, the additional rate of SDLT will apply when an individual acquires a freehold interest in a dwelling, or a leasehold interest in a dwelling which was originally granted for a term exceeding seven years, for a consideration of £40,000 or more, if at the end of the day the individual holds a freehold interest, or a leasehold interest which was originally granted for a term exceeding seven years, in another dwelling (see **4.64–4.68** to determine whether an individual is treated as holding another dwelling for the purposes of the higher rates legislation), and that individual is not replacing his only or main residence. This is the case unless either the interest in the dwelling being acquired, or the interest in the other dwelling held, is subject to a lease with more than 21 years to run.

Exemption if the purchaser already holds an interest in the purchased dwelling

4.71 A 'chargeable transaction' which would **but for this exemption** be a higher rates transaction under *FA 2003, Sch 4ZA, para 3* (see **4.70**) will not be a higher rates transaction if the purchaser already held a 'major interest' (see **4.11**) in the purchased dwelling immediately before the 'effective date' (see **4.91**) of the transaction under which the additional interest in the dwelling is acquired, and the purchased dwelling had been the purchaser's only or main residence throughout the period of three years ending with the 'effective date' (see **4.8**) of the transaction under which the additional interest in the dwelling is acquired. This exemption can be found in *FA 2003, Sch 4ZA, para 7A* and was introduced by *FA 2018, Sch 11, para 3.*

This exemption does not apply in the following circumstances:

- the interest already held in the dwelling is a leasehold interest and, immediately before the 'effective date' (see **4.91**) of the transaction under which the additional interest is acquired the lease has a remaining term of less than 21 years; or
- if immediately before the 'effective date' (see **4.91**) of the transaction under which the additional interest is acquired the purchaser is beneficially entitled to the existing interest in the dwelling as a joint tenant and there are four or more other joint tenants; or

- if immediately before the 'effective date' (see **4.91**) of the transaction under which the additional interest is acquired the purchaser is beneficially entitled as a tenant in common or coparcener to less than a quarter of the interest in the dwelling.

This exemption applies to transactions with an 'effective date' (see **4.91**) on or after 22 November 2017.

This exemption will therefore only apply if the purchaser does not have a 'major interest' (see **4.11**) in another dwelling at the end of the day which is the 'effective date' of the transaction under which the purchased dwelling is acquired.

Replacement of main residence test

4.72 The replacement of main residence test can be satisfied by either (a) a disposal of an individual's main residence before, or on the day that, the new main residence is acquired, or (b) the new main residence is acquired first and the disposal of the previous main residence takes place at a later date.

Disposal of the current main residence on or before the date of acquisition of the new main residence

4.73 For these purposes an individual is replacing his only or main residence if the following conditions are satisfied (*FA 2003, Sch 4ZA, para 3(6)*):

- on the 'effective date' (see **4.91**) of the transaction the purchaser intends to use 'the purchased dwelling' as his, or her, only or main residence,
- in the three-year period prior to the 'effective date' (see **4.91**) of the transaction the purchaser (or the purchaser's spouse or civil partner at the time of the earlier disposal) disposed of a 'major interest' (see **4.11**) in another dwelling which was the purchaser's only or main residence at any time during that three-year period,
- immediately after the 'effective date' (see **4.91**) of the transaction disposing of the previous only or main residence neither the purchaser nor the purchaser's spouse or civil partner had a 'major interest' (see **4.11**) in the sold dwelling. This requirement does not apply in relation to a spouse or civil partner of the purchaser if the two of them were not living together (FA *2003, Sch 4ZA, para 9(3))* on the 'effective date' of the transaction disposing of the previous only or main residence. (Note: This requirement, found in *FA 2003, Sch 4ZA, para 3(6)(ba)* and *(6A)*, is an anti-abuse provision introduced by *FA 2018, Sch 11,*

para 2(2) and *(3)* to prevent the additional rate of SDLT being avoided in circumstances where the purchaser, their spouse or civil partner retain an interest in the previous only or main residence.) The anti-avoidance provision applies to transactions with an 'effective date' (see **4.91**) on or after 22 November 2017. There are transitional provisions excluding transactions effected under a contract entered into and 'substantially performed' (see **4.91**) before 22 November 2017 or effected under a contract entered into before 22 November 2017 but not substantially performed before that date provided (a) there is no variation of the contract, or assignment of rights under the contract on or after 22 November 2017, (b) the transaction is not effected in consequence of the exercise on or after 22 November 2017 of any option, right of pre-emption or similar right, or (c) on or after 22 November 2017 there is no assignment, sub-sale or other transaction relating to the dwelling as a result of which a person other than the purchaser under the contract becomes entitled to call for a conveyance.

- at no time during the period between the disposal of the other dwelling and the acquisition of 'the purchased dwelling' has the purchaser (or the purchaser's spouse or civil partner at the time of the acquisition) acquired a 'major interest' (see **4.11**) in any other dwelling with the intention of it being the purchaser's only or main residence.

It is important to note that the three-year look back period does not apply for purchases of dwellings on or before 26 November 2018, ie the date which is three years after the introduction of the additional SDLT rate was announced by the Chancellor (*FA 2016, s 128(8)* and *(9)*). This is a transitional provision, which ensures that individuals who disposed of their main residence before the announcement of the higher rates on 25 November 2015 are not disadvantaged. Thus an individual who disposed of their main residence say, five years ago, will be treated as replacing their main residence where the 'purchased dwelling' was acquired on or before 26 November 2018. The three-year look back period only applies to 'purchased dwellings' acquired on or after 27 November 2018.

It is only the first acquisition of a new main residence which counts as a replacement. Consequently, if two or more main residences are acquired within three years of a disposal, or on or before 26 November 2018, it will be the first main residence acquired which will be a replacement.

If an individual rents a dwelling between the disposal of their main residence and the purchase of the replacement this will not prevent the purchase being a replacement provided the rental period is not more than seven years (*FA 2003, Sch 4ZA, para 2(4)*).

Example 4.14

Isobel buys a dwelling which she intends to use as her main residence. The 'effective date' (see **4.91**) of the transaction is 31 January 2020. If Isobel (or her spouse or civil partner) had sold a dwelling at any time on or after 1 February 2017 then the acquisition may be a replacement of her main residence. The dwelling would have to have been Isobel's only or main residence at some time during the three-year period 1 February 2017 to 31 January 2020. She must not have acquired another new main residence after the disposal and before the acquisition on 31 January 2020.

If Isobel had acquired her new dwelling on 30 September 2018 then the three-year look back period would not apply and the requirement would simply be that she had disposed of a previous main residence at some time on or before 30 September 2018. She must still not have acquired another main residence after the disposal and before the purchase of the new main residence on 30 September 2018. This is because the three-year look back period does not apply for purchases of dwellings on or before 26 November 2018: see **4.61**.

Disposal of the current main residence after the date of acquisition of the new main residence

4.74 Where the individual has not disposed of their current only or main residence by the end of the day on which they acquire 'the purchased dwelling', which they intend to be their only or main residence, 'the purchased dwelling' will be a replacement for their only or main residence if the following conditions are satisfied (*FA 2003, Sch 4ZA, para 3(7)*):

- the purchaser intends 'the purchased dwelling' to be his, or her, only or main residence;
- in the three-year period starting on the day after the 'effective date' (see **4.91**) of the acquisition of 'the purchased dwelling' the purchaser (or the purchaser's spouse or civil partner at the time of the disposal) disposes of a 'major interest' (see **4.11**) in another dwelling which at any time during the three-year period ending with the 'effective date' (see **4.91**) of the acquisition of 'the purchased dwelling' was the purchaser's only or main residence.

  However, a new *s 77*, amending *FA 2003, Sch 4ZA*, was introduced at the Report Stage of the *Finance Act 2020* to extend the three-year time period where there are 'exceptional circumstances that could not reasonably have been foreseen' which prevented the sale of the previous main residence within the prescribed three-year period. In such circumstances the three-year period is extended to such longer period as HMRC may allow in response to an application made in accordance with new *FA 2003, Sch 4ZA, para 3(7B)*. The Covid-19 pandemic will be 'exceptional circumstances that could not reasonably have been foreseen' for these purposes. The extension of the three-year time limit will only apply if the new main residence was purchased on or after 1 January 2017, so that the three-year period ended on or after 1 January 2020. On 3 June 2020, SDLTM09807 was introduced, which outlines HMRC's views as to what will constitute 'exceptional circumstances that could not reasonably have been foreseen' and it is specifically stated that such circumstances might include:

– being prevented from selling the property owing to government guidance during the Covid-19 pandemic; or

– other action taken by a public authority preventing the sale of the property.

HMRC make it clear that: 'A mere change of intention of any party to the transaction at a late stage, a shortage of funds, or deciding not to sell the property in anticipation of making a loss (for example during a downturn in the market) will not be regarded as exceptional circumstances, rather they are sorts of events that occur in the ordinary course of buying and selling property.'

The three-year time limit will only be extended if the previous main residence is sold as soon as reasonably possible after the exceptional circumstances no longer apply.

The previous main residence must be sold before HMRC will consider whether there were exceptional circumstances. Each case will be considered on its own merits and there is no pre-transaction clearance facility.

If it is considered that exceptional circumstances apply to the disposal of a previous main residence outside of the three-year time period, a claim should be made for a repayment of the higher rate SDLT (see **4.84** for details of the information which should be provided to HMRC when making the repayment claim); and

- immediately after the 'effective date' (see **4.91**) of the transaction disposing of the previous only or main residence neither the purchaser nor the purchaser's spouse or civil partner had a 'major interest' (see **4.11**) in the sold dwelling. This requirement does not apply in relation to a spouse or civil partner of the purchaser if the two of them were not living together (*FA 2003, Sch 4ZA, para 9(3)*) on the 'effective date' of the transaction disposing of the previous only or main residence. (Note: This requirement, found in *FA 2003, Sch 4ZA, para 3(7)(ba)* and *(8)*, is an anti-abuse provision introduced by *FA 2018, Sch 11, para 2(4)* and *(5)* to prevent the additional rate of SDLT being avoided in circumstances where the purchaser, their spouse or civil partner retain an interest in the previous only or main residence.) The anti-avoidance provision applies to transactions with an 'effective date' (see **4.91**) on or after 22 November 2017. There are transitional provisions excluding transactions effected under a contract entered into and 'substantially performed' (see **4.91**) before 22 November 2017 or effected under a contract entered into before 22 November 2017 but not substantially performed before that date provided (a) there is no variation of the contract, or assignment of rights under the contract on or after 22 November 2017, (b) the transaction is not effected in consequence of the exercise on or after 22 November 2017 of any option, right of pre-emption or similar right, or (c) on or after 22 November 2017 there is no assignment, sub-sale or other transaction relating to the dwelling as a result of which a person other than the purchaser under the contract becomes entitled to call for a conveyance.

Where a new dwelling does become a replacement for the purchaser's only or main residence because the purchaser's previous only or main residence is disposed of within the three-year period following the acquisition of 'the purchased dwelling', the land transaction return in respect of the acquisition of the 'purchased dwelling' may be amended to show that the additional rate of SDLT no longer applies, and the amount of the additional rate SDLT may be reclaimed (*FA 2003, Sch 4ZA, para 8(3)*). Where the 'effective date' (see **4.91**) of the disposal is on or after 29 October 2018 the amendment to the land transaction return must be made within the period of 12 months beginning with:

- the effective date (see **4.91**) of the disposal of the property which was previously the purchaser's only or main residence, or
- **if later**, the date by which the land transaction return, in relation to the acquisition of the 'purchased dwelling', had to be filed.

Where the 'effective date' (see **4.91**) of the disposal is before 29 October 2018 the amendment to the land transaction return must be made within the following periods, whichever expires later:

- the period of three months starting with the 'effective date' (see **4.91**) of the disposal of the property which was previously the purchaser's only or main residence; and
- the period of 12 months starting with the date by which the land transaction return, in relation to the acquisition of the 'purchased dwelling', had to be filed.

Where the new main residence is acquired first, but the disposal of the previous main residence takes place before the land transaction return is filed notifying the acquisition of the new main residence, that land transaction return should be filed on the basis that the higher rates of SDLT do not apply, as the individual is replacing their only or main residence.

Example 4.15

Diana acquires a freehold interest in a new main residence on 30 June 2020 for a consideration of £450,000 but retains her freehold ownership of her previous main residence at the end of that day, and that property is worth £300,000. Neither the freehold interest acquired, nor the freehold interest retained, are subject to a lease with more than 21 years to run. The conditions set out in scenario 1 above are satisfied and the acquisition of the new freehold interest is taxed at the higher rates. The SDLT payable is as follows:

Purchase Price (£)	**Rate** (%)	**SDLT** (£)
125,000	3	3,750
125,000	5	6,250
200,000	8	16,000
450,000		26,000

If Diana sells her previous main residence at any time during the 3 year period to 30 June 2023 then the purchase of the new main residence will cease to be a 'higher rates transaction' and Diana can amend the SDLT return on the original transaction and claim back the additional rate SDLT paid. The SDLT payable if the additional rates do not apply is as follows:

Purchase Price (£)	**Rate** (%)	**SDLT** (£)
125,000	0	Nil
125,000	2	2,500
200,000	5	10,000
450,000		12,500

Diana can therefore claim a refund of £13,500 (£26,000 – £12,500).

If a disposal of a previous main residence following the purchase of a new main residence results in the purchase of the new main residence not being chargeable to the SDLT higher rates, as described above, that disposal cannot then be used in deciding if a later purchase of a dwelling is a replacement of a main residence (*FA 2003, Sch 4ZA, para 8(2)*).

What is an individual's main residence?

4.75 There is no definition of only or main residence in the legislation. If the individual lives at only one dwelling that will be their only or main residence. The HMRC Guidance Note (November 2016) indicates at 3.31 that where an individual lives at more than one dwelling all of the facts and circumstances of the case in question must be considered to determine which dwelling is the main residence. The main residence is not necessarily the dwelling where the individual spends the majority of their time although frequently it will be. At SDLTM09812 there is a list of points to be considered in determining which dwelling is an individual's main residence:

- If the individual is married or in a civil partnership, where does the family spend its time?
- If the individual has children, where do they go to school?
- At which residence is the individual registered to vote?
- Where is the individual's place of work?
- How is each residence furnished?
- Which address is used for correspondence?
- Where is the individual registered with a doctor/dentist?
- At which address is the individual's car registered and insured?
- Which address is the main residence for council tax?

There are two parts which need to be tested in determining whether or not an individual is replacing their main residence. The first part relates to the dwelling which has been sold in the three-year period either side of the acquisition and it will be a question of objective fact as to whether or not that dwelling was the individual's only or main residence. The second part relates to 'the purchased dwelling'. In this case it will be a question of the intention of the purchaser at the time of the acquisition. At SDLTM09812 it is stated:

> 'The intention test will not only be met if there is an intent to immediately occupy, if some works are to be undertaken before occupation commences then this does not prevent the test from being met. If the dwelling is intended to be put to other uses, for example as a source of income, then the intention test will not be met. There may be rare cases of the purchaser's genuine intention at the time of purchase being frustrated by events.'

Therefore, the fact that the individual does not move into 'the purchased dwelling' because work is to be carried out on the property will not prevent a property from being an individual's main residence. However, if the initial intention is to let the property out the main residence test will not be satisfied.

Scenario 2 – companies and trusts – single dwelling transaction (FA 2003, Sch 4ZA, para 4)

4.76 A 'chargeable transaction' (see **4.14**) is a 'higher rates transaction' if each of the following conditions are satisfied:

- the purchaser is not an individual (eg the purchaser is a company, the trustees of certain trusts, for example a discretionary trust (see **4.81**), etc);
- the 'chargeable interest' (see **4.11**) acquired consists of a 'major interest' (see **4.11**) in a single dwelling (which excludes any lease originally granted for a term of seven years or less), referred to as 'the purchased dwelling';
- the 'chargeable consideration' (see **4.19**) given for the transaction is £40,000 or more; and
- on the 'effective date' (see **4.91**) of the transaction 'the purchased dwelling' is not subject to a lease which at that date has an unexpired term of more than 21 years (eg where a freehold interest is being acquired that interest is not subject to a lease which has more than 21 years to run at the 'effective date' (see **4.91**) of the transaction).

This means that the additional rate of SDLT will apply where, for example, on or after 1 April 2016, a company acquires a 'major interest' (see **4.11**) in a single dwelling for chargeable consideration of £40,000 or more irrespective of whether or not it holds any other dwellings, ie the additional rate of SDLT applies to first purchases, and all subsequent purchases, of dwellings by companies and other non-individuals. This assumes that the interest in the dwelling acquired is not subject to a lease with more than 21 years to run.

Scenario 3 – individual – multiple dwelling transactions (FA 2003, Sch 4ZA, para 5)

4.77 A 'chargeable transaction' (see **4.14**) is a 'higher rates transaction' if each of the following conditions are satisfied:

- the purchaser is an individual;
- the 'chargeable interest' (see **4.11**) acquired consists of a 'major interest' (see **4.11**) in two or more dwellings, referred to as 'the purchased dwellings';
- the portion of the 'chargeable consideration' (see **4.19**) which is attributable on a just and reasonable basis to each of at **least two** of 'the purchased dwellings' is £40,000 or more;

- on the 'effective date' (see **4.91**) of the transaction at **least two** of 'the purchased dwellings' are not subject to a lease which at that date has an unexpired term of more than 21 years (eg where a freehold interest is being acquired that interest is not subject to a lease which has more than 21 years to run at the 'effective date' of the transaction); and
- at **least two** of the purchased dwellings are not 'subsidiary' to any of the other purchased dwellings. For these purposes dwelling 'A' is subsidiary to dwelling 'B' if (a) dwelling 'A' is located within the grounds of, or within the same building as, dwelling 'B', and (b) the amount of the 'chargeable consideration' (see **4.19**) attributed to dwelling 'B' on a just and reasonable basis is greater than or equal to two thirds of the amount of the 'chargeable consideration' attributed, on a just and reasonable basis, and on a combined basis, to the acquisition of dwelling 'A' and 'B' together with any other purchased dwellings located within the grounds of, or within the same building as, dwelling 'B'. This is referred to as the 'granny flat exception' and is designed to take self-contained dwellings, such as granny flats, etc out of the higher rate charge in appropriate circumstances.

Where two or more dwellings are acquired under a *single transaction* the legislation does not allow there to be a combination of higher rate and 'normal' residential rate transactions, and the transaction will either be a 'higher rates transaction' or it won't. Thus if two or more dwellings are purchased in the same transaction, and at least two of those dwellings satisfy the conditions detailed above, the transaction will be a 'higher rates transaction', and the higher rates will apply to all of the dwellings acquired under the transaction. This is irrespective of whether the individual owns an interest in another dwelling at the end of the day on which the acquisition is made, or whether one of the purchased dwellings replaces a main residence.

The legislation does not define what is meant by 'a single transaction' but it is considered that it means one contract between the same vendor and purchaser (and not including parties connected with the vendor and purchaser) for the acquisition of the agreed number of properties. Thus if two or more dwellings are to be acquired from the same vendor, and those dwellings satisfy the conditions above, and one of the dwellings to be acquired is replacing, or may become a replacement for, the individual's only or main residence, that dwelling should be acquired under a separate contract, which is legally independent from any of the other contracts, such that the higher rate should not apply to its acquisition (see **4.72**), or that in due course, on a disposal of the previous main residence, a subsequent claim can be made that the higher rates do not apply (see **4.74**).

It should be noted that Scenario 4 below may apply if only one of the dwellings acquired in a single transaction are acquired for a consideration of £40,000 or more.

Scenario 4 – individual – multiple dwelling transactions (FA 2003, Sch 4ZA, para 6)

4.78 A 'chargeable transaction' (see **4.14**) is a 'higher rates transaction' if each of the following conditions are satisfied:

- the purchaser is an individual;
- the 'chargeable interests' (see **4.11**) acquired consists of a 'major interest' (see **4.11**) in two or more dwellings, referred to as 'the purchased dwellings';
- there is only one 'purchased dwelling' to which 'chargeable consideration' (see **4.19**) of £40,000 or more is attributed on a just and reasonable basis;
- on the 'effective date' (see **4.91**) of the transaction 'the purchased dwelling' acquired for £40,000 or more is not subject to a lease which at that date has an unexpired term of more than 21 years (eg where a freehold interest is being acquired that interest is not subject to a lease which has more than 21 years to run at the 'effective date' of the transaction);
- the purchased dwelling in respect of which the conditions in the two bullet points immediately above are satisfied is not a replacement for the purchaser's only or main residence (see **4.71**);
- at least one of the 'purchased dwellings' must not be 'subsidiary' to any of the other purchased dwellings. For these purposes dwelling 'A' is subsidiary to dwelling 'B' if (a) dwelling 'A' is located within the grounds of, or within the same building as, dwelling 'B', and (b) the amount of the 'chargeable consideration' (see **4.19**) attributed to dwelling 'B' on a just and reasonable basis is greater than or equal to two thirds of the amount of the 'chargeable consideration' attributed, on a just and reasonable basis, and on a combined basis, to the acquisition of dwelling 'A' and 'B' together with any other purchased dwellings located within the grounds of, or within that same building as, dwelling 'B'. This is referred to as the 'granny flat exception' and is designed to take self-contained dwellings, such as granny flats etc, out of the higher rate charge in appropriate circumstances; and
- at the end of the day which is the 'effective date' of the transaction the purchaser has, or is treated as having (see **4.64–4.68**), a 'major interest' (see **4.11**) in a dwelling, other than one of 'the purchased dwellings', which has a market value of £40,000 or more, and the interest in that other dwelling is not subject to a lease with an unexpired term of more than 21 years.

This scenario applies where the purchaser is an individual acquiring more than one dwelling in a single transaction but only one of the dwellings is acquired for chargeable consideration of £40,000 or more and that dwelling is not subject to a lease which has an unexpired term of more than 21 years. In these circumstances the transaction will be a 'higher rates transaction' only if the dwelling acquired for £40,000 or more is not a replacement for the purchaser's only or main residence and the purchaser already holds, or is treated as holding (see **4.64–4.68**) an unexpired term of more than 21 years.

It should be noted that Scenario 3 above may apply if more than one of the dwellings acquired in a single transaction are acquired for a consideration of £40,000 or more.

Exemption if the purchaser already holds an interest in the purchased dwelling

4.79 A 'chargeable transaction' which would **but for this exemption** be a higher rates transaction under *FA 2003, Sch 4ZA, para 6* (see **4.78**) will not be a higher rates transaction if the purchaser already held a 'major interest' (see **4.11**) in the purchased dwelling immediately before the 'effective date' (see **4.91**) of the transaction under which the additional interest in the dwelling is acquired, and the purchased dwelling had been the purchaser's only or main residence throughout the period of three years ending with the 'effective date' (see **4.91**) of the transaction under which the additional interest in the dwelling is acquired. This exemption can be found in *FA 2003, Sch 4ZA, para 7A* and was introduced by *FA 2018, Sch 11, para 3*.

This exemption does not apply in the following circumstances:

- the interest already held in the dwelling is a leasehold interest and, immediately before the 'effective date' (see **4.74**) of the transaction under which the additional interest is acquired the lease has a remaining term of less than 21 years; or
- if immediately before the 'effective date' (see **4.91**) of the transaction under which the additional interest is acquired the purchaser is beneficially entitled to the existing interest in the dwelling as a joint tenant and there are four or more other joint tenants; or
- if immediately before the 'effective date' (see **4.91**) of the transaction under which the additional interest is acquired the purchaser is beneficially entitled as a tenant in common or coparcener to less than a quarter of the interest in the dwelling.

This exemption applies to transactions with an 'effective date' (see **4.91**) on or after 22 November 2017.

This exemption will therefore only apply if the purchaser does not have a 'major interest' (see **4.11**) in another dwelling at the end of the day which is the 'effective date' of the transaction under which the purchased dwelling is acquired.

Scenario 5 – companies and trusts – multiple dwelling transactions (FA 2003, Sch 4ZA, para 7)

4.80 A 'chargeable transaction' (see **4.14**) is a 'higher rates transaction' if each of the following conditions are satisfied:

- the purchaser is not an individual (eg the purchaser is a company, the trustees of certain trusts, for example, a discretionary trust (see **4.81**), etc),
- the 'chargeable interest' (see **4.11**) acquired consists of a 'major interest' (see **4.11**) in two or more dwellings, referred to as 'the purchased dwellings',
- the 'chargeable consideration' (see **4.19**) which is attributable on a just and reasonable basis to at least one of 'the purchased dwellings' is £40,000 or more,
- on the 'effective date' (see **4.91**) of the transaction at least one of 'the purchased dwellings' is not subject to a lease which at that date has an unexpired term of more than 21 years (eg where a freehold interest is being acquired that interest is not subject to a lease which has more than 21 years to run at the 'effective date' of the transaction).

Under this scenario, the additional rate of SDLT will apply if, for example, in a single transaction, on or after 1 April 2016, a company acquires a 'major interest' (see **4.11**) in two or more dwellings and the 'chargeable consideration' attributed, on a just and reasonable basis, to at least one of those dwellings is £40,000 or more and at least one of the dwellings is not subject to a lease which has an unexpired term of more than 21 years. The higher rate will apply irrespective of whether or not the company holds any other dwellings.

The differences between Scenarios 2 and 5 are that in Scenario 5 more than one dwelling is being acquired and the 'chargeable consideration' is attributed to the dwellings on a just and reasonable basis, whereas in Scenario 2 there is no need for an attribution of the 'chargeable consideration' as only a single dwelling is acquired.

Trustees purchasing dwellings

4.81 The trustee(s) of a 'bare trust' (*FA 2003, Sch 16, para 1(2)*, ie a trust under which the beneficiary is absolutely entitled to the interest in the dwelling as against the trustee or would be absolutely entitled but for disability or age which prevents the beneficiary from holding legal title) is ignored and the beneficiary is treated as the purchaser for the purposes of the additional rates legislation (*FA 2003, Sch 16, para 3(1)*, and *Sch 4ZA, para 10(2)* and *(3)*).

The trustee(s) of a trust under which the beneficiary is entitled to (a) occupy the dwelling for life, or (b) income earned in respect of the dwelling (referred to below as a 'trust for life or income'), is also ignored, meaning that, for the purposes of the higher rates legislation, the beneficiary with the relevant interest in the trust is treated as the purchaser, and the trustee is treated as not being the purchaser (*FA 2003, Sch 4ZA, para 10(1)* and *(3)*). For these purposes it does not matter whether one, or more than one, beneficiary is entitled as described in (a) and (b) above. Consequently, under Scenario 1 considered at **4.70**, if the beneficiary of a 'trust for life or income' owns another interest in a dwelling at the end of the day on which the new dwelling is acquired by the trustees, and that interest is worth £40,000 or more, and is not subject to a lease with more than 21 years to run, then the trustee's acquisition of the dwelling will be a 'higher rates transaction' unless the trustee's purchase is replacing the beneficiary's main residence (**4.72** et seq).

The trustee(s) of a trust which is not a 'bare trust' or 'a trust for life or income' is treated as the purchaser of the 'major interest' (see **4.11**) in the dwelling, and the transaction will be a 'higher rates transaction', if the conditions in scenario 2 or 5 above are satisfied (*FA 2003, Sch 4ZA, para 13*) (note that if the trustee(s) is an individual the condition that the purchaser is not an individual is ignored in determining whether the conditions in scenario 2 or 5 above are satisfied (*FA 2003, Sch 4ZA, para 13(2)*). For example, for the purposes of the higher rates legislation, the trustees of a discretionary trust will be treated as the purchaser of any 'major interest' in a dwelling acquired by them, in their capacity as trustees of that trust, and the transaction will be a higher rates transaction if the conditions in either scenario 2 or 5 (see **4.76** and **4.80**) are satisfied.

Example 4.16

Cameron and Fraser are trustees of a trust and on 1 September 2020 they use the trust funds to purchase a dwelling for £300,000. The terms of the trust entitle an individual beneficiary, Amanda, to occupy the dwelling for life. Cameron and Fraser must consider whether the higher rates of SDLT would apply as if Amanda were purchasing the dwelling. Consequently, if Amanda has a 'major interest' in another dwelling on the 'effective date' (see **4.91**) of the acquisition of the new dwelling by the trustees, and the new dwelling is not a replacement of Amanda's main residence, then the higher rates will apply to the purchase of the new dwelling by the trustees.

Example 4.17

Blair and Nicola are trustees of a trust which enables them to apply the income from the trust's assets at their discretion amongst a class of beneficiaries. Using trust funds, Blair and Nicola acquire a freehold interest in a dwelling on 25 November 2020 for a consideration of £850,000. The trustees are liable to pay the higher rates of SDLT if the conditions outlined in Scenario 2 (see **4.72**) (*FA 2003, Sch 4ZA, para 4*) are satisfied. Those conditions are as follows:

- the purchaser is not an individual – Blair and Nicola are purchasing the dwelling as trustees of the trust and, under the terms of the trust no beneficiary is entitled to (a) occupy the dwelling for life, or (b) the income earned in respect of the dwelling, and the trust is not a 'bare trust'. Consequently, *FA 2003, Sch 4ZA, para13(1)* and *(2)* requires that the condition that the purchaser is not an individual be ignored in determining whether the transaction is liable to the higher rates of SDLT;
- the 'chargeable interest' (see **4.11**) acquired consists of a 'major interest' (see **4.11**) in a single dwelling – this condition is satisfied as a freehold interest in the dwelling is being acquired;
- the 'chargeable consideration' (see **4.19**) given for the dwelling is £40,000 or more – this condition is satisfied as the consideration given for the dwelling is £850,000; and
- on the 'effective date' (see **4.91**) of the acquisition of the dwelling it is not subject to a lease with more than 21 years to run – this condition is satisfied as the trustees are acquiring the unencumbered freehold interest in the property.

All of the conditions in *FA 2003, Sch 4ZA, para 4* are therefore satisfied and Blair and Nicola, acting as trustees of the trust, must pay SDLT at the higher rates and the liability is calculated as follows:

Purchase Price (£)	**Rate (%)**	**SDLT (£)**
125,000	3	3,750
125,000	5	6,250
600,000	8	48,000
850,000		58,000

The trustees must therefore file a land transaction return, and pay the SDLT liability, by 9 December 2020, entering code '04' in question 1 of the land transaction return denoting that the higher rate of SDLT applies to the transaction.

Interaction with multiple dwellings relief

4.82 Where two or more dwellings are acquired as part of a single transaction, or under a number of 'linked transactions' (see **4.86**), it may be possible to reduce the aggregate SDLT liability by making a claim for multiple dwellings relief. The higher rates of SDLT will apply to claims for multiple dwellings relief (see **5.57**) if the relevant conditions in any of scenarios 1–5 (see **4.70–4.80**) apply. If, as part of a single transaction, six or more dwellings are acquired, the SDLT rates for non-residential or mixed-use transactions will apply (see **4.38**). In such circumstances the purchaser can therefore choose whether to apply the non-residential rates by not making a claim for multiple dwellings relief. However, see Example 4.20 where a claim for multiple dwellings relief is made in relation to linked transactions.

Example 4.18

Ewan purchases a block of eight flats for £750,000. If a claim for multiple dwellings relief is made, the average consideration per flat would be £93,750 and the SDLT payable would be £22,500 (average price of £93,750 × 3% × 8 flats – a 3% SDLT rate applies to the purchase of a dwelling for £93,750 as the additional SDLT rate applies). If no claim is made for multiple dwellings relief then the non-residential SDLT rates will apply (six or more dwellings are being acquired as part of a single transaction) as follows:

Purchase Price (£)	**Rate (%)**	**SDLT (£)**
150,000	0	Nil
100,000	2	2,000
500,000	5	25,000
750,000		27,000

In this case it would be beneficial to make a claim for multiple dwellings relief as this would reduce the SDLT liability from £27,000 to £22,500.

Filing a return to which the higher SDLT rate applies

4.83 As for any other 'chargeable transaction' (see **4.14**) a return for a 'higher rates transaction' which has an 'effective date' (see **4.91**) on or after 1 March 2019, or an 'effective date' prior to 1 March 2019 but the transaction became notifiable on or after 1 March 2019, must be filed within 14 days of the 'effective date' of the transaction (see **8.6**). Question 1 on form SDLT 1, on 'type of property', should be completed as code '04' which means that the higher rate of SDLT applies. Payment of the SDLT is made in exactly the same way as that for any other 'chargeable transaction' (see **8.29**).

If the 'effective date' (see **4.91**) of the 'higher rates transaction' was before 1 March 2019, and the transaction became notifiable before 1 March 2019, the land transaction return need only have been filed 30 days, rather than 14 days, after the 'effective date'.

Claiming a repayment of higher rate SDLT

4.84 If a dwelling previously used by a purchaser as their main residence is sold within three years of the 'effective date' (see **4.91**) of the acquisition of a new main residence a refund of the amount of the additional rate of SDLT can be claimed (see **4.74**). If the 'effective date' of the sale of the previous main residence is on or after 29 October 2018 the repayment needs to be reclaimed by the later of: (a) one year from the date of sale of the previous main residence; and (b) one year from the date on which the land transaction return notifying the acquisition of the new main residence had to be filed (*FA 2003, Sch 4ZA, para 8(3)* as amended by *FA 2019, s 44(4)*).

If the 'effective date' (see **4.91**) of the sale of the previous main residence was before 29 October 2018 the repayment had to be reclaimed by the later of (a) three months from the date of sale of the previous main residence, and (b) one year from the date on which the land transaction return notifying the acquisition of the new main residence had to be filed (*FA 2003, Sch 4ZA, para 8(3)*).

The online SDLT calculator at www.gov.uk can be used to calculate the amount of the refund.

Guidance on claiming a refund of the higher rate SDLT is available on www.gov.uk/guidance/stamp-duty-land-tax-online-returns.

The refund can be claimed by completing an SDLT repayment request form available on www.gov.uk at www.gov.uk/government/publications/stamp-duty-land-tax-apply-for-a-repayment-of-the-higher-rates-for-additional-properties. The repayment request form can both be completed and filed online (sign in using Government Gateway) or completed online and the summary printed and posted to HMRC Birmingham Stamp Office (see **Appendix A**).

The following information will be required to complete the SDLT repayment request form:

- the SDLT UTRN for the land transaction return notifying the purchase of the new main residence, and
- the name of the purchaser of the property which has now been sold.

If the SDLT repayment request form is completed by an agent, and the refund is to be paid to that agent, then a signed letter of consent from the purchaser should be attached to the form.

HMRC aim to process all refunds within 15 working days of receiving the repayment request form. HMRC will issue the refund by payable order or will issue a letter to explain why the refund request has not been successful.

Where the previous main residence is sold on or after 1 January 2020, and outside the three-year period due to 'exceptional circumstances that could not reasonably have been foreseen' (see **4.74**), the seller of the property should write to HMRC with an explanation of why they were unable to sell their previous main residence within the three-year period and provide the following information:

- the name, address and daytime telephone number of the person making the request, (either the purchaser of the property which attracted the higher rate of SDLT or their agent);
- the purchaser's name and address, if they are not the person making the request;
- details of the property that attracted the higher rates of SDLT, including the effective date of purchase and the SDLT unique transaction reference number;
- details of the previous main residence that has been sold, including the effective date of sale, the address of the property and the name of the buyer;
- the amount of tax paid on the property that attracted the higher rate of SDLT;
- the amount of the requested repayment of tax; and
- the bank account and sort code details of the person to receive the payment.

If the repayment is to go to an agent rather than the purchaser, HMRC will need a signed letter of consent from the purchaser. If an agent is making the request, HMRC also require a signed letter of consent from the purchaser.

Transitional rules

4.85 If the relevant conditions are satisfied the higher rates of SDLT will apply to all 'land transactions' (see **4.7**) with an 'effective date' (see **4.91**) on or after 1 April 2016 (*FA 2016, s 117(5)*).

However, the higher rates of SDLT do not apply where the contract for the 'land transaction' (see **4.7**) was (a) entered into and 'substantially performed' (see **4.91**) before 26 November 2015, or (b) entered into before 26 November 2015 and not excluded as described below (FA 2016, s 117(6)).

For these purposes a contract entered into before 26 November 2015 but not 'substantially performed' (see **4.91**) before that date is excluded, and therefore the higher rates of SDLT apply, if the following conditions are satisfied:

- there is a variation of the contract, or assignment of rights under the contract, on or after 26 November 2015;
- the transaction is effected in consequence of the exercise, on or after 26 November 2015, of any option, right of pre-emption or similar right; or
- on or after 26 November 2015 there is an assignment, sub-sale or other transaction relating to the whole or part of the land interest acquired under the contract as a result of which a person other than the purchaser under the original contract becomes entitled to call for a conveyance.

For these purposes a variation to a contract would include a change to:

- the land being purchased;
- the parties to the contract;
- the contractual consideration; or
- the term length in an agreement for a lease.

However, some changes, for example a change to the contractual completion date, should be considered too insignificant to be treated as a variation to the contract.

Example 4.19

Hamish exchanged contracts with a construction company on 11 November 2015 for the purchase of four flats, for a consideration of £1,000,000, which he intends to let to third parties. He also jointly owns a property with his wife, which is his only residence. On 11 August 2018 Hamish varied the contract to add his wife as a joint purchaser of the flats. Despite the fact that the contract was entered into before 26 November 2015 Hamish will not be able to benefit from the transitional rules as the contract was varied after 25 November 2015 (*FA 2016, s 117(6)(b)* and *(7)(a)*). The higher rates of SDLT will therefore apply to the transaction.

Linked transactions – higher rate of SDLT

4.86 Transactions are linked if they form part of a single scheme, arrangement or series of transactions between the same vendor and purchaser or, in either case, persons connected with them (*FA 2003, s 108:* see **4.89**). Connected persons are as defined in *CTA 2010, s 1122*. HMRC make it clear at SDLTM09766 that if an individual acquires two or more dwellings in a *single transaction* the legislation does not permit the acquisition of one dwelling to be charged at the normal rates and the acquisition of another dwelling to be charged at the higher rates. However, neither the legislation nor the SDLT Manual makes it clear how linked transactions are treated if, for example, one transaction is chargeable at normal rates and the second transaction at higher rates. The calculation is further complicated if a claim for multiple dwellings relief is made in relation to the linked transactions. It is understood however that the SDLT liability should be calculated as set out below in Example 4.20.

Example 4.20

On 11 March 2020, under separate and legally independent contracts, Campbell agrees to acquire two houses from a developer one of which he intends to use as his main residence and the other he will let out to third parties. On 14 August 2020 Campbell sells his previous main residence and completes the contract for the purchase of his new main residence for a consideration of £450,000. On 24 November 2020 Campbell completes the purchase of the buy-to-let property for a consideration of £550,000.

Campbell must file a land transaction return, and pay the SDLT, on the acquisition of his new main residence by 28 August 2020. As Campbell is replacing his main residence the normal SDLT rates apply and the liability is calculated as follows:

Purchase Price (£)	Rate (%)	SDLT (£)
125,000	0	Nil
125,000	2	2,500
200,000	5	10,000
450,000		12,500

Following completion of the acquisition of the buy-to-let property on 24 November 2020 Campbell must file a land transaction in relation to that transaction, by 8 December 2020, and pay SDLT at the higher rates as the dwelling is being acquired to let and Campbell is not replacing his main residence. As the purchase of the main residence and the buy-to-let properties are 'linked transactions' (see **4.99**) the SDLT liability is calculated as follows:

Aggregated Purchase Price (£)	Rate (%)	SDLT (£)
125,000	3	3,750
125,000	5	6,250
675,000	8	54,000
75,000	13	9,750
1,000,000		73,750

The SDLT payable in relation to the buy-to-let property would therefore be £40,562 (£550,000/£1,000,000 × £73,750).

The revised calculation of the SDLT liability in relation to the new main residence, using the normal rates of SDLT, would be as follows:

Aggregated Purchase Price (£)	Rate (%)	SDLT (£)
125,000	0	Nil
125,000	2	2,500
675,000	5	33,750
75,000	10	7,500
1,000,000		43,750

The amended SDLT liability in relation to the acquisition of the new main residence would therefore be £19,687 (£450,000/£1,000,000 × £43,750). The total SDLT payable would therefore be £60,249 (£40,562 + £19,687).

However, if Campbell makes a claim for multiple dwellings relief it is understood that the SDLT liability should be calculated as set out below.

The average consideration per house would be £500,000 and the SDLT payable at the higher rates would be as follows:

Purchase Price (£)	Rate (%)	SDLT (£)
125,000	3	3,750
125,000	5	6,250
250,000	8	20,000
500,000		30,000

The total SDLT payable would therefore be £60,000 (£30,000 × 2 houses) and the amount payable on the buy-to-let property would be £33,000 (£550,000/£1,000,000 × £60,000).

The SDLT payable at the normal rates based on an average consideration per house would be as follows:

Purchase Price (£)	**Rate (%)**	**SDLT (£)**
125,000	0	NIL
125,000	2	2,500
250,000	5	12,500
500,000		15,000

The total SDLT payable would therefore be £30,000 (£15,000 × 2 houses) and the amount payable on the replacement main residence would be £13,500 (£450,000/£1,000,000 × £30,000).

The total SDLT payable if a multiple dwellings relief claim is made would therefore be £46,500 (£33,000 + 13,500), which compares to a liability of £60,249 if no claim for multiple dwellings relief is made. It is therefore beneficial for Campbell to make a multiple dwellings relief claim.

Campbell must file an amended land transaction return by 8 December 2020, in relation to the purchase of his new main residence and pay the additional SDLT due of £1,000 (£13,500 – £12,500).

He must also file a land transaction return by 8 December 2020 in relation to the purchase of the buy-to-let property and pay the SDLT due of £33,000.

The above is the author's understanding of how the calculation should be carried out in relation to linked transactions; however, until the matter is clarified by HMRC, it is suggested that confirmation of the calculation methodology be obtained from HMRC.

Enveloped residential properties

4.87 A 15% rate applies where an interest in a single dwelling is acquired, for actual or deemed chargeable consideration of more than the '*threshold*', by a company, by a partnership whose partners include one or more companies, or on behalf of a collective investment scheme. Initially the '*threshold*' was £2 million for acquisitions with an effective date of 21 March 2012 or later. *FA 2014, s 111* lowered the '*threshold*' to £500,000 for acquisitions with an effective date of 20 March 2014 or later. In both cases transitional provisions protect transactions under contracts entered into before the relevant date, subject to stringent anti-avoidance conditions.

'Dwelling' is defined so as to exclude buildings such as student halls of residence, care homes and the like. There are provisions for apportionment where a single transaction includes interests in dwellings and other properties. It is not possible to take advantage of the relief for transfers of multiple dwellings to reduce the rate charged (see **5.57**). Anti-avoidance provisions do seek to prevent avoidance of the higher rate by fragmenting the purchase (*s 55A* and *Sch 4A*, inserted into *FA 2003* by *FA 2012, Sch 34*).

It seems that *FA 2003, s 116(7)* – reclassification of residential property as non-residential where six or more properties are transferred in a single transaction – has no application in determining whether the 15% rate applies to a transaction. This is because the 15% rate applies to the acquisition of an interest in a single dwelling for a chargeable consideration of more than £500,000, and it is irrelevant whether the acquisition of that single dwelling is part of a single transaction under which five or more other separate dwellings are acquired, such that *s 116(7)* would reclassify the transaction as an acquisition of non-residential property.

The stated purpose of this provision is to discourage the 'enveloping' of high-value residential properties within corporate shells, a practice which allows future transfers free of SDLT. As such, it may be regarded as an anti-avoidance provision. The provision had no direct effect on the large number of properties already held in this way at 21 March 2012. However, in addition to the one-off charge on purchase of the property, an annual charge on such properties was introduced from 1 April 2013 – the Annual Tax on Enveloped Properties (ATED). This applies to properties already in corporate ownership before the provisions were enacted as well as future acquisitions. A brief outline of the ATED regime is set out at **4.93** – more detail can be found in *Property Taxes 2020/21* (Bloomsbury Professional).

4.88 When the 15% rate was first introduced, the only specific exemptions were for a purchase by a company or partnership in the course of a bona fide property development business which it (or a group company) had carried on for at least two years prior to the purchase and for a purchase by a company acting as trustee of a settlement. Bodies already qualifying for relief from SDLT – for example charities, provided the property is acquired for charitable use – escaped the charge as charities relief could be claimed. However concern was expressed that this anti-avoidance measure penalised legitimate investment in residential property. In the 2012 Finance Bill debates, the government said that the Treasury was in conversations with 'a number of affected interested parties' and that these conversations would inform the coverage of the annual charge and, possibly, of the 15% rate itself.

Finance Act 2013, s 196 and *Sch 40* amended the relief for property developers and introduced a range of further reliefs. *Finance Act 2016, ss 129–131* then introduced a further range of reliefs, and amended some of the existing reliefs, for transactions with an 'effective date' which falls after 31 March 2016.

With effect from 1 April 2016 relief is provided for acquisitions of chargeable interests exclusively for one or more of the following purposes (references are to paragraphs of *FA 2003, Sch 4A*, amended or inserted by *FA 2013, Sch 40* and *Finance Act 2016 ss 129–131*):

- exploitation of the chargeable interest as a source of rents or other receipts (other than 'excluded rents') in the course of a qualifying property rental business *(para 5(1)(a))*;
- use of the chargeable interest as business premises for the purposes of a qualifying property-rental business (other than one giving rise to income wholly or mainly consisting of 'excluded rents') (*para 5(1)(aa)*);
- use of the chargeable interest for the purposes of a 'relievable trade'. A 'relievable trade' is a trade that is run on a commercial basis and with a view to a profit (*para 5(1)(ab)*).
- development or redevelopment of the chargeable interest followed by (i) resale in the course of a property development trade, or (ii) exploitation as a source of non-excluded rents or other receipts in the course of a qualifying property rental business, or (iii) use as business premises for a qualifying property-rental business, or (iv) use for the purposes of a relievable trade (*para 5(1)(b)*);
- use of the chargeable interest in the course of a trading activity which includes opening the property to the public *(para 5B)*;
- the purchaser of the chargeable interest is a financial institution provided the dwelling was acquired in the course of a lending activity and is to be resold *(para 5C)*;
- the purchaser of the chargeable interest is an 'authorised plan provider' who acquires the chargeable interest under a regulated home-reversion plan into which the purchaser enters as a plan provider. A regulated home-reversion plan is a plan under which an individual sells all or part of their home to the plan provider in return for an annuity or lump sum and a life tenancy. This relief can be withdrawn if within three years of the 'effective date' (see **4.91**) of the transaction the purchaser holds the chargeable interest for a purpose other than for the regulated home reversion plan (*para 5CA*);
- occupation of the chargeable interest by certain employees or partners working in a trade or property rental business (see *FA 2016, s 131(2)*) carried on by the property owner (or a group company), provided the employee/partner has a less than 10% interest in the business *(para 5D)*;

- the chargeable interest acquired is in or over a flat that is one of at least three flats in the same premises and is acquired by a tenants' management company and intended for occupation by a caretaker. This relief can be withdrawn if within three years of the 'effective date' (see **4.91**) of the transaction the purchaser holds the flat other than for the use of the caretaker (*para 5EA*);
- a farmhouse occupied by someone working on the farm (or a former long-serving farm worker) *(5F)*.

A 'qualifying property rental business' is a property rental business that is run on a commercial basis and with a view to profit and 'excluded rents' means rents in respect of (a) an electric-line wayleave, (b) the siting of a pipeline for gas or oil, (c) the siting of a mast or similar structure designed for use in a mobile telephone network or other system of electronic communication, or (d) the siting of a wind turbine (*FA 2003, Sch 4A, para 5(3)*).

Inevitably there are detailed conditions governing the reliefs, in an attempt to ensure that they cannot be misused. The reliefs parallel those available in relation to the annual tax on residential properties known as annual tax on enveloped dwellings (ATED) (see **4.94**). However, the reliefs from ATED apply from the inception of the tax. It was difficult to see why the reliefs from the 15% rate were not made retrospective so that they, too, applied from the introduction of that rate. However, this was not done and the *Finance Act 2013* changes to the reliefs applied only from 17 July 2013.

LINKED TRANSACTIONS

4.89 If two or more transactions are linked, the consideration for all of the linked transactions is aggregated to determine the rates of SDLT. Transactions are linked if they form part of a single scheme, arrangement or series of transactions between the same vendor and purchaser or, in either case, persons connected with them (*FA 2003, s 108*). Connected persons are as defined in *CTA 2010, s 1122* (previously *ICTA 1988, s 839*). Whether transactions are linked is a question of fact, but transactions between the same vendor and purchaser which occur at similar times are likely to be presumed to be linked unless there is evidence to the contrary. See HMRC Stamp Taxes Newsletter: April 2020 for HMRC's views as to how to decide whether transactions are 'linked' for the purposes of *FA 2003, s 108*. In *Attorney General v Cohen* [1936] 2 KB 246, [1936] 1 All ER 583, several purchases of properties by the same purchaser from the same vendor at auction were held not to be part of a series of transactions, because each property was the subject of a separate bidding process.

In the case of linked acquisitions of residential properties, the amount of the SDLT liability may then be reduced if multiple dwellings relief is claimed (see **5.57**).

Example 4.21—Linked transactions

Over coffee, Tanya agrees to buy two houses, located in different towns, from Gerald – the first for £160,000, and the second for £400,000. Different solicitors are engaged to deal with the two purchases, and separate contracts are entered into for each purchase. Tanya already owns a property which is her main residence and is buying the two houses as buy-to-let properties. The acquisition of the first house is completed on 10 January 2020 without prior substantial performance, but the second is delayed, while old Land Registry entries are investigated, and does not complete (again, without prior substantial performance) until 15 June 2020.

Tanya must file a land transaction return in relation to the purchase of the first house by 24 January 2020 and pay SDLT, based on the higher rates as she is not replacing her main residence, calculated as follows:

Purchase Price (£)	**Rate (%)**	**SDLT (£)**
125,000	3	3,750
35,000	5	1,750
160,000		5,500

Following completion of the acquisition of the second house on 15 June 2020, Tanya must file a land transaction in relation to that transaction by 29 June 2020, and pay SDLT at the higher rates as the dwelling is being acquired for the purposes of buy-to-let. As the purchase of the two houses are 'linked transactions' (see **4.99**) the SDLT liability is calculated as follows:

Aggregate Purchase Price (£)	**Rate (%)**	**SDLT (£)**
125,000	3	3,750
125,000	5	6,250
310,000	8	24,800
560,000		34,800

The SDLT payable in relation to the second house is therefore £24,857 (£400,000/£560,000 × £34,800).

Tanya must also file an amended land transaction return by 15 July 2020 (*FA 2003, s 81(1A)* as introduced by *FA 2019, s 46(5)*), in relation to the purchase of the first house with the amended SDLT liability calculated at £9,943 (£160,000/£560,000 × £34,800). Tanya must therefore pay additional SDLT of £4,443 (£9,943 – £5,500).

However, if Tanya claims multiple dwellings relief (see **5.57**) the aggregate SDLT liability then falls to £24,800 with SDLT of £7,086 payable on the first house and £17,714 payable on the second.

Example 4.22—Transactions not linked

Gerald attends an auction where he successfully bids for two houses in the same street, which are sold as separate lots. Gerald pays £110,000 for one and £115,000 for the other. Gerald already owns another property which he uses as his main residence and he acquires the two houses as buy-to-let properties. After the auction, he discovers the vendor is the same for both houses. The transactions are not linked, because each purchase was agreed totally independently of the other. SDLT is payable on both purchases at a rate of 3% as the higher rates of SDLT apply since Gerald is not replacing his main residence.

TIMING OF OBLIGATIONS

4.90 In general, payment of any SDLT must be made and SDLT returns must be submitted within 14 days of the 'effective date' (see **4.91**) of the transaction. The processes for making a return and payment, together with details of the circumstances in which further returns may be needed, are set out in **Chapter 8**.

If the 'effective date' (see **4.91**) of the transaction was before 1 March 2019, and the transaction became notifiable before 1 March 2019, the SDLT filing and payment window was 30 days rather than 14 days from the 'effective date' of the transaction.

The effective date

4.91 There is more than one statutory attempt to define the effective date, covering separate specific circumstances, but they all seek to achieve the same overall result (*FA 2003, ss 119, 44(4)*). In essence, the effective date for a transaction is the earlier of:

- the date of legal completion – that is, the date of execution of the conveyance, lease or other document giving the transaction final legal effect, and

- the date on which the transaction is 'substantially performed'. This date depends on the nature of the transaction and is the earlier of the following:
  - the date on which a substantial amount of any consideration is paid. If the consideration includes payment of rent, this is the earlier of the date on which the first payment of rent is made and the date on which a substantial amount of any other consideration is paid. For consideration other than rent, a 'substantial amount' means substantially the whole. Although not set out in the statute, HMRC consider that 90% or more is substantially the whole, but reserves the right to argue for a smaller proportion if they believe avoidance of SDLT is involved; and
  - the date on which the purchaser takes possession of the whole or substantially the whole of the property. 'Possession' is not comprehensively defined, but is considered further below.

Particular care is needed when non-monetary consideration is given. For example in an exchange, each person's purchase may be substantially performed at the earlier of taking possession of their purchase or completing the sale of the other property.

Example 4.23—Sale and leaseback timing

Mark agrees to sell his freehold workshop to Luke. In return, Luke agrees to redevelop the site and grant Mark a 100-year lease of a new workshop in the new development. The 100-year lease will be granted for a peppercorn rent and no premium. The development will include new offices, which Luke will lease to third parties to pay for the overall redevelopment and (he hopes) give him a profit. The sale to Luke is completed on 1 March 2020 without prior substantial performance and Mark moves his activities into temporary accommodation. The development is completed and Mark's new lease is granted on 1 May 2021. Clearly Luke must make an SDLT return and pay tax on his purchase of the freehold by 15 March 2020. Mark does not receive the benefit of his lease until 1 May 2021. However, he has paid the full consideration for this lease on 1 March 2020, by transferring the freehold to Luke. Therefore, his agreement for lease was substantially performed on that date and he too must make an SDLT return and pay tax by 15 March 2020. As noted at **5.41,** HMRC do not consider that sale and leaseback relief is available because of the redevelopment between the sale and the leaseback. The requirement to complete a return and pay tax so early is not entirely reasonable and HMRC may agree in this situation to have regard to the 'possession' test and accept that the effective date should be the date of grant of the leaseback. However, that would appear to be a concession and should not be relied on without specific agreement from HMRC. It would be safer to submit the return and pay the tax within 14 days after the transfer of the freehold.

Possession

4.92 The term 'possession' has a long legal history and cannot readily be comprehensively defined. The following explanation sets out the view which HMRC are understood to take. The purchaser takes possession of the property when he first occupies or uses it, or becomes entitled to occupy or use it. This is not restricted to the time when the purchaser finally moves in, but may include, for example, having the right to enter the property for the purpose of fitting out. However, a person also has possession if he receives rents or other profits from the land or has the right to receive them. It does not matter whether any of these occurs under the terms of the contract governing the transaction, or under some other arrangement such as a temporary licence or lease. However, if the purchaser already has possession of the property under one interest before entering into a land transaction to acquire a different interest in the same property, the prior possession will not itself cause the later transaction to be substantially performed (SDLTM07900).

Example 4.24—Occupation under previous interest

William occupies an office building under a lease which has 25 years to run. The current rent is £100,000 per year, payable quarterly in advance. His landlord is Vera, who owns the freehold. William agrees to buy the freehold from Vera for £750,000, subject to satisfactory structural survey etc. The agreement provides that William will pay a deposit of £75,000 on signing, a further instalment of £300,000 within 10 days of delivery of the structural survey, and the balance of £375,000 on final completion. The agreement also provides that the final instalment will be reduced by any rent which William pays and which relates to the period after delivery of the structural survey. William occupies and therefore has possession of the property immediately after the agreement is signed. However, he occupies under the terms of the existing lease and not as a result of entering into the agreement to buy the freehold. Therefore, the agreement is not regarded as substantially performed by reason of William's occupation. 50% of the purchase price is paid prior to completion, or possibly slightly more because of the adjustment of the final instalment to allow for rent paid; since this is less than 90%, the agreement will not be regarded as substantially performed until the remaining 50% is paid, on completion.

Example 4.25—Receipt of rents as substantial performance

The same fact pattern applies as in the previous example, except that William's property-holding company Uppercase Ltd, rather than William himself, agrees to buy the freehold from Vera. As part of the agreement, Uppercase Ltd is entitled to receive all rent payable on the property from the date the structural survey is delivered and the £300,000 is paid. The agreement will be regarded as substantially performed no later than the date the structural survey is delivered and the £300,000 is paid, because at that time Uppercase Ltd will become entitled to receive rents.

Transitional provisions

4.93 SDLT was introduced on 1 December 2003, and transactions commenced from that date are wholly within the SDLT rules. Where the contract was entered into on or before 30 November 2003, the transaction may be subject to stamp duty, SDLT or both, as set out below (*FA 2003, Sch 19*). *FA 2003* received Royal Assent on 10 July 2003:

(1) **Contract entered into on or before 10 July 2003**: Subject to stamp duty only, no matter when substantially performed or completed. However, if the contract is varied or assigned after 10 July 2003 or given effect as a result of the exercise of an option or similar right after that date, it is effectively treated as entered into on the date of variation/assignment/exercise.

(2) **Contract entered into after 10 July 2003**:

    (a) **Contract completed on or before 30 November 2003**: subject to stamp duty only;

    (b) **Contract completed after 30 November 2003**: subject to SDLT, but the contract may also have been subject to stamp duty under *FA 2002, s 115*, in which case credit is given for any stamp duty paid.

For these transactions liability to stamp duty or SDLT is not affected by when the transaction was 'substantially performed', as this phrase has no meaning in the context of stamp duty. However, this does affect the 'effective date' (see **4.91**) and therefore the date on which SDLT is payable. If the transaction is subject to SDLT but the contract was substantially performed before 1 December 2003, the effective date is the date of completion. If the contract is substantially performed after 30 November 2003, the effective date is, as normal, the earlier of substantial performance and completion.

As SDLT is now more than 16 years old, there may now be few uncompleted transactions to which these transitional rules may apply. However, particular care should be taken in unwinding old structures which may have been set up for stamp duty planning purposes, see **13.26** et seq.

Example 4.26—Application of transitional provisions

On 1 June 2001, Propco Ltd contracted to buy a commercial property Q which was under construction, for £9.5 million. The vendor had previously bought the site using the 'resting on contract' planning (see **13.29**), so title was held by two nominee companies. On 1 August 2003, Propco assigned the purchase contract to its parent company, Holdco. Continuing the planning, Holdco paid the purchase price to the vendor on 30 September 2003 and took a transfer of the shares in the nominee companies. As a result, the transaction had been substantially performed within the SDLT meaning of that term, but not completed and no stamp duty had been paid.

On 1 March 2020, as part of an exercise to 'tidy up' the Holdco group before a stock market listing, title to site Q is transferred from the nominee companies to Holdco. This effectively completes the original purchase contract entered into in 2001 and, but for the SDLT transitional provisions, would give rise to a stamp duty charge.

Although the contract was entered into before 11 July 2003, it was assigned after that date and so is treated as having been entered into on the date of assignment (1 August 2003), which is after 10 July 2003. It was completed after 30 November 2003, and so is within (2)(b) in **4.93,** ie the transaction is subject to SDLT. The effective date is 1 March 2020 (date of completion) and SDLT is payable, and a return due, on or before 15 March 2020.

ANNUAL TAX ON ENVELOPED DWELLINGS (ATED)

4.94 *Finance Act 2013, Pt 3* (*ss 94–174* and *Schs 33–35*) introduced a new tax known as annual tax on enveloped dwellings, or ATED. A brief account of this tax is included here because:

- the tax was introduced partly in response to the alleged avoidance of SDLT by transferring shares of companies which held residential property;
- the rules for administration of the tax have been derived from those relating to SDLT; and
- administration of the tax has become the responsibility of the section of HMRC which also deals with SDLT.

The following description is no more than an outline, primarily to allow readers to determine whether there is a risk that the tax may apply to a particular situation. A more detailed, in-depth explanation may be found in *Property*

Taxes 2020/21 (Bloomsbury Professional). Section and schedule references in this part are to *Finance Act 2013* unless otherwise indicated.

4.95 The key attributes of ATED are as follows:

1. the tax applies when an interest in a single dwelling, with a value of more than the '*threshold*', is held by a company, partnership or collective investment scheme at any time in the 'chargeable period'. It applies to a partnership only if the partners include one or more companies;
2. the tax applies to 'chargeable periods', being years from 1 April to 31 March. The first chargeable period for properties with a value of more than £2 million was that commencing 1 April 2013. The first chargeable period for lower value properties commenced on 1 April 2015 in relation to properties with a value of more than £1 million but not more than £2 million and from 1 April 2016 to properties with a value of more than £500,000 but not more than £1 million;
3. the amount of tax payable for each chargeable period depends on:
    a. the value of the interest in the dwelling; and
    b. whether the interest is held for the whole chargeable period;
4. it is a self-assessment tax;
5. there are reliefs for properties held by certain entities;
6. there are anti-avoidance provisions; and
7. interest, penalty and enforcement rules apply and are similar to those applying to SDLT.

Single dwelling

4.96 There is a detailed definition of 'single dwelling interest' (*s 108*), designed to prevent mitigation of the tax. If more than one dwelling is held, each must be evaluated separately. Specific rules attempt to deal with single or linked buildings which may be regarded as a single dwelling or more than one dwelling (*s 112, s 116, s 117*). There is no provision equivalent to SDLT multiple dwellings relief (see **5.57**) to average the values of the properties.

Amount of tax

4.97 The tax is based on the market value of the interest held, initially on 1 April 2012 or on the first day on which the tax applies to the company, etc if later. The market value must then be reappraised every fifth anniversary of 1 April 2012, although the reappraised valuation does not apply in determining the tax payable for the chargeable period beginning with that five-yearly valuation date (*FA 2003, s 102(2A)*, inserted by *FA 2015, s 71)*. This is to ensure that there is sufficient time to obtain the five-yearly valuation before the ATED return has to be filed and applies for chargeable periods beginning on or after 1 April 2015. This means that the market value of dwellings within the ATED regime on 1 April 2012 should have been reappraised on 1 April 2017 with the updated valuation applying for the chargeable period 1 April 2018 to 31 March 2019. However, if there is an acquisition or part-disposal with consideration of £40,000 or more this also gives rise to the need to reappraise the market value (*s 102, s 103*).

The amounts of tax shown in the table below are those which apply for the years commencing 1 April 2019 and 1 April 2020. It is specifically provided that the ATED charge will be increased each year in line with increases in the Consumer Price Index to the previous September, rounded down to the next £50 (*s 101*). However, the government raised the ATED charges for the year commencing on 1 April 2015, for properties with a value of more than £2 million, by 50% above inflation. Consequently, the annual increase of the ATED charge, in line with any increase in the Consumer Price Index under *s 101*, did not apply in relation to the chargeable period beginning on 1 April 2015. The change in the Consumer Price Index to September 2015 was negative and therefore the ATED charges for 2016/17 were unchanged from the 2015/16 charges.

Value	**Tax 2019/20**	**Tax 2020/21**
More than £500,000 but not more than £1 million[a]	£3,650	£3,700
More than £1 million but not more than £2 million[b]	£7,400	£7,500
More than £2 million but not more than £5 million	£24,800	£25,200
More than £5 million but not more than £10 million	£57,900	£58,850
More than £10 million but not more than £20 million	£116,100	£118,050
More than £20 million	£232,350	£236,250

(a) Charge first applied for periods commencing 1 April 2016 or later, see *FA 2014, s 110*.
(b) Charge first applied for periods commencing 1 April 2015 or later, see *FA 2014, s 109*.

Where the tax applies for only part of the chargeable period, for example because the property is acquired or disposed of partway through the year, the amount payable is pro-rated on a daily basis. Tax is initially payable on the assumption that the property will be held from the start of the year or later date of acquisition until the end of the year.

If the property is disposed of before the end of the year (or if its value falls so as to reduce the tax, or if a relief begins to apply), it is possible to apply for repayment of the tax overpaid. That application may be made during or up to one year after the end of, the chargeable period by amending the original return. This means there is effectively a one-year time limit on making such a claim (*s 100*).

Self-assessment

4.98 An obligation to submit a return and pay tax generally arises within 30 days of the start of the chargeable period. If the tax begins to apply to a company, partnership or collective investment scheme part way through a chargeable period (eg because a property is acquired), the return and payment obligations generally arise 30 days after the date of the event which causes the tax to apply (*s 159, s 163*). However the deadline for making the first return in relation to properties with a value of more than £2 million was 1 October 2013 and the deadline for the first tax payment was 31 October 2013, or in each case 30 days after the date of the event which first caused the tax to apply if that was later. (*Sch 35, Pt 2*). Similarly, for properties with a value of more than £1 million but less than £2 million the first return was not due until 1 October 2015 nor payment before 31 October 2015. However, this concession was not extended to properties with a value of more than £500,000 but not more than £1 million. First return and payment obligations for such properties caught by the rules on 1 April 2016 were due by 30 April 2016.

Where a company, partnership or collective investment scheme is claiming a relief (see **4.99**) from ATED, it must do so by submitting a return (*FA 2013, s 100*). Since 1 April 2015 it has been possible to file a simplified return called a 'relief declaration return' which must specify the type of relief being claimed but does not need to contain information identifying the particular property (or properties) in relation to which the relief is being claimed or their valuation (*FA 2013, s 159A* inserted by *FA 2015, s 73(3)*). A 'relief declaration return' can be made in respect of more than one property but can only be in relation to one particular relief, ie separate returns must be filed if different reliefs are being claimed for different properties. The return will be treated as made in respect of any property held by the company, partnership or collective investment scheme which is within the charge to ATED, is relievable from the charge to ATED by virtue of the relief specified in the return and there is no day in the chargeable period, prior to the submission of the 'relief declaration return', in relation to which the property is not relieved from the charge to ATED.

Reliefs

4.99 Reliefs are provided for:

- dwellings held by property traders and developers or property rental business (*s 133, s 134, s 138, s 139, s 141*);
- those opened to the public in the course of a trading activity (*s 137*);

- financial institutions, provided the dwelling was acquired in the course of a lending activity and is to be disposed of without undue delay (*s 143*);
- a dwelling held by an 'authorised plan provider' who has entered into a regulated home-reversion plan relating to the single-dwelling interest and on which the 'occupation condition' is satisfied. A regulated home-reversion plan is a plan under which an individual sells all or part of their home to the plan provider in return for an annuity or lump sum and a life tenancy. The 'occupation condition', if no 'qualifying termination event' (*Financial Services and Markets Regulated Activities Order 2001 (SI 2001/544), art 63B*) has occurred, is that the person who was originally entitled to occupy the dwelling under the regulated home reversion plan is still entitled to do so. If a 'qualifying termination event' (*Financial Services and Markets Regulated Activities Order 2001 (SI 2001/544), art 63B*) has occurred the 'occupation condition' is that the single dwelling interest is being held with the intention that it will be sold without delay and no non-qualifying individual is permitted to occupy the dwelling. This relief applies for chargeable periods beginning on or after 1 April 2016 (*s 144A*);
- a dwelling, which is a flat, is held by a company ('the management company') for the purposes of caretaker accommodation, the flat is contained in premises which also contain two or more other flats, the tenants of at least two of the flats in the premises are members of the management company, the management company owns the freehold of the premises and the management company is not carrying on a trade or property rental business. This relief applies for chargeable periods beginning on or after 1 April 2016 (*s 147A*);
- providers of social housing (*s 150*);
- charities (*s 151*);
- properties occupied by certain employees or partners working in a trade or qualifying property rental business (see *FA 2016, s 135(3)* – the amendment to include qualifying property rental businesses applies for chargeable periods beginning on or after 1 April 2016) carried on by the property owner (or a group company), provided the employee/partner has a less than 10% interest in the business (*s 145*); and
- farmhouses occupied by someone working on the farm (or a former long-serving farm worker) (*s 148*).

Anti-avoidance provisions

4.100 The rules have been carefully framed throughout in an attempt to provide complete certainty and to prevent avoidance. This accounts for a high proportion of the 80 pages of legislation. In addition to the general attempt to define closely how and when the tax applies, there are specific provisions to prevent reduction of the value of a dwelling by fragmenting ownership between different people (*s 109, s 110*) or by physically dividing the dwelling into separate parts (*s 115*).

The tax is within the DOTAS rules (see **9.26** for application to SDLT), and its application to the tax is set out in the *Annual Tax on Enveloped Dwellings Avoidance Schemes (Prescribed Descriptions of Arrangements) Regulations 2013 (SI 2013/2571)*.

The main effect of the regulations is to add ATED to the taxes covered by the DOTAS regulations. As a result, the general requirements for promoters and users to provide information to HMRC, often within very short time limits, would apply to arrangements expected to provide an advantage in relation to ATED. There is a very wide description of the kind of arrangement which is caught, being any arrangement under which:

- a company, partnership or collective investment scheme ceases to meet the ownership condition in respect to the chargeable interest;
- the taxable value of the chargeable interest is reduced to £500,000 or less (prior to 1 April 2016 the limit was £1 million); or
- the taxable value of the chargeable interest is reduced with the consequence that the chargeable interest falls within a lower tax band than it otherwise would.

Certain arrangements are then excluded from the obligation to disclose, including an arrangement under which the transfer constitutes a settlement. It is not clear why such arrangements should be excluded, unless HMRC feel that avoidance arrangements involving such transfers are already blocked.

A separate version of form AAG4 (AAG4 (ATED)) is provided for notification of use of a scheme (see www.hmrc.gov.uk/aiu/form-aag4-kana.htm).

The tax is also subject to the general anti-abuse rule in *FA 2013, ss 206–215* (see **9.3**).

Administration and compliance

4.101 As with other taxes, there are requirements for the taxpayer to keep records (*Sch 33, pt 2*), interest is charged on late paid tax and penalties are chargeable if returns are late or incorrect (*Sch 34, pt 2*). HMRC have power to carry out enquiries (*Sch 33, pt 3*), correct errors in returns and to make determinations of tax payable or assessments as necessary (*Sch 33, pts 4* and *5*). The provisions governing enquiries into returns and settlement of disputes are similar to those for SDLT (for which see **8.36** et seq). Routine assessments cannot normally be made more than four years after the end of the chargeable period, or six years if to recover tax lost as a result of carelessness. However this is extended to 20 years in cases attributable to the deliberate action of the taxpayer, or where there has been a failure to make a return or provide information required under the DOTAS rules (*Sch 33, para 25(3)*).

The SDLT rules on collection and recovery of the tax (*FA 2003, Sch 12*) are directly applied to this tax (see **8.35**). HMRC provided some guidance on administrative aspects of ATED in Stamp Taxes Bulletin 1/2014, which can be viewed in the UK Government Web Archive.

4.102 The tax is charged because the property is located in the UK. The tax continues to apply to properties located in Scotland and Wales despite the fact that SDLT no longer applies to properties situated in those countries. The location of the company, etc which owns the property is irrelevant. In the case of SDLT, LBTT and LTT there is a practical need to deal with any liability because it should not be possible to register ownership of the property at the land registries until this has been done. There is no equivalent requirement attached to the payment of ATED. There must therefore be some risk that non-UK companies with no UK presence other than ownership of a dwelling will fail to comply with ATED obligations.

4.103 It may be decided to transfer the property out of the company to prevent future liability to ATED. Care is needed if this is to be done without creating a liability to SDLT (assuming the property is located in either England or Northern Ireland). Provided the company is debt free, the property can be transferred as a distribution in the winding up of the company and no SDLT charge will normally arise. However, if the company has debt – typically in the form of a mortgage secured on the property – transfer in return for the shareholder taking on the debt will be a transfer for consideration and liable to SDLT. HMRC have confirmed that, where the debt is owed to the shareholder so that it simply disappears when the company is wound up and the property transferred to the shareholder, this will not be regarded as giving consideration. However, if there is a third-party debt and the shareholder provides funds for it to be paid off (whether by loan, gift or by subscription for further shares), HMRC will consider whether *FA 2003, s 75A* applies (see **9.4** et seq). If they consider that the provision of funds to pay off third-party debt is 'involved in connection with the disposal' of the property to the shareholder, they will seek to apply *s 75A* and charge SDLT as if the third-party debt had been assumed by the shareholder. See SDLTM04042 for details of HMRC's views on this matter. Following the decision of the Supreme Court in *Project Blue Limited v HMRC* [2018] UKSC 30 in June 2018, and the updates to *FA 2003, s 75A* HMRC guidance published on 15 January 2020, the guidance in SDLTM04042 is currently under review by HMRC, who have undertaken to carry out that review at the earliest opportunity.

Chapter 5

SDLT Reliefs

INTRODUCTION

5.1 Some transactions are automatically exempt from an obligation to notify HMRC and do not give rise to any SDLT charge. The legislation labels some (but not all) of these as 'exempt transactions'. In this book, the term 'exemption' is applied to all such cases. Even where an exemption applies, so that there is no liability to pay SDLT or submit a return, the taxpayer is still required to keep appropriate records and documents for up to six years (see **8.62**). However, it should be noted that the requirement to 'self-certify' transactions as exempt, using form SDLT60, was abolished by *FA 2008, Sch 30* with effect from 12 March 2008. Land Registries should now agree to register exempt transactions on the basis of a statement by the purchaser that the transaction is exempt from SDLT.

5.2 In contrast, there are many reliefs reducing or eliminating SDLT liabilities that would otherwise arise. Such reliefs do not apply automatically (despite the fact that, in many cases, the legislation describes qualifying transactions as 'exempt from charge'), but must be claimed by submission of an SDLT return (see **8.2**, *FA 2003, s 62(3)* and SDLTM20010). The relief is claimed in the return by putting appropriate codes in boxes; the form provides no space for disclosure of further information explaining the circumstances surrounding the claim. Many reliefs are hedged around with complex anti-avoidance rules, which create genuine uncertainty as to their availability.

5.3 It is often desirable to provide further information in order to ensure full disclosure and reduce the risk that HMRC may reject the claim and make a 'discovery' assessment up to six years later. As a result, it has become commonplace to submit further information by way of letter when the SDLT return is completed (see **8.47**). HMRC have acknowledged this process in informal discussion, but do not appear to have issued any formal guidance on the matter.

5.4 There are several reliefs which are subject to retrospective withdrawal ('clawback') if certain events occur, as explained below in the descriptions of the reliefs. In these cases, it is necessary to keep track of both the property and the owner(s), in order to be able to make necessary returns and payments should clawback apply. Special rules apply where the interest disposed of is a lease, on grant of which group relief (or one of a list of other reliefs) was claimed. If nothing has already happened to cause clawback of that relief, the first transfer of the lease which does not itself qualify for one of the specified list of reliefs is treated as the grant of a new lease for the remaining term of the actual lease and at the rent payable by the transferee. SDLT is chargeable on the transferee accordingly (*FA 2003, Sch 17A, para 11*). See **6.17** et seq for an explanation of this and an example.

5.5 Finally, to add to the confusion, there is a provision which is generally regarded as a relief but strictly is simply a computational rule. This is the so-called 'PFI relief' in *FA 2003, Sch 4, para 17* (see **5.17**). This rule exempts certain consideration from charge, applies automatically (like an exemption) but still requires submission of a return (like a relief).

Originally 'sub-sale relief', was also a computational provision which applied automatically to disregard all except the final step in certain series of transfers. However, *FA 2013, s 195* replaced this with a true relief, requiring a claim in a land transaction return (see **5.8**).

5.6 In this chapter, reliefs with a wide application are dealt with in some detail, but those with relatively narrow or specialised application are dealt with only briefly, the most specialised being summarised in table form. Reliefs which have been abolished or virtually abolished are mentioned at the end of the chapter. A few reliefs which apply specifically to leases are dealt with in **Chapter 6** (see **6.81** et seq).

EXEMPTIONS

5.7 The main exemptions are listed in *FA 2003, s 77A* and *Sch 3*, as follows:

(1) A transaction for which there is no chargeable consideration is exempt (*FA 2003, Sch 3, para 1*). Chargeable consideration is defined in *FA 2003, Sch 4* (see **4.19**). If there is no actual consideration in money or money's worth, there will be no chargeable consideration unless *FA 2003, s 53* (purchaser is connected company; see **4.30**), or *FA 2003, Sch 15* (transfers involving partnerships; see **Chapter 7**), or *FA 2003, Sch 4, para 12(1)(c)* (land transaction entered into by reason of employment), apply. Additionally, *FA 2003, Sch 4* provides for certain amounts to be ignored where they might otherwise be regarded as consideration, see **4.36**.

(2) The grant of a lease to a tenant by a relevant housing provider (RHP) for an indefinite term or in circumstances where the lease is terminable

by notice of a month or less is exempt provided certain other conditions are satisfied (*FA 2003, Sch 3, para 2*). For these purposes a 'relevant housing provider' is a non-profit registered provider of social housing or a registered social landlord. Detailed review of the rules affecting RHPs is beyond the scope of this book, but it seems likely in practice that any transaction which might qualify for this exemption may also be exempt under the '*de minimis* consideration' rules; see (7) below.

(3) A transfer between parties to a marriage or civil partnership in connection with dissolution of the marriage or partnership or separation of the parties (whether in pursuance of a court order or by agreement) is exempt (*FA 2003, Sch 3, paras 3* and *'second 3A'*, an apparent glitch in numbering of the statute).

(4) A transfer of property to a beneficiary under a will or intestacy is exempt, provided the transferee gives no consideration other than the assumption of any debt secured on the property. If other consideration *is* given, the assumption of any secured debt does not count as consideration in calculating the SDLT charge (*FA 2003, Sch 3, first para 3A*). Similarly, a variation of a will within two years of death (eg by way of a family deed of arrangement) is exempt, provided no consideration is given other than agreement to other variations (*FA 2003, Sch 3, para 4*).

(5) A transfer not involving the grant of a lease is exempt if the chargeable consideration (together with the consideration for any linked transactions; see **4.84**) is less than £40,000 (*FA 2003, s 77A(1.2), (1.4)*). The figure of £40,000 seems somewhat arbitrary – it is difficult to see why it should not be increased to match the threshold below which no SDLT is chargeable. Note that the consideration must be less than £40,000, not '£40,000 or less'.

(6) The grant of a lease for a term of seven years or more is exempt if the chargeable consideration other than rent is less than £40,000 and the rent is less than £1,000 per annum (*FA 2003, s 77A(1.3)*). This exemption does not specifically require aggregation of chargeable consideration of linked transactions. It may be that HMRC would argue that the need to aggregate is implied by the general provisions of *FA 2003, s 55(4)* but it is by no means clear that this would be correct.

(7) The grant of a lease for a term of less than seven years is exempt, provided the chargeable consideration does not exceed the zero rate threshold – that is, provided no tax is chargeable and no tax would be chargeable but for availability of a relief (*FA 2003, s 77A(1.5), (2)*). In relation to rent no tax will be chargeable if the aggregate of the net present value of the rent (see **6.47** et seq) is £125,000 or less (residential property) or £150,000 or less (non-residential property). For any consideration other than rent (ie a premium), no tax will be chargeable if the amount of the consideration other than rent is £125,000 or less (residential property)

or £150,000 or less (non-residential property) (see **4.37**). The higher SDLT rate for additional dwellings and dwellings purchased by companies and other non-individual purchasers (see **4.56**) does not apply to the grant of a lease for less than seven years, as it only applies where a 'major interest' in a dwelling is acquired, and a lease granted for a term of less than seven years is not a 'major interest' (see **4.11**) for the purposes of the higher SDLT rates legislation (*FA 2003, Sch 4ZA, para 2(4)*).

(8) The assignment or surrender of a lease which was originally granted for a term of less than seven years, where the chargeable consideration for the assignment or surrender does not exceed the zero rate threshold, is exempt.

SUB-SALE RELIEF

5.8 As originally enacted, *FA 2003, s 45* was not a true relief; it was a computational provision which applied automatically if the conditions were satisfied. However, the original provisions were widely exploited, using structures which gave economic ownership of property while qualifying for sub-sale treatment. *FA 2013, s 195* replaced these provisions with a true relief which has to be claimed in a land transaction return. The relief is designed to prevent avoidance while retaining the same overall tax effect for 'genuine' cases. At the same time *FA 2013, s 194* amended the original provisions with retrospective effect to counter some specific avoidance arrangements (see **5.16**). An attempt to challenge the legitimacy of the retrospective change, by way of judicial review, was blocked by the court (*R (on the application of St Matthews (West) Ltd and others) v HMRC*, High Court, judgment 6 June 2014).

5.9 Sub-sale relief can apply where:

- A agrees to transfer property to B but,
- before that contract is completed or substantially performed, B agrees to transfer all or part of the same property to C, and either
  - B drops out so that substantial performance and completion occurs directly between A and C, or
  - the A–B contract is substantially performed and completed at the same time as, and in connection with, respective substantial performance and completion of the B–C contract.

The relief is often relied on in arrangements to finance speculative developments. A builder may find it difficult to borrow the full cost of a development without certainty of selling a proportion of the apartments or units. If apartments or units are sold 'off plan' to investors, the builder will be able to borrow more easily. When the development is completed, the investors may sell the apartments or units on, without taking possession as illustrated in Example 5.1. A form of sub-sale relief had long been available under stamp duty. When SDLT was introduced in 2003, the initial proposals did not include sub-sale relief. However the importance of this to the construction industry was sufficient to persuade the government to include the relief.

5.10 Under the old rules, the A to B agreement was ignored for SDLT purposes, to the extent that the property passed to C. In respect of the property transferred to C, SDLT obligations arose only in relation to the A to C or B to C transfer (*FA 2003, s 45*, before amendment by *FA 2013*). Because this was an automatic treatment if the transaction qualified, there was neither need nor facility for B to make a return or claim relief or exemption. If the whole property was transferred to C, SDLT was charged only on the overall total amount which C paid to A and/or B. If only part of the property was transferred to C, B also paid SDLT in respect of the part retained.

The new pre-completion transaction rules

5.11 The new rules, which are substantially longer than the old, are in *FA 2003, Sch 2A*. The greater length and complexity attracted criticism from business and advisers but also from MPs during the Finance Bill debates, but no simplification was offered by the government. HMRC provide guidance at SDLTM21500 et seq.

The new rules apply to transactions entered into on or after 17 July 2013. Paragraph numbers in this explanation refer to *Sch 2A* unless otherwise stated. The technical operation of the rules has been completely recast in order to combat avoidance. However in straightforward cases the overall effect should be unchanged, save that B will now normally have to make a land transaction return and claim relief.

5.12 The rules distinguish between two forms of sub sale. An 'assignment of rights' occurs when B drops out of the transaction so that C gains the rights and obligations of B in relation to the original contract. Performance and completion of the transaction then takes place directly between A and C. A 'free standing transfer' takes place when the A to B contract remains in place and is performed and completed between A and B, but the property is transferred on to C under a separate agreement.

- In the case of an assignment of rights, the A to B agreement is regarded as substantially performed/completed by C and liability to tax in respect of that agreement now falls on C. C therefore is responsible for notifying the transaction and paying the liability. In addition, B is regarded as entering into a notional land transaction on the same terms as provided in the original A to B agreement (*para 5*). Unless excepted under other provisions (eg if the transaction is exempt, see **5.7**) B must notify HMRC of the notional transaction by submission of a land transaction return. See **8.6** in relation to notifying transactions.

- In the case of a freestanding transaction, both the A to B transaction and the B to C transaction are subject to SDLT. *Sch 2A* does not specifically state that the A to B transaction is subject to SDLT. However (in contrast with the old rules) there is no longer any provision disregarding this transaction and since it is substantially performed/completed, it remains subject to SDLT on general principles. Therefore both B and C must notify the transaction by submission of land transaction returns, unless excepted under other provisions such as application of an exemption (see **5.7**).

In both cases, provided the appropriate conditions are satisfied, B can claim relief from SDLT in the return, in respect of the part sub-sold to C (*paras 15, 16*). Apart from actually being a step in a sub sale, the main condition to be satisfied is that the transaction does not form part of any tax avoidance arrangements (*para 18*). In this context 'tax' is not separately defined and so must be taken to mean only SDLT (*FA 2003, s 121*). Relief is also denied if the second (or final) transfer qualifies for relief under *FA 2003, ss 71A–73* (alternative property finance, see **5.37** onwards). In contrast with the old version of sub-sale relief, there is no specific denial of relief if the B to C transfer qualifies for group, reconstruction or acquisition relief (see **5.20**). It is assumed that HMRC are content to rely on the specific rules for those reliefs and/or general anti-avoidance rules to prevent such a combination of reliefs.

As before the rules allow for successive sub sales, with each intermediate purchaser being responsible for notifying the transaction and for each, other than the final purchaser, potentially able to claim relief. In the case of an assignment of rights, if only part of the land is sub sold, the original A to B agreement is regarded as divided into two, covering the part sub sold and the part retained (*para 7*). The consideration must be apportioned between the two (or more) parts on a just and reasonable basis (*FA 2003, Sch 4, para 4*).

5.13 Most of *Sch 2A* effectively consists of anti-avoidance measures, designed to ensure that SDLT is payable on the full economic consideration given. Terms and expressions are closely defined in an attempt to remove any doubt. A new rule imposes a minimum consideration which C is deemed to give if B and C are connected (as defined in *Corporation Tax Act 2010, s 1122*) or not acting at arm's length. Under this rule the consideration given by C is deemed to be the greatest of:

- the actual consideration given by C;

- the consideration to be given under the original A to B agreement; and
- the total net amount of consideration given by B and C.

In relation to the final bullet point above, the net amount of consideration is the amount given minus any amount received from someone else. Where only part of the original land is sub sold, amounts are apportioned accordingly. The rules are modified where there are successive sub sales. The net amount of consideration referred to in the final bullet point above becomes the total net amount given by C and all intermediate purchasers who are connected with (or not acting at arm's length with) C. The consideration referred to in the second bullet point above becomes the consideration to be given by the first intermediate purchaser in the chain who is connected with, or not acting at arms' length with C (*paras 12–14*).

5.14 Under *para 19*, the Treasury can make regulations to amend the legislation, in order to exempt certain purchasers (B in the narrative above) from making returns or from needing to claim relief. As at 30 April 2020 no such regulations had been made.

5.15 Early in the SDLT era, a mechanism exploited sub sale treatment to avoid or defer SDLT on substantial performance, using 'alternative contracts'. These provided for the land to be transferred to the original purchaser or a third party, the main idea being that the original purchaser would never gain an interest in land and so would not have to pay SDLT. It is not clear that the planning worked, but *FA 2003, ss 44A* and *45A* were enacted to put the matter beyond doubt and ensure the SDLT liability arose as soon as the original contract was substantially performed.

Retrospective changes to old rules

5.16 Despite the provisions referred to in **5.15**, the old version of sub-sale relief was widely relied on in various attempts to mitigate SDLT. Pending amendment of the rules for sub-sale relief by *FA 2013*, it was announced at the time of the 2012 Budget that any remaining such arrangements would be countered by legislation with retrospective effect back to 21 March 2012. *FA 2012, s 213* amended the DOTAS rules to require re-disclosure of schemes using sub-sale relief. This was to ensure that the users of such schemes were also required to notify HMRC (see **9.38**). From 21 March 2012, the grant or assignment of an option was prevented from qualifying as a sub sale or assignment (*FA 2012, s 212*).

FA 2013, s 194 amended the old version of *FA 2003, s 45* to deny relief for the A to B transfer where the B to C transfer was substantially performed but not completed at the same time as the A to B transfer and B remained in possession of the property, and it was reasonable to conclude that a main purpose of the arrangements was the obtaining of a tax advantage for B. This was to counter a specific arrangement under which B, the real purchaser, agreed to sub-sell the property to another party, C, for a very small sum but with completion delayed for a century or more. Because the legislation was retrospective, those who had used this arrangement were given until 30 September 2013 to submit a land transaction return disclosing the liability and to pay the tax. If this deadline was met, no penalty would be charged (although interest would be payable on the tax).

In an amendment introduced by the government during the Committee stage of the Finance Bill, *FA 2003, s 45* was further amended to counter a recently identified scheme using options, which claimed to escape the restrictions imposed by *FA 2012, s 210* mentioned above.

Example 5.1—Sub sales

Buildquick Ltd proposes to build a block of apartments. Richman, who has an impeccable credit record and is not connected with Buildquick, agrees to buy six apartments for a total price of £1.5 million (ie £250,000 each). Each apartment will be acquired under a separate, and legally independent, agreement to facilitate the onward sale, by Richman, to third parties. It is therefore considered that the acquisition of each apartment will be a separate transaction (as there are separate agreements) and consequently *FA 2003, s 116(7)* (which applies where six or more dwellings are acquired as part of a single transaction and treats such a transaction as the acquisition of non-residential property) will not apply to treat the acquisition of the apartments as an acquisition of non-residential property (see **4.47**).

The agreements allow Buildquick to borrow from its usual bank to fund construction. Richman pays the customary 10% deposit. The agreements have not yet been completed or substantially performed, so no SDLT obligations have yet arisen.

As completion of construction approaches, Richman's agent begins marketing the apartments. Sales of the first two are agreed to unconnected individuals at £270,000 each. In each case, the purchaser pays Richman's agent a deposit of 10%. At this stage, no SDLT obligations have arisen.

The apartments are finished and the time for completion of the sales arrives. At the last minute, an unconnected buyer is found for a third apartment, at a price of £240,000. Sales of the first three apartments to Richman are substantially performed and completed at the same time as the onward sales to the unconnected purchasers. The purchases by Richman give rise to the obligation to complete a land transaction return but he should be able to claim relief under *FA 2003, Sch 2A, para 16* so that no tax arises. SDLT is chargeable only on the ultimate purchasers. Since these ultimate purchasers are not connected with each other or with Richman, SDLT is chargeable on each at the rates appropriate to the amount paid – that is, 0%, 2% and 5% on each of two purchases at £270,000 and 0% and 2% on the third purchase at £240,000. This assumes that the ultimate purchasers are not liable to pay the 3% additional rate of SDLT on their acquisitions of the flats (see **4.56** et seq). The amount paid by Richman is irrelevant in calculating the SDLT liability of the third party purchasers.

Richman completes the purchase of the fourth and fifth apartments in his own name, with the intention of letting them out at rent. He assigns the benefit of the contract to purchase the sixth apartment to his sister, who pays £10,000 for the benefit of the contract, and pays Buildquick the balance of the original purchase price, £225,000, to complete the purchase. The arrangements relating to the fourth, fifth and sixth apartments give rise to SDLT issues as follows:

- Although the market value of the sixth apartment is probably at least the £240,000 paid by the last-minute purchaser of the third, the total amount paid by the sister is only £235,000 (£10,000 to Richman for transfer of the contract and £225,000 to Buildquick to complete). However, Richman has paid a £25,000 deposit. Since Richman is connected with his sister, the minimum consideration rule comes into play (*para 12*). The three figures to consider are:

    1. the total amount of consideration given by the sister (£235,000);
    2. the amount payable under the original agreement between Richman and Buildquick (£250,000); and
    3. the total net amount paid by Richman (£25,000 deposit less £10,000 received from sister = £15,000) and his sister (£235,000).

    The second and third amounts are the same, £250,000 and are larger than the first amount. So the sister pays SDLT on £250,000. The new rules remove one ambiguity; under the old version of s *45*, it could have been argued that SDLT was due on the gross amount paid by Richman and his sister, totalling £260,000 – although this would have been greater than the real net cost of the apartment.

- The purchases of apartments four and five by Richman and the purchase of the sixth by his sister are linked transactions (see **4.99**). The consideration must therefore be aggregated to determine the SDLT rate. The aggregate consideration is £750,000 so prima facie the SDLT rates which apply should be 3%, 5% and 8%. This is on the basis that both Richman and his sister already own separate properties which they use as their main residence, and the apartments are being acquired as buy-to-let properties, such that the higher rates of SDLT apply (see **4.56**). However, if Richman and his sister choose to make a claim, the purchases should qualify for multiple dwellings relief under *FA 2003, Sch 6B* (see **5.57**). In this case the rates of SDLT are determined by the average cost of the apartments – £250,000 – and the SDLT higher rates that will apply will therefore be 3% and 5%.

PFI RELIEF

5.17 This is the calculation provision which looks like a hybrid exemption/relief, referred to at **5.5**. Although popularly referred to as PFI relief, *FA 2003, Sch 4, para 17* does not necessarily apply to all PFI-type transactions, nor does it necessarily remove all liability. It merely excludes certain amounts from the calculation of chargeable consideration where:

(1) there is a transfer of land (which may include the grant of a lease) from a 'qualifying body' (A) to a non-qualifying body (B), and

(2) a lease back of that land to A, and

(3) an agreement for B to provide services to, or carry out works for A, to be paid for at least in part in money.

5.18 'Qualifying bodies' include public bodies within *FA 2003, s 66* (broadly, local and central government organisations, health authorities and other statutory bodies, but the list in s *66* should be checked in any individual case). They also include entities operating Higher and Further Education establishments and Academies – the list in *FA 2003, Sch 4, para 17(2)* should be checked where appropriate.

5.19 Where the relief applies, the chargeable consideration for the initial transfer of land does not include the value of the lease-back or the carrying out of works or provision of services by B. The chargeable consideration for the lease-back does not include the initial transfer of land, any transfer of other land from A to B, or the payment of money by A to B. This may mean that there is no chargeable consideration for any of the land transfers; however, PFI-type transactions are often more complex than the relief appears to envisage, and each transaction must be analysed carefully to establish whether the precise conditions have been met for all consideration to be excluded from charge.

Example 5.2—PFI relief

Anytown Unitary Authority (A) needs a new building for council offices and a public library. This is to be built on a site mostly owned by A. Buildit plc (B) owns a small piece of land adjacent to this site, which is needed for access. It is agreed that:

(1) B will transfer the freehold of the small piece of land to A;

(2) A will grant B a 25-year lease of the whole site at a peppercorn rent;

(3) B will construct the building to A's specification;

(4) B will lease the building back to A for 25 years less one day, on the basis that B will manage the building (cleaning, maintenance, security etc);

(5) A will pay B a 'unitary charge' each year for provision of the building and services; and

(6) in addition, A will transfer to B the freehold of an old library site, on which B hopes to develop luxury apartments for sale.

Items 3 and 4 do not count as chargeable consideration for the grant of the lease at 2. Items 2, 5 and 6 do not count as chargeable consideration for the grant of the lease at 4. However, the transfer at 1 is not within the relieving provisions and is potentially subject to SDLT. If A is not able to claim any other relief or exemption, it will be necessary to establish how much of the value of 2, 5 and 6 should be attributed as consideration for the transfer at 1, and SDLT will be charged on this. The natural assumption will be that the consideration is the same as the market value of the small piece of land, unless analysis of the figures suggests otherwise. Central government bodies and some others, such as strategic health authorities, have the benefit of blanket SDLT reliefs, but reliefs available to the various local authorities are more limited and probably do not apply here.

GROUP, RECONSTRUCTION AND ACQUISITION RELIEFS

5.20 These reliefs are dealt with together because they appear together in *FA 2003, Sch 7* and many of the conditions and anti-avoidance provisions are similar. The basic operation of each relief is outlined separately below, with an account of the conditions which apply to the particular relief. This is followed by discussion of an anti-avoidance provision which is common to all three reliefs. Finally, there is a review of the circumstances in which each relief may be retrospectively withdrawn (clawed back) as a result of events after the initial transaction.

5.21 The reliefs apply to transactions involving 'companies' (*FA 2003, Sch 7, paras 1, 7* and *8*). There are no restrictions as to residence or place of incorporation of the companies, providing they can be recognised as bodies corporate. In relation to group relief, with the possible exception of the top company of a group, they must have 'issued ordinary share capital' or its equivalent. This can cause difficulties in relation to some overseas entities, where their 'corporate' nature may be open to question or which may have no concept of shares or share capital. In any case of doubt, it is possible to ask the opinion of HMRC. However, if it is not a type of body on which they have previously opined, HMRC are likely to demand an appropriate legal opinion from a lawyer in the relevant country (paid for, inevitably, by the taxpayer).

5.22 Relief may not be due, or in some cases may be withdrawn, if there are 'arrangements' for certain events to happen – the specific events are mentioned in relation to each relief below. The legislation makes it clear that 'arrangements' may exist even though there is no legal commitment by the parties (*FA 2003, Sch 7, para 2(5)*); in relation to stamp duty, HMRC gave their view that arrangements exist where it is intended that the event will happen and there is no likelihood in practice that it will not (see SP 3/98, para 6); however, in Inland Revenue Tax Bulletin Issue 70 (April 2004 – '*Stamp Duty Land Tax: Group Relief*') HMRC make the point that the term 'arrangements' was not defined for the purposes of stamp duty and 'Under this new definition [*FA 2003, Sch 7, para 2(5)*] "arrangements" will include schemes, arrangements or understandings not in writing and the existence of arrangements in a particular claim will depend on a consideration of all of the facts relating to the claim and the surrounding circumstances' (para 19). The guidance goes on to state at para 34 that '... the practical likelihood of the scheme being carried through is not in itself relevant.' A link to the article in Inland Revenue Tax Bulletin Issue 70 can be found at SDLTM23011. This seems to be an attempt by HMRC to suggest that the term 'arrangements' may have a wider meaning for the purposes of SDLT than it does for stamp duty purposes. However, in the view of the author, this is probably not the case and similar criteria to that used in determining whether an 'arrangement' exists for stamp duty should apply in relation to SDLT. The legislation which denies the availability of the relief if a disqualifying arrangement is in existence should, like any other statutory provision, be interpreted purposively, with the relief only being denied if the arrangement is designed to avoid SDLT.

Group relief

5.23 Group relief removes any SDLT charge on land transactions between companies (ie bodies corporate) which are members of the same group (*FA 2003, Sch 7, para 1*). To be members of the same group, one company must be the 75% subsidiary (direct or indirect) of the other, or each must be the 75% subsidiary of a third company. For A to be the 75% subsidiary of B, B must be:

(a) the beneficial owner of not less than 75% of the issued ordinary share capital of A;

(b) beneficially entitled to at least 75% of any profits of A available for distribution to equity holders; and

(c) beneficially entitled to at least 75% of any assets of A available for distribution to equity holders on a winding up.

Where ownership is indirect, proportions are to be calculated in the normal algebraic manner under *Corporation Tax Act 2010 (CTA 2010), ss 1155–1157*. Rights of equity holders are measured in accordance with *CTA 2010, Pt 5*, Chapter 6 (omitting references to arrangements which might affect future rights if put into effect). If shares in a particular company are not identical as to par value and rights, or if creditors have greater rights than payment of the relevant debts, it will be necessary to consider the impact of this chapter.

Example 5.3

Fred, an individual, owns 100% of the shares of Gill Ltd and 100% of the shares of Irene Ltd. Gill Ltd owns 90% of the shares of Jack Ltd and 75% of the shares of Kerri Ltd. Irene Ltd owns the other 10% of Jack Ltd and 20% of Harry Ltd. Jack Ltd owns the remaining 80% of Harry Ltd. Fred's business partner Leo owns the remaining 25% of shares in Kerri Ltd. All shares are ordinary, same class and denomination, and there are no share options or other instruments which might change relative entitlement to dividends or asset distribution in a winding up. The structure is therefore as follows:

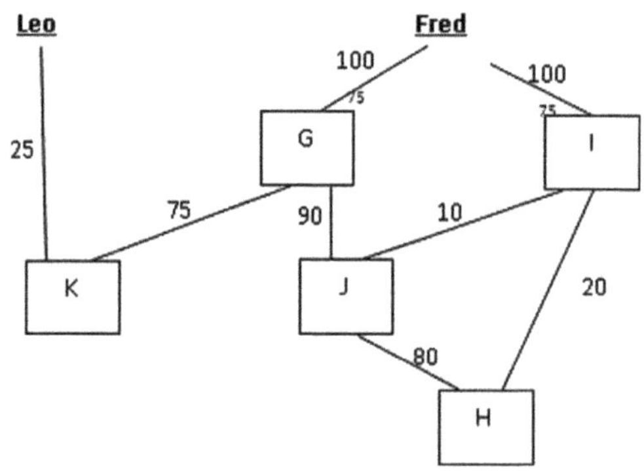

Clearly, Fred ultimately controls all of the companies, so they are connected for the purposes of *Corporation Tax Act 2010, s 1122*. This has implications for the measurement of consideration for any land transactions between them (see **4.30**). However, they are not all members of the same group. J and H form a group, so transfers between them are capable of qualifying for group relief. Equally G, J and K form a group, and transfers between them may qualify for relief. However, H is not grouped with G or K. This is because G has (indirect) beneficial ownership of only 72% (90% × 80%) of H, the other 28% being owned directly and indirectly by I (and I is not grouped with any of the other companies). Note that J is separately grouped with both H, and G and K.

In contrast with some direct tax provisions, it is acceptable for SDLT purposes for a company to be a member of more than one group in this way. Although H and G (or K) are not directly grouped, it appears at first glance that it should be possible to transfer land between them free of SDLT, for example by G making the transfer first to J, and then J transferring onwards to H. However, group relief is surrounded by anti-avoidance provisions (see **5.28**), and it is highly likely that these would apply to such a sequence, potentially denying relief on both transfers and leading to a higher charge than would have applied to a direct transfer.

Treatment of LLP – company or partnership?

5.24 There is a conflict between possible treatments of a limited liability partnership (LLP). For most purposes, an LLP is regarded as a body corporate. On this basis, it can be the top company of a group for group relief purposes, and transfers between companies owned by the LLP may qualify for SDLT group relief. An LLP cannot be a subsidiary within a group, because it does not have issued ordinary share capital; and as it cannot be looked through as it is a body corporate, it therefore breaks any group structure, isolating companies above it in the structure from those below. Therefore, group relief cannot be available for a transfer to (or from) a subsidiary company, from (or to) a partner or other company above the LLP in the structure, **even if all companies are substantively in the same corporate group.**

However, the special rules governing the application of SDLT to partnerships (see **Chapter 7**) state that any chargeable interest held by a partnership (which includes an LLP) is regarded as held not by the partnership but by the partners (*FA 2003, Sch 15, para 2(1)(a)*). Therefore, group relief is not available for a transfer of property from (or to) an LLP to (or from) a corporate partner, because this is regarded as a transfer from (or to) all of the partners, unless the partners are all members of the same group. A transfer of property from a subsidiary of the LLP to the LLP itself cannot qualify for group relief even if the partners in the LLP are all members of the same group. This is because such a transfer is regarded as a transfer to the partners, and the partners cannot be grouped with the subsidiary of the LLP because the presence of the LLP breaks the group relationship. The provisions at *FA 2003, Sch 15, para 2* which treat partnership property as owned by the partners, do not apply to treat shares owned by the LLP as owned by the partners. This is an unreasonable and potentially unfair consequence of treating the LLP differently in relation to ownership of property and of shares.

After some uncertainty, HMRC eventually confirmed this interpretation in guidance published on 11 December 2014 (see www.hmrc.gov.uk/so/group-rel-sdlt-sd.htm).

Example 5.4

Companies B and C are 100% owned by company D. B and C are equal partners in an LLP. The LLP owns 100% of the shares in company E. The presence of the LLP means that, for SDLT purposes, E is not grouped with B, C or D. A transfer of property from E to the LLP will not qualify for group relief because it will be treated as a transfer to B and C. Similarly, a transfer from E to any of B, C or D will not qualify for group relief. However, a transfer between any pair of B, C, D or the LLP may qualify for relief.

Arrangements

5.25 In accordance with *FA 2003, Sch 7, para 2*, group relief is not available if, at the time of the transfer, there are 'arrangements' under which:

- at that or a later time, a person could obtain control of the purchaser but not the vendor. This condition may be breached if a third party has options to acquire or subscribe for shares of the purchaser, for example. However, if the arrangements are part of a scheme of reconstruction which itself will qualify for stamp duty relief under *FA 1986, s 75*, relief will not be denied (see SDLTM23035); or
- any part of the consideration is to be provided or received by someone other than a group member. In principle, this could lead to denial of relief where, for example, the purchaser borrows funds from a bank. In Inland Revenue Tax Bulletin Issue 70 (April 2004) HMRC state that borrowing on ordinary commercial terms to fund an intra-group transfer would not normally lead to denial of relief (para 29). In addition HMRC indicate that they will consider all of the facts and interpret this provision as not denying relief unless loan finance is provided as part of a scheme to save SDLT when the property leaves the SDLT group (para 27); or
- the companies are to cease to be members of the same group by reason of the purchaser leaving the group. It is not generally a problem if there are arrangements under which the vendor is to leave the group. However, arrangements even for this must not be too far advanced, or beneficial ownership of relevant shares may already be lost and the group broken before the time of the transfer.
- In addition group relief is not available if: (a) the transaction is not carried out for bona fide commercial reasons; or (b) the transaction forms part of arrangements of which the main purpose, or one of the main purposes, is the avoidance of liability to tax. This anti-avoidance provision is considered further at **5.28**.

Reconstruction relief

5.26 Reconstruction relief removes any SDLT charge on land transactions in the course of a qualifying reconstruction under which one company, A, acquires all or part of the undertaking of another, B (*FA 2003, Sch 7, para 7*). The reconstruction qualifies if:

(1) the consideration includes the issue of non-redeemable shares in A to all of the shareholders of B;

(2) there is no other consideration, except that A is permitted to assume or discharge debt of B;

(3) the shareholders of B before the transaction end up owning identical proportions (or as near as is possible) of company A; and

(4) the transaction is for bona fide commercial purposes, without a main purpose of avoiding tax.

See **5.28** for a discussion of the last of these conditions.

This relief is the SDLT equivalent of stamp duty relief under *FA 1986, s 75* (confusingly headed 'acquisitions: reliefs' in the legislation), and the stamp duty case law relating to the term 'undertaking' applies here too. The HMRC view on this is set out in SDLTM23201. Broadly, there must be some form of active business originally carried on by B and subsequently continued by A – a mere transfer of assets which are passively held or subsequently used by A for a different purpose will not qualify.

Acquisition relief

5.27 Acquisition relief is the SDLT equivalent of stamp duty relief under *FA 1986, s 76*. It reduces the rate of SDLT chargeable to 0.5% where a company, A, acquires all or part of the undertaking of another, B, and relevant other conditions are met (*FA 2003, Sch 7, para 8*). The conditions are

(1) the consideration includes the issue of non-redeemable shares in A to B, or to any or all of the shareholders of B,

(2) the only other consideration (if any) comprises one or both of:

- payment of cash not exceeding 10% of the nominal value of the shares issued, and

- the assumption or discharge by A of liabilities of B,

(3) A is not associated with any company which is party to 'arrangements' with B relating to the shares issued by A, and

(4) the main activity of the undertaking consists of a trade other than property dealing or development.

Condition (3) is intended to prevent relief where the parties agree in advance that B will sell the newly issued shares to a member of A's group or other associated company, so that as far as B is concerned the sale of the undertaking is effectively for cash. However, the condition can cause difficulties in relatively innocent circumstances, where A and B are themselves associated perhaps because they are held by members of the same family, and shareholder agreements give pre-emption rights where one shareholder wishes to exit. All such transfers require careful detailed analysis to establish whether the relief applies; in general, HMRC seem reluctant to provide guidance on whether particular arrangements fall foul of this condition.

Condition (4), which was added in 2005, means that the relief does not apply to the transfer of a property letting business (not a trade) or a property development activity. The relief is, however, potentially useful in relation to the transfer of a trade where property forms a large proportion of the fixed assets – for example, retailing, pub or hotel operations.

Anti-avoidance provision

5.28 Each relief is additionally subject to the condition that the transaction must be for bona fide commercial purposes, without the avoidance of tax forming a main purpose. 'Tax' here means stamp duty, SDLT, income tax, corporation tax or capital gains tax. This condition is effectively a general anti-avoidance provision. There is no legislative guidance as to its scope, and doubt over this has led to significant uncertainty as to whether relief is due. In response to widespread disquiet, HMRC produced a 'white list' of transactions which would not normally be regarded as falling foul of this condition. The list can be found at SDLTM23040. However, the list itself is heavily caveated and gives limited comfort in the context of real commercial transactions. HMRC have also confirmed that group relief would not be denied merely because one company obtained a tax advantage by implementing the transactions detailed below, even if the transactions formed part of the same arrangements:

(1) a group, acquiring from a third party, a company which held property; then

(2) transferring the property held by the acquired company within the wider group; potentially followed by

(3) the liquidation, winding-up or striking-off of the acquired company after the transfer of the property within the wider group.

This confirmation is now set out in SDLTM23040 but includes the added warning that the presence of steps in addition to those detailed above may indicate, when taken together, that there are arrangements of which the main purpose, or one of the main purposes, is avoidance of tax, so that group relief would be denied. For example, see **9.8** for commentary on the decision of the First-tier Tribunal (Tax) in *(1) Hannover Leasing Wachstumswerte Europa Beteiligungsgesellschaft mbH; (2) Hanover Leasing Wachstumswerte Europa VI GmbH & Co KG v HMRC* [2019] UKFTT 262.

Clawback of relief

5.29 Even where a transaction initially qualifies for one of these reliefs, in certain circumstances the relief may be retrospectively withdrawn, leading to the crystallisation of the SDLT charge originally relieved. Because SDLT is a self-assessment tax, it is for the taxpayer to detect and disclose any situation in which a clawback arises (*FA 2003, s 81* – 'Further return where relief withdrawn'). Where one of these reliefs has been claimed, it is therefore important to put in place arrangements to monitor ownership of the property, and of the companies involved in the original claim, for an appropriate period, which is generally three years.

Clawback of group relief

5.30 Group relief is clawed back if the purchaser, while it or a 'relevant associated company' still owns the property (or an interest derived from it), ceases to be a member of the same group as the vendor, either within three years of the 'effective date' (see **4.91**) of the property transfer, or later but under arrangements entered into within that three-year period. A 'relevant associated company' is any other member of the group which leaves the group 'in consequence of' the purchaser leaving. This provision prevents an otherwise simple avoidance arrangement, under which the purchaser transfers the property to a wholly-owned subsidiary before both purchaser and subsidiary leave the vendor's group and the purchaser is thus able to claim that it no longer holds any interest in the property. If the interest which the purchaser (or a relevant associated company) still holds is less than the interest originally transferred, a pro rata amount of the relief is withdrawn (*FA 2003, Sch 7, para 3*).

Example 5.5

Xerxes Ltd owns 100% of the shares of Yolande Ltd and Zeb Ltd. On 2 March 2020, Y transfers to Z a freehold interest in a commercial property worth £800,000, and group relief from SDLT is claimed. In September 2020, Z grants a capital lease of part of the property to a third party, in return for a premium of £600,000 and a peppercorn rent. It is agreed that the value of the part thus disposed of is three-quarters of the value of the whole property. On 24 February 2021, X sells 50% of the shares of Z to another third party, in the course of setting up a joint venture. Z therefore leaves the X group while still holding an interest in the property with a value of one quarter of the value of the whole property. The SDLT payable is, therefore, one quarter of the SDLT which would have been payable on the original transfer on 2 March 2020, if group relief had not been claimed. The SDLT on the original transfer would have been calculated as follows:

Purchase Price (£)	**Rate (%)**	**SDLT (£)**
150,000	0	NIL
100,000	2	2,000
550,000	5	27,500
800,000		29,500

Consequently, the amount chargeable under the clawback is one quarter of £29,500 or £7,375.

Note the SDLT is *not* calculated as if there was a transfer of a property with a value of one quarter of the original; in the present case, such a calculation would give a liability of £1,000 – but, sadly, this is not how the clawback operates! However, even if SDLT rates or thresholds have subsequently changed, the clawback is still calculated on the basis of rates and thresholds which applied at the time of the original transfer.

5.31 Group relief is not clawed back where the purchaser leaves the vendor's group (*FA 2003, Sch 7, para 4*):

- as a result of the winding up of the vendor or a company above the vendor in the group;
- in the course of a reconstruction which itself qualifies for relief under *FA 1986, s 75*, as a result of which the purchaser becomes a member of the same group as the 'acquiring company'; or
- in the course of a qualifying demutualisation of an insurance company.

5.32 Group relief is not clawed back if it is the vendor which leaves the group rather than the purchaser. This allows a group to remove property which it wishes to keep from a subsidiary which is to be disposed of. However, if there is subsequently a change of control of the purchaser within three years of the original transfer, the purchaser is at that time treated as leaving the vendor's group, and clawback applies accordingly (*FA 2003, Sch 7, para 4ZA*). See **5.34** for discussion of what amounts to a change of control. There are complex anti-avoidance provisions designed to ensure the 'change of control' rules apply as intended, where successive transfers of the property might otherwise lead to doubt as to their application. Although it is not clear why, the winding up of the purchaser is also treated as a change of control (*FA 2003, Sch 7, paras 4ZA, 4A*).

However, if the purchaser ceases to be a member of the same group as the vendor as a consequence of the vendor being wound up, or a company above the vendor being wound up, so that group relief is not clawed back (see **5.31**), it is understood that HMRC accept that a subsequent change of control of the purchaser will not cause the group relief to be clawed back under *FA 2003, Sch 7, para 4ZA*.

Clawback of reconstruction or acquisition relief

5.33 These reliefs are clawed back if, within three years of the 'effective date' (see **4.91**) of the property transfer, or later under arrangements entered into within that three-year period:

- control of the acquiring company changes; and
- that company or a relevant associated company holds the property or an interest derived from it (*FA 2003, Sch 7, para 9*).

A 'relevant associated company' is a company controlled by the acquiring company immediately before the change in control, control of which changes as a consequence of the change in control of the acquiring company. If only part of the property, or a lesser interest derived from it, is held, an amount of relief is withdrawn pro rata to the relative values of the whole property and the part or interest still held. The calculation is analogous with that for withdrawal of group relief (see Example 5.5).

Change of control

5.34 In many cases, a change of control is easily identified – for example, when a majority shareholder sells all of its shares to a third party. However, a change of control may be very difficult to identify or define in some circumstances and, in the case of a publicly traded company, may be subject to the whim of the market. In the 2003 Finance Bill debates, the government stated that normal market transactions in shares which are publicly traded would not be regarded as giving rise to a change in control (see *Hansard*, Standing Committee B, 10 June 2003, col 425). However, this leaves open the possibility that the transfer of a minority shareholding in a company whose shares are not publicly traded may still give rise to a change of control, since the company would then be controlled by a different group of people.

5.35 There is no clawback of reconstruction or acquisition relief where control of the acquiring company changes for one of the following reasons:

(1) as a result of transactions in connection with divorce etc or distribution of an estate, as set out in (3) and (4) at **5.7** (*FA 2003, Sch 7, para 10(2)* and *(3)*),

(2) as a result of a transfer of shares which itself qualifies for group relief under *FA 1930, s 42 (FA 2003, Sch 7, para 10(4))* or share acquisition relief under *FA 1986, s 77* (*FA 2003, Sch 7, para 10(5)*) (see **11.9** et seq), or

(3) purely as a result of a loan creditor becoming or ceasing to be treated as having control (*FA 2003, Sch 7, para 10(6))*. This may happen, for example, when a loan creditor gains additional rights if the company defaults on payments under the loan.

There are anti-avoidance provisions to ensure that, where (2) above applies to prevent clawback, subsequent transactions leading to the relevant company either leaving the group or suffering a change of control within the original three-year period (or later under arrangements entered into within the period) will lead to clawback (*FA 2003, Sch 7, para 11*).

5.36 In relation to the clawback of all three reliefs, if the company liable to pay the tax fails to pay within six months of the due date, there are provisions (*FA 2003, Sch 7, paras 5, 12*) allowing tax to be recovered from:

- any company which was above the liable company in a group structure at any time between the original transfer and the event leading to clawback,
- a controlling director of the company liable to pay the tax or any other company having control of it, or
- in the case of group relief, the vendor.

Purchasers of companies should be aware of the risk of liability under these provisions and should seek appropriate protection in the form of warranties, indemnities, retentions etc.

OTHER MAJOR RELIEFS

Alternative finance reliefs

5.37 A series of reliefs has been introduced in an attempt to ensure that additional SDLT liabilities do not arise on property transactions where funding is structured in such a way as to avoid payment of interest. The need to avoid interest typically arises from specific beliefs, particularly the acceptance of *Shari'ah* principles; however, availability of the reliefs depends only on the nature of the transaction and participants, and not on subscription to any particular set of beliefs. The reliefs fall into two groups. The first (*FA 2003, ss 71A–73B*) relates to the purchase or ownership of property where, in other circumstances, mortgage finance might be obtained; these are dealt with in more detail below. The second (*FA 2003, Sch 61, paras 6–9*) relates to property-backed investment bonds. Review of the reliefs available to those involved in the issue and management of such bonds is beyond the scope of this book; it is sufficient to note that a portfolio investor in qualifying bonds, although in fact gaining a direct interest in the underlying property, is deemed not to have such an interest for SDLT purposes (*FA 2009, Sch 61, para 2*). This does not apply if the investor, together with connected persons, has the right of management and control of the underlying property (eg by virtue of the proportion of bonds held). Careful fact gathering and analysis may therefore be required where anything more than an obvious minority of bonds is held, and especially where family members or connected companies may hold investments in the same products. This difficulty is acknowledged in the legislation. If connected persons obtain control inadvertently, the favourable tax treatment is not lost, provided the control is not in fact exercised and holdings are reduced to remove that control once the issue has come to light (*FA 2009, Sch 61, paras 3–4*).

5.38 The reliefs relating to purchase or ownership of property envisage two forms of transaction. In the first (*s 71A*), under arrangements with the ultimate or intended owner ('Owner'), a financial institution ('Bank') purchases a freehold or leasehold property, leases it to Owner and grants Owner a right (the 'option') to require Bank to transfer the original freehold or leasehold interest to Owner. The terms of the lease and option typically ensure that Bank receives the same economic return as if it had provided mortgage finance secured on the property. If the relief applies, the lease to Owner and the final transfer to Owner under the option are relieved from SDLT. Partial transfers to Owner under the option during the course of the arrangement (eg as a result of Owner making capital payments) are exempt from SDLT. As a result, the only SDLT payable is on the initial purchase by Bank, which is equivalent to what would happen if Owner purchased the property from a third party with the aid of conventional mortgage finance. However, if Bank buys the property from Owner, that purchase is also relieved from SDLT. In this situation, no SDLT is payable on the overall transaction, reflecting the position where a property owner obtains a loan secured on property already held.

The second form of transaction (*s 73*) envisages purchase of the property by Bank and onward sale to Owner, the onward sale typically being on instalment terms designed to replicate the economics of a repayment mortgage. If the relief applies, the onward sale to Owner is relieved from SDLT. Again, if the purchase by Bank is itself from Owner, that transaction is also eligible for relief.

There were provisions to ensure that the reliefs applied with the same overall effect where the property was located in Scotland (*ss 72, 72A*). However, following the introduction of LBTT with effect from 1 April 2015, these provisions were repealed by *Scotland Act 2012, Sch 3, paras 2* and *10* from that date.

However, relief is denied if, at the time of the transaction, there are arrangements to transfer control of the financial institution. This is an anti-avoidance provision, to counter the possibility of a bank setting up a subsidiary to enter into the transaction, with every intention of then selling the subsidiary to the erstwhile purchaser of the property. Further anti-avoidance provisions (*s 73A*) seek to prevent the combination of these reliefs with group, reconstruction and acquisitions reliefs described above, to obtain an overall tax advantage.

The legislation originally relied on a very wide definition of Financial Institution set out in *FA 2005, s 46*, which included licensed credit brokers. The potential tax savings in some transactions were such that it was worthwhile to set up such a credit broker to take advantage of the relief. To counter this, a narrower definition of Financial Institution was imported from *ITA 2007, s 564B* by *FA 2011, Sch 21, para 3* with effect from 24 March 2011. It also includes, for transactions with an effective date on or after 25 March 2015, any person with permission under the *Financial Services and Markets Act 2000, Pt 4A* to enter into regulated 'home purchase plans' as 'home purchase provider' (*FA 2003, s 73BA(3)*, inserted by *FA 2015, s 68(2)*).

5.39 The interest held by Bank is an exempt interest (*s 73B*). This means any transfer to another financial institution (eg if the bank sells its loan book) will not give rise to an SDLT charge.

Sale and leaseback relief

5.40 If A transfers a property to B (or grants a lease to B) (the Sale), and out of the interest transferred B grants a lease back to A (the Leaseback), relief from SDLT is available on the leaseback provided certain conditions (see **5.41**) are satisfied (*FA 2003, s 57A*). The purpose of the relief is to facilitate transfer of properties from occupiers to investors. Absent the relief, it might be possible for the same effect to be achieved in some cases by A first granting a lease to a group company, with SDLT group relief being claimed on the grant of the lease, then transferring the property, subject to this lease, to B. However, the relief allows a simpler process and resolves doubts as to whether anti-avoidance provisions might otherwise apply.

The relief itself does not reduce the SDLT charge on the original transfer from A to B. However, if the original transfer agreement requires the leaseback to be granted and if this requirement reduces the value of the interest originally transferred, SDLT will be charged on that original transfer, only on the reduced value. HMRC's original agreement with this view is made clear in an article at www.hmrc.gov.uk/so/exchanges.htm, referred to in Stamp Taxes Bulletin 2/2011, see www.hmrc.gov.uk/so/bulletin-22011.htm. Their continued agreement is confirmed at SDLTM04020a Example 3.

Example 5.6

Matthew owns freehold premises comprising a shop with apartment over, valued at £500,000. He sells the premises to Cassandra for £200,000 cash. The sale agreement requires Cassandra to grant a 100-year lease of the apartment back to Matthew at a peppercorn rent. No SDLT will arise on the 100-year lease as sale and leaseback relief should be available. Assuming the transaction is at arm's length, it is reasonable to regard £200,000 as representing the current value of the premises subject to the requirement to lease the apartment back, so Cassandra should have to pay SDLT on that amount.

5.41 The relief should still be available even if, for some reason, no SDLT is payable on the original transfer, but A and B must not be members of the same group and the transfer to B must not be a sub sale or a 'pre-completion transaction' within the meaning of *FA 2003, Sch 2A* (transactions entered into before completion of contract) (*FA 2003, s 57A(3)(c)* and *(d)*) (see **5.8** et seq as to the meaning of sub sale and 'pre-completion transaction'). The transactions must be entered into in consideration of each other, so it would be wise to have this overtly stated in the documents (*FA 2003, s 57A(3)(a)*). The only other consideration permitted for the original transfer is the payment of money or the assumption, satisfaction or release of a debt (or both) (*FA 2003, s 57A(3)(b)*). Thus, the relief is not available if, for example, in consideration of the first transfer, B also agrees to provide A with services in addition to granting the leaseback to A out of the original property. However, subject to the possible application of the general anti-avoidance rules (see **9.3** et seq), it may be possible to agree the provision of services under a separate contract for cash consideration payable by A but left outstanding as a debt. The transfer from A to B could possibly then be partly in satisfaction of the debt, which is within the terms of the relief.

It appears to be HMRC's view that if A transfers a property to B in return for B agreeing to redevelop it and then grant a leaseback of part of the developed property, this does not come within the terms of the relief. It is understood that they consider that the agreement to redevelop the property (or procure its redevelopment) is non-financial consideration for the original sale. B would be able to take account of the obligation to grant a lease to A in valuing the original transfer, but A would not be entitled to sale and leaseback relief and would pay SDLT on the full market value of the leaseback from B.

Social housing, right to buy and shared ownership

5.42 This group of reliefs applies to a limited range of acquisitions by providers of social housing and qualifying leases/sales to their tenants.

The *Housing and Regeneration Act 2008* refers to registered providers of social housing and for SDLT purposes a 'relevant housing provider' (RHP) is defined as either a non-profit registered provider of social housing or a registered social landlord (*FA 2003, s 71(1A)*). An acquisition by an RHP qualifies for complete relief from SDLT if:

(1) the majority of its trustees/board members/management committee members are tenants (*FA 2003, s 71(1)(a)* and *(2)*), or

(2) the vendor is an RHP, a housing action trust or a qualifying local or central government body (see list at SDLTM27500) (*FA 2003, s 71(1)(b)*), or

(3) the transaction is partly or wholly funded with a grant or other financial assistance from the National Lottery or pursuant to one of the *Housing Acts* (*FA 2003, s 71(1)(c)* and *(4)*).

Profit-making registered providers of social housing are also able to benefit from the relief, but only if condition (3) above is satisfied (*FA 2003, s 71(1A)*).

5.43 Certain tenants are entitled to buy their homes from their public sector landlord (or from a successor body under a preserved right) at a discount to market value. The sale conditions normally include a contingent liability to repay the discount if the purchaser re-sells within a certain period. Under normal SDLT rules, this contingent further consideration should be charged to SDLT (see **4.20**). *FA 2003, Sch 9, para 1* provides that the contingent consideration does not count as consideration for SDLT purposes. This is expressed as a computational provision rather than a relief, but it is the view of HMRC that a claim to relief is required on an SDLT return, entering code 22 in Section 9 of the form. The return should be completed showing the actual consideration paid and not including the contingent amount. *FA 2003, Sch 9, para 1(3)* contains a comprehensive list of relevant 'public sector bodies', which are mainly central and local government entities and social housing bodies.

5.44 *FA 2003, Sch 9, paras 2–12* provide a treatment which may provide partial relief from SDLT for the tenant who buys an interest in his or her home under 'shared ownership' arrangements. The normal 'shared ownership' arrangement is for the tenant to enter into a lease, paying a premium (representing part ownership of the property) and rent (for the part not purchased). The treatment is available where the tenant has a right to purchase further shares by making capital payments leading to a reduction in rent ('staircasing') and/or, where the freehold reversion is available, has the right eventually to purchase it. Where staircasing is allowed, the lease must state the minimum rent which can be payable as a result of maximum staircasing without acquiring the freehold. The rules relating to this relief are complex. The following paragraphs provide a summary, but it will be important to check the terms of the lease and the status of the parties in detail against the legislation to be sure that the relief is available.

In the absence of any special treatment, SDLT would be potentially chargeable on both the premium and the rent, and further SDLT could be chargeable on later 'staircasing' transactions. This could lead to an element of double charge, since the capital payment on the staircasing transaction would relate to the same interest in the property as the initial SDLT payment on the rent. To avoid such problems, the tenant may elect to have SDLT charged on the full value of the property at the time of the initial transaction. 'Full value' here means market value, or the discounted value where the tenant is entitled to buy at a discount. Equivalent treatment is available for 'shared ownership trust' arrangements often used in relation to blocks of apartments where individual ownership of the freehold reversion is not possible.

5.45 If this election is made, SDLT is not chargeable on the rent, nor is it chargeable on subsequent staircasing transactions and/or the eventual purchase of the freehold. Even if no election is made, staircasing transactions are not subject to SDLT, provided the total share of the property owned by the tenant does not exceed 80%. Any subsequent staircasing purchases which take the proportion owned above 80% and any purchase of the freehold reversion remain subject to SDLT. Whether the election is made or not, the normal 'linked transactions' rules are modified so that the consideration for later transactions is not aggregated with that for the original grant in determining the rate of tax on the original grant. This means the later transactions do not lead to the need to reconsider the tax charged on the original grant. However, if no election is made, the consideration for all transactions (including the grant of the original lease) is aggregated in order to determine the rate of SDLT payable on staircasing transactions which leave the tenant with more than 80% of the property and on acquisition of the freehold reversion.

Election to apply the 'full value' treatment must be made in the SDLT return, or by amendment of the return within 12 months of the due date of the return. Guidance on completion of the standard SDLT1 return form in these circumstances is at SDLTM27080. HMRC instruct that the election is made by showing the market value of the property as the consideration in Box 22, although it seems likely that this should say the 'full value' as defined above, since this is the amount by reference to which the SDLT liability will be calculated. If there is thought to be any uncertainty, the election could also be notified by letter to Birmingham Stamp Office (see **Appendix A**), quoting the UTRN of the return. Careful review of the circumstances is required because the election, once made, is irrevocable.

Example 5.7

On 11 March 2020 Stanley and Oliver enter into identical 100-year shared ownership leases with the Holly Wood Housing Trust. Neither Stanley nor Oliver owns any other properties and therefore the higher rates of SDLT would not apply to the transactions. They each pay an initial premium of £100,000 (which is considered to give them each a 50% share in their property) and rent of £5,000 per annum which is subject to yearly adjustment in line with the Consumer Price Index. They have the option to increase their ownership at the end of each year in multiples of 10% of the total value of the property. The minimum annual rent, which would apply if the tenant held 90% of the property, would be £500. Any acquisition which would take ownership above 90% necessarily includes acquisition of the freehold. Stanley elects to apply the 'full value' SDLT treatment; Oliver does not. After four years, they each opt to acquire a further 30% interest, paying £36,000 (based on the then market value) and reducing rent accordingly. At the end of the sixth year, they each buy a further 10% for £13,000. Finally, at the end of year eight, they each buy the remaining 10% including the freehold reversion, for £14,000. Neither qualifies for any special treatment. Their SDLT positions are as follows:

	Stanley	**Oliver**
Initial purchase	Full value is £200,000, SDLT payable at 0% and 2% = £1,500. The NPV of the minimum rent is £13,827, which is below the £125,000 threshold, so no SDLT is payable on it.	Lease premium £100,000 and NPV of rent £138,276, so no SDLT on premium and £132 on rent. The indexing of the rent is ignored for SDLT purposes, so this is treated as a flat £5,000 per annum rent.
30% addition, taking total ownership to 80%	No liability; no SDLT return required.	No liability; no SDLT return required.
10% addition	No liability; no SDLT return required.	Aggregate of capital sums paid to date (£100,000 + £36,000 + £13,000) = £149,000, so the 0% and 2% rates apply. SDLT payable on £24,000 at 2% = £480. SDLT return required.
Final 10% purchase including freehold	No liability, but SDLT return must be submitted (see SDLTM27080).	Aggregate of capital sums paid to date (£149,000 + £14,000) = £163,000, so 2% rate still applies. SDLT payable on £14,000 at 2% = £280. SDLT return required.

Overall, Stanley pays SDLT of £1,500, Oliver pays £892 but has to complete an extra SDLT return. Economically, it would not appear to be worthwhile to make an election. However, this depends on the precise facts. In particular, Oliver faces the risk of substantial increases in value or changes in SDLT rules, leading to a higher SDLT cost. Note that, if the final purchase had pushed the aggregate consideration over £250,000, the 2% and 5% SDLT rates would have applied to the last purchase as it is fully linked to the penultimate purchase (see **4.99**).

5.46 The final relief in this section is in *FA 2003, Sch 9, paras 13–14* (introduced by *FA 2009, s 82*) and concerns 'rent to mortgage' and 'rent to loan' transactions. These are transactions where individuals initially rent a property under an assured shorthold tenancy, perhaps while saving for a deposit, and subsequently purchase an interest under a shared ownership lease or trust. The relief provides that the shorthold tenancy and the shared ownership lease/trust arrangement are not linked with each other, and that the effective date (see **4.91**) of the shared ownership transaction is determined without regard to the shorthold tenancy. This ensures that no SDLT disadvantage arises from the fact that the tenant initially occupies under a pure rental lease.

Relief for first-time buyers

5.47 A relief is available, from 22 November 2017, where a 'first-time buyer' (see **5.51**) purchases their first home and the 'chargeable consideration' (see **4.19**) is not more than £500,000. If the relief is available, the rate of SDLT on the first £300,000 of consideration is 0% and on any balance of the consideration up to £500,000 the rate of SDLT is 5%. If the consideration for the transaction (or a series of 'linked transactions' (see **4.99**)) exceeds £500,000 no relief is available, and the normal rates of SDLT apply (see **4.37** et seq). The legislation dealing with the relief can be found in *FA 2003, s 57B* and *Sch 6ZA* (introduced by *FA 2018, s 41*). The relief must be claimed in a land transaction return or in an amendment to a land transaction return (see **5.54**).

Example 5.8

Rory, who has previously lived in his parent's house, agrees to acquire the freehold interest in a house in Manchester for a consideration of £480,000. As this is the first house which Rory has ever purchased he is able to claim the first-time buyer's relief and the SDLT payable is calculated as follows:

Chargeable Consideration	*Rate*	*SDLT*
	%	£
On the first £300,000 of the purchase price	0	Nil
On the remaining £180,000	5	9,000
Total SDLT payable		9,000

If the relief for first-time buyers had not been available the SDLT payable would have amounted to £14,000 and therefore, in this example, claiming the relief reduces the SDLT liability by £5,000.

If the purchase price of the house had been, say, £505,000, the relief for first-time buyers would not have been available (as the consideration exceeds £500,000) and the SDLT payable would have been calculated as follows:

Chargeable Consideration	*Rate*	*SDLT*
	%	£
First £125,000	0	Nil
Next £125,000	2	2,500
Balance of £255,000	5	12,750
Total SDLT payable		15,250

5.48 As with all SDLT reliefs a number of conditions must be satisfied if the relief for first-time buyers is to be available. In outline the relief will be available in the following circumstances:

(a) an interest in a single dwelling is being acquired;

(b) the consideration given for the acquisition is not more than £500,000;

(c) the purchaser is an individual or, if there is more than one purchaser, each of the purchasers is an individual;

(d) the purchaser is a first-time buyer intending to occupy the dwelling as their only or main residence or, if there is more than one purchaser, each of the purchasers is a first-time buyer and intends to occupy the dwelling as their only or main residence;

(e) the 'effective date' (see **4.91**) of the transaction is on or after 22 November 2017; and

(f) the purchase of the single dwelling is not 'linked' (see **4.89**) with any other 'land transaction' (see **4.7**) other than a transaction (or transactions) to acquire garden or grounds which form part of the purchased dwelling or for the acquisition of an interest in or rights over land which subsists for the benefit of the dwelling being acquired or its garden or grounds.

These conditions are considered in more detail below.

5.49

(1) Purchase of a single dwelling (*FA 2003, Sch 6ZA, para 1(2)*)

The relief is only available if a single dwelling is being acquired and it is not available if more than one dwelling is being acquired in a single transaction. It will be a question of fact as to whether or not more than one dwelling is being acquired. HMRC's view is that 'A self-contained part of a building will be a separate dwelling if the residents of that part can live independently of the residents of the rest of the building, including independent access and domestic facilities.' (HMRC Guidance Note 'Stamp Duty Land Tax: Relief for first time buyers' (22 November 2017)).

The 'chargeable interest' (see **4.14**) acquired must be a 'major interest' (see **4.11**) in a single dwelling. For these purposes 'major interest' will cover the acquisition of either a freehold or leasehold interest. However, a lease which has less than 21 years to run at the start of the day after the 'effective date' (see **4.91**) of the transaction is specifically excluded from the definition of a 'major interest' (*FA 2003, Sch 6ZA, para 8*). This means that the relief for first-time buyers will not apply to the assignment of an existing lease with 21 years or less to run or the grant of a new lease for 21 years or less.

What counts as a dwelling for the purposes of the relief is set out in *FA 2003, Sch 6ZA, para 9*. A dwelling means a building which is used or suitable for use as a single dwelling, or is in the process of being constructed or adapted for use as a single dwelling (*FA 2003, Sch 6ZA, para 9(2)*). It also includes associated gardens, grounds, outbuildings and other rights which subsist for the benefit of the dwelling, for example access rights across adjacent property (*FA 2003, Sch 6ZA, para 9(3)* and *(4)*).

An off-plan purchase will count as a single dwelling for the purposes of the relief provided:

(a) contracts have been exchanged for the purchase of a building, or part of a building, which is to be constructed or adapted for use as a single dwelling;

(b) the contract is 'substantially performed' (see **4.91**); and

(c) at the time the contract is 'substantially performed' (see **4.91**) the construction or adaption of the building has not yet begun.

Holiday homes and furnished holiday lettings which are suitable for use as dwellings will come within the meaning of dwelling for the purposes of the relief.

Certain types of properties which are included within the definition of 'residential property' for SDLT purposes (see **4.38**) are not within the definition of 'dwelling' for the purposes of the relief for first-time buyers. The types of properties excluded are those used to provide residential accommodation for school pupils, purpose-built student accommodation, purpose-built accommodation for members of the armed forces and an institution that is the sole or main residence of at least 90% of its residents and does not fall within any of the purposes within *FA 2003, s 116(3)*: see **4.38** (*FA 2003, Sch 6ZA, paras (7)* and *(8)*).

5.50

(2) The 'relevant consideration' for the transaction must not be more than £500,000 (*FA 2003, Sch 6ZA, para 1(3)*)

The term 'relevant consideration' is defined in *FA 2003, Sch 6ZA, para 7*. If the transaction is not one of a number of 'linked transactions' (see **4.89** et seq) the 'relevant consideration' is simply the 'chargeable consideration' (see **4.19**) given for the single dwelling (*FA 2003, Sch 6ZA, para 7(a)*). Alternatively, if the transaction is one of a number of linked transactions (see **4.89**) the 'relevant consideration' is the aggregate 'chargeable consideration' (see **4.19**) given for all of those linked transactions. However, if the transaction is 'linked' to one or more other transactions, the relief for first-time buyers will only be available if the other 'linked' transactions relate solely to the acquisition of garden, grounds or outbuildings and other rights which subsist for the benefit of the dwelling being acquired (see **5.52**) (*FA 2003, Sch 6ZA, para 1(5)* and *(6)*).

If the aggregate consideration for all of the 'linked transactions' (see **4.89**) exceeds £500,000 none of the transactions will qualify for the relief for first-time buyers.

5.51

(3) The purchaser or, if there is more than one purchaser, each of the purchasers, must be first-time buyers intending to occupy the dwelling as their only or main residence (*FA 2003, Sch 6ZA, para 1(4)*)

The relief is only available if the purchaser, or if there is more than one purchaser, each of the purchasers, is an individual. If any of the purchasers is a company or other non-natural person, the relief is not available.

Each of the purchasers must be a 'first-time buyer' and the meaning of the term 'first-time buyer' can be found at *FA 2003, Sch 6ZA, para 6*. To be a 'first-time buyer' an individual must not have previously been a purchaser, either alone or along with others, of a 'major interest' (see **5.49**) in a dwelling located anywhere in the world. This would include any previous acquisition of an interest in a dwelling as a result of an inheritance, or by a financial institution on behalf of a person under an alternative finance scheme (see **5.37** et seq).

The previous acquisition of a lease, either by grant or assignment, is ignored for the purposes of this restriction provided the lease had less than 21 years to run at the start of the day after the date on which it was acquired (*FA 2003, Sch 6ZA, para 6(2)*).

If the purchaser has previously acquired a dwelling as a trustee of a trust that acquisition will not cause the relief to be denied unless the purchaser was also a beneficiary of the trust (HMRC Guidance Note – 22 November 2017 – Stamp Duty Land Tax: Relief for first-time buyers).

A previous acquisition by the purchaser of 'non-residential property' (see **4.38**) or 'mixed-use property' (see **4.38**) will not cause the relief to be denied, provided the property did not include a dwelling. A mixed-use property is one which includes both residential and non-residential property.

All of the purchasers must intend to occupy the dwelling as their only or main residence. There is no definition of only or main residence in the legislation. The HMRC Guidance Note 'Stamp Duty Land Tax: Relief for first time buyers' (22 November 2017) states that:

> 'In cases where an individual resides at only one dwelling, that will be their only or main residence. There may be cases where an individual first-time buyer intends to continue to reside at another dwelling following the purchase of a dwelling, for example the individual maintains a home that they rent from someone else and intends to continue to do so indefinitely. In such cases, all of the facts and circumstances of the case should be considered to determine whether the individual intends the purchased dwelling to be their main residence.'

The purchaser does not need to occupy the dwelling immediately after its acquisition. However, at the 'effective date' (see **4.91**) of the transaction the purchaser must have a clear intention to occupy the dwelling as their only or main residence even if circumstances are such that it is not possible or practical to take occupation immediately (eg the dwelling may require refurbishment).

5.52

(4) Linked transactions (*FA 2003, Sch 6ZA, paras 1(5),1(6), 2* and *5*)

If the purchase of the dwelling is 'linked' (see **4.89**) to another transaction, the relief is not available unless the linked transaction relates solely to the acquisition of garden or grounds which form part of the acquired dwelling or for the acquisition of an interest in or rights over land which subsists for the benefit of the dwelling being acquired or its garden or grounds.

Where the acquisition of an interest in a single dwelling is eligible for the relief for first-time buyers (the 'main transaction'), that relief is also available in relation to one or more 'linked transactions' (see **4.89**) for the acquisition of garden or grounds which form part of the acquired dwelling or for the acquisition of an interest in or rights over land which subsists for the benefit of the dwelling being acquired or its garden or grounds, but only if each of the purchasers under the 'linked transaction' are also purchasers in relation to the main transaction (*FA 2003, Sch 6ZA, para 2*).

A subsequent 'linked transaction' (see **4.89**) may mean that a transaction (or transactions) which originally qualified for the relief no longer qualify and, in these circumstances, the relief is withdrawn (*FA 2003, Sch 6ZA, para 5*). This could happen in the following circumstances:

(a) there is a subsequent 'linked transaction' (see **4.89**) which involves the acquisition of a 'chargeable interest' which is not garden or grounds which form part of the acquired dwelling or an interest in or rights over land which subsists for the benefit of the dwelling being acquired or its garden or grounds; or

(b) there is a subsequent 'linked transaction' the consideration for which, when added to the consideration for all of the other linked transactions, means that the 'relevant consideration' (see **5.50**) exceeds £500,000.

If the 'linked transactions' all occur on the same day then the relief for first-time buyers should be claimed if all of the conditions are satisfied.

If a subsequent 'linked transaction' occurs before the land transaction return for the original transaction is filed with HMRC then account should be taken of all of the transactions which have taken place, including that linked transaction, in determining whether or not the relief is available.

Finally, where a subsequent 'linked transaction' occurs after the land transaction return for the original transaction has been submitted to HMRC, and that 'linked transaction' causes the relief for first-time buyers to be withdrawn, a further return (see **8.15** et seq) must be submitted to HMRC in relation to the original transaction. The further return will recalculate the SDLT payable in relation to the earlier transaction on the basis that the relief is withdrawn.

A subsequent 'linked transaction' may not cause the relief for first-time buyers to be withdrawn but may result in additional SDLT becoming payable on the original transaction, as the SDLT payable on the aggregate consideration for all 'linked transactions' is apportioned between the transactions based on the 'chargeable consideration' for each transaction (see Example 5.9). In these circumstances a further return would need to be filed in relation to the original transaction with the amended SDLT liability being calculated based on the increase in the 'relevant consideration' (see **5.50**).

In either case the further return must be submitted to HMRC within 30 days of the 'effective date' (see **4.91**) of the later transaction and the additional SDLT must be paid within that same 30-day period (see **8.15** et seq). The time limit to notify and pay the tax remains at 30 days even if the 'effective date' (see **4.91**) of the transaction is on or after 1 March 2019 in accordance with *FA 2003, s 81A(1A)* as introduced by *FA 2019, s 46(5)*, on the basis that the original transaction will have been notified and the first-time buyers relief claimed.

Example 5.9

The facts are as in Example 5.8 however as part of the original contract Rory had agreed to pay the vendor an additional £10,000 for the freehold interest in grounds forming part of the dwelling being acquired. The acquisition of the grounds does not complete until after the land transaction return in relation to the acquisition of the dwelling has been submitted to HMRC. The original acquisition of the dwelling and the subsequent acquisition of the grounds will be 'linked transactions' (see **4.89**) and the SDLT liability, claiming relief for first-time buyers, is calculated as follows:

Chargeable Consideration	*Rate*	*SDLT*
	%	£
On the first £300,000 of the purchase price	0	Nil
On the remaining £190,000	5	9,500
Total SDLT payable		9,500

The SDLT payable in relation to the acquisition of the grounds is therefore £194 (£10,000/£490,000 × £9,500).

Rory must also file an amended land transaction return in relation to the original purchase of the dwelling with the SDLT liability calculated at £9,306 (£480,000/£490,000 × £9,500) and pay the additional SDLT due of £306.

5.53 The relief applies to acquisitions of single dwellings with an 'effective date' (see **4.91**) on or after 22 November 2017. It makes no difference whether or not a contract was entered into before, on or after 22 November 2017. As long as the 'effective date' of the transaction is on or after 22 November 2017 then the relief will be available provided the conditions detailed above are satisfied. However, in determining whether or not the relief will be available for the acquisition of a single dwelling, with an 'effective date' on or after 22 November 2017, account will have to be taken of any transactions which are 'linked' to that acquisition and which had an 'effective date' before 22 November 2017.

5.54 The relief for first-time buyers must be claimed in a land transaction return or an amendment to that return (*FA 2003, Sch 6ZA, para 1(1)*). The claim is made by entering code 32 at question 1.9 in the land transaction return. If the land transaction return is submitted online (see **8.9**) the software will calculate the SDLT payable using the rates applicable to relief for first-time buyers (see **5.47**). The exception is where the transaction is the grant of a new lease in which circumstances the lease calculator on the HMRC website (www.tax.service.gov.uk/calculate-stamp-duty-land-tax) should be used to work out the SDLT payable and the amount of the tax should then be entered at Question 1.14 of the land transaction return.

5.55

Interaction with other SDLT rules

The relief for first-time buyers cannot be claimed if the 'chargeable transaction' (see **4.14**) under which the single dwelling is acquired is a 'higher rates transaction' (see **4.56** et seq) (*FA 2003, Sch 6ZA, para 1(7)*). This could occur, for example, where an individual acquires their first home in their own name but, immediately following that acquisition, the individual's spouse owns a property which the couple previously used as their main residence but is now to be let out (see **4.61**).

As originally enacted the relief for first-time buyers was only available in relation to the grant of a shared ownership lease (see **5.44** et seq) where the tenant had elected to have SDLT charged on the market value of the single dwelling at the time of the initial transaction (*FA 2018, s 41(5)*). If the market value treatment did not apply the relief for first-time buyers could not be claimed in relation to any of the transactions involved in the shared ownership scheme. However, *FA 2019, ss 42* and *43* extended the first-time buyer's relief to purchasers of shared ownership properties who do not elect to pay SDLT on the market value of the whole of the property when they purchase their first share. The extension of the relief applies retrospectively from 22 November 2017, meaning that a repayment can be claimed by those who have paid SDLT on the acquisition of a shared ownership lease on or after 22 November 2017 but who now qualify for the first-time buyer's relief. The time limit for making such a repayment claim, for those who completed their transaction before 29 October 2018, was extended to 28 October 2019 (*FA 2019, s 43*). The relief will be applied to the first share purchased, where the market value of the shared ownership property is £500,000 or less. First-time buyers will pay no SDLT where they pay £300,000 or less for the first share. Those paying between £300,000 and £500,000 for their first share will pay SDLT at 5% on the amount in excess of £300,000. The relief will also apply to any SDLT due on rental payments but will not apply to the purchase of any further shares in the property. First-time buyers purchasing a shared ownership property whose market value is more than £500,000 will not be entitled to any relief and will pay SDLT at the normal rates (see **4.37**).

If a single dwelling is acquired under an 'alternative finance arrangement' (see **5.37** et seq) entered into between an individual and a financial institution a claim can be made for relief for first-time buyers. In such circumstances the individual who is entitled to occupy the property is treated as the purchaser in relation to the transaction for the purposes of *FA 2003, Sch 6ZA, para 1(4)* (requirement that each of the purchasers intends to occupy the dwelling as their only or main residence) and *FA 2003, Sch 6ZA, para 2(2)* (relief may only be claimed for any 'chargeable transaction' (see **4.14**) that is linked to a transaction which is eligible for the relief (the 'main transaction') if each of the purchasers under the linked transaction is also a purchaser in relation to the 'main transaction' (*FA 2003, Sch 6ZA, para 3*)).

SPECIALIST AND MINOR RELIEFS

House trader relief

5.56 Full relief from SDLT is available for certain acquisitions of residential property from individuals who are buying another property. The acquisition may be made by a house building company from which the individual is buying a new dwelling, or by a property trader whose business includes buying such properties from individuals. Relief is also available for an acquisition by such a company, whether or not the replacement home is new, if arrangements to sell the old home have broken down or if the individual is moving due to relocation of employment. In the latter case, it is also possible for the employer to acquire the old home free of SDLT. Finally, relief is also available where the property is acquired by an appropriate trader from personal representatives of a deceased person.

The aims of the relief are to improve liquidity in the housing market and to assist with mobility of labour. Conditions apply to ensure the property really was used as the individual's residence, and to guard against exploitation by property developers who may buy property with the intention of refurbishing or redeveloping for onward sale (*FA 2003, s 58A, Sch 6A*).

Transfers involving multiple dwellings

5.57 A further relief introduced by *FA 2011* with effect from 19 July 2011 aims to encourage investment in residential property for letting (*FA 2003, Sch 6B*). The relief may be claimed if the main subject matter of a transaction, or of a number of linked transactions, comprises interests in more than one dwelling. Subject to satisfaction of detailed conditions, the relief may reduce the amount of SDLT chargeable on consideration other than rent.

The 3% additional rate of SDLT on the acquisition of additional dwellings and dwellings purchased by companies will apply to a claim for multiple dwellings relief if the relevant conditions are satisfied (see **4.56** et seq). If, as part of a single transaction, six or more dwellings are acquired, the SDLT rates for non-residential or mixed use transactions will apply (see **4.38**). In such circumstances the purchaser can therefore choose whether to apply the non-residential rates by not making a claim for multiple dwellings relief.

Where a claim for multiple dwellings relief is made the first stage in calculating the SDLT chargeable is to divide the aggregate consideration attributable to interests in dwellings by the number of dwellings to give an average consideration per dwelling. The SDLT chargeable on the acquisition of a residential property for the amount of the average consideration per dwelling is then calculated, and the amount so determined is then multiplied by the number of dwellings actually acquired, to give the amount of the SDLT chargeable in relation to dwellings (*FA 2003, Sch 6B, para 5(1))*. The actual values of the individual properties do not matter – only the average is important. However, the relief cannot reduce the amount of the SDLT chargeable below 1% of the consideration attributable to dwellings (*FA 2003, Sch 6B, para 5(2))*. Following the introduction of the 3% additional rate of SDLT on the acquisition of additional dwellings and dwellings purchased by companies (see **4.56**) the circumstances in which this *de minimis* rate of SDLT might apply are significantly reduced. The relief must be claimed in an SDLT return or an amended return (*FA 2003, Sch 6B, para 4(1))*. The relief is not available if relief could be claimed under *FA 2003, Sch 7* (group and reconstruction reliefs) or *FA 2003, Sch 8* (charities relief), or if any of those reliefs has been claimed and withdrawn (*FA 2003, Sch 6B, para 2(4)(b))*. The relief does not apply to the acquisition of a dwelling to which the 15% SDLT rate applies as described in **4.87** (*FA 2003, Sch 6B, para 2(4)(aa))*. In addition the relief is not available for transactions within *FA 2003, s 74*, which deals with collective purchases of freehold by leaseholders (*FA 2003, Sch 6B, para 2(4)(a)*). Finally the relief is denied if the transaction is linked with another with an 'effective date' (see **4.63**) before 19 July 2011(*FA 2011, Sch 22, para 9*).

Example 5.10A

On 14 August 2020 Property Holdings plc (P) purchases the freeholds of five new houses from Housebuilder plc (H) for total consideration of £1.1 million. SDLT would be chargeable at the 3% additional rate (see **4.56 et seq**) and, in the absence of a claim for multiple dwellings relief, the amount payable would be £86,750 calculated as follows:

Purchase price	Rate	SDLT chargeable
£	%	£
125,000	3	3,750
125,000	5	6,250
675,000	8	54,000
175,000	13	22,750
1,100,000		86,750

If multiple dwellings relief is claimed, the amount of the SDLT chargeable is calculated as follows:

The average consideration per dwelling is £1,100,000 divided by 5 giving an amount of £220,000 and the SDLT chargeable on a purchase of a residential property for a consideration of £220,000 is as follows:

Purchase price	Rate	SDLT chargeable
£	%	£
125,000	3	3,750
95,000	5	4,750
220,000		8,500

The SDLT chargeable in relation to the consideration for dwellings is therefore initially calculated as £42,500, being £8,500 multiplied by the number of dwellings of five.

The SDLT chargeable in relation to the consideration for dwellings can never be less than 1% of the consideration attributable to dwellings, which in this case is £11,000 (1% of £1,100,000).

Consequently, the SDLT chargeable in relation to the consideration payable for the dwellings is £42,500, on the basis that a claim for multiple dwellings relief is made.

If there is a change of circumstances within three years of the effective date of the transaction (or before an onward disposal to an unrelated party if sooner), and if the new circumstances would have led to a higher tax charge at the time of the original transaction, in relation to the five dwellings qualifying for multiple dwellings relief, a further SDLT return must be made and the additional tax paid within 30 days of the change of circumstances (*FA 2003, Sch 6B, para 6:* see Example 5.11).

The relief may also apply if the transaction includes property which does not count as a dwelling. Consideration must then be apportioned on a just and reasonable basis between the dwellings and the other property. The relief is applied to the consideration apportioned to the dwellings. SDLT is charged on the consideration apportioned to the other property as the appropriate fraction of the amount of SDLT which would have been chargeable had no claim been made for multiple dwellings relief.

Example 5.10B

As part of the same transaction (ie under a single contract), P also purchases three shop units from H. The total consideration is £1.55 million, of which £1.1 million is justly apportioned to the houses and £450,000 to the shops. In the absence of a claim for multiple dwellings relief SDLT on the house purchases is not charged at the higher rates as the transaction is the acquisition of non-residential property (ie both residential and non-residential property is being acquired as part of the same transaction) and therefore the SDLT rates for non-residential or mixed use property are used to calculate the SDLT charge (see **4.56** et seq).

As detailed above, on the basis that the transaction does not comprise entirely of residential property, as it includes the acquisition of the shops, the transaction is taxed as the acquisition of non-residential property (*FA 2003, s 55(2)(b)*). The SDLT payable on the total consideration of £1.55 million is calculated as follows:

Purchase Price (£)	**Rate (%)**	**SDLT (£)**
150,000	0	Nil
100,000	2	2,000
1,300,000	5	65,000
1,550,000		67,000

The SDLT chargeable, in the absence of a claim for multiple dwellings relief, would therefore be £67,000.

The SDLT chargeable on the shops is then calculated as follows:

£450,000/£1,550,000 × £67,000 = £19,452

The SDLT chargeable on the five houses is then calculated as follows:

£1,100,000/£1,550,000 × £67,000 = £47,548.

However, if a claim for multiple dwellings relief is made in relation to the acquisition of the five houses the SDLT payable on acquisition of those houses can be reduced to £42,500 (see Example 5.10A). It should be noted that the higher rates of SDLT will apply where a claim for multiple dwellings relief is made as the purchaser is a company and the liability is calculated on the basis of an acquisition of wholly residential property (*FA 2003, Sch 6B, para(1)*).

The total SDLT on the transaction is therefore £42,500 plus £19,452, or £61,952.

For the purposes of multiple dwellings relief 'dwelling' means a building or part of a building used or suitable for use as a dwelling or in the process of being constructed or adapted for such use, together with any garden or other grounds to be enjoyed with it (see SDLTM29955). Land that subsists, or is to subsist, for the benefit of the dwelling is to be taken to be part of the dwelling for the purposes of the relief. At SDLTM29955 HMRC state: 'This applies to an interest in land which is not contiguous [ie does not share a common border] with the dwelling and its garden or grounds: for example, a separate lease of a garage in a block.' It may also include property which is to be constructed or adapted as a dwelling but where work has not yet commenced – but only if the SDLT arises on 'substantial performance' of a contract (see **4.9**). However, if the dwelling acquired is subject to a lease the term of which was 21 years or more when originally granted, a superior interest to that lease does not count as a dwelling (*FA 2003, Sch 6B, para 2(6)*). This restriction on the availability of the relief does not apply, for transactions with an effective date on or after 26 March 2015, if all of the following conditions are satisfied (*FA 2003, Sch 6B, para 2(7)*, inserted by *FA 2015, s 69(1)*):

(a) the vendor is a 'qualifying body' (which term includes housing authority, housing association – see *FA 2003, Sch 9, para* 5);

(b) the transaction is a sale under a sale and leaseback arrangement within the meaning of *FA 2003, s 57A(2)*;

(c) the sale transaction is the grant of a new lease; and

(d) the leaseback is exempt under *FA 2003, s 57A* (see **5.40** et seq).

FA *2003, s 116(7)* (six or more residential properties to be treated as non-residential) is specifically stated not to apply to properties in respect of which multiple dwellings relief is claimed (*FA 2003, Sch 6B, para 7(7)*). However in a mixed transaction it will still apply in calculating the SDLT chargeable on those properties in respect of which multiple dwellings relief is not due.

Example 5.10C

On 30 November 2020, P Ltd, a property investment company, agrees to purchase six houses from H as part of a single transaction, in circumstances where H has leased three of them to tenants under 99-year leases. In the absence of a claim for multiple dwellings relief, as six dwellings are being acquired under a single transaction *FA 2003, s 116(7)* would apply and the transaction would be treated as the acquisition of non-residential property. However, P Ltd should consider whether a claim for multiple dwellings relief would be advantageous. The consideration justly attributable to the three unoccupied houses is £1 million, with £100,000 attributable to the three leased houses. Multiple dwellings relief only applies to the three unoccupied houses (as the other properties are subject to leases which were originally granted for a term of 21 years or more – *FA 2003, Sch 6B, para 2(6)*), and the amount of the SDLT chargeable is calculated as follows:

The average consideration per dwelling is £1,000,000 divided by three giving an amount of £333,333, and the SDLT chargeable on a purchase of a residential property for a consideration of £333,333 is as follows:

Purchase Price	Rate	SDLT Chargeable
£	%	£
125,000	3	3,750
125,000	5	6,250
83,333	8	6,667
333,333		16,667

The SDLT chargeable in relation to the consideration for dwellings is therefore initially calculated as £50,001, being £16,667 multiplied by the number of dwellings of three.

As 1% of the consideration attributable to dwellings would be £10,000 (£1,000,000 × 1%) the SDLT chargeable in relation to dwellings is £50,001, as that amount is greater than £10,000.

The SDLT chargeable in relation to those houses which do not qualify for relief is then calculated as follows.

As indicated above, as the transaction comprises the acquisition of six residential properties as part of a single transaction the houses are treated as being non-residential property (*FA 2003, s 116(7)*). The SDLT payable on consideration of £1,100,000 in a non-residential property transaction is as follows:

Purchase Price (£)	**Rate (%)**	**SDLT (£)**
150,000	0	Nil
100,000	2	2,000
850,000	5	42,500
1,100,000		44,500

The SDLT chargeable in the absence of a claim for multiple dwellings relief would therefore have been £44,500. As this is less than the SDLT liability on the purchase of the three houses, assuming a claim for multiple dwellings relief is made, there is no benefit in making that claim, and the transaction should be taxed using the non-residential rates of SDLT, resulting in a liability of £44,500.

Example 5.11

On 1 April 2020, Cupid Ltd pays Venus £800,000 for a building on which work has started to convert it into four flats, on the basis that Cupid Ltd will finish the conversion work. The 3% additional rate will apply as the transaction involves a company acquiring residential property (see **4.56** et seq). Consequently, Cupid Ltd pays SDLT calculated as follows:

The average consideration per dwelling is £800,000 divided by 4 giving an amount of £200,000, and the SDLT chargeable on a purchase of residential property for a consideration of £200,000 is as follows:

Purchase Price	Rate	SDLT Chargeable
£	%	£
125,000	3	3,750
75,000	5	3,750
200,000		7,500

The SDLT chargeable in relation to the acquisition of the building is therefore initially calculated as £30,000, being £7,500 multiplied by the number of proposed dwellings of four.

The minimum rate of SDLT does not apply as 1% of the consideration attributable to dwellings would be £8,000 (£800,000 × 1%) and the SDLT chargeable in relation to the transaction is £30,000 (*FA 2003, Sch 6B, para 5(2)*).

Work progresses slowly and, two years later, Cupid Ltd decides to revise the design and create just two larger flats. If the original plan had been to create only two flats the SDLT chargeable would have been calculated as follows:

The average consideration per dwelling is now £800,000 divided by two, giving an amount of £400,000, and the SDLT chargeable on a purchase of a residential property for a consideration of £400,000 is as follows:

Purchase Price	Rate	SDLT chargeable
£	%	£
125,000	3	3,750
125,000	5	6,250
150,000	8	12,000
400,000		22,000

The revised amount of SDLT chargeable on the acquisition of the building is £44,000, being £22,000 multiplied by two. Within 30 days of Cupid Ltd deciding to create only two flats, he must make a further SDLT return and pay the additional tax of £14,000 (£44,000 – £30,000).

Charities relief

5.58 There are three ways in which an acquisition by a charity or charitable trust may be relieved from charge, as follows:

(1) Relief is available if the whole property is to be held for 'qualifying charitable purposes'. This means either furtherance of the charity's charitable purposes or as an investment to produce profits to be used for those charitable purposes (*FA 2003, Sch 8, para 1*).

(2) Alternatively, full relief is still available if less than all, but more than 50% by value, of the property is to be held for qualifying charitable purposes, but the clawback rules are then different (*FA 2003, Sch 8, para 3*).

(3) Originally HMRC took the view that, where a charity acquired property jointly with a non-charity, no relief was due. However, in *The Pollen Estate Trustee Company Limited and King's College London v HM Revenue & Customs* (June 2013), the Court of Appeal held that the charity was entitled to relief from its share of the total SDLT charge, provided the other conditions for relief were met. The Court confirmed that SDLT payable in respect of the non-charity's share of the property should be calculated at the rate applicable to the whole consideration. In an attempt to ensure clarity, *FA 2014, s 113* and *Sch 23* introduced *FA 2003, Sch 8, paras 3A* to *3C* with effect from 17 July 2014. These paragraphs give relief where one or more charities purchase property with one or more non-charities, provided the property is acquired by

them as tenants in common. The relief given is the proportion of the total charge equal to the lower of the proportion of the property owned by the charity and the proportion of the purchase consideration provided by the charity. Because the relief is given in terms of tax rather than by disregarding consideration, the rates of SDLT are determined by the total consideration given by all parties. Relief is available whether the whole or more than 50% by value of the charity's interest is to be held for qualifying charitable purposes. However the clawback rules are different in those two cases as noted at **5.59.**

The changes do not directly deal with joint acquisition by two or more charities (without involvement of a non-charity). It is thought HMRC may accept the general legislative principle that the singular includes the plural to grant relief but complications may arise in relation to clawback where one charity qualifies for relief under (1) above and the other under (2).

5.59 In all cases, relief is denied if the transaction was entered into for the purpose of avoiding SDLT (*FA 2003, Sch 8, para 1(3)*). Relief is clawed back if, either within three years of the acquisition, or later under arrangements entered into within the three-year period, a 'disqualifying event' occurs and the charity still holds the property or an interest derived from it.

If relief was obtained under (1) in **5.58**, 'disqualifying event' means either the charity ceasing to be established for charitable purposes only, or the charity beginning to use the property, or any interest derived from it, for non-charitable purposes. If only part of the property is still held when the disqualifying event occurs, or if only part becomes used for non-charitable purposes, an appropriate proportion of the relief is withdrawn.

Alternatively, if relief was obtained under (2) in **5.58**, 'disqualifying event' *additionally* includes any transfer of all or part of the land, or the grant of a lease at a premium or at a rent of less than £1,000 per year, unless that transfer or grant is made in furtherance of the charitable purposes of the charity.

If relief is obtained under (3) in **5.58**, the same definitions of disqualifying event are applied, depending on whether the whole of the charity's share, or only part, was originally to be held for qualifying charitable purposes.

5.60 From 1 April 2012, the provisions of *FA 2010, Sch 10* apply to determine whether an organisation qualifies as a 'charity' for the purposes of stamp taxes, including SDLT. *Sch 10* requires that the charity be:

- established for charitable purposes only;
- subject to the courts in the UK, elsewhere in the EU, Iceland, Liechtenstein or Norway;

- registered with the Charity Commission or another regulator, if the laws of the home territory so require; and
- administered by 'fit and proper persons'.

These rules are designed to prevent abuses of charitable status (see www.hmrc.gov.uk/charities/tax/recognition.htm).

Example 5.12

On 1 December 2020, the Q Charitable Trust buys freehold land for £1 million, with the intention of constructing a new operations centre for its own use on three quarters (by area) of the site and selling the other quarter to an unrelated company, R, for a previously negotiated price of £300,000. Because the property is not to be used wholly for charitable purposes, full SDLT relief of £39,500 is claimed under *FA 2003, Sch 8, para 3*, as set out under (2) in **5.58** above. The sale to R falls through, but on 1 May 2021, a slightly different plot is sold to another unrelated buyer, S, for £350,000. It is agreed with HMRC that the value of the plot sold is one quarter of the value of the whole site. At this point, one quarter of the relief previously granted is clawed back, and Q must complete a new SDLT return disclosing the charge and making payment. The SDLT payable is one quarter of the SDLT of £39,500 in relation to which relief was claimed, ie £9,875. The SDLT clawed back is based on the appropriate proportion of the SDLT which would have been payable in the absence of a claim for charities relief and *not* the SDLT which would be payable based on the value of the plot disposed of alone.

Note that, if Q had intended to use the whole site for its charitable purposes at the time of acquisition and thus claimed relief under *FA 2003, Sch 8, para 1*, as set out under (1) above, but subsequently decided to sell the plot to S, this disposal would not have led to any clawback of relief.

Construction proceeds slowly but, as a result of changes in practice at Q during the development period, the operations centre is larger than needed. On 1 November 2021, Q agrees to grant a 25-year lease of one floor to an unrelated company, T, at a premium of £800,000 and a peppercorn rent. The premium is paid and T occupies on 31 March 2022. It is agreed with HMRC that the value of the floor leased out is 40% of the value of the original site acquired for £1 million. At this point, 40% of the relief originally granted and not yet withdrawn is now clawed back – that is 40% of £39,500, or £15,800. At this point, Q owns less than 50% of the original site. This is not a problem as, when the relief was claimed, Q intended to use more than 50% for its charitable purposes. However, given the amount finally disposed of, there may be some risk that HMRC would challenge the original intention.

Incorporation of a limited liability partnership

5.61 Relief is available where partnership property is transferred to a limited liability partnership (LLP) from some other form of partnership or from the partners, on incorporation of the LLP (*FA 2003, s 65)*. The relief only applies to a straightforward change of form from another kind of partnership, with no change in partners or their relative interests in the partnership. To qualify, the transfer must happen within 12 months of the date of incorporation of the LLP. In the absence of the relief, the special partnership rules discussed at **7.13** et seq would apply such that, on a transfer from another form of partnership to the LLP, with no change of partners or their relative interests in the partnership, no charge to SDLT would be expected to arise. However, a claim under *FA 2003, s 65* is generally seen as a simpler method of claiming relief assuming the requisite conditions are satisfied. There is an apparent conflict with the rule in *FA 2003, s 53* (see **4.30**) that the chargeable consideration for a transfer to a connected company (because an LLP is a body corporate and is therefore a 'company' for the purposes of *FA 2003, s 53*) is an amount not less than the market value of the property. However, HMRC have confirmed at SDLTM 34170 that the special partnership rules take precedence over *FA 2003, s 53*.

Treatment of COACSs for SDLT purposes and seeding relief for PAIFs and COACSs

5.62 Property Authorised Investment Funds (PAIFs) have been available since 2008 and are a form of regulated property fund, structured as an open-ended investment company, which are tax efficient.

Co-ownership Authorised Contractual Schemes (COACSs) were established by the *Collective Investment in Transferable Securities (Contractual Scheme) Regulations 2013*, and are a form of tax-transparent fund which was introduced to strengthen the UK's attractiveness as a location for funds.

FA 2016, s 133 and *Sch 16* sets out how COACS are to be treated for SDLT purposes and also introduces a seeding relief for both PAIFs and COACSs.

5.63 For the purposes of SDLT (with the exception of group relief, reconstruction relief and acquisition relief) a COACS is treated as if it were a company and the rights of the participants in the COACS are treated as though they were shares in the company (*FA 2003, s 102A* introduced by *FA 2016, Sch 16, para 1*). This means that the units in a COACS can be transferred without any charge to SDLT subject to any withdrawal of SDLT seeding relief which is discussed in **5.66** below. Consequently, as a transfer of units in a COACS should not be chargeable to either stamp duty reserve tax or stamp duty (*FA 1986, s 90(7B)* and *FA 1999, Sch 13, para 25A*), such a transfer can be made free of all stamp taxes.

The definition of COACS in the *Financial Services and Markets Act 2000, s 261D(1)* is extended to include other contractual schemes established under the law of a European Economic Area (EEA) state other than the UK.

Where a COACS enters into a land transaction, it, and not the participants in the COACS, is the purchaser, and in relation to the filing of land transaction returns, HMRC enquiries, assessments, liability for SDLT and deferment applications the operator of the COACS is treated as the purchaser (*FA 2003, s 102A(11)*).

5.64 *FA 2003, 65A* and *Sch 7A* (introduced by *FA 2016, Sch 16, para 3*) provides an SDLT seeding relief (the initial transfer of properties into the investment vehicle) for transfers of a major interest in property (ie freehold and leasehold interests in land) to both COACSs and PAIFs. The reliefs must be claimed in a land transaction return, or an amendment to a land transaction return, which must be accompanied by a notice to HMRC confirming that the purchaser is either a PAIF or a COACS, or an equivalent body established in the EEA.

The relief is only available during the 'seeding period' which starts on the date the PAIF or COACS is first seeded (provided it has not yet been opened up to investors) until the earlier of: (a) the date that a person who was not a seed investor transfers non-property assets to the PAIF or COACS; and (b) 18 months from the date the PAIF or COACS was first seeded.

5.65 It is beyond the scope of this book to consider the seeding reliefs in detail; however, both reliefs are subject to two-part anti-avoidance motive tests which require that the transfer of the major interest in land to the PAIF or COACS is effected for bona fide commercial reasons and does not form part of an arrangement of which the main purpose, or one of the main purposes, is the avoidance of liability to stamp duty, income tax, corporation tax, capital gains tax or SDLT. In addition, at the 'effective date' (see **4.91**) of the transfer of the major interest in land to the PAIF or COACS, there must be no arrangement in place which would, or could, result in a subsequent withdrawal of seeding relief on a disposal of units in the PAIF or COACS.

5.66 The seeding relief is withdrawn if, in certain circumstances: (a) the fund ceases to be a PAIF or COACS within a specified period; or (b) the portfolio test is not met (for non-residential property the PAIF or COACS must hold at least ten seeded interests in land and the chargeable consideration attributable to all the seeded interests must be at least £100 million with a maximum of 10% attributable to residential property. In relation to residential property the PAIF or COACS must hold at least 100 seeded interests with a chargeable consideration attributable to all of the seeded interests of at least £100 million); or (c) there is a disposal of certain units by a vendor and those units related to a seeding transaction; or (d) a non-qualifying individual is permitted to occupy a dwelling in relation to which seeding relief is claimed; or (e) in relation to a COACS only (the test is implicit in relation to a PAIF) if the genuine diversity of ownership condition is not met during a specified period.

5.67 Claiming seeding relief in relation to a PAIF or COACS, and understanding when the reliefs may be withdrawn, is a highly specialised area and the commentary above only provides an outline of the conditions to be satisfied and the anti-avoidance measures which are in place to prevent the relief from being abused. In all cases the author would recommend that professional advice be taken in relation to any such claim.

Reliefs for other specified bodies and transfers

5.68 Relief is available for acquisitions in a range of transactions by other bodies, specified either individually or by class. These are listed below; most are very specialised. Relief is usually subject to conditions, so it is essential to consult the relevant legislation and/or take expert advice before claiming the relief. In general, the relief is claimed by inserting '28' (other reliefs) at the appropriate point in the SDLT return (see **8.23**). In addition, specific relief is often provided in legislation other than *Finance Acts*, in respect of transfers in the course of government-sponsored projects. It is, therefore, generally worth checking such legislation in these cases or, if involved early enough in the process, lobbying for such relief to be provided. Much of the legislation noted below pre-dates SDLT and originally granted stamp duty relief, but it has been amended, largely by statutory instrument under *FA 2003, s 123(3)*. There is a list of miscellaneous reliefs not in the SDLT legislation at SDLTM29600, accessible at www.hmrc.gov.uk/manuals/sdltmanual/sdltm29600.htm.

Qualifying transfer	**Legislation and notes**
Transfer on compulsory purchase facilitating development	*FA 2003, s 60*; relief applies to planning authority or other person making the compulsory purchase order
Transfer to a public authority to comply with planning obligations, for example under *Town and Country Planning Act 1990, s 106*	*FA 2003, s 61*
Between 'public bodies' (local and national government bodies, National Health Service bodies, their wholly-owned subsidiary companies and other statutory bodies), on reorganisation*	*FA 2003, s 66* (see detailed list in legislation) References to NHS bodies are probably redundant (see below)
Between Local Constituency Associations on reorganisation of parliamentary constituencies	*FA 2003, s 67*

Qualifying transfer	Legislation and notes
Acquisition by British Museum, Natural History Museum, and other specified similar bodies; certain transfers to 'heritage bodies' of property accepted in payment of tax	*FA 2003, s 69*; *National Heritage Act 1980, s 11A**
On demutualisation of an insurance company or a building society	*FA 2003, ss 63, 64* (provided the demutualisation satisfies conditions; see legislation)
On merger of building societies or transfer of business*	*Building Societies Act 1986, s 109A*
Acquisition by NHS Trusts, Foundation Trusts and similar bodies in the UK*, including new bodies established under current and proposed reforms of the NHS	*Health and Social Care (Community Health & Standards) Act 2003, s 33(2)*; *FA 2003, s 67A*, inserted by *FA 2012, s 216*
Acquisition by designated visiting armed forces or NATO headquarters*	*FA 1960, s 74A*
Transfers in the course of an amalgamation of friendly societies or transfer of friendly society business*	*Friendly Societies Acts 1974* and *1992, s 105A* in each case
Certain transfers in relation to roads, airports and lighthouses*	*Highways Act 1980, s 281A*; *Airports Act 1986, s 76A*; *Merchant Shipping Act 1995, s 221*
Certain transfers relating to inclosures and common land*	*Inclosure Act 1845, s 163A*; *Metropolitan Commons Act 1866, s 33*

* These reliefs are subject to the modified rules on subsequent disposal of a lease; see **6.17**.

OBSOLETE RELIEFS

Disadvantaged areas relief

5.69 This relief, in *FA 2003, s 57* and *Sch 6*, originally allowed complete relief from SDLT on transfer of property in some 2,000 specified areas of the UK which, on the basis of rather old census information, were regarded as disadvantaged. They included areas which had subsequently become desirable and valuable, in particular a number of high-profile shopping centres which were therefore quickly transferred into special purpose companies, allowing future transfers of those companies free of SDLT. The relief was modified by *FA 2005, s 96* to apply only to wholly residential property where the consideration did not exceed £150,000. Since there was a general threshold of £125,000 below which SDLT was not chargeable on residential property, and there were various temporary increases in this threshold, in practice disadvantaged areas relief applied to few transactions. The government recognised this fact and *FA 2012* abolished the relief from 6 April 2013. This is subject to retention of the relief under certain circumstances for completion of contracts entered into on or before 16 March 2005.

Unit trust seeding relief

5.70 This relief, originally in *FA 2003, s 64A* but now abolished, allowed transfer of property to a new unit trust in return for the issue of units, without SDLT cost. Its purpose was to allow bodies such as investment and pension funds to turn fundamentally illiquid property investments into tradable units, in order to comply with new regulations relating to the structure of their balance sheets. However, the relief was loosely drawn and allowed many owners to transfer properties to essentially privately held, non-UK unit trusts. It was then possible for effective ownership of the properties to be transferred free of stamp tax by transfer of the units. Many properties are still held in this way. The relief was withdrawn by *FA 2006*; unusually, the 2006 Budget announcement specified that the withdrawal took effect from 2pm on Budget day, in an attempt to prevent a last-minute scramble to take advantage of the relief.

First-time buyer's relief (ceased to apply from 24 March 2012)

5.71 *FA 2003, s 57AA*, introduced by *FA 2010, s 6*, provided a time-limited relief for the first purchase of a wholly residential property by a person or persons ('first-time buyer/s') who had not previously been a 'purchaser' of a residential property. The relief was available for purchases with an effective date between 25 March 2010 and 24 March 2012 inclusive. It applied if the consideration for the purchase exceeded £125,000 but did not exceed £250,000. It therefore only applied to purchases which would otherwise have been subject to SDLT at 1%. No relief was available if the price exceeded £250,000 – there was no question of partial relief. The relief also applied to appropriate acquisitions under 'alternative finance' arrangements (see **5.37**), removing the single charge to SDLT which would otherwise remain after application of the alternative finance reliefs. Strangely, the relief did not overtly specify that the first-time buyers must be one or more individuals, but this was perhaps implied by the condition that the property had to be for occupation by the buyer(s) as their only or main residence. If the transaction was the grant of a lease or the acquisition of a second-hand lease, the lease had to have at least 21 years to run. The relief was denied if the acquisition was linked with any others. To claim the relief, an SDLT return had to be completed and code 32 entered in Section 9. A new form of relief for first-time buyers has now been introduced for transactions with an 'effective date' (see **4.91**) on or after 22 November 2017 (see **5.47** et seq).

Zero carbon homes relief

5.72 This relief in *FA 2003, s 58B* was introduced by *FA 2007*. It applied for a limited period of five years from 1 October 2007 and so expired on 30 September 2012. Full relief from SDLT was available on the first acquisition of a dwelling which was a 'zero carbon home' and with a price not exceeding £500,000. For more expensive homes, the SDLT bill was reduced by £15,000 (being the SDLT on a £500,000 home). Zero carbon was defined by reference to zero net carbon dioxide emissions over the course of a year, and therefore effectively required the dwelling to generate power for return to the national grid to compensate for energy used. 'First acquisition' meant acquisition on or before first occupation. As initially drafted, the relief applied only to houses which were separate buildings, but it was realised that, in the immediate future at least, the only dwellings with any practical hope of being 'zero carbon' would be flats. The relief was therefore modified, with retrospective effect, to include parts of buildings. Detailed regulations provided a mechanism for assessment and certification of qualifying homes – it was considered that this could easily be combined with the normal energy efficiency assessment required for new homes under Building Regulations (*FA 2003, ss 58B, 58C*; *SI 2007/3437*). To claim this relief, code 30 had to be entered in Section 9 of the SDLT return.

The relief only applied to the first acquisition of a new dwelling. It did not, therefore, encourage the modification of existing homes to improve their energy efficiency.

Chapter 6

SDLT and Leases

INTRODUCTION

6.1 Each of the grant, variation, assignment and surrender of a lease is a 'land transaction' and therefore potentially gives rise to SDLT obligations as set out in **Chapter 4**. As with other UK land transactions, there may be obligations to make or amend SDLT returns even if no liability arises (see **8.2**). However, where leases are concerned, the general rules are substantially amended and generally made more complex. There are special rules for calculation of SDLT on rent in *FA 2003, Sch 5*, but the main technical provisions are in *FA 2003, Sch 17A*. This schedule was inserted after enactment of the main SDLT rules and has itself been amended several times in an attempt to make the rules easier to apply whilst guarding against avoidance.

Obligations may arise at various times, such as when a payment is made, on first occupation, when rent amounts are agreed or changed, and even when the lease itself is formally executed. They may also arise in connection with arrangements which are not normally regarded as giving rise to a lease – for example, informal occupation or periodic tenancies – and on less formal changes, even if not documented as a variation etc. It is, therefore, important to establish clearly the nature of the transaction.

The four key questions to address are the same as for other transactions; but, in relation to leases, the fourth question is likely to require the most attention:

- What SDLT obligations and liabilities may arise?
- At what time do SDLT obligations and liabilities arise?
- What reliefs, if any, are available?
- What special rules may affect this transaction?

It has been recognised that some aspects of the rules are oppressively complex. *FA 2013, Sch 41* provided some simplification by abolishing rules relating to abnormal rent increases (see **6.27** for explanation of the old rules), and making the rules relating to substantial performance of a lease before execution (see **4.91** and **6.74**) and leases which continue after a fixed term (see **6.13**) more logical. These changes were welcome, but the rules remain complex and there is undoubtedly scope for further simplification.

6.2 In general, a lease granted before 1 December 2003 is exclusively within the old stamp duty regime. SDLT will only arise in connection with such a lease if an event occurs which is treated as the grant of a new lease – a renewal or extension of the term or a variation which in law amounts to the surrender and re-grant of the lease (SDLTM 10025). Other changes such as an increase in rent after the first five years of the term of a lease will not give rise to an SDLT charge (see SDLTM10025 and SDLTM15010).

6.3 SDLT may be chargeable on both rent and any real or deemed premium.

On the grant of a new lease, SDLT is charged on any real or deemed premium on the same basis as it is charged on consideration given for any other 'land transaction' (see **4.7** and **4.37**).

Like other forms of 'chargeable consideration' (see **4.19** et seq), the rates and bands at which SDLT is charged on consideration consisting of rent depends on the amount of the chargeable consideration, and whether the transaction is a residential property transaction or a non-residential property transaction.

Until 16 March 2016 the bands and rates of SDLT applying to rent, on the grant of a new lease over residential property and over non-residential property were the same and were as follows:

Net present value of rent (£)	**Rate (%)**
Up to 150,000	0
Over 150,000	1

The above bands and rates continue to apply to rent on the grant of a new lease over residential property.

However, for transactions with an 'effective date' (see **4.91** and **6.74**) on or after 17 March 2016 the following bands and rates apply to rent on the grant of a new lease over non-residential property (*FA 2016, s 116(9)*):

Net present value of rent (£)	**Rate (%)**
Up to 150,000	0
Over 150,001 to £5,000,000	1
Over £5,000,000	2

In relation to the rates and bands applying to rent payable under a lease of non-residential or mixed-use property there are transitional rules, which provide that where an agreement for lease was entered into before 17 March 2016, but the agreement was not completed until on or after 17 March 2016, then provided that there is no event of the kind listed in *FA 2016, s 116(15)*, which results in the effect of the agreement being different from the effect of the agreement when first entered into, the purchaser can elect to pay SDLT based on the old rates and bands (*FA 2016, s 116(13)(b)* and *(15)*). Similarly, where the agreement for lease was entered into and substantially performed (see **4.9**) but not completed (see **4.91** and **6.74**) before 17 March 2016 then the purchaser can elect to apply the old rates and bands to the completion transaction taking place on or after 17 March 2016 (*FA 2016, s 116(13)(a)*). To choose to pay SDLT based on the old rates and bands the purchaser just enters the appropriate amount of SDLT in box 14 and 25 of the land transaction return.

The grant of a new lease is a residential property transaction if the property over which the lease is granted consists *entirely* of residential property (see **4.56** et seq) or, if the grant of the lease is one of a number of linked transactions (see **4.99**), the chargeable interests acquired under each linked transaction, and the properties over which any new lease is granted, consist *entirely* of residential property (*FA 2003, s 55(1B), (1C), (3)* and *(4)*).

The grant of a new lease is a non-residential property transaction if the property over which the lease is granted either consists of, or includes, non-residential property. If the grant of the new lease is one of a number of linked transactions (see **4.99**), it will be a non-residential property transaction if the chargeable interests acquired under any of the linked transactions, and the properties over which any new lease is granted, consist of, or include, an interest in non-residential property (*FA 2003, s 55(2), (3)* and *(4)*).

The grant of a new lease is a mixed use property transaction if the property over which the lease is granted consists of, or includes, both residential and non-residential property. If the grant of the new lease is one of a number of linked transactions (see **4.99**), it will be a mixed use property transaction if the chargeable interests acquired under any of the linked transactions, and the properties over which any new leases are granted, consists of, or include both residential and non-residential property (*FA 2003, s 55(2), (3)* and *(4)*).

Thus the tax rates and bands in relation to rent for residential property will only be applicable if the property, or properties, over which the lease is granted consist(s) *entirely* of residential property, and the grant of the lease is not 'linked' (see **4.99**) with any 'chargeable transaction' (see **4.14**) over non-residential or mixed use property.

For transactions with an 'effective date' (see **4.91** and **6.74**) on or before 16 March 2016, where the rent payable under a lease of non-residential property was £1,000 or more per annum there was no zero rate band in respect of any consideration other than rent. Consequently, any premium payable under such a lease, in an amount of up to £150,000, was taxed at a rate of 1% (*FA 2003, Sch 5, para 9A*). However, this rule was abolished, subject to the transitional provisions discussed above, for any transaction with an 'effective date' (see **4.99** and **6.74**) on or after 17 March 2016 (*FA 2016, s 116(11)*). This therefore means that from that date the £150,000 zero rate band applies when calculating the SDLT chargeable on a premium payable on the grant of a lease of non-residential property.

SDLT obligations fall on the 'purchaser'. In most cases, this will be the tenant/lessee but, where a lease is surrendered or varied to shorten the term, the landlord/lessor is the purchaser (*FA 2003, s 43, Sch 17A, para 15A*).

6.4 The general rules relating to timing and notification of liability, availability of reliefs and disclosure of information apply to lease transactions. Specific rules for calculating the SDLT liability and modifications to other general rules are dealt with in detail by way of examples in the text which follows.

6.5 Sometimes, liabilities will arise at a future time on a lease granted now, or now on a lease granted years ago, especially where the lease is transferred to another tenant. It may, therefore, be important to obtain and retain the full detailed history of a lease, and of previous leases of the same premises if they are linked with the present lease (see **6.58**).

EVENTS GIVING RISE TO SDLT OBLIGATIONS AND LIABILITIES

New lease

6.6 SDLT may arise on entering into a lease (*FA 2003, s 43(3)(a)*). It is common for the parties initially to enter into an agreement for lease, the definitive lease being executed later, after all necessary details have been settled. The agreement may be acted on before the definitive lease is executed (eg by payment of rent or the tenant having access to the premises). The general SDLT concept of 'substantial performance' applies to an agreement for lease (see, eg *FA 2003, s 44(7)*). SDLT obligations may therefore arise when the agreement is acted on and when the definitive lease is executed – see **4.99** and **6.74**.

As a general principle an amount payable in respect of a period before a lease commences (or is treated as commencing) cannot be regarded as rent even if it is expressed as such (see SDLTM11010). Provided it really is consideration for the lease, any such amount will be treated as a premium. This may occur, for example, when negotiations between landlord and putative tenant have been delayed and the landlord is able to demand 'rent' for an earlier period before the tenant took occupation or signed the lease (see Example 6.3 for an illustration of this). More usually, the payment of such an amount (or earlier taking possession of the property) will trigger the commencement of a notional lease, as explained at **4.99** and **6.74**, and the amount paid will be respected as rent for that notional lease.

The one exception arises on renewal of a lease originally entered into within the SDLT regime; see **6.65** and Example 6.23C.

New lease for seven years or more

6.7 For non-lease transactions, there is no requirement to make an SDLT return if the chargeable consideration is less than £40,000 (*FA 2003, s 77A(1)*). Where a lease for seven years or more is granted, this exemption from making a return only applies if the annual rent is also less than £1,000. This was logical for a non-residential lease granted on or before 16 March 2016 (see **6.3**) involving both rent and premium because, if the annual rent was £1,000 or more, there was no 'zero rate band' for the premium and any premium, however small, gave rise to an SDLT liability (*FA 2003, Sch 5, para 9A*). However, this rule was abolished for transactions with an 'effective date' (see **4.99** and **6.74**) on or after 17 March 2016. Therefore the continuing requirement that the rent must be less than £1,000 per annum, otherwise the grant of the lease is notifiable, would now seem to have little logic.

Example 6.1—Rent and premium below threshold, notifiable

On 1 January 2021, Methuselah enters into a 250-year lease as tenant on a plot of farmland at a yearly rent of £5,200, subject to revision every five years in line with movement in the Retail Price Index. A premium of £35,000 is payable under the terms of the lease. The tenant has the right to terminate the lease at any time after 1 January 2041. Increases in rent in line with the Retail Price Index are ignored for SDLT purposes (see **6.37**), so this is treated as a lease at a fixed rent of £5,200 per annum. The NPV of the rent is £148,542, which is below the threshold of £150,000 so no SDLT is payable on the rent. Equally no SDLT is payable on the premium as it is below the £150,000 threshold, and below the £40,000 threshold above which non-lease transactions must be notified. Nonetheless, an SDLT return must be submitted within 14 days of execution or earlier substantial performance of the lease, as the rent payable under the lease is not less than £1,000 per annum.

New lease for less than seven years

6.8 The grant of a lease for less than seven years does not have to be notified unless the consideration (rent and/or premium) exceeds the relevant zero rate band. The relevant zero rate band for consideration other than rent is up to £125,000 for residential property and up to £150,000 for non-residential property. For rent the zero rate band applies to an aggregate NPV of up to £125,000 for residential property and up to £150,000 for non-residential property.

Example 6.2—Rent and premium below threshold, not notifiable

On 30 June 2020 Moira grants Nathan a six-year lease of a house (single residence) for a premium of £30,000 and an annual rent of £10,000. The NPV of the rent is clearly below the residential threshold for rent (£125,000), and the premium is within the zero rate band (also £125,000). The higher rates of SDLT (see **4.56**) do not apply as a lease granted for a term of less than seven years is not a 'major interest' (see **4.11**) for the purposes of *FA 2003, Sch 4ZA* (*FA 2003, Sch 4ZA, para 2(4)*). Since the lease is for less than seven years and no tax is payable on either rent or premium, no SDLT return or other notification is required.

Example 6.3—Liability on NPV of rent: rent paid for period prior to grant of lease

On 1 March 2020, Craig agrees to grant a five-year lease of a shop to Laura for rent of £50,000 per annum, payable quarterly in advance. It is agreed that the lease will commence on 1 April 2020. However, a dispute over the detailed terms and conditions means the lease is not executed until 1 May 2020. Laura makes the first rent payment, for the period 1 April to 30 June 2020, on 1 May 2020, and takes possession of the shop on the same day. Since nothing happens to cause the agreement to be substantially performed before the lease is executed, the lease is deemed to commence on the date of execution and not at the (earlier) alleged start date – so, for SDLT purposes this is a 4-year, 11-month lease commencing on 1 May 2020. Although £4,167 (£50,000/12 months) of rent is expressed as being for the period 1 to 30 April 2020, rent cannot in fact relate to a period before the lease begins (see **6.6**) (the one exception to this rule arises when a lease, originally executed under SDLT, is renewed – see **6.65** and Example 6.23C). It is HMRC's view that this amount must therefore be regarded as a premium for the lease. The NPV of the aggregate rent payable over the term of the lease is £222,244 and SDLT of £722 is payable on that amount of rent. No SDLT is payable on the deemed premium of £4,167 as it is below the £150,000 threshold. Laura must file a land transaction return, and pay the SDLT due of £722, by 15 May 2020.

Licence to occupy and informal arrangements

6.9 A licence to occupy land is not a 'chargeable interest' (*FA 2003, s 48(2)(b)*), so no SDLT obligations arise on entering into or terminating a licence. However, HMRC warn that the nature of an interest in land is not determined by calling it a 'licence'; in any case of doubt, appropriate legal advice should be sought. A tenancy giving exclusive occupation of a property is more than a licence and is potentially subject to SDLT.

6.10 Normally, a transaction creating a tenancy is reduced to writing, but it is possible for a tenancy to be implied by the actions of the parties. No liability should arise on a tenancy at will (*FA 2003, s 48(2)(c)*, see SDLTM 10050), but over time this may develop into a periodic tenancy which is potentially within the charge. However, it may be that the arrangement commenced before 1 December 2003 (the date on which SDLT was introduced). In that case, no SDLT obligations should arise unless and until the arrangement is varied. It is suggested that appropriate legal advice should be taken to establish the status of any such arrangements.

6.11 HMRC's draft guidance on SDLT and partnerships originally suggested that, if a partnership informally occupied a property owned by a partner, the property should be regarded as belonging to the partnership rather than simply let to it. An article in SDLT Technical News 5 (August 2007) announced the more reasonable view that this would depend on the facts of the individual case (see **7.43**). The final guidance on SDLT and partnerships (SDLTM33000 et seq) is silent on the matter.

Lease for an indefinite term and holding over

6.12 A periodic tenancy (ie a tenancy which continues for successive periods until the tenant gives the landlord notification that they want to end the tenancy), whether or not reduced to writing, is probably the most common example of a 'lease for an indefinite term' (*FA 2003, Sch 17A, para 4*). Such a lease, assuming it comes into existence on or after 1 December 2003 (the date on which SDLT was introduced), is treated in the first instance as a lease for one year. If it continues beyond the end of the first year, it is treated as having been a lease for two years from the outset. At the commencement of each successive year thereafter, it is treated as having been, from the outset, a lease for one year longer than at the commencement of the previous year.

Following each one-year extension any SDLT obligations must then be dealt with within either 14 days or 30 days after the end of the previous deemed fixed period as described below. Thus if the lease for an indefinite term is deemed to have a fixed period to, say, 28 August 2020, but the lease continues beyond that date, the lease is then treated as having a deemed fixed period to 28 August 2021, and any SDLT obligations, arising from that deemed one-year extension to 28 August 2021, must be dealt with within either 14 days or 30 days of 28 August 2020 as described below.

The 'effective date' (see 4.99 and 6.74) of the grant of the lease is on or after 1 March 2019, or the lease only becomes notifiable on or after 1 March 2019

If the effect of treating the lease as extended by one year is that the transaction becomes notifiable, when it was not previously notifiable, the lessee must deliver a return within 14 days of the end of the previous deemed fixed period (*FA 2003, Sch 17A, para 4(3)* as amended by *FA 2019, s 46(8)(b)*).

However, if the effect of treating the lease as extended by one year is that tax is payable in respect of the transaction where none was payable before, but the transaction has previously been notified, or additional tax is payable in relation to the transaction, the lessee must deliver a further return within 30 days of the end of the previous deemed fixed period (*FA 2003, Sch 17A, para 4(3A)* as introduced by *FA 2019, s 46(8)(b)*).

For the purposes of both *FA 2003, Sch 17A, para 4(3)* and *para 4(3A)* any tax or additional tax payable is calculated using the SDLT rates and bands as at the 'effective date' (see **4.99** and **6.74**) of the grant of the lease (*FA 2003, Sch 17A, para 4(3B)* as introduced by *FA 2019, s 46(8)(b)*).

Where the lessee is required to deliver a return under *FA 2003, Sch 17A, para 4(3)*, or a further return under *para 4(3A)*, that return must include a self-assessment of the tax chargeable based on the information in the return and the tax, or additional tax, must be paid not later than the date by which the return must be filed (*FA 2003, Sch 17A, para 4(3C)* as introduced by *FA 2019, s 46(8)(b)*).

The 'effective date' of the grant of the lease is before 1 March 2019 and the grant of the lease became notifiable before 1 March 2019

If the effect of treating the lease as extended by one year is that tax is payable in respect of the transaction where none was payable before, or that additional tax is payable in relation to the transaction, the lessee must deliver a return within 30 days of the end of the previous deemed fixed period. The return must include a self-assessment of the amount of the tax chargeable on the basis of the information contained in the return and the tax, or additional tax, must be paid not later than the filing date for the return (*FA 2003, Sch 17A, para 4(3)* prior to amendment by *FA 2019, s 46(8)(b)*).

The above treatment of a lease for an indefinite term (irrespective of the 'effective date' of the grant of the lease) contrasts with the treatment of leases for a fixed term which continue after the end of that fixed term where, for periods beginning on or after 17 July 2013, the SDLT obligations are postponed until 30 days after the end of the one-year extension (see **6.13**).

There is no adjustment if the lease for an indefinite term ends before the end of a year in respect of which SDLT has been paid (eg the tenant vacates the premises or alternatively enters into a fixed-term lease in place of the periodic tenancy). However, if the lease for an indefinite term is superseded by a fixed-term lease, allowance should be available in calculating the SDLT on the fixed-term lease, in respect of SDLT paid on the lease for an indefinite term for the overlap period, see **6.83**.

Commonly, particularly in relation to residential tenancies, the rent will not be high enough to produce any SDLT liability in the early years. However, as time passes and the lease 'grows' in length, SDLT obligations may arise. Although the notification requirements for leases under and over seven years are different, it is specifically provided that a lease for an indefinite term (eg a periodic tenancy) does not become notifiable purely as a result of passing the seven-year mark (*FA 2003, Sch 17A, para 4(4A)*).

None of the above applies to a lease for an indefinite term which came into existence before 1 December 2003, unless it is varied in such a way as to bring it within the SDLT regime (see **6.2** but note that continuation from one year to the next in accordance with the written or implied terms of the lease does not amount to a renewal or extension of the term).

A tenancy at will (ie a property tenure without a written agreement that can be terminated at any time by either the tenant or the landlord) is also specifically stated to be a lease for an indefinite term (*FA 2003, Sch 17A, para (5)(b)*). This seems a bizarre provision, given that a tenancy at will is outside the charge to SDLT (*FA 2003, s 48(2)(c)(i)*), as noted at **6.10**.

Example 6.4—Lease for indefinite term

On 1 September 2013 Quirinius took on a tenancy of a commercial unit. Under the terms of the tenancy Quirinius paid a quarterly rental of £7,500 including VAT, rent to be increased at each anniversary of the tenancy in line with the Retail Price Index. The tenancy may be terminated by either party on giving one quarter's notice on the due date of a rental payment.

The tenancy was initially treated as a lease for one year at an annual rent of £30,000. No SDLT was due as the NPV of the rent was below £150,000. There was no obligation to make a return because the lease was for less than seven years and no tax was due. On 1 September 2014 the continuing tenancy was treated as having been a lease for two years from the outset, at an annual rent of £30,000. The increase in rent in line with the RPI is ignored (*FA 2003, Sch 17A, para 7(5)*). Again, no SDLT liability arose and no return was required. The same applied at 1 September in each of 2015, 2016 and 2017. At 1 September 2018, the lease was deemed to have been for six years from 1 September 2013 to 31 August 2019. The NPV of the rent (at £30,000 per year ignoring RPI increases) on the deemed six-year lease was £159,856. As this was over the £150,000 threshold for an SDLT liability to arise a Land Transaction Return was submitted and SDLT was paid at 1% of £9,856 (see **6.47** et seq for calculation principles). The Land Transaction Return was due, and the SDLT was payable, by 30 September 2018, that is 30 days after the end of the previous fixed term on 31 August 2018 (*FA 2003, Sch 17A, para 4(3)*).

If the tenancy had then been terminated during the sixth year – say on 28 February 2019, so that in total it had lasted five years and six months – there would have been no refund of the SDLT. This is the case even though a fixed-term lease for the same period and rent would not have given rise to any SDLT liability, as the NPV of the rent would have been below the £150,000 threshold.

If the tenancy had not become notifiable until, say, 1 September 2019 then the Land Transaction Return would have been due, and the tax payable, by 14 September 2019 (*FA 2003, Sch 17A, para 4(3)* as amended by *FA 2019, s 46(8)(b)*).

The tenancy continues. At 1 September 2019 it is regarded as becoming a lease for seven years (from 1 September 2013 to 31 August 2020). The NPV of the rent is £183,436. SDLT liability arises on the increase in NPV of the rent in comparison with the previous year (SDLT is 1% of (£183,436 – £159,856) and a land transaction return is required. The return is due and the SDLT is payable by 30 September 2019, which is 30 days after the end of the deemed fixed period on 31 August 2019. As the transaction had become notifiable before 1 March 2019 (in this case by 30 September 2018) the deadline for filing the further return is 30 days after 31 August 2019 in accordance with *FA 2003, Sch 17A, para 4(3)* prior to its amendment by *FA 2019, s 46(8)(b)*.

However, in January 2020 Quirinius and the landlord enter into negotiations to replace the tenancy with a new ten-year lease. Terms are agreed and the new lease is executed (with no prior agreement) on 28 February 2020. Rent of £15,000 plus the RPI increase is paid in respect of the six months to 28 February 2020, in accordance with the terms of the tenancy. The tenancy is treated as ending on the date of actual termination but there is no ability to claim a refund for the SDLT paid on the rent for the period 1 March 2020 to 31 August 2020. However, as the periodic tenancy has been superseded by a fixed-term lease, allowance should be available in calculating the SDLT on the fixed-term lease, in respect of SDLT paid on the periodic tenancy for the overlap period (ie the period 1 March 2020 to 31 August 2020), see **6.83**. The Land Transaction Return, and payment of any SDLT in respect of the new lease, is due by 14 March 2020 (*FA 2003, s 76(1)* as amended by *FA 2019, s 46(2)*).

Lease for an indefinite term and holding over

6.13 A tenant may remain in occupation after the end of a fixed-term lease ('holding over'), continuing to pay rent, perhaps while a new lease is negotiated. The precise SDLT consequences of holding over will depend on whether the old lease was granted under the stamp duty or SDLT regimes and the terms of any new lease. This is one area in which helpful amendments were made by *FA 2013* – see *FA 2003, Sch 17A, paras 3, 3A* as amended.

In principle, periods of holding over are treated in the same way as the second and subsequent years of a lease for an indefinite term (see **6.12**), however the deadlines for filing returns, or further returns, and for paying any SDLT, or additional SDLT, are different.

The old lease for a fixed term is effectively deemed to remain in force, growing in length one year at a time (*FA 2003, Sch 17A, para 3(2)*):

The 'effective date' (see 4.64 and 6.47) of the grant of the fixed-term lease is prior to 1 March 2019 and the lease becomes notifiable before 1 March 2019

If the old lease was subject to SDLT, reporting and payment obligations arise in respect of each one year deemed extension. Prior to 17 July 2013 these obligations had to be dealt with within 30 days of the start of each one-year period of holding over. From 17 July 2013 the obligations are postponed to 30 days after the end of each one-year period (or within 30 days of the end of the period of holding over if sooner).

The 'effective date' (see 4.64 and 6.47) of the grant of the lease is on or after 1 March 2019, or the 'effective date' of the grant of the lease is before 1 March 2019 but the lease only becomes notifiable on or after 1 March 2019

If the effect of the lease growing by one year is that the transaction becomes notifiable, in circumstances where it was not previously notifiable, the lessee must deliver a return, and pay any SDLT due, within 14 days after the end of the one-year lease extension (*FA 2003, Sch 17A, para 3(3)* as amended by *FA 2019, s 46(8)(a)*).

However, if the transaction has already been notified, but the effect of the lease growing by one year is that tax is payable where none was payable before, or additional tax is payable in respect of the transaction, the lessee must deliver a further return in respect of the transaction, within 30 days after the end of the one-year extension (*FA 2003, Sch 17A, para 3(3ZA)* as introduced by *FA 2019, s 46(8)(a)*).

For the purposes of both *FA 2003, Sch 17A, para 3(3)* and *para 3(3ZA)* any tax or additional tax payable is calculated using the SDLT rates and bands as at the 'effective date' (see **4.99** and **6.74**) of the grant of the fixed-term lease (*FA 2003,Sch 17A, para 3(3ZB)* as introduced by *FA 2019, s 46(8)(a)*).

Where the lessee is required to deliver a return under *FA 2003, Sch 17A, para 3(3)*, or a further return under *para 3(3ZA)*, that return must include a self-assessment of the tax chargeable based on the information in the return and the tax, or additional tax, must be paid not later than the date by which the return must be filed (*FA 2003,Sch 17A, para 3(3ZC)* as introduced by *FA 2019, s 46(8)(a)*).

Grant of fixed-term lease subject to stamp duty

If the old lease was subject to stamp duty, the deemed extensions do not give rise to SDLT obligations unless there is an increase in rent which was not provided for in the original lease, or there are other changes which may be deemed to give rise to a new lease or agreement for lease (see **6.22**).

The above treatments of a lease for a fixed term may be modified if the period of holding over is followed by the execution of a new lease of substantially the same premises to the same tenant. For details of the treatment of lease renewals see **6.64**.

Airspace and roof-space leases – renewables and telecoms

6.14 A lease of roof-space or airspace for installation of solar panels, wind turbines or telecom masts is potentially chargeable just like any other lease. The installation of the equipment will not normally count as consideration, even though required under the terms of the lease, because it will normally fall within *FA 2003, Sch 4, para 10* (see **4.26**). Any cash premium or rent payable under the lease will be chargeable in the normal way. In relation to renewable energy, such leases often provide a right for electricity to be provided to the owner or occupier of the building either free or at reduced price. This right, being consideration in money's worth, must be valued at the effective date of the lease and included as a premium. The ongoing supply of electricity under the lease does not count as rent.

In *Stamp Taxes Bulletin 1/2014* (see www.hmrc.gov.uk/so/bulletin01-2014.pdf) HMRC comment that in most cases the value of the right to electricity will fall below the £40,000 notification threshold and no SDLT return will be required. However, this may not be so for larger installations, perhaps on commercial premises, and HMRC regard it as the responsibility of the taxpayer to check the point.

In the case of domestic solar panels, the common alternative arrangement is that the homeowner buys the panels and receives the full benefit of electricity generated either through free use or payment for feeding back into the grid. No lease is involved in this situation and no SDLT obligations arise.

Transfer of a lease or agreement for lease

6.15 In a straightforward case, the transfer of an existing lease to a new tenant (with no other change in terms and conditions) will be subject to SDLT in the same way as the transfer of any other interest in land. The new tenant will be subject to SDLT on any consideration given: (a) to the outgoing tenant; and (b) to the landlord (apart from ordinary rent) – for example, a lump sum paid to persuade the landlord to consent to the transfer. However, neither the rent payable under the lease nor any premium paid to the landlord by the outgoing tenant (eg in return for the landlord agreeing to release the tenant from the lease) will figure in the new tenant's SDLT liability. Equally, the assumption of normal tenant's obligations and undertakings (such as to maintain the property) do not count as consideration (*FA 2003, Sch 17A, para 17*). There are provisions at *FA 2003, Sch 17A, para 12A* designed to ensure that the assignment of an agreement for lease, rather than the lease itself, produces the same overall SDLT liability.

Liabilities which fall on transferee

6.16 Many cases are not straightforward, and it is always necessary for the new tenant to understand the full history of the lease, in order to determine whether the transfer, or the nature of the lease itself, may give rise to other SDLT liabilities and obligations. Additional obligations may arise in two situations. The first is where the rent was uncertain or variable when the lease was granted. If the lease is transferred to a new tenant before the SDLT liability is resolved, the new tenant inherits the obligation to make any necessary disclosures or further returns and to pay any additional SDLT once the uncertainty is resolved. See **6.37** et seq for an explanation of those obligations.

Relief claimed on original grant of lease

6.17 The second situation where the new tenant may incur unexpected liabilities is where one of a specified list of reliefs (see **6.20**) was claimed when the lease was granted (*FA 2003, Sch 17A, para 11*). If nothing has already happened to cause clawback of that relief, the first transfer of the lease which does not itself qualify for one of the specified list of reliefs is treated as the grant of a new lease for the remaining term of the actual lease and at the rent payable by the transferee. This means, for example, if there have been any rent increases between the dates of original grant and transfer, the current (higher) rent will be taken into account in calculating any SDLT payable. SDLT is also payable, in the normal way, on any premium which the new tenant pays to the landlord. HMRC consider that any amount paid by the new tenant to the outgoing tenant in respect of the transfer is also within the charge to SDLT, as would be the case for a straightforward transfer of a lease on which no relief had previously been claimed. It is logical that this should be the case, but it is by no means clear that the wording of the legislation supports this view.

6.18 SDLT is chargeable on the transferee, and not on the original lessee who claimed the relief. Therefore, strictly, this is not a clawback, it is merely a modification of the normal rules for determining a purchaser's SDLT liability. However, as the example below demonstrates, in practice the rules do lead to an effective clawback of part of the relief previously claimed, even though it is the new owner/tenant who has responsibility for the resulting SDLT.

6.19 The rules are not subject to any kind of time limitation: they apply on a disposal of the lease at any time in its life. Anyone acquiring a second-hand lease should check whether it will be subject to these special rules and seek protection from unexpected SDLT liabilities by way of warranties, indemnities, retentions or whatever may be thought appropriate.

6.20 The special rules apply where any of the following has been claimed on the grant of a lease:

(1) group, reconstruction or acquisition relief,

(2) sale and leaseback relief,

(3) charities relief,

(4) relief for transfers involving public bodies, or

(5) any relief brought forward from the stamp duty rules by regulations under *FA 2003, s 123(3)*.

Care must be taken in relation to the last of these, as many of the reliefs mentioned in the table at **5.68** fall into this category.

However, the special rules do not apply if the transfer itself qualifies for any of the reliefs in the list (not necessarily the same relief as that previously claimed), provided the transferee claims the relief in an SDLT return.

Example 6.5—Transfer of lease after relief claimed

On 1 March 2013, V plc granted a 25-year lease over commercial property to its subsidiary W Ltd at a rent of £100,000 per annum, subject to five-yearly upwards-only rent reviews. Group relief was claimed. On 1 March 2018, the scheduled rent review leads to a rent increase, to £110,000. On 1 June 2020,

W Ltd transfers the lease to an unrelated company X Ltd. X Ltd pays W Ltd £180,000 for the transfer and takes over all of the other terms and conditions of the lease.

X Ltd is not entitled to any relief in the list mentioned above, so the transfer is treated as the grant of a new lease for the remaining 17 years 9 months of the term, at an initial yearly rent of £110,000. This charge effectively claws back part of the relief claimed by W Ltd when the lease was first granted. In this example, it is worse than a simple clawback because it also takes account of the new, higher rent. In addition, in this example, X Ltd pays a sum to W Ltd for the transfer, and this will be subject to SDLT as if it was a premium. The SDLT chargeable on the premium would be £600 (£150,000 at 0% plus £30,000 at 2%). This particular example is worse than that. When X Ltd takes on the lease, a further rent review is due in less than five years. Therefore, the acquisition is treated as a grant of a lease for uncertain or variable rent. It will be necessary for X Ltd to review the position when the rent review occurs, submitting a further SDLT return and paying further SDLT as appropriate (see Example 6.12).

Shared ownership leases

6.21 In the context of affordable/social housing, arrangements are often made for the purchase of a part share in a dwelling. The purchaser then occupies the rest of the dwelling under a lease or tenancy. There are specific provisions (*FA 2003, Sch 9*) designed to remove or minimise any SDLT charge on such arrangements, and these are explained at **5.42** in relation to reliefs.

Variation of existing lease

6.22 The original rules dealing with the variation of an existing lease were substantially rewritten in 2006. A variation may give rise to SDLT obligations, depending on:

- the precise nature of the variation, including whether, in law, it amounts to a surrender and re-grant;
- whether either party gives consideration or is deemed to give consideration;
- when the variation occurs relative to the date(s) on which the term of the original lease began or was deemed to have begun (see **6.24–6.26**); and
- whether the original lease was granted under the stamp duty or SDLT regime.

Examples of variations

Increase in rent within first five years

6.23 An increase in rent in accordance with the terms of the lease (eg as a result of a rent review) does *not* arise from a variation. However, where such a change in the rent is possible within the first five years of the term, the rent will have been regarded as uncertain at the inception of the lease. This will have given rise to particular SDLT reporting obligations (see **6.37**).

6.24 A lease may be varied to increase the rent – that is, other than in accordance with the original terms of the lease. If this happens with effect from a date within five years of the beginning of the term, a new notional lease is normally deemed to be granted, covering the period from the effective date of the rent increase to the end of the original lease. The rent for the new notional lease is equal to the increase. This notional lease is then subject to SDLT (*FA 2003, Sch 17A, para 13*). The new notional lease may be linked with the original lease but is not necessarily so – this is a question of fact. These rules are disapplied where the variation arises from certain provisions relating to agricultural tenancies and holdings. In such cases, a variation has no immediate SDLT consequences.

Example 6.6—Rent increase in first five years

On 1 July 2016, Giovanni entered into a new ten-year lease of a storage and distribution depot at a yearly rent of £25,000 and no premium, with a market rent review due on 1 July 2021. An SDLT return was submitted accordingly. The lease restricted activities in the premises to storage, repackaging and distribution. Giovanni always intended in due course to carry out repairs of faulty goods returned to the depot (and had mentioned this to the landlord when taking the lease on). The landlord agrees to vary the lease to permit this, in return for an increase in rent to £28,000 from 1 January 2020. An additional lease is deemed to come into existence on that date, for a term equal to the remaining 6.5 years of the original lease and at a yearly rent of £3,000. Giovanni must decide whether any SDLT arises on this deemed additional lease and, if so, must submit a further SDLT return accordingly. Since it was always expected that the lease would be varied in this way, it seems likely that the original lease and the deemed additional lease are linked. On this basis, additional SDLT will arise on the deemed lease; see **6.61** and Example 6.22. HMRC appear to accept that the deemed additional lease should not be regarded as of uncertain or variable rent, even though a market rent review is due in respect of the (real) lease just 18 months later.

Increase in rent after first five years

6.25 If the original lease was granted before 1 December 2003, or after that date but with the benefit of the implementation transition provisions (see **4.93**), it will have been subject to the stamp duty regime. A variation to increase the rent after the first five years of the term will not be subject to SDLT, provided it is, in law, a mere variation and not the grant of a new lease (SDLTM10025).

Example 6.7—Original lease under stamp duty

Lucy is tenant of a 1960s office building under a 25-year lease which was granted on 1 January 2000. Rent is increased every five years in line with inflation and is currently below the market rent for an equivalent modern building. The building requires significant work to bring it up to current standards. Lucy agrees to a variation of the lease to provide for market level rent reviews at 1 January 2015 and 2020. In return, the landlord agrees to arrange and fund refurbishment of the building. Because the lease was granted under the stamp duty rules, this variation has no SDLT or stamp duty consequences.

6.26 An increase in rent after the first five years, whether as a result of a rent review, variation or any other matter short of renewal, extension of term or surrender and re-grant, is also ignored if the original lease was subject to SDLT, provided the increase takes effect on or after 17 July 2013 (*FA 2013, Sch 41, para 7*). Prior to that date it was necessary to consider whether the increase was 'abnormal'. The old rules are outlined briefly at **6.27.** If, exceptionally, there is a current need to consider whether SDLT liabilities arise on a rent increase taking effect before 17 July 2013, previous editions of this book should be consulted for guidance. In the Finance Bill debates the government explained that the old rules were being abolished because it was accepted that SDLT avoidance by artificially depressing rent for the first five years of a lease was unlikely to happen. However they made it clear that the matter would be reconsidered should evidence of such avoidance emerge. In practice, it seems likely that it would be possible for HMRC to rely on the GAAR to counter any such avoidance, see **9.3**.

Abnormal rent increases – old rules

6.27 The concept of abnormal rent increases only applied to rent increases on leases granted or deemed granted within the SDLT regime, which took effect after the first five years of the lease and before 17 July 2013. The general principle was that a rent increase was abnormal if the new rent was greater than the 'rent previously taxed' by more than 20% (measured on a straight-line basis) for each complete year elapsed since the starting date for the rent previously taxed. The rent previously taxed was the last rent by reference to which SDLT had been charged. A five-step calculation was necessary to determine the matter. If there was an abnormal increase in rent, this was deemed to give rise to a new lease, running in parallel with the old, for the amount of rent which had not previously been subjected to SDLT. This notional lease was deemed to have been granted on the day on which the new higher rent first became payable (which may not be the same as the date from which the new rent took effect).

Decrease in rent

6.28 A decrease in rent is specifically treated as an acquisition of a chargeable interest by the tenant (*FA 2003, Sch 17A, para 15A(1)*). If the tenant gives or is deemed to give consideration, this will be within the charge to SDLT. Normal compliance rules apply – if no consideration is given or deemed to be given, or if the consideration (either actual or deemed) is below £40,000, there will be no need to notify HMRC; otherwise, an SDLT return will be required, even if no tax is actually payable.

Decrease in term

6.29 If a lease is varied to decrease the term, this is treated as the acquisition of a chargeable interest by the landlord (*FA 2003, Sch 17A, para 15A(2)*). If the landlord gives or is deemed to give any consideration, this will be within the charge to SDLT. However, if the tenant gives consideration, for example in order to have the term of an onerous lease reduced, this will not be subject to SDLT.

Other variations

6.30 The most common types of variation of a lease are covered by specific rules as set out in preceding paragraphs. All other variations are treated as the acquisition of a chargeable interest by the tenant only if the tenant gives (or is deemed to give) consideration in money or money's worth (*FA 2003, Sch 17A, para 15A(1A)*). Other variations are specifically excluded from the scope of SDLT (*FA 2003, s 43(3)(d)*).

Surrender

6.31 The surrender of a lease is the acquisition of a chargeable interest by the landlord (*FA 2003, s 43(3)(b)*). Therefore, if the landlord gives or is deemed to give chargeable consideration, this will be within the scope of SDLT.

Surrender and re-grant

6.32 Whether a variation of a lease amounts to a surrender and re-grant is a matter of law and, in any case of doubt, appropriate legal advice should be sought. However, it is generally true that a variation which does not overtly state that the old lease is surrendered is not likely to amount to a surrender and re-grant unless it varies the term or the extent of the premises demised.

Where a surrender and re-grant occurs, SDLT is chargeable in respect of rent under the new lease in the normal way. Any obligation to notify the transaction and pay SDLT falls on the tenant.

6.33 If the original lease was granted under the stamp duty regime, no credit is given for any stamp duty previously paid. For this reason, it is generally best to avoid surrender and re-grant of a lease at rent where the old lease was granted under the stamp duty regime.

6.34 However, if the original lease was granted under the SDLT regime, and if the premises under the two leases are 'the same or substantially the same', credit may be available in respect of rent for the 'overlap period'; see **6.83**.

6.35 Where rent under the new lease is variable or uncertain, it should be noted that the overlap relief is ignored in measuring the highest 12-month rent in the first five years, in order to determine the deemed rent for Year 6 onwards. The surrender of the old lease does not count as chargeable consideration for the grant of the new, nor does the grant of the new count as chargeable consideration for the surrender of the old (*FA 2003, Sch 17A, para 16*). If the landlord gives chargeable consideration for the surrender of the old lease other than the grant of the new lease, or is deemed to give such consideration, it may be necessary for the landlord to notify the surrender as a separate transaction and pay any SDLT arising on that.

Example 6.8—Superseding lease, no credit for stamp duty

The facts are as in Example 6.7 above. However, the landlord is only prepared to fund the refurbishment if Lucy agrees to a longer lease. Therefore, on 1 January 2015, the original lease is surrendered in return for a new 15-year lease at a market rent and with five-yearly market rent reviews. SDLT is payable on this in the normal way. Because the original lease was dealt with under the stamp duty rules, no credit is available for the stamp duty already paid in respect of the 'unused' period of the old lease. The SDLT liability would be lower if the parties agreed to amend the old lease, as in the original example, and at the same time enter into a 'reversionary lease' to cover the period from expiry of the old lease (31 December 2025) to the intended end date of the new lease (see **6.36**).

Example 6.9—Superseding lease, credit for SDLT

The facts are as in Example 6.6 above. However, shortly after the 1 July 2021 rent review (which increases the yearly rent to £35,000), Giovanni concludes that the use of the premises would be enhanced if a small patch of land to the side were added to the lease. The lease is amended on 1 October 2021 to include this, with no additional rent payable. At the same time, the term of the lease is extended by five years to 30 June 2031. This extension of both term and premises is deemed to be a surrender and re-grant of the lease. It is considered that the additional land is small enough for the old and new leases to be regarded as leases of 'substantially the same' premises. SDLT is payable on the 'new' lease, which is for 9 years 9 months at a rent of £35,000 per annum, but credit is given for the £28,000 per annum rent which would have been payable under the old lease (including the deemed additional lease at rent of £3,000 per annum) for the period to 30 June 2026. The rent (before discounting to NPV) to be taken into account in the SDLT calculation for each year of the new lease is as follows:

Period	**Calculation**	**Deemed rent (£)**
Each of 5 years to 30/9/2026	35,000 – 28,000	7,000
Each of 4 years to 30/9/2030	–	35,000
Period to 30/6/2031	9 months at 35,000 pa	26,750

The highest deemed rent in any 12-month period in the first five years of the new lease appears to be £7,000; however, the credit for rent under the old lease is ignored in determining this 'highest rent' figure, so the deemed rent for periods after the end of the overlap period reverts to the highest figure before relief, which is £35,000 in this case.

Reversionary leases

6.36 Varying a lease to increase the term amounts, in law, to a surrender and re-grant, and is subject to SDLT accordingly, as set out above. Sometimes, an alternative is for the parties to enter into a further lease of the premises, covering the period from expiry of the current lease to the desired later expiry date. When this happens, the lease is granted before its start date. The 'effective date' (see **4.99** and **6.74**) for SDLT purposes is the date of grant, not the commencement date. However, the commencement date is used in calculating the NPV of rents, so no benefit is gained from the fact that rent will not become payable under the new lease until some future date. The original and reversionary leases may be successive linked leases if the reversionary lease was contemplated when the original lease was implemented (see **6.59**). However, this is a question of fact and the leases are not necessarily linked.

Example 6.10—Reversionary lease

Gwen occupies a shop unit under a ten-year lease which expires on 30 September 2021. She wants to remain in occupation beyond this date and, on 1 December 2020, a reversionary lease is executed for a further ten years from 1 October 2021 at a rent of £20,000 per annum. Gwen must submit an SDLT return no later than 15 December 2020 and pay any SDLT due on the new lease by the same date. The NPV of the rents, calculated using 1 October 2021 as the start date, is £166,332. The lease is not linked with the old lease or any other, so the SDLT payable is 1% of £(166,332 – 150,000), which is £163.

ONGOING OBLIGATIONS

SDLT liability not finally determined when lease was granted

6.37 Sometimes, when a lease is granted, the rent for the first five years is actually or potentially variable or uncertain – for example, because the rent depends on the tenant's business results or there is a rent review scheduled within the first five years. (Note, however, that rent increases in line with the Retail Price Index are ignored (*FA 2003, Sch 17A, para 7(5)*).) In such cases, it is not possible finally to determine the SDLT liability until the uncertainty is resolved, potentially after the end of the first five years. Once the rent for the first five years is known, the deemed rent for the rest of the lease can be determined (see **6.48**). Any uncertainty or variability after the end of Year 5 is ignored. As with other land transactions, the return must initially be completed on the basis of a reasonable estimate. The return must then be amended once the consideration is finally determined (*FA 2003, Sch 17A, paras 7, 8*).

Example 6.11—Variable or uncertain rent

On 23 April 2020, Richard grants Harold a 25-year lease of the site for a theme park. The lease requires Harold to construct and open the theme park within two years of grant. No premium is payable. Rent is set at a base level of £10,000 per year but, from Year 4 onwards, the rent is to be 5% of the turnover of the park, if this is higher than £10,000 (additional rent based on turnover to be estimated and paid quarterly with adjustment at the year-end). Reasonably conservative business projections indicate that 5% of turnover will be £8,000 in Year 4 and £12,000 in Year 5.

By 7 May 2020, Harold must submit an SDLT return on the basis of a reasonable estimate of rent, and it seems that £10,000 for Years 1 to 4 and £12,000 for Year 5 would be justifiable. Once the rent for Years 4 and 5 is finally determined (presumably, fairly early during Year 6), Harold must consider whether a further return is required. If the actual rent exceeds the estimate used in the original return, a further return must be submitted and additional SDLT paid. If the actual rent is less than the estimate, Harold is entitled (but not required) to submit an amended return and claim repayment of any SDLT overpaid. See **8.17** for details of submission of further or amended returns.

6.38 Prior to 17 July 2013, potential difficulties arose when a tenant took possession on the basis of an agreement for lease, the final lease being granted some time later, perhaps once minor details had been settled. Such a lease will often be expressed as commencing from the date on which the tenant takes possession with a rent review five years from that date. Previously, for SDLT purposes, the final lease would have been treated as beginning on the date of grant and the first rent review would have been due less than five years later. Hence, a lease with normal five-yearly rent reviews and no other uncertainty over rent would nonetheless often have been treated as a lease with variable or uncertain rent for SDLT purposes. The rules were amended by *FA 2013, Sch 41, para 6* with effect from 17 July 2013 to provide that the final lease is treated as commencing on the date of substantial performance, which will generally coincide with the commencement date stated in the lease. This should prevent such leases, with normal five-yearly rent reviews, being treated as having variable or uncertain rent.

Example 6.12—Rent review within five years of final execution

Tom enters into an agreement for a 12-year lease of a workshop and the agreement is substantially performed by Tom taking possession on 1 November 2020. The lease is finally executed on 20 February 2021, is expressed as ending on 31 October 2032, and provides for rent reviews at 1 November 2025 and 2030.

Under the old rules the term of the lease would have been treated as commencing when it was executed on 20 February 2021. The first rent review falls within five years of this date, so the lease would have been regarded as being at an uncertain or variable rent. When the first rent review was settled, it would have been necessary to review the original SDLT return and calculation. If (as is likely) this would have led to a greater SDLT liability than originally disclosed, a further return would have had to be made and additional SDLT be paid.

The new rules apply to leases with an effective date on or after 17 July 2013 – that is, which are executed, or substantially performed if earlier, on or after that date. The old rules continue to apply to leases which were substantially performed before 17 July 2013, even if they are finally executed on or after that date.

Under the new rules, the term of the lease is treated as commencing on 1 November 2020. The first rent review falls at least five years after this date so the rent is not regarded as variable or uncertain. SDLT obligations can be dealt with on the basis of the starting rent alone and no further action will be necessary when the rent reviews occur.

6.39 Care is needed when the date of the first rent review falls in the final quarter of the fifth year of the term. This may occur, for example, when rent is payable on traditional quarter days but the lease commences on some other date. In this situation, it may be possible to treat the first rent review as falling five years after commencement of the lease, so that the variable or uncertain rent provisions do not apply (*FA 2003, Sch 17A, para 7A*). However, in applying this rule, it appears that the precise wording of the lease will be important. The lease must provide that the first rent review is due five years after a specified date which itself falls within the three months before the commencement of the lease. It appears that, if the lease merely states 'the first rent review will be on [date within the last quarter of the first five years]', without specifically referring to a date within the three months before the lease began, the rule will not apply and the lease will be treated as having variable or uncertain rent. There does not appear to be any policy reason for this restriction, so it may simply be a case of poorly worded legislation. It is not known whether HMRC allow any flexibility in applying this rule.

Example 6.13—Rent review in final quarter of Year 5

Sales Ltd leases a shop unit from Retail Mall plc for ten years from 1 January 2021. Sales Ltd takes possession on 1 January 2021 but the lease is not finally executed until 10 February 2021. The lease provides for a rent review after five years and, to fit with Retail Mall's other leases, this is due on 25 December 2025. Sales Ltd must make an SDLT return no later than 15 January 2021. Providing the rent review clause of the lease is appropriately worded (on the lines of 'the rent review shall occur five years after 25 December 2020'), the fact that it falls before the fifth anniversary of both substantial performance of the agreement and grant of the lease itself will not cause the rent to be regarded as variable or uncertain.

As a result of the changes introduced by *FA 2013, Sch 41, para 6*, it no longer matters exactly when the final lease is executed, provided it is before the first rent review.

MAKING AND AMENDING SDLT RETURNS

6.40 SDLT returns relating to lease transactions are made and amended in just the same ways as for other UK land transactions; see **Chapter 8**. Some forms/sections of the return apply only to transactions involving leases.

If the return is completed online, these sections only appear if appropriate entries are made in the early sections to indicate that leases are involved. This is set out more fully in **Chapter 8**. As with other transactions, there is generally no prescribed form for amending a return, and amendments are made by writing to SDLT Compliance at Birmingham Stamp Office (see **Appendix A**). HMRC do say that minor amendments may be notified by telephone, but written communications have the advantage of leaving a record.

CALCULATING THE LIABILITY

What is consideration?

6.41 SDLT is charged on 'chargeable consideration' which is defined for leases, as for other transactions, as 'any consideration in money or money's worth given … by the purchaser or a person connected with him' (*FA 2003, Sch 4, para 1*). In relation to the grant or variation of a lease, consideration may be in the form of rent and/or premium. Since the tax treatments of the two forms of consideration differ, it is important to distinguish between them (see **6.44**). In relation to both rent and premium, the usual valuation rules apply to consideration other than in cash and to consideration in a currency other than sterling (see **4.19**), as do the limited exemptions where the consideration includes the carrying out of works (see **4.26**) or the transaction qualifies for 'PFI relief' (see **5.17**).

6.42 When a lease is surrendered in consideration for the grant of another lease, the surrender and grant do not count as consideration for each other (*FA 2003, Sch 17A, para 16*). The acceptance of normal tenant's obligations other than payment of rent and premium does not count as consideration when a lease is granted (*FA 2003, Sch 17A, para 10*). The acceptance of such obligations *including* payment of rent does not count as consideration for the transfer of a lease (*FA 2003, Sch 17A, para 17*).

Rent

6.43 There is no comprehensive definition of rent, so it must be taken as having its ordinary commercial meaning of consideration paid by a tenant, usually periodically, for use or occupation of the property. Where rent is payable other than in sterling cash, it must be valued in the same way as other consideration, at the effective date of the lease; see **4.19**. A single sum expressed as payable in respect of rent and other matters, without apportionment, is to be treated as entirely rent (*FA 2003, Sch 17A, para 6*). To minimise the SDLT payable, it may therefore be important to ensure that 'inclusive' rents are overtly apportioned, in the terms and conditions of the lease, between rent proper and other items such as insurance, cleaning and maintenance. At SDLTM11015, HMRC state that:

> 'Service charges payable from tenant to landlord are a payment for the services the tenant will use during the lease. As such, service charges are not rent and therefore are not chargeable consideration for SDLT purposes and are excluded from the calculation of tax as long as the payment of the service charge has been either:
>
> - provided for in the lease as a separate figure or
> - expressed in the lease as part of an inclusive rent payment and apportioned on a just reasonable basis.
>
> The fact that a service charge is reserved in a lease as rent does not make it rent for SDLT purposes'.

In practice, therefore, HMRC seem willing to accept a reasonable apportionment even where this is not explicit in the lease. The apportionment, whether explicit in the lease or negotiated with HMRC, must be on a just and reasonable basis (*FA 2003, Sch 4, para 4*).

Example 6.14

Albert leases an office suite in a larger building owned by Big Office Co Ltd on a ten-year lease, terminable by either party on one year's notice. The rent is £30,000 per annum plus a proportionate share of an insurance premium paid by Big Office and covering the whole building. The rent includes heating/air conditioning and regular cleaning, but amounts are not allocated to these in the lease. Light and power are separately metered and charged. The insurance premium is clearly identified and, since it merely passes on actual cost, is presumably 'just and reasonable', so it will not form part of the rent for SDLT purposes. Since the remaining rent is not allocated between real rent and matters such as cleaning and heating, strictly it is all rent for SDLT purposes. The parties would be well advised to insert a reasonable allocation into the lease. However, even in the absence of numbers in the lease itself, HMRC may be persuaded to accept an allocation. They may require evidence from Big Office to support amounts allocated to non-chargeable matters.

6.44 An anti-avoidance provision at *FA 2003, Sch 17A, para 18A* is designed to prevent a premium being disguised as rent, which would normally give rise to a lower SDLT liability. If the tenant pays any loan or deposit in excess of a normal 'rent deposit', the loan or deposit is to be taxed as a premium, even though it may be repayable (typically by offset against rent payments as they fall due).

New leases

6.45 When a new lease is granted or deemed to be granted, SDLT must be calculated separately on any rent and on any premium or deemed premium (*FA 2003, Sch 5*). The two components are then simply added to give the SDLT liability. As in other cases, any VAT chargeable must be included in both rent and premium. However, if VAT arises as a result of the landlord exercising the 'option to tax' *after* the 'effective date' (see **4.99** and **6.74**) of the transaction, this does not have to be taken into account (*FA 2003, Sch 4, para 2*).

SDLT on a premium

6.46 A premium is subject to SDLT at normal rates up to 12% on a progressive basis for a transaction consisting entirely of residential property (however the higher rates of SDLT of up to 15%, on a progressive basis, for additional dwellings and dwellings purchased by companies, may apply (see **4.56**) or a slab rate of 15% could apply in certain circumstances (see **4.87**)) and up to 5% on a progressive basis for any other lump sum payment for an interest in land which is non-residential property (see **4.37**). For transactions with an 'effective date' (see **4.99** and **6.74**) on or before 16 March 2016, if a lease of non-residential property was subject to a rent of £1,000 or more per annum, the zero tax rate for a premium up to £150,000 was replaced by a 1% rate. However, this rule was abolished by *FA 2016, s 116(11)*. This means that for a lease of non-residential property, granted on or after 17 March 2016, SDLT will only be payable on a premium if the amount of that premium exceeds £150,000.

For first-time buyer's relief (see **5.47** et seq) to be available the 'chargeable interest' (see **4.14**) acquired must be a 'major interest' (see **4.11**) in a single dwelling. For these purposes 'major interest' will include the grant of a new lease. However, a lease which has less than 21 years to run at the start of the day after the 'effective date' (see **4.99** and **6.74**) of the transaction is specifically excluded from the definition of a 'major interest' (*FA 2003, Sch 6ZA, para 8*). This means that the relief for first-time buyers will not apply to the grant of a new lease for 21 years or less.

SDLT on rent

6.47 To calculate the SDLT on the rent, it is first necessary to establish the amount of rent to be taken into account for each year of the lease. If the lease is no longer than five years, the rent for SDLT purposes is simply the actual rent. As noted at **6.37**, if these amounts are not determined at the 'effective date' (see **4.99** and **6.74**) of the lease, SDLT must be paid based on a reasonable estimate. A further return must be made, with payment of any additional SDLT, once the amounts are finally determined. If the final figures indicate that SDLT has been overpaid, an amendment to the return may be submitted and any overpayment reclaimed, but this is not compulsory.

Rent after fifth year

6.48 If the lease is longer than five years but the rent is fixed and at a constant rate throughout the term, again SDLT is based on the actual rent. However, this is probably unusual since most leases for more than five years are likely to provide for rent reviews. If the lease provides for the rent to change over the term for any reason, whether certainly or contingently, the following rules apply to determine the rent for SDLT purposes (*FA 2003, Sch 17A, para 7*):

(1) For the first five years, the actual rent is used.

(2) For each year after the first five, the rent is assumed to be equal to the highest rent for any consecutive 12-month period in the first five years.

This means that an abnormal 'spike' in the rent in the first five years can lead to a very large increase in SDLT payable, as the highest 12-month rent in those early years will form the basis of the deemed rent for later years (see Examples 6.16 and 6.19).

6.49 The rule applies even if the actual rent is known for periods after the first five years, so known increases after the first five years are ignored (see Example 6.15).

Example 6.15—Actual rent after Year 5 ignored

Amy grants Toni a 20-year lease of a shop at an initial rent of £10,000 per annum. The lease is executed on the start date without prior substantial performance. The lease provides for five-yearly rent reviews, with the rent increasing by at least 50% at each review, or to market rent if higher. It is therefore known that the rent will be at least £15,000, £22,500 and £33,750 per annum from the start of Years 6, 11 and 16 respectively. However, for the purposes of the SDLT return at the start of the lease, the rent is treated as £10,000 per annum throughout the term of the lease. This is because the rent is £10,000 per annum for the first five years (rule 1), and the highest 12-month rent in the first five years is also £10,000 (rule 2).

Example 6.16—Effect of brief spike in rent in first five years

Julie granted an eight-year lease of a restaurant to Ken, commencing on 1 December 2020. The lease was executed on the start date without prior substantial performance. No premium was payable. Rent is £10,000 per quarter inc VAT but, for any quarter in which the restaurant turnover exceeds £100,000, the next quarter's rent is increased by one-tenth of the excess. Over the first five years, the restaurant turnover exceeds £100,000 only in the quarters ending 31 May 2021 (when the rent for the following quarter is agreed at £11,000) and 28 February 2022 (when the rent for the following quarter is £12,300). These increases are not known when the lease is executed, and an initial return is submitted on the basis that the rent is £10,000 per quarter (£40,000 per annum) throughout. At the end of the first five years, a further return is required, with SDLT based on the following rent figures:

Year 1	£41,000	Three quarters at £10,000 plus one at £11,000
Year 2	£42,300	Three quarters at £10,000 plus one at £12,300
Each of Years 3 to 5	£40,000	Four quarters at £10,000
Each of Years 6 to 8	£43,300	This is the rent for the 12 months from 1 June 2021 to 31 May 2022, being the highest rent for any 12-month period in the first five years.

6.50 Once the rent for each year is determined (or estimated if uncertain at the outset), the net present value (NPV) of that rent over the life of the lease must be calculated, using the formula and discount rate specified in the legislation (*FA 2003, Sch 5, paras 3, 8*). Since the inception of SDLT, the discount rate has been 3.5%, but in future this may be varied by regulation. For these purposes, the length of the lease is taken as the term specified in the lease, ignoring any break clauses, other right to terminate early, or any right to extend or renew. However, if any right to extend or renew is subsequently exercised, the resulting further lease or extension may be linked with the original lease, whether successively or not; see **6.58** et seq.

6.51 In simple terms, the rent for the first 12 months is divided by 1.035 to give its discounted value, the rent for the second 12 months is divided by $(1.035)^2$, and so on to the end of the term of the lease. The discounted rent figures for all years are then totalled. If this total does not exceed the relevant threshold (currently £150,000 for non-residential or mixed property, or £125,000 for residential property: *FA 2003, Sch 5, para 2*), no SDLT is chargeable on the rent. The rates and bands used to calculate the SDLT liability on rent, for both residential property and non-residential or mixed use property, are set out at **6.3**.

6.52 It should not be unduly difficult to set up a spreadsheet to perform SDLT calculations for leases. However, an SDLT calculator for this purpose is provided on the HMRC website at www.gov.uk/stamp-duty-land-tax. The HMRC calculator works for most cases, provided the correct information is input, and its use is recommended. However, it is purely a mechanical aid. It will not detect whether the correct information is entered, and HMRC have made it clear that they will hold the taxpayer responsible if the calculator gives incorrect answers because incorrect information has been entered. Therefore, it is important to have a full understanding of the nature of the transaction when entering information into the calculator, to guard against errors. A copy of the output (printed or electronic) should be retained in case of any future query.

Example 6.17—Calculation of NPV

On 1 May 2019, Jeremy agrees to grant Kate a ten-year lease of a hotel at an annual rent of £25,000 inc VAT and for a premium of £250,000. There is an upwards-only rent review on the fifth anniversary. The lease is granted on 1 July 2019 without previously having been substantially performed. The 'effective date' (see **4.99** and **6.74**) is therefore 1 July 2019, and the rent review is due on 1 July 2024. The SDLT can be calculated manually as follows:

Year	**Actual rent for SDLT purposes**	**Discounted rent**
1	£25,000	£24,154
2	£25,000	£23,337
3	£25,000	£22,548
4	£25,000	£21,786
5	£25,000	£21,049
6	£25,000	£20,337
7	£25,000	£19,649
8	£25,000	£18,985
9	£25,000	£18,343
10	£25,000	£17,722
Total discounted rent		£207,910
Less zero rate band		(£150,000)
SDLT charged at 1% on		£57,910
SDLT on rent		£579
SDLT on premium: £250,000 (£150,000 at 0% + £100,000 at 2%)		£2,000
Total SDLT (on rent and premium)		£2,579

6.53 Alternatively, the HMRC calculator may be used. This has a series of input screens, as follows:

First screen:

On the first screen 'Leasehold' should be selected as the transaction comprises the grant of a new lease after which 'continue' should be selected.

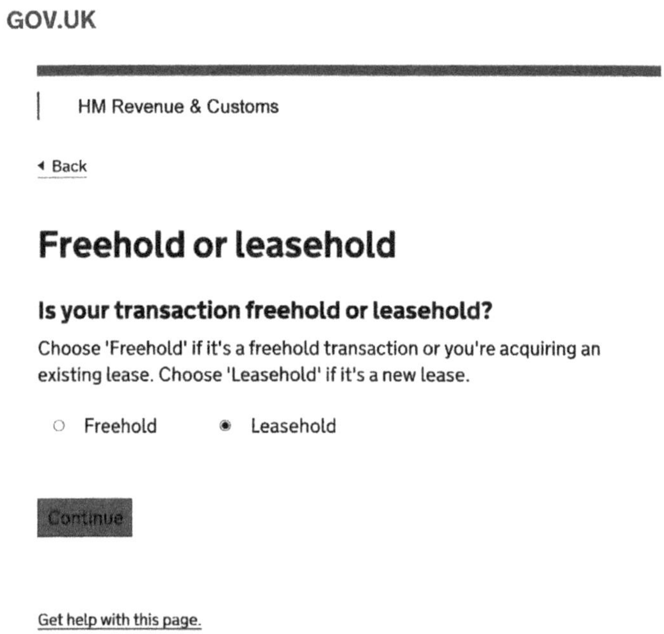

Second screen:

As the new lease is being granted over a hotel, 'Non-residential' should be selected after which 'continue' should be selected.

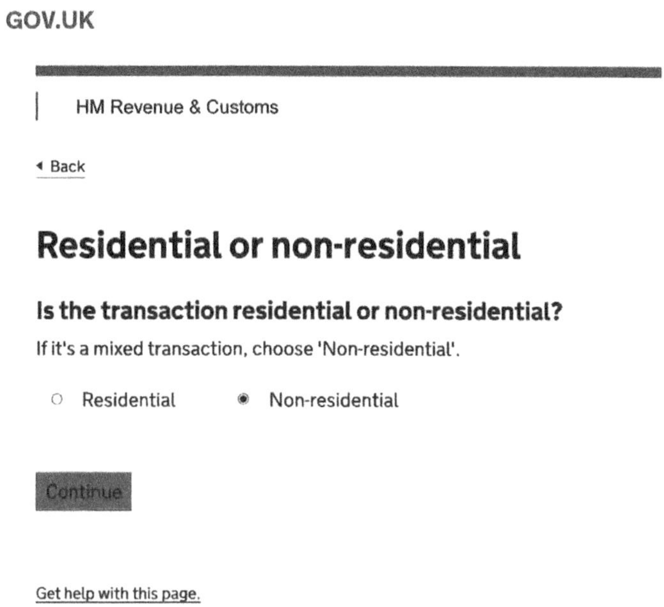

GOV.UK

HM Revenue & Customs

◂ Back

Residential or non-residential

Is the transaction residential or non-residential?

If it's a mixed transaction, choose 'Non-residential'.

○ Residential ◉ Non-residential

Continue

Get help with this page.

On the third screen insertion of the effective date (see **4.99** and **6.74**) and clicking ‘continue’ leads to the next three screens, as shown below: the first is headed ‘Lease dates’, in which the start and end dates of the lease are entered, the second is headed ‘Lease premium’ in which the amount of any premium is entered; and the third is headed ‘Rent’ in which the rent for the first five years of the term of the lease is entered.

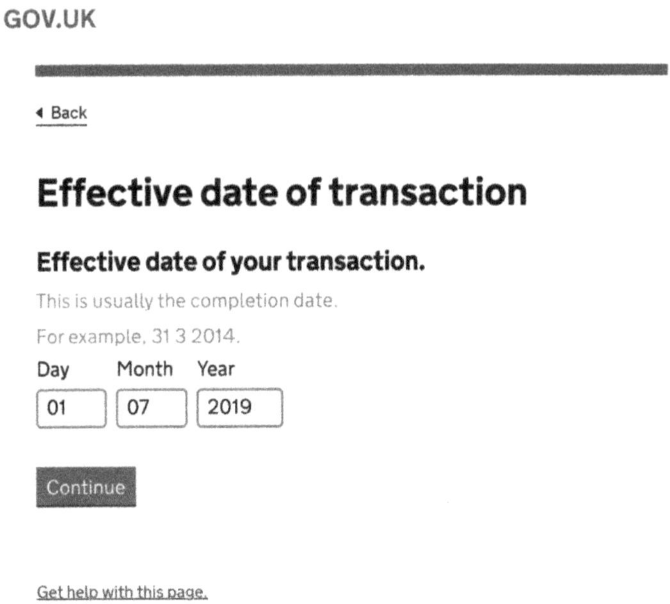

GOV.UK

Back

Effective date of transaction

Effective date of your transaction.

This is usually the completion date.

For example, 31 3 2014.

Day	Month	Year
01	07	2019

Continue

Get help with this page.

GOV.UK

◂ Back

Lease dates

Start date shown in your lease.

This is the date your term starts.

For example, 31 3 2014.

Day	Month	Year
01	07	2019

End date shown in your lease.

This is the date your term ends.

For example, 31 3 2017.

Day	Month	Year
30	06	2029

Continue

Get help with this page.

GOV.UK

HM Revenue & Customs

◂ Back

Lease premium

Total premium payable.

Find this in your lease.

£ 250000

Is your lease premium less than £40,000?

Continue

Get help with this page.

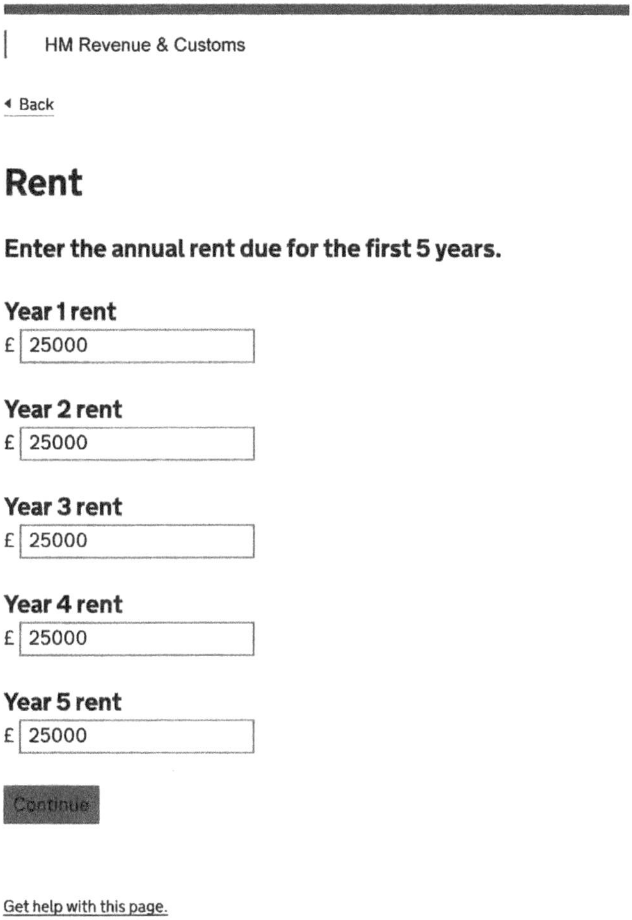

HM Revenue & Customs

◂ Back

Rent

Enter the annual rent due for the first 5 years.

Year 1 rent

£ 25000

Year 2 rent

£ 25000

Year 3 rent

£ 25000

Year 4 rent

£ 25000

Year 5 rent

£ 25000

Continue

Get help with this page.

6.54 As discussed at **6.46,** where the grant of a lease over non-residential property (see **4.38**) had an 'effective date' (see **4.99** and **6.74**) on or before 16 March 2016, and that lease was subject to a rent of £1,000 or more per annum (referred to as the 'relevant rent' in *FA 2003, Sch 5, para 9A*), the zero tax rate for a premium of up to £150,000 was replaced by a 1% rate. However, this rule was abolished by *FA 2016, s 116(11)* for leases granted on or after 17 March 2016. Consequently, as the lease in Example 6.17 was granted on 1 July 2019 the premium benefits from the zero rate band of £150,000 and the SDLT chargeable on the premium is £2,000 (£150,000 at 0% plus £100,000 at 2%).

Example 6.18—Use of HMRC calculator

Using the numbers from Example 6.17 above, the output from the calculator is:

GOV.UK

◂ Back

Check your answers

Start again (https://www.gov.uk/calculate-stamp-duty-land-tax)

Freehold or leasehold	Leasehold	Change
Residential or non-residential	Non-residential	Change
Effective date of transaction	1 July 2019	Change
Start date as specified in lease	1 July 2019	Change
End date as specified in lease	30 June 2029	Change
Term of lease	10 years 0 days	
Premium	£250,000	Change
Year 1 rent	£25,000	Change
Year 2 rent	£25,000	Change
Year 3 rent	£25,000	Change
Year 4 rent	£25,000	Change

Year 5 rent	£25,000	Change
Highest 12 monthly rent	£50,000	

Calculate your SDLT

Get help with this page.

GOV.UK

◂ Back

Result

Results based on SDLT rules from 17 March 2016

Total amount of tax for this transaction	£3,762	
Net present value	£326,291	
SDLT on rent	£1,762	Detail
SDLT on premium	£2,000	Detail

Results based on SDLT rules before 17 March 2016

You may be entitled to pay SDLT using the old rules if you exchanged contracts before 17 March 2016.

Total amount of tax for this transaction	£4,262	
Net present value	£326,291	
SDLT on rent	£1,762	Detail
SDLT on premium (1%)	£2,500	

You can print your calculation.

Or you can start again (https://www.gov.uk/calculate-stamp-duty-land-tax).

Go to the GOV.UK homepage for SDLT.

What did you think of this service? (https://www.gov.uk/feedback-survey/?origin=SDLTC)

6.55 Note that the 'Check your answers' screen shows all of the entries made on the input screens, so it is easy to check there have been no transcription errors. The results based on the SDLT rules before 17 March 2016 have no application as the agreement to enter into the lease was made on 1 May 2019, ie after 16 March 2016, and therefore the transitional rules (see **6.3**) are not in point.

Example 6.19—HMRC calculator, spike in early rentals

Facts are as in Example 6.17, except that the rent for the period from 1 July 2020 to 30 June 2021 is doubled to £50,000 in recognition of expected better business from a major international sporting tournament. This means that the rent for Year 2 will be £50,000, and that will be the highest rent for any consecutive 12 months in the first five years of the term of the lease. The output from the calculator is as follows:

GOV.UK

◂ Back

Check your answers

Start again (https://www.gov.uk/calculate-stamp-duty-land-tax)

Freehold or leasehold	Leasehold	Change
Residential or non-residential	Non-residential	Change
Effective date of transaction	1 July 2019	Change
Start date as specified in lease	1 July 2019	Change
End date as specified in lease	30 June 2029	Change
Term of lease	10 years 0 days	
Premium	£250,000	Change
Year 1 rent	£25,000	Change
Year 2 rent	£50,000	Change
Year 3 rent	£25,000	Change
Year 4 rent	£25,000	Change

Year 5 rent	£25,000	Change
Highest 12 monthly rent	£25,000	

Calculate your SDLT

Get help with this page.

GOV.UK

◂ Back

Result

Results based on SDLT rules from 17 March 2016

Total amount of tax for this transaction	£2,579	
Net present value	£207,915	
SDLT on rent	£579	Detail
SDLT on premium	£2,000	Detail

Results based on SDLT rules before 17 March 2016

You may be entitled to pay SDLT using the old rules if you exchanged contracts before 17 March 2016.

Total amount of tax for this transaction	£3,079	
Net present value	£207,915	
SDLT on rent	£579	Detail
SDLT on premium (1%)	£2,500	

You can print your calculation.

Or you can start again (https://www.gov.uk/calculate-stamp-duty-land-tax).

Go to the GOV.UK homepage for SDLT.

What did you think of this service? (https://www.gov.uk/feedback-survey/?origin=SDLTC)

6.56 The substantial increase in the SDLT charge on the rental element illustrates the effect of a temporary increase in rent during the first five years, as rent for every year after the first five is assumed to be equal to the highest rent for *any* consecutive 12-month period in the first five years. Where rent is variable during the first five years, it is important to establish the precise manner of variation and the correct attribution of rent to each period, as specified by the lease (*FA 2003, Sch 17A, para 7*; see **6.73**).

The results based on the SDLT rules before 17 March 2016 are not relevant as the agreement to enter into the lease was made on 1 May 2019, ie after 16 March 2016 and the transitional provisions (see **6.3**) have no application.

Connected company rule

6.57 The normal rule applies, that if the 'purchaser' (the lessee or, in the case of a surrender, the landlord) is a company connected with the other party, the consideration is taken to be at least equal to the market value of the lease in question (*FA 2003, s 53*). Note that it does not matter whether the 'vendor' is a company, individual or other entity. Application of the rule depends only on the 'purchaser' being a company which is connected with the 'vendor'. This is subject to the same exceptions as apply to other transactions (see **4.29**). Where this rule applies to the grant of a lease, it does not lead to any deemed adjustment of the actual rent. If the rent charged under the lease is less than a full market rent, it is assumed that the lease will have a capital value. The amount of this capital value is taxed as a deemed premium.

Example 6.20—Lease to connected company

On 24 June 2020 Maria grants to her family trading company, PPM Ltd, a ten-year lease of a barn on her farm, for use as a storage facility. The lease is at a flat rent of £5,000 per annum with no provision for rent reviews. The NPV of rent over the life of the lease is clearly below the £150,000 threshold. However, it is acknowledged that a current market rent would be £30,000 and a lease at the actual rent of £5,000 would command a market premium of £200,000. The lease is therefore subject to SDLT on this premium and the SDLT chargeable is £1,000 (£150,000 at 0% plus £50,000 at 2%). It is worth noting that, if the rent had been set at a market level of £30,000 so that there was no deemed premium, the NPV of the rent would have been £249,498 and the SDLT payable would have been £994, almost the same as that payable based on the deemed premium. PPM Ltd must file an SDLT return and pay the SDLT due of £1,000, by 8 July 2020.

Linked transactions

6.58 Lease transactions may be 'linked' with other UK land transactions (whether or not involving other leases) if they form part of a single scheme, arrangement or series of transactions between the same vendor and purchaser or persons connected with them (*FA 2003, s 108*; see **4.89**). There are two distinct ways in which lease transactions may be linked, and each has its own implications.

Successive linked leases

6.59 If successive leases of substantially the same premises are granted, and if those leases are linked, the second and subsequent leases are effectively treated as extending the earlier lease (*FA 2003, Sch 17A, para 5*). As each lease in the series after the first is granted (or substantially performed), any SDLT return made in respect of the earlier lease must be amended to show details for what is now deemed to be a longer lease, and any additional SDLT must be paid. Additional SDLT may arise in relation to rent (the NPV of the rent will have increased because the deemed lease is for a longer period) and/or premium (if a further premium is paid, the premiums must be aggregated both to determine the rates of tax and to calculate the amount of tax).

Example 6.21—Successive linked leases

Harriet granted Ian a five-year lease of a warehouse commencing 1 September 2015 for a premium of £130,000 and a yearly rent of £50,000. The lease was executed on the start date without prior substantial performance. The lease agreement included an option for Ian to take a further five-year lease commencing on 1 September 2020 at the same rent, on payment of a further premium of £130,000. Ian exercises the option; the second lease is executed on 1 August 2020 (ie one month before commencement) and the additional premium is paid on 1 September 2020.

During September 2015, Ian submitted an SDLT return for the five-year lease, with premium £130,000 and yearly rent of £50,000. The total SDLT paid was £2,057, comprising £1,300 on the premium (charged at 1% because the rent is £1,000 or more and the effective date of the grant of the lease is on or before 16 March 2016: see **6.46**) and £757 on the rent. A further SDLT return is needed in respect of the second lease. The leases are linked, so there is deemed to be a ten-year lease at a flat rental of £50,000 per annum and a premium of £260,000, commencing 1 September 2015. The SDLT on such a lease is £10,458, comprising £7,800 on the premium (at 3%) and £2,658 on the rent. The SDLT paid on the original lease is deducted, leaving £8,401 payable as a result of the second lease. Although the second lease is not 'substantially performed' early, it is executed one month before commencement, so the further SDLT return and payment are due 30 days after execution, that is no later than 31 August 2020 (*FA 2003, s 81A(1)* prior to its amendment by *FA 2019, s 46(5)* as the grant of the original lease was notified before 1 March 2019). As the leases are linked, such that there is deemed to be a single lease, for a term of ten years, commencing on 1 September 2015, it is the SDLT bands and rates which applied on 1 September 2015 which are used to calculate the SDLT on the 'extended' lease, and not those which applied on 1 August 2020 when the second lease was granted.

6.60 Successive leases are not necessarily linked. If, when the first lease was granted, there was no agreement (explicit or implied) that the next lease would be granted, and if the next lease was negotiated independently of the first, they are not likely to be linked. However, if the first lease contained an option for the grant of a further lease, they probably are linked. HMRC tend to assume that successive leases are linked unless there is clear evidence to the contrary.

Other linked leases

6.61 Leases of different premises may be linked – for example, a tenant may take on leases of two shops in different towns from the same landlord, negotiated as a single deal. Additionally, any deemed lease arising from an abnormal increase in rent prior to 17 July 2013 (see **6.26**) was automatically linked with the original lease and with any previous such deemed leases (*FA 2003, Sch 17A, para 14(5)(b)*). However, where a deemed lease runs in parallel with the original lease, the two cannot be 'successive'. The deemed lease arising from a variation to increase rent within the first five years of a lease is not automatically linked with the original lease – this is a matter to be determined in the light of the facts. For example, if the rent increase is a result of a statutory rent review, the leases are unlikely to be linked; if the increase relates to improvements of the premises contemplated when the lease was originally executed, the leases are likely to be linked.

6.62 Where leases are linked and the 'successive leases' rules do not apply (eg leases of two properties agreed between the same parties as part of a single transaction), any premiums are aggregated to determine the correct rate of SDLT, which is then applied separately to each premium. The NPV of the rents under the leases are also aggregated to give a figure for total NPV (TNPV), and the tax on this is calculated in the normal way. The tax applicable to each lease is then calculated by applying the fraction NPV (for the individual lease)/TNPV to the overall tax on rent.

6.63 If the linked leases do not have the same 'effective date' (see **4.99** and **6.74**) (or if some are and some are not wholly residential), and if, as a result, the zero rate threshold would be different for the separate leases, the tax on the TNPV must be calculated afresh for each lease before applying the NPV/TNPV fraction (*FA 2003, Sch 5, para 2*). This complexity means it is not possible to use the SDLT calculator on the HMRC website to make a direct calculation of the SDLT due on the leases. However, the calculator can still be used to calculate the NPVs for the individual leases, the remainder of the calculation then being performed manually.

Example 6.22—Non-successive linked leases calculation

The facts are as in Examples 6.6 and 6.9 above. The NPV of rent under the original lease is £207,915 and the SDLT paid was £579. The NPV of the deemed additional lease is £21,712, so the aggregate NPV is £229,627. The SDLT payable on a lease with this rental NPV is 1% of £(229,627 – 150,000), which is £796. Thresholds and rates are the same for both actual and deemed lease, so this calculation is appropriate for both leases. The revised SDLT attributable to the original lease is £796 × £207,915/£229,627, which is £720, and the SDLT attributable to the deemed additional lease is £796 × £21,712/£229,627, which is £75 (the £1 overall reduction arises from rounding and seems to be acceptable). As a stand-alone lease, the deemed lease arising from the rent increase would not have given rise to any SDLT charge but, because it is linked with the original lease, a charge arises.

LEASE RENEWALS AND EXTENSIONS

6.64 The interaction between the SDLT rules and commercial practice often leads to complexity when a lease is renewed, or where a lease for an indefinite term (see **6.12**) is replaced by a fixed-term lease. This complexity has been reduced (but by no means eliminated) by amendments made by *FA 2013, Sch 41*. In some cases the costs of compliance remain greater than the amount of tax payable. Inevitably, the tax payable will depend on the rent (and premium, if any) payable under the new lease and its length. However, the tax may also depend on matters such as:

- when the *old* lease was executed (or is treated as having been executed in the case of a lease for indefinite term);
- whether the old lease had a fixed term and if so,
- whether there has been a period of 'holding over' between expiry of the old lease and finalisation of the new; and
- how the parties agree to treat the holding-over period.

A period of holding over occurs when the tenant remains in occupation after a lease has expired, usually while a new lease is negotiated (see **6.13**).

Information required

6.65 The answers to the following questions will be important in determining the SDLT consequences of a renewal of a lease:

- Was the old lease subject to stamp duty or SDLT?
- Did the new lease take effect before expiry of the old (is there an overlap in the periods of the lease)?
- If not, did the parties enter into an agreement for lease, which was substantially performed before the new lease was finally executed?
- When is the new lease stated to begin?
- Was there a gap between the end of the old lease and the finalisation of the agreement for the new lease (or execution of the new lease if there was no pre-execution agreement), during which the tenant remained in occupation?
- If there was a gap, was it less than one year, or alternatively a year or more?
- Are the old and new leases linked (see **6.58**)?

The following paragraphs and examples deal with the SDLT consequences for each possible combination of answers to these questions.

Old lease under SDLT

New lease granted on or before expiry of old fixed-term lease

6.66 If the new lease is stated to take effect immediately after the end of the old, is executed before or immediately on expiry of the old and is not linked with the old (see **6.58**), SDLT is payable as if the new lease is a simple stand-alone lease for the term and consideration stated in the lease. If the new lease is linked with the old, this affects the calculation of SDLT (see **6.59** and Example 6.21) but not the timing of SDLT obligations.

If the new lease is executed before the end of the old, the new lease is a reversionary lease (see SDLTM17070). It is important then to consider timing – SDLT obligations arise 14 days after the date of execution of the new lease, not 14 days after the start date. This assumes that the 'effective date' (see **4.99** and **6.74**) of the new lease is on or after 1 March 2019, or that the lease had only become notifiable on or after 1 March 2019. If the 'effective date' is before 1 March 2019, and the lease became notifiable before 1 March 2019, the SDLT obligations arose 30 days after the date of execution of the new lease (*FA 2019, s 46(10)*). See Example 6.23A.

If the new lease takes effect before the end of the old, credit may be available against the SDLT payable, for SDLT paid on the old lease for the overlap period – see Example 6.23B, and Example 6.9 for the calculation of overlap relief.

New lease granted after expiry of old fixed-term lease

New lease expressed as beginning immediately on expiry of old

6.67 If the tenant remains in occupation throughout and the new lease is expressed as commencing immediately on expiry of the old, it will be treated as commencing on that date no matter when actually executed (*FA 2003, Sch 17A, para 9A(2)*). This treatment is in contrast with the SDLT treatment of a completely new lease, where the term cannot be treated as beginning before the lease is executed. See Example 6.23C.

Gap between expiry of old lease and stated start date of new

6.68 For old leases which expire on or after 17 July 2013, provided the term of the new lease is expressed as beginning at some time during the one-year period beginning with the date of expiry of the old, it will still be treated for SDLT purposes as beginning immediately on expiry of the old lease (*FA 2003, Sch 17A, para 3A(1),(2)* and *(3)*). In other words any period of holding over before the lease is expressed as beginning, amounting to less than one year, will be added to the term of the new lease for SDLT purposes. Accordingly, no separate return will be required for the period of holding over.

The most likely scenario is that a new lease will be executed within one year after the date of expiry of the old lease. If the new lease is not executed until more than one year after expiry of the old and if it is not expressed as beginning immediately on expiry of the old, any complete years of holding over will be dealt with as explained in **6.13**.

Once the new lease is finally executed, and provided the latest complete year of holding over commences on or after 17 July 2013, the new lease is treated for SDLT purposes as beginning immediately after the end of the last complete year of holding over (*FA 2003, Sch 17A, para 3A(5)*). Accordingly no SDLT obligations arise in respect of the final part year of holding over, but that part year is added to the term of the new lease for the purpose of calculating the SDLT on the new lease. The SDLT obligations in respect of the new lease arise 14 days after the date the new lease begins, which will normally be the date of execution. This assumes that the 'effective date' of the grant of the new lease is on or after 1 March 2019, or the new lease only becomes notifiable on or after 1 March 2019. If the new lease was notifiable before 1 March 2019 the SDLT obligations arise 30 days after the new lease begins.

For leases which expired prior to 17 July 2013, if the new lease was expressed as beginning later than immediately after expiry of the old, the new lease was treated for SDLT purposes as beginning on the date on which it was executed (or the date on which it was stated to begin if later). This then gave rise to a period of holding over between expiry of the old lease and the 'effective date' (see **4.99** and **6.74**) of the new lease, which was dealt with for SDLT purposes as explained at **6.13**. On the grant of the new lease, overlap relief would normally be available in respect of any part of a deemed one-year extension on which tax had been paid but which had not expired. These fruitless complications were swept away by the *FA 2013* changes where old leases expire on or after 17 July 2013 or where leases expired before that date but the latest one-year period of holding over commenced on or after that date. However the old rules continued to apply until 17 July 2014, where old leases expired in the year up to 17 July 2013 and new leases were still under negotiation.

New lease superseding old lease for indefinite term

6.69 The new lease will be subject to SDLT as a simple stand-alone lease for a term commencing on the date of execution or later stated start date or, if earlier, the date of substantial performance (see **4.99** and **6.74**) of any agreement for lease. Note however that occupation of the property under the earlier lease for indefinite term will not cause substantial performance of any agreement for the new lease. If SDLT has been paid on the lease for indefinite term for a period which is partly included in the term of the new lease, it should be possible to claim overlap relief in respect of that part – see **6.83**.

Old lease under stamp duty

6.70 SDLT is payable as if the new lease is a simple stand-alone lease for the term and consideration stated in the lease. The new lease cannot be treated as linked with the old. The main complication arises from the fact that 'rent' for a period before the effective start date of the new lease is treated as a premium as set out at **6.6**.

New lease granted on or before expiry of old fixed-term lease

6.71 If the new lease is executed before the end of the old, the new lease is a reversionary lease (see SDLTM17070). It is important then to consider timing – SDLT obligations arise 14 days after the date of execution of the new lease, not 14 days after the start date. This assumes that the 'effective date' (see **4.99** and **6.74**) of the new lease is on or after 1 March 2019, or that the new lease only became notifiable on or after 1 March 2019. If the 'effective date' is before 1 March 2019, and the new lease became notifiable before 1 March 2019, the SDLT obligations arose 30 days after the date of execution of the new lease. See Example 6.23A – the same principles apply even though the old lease was subject to stamp duty.

If the new lease takes effect before the end of the old, no credit is available against the SDLT payable, for stamp duty paid on the old lease for the overlap period.

New lease granted after expiry of old fixed-term lease

6.72 If the tenant has simply remained in occupation during the period of holding over, paying rent as if the old lease has continued, this period will be treated as a continuation of the old lease as described at **6.2**. No SDLT obligations will arise in respect of this period. The new lease will be treated as beginning on the date on which it is executed, or 'substantially performed' (see **4.99** and **6.74**) if earlier. A payment of rent under the new lease will be regarded as substantial performance, but the lease will not be regarded as substantially performed merely because the tenant is in occupation/has possession under the deemed continuation of the old lease (see SDLTM07900).

The lease may be expressed as beginning on a date earlier than the date of execution or substantial performance. However, in this case, because the old lease was not subject to SDLT, the treatment outlined in para **6.67** will not apply. Instead the general rule will apply and the lease will not be treated as beginning earlier than the date of execution or earlier substantial performance. Any rent reserved under the new lease which is expressed as being for a period before the deemed start of the lease, will be treated as a premium. Such amounts are often small and usually below the thresholds for payment of SDLT (£125,000 for residential property, £150,000 for non-residential or mixed property, see **4.37**).

If, exceptionally, any action is taken before the new lease is agreed, which would itself be regarded in property law as a surrender and re-grant (eg a significant change in the premises leased or an explicit agreement to extend the lease for a further fixed term), this is also likely to be regarded as the grant of a new lease for SDLT purposes. In such cases, further advice will be required, preferably taken in advance, based on a detailed analysis of the fact pattern. However a mere increase in rent paid in respect of the period of holding over, even if not provided for in the old lease, will not normally give rise to a new deemed lease for the period in question.

Lease renewal examples

6.73 The following examples are referred to in paras **6.65** to **6.72**.

General fact pattern

ServiceCo occupies a commercial unit under a lease from an unrelated Propco. When the old lease was granted (more than five years ago) there was no agreement between the parties as to whether the lease would be renewed and the old lease does not include any option to renew. The lease expires on 31 December 2020, at which time the annual rent is £100,000 including VAT. A new lease is negotiated, the commercial terms being for seven years from 1 January 2021 (except where noted below) at yearly rent of £120,000 including VAT. No separate premium is payable. There is a rent review due on 1 January 2026.

Example 6.23A

New lease is negotiated in advance and executed on 1 December 2020 to take effect on 1 January 2021. There are no complications, the HMRC calculator gives the NPV of the rent as £733,745, and the SDLT payable as £5,837. The rent review will not occur during the first five years of the lease and so can be ignored. The calculation of SDLT is based on the lease commencing on 1 January 2021. However, because the lease was executed on 1 December 2020, the SDLT return and tax payment are due within 14 days of this date (ie by 15 December 2020), which is before the lease period commences. It does not matter whether the old lease was subject to stamp duty or SDLT (this would matter if the leases could be regarded as linked, see **6.58**).

Example 6.23B

As Example 6.23A, except lease was executed on 1 July 2020 and took immediate effect, displacing the old lease. The new lease is again for seven years (ie it expires in this case on 30 June 2027). The SDLT return and tax payment were due by 15 July 2020.

(i) If the old lease was a stamp duty lease, the basic calculation is the same as for Example 6.23A; no allowance is given in respect of the unexpired six months of old lease displaced by the new lease.

(ii) If the old lease was an SDLT lease, an allowance is given in the SDLT calculation for the £50,000 rent which would have been paid under the old lease for the period from 1 July to 31 December 2020. See Example 6.9 for the method of calculation. The rent for the first year of the new lease is therefore taken to be £70,000 (ie £120,000 less the £50,000 'allowance'). The HMRC calculator gives the NPV of the rent as £685,436 and the tax payable as £5,354.

Example 6.23C

New lease is finally executed on 1 July 2021, stated to be for seven years from 1 January 2021 at yearly rent of £120,000 but silent on matter of payment of rent for period before execution. ServiceCo has continued paying rent at yearly rate of £100,000 but pays an extra £10,000 immediately before the new lease is executed, to bring the yearly rate for the period of holding over (1 January to 30 June 2021) up to the new rent.

(i) Both parties are satisfied that the extra payment is in respect of occupation during the period of holding over and is not an inducement to the landlord to enter into the new lease.

  (a) If the old lease was under stamp duty, continued occupation after expiry is treated as an extension of that lease which is not subject to SDLT on either the rent paid at the 'old' rate or the retrospective £10,000 rent increase.

  (b) If the old lease was under SDLT, continued occupation is, in the first instance, regarded as an extension of the old lease. Because the old lease expired after 17 July 2013 and the new lease is stated to commence immediately after expiry of the old, the new lease is treated as starting on 1 January 2021. The SDLT is based on an NPV of rent of £733,754, as in Example 6.23A. No further liability or obligations arise in respect of the period of holding over.

  (c) The same analysis would apply if the new lease was stated to commence on some date after 1 January 2021 – for example on 1 July 2020, the date of execution – such that there was acknowledged to be a gap between the end of the old lease and the start of the new.

(ii) The parties acknowledge that the extra £10,000 payment was made to persuade Propco to grant the new lease.

  (a) If the old lease was under stamp duty, the continued payment of rent at the old rate during the period of holding over is treated as an extension of the old lease, with no SDLT consequences. However, the additional £10,000 is treated as a premium for the new lease. No SDLT is chargeable on the deemed premium of £10,000 as it falls within the £150,000 zero rate band. The same analysis would apply if the new lease was stated to commence on a date after 1 January 2021 because the lease cannot be regarded as beginning before the date of execution or earlier substantial performance (see **4.99** and **6.74**).

(b) If the old lease was under SDLT, the new lease is treated as beginning on the stated start date of 1 January 2021 and for a period of seven years. The £60,000 rent paid in respect of occupation in the six months to 30 June 2021 is taken into account as rent under the new lease, irrespective of whether the payment is acknowledged as being in respect of the new lease (*FA 2003, Sch 17A, para 9A*). However, SDLT, obligations arise on 15 July 2021 being 14 days after execution (or earlier substantial performance) of the new lease (*FA 2003, s 76(1)* as amended by *FA 2019, s 46(2)*).

Example 6.23D

New lease is finally executed on 1 July 2022, stated to be for seven years from 1 July 2022, so there is an 18-month gap between expiry of the old lease and stated commencement date of the new. Yearly rent is £120,000 but lease is silent on the matter of the payment of rent for the period before execution. ServiceCo has continued paying rent at yearly rate of £100,000 but pays an extra £30,000 immediately before lease is executed, to bring the yearly rate for the period of holding over (1 January 2021 to 30 June 2022) up to the new rent. If the old lease was under stamp duty, the treatment is covered under Examples 6.23C(i) and 6.23C(ii) above. If the old lease was under SDLT, the treatment of the period of holding over is as follows:

- If, in law, the old lease is treated as continuing (eg under provisions of the landlord and tenant legislation), the continued occupation is treated initially as a one-year extension of the old lease. This is likely to lead to the need to recalculate the SDLT payable on that old lease (see **6.17**). An amended return and payment of any additional SDLT will be due by 30 January 2021 (*FA 2003, Sch 17A, para 3(3)* prior to amendment by *FA 2019, s 46(8)(a)*). However, the additional £20,000 rent for the period will not be taken into account in calculating the additional SDLT.
- The eventual execution of the new lease brings a retrospective end to the deemed continuation of the old lease. This is treated as ending on 31 December 2021 (one year after the actual termination date) and the new lease as beginning on 1 January 2022 (*FA 2003, Sch 17A, para 3A(5)*). As a result the new lease is deemed to have a period of 7 years 6 months, with rent of £120,000 per annum. The SDLT return and tax payment are due by 15 July 2022 despite the deemed start date of 1 January 2022 (*FA 2003, s 76(1)* as amended by *FA 2019, s 46(2)*).
- If, exceptionally, the foregoing does not apply (perhaps because the lease dis-applied the relevant landlord and tenant provisions), it is likely that an implied new tenancy, a lease for an indefinite term, arises for the interim period. This will be separately subject to SDLT as described at **6.12**, but will probably be linked to the new lease, forming a pair of successive leases. SDLT obligations in respect of the first one-year period will have

to be dealt with by 14 January 2021 (14 days after the start of the implied tenancy) and those for the second year by 14 January 2022. Credit should then be available for SDLT paid in respect of the six months from 1 July 2022 when calculating the SDLT on the new lease. Overall therefore, apart from bringing deadlines forward, this should have the same net effect as the lease being stated as beginning on 1 January 2021, as in Example 6.23C(ii)(b). In the present case, the landlord's acceptance of continued rent payment suggests this would be the case. However, it would save the need to even consider the matter if the new lease was expressed as beginning immediately after expiry of the old!

- Finally, it may be that the tenant's continued occupation is an act of trespass, or is under a tenancy at will. Such occupation has no SDLT consequences. However, it is likely to be difficult to demonstrate that this is the basis of occupation given that rent is paid and accepted during the period of occupation and a new lease is eventually executed.

WHEN DO SDLT OBLIGATIONS ARISE?

Grant of a lease

6.74 The concepts of 'substantial performance' and 'effective date' (see **4.99**) apply to transactions involving leases, but with some specific 'trigger points'. In the case of a new lease, there are typically several stages which may occur at different times. The first SDLT liability and obligation to submit a return will arise 14 days (*FA 2003, s 76(1)*) after the earlier of:

- the lease proper being executed, and
- the agreement for lease being substantially performed.

Substantial performance occurs on the earliest of:

- the first payment of rent being made,
- substantially the whole of any consideration other than rent (eg a premium) being paid, and
- the tenant taking possession of substantially the whole of the premises.

The tenant will be regarded as taking possession if he occupies the premises, including for the purpose of fitting out, or if he becomes entitled to enjoy other benefits of tenancy such as receipt of rent from a sub-tenant (see **4.9**). Where an agreement for lease is substantially performed before the lease is granted, this is deemed to be the grant of a notional lease on the terms provided for in the agreement. The 'effective date' of the grant of the notional lease is the date of substantial performance (*FA 2003, para 12A, Sch 17A*).

When SDLT obligations have arisen on a notional lease as a result of substantial performance of the agreement, the subsequent grant of the real lease is also potentially subject to SDLT.

The requirement to submit the return within 14 days applies if the 'effective date' (see **4.99**) of the grant of the lease is on or after 1 March 2019, or the 'effective date' of the grant of the lease is before 1 March 2019 but the lease only became notifiable on or after 1 March 2019. If the grant of the lease became notifiable before 1 March 2019 the SDLT filing and payment obligations arise 30 days, rather than 14 days, after the occurrence of the triggering events outlined in the bullet points in this **6.74**.

Leases with an effective date before 17 July 2013

6.75 For leases with an 'effective date' before 17 July 2013, when the real lease is granted, the notional lease is deemed to be surrendered and overlap relief (see **6.82** and Example 6.9) is given for SDLT paid on the notional lease. The practical effect is that, provided the lease is for the same rent and term (and premium, if any) as envisaged in the agreement for lease, no further SDLT is payable. In this case, by virtue of the combined effect of *FA 2003, s 77A(3)* and *Sch 17A, para 9*, no further notification to HMRC is required. However, difficulty can arise if the rent is uncertain, variable or payable in a currency other than sterling:

> First, if rent is payable in another currency and the exchange rate moves between substantial performance and completion, the sterling equivalent of the rent will differ at the two dates. If the sterling equivalent increases, extra SDLT will be payable. If the sterling equivalent decreases, no refund of SDLT will be due.
>
> Second, for SDLT purposes, the term of the lease will normally be regarded as beginning no earlier than the date of grant. This may result in a rent review falling within the first five years of the term, making the rent 'uncertain' (see **6.37**). It may also be important in determining such matters as when further returns are required if rent is variable or uncertain (see **6.78**). The exception to this rule occurs when a lease originally executed under SDLT is renewed, see **6.67**.

Leases with effective date on or after 17 July 2013

6.76 The position has been simplified for leases with an 'effective date' on or after 17 July 2013. When the real lease is granted, the notional lease is deemed to be a real lease granted on the date of substantial performance of the agreement and ending on the end date of the actual lease. The rent and premium are as given in the actual lease. A further return is required only if further tax is payable on grant of the actual lease, for example because the rent, premium or term of the lease are greater than was taken into account in the original return. The lease is regarded as beginning at the 'effective date' (see **4.99** and **6.74**) of the lease, so the issue relating to uncertain rent, mentioned in **6.75** above, no longer arises.

Deferral of SDLT

6.77 If (perhaps unusually) any amount of a premium is contingent or uncertain at the 'effective date' (see **4.99** and **6.74**) and will not be payable until more than six months after the effective date, the lessee may apply to HMRC to defer payment of an appropriate amount of SDLT in the same way as for other land transactions (see **8.31**). However, it is not possible to apply to defer payment of SDLT arising in respect of rent, even if the amount of rent is uncertain at the 'effective date'. This means that, if final settlement of the rent leads to a further SDLT liability, say at the end of the first five years of the lease, interest will be chargeable on that SDLT from the original due date (14 days after the 'effective date' of the grant of the lease assuming the effective date is on or after 1 March 2019, or that the lease only became notifiable on or after 1 March 2019. If the lease became notifiable before 1 March 2019 the deadline is 30 days rather than 14 days).

Uncertain or variable rent

6.78 The rent for the first five years of the lease may not be finally ascertained at the outset (eg because the rent is based on results of a business or because there is a rent review within the first five years) – see **6.37** et seq. However, it remains necessary to submit returns and pay SDLT by the requisite deadline and any SDLT payable must be calculated on the basis of a 'reasonable estimate' of the rent (*FA 2003, s 51(2)*).

Notification of the grant of the lease if notification thresholds breached (see 5.7 – points (6) and (7))

Where the 'effective date' (see **4.99** and **6.74**) of the grant of the lease is before 1 March 2019, and the grant of the lease was notifiable before 1 March 2019, the land transaction return must be filed and tax paid within 30 days of the 'effective date' (*FA 2003, s 76(1)* prior to amendment by *FA 2019, s 46(2)*).

However, where the 'effective date' (see **4.99** and **6.74**) of the grant of the lease is on or after 1 March 2019, or the 'effective date' of the grant of the lease was before 1 March 2019 but the grant of the lease only became notifiable on or after 1 March 2019, the land transaction return must be filed and any tax paid within 14 days of the 'effective date' (*FA 2003, s 76(1) as* amended by *FA 2019, s 46(2)*).

Notification when rent for first five years of term of lease ascertained

Details must then be notified, and any additional SDLT paid, as a result of: (a) the rent for the first five years being finally ascertained; or (b) the end of the fifth year of the term of the lease being reached, whichever happens earlier.

The 'effective date' of the grant of the lease is before 1 March 2019 and the grant of the lease becomes notifiable before 1 March 2019

In this case the revised rents must be notified, and any additional SDLT paid, within 30 days of the earlier of: (a) the rent for the first five years of the term of the lease being finally ascertained; and (b) the end of the fifth year of the term of the lease being reached (*FA 2003, Sch 17A, para 8(3)* prior to amendment by *FA 2019, s 46(8)(c)*).

The rent for the first five years may not have been finally determined when the five-year deadline arrives (eg it may depend on the profits of a period for which accounts have not yet been finalised). In that case, it may be necessary at the five-year point to submit a further return on the basis of a revised reasonable estimate, and further amend this once the rent is finally determined.

In either case the 'relevant date' (*FA 2003, s 87(3)*) for interest on overdue tax purposes remains the 'effective date' of the grant of the lease, and interest will be charged on any SDLT paid more than 30 days after that date (*FA 2003, s 87(1)* and *(3)(c)* prior to the amendments by *FA 2019, s 46(7)* having effect).

The 'effective date' (see 4.99 and 6.74) of the grant of the lease is on or after 1 March 2019, or the effective date of the grant of the lease was before 1 March 2019 but the lease only became notifiable on or after 1 March 2019.

In these circumstances the deadline for providing details of the revised rents, and paying any additional tax due, depends upon whether or not the grant of the lease has already been notified to HMRC.

If the effect of the revision to the rents is that the transaction becomes notifiable, when it was not previously notifiable, the lessee must file a return within 14 days of: (a) the rent for the first five years of the term of the lease being finally ascertained; or (b) the end of the fifth year of the term of the lease being reached, whichever is earlier (*FA 2003, Sch 17A, para 8(3)* as amended by *FA 2019, s 46(8)(c)*).

However, if the grant of the lease has already been notified, but the effect of the revised rents is that tax is payable where none was payable before, or that additional tax is payable in respect of the transaction, the lessee must file a further return within 30 days of: (a) the rent for the first five years of the term of the lease being finally ascertained; or (b) the end of the fifth year of the term of the lease being reached, whichever is earlier (*FA 2003, Sch 17A, para 8(3A)* as introduced by *FA 2019, s 46(8)(c)*).

As discussed above the rent for the first five years may not have been finally determined when the five-year deadline arrives (eg it may depend on the profits of a period for which accounts have not yet been finalised). In that case, it may be necessary at the five-year point to submit a further return on the basis of a revised reasonable estimate, and further amend this once the rent is finally determined.

In either case the 'relevant date' (*FA 2003, s 87(3)*) for interest on overdue tax purposes remains the 'effective date' of the grant of the lease, and interest will be charged on any SDLT paid more than 14 days after that date (*FA 2003, s 87(1A)* as introduced by *FA 2019, s 46(7)*).

For the purposes of both *FA 2003, Sch 17A, para 8(3)* and *para 8(3A)* any tax or additional tax payable is calculated using the SDLT rates and bands as at the 'effective date' (see **4.99** and **6.74**) of the grant of the lease (*FA 2003, Sch 17A, para 8(3B)* as introduced by *FA 2019, s 46(8)(c)*).

Where the lessee is required to deliver a return under *FA 2003, Sch 17A, para 8(3)*, or a further return under *para 8(3A)*, that return must include a self-assessment of the tax chargeable based on the information in the return and the tax, or additional tax, must be paid not later than the date by which the return must be filed (*FA 2003, Sch 17A, para 8(3B)* as introduced by *FA 2019, s 46(8)(c)*).

Example 6.24—Timing of returns and tax payments

The facts are as in Example 6.16 above. Ken must submit an SDLT return and pay SDLT no later than 15 December 2020. At that time, he must make a reasonable estimate of what the rent will be, and it seems likely that his estimate will be £10,000 per quarter. The total rent payable over the first five years (and, therefore, the final SDLT liability) will not be known until some time after the end of the first five years. Because the actual rent is higher than the estimate, Ken must submit a further return by 30 December 2025 (ie within 30 days of the end of the first five years – *FA 2003, Sch 17A, para 8(3A)* as introduced by *FA 2019, s 46(8)(c)*), self-assessing the additional SDLT, which must be paid by the same date. If the correct figures are not known by this due date, Ken must make a reasonable estimate, and then correct the return once the actual numbers are known. If any of this leads to additional SDLT being paid after 15 December 2020, interest will be charged on this additional tax from that date.

Informal occupation and holding over

6.79 It can be difficult to establish when SDLT obligations arise in cases of informal occupation. It is essential to establish the precise legal nature of the occupation. A periodic tenancy is initially regarded as a lease for one year. If the annual rent exceeds the relevant threshold, SDLT obligations arise 14 days (30 days if the grant of the tenancy was notifiable before 1 March 2019) after commencement. If the tenancy continues beyond one year, it is treated as a lease for two years, then three years and so on. At the commencement of each further year, it is necessary to consider whether the cumulative rent and/or period are sufficient to give rise to SDLT notification or payment obligations. If so, those obligations arise either 14 or 30 days after the start of the year in question as described in **6.12**.

In some cases, the position may be similar where a tenant remains in occupation after the end of the lease. However, where the tenant is 'holding over' while a new lease is negotiated, the precise nature and timing of SDLT obligations in respect of the holding-over period depend on the provisions of the new lease (see **6.64** et seq).

Variation or surrender of a lease

6.80 There are no special rules relating to the time for notifying and paying SDLT on the variation or surrender of a lease. The obligations arise 14 days (assuming that the 'effective date' of the transaction is on or after 1 March 2019 or that the transaction only became notifiable on or after 1 March 2019) after the earlier of:

- completion of the formalities giving effect to the variation (eg the parties executing the relevant document), and
- 'substantial performance' of the variation.

The meaning of substantial performance is as set out in **4.99** and **6.74**.

If the 'effective date' of the variation or surrender was before 1 March 2019, and the transaction became notifiable before 1 March 2019, the notification and payment obligations arise 30 days, rather than 14 days, after the earlier of:

- completion of the formalities giving effect to the variation (eg the parties executing the relevant document), and
- 'substantial performance' of the variation.

RELIEFS

6.81 In general, reliefs and exemptions available for other UK land transactions also apply to transactions involving leases – see **Chapter 5** in respect of reliefs. Some of the reliefs are modified for lease transactions, particularly in relation to possible future clawback of the relief. There are a few additional reliefs which only apply to lease transactions.

Sale (or lease) and leaseback relief

6.82 Where a vendor sells or leases a 'major interest' (see **4.11**) in a property to a purchaser and, in consideration (wholly or partly), the purchaser grants a lease (the 'leaseback') to the vendor out of that major interest, the leaseback may be exempt from SDLT (*FA 2003, s 57A*). The only other consideration permitted for the initial sale/lease (which must not be a sub sale, see **5.8**) is cash and/or assumption, satisfaction or release of a debt; the vendor and purchaser must not be companies in a group relationship, such that they could qualify for group relief.

A fairly commonplace commercial arrangement is for an owner to transfer a property to a developer in return for the developer redeveloping the site and granting the owner a long lease of part of the new development. The developer recoups his cost and makes a profit by selling the rest of the development to third parties. It is understood that HMRC consider that the lease back to the owner does not qualify for sale and leaseback relief, because the developer's agreement to redevelop the site amounts to non-qualifying consideration. SDLT is therefore due on both the original sale to the developer and the lease back to the owner.

Overlap relief

6.83 This is mentioned at **6.34**, and applies if a lease is granted which supersedes a previous lease of substantially the same premises, which itself was subject to the SDLT regime. In calculating SDLT on the new lease, the rent for the 'overlap period' (ie the period which would have been covered by the old lease but is now covered by the new) is reduced by the rent which would have been paid under the old lease if that had been left to run its course (*FA 2003, Sch 17A, para 9*). This is not strictly a relief, it is a statutory treatment. Therefore it is not necessary to claim the 'relief' by answering question 9 of the SDLT1 return form 'yes' and entering a code. It is sufficient, when calculating SDLT on the new lease, to reduce the rent by the rent which would have been paid under the old lease. The relief may also apply where the new lease is granted to someone who acted as guarantor under the original lease, or in certain circumstances where the new lease is granted to someone who was a sub-tenant of the original lessee.

This relief is in addition to the general principle set out in *FA 2003, Sch 17A, para 16* that, where a lease is surrendered in consideration of the grant of another, neither the surrender nor the grant counts as consideration for the other.

Exercise of collective rights by tenants of flats

6.84 Tenants holding long leases of flats may have the right to gain control of the freehold. This may be achieved, for example, by the tenants jointly forming a company or other entity to buy the freehold. Although the amount paid by any individual tenant may not be large enough to give rise to any SDLT liability, the total amount payable by the company may be very large, possibly attracting SDLT at the top rate. This is clearly unfair in comparison with a leaseholder of an equivalent single house, who may be able to buy the freehold as an individual without triggering an SDLT charge. *FA 2003, s 74* provides a relief, under which the rate of SDLT to be applied is determined by dividing the total consideration payable by the company or other entity by the number of flats involved. In its original form, the relief only applied to a specific type of company expected to be established under the *Leasehold Reform, Housing and Urban Development Act 1993*. Unfortunately, the provisions of that Act allowing formation of such companies have never been brought into effect, so this relief was ineffective until amended by *FA 2009, s 80*. The form of entity buying the freehold is now not specified. An explanation of the relief can be found at SDLTM28500.

Chapter 7

SDLT and Partnerships

INTRODUCTION

7.1 The main legislation specifically dealing with partnerships is in *FA 2003, Sch 15*. *Part 1 (FA 2003, Sch 15, paras 1–4)* and *Part 2 (FA 2003, Sch 15, paras 5–8)* set out general provisions, including confirmation of the treatment of an ordinary acquisition of a chargeable interest from an unconnected vendor. *Part 3 (FA 2003, Sch 15, paras 9–40)* was inserted by *FA 2004* and contains the detailed rules applying SDLT to almost all other transactions of partnerships which own, acquire or dispose of chargeable interests. The heading, suggesting that the *Part 3* provisions only apply in 'special' circumstances, is misleading!

7.2 The UK tax system has always had difficulty working out how to deal with partnerships – in particular, whether to treat them as separate entities distinct from their members or as mere aggregations of separately taxed members – and SDLT continues that uncertainty. When SDLT was introduced, many partnership transactions were initially left entirely within the stamp duty rules, while the government tried to work out how best to deal with them under SDLT. Since the enactment of *FA 2004*, SDLT has generally applied to transactions by partnerships or partners, but with modification of and additions to the general rules. Substantial changes were made to the rules by *FA 2006*, *FA 2007* and *FA 2008*. The last of these amended the *FA 2007* changes with retrospective effect when it was realised that the earlier provisions caused major problems for some very large, widely held property investment vehicles.

7.3 This difficulty and uncertainty is reflected in the fact that HMRC issued guidance in draft, in conjunction with the enactment of *FA 2004*, but only finalised it and included it in the Stamp Duty Land Tax Manual in March 2011. HMRC's guidance on partnerships can be found at SDLTM33000 to SDLTM34800.

7.4 Three types of UK-based partnership are recognised:

- a (general) partnership within the *Partnership Act 1890*;
- a limited partnership (LP) registered under the *Limited Partnerships Act 1907*; and

- a limited liability partnership (LLP) formed under the *Limited Liability Partnerships Act 2000* or the Northern Ireland equivalent.

The SDLT rules seek to treat all three types of entity in the same way; they also apply the same treatment to any 'firm or entity of a similar character' formed under the laws of another country. Difficulties arise because the three types of entity listed above and many equivalent overseas entities have quite different legal and commercial characteristics. As a result, the SDLT treatment of a particular transaction may be logical in one case (say, involving a general partnership) but less so in another (say, involving an LLP). These differences have been a factor in the use of partnerships to mitigate SDLT costs, and many of the special rules which now apply were originally intended to combat perceived avoidance. Particular issues arise from the fact that LLPs (together with Scottish LPs and many overseas equivalents) are bodies corporate for the purposes of general law and many other tax purposes (LLPs) and/or have separate legal personality (Scottish LPs), but are treated as 'transparent' as regards ownership of land for SDLT purposes (see, for example, **5.24**).

GENERAL PRINCIPLES AND ORDINARY TRANSACTIONS

General principles

7.5 Property held by or on behalf of a partnership is treated as held by or on behalf of the partners (and not the partnership); a land transaction entered into for the purposes of a partnership is treated as entered into by or on behalf of the partners (and not the partnership); this is so even if the partnership is regarded as a body corporate or other legal entity for other purposes, such as ability to enter into contracts and to own property (*FA 2003, Sch 15, para 2*). However, the partners at the effective date (**4.91**) of the transaction have joint and several liability for payment of any tax (*FA 2003, Sch 15, paras 6, 7*). They also have responsibility, in some circumstances together with any partners who join after the effective date, for payment of any penalty, for example for failure to make a return or notify liability. Although this means all partners have responsibility for compliance, they may nominate 'representative partners' to act on behalf of the partnership. Any such nomination must be notified to HMRC (*FA 2003, Sch 15, para 8*).

7.6 If there is a change in the membership of a partnership, it is nonetheless treated as the same continuing partnership, provided at least one member before the change remains a member afterwards (*FA 2003, Sch 15, para 3*). Thus, despite the assertions in the previous paragraph, there are ways in which a partnership is treated as a separate entity.

Partnership share

7.7 In order to calculate the chargeable consideration for many partnership transactions, or even in some cases to determine whether a chargeable transaction has occurred, it is necessary to know the shares which the different partners have in the partnership. For most SDLT purposes, a partner's share in a partnership is defined as the proportion in which he is entitled to share in the **income profits** of the partnership at the effective date (**4.91**) of the transaction (*FA 2003, Sch 15, para 34(2)*). When property is transferred out of a partnership, a more complicated definition applies, although in many cases it produces the same result (see **7.23**). Entitlement to capital, or to capital profits, does not enter into the calculation. The definition causes practical difficulties – partnerships often decide the precise sharing of profits after the year-end, once total profits and the contribution of each partner to them are known. In such cases, it may be necessary to complete an SDLT return and pay tax based on estimated shares, then amend the return once profit shares are finally settled. Since profit shares do not normally vary from day to day, the reference to the 'effective date' is usually taken to mean the accounting period containing the effective date.

Ordinary transactions

7.8 If a partnership (or a partner on behalf of a partnership) enters into a land transaction with a person who is completely at arm's length, that transaction is treated in the same way as an equivalent transaction not involving a partnership. The only modification is that the partners have joint and several responsibility for any compliance matters. A person is completely at arm's length if he is neither a partner (whether current, joining or departing) nor connected with a partner. Connected for these purposes is as defined by *Corporation Tax Act 2010 (CTA 2010), s 1122*, although the automatic connection of partners with each other is omitted. It follows that, for such an arm's-length transaction, SDLT is generally chargeable by reference to the value of the actual consideration, and it is only necessary to consider the market value of the property itself where that would be required for a non-partnership transaction (eg for exchanges of property interests).

SPECIAL PROVISIONS

7.9 The application of the SDLT rules to arm's-length transactions is relatively straightforward. Complications arise when there is a connection between the partnership and the other party, ie where the other party is a partner (current, departing or joining) or is connected with a partner. It is necessary to consider separately the implications of the partnership acquiring or disposing of property, including modification of an existing interest where that would be treated as an acquisition or disposal under general SDLT rules. It is also necessary to consider the implications of changes in the membership or relative interests of the members in a partnership which owns property; in certain cases, such changes are deemed to give rise to a corresponding transfer of property interests between partners.

7.10 In general, when partnership transactions are subject to the 'special provisions', SDLT is charged by reference to the market value of the property interest in question and the proportion of the property which is deemed to be transferred. In the original version of the legislation, any actual consideration given was also taken into account. The rules were amended in 2006 to remove this link. Actual consideration (other than any change in partnership share) is now irrelevant in these cases. However, there are many anti-avoidance rules; in some circumstances, amounts which are commercially equivalent to consideration may trigger these (see **7.17**).

7.11 The legislation sets out formulae which must be applied to the market value of the property in question to determine the deemed consideration for the transaction. The formulae appear complex, but are generally seeking to achieve a relatively simple overall effect, which is to ensure that tax is charged on the economic transfer of value which takes place.

Example 7.1—Simple partnership case

Eric and Ernest are in a general partnership, sharing income and capital profits equally. They agree to admit Eddie as an equal partner (so each partner has a one-third share in profits, losses and assets) in return for Eddie agreeing, *inter alia*, to contribute freehold premises to the partnership. The property is transferred to Eric and Eddie jointly to hold on trust for the partnership (this is a normal arrangement, because a general partnership is not a body capable of holding the title to land). In the absence of any other complicating factors, SDLT is chargeable by reference to two-thirds of the market value of the property. This is the proportion which has economically changed hands by transfer to the other partners; Eddie still has a one-third interest in the property through his membership of the partnership, so no SDLT is charged on that proportion.

7.12 Inevitably, real transactions do include complicating factors, and HMRC are keen to minimise avoidance. Therefore, the basic formulae are supplemented by definitions and rules for special cases which must be taken into account. It would not be safe to assume that the simple apportionment set out above gives the correct SDLT charge, without checking the specific facts of the case against the detailed rules. Many changes to the rules are attempts to combat perceived avoidance, especially attempts to combine the partnership rules with reliefs (eg sub-sale relief, see **5.8**) and other special provisions to mitigate SDLT costs.

Acquisition by a partnership

7.13 Under *FA 2003, Sch 15, para 10*, when a chargeable interest is acquired by a partnership from a partner, or from a person who becomes a partner as a result, or from a person who is connected with either, SDLT is charged on deemed consideration equal to:

$$MV \times (100 - SLP)\%$$

where MV is the market value of the chargeable interest at the effective date of the transfer, and SLP is the 'sum of the lower proportions'. A five-step calculation is required to determine SLP, set out in the legislation (*para 12*) as follows:

(1) Identify the 'relevant owner(s)'. These are persons who have an interest in the property immediately before it is transferred and are partners or connected with partners immediately after the property is transferred.

(2) For each relevant owner, identify the 'corresponding partner(s)'. These are persons who are partners immediately after the transfer and who are relevant owners or are individuals connected with relevant owners. For these purposes, a company may be regarded as an individual connected with a relevant owner *only* if it holds property as trustee and is connected by virtue of *CTA 2010, s 1122(6)* (trustee connected with settlor etc).

(3) For each relevant owner, take the proportion of the property to which he is entitled immediately before the transfer and apportion it between any one or more of his corresponding partners. Where a relevant owner has more than one corresponding partner, the apportionment may be performed in whatever manner gives the best result.

(4) Find the 'lower proportion' for each person who is a corresponding partner in relation to one or more relevant owners. The lower proportion is the lower of:

   (a) the proportion apportioned to him under (3) above, and

   (b) his partnership share immediately after the transfer.

(5) Add together the lower proportions for each partner who is a corresponding partner. This is the SLP.

Example 7.2—Calculating the sum of the lower proportions

Alfred, Betty and Carl are in partnership, sharing income profits 40%, 40% and 20% respectively. Betty and Carl are sister and brother; apart from the partnership, Alfred is not related to or connected with Betty or Carl. The partners agree to buy a building from Danielle, who is Betty and Carl's sister, for £500,000. The calculation steps are as follows:

(1) The only relevant owner is Danielle, because she owns 100% of the property before the transfer.

(2) Betty and Carl are corresponding partners because they are individuals connected with the only relevant owner, their sister Danielle.

(3) Danielle was entitled to 100% of the property before the transfer. We choose to apportion this 50% to each corresponding partner, Betty and Carl.

(4) For Betty, her partnership share immediately after the transaction is 40%, and the proportion apportioned to her under (3) is 50%, so her lower proportion is 40%; for Carl, his partnership share immediately after the transaction is 20%, and the proportion apportioned to him under (3) above is 50%, so his lower proportion is 20%.

(5) The sum of the lower proportions is 40% (Betty) plus 20% (Carl), which is 60%.

The consideration for SDLT purposes is therefore MV × (100 – 60)%, or 40% of the market value, ie £200,000. In this relatively simple case, it can be seen that this represents the proportion of the property effectively transferred to Alfred, the partner who is not connected with the original owner of the property.

7.14 In most cases before the transfer, the property will be owned by one person, so there will be only one relevant owner. If two or more persons own a property as beneficial joint tenants, they are treated as owning as tenants in common, in equal shares.

Connected companies

7.15 The restriction to individuals in step (2) detailed in **7.13** was introduced by *FA 2007, s 72*, and is designed to prevent the use of a partnership arrangement to transfer property to a connected company without suffering SDLT on the full market value of the property. Other anti-avoidance rules are dealt with at **7.17** and **7.27**.

Example 7.3—Partnership including connected company

Derek sets up a company, Fiddler Ltd, in which he is the sole shareholder. Derek and Fiddler Ltd form a limited partnership in which Derek is the limited partner with a 1% share and Fiddler Ltd is the general partner with a 99% share. Derek transfers a valuable property to the partnership. The steps to calculate the proportion of market value on which SDLT is charged are as follows:

(1) Derek is the only relevant owner with 100%.

(2) Derek is also the only corresponding partner. Fiddler Ltd cannot be a corresponding partner, as it is not an individual.

(3) Therefore, Derek's 100% ownership before the transfer must be apportioned 100% to Derek as corresponding partner after the transfer.

(4) Derek's partnership share immediately after the transfer is only 1%, so his lower proportion is 1%; Fiddler Ltd is not a corresponding partner, so it does not figure in the calculation.

(5) The SLP is therefore 1%, and SDLT is chargeable on the 99% of the market value effectively transferred to Fiddler Ltd.

Lease at rent and other transactions

7.16 The same principle applies where the acquisition takes the form of the grant of a lease at rent to the partnership from a partner or person connected with a partner. In that case, the calculation set out above is applied to each year's rent. The resulting apportioned rent figures are then used to calculate the SDLT on the net present value (NPV) of the rent in the normal way (see **6.50**). The same principle also applies where there is a variation of a lease or other chargeable interest which, on normal principles, is regarded as an acquisition by the partnership from a partner or person connected with a partner.

Example 7.4—Lease at rent, partnership shares vary

Twin sisters Gloria and Grace carry on a market research business in partnership with Harry, with whom they are not otherwise connected. Partnership profit-sharing ratios are adjusted at the end of each year in accordance with the partnership deed, using a formula which takes account of matters such as business won, hours worked etc. Gloria grants a 20-year lease to the partnership (strictly, to the partners jointly to hold on behalf of the partnership) at a time when the profit-sharing ratios are 25% to Gloria, 40% to Grace and 35% to Harry. The lease is for a rent of £25,000 per annum (thought to be market rent) and no premium, with a market rent review at the end of every fifth year. The partnership has the option to surrender the lease at each rent review date. The calculation steps are as follows:

(1) Gloria is the only relevant owner, owning 100% of the property before the grant of the lease.

(2) Gloria and Grace are corresponding partners, as they are the relevant owner or an individual connected with the relevant owner.

(3) Gloria's 100% ownership of the property before the grant of the lease is apportioned between Gloria and Grace – we choose to apportion 50% to each.

(4) Gloria's partnership share immediately after the grant of the lease is 25%, and Grace's is 40%. In each case, this is less than the apportioned ownership under (3), so in each case the partnership share is the lower proportion.

(5) Therefore the SLP is 25% + 40% = 65%, and the NPV of the remaining 35% of the rent, ie £8,750 per annum, is subject to SDLT. In this particular case, the NPV is less than £150,000, so no SDLT will be payable, but it will be necessary to submit an SDLT return (see **8.2**).

Two years later, the partners agree that the estimate of the market rent was wrong and it should have been £35,000 per annum. They therefore agree to vary the lease to increase the rent to this sum with effect from the start of the third year. At that time, the profit-sharing ratios are Gloria 30%, Grace 30% and Harry 40%. The variation to increase the rent is treated as the grant of a further lease for the remaining 18 years at a rent equal to the increase, which is £10,000 per annum – see **6.24** in this regard. Carrying out the SLP calculation shows that the NPV of 40% of this rent, or £4,000 per annum, is subject to SDLT. On its own, this would be too little to give rise to an SDLT cost. However, in this case, the deemed further lease is probably linked with the original lease (see **6.58** et seq). As a result, SDLT will be payable on both the original lease and the deemed further lease as a result of this rent increase. See Example 6.22 for an illustration of the calculation required.

Withdrawal of money after acquisition of property

7.17 The transfer of property from a partner or person connected with a partner to a partnership marks the start of a three-year period within which certain other events can lead to a further SDLT charge (*FA 2003, Sch 15, para 17A*). If, during that period, the partner concerned (ie the partner who transferred the property or the partner who is connected with the person who transferred the property) withdraws from the partnership money or money's worth which does not represent income profit, but:

- is capital withdrawn from the partners' capital account, or
- arises from the partner reducing his interest or ceasing to be a partner,

the withdrawal is treated as a chargeable land transaction. Where the original transfer was from a person connected with a partner, withdrawal of value by either the partner or any person connected with the partner is treated as a chargeable transaction. However, presumably, the connected person would have also to be a partner to be able legitimately to withdraw capital etc.

If the partner (or, where the original transfer was from a person connected with a partner, the partner or a person connected with the partner) has made a loan to the partnership, the repayment of any of the loan or a withdrawal of any amount by that person which does not represent income profit of the partnership is also treated as a chargeable land transaction.

In either case, the chargeable consideration is the smaller of:

- the amount withdrawn from or repaid by the partnership, and
- the market value of the land at the date of the original land transfer, reduced by any amount which has already been charged to SDLT.

If the withdrawal of money or money's worth is also subject to SDLT as a transfer of an interest in a 'property-investment partnership' (PIP) (see **7.30**), the SDLT charged under the 'withdrawal of money' provision is reduced by the amount of any charge under the 'transfer of an interest in a PIP' provision (*FA 2003, Sch 15, para 17A(8)*). If a '*paragraph 12A* election' (see **7.38**) has been made in respect of the property transfer, no SDLT arises on a subsequent withdrawal of value.

Example 7.5—Repayment of loan after transfer

Using the facts as in Example 7.2, the partnership does not have enough ready cash to pay the whole price of the building purchased from Danielle, so it is agreed that £350,000 will be left outstanding as a loan from Danielle to the partnership, with interest being charged at 2% above the Bank of England base rate, payable monthly in arrears. The loan arrangement has no effect on the SDLT charge on the initial transfer of the property to the partnership. One year later, after a purge on debtors, the partnership has enough cash and pays off the loan. The loan repayment is taken to be a land transaction, and SDLT is chargeable on the partnership. However, SDLT was paid on £200,000 when the property, with a value of £500,000, was transferred to the partnership. The chargeable consideration for the deemed land transaction cannot exceed the part of that market value which has not yet been taxed. So, SDLT is chargeable on £300,000, and not on the full £350,000 loan repayment. Note that this limitation is assessed by considering the market value of the property when it was transferred, and not the value at the time of the loan repayment or other withdrawal of value.

Had the partnership borrowed from a bank at the outset and paid Danielle in full, the SDLT charge on the original land transfer would still have been based on £200,000, but the subsequent repayment of the bank debt would not have given rise to an SDLT charge. It is difficult to see any policy reason for this discrimination, which therefore looks rather like a poorly directed anti-avoidance provision.

Transfer to a PIP may also involve a transfer of a partnership interest

7.18 The charge on the partnership when a new or existing partner (or someone connected with him) transfers a chargeable interest to the partnership does not depend on the amount or form of consideration given by the partnership. As suggested in Example 7.1, the consideration could take the form of admitting a new partner or increasing a partner's share. This acquisition of, or increase in, partnership share will be regarded as a transfer of an interest in a partnership. If the partnership is a property investment partnership (PIP), this transfer will be separately subject to SDLT (see **7.30**), chargeable on the new partner or the partner whose share has increased. This is in addition to the charge on the partnership arising from the acquisition of the property. The transaction is an exchange. This fact should not affect the calculation of SDLT because, both in transactions between a partnership and its partners (or persons connected with them) and in an exchange, SDLT is calculated by reference to the market value of the chargeable interests acquired (albeit indirectly, where a partnership interest is acquired) rather than the consideration given. As noted below (see **7.34** and **7.36**), the newly transferred property is not taken into account in determining the SDLT charge on the transfer of the partnership interest, so there is no double charge.

Example 7.6—Admission of partner, transfer of property

X Ltd and Y Ltd are limited partners in Spendit LP, a limited partnership which owns shopping centres and is clearly a PIP. The general partner is a Jersey-registered company with a negligible partnership share. X Ltd has a 40% partnership share, and Y Ltd has 60%. The shopping centres are worth £100 million. It is agreed that Z Ltd will be admitted as a limited partner with a partnership share of 30%, so that X Ltd's share drops to 28% and Y Ltd's to 42%. By way of payment, Z Ltd will transfer a further shopping centre to

Spendit LP, with a value of £45 million. Apart from membership of Spendit LP, there are no other connections between X Ltd, Y Ltd and Z Ltd.

- **Transfer of property to Spendit**: The calculation set out at **7.13** shows that Spendit is liable for SDLT on 70% of the £45 million value of the property brought to the partnership by Z Ltd.
- **Transfer of partnership share to Z Ltd**: Z Ltd is deemed to have acquired an interest in the 'relevant partnership property' owned by Spendit before Z Ltd joined. The consideration is the market value of the property multiplied by the partnership interest acquired, ie 30%. Whether the shopping centres already owned by Spendit are relevant partnership property will depend on their history, and the question of whether the transfer to Z Ltd is 'Type A' or 'Type B' (see **7.33** and **7.35**).

Disposal by a partnership

7.19 A disposal of a chargeable interest by a partnership should not directly give rise to any SDLT obligations for the partnership; it is for the purchaser to deal with any SDLT. If the disposal is to an unrelated third party, the purchaser will be liable for SDLT in the normal way, based on consideration given. However, if the disposal is to a partner or a person who has been one of the partners or to a person connected with a partner or a person who has been one of the partners, special rules come into play (*FA 2003, Sch 15, para 18*). These are similar to those outlined in the previous paragraph; their purpose is to ensure the purchaser pays SDLT only on the proportion of the property which he and/or connected individual partners did not already own indirectly through membership of the partnership. As in the previous paragraphs, SDLT is charged on deemed consideration equal to:

$$MV \times (100 - SLP)\%$$

where MV is the market value of the chargeable interest at the effective date of the transfer, and SLP is the 'sum of the lower proportions'. Again, a five-step calculation is required to determine SLP, set out in the legislation (*FA 2003, Sch 15, para 20*) as follows:

(1) Identify the 'relevant owner(s)'. These are persons who have an interest in the property immediately after it is transferred and are partners or connected with partners immediately before the property is transferred.

(2) For each relevant owner, identify the 'corresponding partner(s)'. These are persons who are partners immediately before the transfer and who are relevant owners or are individuals connected with relevant owners. For these purposes, a company may be regarded as an individual connected with a relevant owner *only* if it holds property as trustee and is connected by virtue of *CTA 2010, s 1122(6)* (trustee connected with settlor etc).

(3) For each relevant owner, take the proportion of the property to which he is entitled immediately after the transfer and apportion it between any one or more of his corresponding partners. Where a relevant owner has more than one corresponding partner, the apportionment may be performed in whatever manner gives the best result.

(4) Find the 'lower proportion' for each person who is a corresponding partner in relation to one or more relevant owners. The lower proportion is the lower of:

  (a) the proportion apportioned to him under (3) above, and

  (b) his partnership share immediately before the transfer.

(5) Add together the lower proportions for each partner who is a corresponding partner. This is the SLP.

Example 7.7—Transfer of property to partner

Alfred, Betty and Carl are (still) in partnership, sharing income profits 40%, 40% and 20% respectively. Betty and Carl are siblings, Alfred is not related to them. Betty decides to withdraw from the partnership and it is agreed she will take one of the properties in satisfaction of her entitlement to partnership capital. The calculation of Betty's SDLT liability is as follows:

(1) The only relevant owner is Betty, because she owns 100% of the property after the transfer.

(2) Betty and Carl are corresponding partners because they are, or are connected with, the only relevant owner, Betty.

(3) Betty is entitled to 100% of the property after the transfer. We choose to apportion this 50% to each corresponding partner, Betty and Carl.

(4) For Betty, her partnership share immediately before the transaction is 40%, and the proportion apportioned to her under (3) is 50%, so her lower proportion is 40%; for Carl, his partnership share immediately before the transaction is 20%, and the proportion apportioned to him under (3) above is 50%, so his lower proportion is 20%.

(5) The sum of the lower proportions is 40% (Betty) plus 20% (Carl), which is 60%.

The consideration for SDLT purposes is therefore MV × (100 – 60)%, or 40% of the market value. In this simple case, it can be seen that this represents the proportion of the property effectively transferred from the partner who is not connected with the final owner of the property. Again, the same principles apply in relation to rent if the 'transfer' is the grant of a lease at rent.

Example 7.8—Transfer of property to connected company

The initial facts are as in Example 7.7, but it is Alfred who wishes to withdraw from the business. It is decided to wind up the partnership and transfer the properties and other assets to a newly formed company BC Ltd in which Betty and Carl are equal 50% shareholders. It is agreed that BC Ltd will pay for the business and properties by paying Alfred an agreed amount of cash and by issuing shares to Betty and Carl. The calculation of BC Ltd's SDLT liability is analogous to that in Example 7.7:

(1) The only relevant owner is BC Ltd, because it owns 100% of the property after the transfer.

(2) Betty and Carl are corresponding partners because they are connected with the only relevant owner, BC Ltd. This is on the basis that both Betty and Carl will be treated as being connected with BC Ltd by virtue of *Corporation Tax Act 2010, s 1122(3)(b)* which states: 'A company is connected with another person ("A") if – … (b) A together with persons connected with A have control of the company.' As Betty and Carl are both connected with each other, as they are siblings, they are both treated as controlling BC Ltd (*Corporation Tax Act 2010, s 1122(5)(b)*).

The question which then arises is whether Alfred is also treated as having control of BC Ltd, even though he has no equity interest in BC Ltd. *Corporation Tax Act 2010, s 1122(3)(a)* states that: 'A company is connected with another person ("A") if – (a) A has control of the company …'. Control for these purposes is defined in *Corporation Tax Act 2010, s 450*, which broadly provides that a person has control of a company if he exercises direct or indirect control over the company's affairs. For these purposes the rights of any 'associate' of a person are attributed to that person in determining whether that person has control of a company (*Corporation Tax Act 2010, s 451(4)(c)*). *Corporation Tax Act 2010, s 448(1)(a)* provides that any partner of a person is an 'associate' of that person. Consequently, as Alfred is in partnership with Betty and Carl he will be an 'associate' of both, and attributing the rights and powers of Betty and Carl in relation to BC Ltd to Alfred would mean that Alfred would be treated as possessing the whole of the share capital of BC Ltd, and therefore he would be treated as controlling BC Ltd. Therefore, Alfred is connected to BC Ltd by virtue of *Corporation Tax Act 2010, s 1122(3)(a)*, and is consequently a corresponding partner in relation to BC Ltd.

(3) BC Ltd is entitled to 100% of the property after the transfer. We choose to apportion this 40% to Alfred, 40% to Betty and 20% to Carl.

(4) Alfred's partnership share immediately before the transaction is 40%, and the proportion apportioned to him under (3) above is also 40%, so his lower proportion is 40%. For Betty, her partnership share immediately before the transaction is 40%, and the proportion apportioned to her under (3) is 40%, so her lower proportion is 40%; for Carl, his partnership share immediately before the transaction is 20%, and the proportion apportioned to him under (3) above is 20%, so his lower proportion is 20%.

(5) The sum of the lower proportions is 40% Alfred plus 40% (Betty) plus 20% (Carl), which is 100%.

The consideration for SDLT purposes is therefore MV × (100 – 100)%, which is nil. It can therefore be seen that where all of the partners in a partnership are individuals the incorporation of the partnership should not give rise to a charge to SDLT.

There is an apparent conflict with the rule in *FA 2003, s 53* that a transfer to a connected company is deemed to be at not less than market value. However, HMRC have confirmed at SDLTM 34170 that the partnership rules override *FA 2003, s 53*.

7.20 In most cases after the transfer, the property will be owned by one person, so there will be only one relevant owner. If the transfer is to two or more persons as beneficial joint tenants, they are treated as owning as tenants in common, in equal shares.

Transfers between partnerships

7.21 The possibility is recognised that a property may be transferred from one partnership to another and that there may be connections or commonality between the partners. In that case, it is necessary to perform calculations of the chargeable consideration twice: once as set out at **7.13** (transfer to a partnership from connected owner); and once as explained at **7.19** (transfer from a partnership). The chargeable consideration is then to be taken as the higher of the two amounts thus calculated (*FA 2003, Sch 15, para 23*).

7.22 However, the following conditions must be satisfied if *FA 2003, Sch 15, para 23* is to apply:

(1) There must be a transfer of a chargeable interest from one partnership (the 'transferor partnership') to another partnership (the 'transferee partnership'). This means that the partnerships are treated as opaque for the purposes of the legislation and para 2 (which treats any chargeable interest held by a partnership as being held by the partners, and any land

transaction entered into by the partnership as having been entered into by the partners), cannot apply; and

(2) Both *FA 2003, Sch 15, para* 10 (see **7.13**) and *FA 2003, Sch 15, para 18* (see **7.19**) must apply to the transfer of the chargeable interest. For para 10 to apply the transfer must be made by a partner of the transferee partnership, or a person who becomes a partner in the transferee partnership in return for the transfer or, in either case, a person connected with that person. For *FA 2003, Sch 15, para 18* to apply the transfer must be to a person who is or has been a partner in the transferor partnership or to a person connected with a person who is or has been one of the partners in the transferor partnership. For these requirements to be satisfied the partnerships would have to be treated as transparent either under general law or as a result of the application of *FA 2003, Sch 15, para 2* (see above for the impact of *FA 2003, Sch 15, para* 2). Consequently, if it is accepted that *FA 2003, Sch 15, para 2* does not apply to *FA 2003, Sch 15, para 23* (it is not known whether HMRC accept this point) then the partnerships would have to be treated as transparent under general law, which would mean that neither the transferor partnership nor the transferee partnership could be a partnership with separate legal personality such as an LLP, Scottish partnership or a non-UK partnership which had separate legal personality.

It is considered that the better view is that *FA 2003, Sch 15, para 2* does not apply for the purposes of *FA 2003, Sch 15, para 23* and therefore that *FA 2003, Sch 15, para 23* only applies where the transferor partnership and the transferee partnership are partnerships which under general law do not have separate legal personality such as, an English general partnership, an English limited partnership etc. However, given the complexity of the analysis, it is suggested that consideration should be given to seeking a non-statutory clearance from HMRC if there is doubt as to whether *FA 2003, Sch 15, para 23* applies to a transaction.

Partnership share – special rules

7.23 As noted above (see **7.7**), for most SDLT purposes, partnership share is defined as the proportion in which the partner is entitled to share in income profits. A more complex analysis and calculation are required to determine the partnership share of any relevant partner, when this is required for step (4) in the SLP calculation on transfer of a chargeable interest out of a partnership (*FA 2003, Sch 15, para 21*). The complexity arises from an attempt to negate early SDLT mitigation which used partnership structures. In a straightforward case, if stamp duty or SDLT (based on market value or arm's-length consideration) has been paid on all properties acquired after 19 October 2003 and, where necessary, on transfers of partnership interests, the share of any partner should simply be the proportion in which he is entitled to share in income profits. However, to be certain of having the right numbers, it is necessary to work through the following steps:

(1) Check whether the chargeable interest which is the subject of the transfer (or from which any lease is granted, if the transaction is the grant of a lease):

  (a) was transferred to the partnership before 20 October 2003, or

  (b) was transferred to the partnership on or after that date, and either the instrument of transfer has been duly stamped or SDLT has been duly paid on the transfer.

  If neither (a) nor (b) applies, the partnership share of the partner is treated as zero.

(2) Assuming the partnership share is not zero under step (1), find the 'relevant date':

  (a) If (1)(a) applies and the partner was a partner on 19 October 2003, that is the relevant date.

  (b) If (1)(a) applies and the partner became a partner after that date, the date he became a partner is the relevant date.

  (c) If (1)(b) applies and the partner was a partner when the property was transferred to the partnership, the relevant date is the date of that transfer.

  (d) If (1)(b) applies and the partner became a partner after the property was transferred to the partnership, the relevant date is the date he became a partner.

(3) Find the partner's actual partnership share on the relevant date.

(4) Add to the share determined under (3) any increases in the partner's share, where:

  (a) if the increase resulted from a transfer which occurred on or before 22 July 2004, the instrument of transfer has been duly stamped with *ad valorem* stamp duty, and

  (b) if the increase resulted from a transfer which occurred after that date, any SDLT payable in respect of the transfer has been duly paid.

(5) Deduct from the result of (4) any decreases in the partner's partnership share during the period from the day after the relevant date to the day before the date on which the transfer of property out of the partnership occurs.

It can, therefore, be seen that a great deal of historic information may be needed to determine what should be a simple matter of a partner's partnership share.

Transfer from a corporate partnership

7.24 The rules are modified if a property is transferred from a partnership whose members are entirely bodies corporate and the SLP is 75% or more (*FA 2003, Sch 15, para 24*). In this case, no reduction is given for the SLP, and the consideration is deemed to be equal to the market value of the property (and, if the transfer is the grant of a lease at rent, the full NPV of the rent is subject to SDLT). This situation can only occur when the transferee is a partner with a 75% or higher partnership share. In this situation, the only way to reduce the SDLT charge is to claim group relief on the transfer. Group relief is modified for partnership transactions to allow for this (*para 27*; see **7.40**).

Transfer of an interest in a partnership

7.25 Whether a true transfer of an interest in a partnership is possible depends on the law governing the partnership, and the terms of the partnership deed or other agreements governing such matters. In some cases, it may be possible to achieve an effect equivalent to a transfer, only by one partner withdrawing capital or in some other way relinquishing some or all of his entitlement as partner, while another person becomes a partner, introduces new capital or increases his entitlement in some other way. For most transactions, the legislation makes these distinctions irrelevant, defining a transfer of an interest in a partnership as any occasion on which a person acquires or increases a partnership share (*FA 2003, Sch 15, para 36*). This is regarded as a transfer of partnership interest to the person acquiring or increasing partnership share and from the other partners. This is a very wide definition, covering not only situations where a person makes payments to other partners to acquire or increase his partnership share, but also where a person introduces capital on admission to the partnership, such that the actual value of the other partners' interests remains unchanged. The definition of transfer of a partnership interest was introduced from 19 July 2007; prior to that, a definition applied which did refer to changes in the actual value of each partner's interest.

7.26 When the special rules for partnership transactions were first introduced, *any* transfer of a share in any partnership which owned UK property was treated as a transfer of an equivalent share in the UK property. It was eventually accepted that this placed an unnecessary administrative burden on ordinary trading partnerships which happened to own their premises – profit-sharing ratios within large professional partnerships may change several times each year, and each could give rise to complex SDLT calculations as well as the need to value the property held. Therefore, *FA 2006* restricted the scope of the charge on transfers of partnership interests, so that it now only applies to transfers of interests in 'property investment partnerships' (PIPs). As a result, a transfer of an interest in a partnership which is not a PIP will not give rise to SDLT obligations, unless caught by anti-avoidance provisions (see **7.27**).

Transfer pursuant to earlier arrangements

7.27

If:

- a chargeable interest is transferred to a partnership from a partner or person connected with a partner (the **land transfer**),
- that person or partner then transfers any or all of his partnership interest under arrangements which were in existence at the time of the **land transfer**, and
- the partnership transfer would not otherwise be a chargeable transaction,

the partnership transfer is a chargeable land transfer (*FA 2003, Sch 15, para 17*). The partners are treated as the purchaser under this deemed transaction, and the chargeable consideration is the market value of the land at the date of the land transfer multiplied by the proportionate share in the partnership transferred under the arrangements. However, this treatment does not apply if an election is made in respect of the land transfer under *FA 2003, Sch 15, para 12A* (see **7.38**). As in other cases (see **5.25**), arrangements are defined as including any scheme, agreement or understanding, whether or not legally enforceable.

7.28 The practical implication is that, if a partner transfers a chargeable interest to the partnership and shortly after transfers all or part of his partnership interest, HMRC are likely to question whether the transactions are part of a single arrangement. The deemed land transaction arising as a result of such a transfer of an interest in a partnership is notifiable (by completion of an SDLT return) only if the deemed consideration is sufficient for tax to be payable (*FA 2003, Sch 15, para 30*). For example, if the initial property transfer to the partnership did not involve the grant of a lease at rent and if there are no linked transactions, the subsequent transfer of partnership interest will not be notifiable unless the deemed consideration exceeds the zero rate limit of £125,000 or £150,000 for residential or non-residential/mixed property respectively. In relation to the £125,000 limit this assumes that the additional rate of SDLT does not apply (see **4.56**) since, if it did apply, a 3% SDLT charge would arise if the property had a value of £40,000 or more.

Property investment partnerships

7.29 A property investment partnership (PIP) is defined as a partnership whose sole or main activity is investing or dealing in chargeable interests, whether or not the activity includes the carrying out of construction activities on the land (*FA 2003, Sch 15, para 14(8)*). So, a partnership which invests in property in order to receive rent or buys and sells property in order to make a profit (whether as a trade or an investment activity), is a PIP if this is its sole or main activity.

As indicated above the definition of a PIP states that it does not matter whether the activity of the partnership includes the carrying out of 'construction works' on the land that is being held as an investment or being bought and sold. Therefore a partnership whose main activity is investing in or dealing in land will not be excluded from being a PIP merely because it carries out some construction work before any profit is realised. However, as part of the Standing Committee debates on the amendment to the Finance Bill 2003, Sch 7, to restrict the availability of acquisition relief to companies whose main activity is the carrying on of a trade that does not consist wholly or mainly of dealing in chargeable interests the Economic Secretary to the Treasury stated:

> 'I understand that there have been worries that the concept of dealing in chargeable interests is uncertain, a point made by the hon Gentleman. It is unclear, for example, whether a property developer or house builder will be caught. Whilst it is ultimately a question of fact what trade a company is carrying on, I can reassure the Committee that property developers and house builders who derive most of their profits from their work, rather than from buying and selling would not be caught by the measure (*FA 2003, para 8(5A), Sch 7*). Companies that want reassurance about that in relation to their specific trade can approach HMRC to seek clarification.'

On this basis it is understood that HMRC accept that a partnership that generates most of its profits from property development should not be treated as a PIP.

If a partnership carries on more than one activity, some of which do not consist of investing or dealing in chargeable interests, it will be necessary to determine which isthe main activity. In many cases, this may be obvious, but it may be difficult in borderline cases, where the partnership perhaps devotes similar effort to two activities, only one of which is caught, and derives similar levels of profit from them. In such a case, it may be necessary to carry out detailed analysis of time spent on the different activities, capital employed in each and profits derived from each, in order to form a defensible view. Unfortunately, there is no room for compromise or apportionment – the partnership must be classified as wholly a PIP or not a PIP. If a partnership is a PIP, all property held must be considered as potential 'relevant partnership property' (as defined below); there is no exemption for any property which may be held for the purposes of a minority 'non-PIP' purpose.

Transfer of an interest in a PIP

7.30 A transfer of an interest in a PIP is treated as a chargeable transaction if the 'relevant partnership property' (see next paragraph) includes a chargeable interest. The consideration for the chargeable transaction is a proportion of the market value of the relevant partnership property; the proportion is the proportion by which the transferee's partnership share increases. Where the transfer of an interest in a PIP is one side of an exchange, the interest in the PIP is deemed to be a major interest in land if any of the relevant partnership property is a major interest – this then confirms the need to calculate SDLT by reference to the market values of the relevant partnership property (see **4.32**).

Example 7.9—Retirement of partner, linked transactions

DEF Partnership is a PIP with three partners D, E and F, each with a one-third partnership share. There is no connection between the partners other than the fact that they are partners in the DEF partnership. F decides to withdraw and D and E each make an agreed payment to F to acquire his share equally; as a result, the shares of D and E each increase to 50%. This is a Type A transfer (see **7.33**). The relevant partnership property (see **7.31**) has a value of £1.2 million. Each of D and E is treated as the purchaser under a chargeable transaction with consideration of one sixth of £1.2 million, or £200,000 (one sixth being the proportion by which their respective partnership shares increase). In the author's view, the two acquisitions are linked (see **4.84**) because they form a series or composite transaction between the same vendor (F) and purchasers D and E, who are connected within the terms of *CTA 2010, s 1122*. Note that, for the purposes of determining whether transactions are linked, the automatic connection of partners applies. The draft HMRC guidance on partnerships appeared to suggest that the transfers would not be linked but the final guidance does not comment on the issue.

Relevant partnership property

7.31 There are two definitions of relevant partnership property, depending on whether the transfer is classified as Type A or Type B (see **7.33–7.35**). This distinction, with its related rules, is the main concept introduced by the *FA 2008* changes to *FA 2003, Sch 15*. The intention of the legislation is to ensure SDLT is paid where a partnership structure is used to transfer economic ownership of property between partners for consideration. It seeks to avoid difficulties for partnership structures used in widely held property investment schemes or where transfers occur for no consideration (eg normal periodic adjustments of profit-sharing ratios). However, it is necessary to work through the definitions in any particular case. It would not be safe to decide that no SDLT charge arises purely on the basis of the general intention of the legislation. It is important to note that the distinction between Type A and Type B transfers is relevant only for deciding whether the partnership holds relevant partnership property and, if yes, its value. Both types of transfer are potentially subject to SDLT. However, in many Type B transfers, there will be no relevant partnership property and so no SDLT liability.

Market rent leases

7.32 Leases which satisfy certain very stringent conditions are referred to as 'market rent leases' and are always excluded from relevant partnership property. Therefore, if a partnership only holds leases of this kind, no transfer (whether Type A or Type B) will be a chargeable transaction. In practice, such partnerships are likely to be rare. To qualify as a market rent lease, a lease must have been granted for a market rent only (ie no premium and no arrangements for any future premium). Furthermore, either it must be for a term not exceeding five years or, if for a longer term, it must provide for market rent reviews at no longer than five-yearly intervals. Note that the rent review must provide for adjustment to a market rent, which means it must be possible for the rent to fall if market rents have declined. Most rent review clauses provide for upward-only reviews, and such a lease cannot qualify as a market rent lease, even though the inability of the rent to fall may have no practical effect. An anti-avoidance condition requires that there should not have been any amendment to the lease since it was granted which itself leads to the rent being less than a market rent immediately after the transfer of the partnership interest.

Example 7.10—Market rent leases, anti-avoidance rule

Partner X has a 99% share in the XY partnership which is a PIP. X grants a 200-year lease to the partnership at a market rent, with five-yearly market rent reviews. The partnership pays SDLT on the 1% of the NPV of rent, representing the 1% effectively transferred to Partner Y. X then agrees to reduce the rent to a peppercorn. This is a transfer to the partnership (see **6.28**), and the partnership pays SDLT on the 1% of the market value of the transfer (in practice, the value of the transfer is probably close to the market value of the freehold property). The partnership now owns virtually the whole economic value of the freehold property. X then transfers 98% of his partnership share to Y, for consideration. When it was granted, the lease was a market rent lease. But for the prohibition on subsequent amendments, it might still count as a market rent when the partnership share is transferred. The anti-avoidance condition ensures that the lease is not excluded from relevant partnership property. The value of the lease is, therefore, taken into account in determining any SDLT payable on the transfer of the partnership interest.

Type A transfers

7.33 Two situations give rise to a Type A transfer (*FA 2003, Sch 15, para 14(3A), (3B)*). The first occurs when the whole or part of a partner's interest as partner is transferred to another person (whether or not an existing partner) in return for consideration in money or money's worth. For the legislation to make sense, this must mean consideration given to the partner whose interest reduces (or to someone else at that partner's behest). The mere contribution of capital to the partnership by the person who gains partnership share does not amount to the giving of consideration for these purposes. The second occurs when a new partner joins and an existing partner withdraws money or money's worth from the partnership, thereby reducing or extinguishing his partnership share. However, this is not a Type A transfer if the withdrawal of money or money's worth comes from resources available to the partnership prior to the transfer.

Example 7.11—A Type A transfer

The PQR partnership is a PIP with three partners, P, Q and R, sharing profits equally. The partnership holds assets worth £1 million and cash on deposit of £200,000. P decides to retire. At the same time, the other partners decide to admit S as a new partner with a 20% share. S introduces capital of £240,000 for this share. The partnership uses £200,000 of this cash and the £200,000 previously on deposit to pay out P's capital. This is a Type A transfer.

7.34 If the transfer of an interest in a partnership is Type A, all chargeable interests held by the partnership are regarded as relevant partnership property, apart from market rent leases (see **7.32**) and any property transferred to the partnership in connection with the transfer of partnership interest (*FA 2003, Sch 15, para 5*).

Example 7.12—Type A transfer, relevant partnership property

The assets held by the PQR partnership (see Example 7.11) consist of: various plots of freehold building land purchased from third parties at various times and currently valued at £600,000; a long leasehold office transferred from P in 2006 and valued at £200,000; a warehouse leased from a third party; and sundry loose furniture and stock-in-trade valued at £150,000. The warehouse lease is at rent, subject to five-yearly market rent reviews and qualifying as a market rent lease (see **7.32**). However, local rents have increased dramatically since the last rent review 18 months ago. Because this lease has the benefit of three and a half years at the current rent, now substantially below current market levels, it is considered to have a value of £50,000.

The freehold building land and long leasehold offices, total value £800,000, are relevant partnership property for a Type A transfer. However, the warehouse lease is not relevant partnership property and may be ignored. The total partnership share transferred is 33.3%, being the share relinquished by the retiring partner: 20% of this goes to the new partner S for deemed consideration of £160,000 (20% of £800,000); and 6.7% goes to each of the continuing partners Q and R for deemed consideration of £53,336 each.

These are three separate transfers, so the question arises as to whether they are 'linked' (see **4.89**). If they are not linked, S will pay SDLT of £200, being 2% of £10,000; Q and R will pay no SDLT, because the consideration paid by each is below the threshold, but each will have to notify the transaction. If they are linked, the aggregate consideration will be £266,672, and the total SDLT liability will be £2,833 divided between the partners based on the consideration each is deemed to give. It is difficult to see how the transfers to Q and R can be anything other than linked, but aggregation of consideration for these transfers does not in itself give rise to a charge. It may be possible to argue that the transfer to S is not linked with the other transfers because, when the transfers were agreed, S was not a partner and so was not connected with Q and R. To strengthen the position, P, Q and R would be well advised to agree the surrender of 13.3% of P's capital *before* it is agreed to admit S on surrender of P's remaining 20%.

Type B transfers

7.35 Any transfer of an interest in a PIP which is not a Type A transfer is a Type B transfer (*FA 2003, Sch 15, para 14(3C)*). This includes:

- a transfer which is the result of an adjustment of profit-sharing ratios between the partners, with no partner paying any other for the transfer and no new partner being introduced; or
- a transfer which is the result of a partner (X) reducing his share or exiting the partnership, where no payments are made by any other partner and either no new partner is admitted, or, if a new partner is admitted, any amount withdrawn from the partnership by X is paid out of resources which were available to the partnership before the transfer. It is considered that 'resources' here includes previously arranged loan facilities.

Example 7.13—A Type B transfer

The XYZ partnership is a PIP with three partners, Z, Y and Z, sharing profits equally. The partnership holds assets worth £1 million and cash on deposit of £200,000. X decides to retire. It is agreed that X will take £400,000 cash in settlement of his partnership capital and accumulated profits. The partnership borrows £200,000 from its bank to fund this cash payment. Since no new partner has been admitted and no existing partner has paid anything for his increased partnership share, this is not a Type A transfer, so it must be a Type B transfer. Care is needed here. If Y or Z gives any additional security to the bank in relation to the borrowing, this could be interpreted as giving consideration for the additional partnership share acquired on withdrawal of X, making it a Type A transfer. Treatment as Type B will be more secure if the borrowing from the bank is arranged before X decides to retire.

Relevant partnership property for Type B transfers

7.36 In addition to market rent leases, the following property is excluded from relevant partnership property in a Type B transfer (*FA 2003, Sch 15, para 14(5A)*):

- any chargeable interest transferred to the partnership in connection with the transfer of partnership interest. For example, if an incoming partner pays his contribution to capital by transferring a property to the partnership, that property is not relevant partnership property. It is reasonable to exclude this from any SDLT calculation on the transfer of partnership share, since there will be a separate SDLT calculation/charge in respect of this property transfer (see **7.13**);
- any chargeable interest transferred to the partnership on or before 22 July 2004. This is the date from which this kind of partnership transaction was brought within the SDLT regime;
- any chargeable interest not economically attributable to the partnership interest transferred. For example, it may be that other partners have sole rights to profits and proceeds of a property, so that the partner receiving the partnership share gains no interest in that particular property – although this is an arrangement more commonly seen in relation to the premises of professional and trading partnerships than the assets of PIPs;
- any chargeable interest in respect of which an election has been made under *FA 2003, Sch 15, para 12A* (see **7.38**); and
- any other chargeable interest which was not acquired from a partner (existing or newly admitted) or from someone connected with such a partner.

The net result of these exclusions is that relevant partnership property for a Type B transfer consists only of property transferred to the partnership from a partner or connected person, after 22 July 2004, in respect of which no election has been made under *FA 2003, Sch 15, para 12A*, which is not a market rent lease, and which is not held solely for the benefit of partners other than the recipient of the transfer.

Notifying liability

7.37 A land transaction consisting of the transfer of an interest in a PIP is notifiable just like any other land transaction by completion of an SDLT return, but *only* if the deemed consideration, together with that for any linked transactions, is high enough to give rise to an SDLT liability (*FA 2003, Sch 15, para 30*). This contrasts with many other land transactions, where notification is needed even when no SDLT liability arises.

Paragraph 12A election

7.38 Normally, when a property is transferred to a partnership from one or more partners, or persons connected with partners, SDLT is not charged on the full market value, as explained at **7.13**. However, it is possible for a PIP to make an election under *FA 2003, Sch 15, para 12A* to disapply that rule and have SDLT charged on the full market value of the property. The property is thereafter effectively treated as if it had been acquired from an unconnected third party. The election must be made in the SDLT return for the transaction and, once made, is irrevocable.

If the election is made, it will normally increase the amount of SDLT payable immediately, since there will be no reduction in deemed consideration for the part of the property effectively remaining in the ownership of the transferor or his corresponding partner(s). This is not likely to be an attractive option in many cases, but may be worthwhile where the extra SDLT is not very large and it is anticipated that there will in future be Type B transfers of partnership interests. The election will then exclude the property from the calculation of SDLT on such transfers (see **7.36**).

RELIEFS

7.39 For the avoidance of doubt, *FA 2003, Sch 3, para 1* (exemption for transfer for no chargeable consideration) is specifically disapplied to transactions involving partnerships (*para 25(1)*). Apart from that, other reliefs and exemption generally do apply to transfers to and from partnerships, to the extent they would apply to transfers to and from the partners (*FA 2003, Sch 15, para 25(2)*). Additionally, a transfer of an interest in a partnership may qualify for relief if a direct transfer of relevant chargeable interests held by the partnership would have qualified.

7.40 Although group relief under *FA 2003, Sch 7* may apply to transfers involving partnerships, careful analysis of the various relationships will be required. All partnerships are regarded as 'transparent' as far as ownership of chargeable interests is concerned. However, some kinds of partnership are not treated as 'transparent' as far as ownership of shares is concerned:

(1) English general and limited partnerships do not have separate legal personality and are therefore regarded as transparent in relation to share ownership. As a result if all partners in such a partnership are members of a group, any company at least 75% owned by the partnership will also be a member of the group for SDLT purposes. Transfers of chargeable interests between the partners, the partnership and companies owned by the partnership (satisfying the normal 75% ownership test) will potentially qualify for group relief.

(2) All Scottish partnerships and all UK LLPs have separate legal personality and are therefore not transparent in relation to share ownership. Therefore a company owned by such a partnership cannot be in a group with the partners. Transfer of a chargeable interest between one or more partners and a company owned by the partnership cannot qualify for group relief. Furthermore, because chargeable interests held by the partnership itself are treated as owned by the partners (*FA 2003, Sch 15, para 2*), transfers between the partnership and a company which it owns cannot qualify for group relief.

(3) Scottish general and limited partnerships are not bodies corporate and so cannot function as the parent of a group. Therefore two companies, each directly owned by such a partnership, are not grouped with each other and a transfer of a chargeable interest between them cannot qualify for group relief. In contrast, an LLP is a body corporate and can function as the parent of a group. A transfer of a chargeable interest between companies directly or indirectly owned by an LLP may qualify for group relief, subject to satisfying the normal 75% ownership tests. It remains the case however that a transfer directly between the LLP and a company which it owns cannot qualify as explained at (2) above.

HMRC set out their views on these matters in SDLTM34360 to SDLTM34490.

Where group relief does apply, the wording of the provisions is modified to ensure that:

(1) relief is granted by reference to the partnership share of the partner(s) which are in the same group as the transferor/transferee company (*FA 2003, Sch 15, para 27A*), and

(2) in the case of a transfer to a partnership, relief is clawed back if those partners cease to be in the same group as the transferor while the partnership still holds the property or an interest derived from it (*FA 2003, Sch 15, para 27*).

7.41 The wording of charities relief is modified to ensure that it applies only if all of the chargeable interests held by the partnership are held for charitable purposes – that is, there is no partial relief if the partnership holds some properties for charitable purposes and some not (*FA 2003, Sch 15, para 28*).

SUNDRY PROVISIONS

7.42 Stamp duty continues to apply to a document which transfers an interest in a partnership, if that partnership holds stock or marketable securities; see **10.58** (*FA 2003, Sch 15, paras 31–33*).

The acquisition of a partnership interest is only subject to SDLT as set out above (*FA 2003, Sch 15, para 29*). If an interest in a partnership is acquired in some other way, it is not subject to SDLT.

Example 7.14—Non-chargeable acquisition of partnership interest

Cubit LLP is a business advisory partnership with 53 partners, employing 371 staff working out of 11 offices. Cubit has various interests in its office buildings, and a portfolio of business premises which it lets out, but rental income forms only 20 to 30% of its income, the balance coming from advisory and consulting activities. It is therefore considered that Cubit is not a PIP. The partners decide to admit three new partners, two from the existing workforce and one by direct appointment from outside. Each partner contributes £20,000 partnership capital (funded, in the case of the existing staff, by a corresponding loan from the partnership, to be repaid out of profit share) and has an initial profit share of 0.25%.

On the general definition, this amounts to three transfers of partnership interest to the new partners. However, as Cubit is not a PIP, and the transfers are not in connection with the transfer of chargeable interests in UK land, nor are they 'pursuant to earlier arrangements' involving transfers of chargeable interests (*FA 2003, Sch 15, para 17*), the transfers of partnership interests are not within the charge to SDLT.

Partnership property – guidance

7.43 A chargeable interest is partnership property for SDLT purposes if:

(a) it is held by or on behalf of the partnership, or by the members of a partnership; and

(b) it is held for the purposes of the partnership business (*FA 2003, Sch 15 para 34(1)*).

The HMRC guidance on what constitutes partnership property can be found at SDLTM33390. The guidance states as follows:

> 'In practice, whether a chargeable interest is partnership property or not for SDLT purposes will be decided by reference to whether it is partnership property by virtue of section 20 of the Partnership Act 1890. So a chargeable interest acquired, whether by purchase or otherwise, on account of the firm or for the purposes and in the course of the partnership business, will be partnership property for SDLT purposes.
>
> The mere fact that a business is carried on in property belonging to one or more partners does not make that partner's chargeable interest partnership property. Where a chargeable interest is owned by all the partners whether it is partnership property depends on the basis on which it is held by the co-owners.'

Therefore, for a chargeable interest to be partnership property the partnership must either acquire the chargeable interest or the partners must hold the chargeable interest on behalf of the partnership, and the mere fact that the partnership business is carried on from a property belonging to one of the partners will not be sufficient to make that chargeable interest partnership property for SDLT purposes.

Further guidance on the meaning of partnership property can be found at BIM82058.

Retrospective taxation?

7.44 The *FA 2007* changes contained the usual transitional provisions to ensure that they did not apply retrospectively to transactions already started at the time the changes were announced (2pm on 6 December 2006). The *FA 2008* changes then removed those transitional provisions. As a result, it appears that the rules, as amended by *FA 2008*, apply to all transactions, even those commenced before any of the changes were announced. In the, perhaps unlikely, event that completion is taking place of transactions which commenced so long ago, careful analysis will be required to establish whether the current rules lead to greater taxation than would have been the case under the pre-2007 rules and, if so, whether this is retrospective taxation which may be susceptible to challenge.

Chapter 8

SDLT Administration and Compliance

INTRODUCTION

8.1 This chapter deals with questions of what must be notified to HMRC, on whom the responsibility for notification and payment of SDLT falls, and the processes involved. It details deadlines, costs of missing them, and occasions on which payment of SDLT may validly be postponed. It explains how to claim repayment if a payment of SDLT proves excessive. Finally, it reviews the powers which HMRC have to enquire into and amend returns, assess unpaid or underpaid SDLT and seek penalties. The relevant legislation is in *FA 2003, ss 76–99* (including the amendments made by *FA 2019, s 46*) and *Schs 10–14*, and the *SDLT (Administration) Regulations 2003, SI 2003/2837*, as amended by the *SDLT (Administration) (Amendment) Regulations 2011, SI 2011/455* and the *SDLT (Administration) (Amendment) Regulations 2018, SI 2018/1319*. The *SDLT (Electronic Communications) Regulations 2005, SI 2005/844*, govern the electronic submission of SDLT returns. Precise references are given in appropriate paragraphs below.

SDLT is within the regime for disclosure of tax avoidance schemes (DOTAS), but with its own rules for determining what must be disclosed. Responsibilities in relation to DOTAS are dealt with in **Chapter 9**.

NOTIFICATION

What is notifiable, and by whom?

8.2 In general, (real) land transactions (see **4.7** for definition) are notifiable unless exempt. There is a list of exemptions, which also render the transaction non-notifiable, at **5.7**. If none of the exemptions apply, the transaction is notifiable even if no SDLT is payable. It is especially important to note that a transaction is not excused from being notified merely because a relief is available to reduce or remove the SDLT liability – reliefs must be claimed in a return.

Deemed land transactions also give rise to the obligation to notify. In many cases, a real transaction is deemed to be a land transaction (or to be the acquisition of a chargeable interest, which is automatically a land transaction; see **4.7**). Examples include the substantial performance of a contract before completion (see **4.10**), or variation of a lease to reduce the rent or term (see **6.28** and **6.29**). In other cases, actions or events are deemed to amount to transactions which are specifically stated to give rise to an obligation to submit an SDLT return. One example would be on final determination of uncertain consideration or rent, if that leads to further SDLT becoming payable (see **4.20**).

Three cases involving anti-avoidance provisions are specifically stated to be notifiable (*FA 2003, s 77(1)(c), (d)* and *(e)*). These are the deemed transaction on substantial performance of a contract providing for conveyance to a third party (see **5.15**), the 'notional land transaction' under *FA 2003, s 75A* (see **9.4** et seq), and the notional or additional land transaction under *FA 2003,Sch 2A, para 5* (see **5.11** et seq). In each of these cases, most of the exemptions from notification outlined in **5.7** do not apply; so, for example, a deemed transaction under one of these sections is notifiable even if the consideration is below the normal £40,000 notification threshold. However, exemptions from notification *do* apply to secondary transactions in 'alternative finance' arrangements (see **5.39**) and transfers of partnership interests (see **7.37**). It is not clear why the exemptions should apply to some transactions but not to others, and this may simply be the result of poor structuring of the legislation. Making these notional transactions notifiable places responsibility for interpretation and application of the general anti-avoidance rules firmly on the taxpayer.

In relation to timing of obligations, see **4.85** et seq.

Exempt transactions

8.3 If a transaction is exempt, there is no obligation to notify it to HMRC (*FA 2003, s 77A*). However, the taxpayer does still have the obligation to maintain records relating to the transaction for at least six years (see **8.61**). When SDLT was introduced, it was possible for the taxpayer to 'self certify' that the transaction was exempt. The self certificate could then be used as evidence that SDLT obligations had been completed, allowing the land transaction to be registered. Self certificates were abolished by *FA 2008*; when registering an exempt transaction, it is now necessary simply to inform the Land Registry that the transaction is exempt.

8.4 Sometimes, taxpayers choose to complete returns for transactions which appear to be exempt. This is commonly done to guard against future allegations of failure to notify, where exemption is dependent on a treatment of the facts which could be susceptible to challenge. This is considered in more detail at **8.47**.

Responsibility for notifying

8.5 Responsibility for notification and payment of any tax falls on the purchaser (*FA 2003, s 76*; SDLTM00060). The identity of this person is usually self-evident, being the person who gains beneficial ownership of the land interest. However, there are several provisions identifying the purchaser in particular circumstances:

- When property is transferred to a partnership, or where value is withdrawn from a partnership after such a property transfer (see **7.13** and **7.17**), all of the partners are purchasers and have joint and several responsibility for notification. They may nominate one or more responsible partners, but this does not remove the responsibilities of individual partners if the nominated partners fail in their duties (*FA 2003, Sch 15, paras 6–8*).
- When a lease is varied to shorten the term, the landlord is the purchaser. If it is varied to reduce the rent, the tenant is the purchaser (*FA 2003, Sch 17A, para 15A*).
- Where trustees of a settlement other than a bare trust acquire beneficial ownership of a property, they are the purchasers (*FA 2003, Sch 16, para 4*). The obligation to make a return may be discharged by any one or more of the trustees, but subsequent obligations, for example in relation to enquiries by HMRC, then fall on the trustees who signed the return. Where trustees (or nominees) acquire a property under a bare trust, the person on behalf of whom the acquisition is made is normally treated as the purchaser (*FA 2003, Sch 16, para 3(1)*). However, if the acquisition by bare trustees takes the form of the grant of a lease to them, they are treated as purchasers of the whole beneficial interest in the lease (*FA 2003, Sch 16, para 3(2)*; see **4.18**). In origin, this is an anti-avoidance provision.
- Where the Official Solicitor is acting for a person under a disability (eg mental incapacity), the Official Solicitor may notify on behalf of that person (*FA 2003, Sch 10, para 1B*). However, the person for whom the Official Solicitor acts remains the purchaser and therefore is liable for tax, interest and penalties where these arise.

How to notify

8.6 Notification is by submission of a land transaction return (LTR) to HMRC. For transactions with an 'effective date' (see **4.91** and **6.74**) on or after 1 March 2019 the LTR is due within 14 days from the 'effective date' of the transaction (*FA 2003, s 76(1)* as amended by *FA 2019, s 46(2)* – see **4.8**). The new 14-day time limit also applies to transactions with an 'effective date' before 1 March 2019 which only become notifiable on or after 1 March 2019 (*FA 2003, s 76(1)* as amended by *FA 2019, s 46(2)* and *(10)(b)*).

If the 'effective date' (see **4.91** and **6.74**) of the transaction was before 1 March 2019, and the transaction became notifiable before 1 March 2019, then the LTR is due within 30 days from the 'effective date' of the transaction (*FA 2003, s 76(1)* prior to its amendment by *FA 2019, s 46(2)*).

With the aim of making compliance with the revised 14-day time limit easier new forms SDLT3 and SDLT4 were introduced (*The Stamp Duty Land Tax (Administration) (Amendment) Regulations 2018, SI 2018/1319* which were laid before the House of Commons on 10 December 2018 and came into force on 1 March 2019).

Paper forms

8.7 An LTR must be in a form and containing information prescribed by regulations, or in such other form as has been 'approved by the Board', ie HMRC (*FA 2003, Sch 10, para 1*). The principal regulations are the *SDLT (Administration) Regulations 2003, SI 2003/2837*, as amended by the *SDLT (Administration) (Amendment) Regulations 2011, SI 2011/455* and the *SDLT (Administration) (Amendment) Regulations 2018, SI 2018/1319*. The 2011 regulations include a facsimile of the general LTR (form SDLT1) and supplementary forms required in some cases (forms SDLT3 and SDLT4). Form SDLT2 was not amended by the 2011 regulations and so is as included in the 2003 regulations. The 2018 regulations amend the existing regulations in relation to the procedure for applying to defer payment of SDLT in certain cases of contingent or unascertained consideration (see **8.30** et seq) and provide new forms SDLT3 and SDLT4. Facsimiles of the new forms SDLT3 and SDLT4 are included within the 2018 regulations. The forms (including the new forms SDLT3 and SDLT4) are reproduced at **Appendix B**. Form SDLT2 should be completed if there are either more than two purchasers or more than two sellers. Form SDLT3 is filled in if either more than one property is acquired or, there is only one property but it is not possible to fit the full address of the property into the space on the SDLT1 form. Finally form SDLT4, as well as form SDLT1, should be completed in the following circumstances:

- the land or property acquired is mixed-use property (see **4.37**) or non-residential property (see **4.37**);
- the purchaser is a company;
- the transaction relates to the grant of a lease over residential property, or the acquisition of an interest in residential property where there is a lease involved, and there is more than one property;
- the transaction is part of a sale of a business;

- the purchaser has asked HMRC for advice on how the law applies to the transaction by requesting a non-statutory clearance or a post-transaction ruling in accordance with CAP 1 (Clearances and Approval 1) has been requested;
- any part of the consideration other than rent is contingent or uncertain;
- an application has been made, or is to be made, to HMRC to defer SDLT on contingent or uncertain consideration (see **8.31**); and
- there are mineral rights reserved.

The regulations permit use of a different form if approved by HMRC. If paper forms are to be submitted you must use the official HMRC print of the form. Each SDLT1 has a unique reference number (the unique transaction reference number or UTRN), and an original form must be used for each return. Previously, it was acceptable to use photocopies of blank supplementary forms, but HMRC's latest instructions insist on originals of these too. Insistence on a single original paper form causes difficulties in some cases, especially when the required signatories are scattered over several locations or perhaps located overseas; electronic submission may be easier in such cases. Supplies of forms may be obtained from HMRC; see **Appendix A**. Forms must be completed in black ink (*reg 9(1)*) to aid reading by an electronic scanner. Further guidance on the completion of the forms is set out at **8.19** et seq.

It was possible to continue to use the old Forms SDLT3 and SDLT4 to notify a transaction provided the forms were delivered before 1 June 2019 (*SDLT (Administration) (Amendment) Regulations 2018, SI 2018/1319, reg 3).*

8.8 Routine paper returns should be sent to the Stamp Office at the address shown in **Appendix A**. Apart from the return, any supplementary forms, a cheque in payment of the SDLT (if paying by cheque) and a plan (if one is provided), no correspondence or other documents should be included. If paying by cheque it should be made payable to 'HM Revenue and Customs only' followed by the 11-character unique transaction reference number (UTRN). If you are sending a cheque for more than one UTRN, HMRC advise sending a schedule listing each UTRN against each amount. The payslip on the back of the paper return needs to be completed and sent with the cheque. You can include a letter with the payment asking for a receipt from HMRC. For guidance where it is considered necessary to submit other information or documents to HMRC, see **8.47**. HMRC request that the papers be submitted in an A4 or larger envelope, without folding, as folding may cause problems with machine reading. HMRC advise that three working days should be allowed for a cheque to reach them. They also encourage payment by means of 'Faster Payments', 'CHAPS' or 'Bacs' or other electronic means (including debit cards or corporate credit cards) where possible, to minimise the risk of payment going astray. Links to appropriate destination bank account details are at www.hmrc.gov.uk/payinghmrc/stamp-land.htm, which should be consulted whenever payments are made in case account details change.

Electronic returns

8.9 The *SDLT (Electronic Communications) Regulations 2005, SI 2005/844*, permit delivery of LTRs electronically and, on this basis, HMRC offer the facility to submit LTRs via the internet once the person making the submission has registered for the purpose. The forms can be completed and submitted using basic software provided free of charge by HMRC, or by using commercial software which has more features. The forms are fundamentally the same as the paper versions, and the guidance set out below (at para **8.19** et seq) applies equally to the electronic forms. Links to appropriate paragraphs of HMRC's own guidance on completion, equivalent to the guidance for paper returns (see **8.20**), should be available as each section of the return is completed. The online forms are 'intelligent', in that they decide which sections to present for completion in accordance with sections already completed; they should, therefore, make it clear when completion of supplementary forms is required. Part-completed forms can be stored for later finalisation and submission. The software should also check for inconsistencies or omissions and prevent submission if these are found. However, the software will not check for technical errors, so the fact that submission is allowed does not guarantee that the return is correct! The electronic forms are just as restrictive and limited as their paper counterparts, so the same difficulties arise in ensuring adequate disclosure (see **8.19** and **8.47**).

If you have filed the return electronically but wish to pay by cheque then the cheque should be sent to the Stamp Office at the address shown in **Appendix A** enclosing a payslip and quoting a UTRN to avoid delay. You can include a letter with the payment asking for a receipt from HMRC. However, as highlighted at **8.8,** electronic payment is encouraged by HMRC.

8.10 Paper returns have to be signed by the purchaser(s) (*FA 2003, Sch 10, para 1(1)(c)*), but clearly this is not possible for electronic forms. Instead, before an agent is permitted to submit the final return, he must confirm that the purchaser has approved the draft return and that appropriate evidence of this is held. The only fact which is allowed to be missing from the draft approved by the purchaser is the 'effective date' (see **4.91** and **6.74**). This allows the forms to be drafted before completion of the transaction, approved by the purchaser, and then finalised and submitted immediately on the 'effective date' (*FA 2003, Sch 10, para 1A*).

8.11 When a return is submitted online, the HMRC certificate (form SDLT5) is issued automatically and immediately. This contrasts with submission of paper returns, when there may be a delay of several days or even weeks before the SDLT5 is received. The SDLT5 certificate must be submitted to the Land Registry to permit registration of the purchaser's interest or the change brought about by the transaction, so there is a clear advantage in receiving this immediately.

8.12 Before using the online submission facility, it is necessary to register with HMRC, following the process which begins with a link under 'Do it online' on the SDLT Index page of the HMRC website, at www.hmrc.gov.uk/sdlt/index.htm. The process includes waiting for postal delivery of a PIN before the service can be activated, so it is not a good idea to wait until a return is due before registering. HMRC recommend allowing ten working days (21 working days if you are outside of the UK) to register.

Integration of SDLT compliance and registration of land transactions

8.13 It is understood to be a long-held government ambition to integrate collection and routine administration of SDLT with registration of land transactions, leaving HMRC to deal with policy and policing. Prior to 1 April 2015 it was possible for law firms, licensed conveyancers, mortgage lenders, etc for many transactions involving registered land in Scotland, to deliver LTRs via the Registers of Scotland under the ARTL system for Automated Registration of Title to Land. However, in practice, for a variety of reasons, few firms actually used the system. It remains to be seen whether the integration of SDLT compliance and the registration of land in England and Northern Ireland will ever be achieved.

Electronic submission of LTRs may eventually become compulsory but, for the time being, paper forms are still acceptable.

On 8 July 2014 HMRC produced updated guidance on submission of LTRs, in relation to land situated in Scotland, for transactions with an 'effective date' (see **4.74** and **6.74**) both before 1 April 2015 and on or after 1 April 2015 (the date from which Land and Buildings Transaction Tax applies to transactions over land in Scotland), including the facility to have paper forms SDLT5 produced very quickly when necessary. This guidance is available at www.hmrc.gov.uk/sdlt/return/scottish.htm#7.

Computer-generated paper forms

8.14 When SDLT was introduced, as a first step towards automation, it was possible to complete return forms on screen (using software provided by HMRC or independent suppliers) before printing out, signing and submitting the printed copy. Because these computer-generated forms did not bear a unique number (UTRN, see **8.7**), HMRC provided separate numbered payslips for payment of SDLT. The number from the relevant payslip was added to the computer-generated return form and functioned as its UTRN. Software was then developed to summarise information in the forms in a barcode printed on the forms ('2D Bar-coded Forms') which could be machine read more easily. These methods of submitting returns are no longer available; the choice is only between handwritten paper forms and full online submission.

Further and amended returns

8.15 A number of transactions and events, described at various points in this book, give rise to the requirement to submit a further LTR when one has already been submitted for the original transaction, or to amend the original LTR. It is important to follow the correct procedure for amending or submitting further returns (see **8.17** et seq). HMRC have expressed concern that they too often receive a duplicate return with the request to cancel the original, when an amendment or correction is required (see Stamp Taxes Bulletin 1/2014, www.hmrc.gov.uk/so/bulletin01-2014.pdf). In most cases amendments and further returns do not require submission of a further form SDLT1!

Example 8.1—Further return, variable rent

On 11 June 2020 Dave enters into a seven-year lease of a pub; the lease is executed without prior substantial performance of any agreement. The rent is provisionally fixed at £30,000 per annum, but this is to be adjusted at the end of each year using a formula which takes account of turnover in the year just ended. An LTR is submitted within 14 days of the grant of the lease. At the end of the first five years, it is established that the rent has been above £30,000 in all years, so further SDLT is payable. A further return is due within 30 days of the end of the fifth year of the lease (*FA 2003, Sch 17A, para 8(3A)* as introduced by *FA 2019, s 46(8)(c)*). See **8.17** for details of how to make the further return. If the original grant of the lease had not been notifiable because the NPV of the rent was below the £150,000 threshold, however the lease became notifiable as a result of the rent for the first five years being ascertained, an SDLT1 form would have had to be submitted within 14 days of the rent being ascertained (*FA 2003, Sch 17A, para 8(3)* as amended by *FA 2019, s 46(8)(c)*).

Example 8.2—Further return, clawback of relief

Dozy Ltd purchases a property from group company Dee Ltd and submits an LTR on which group relief from SDLT is claimed. Two years later, on

28 August 2020, Dozy Ltd, while still owning the property, is sold to a third party. Dozy Ltd must make a further return reporting the withdrawal of group relief within 30 days of whichever step leads to its old parent group ceasing to have beneficial ownership of its shares (*FA 2003, s 81(a)*). See **8.17** for details of how to make the further return.

Example 8.3—Further return, final determination of consideration

On 25 November 2020 Beaky Ltd buys a property from a connected company Mick Ltd and files an LTR, paying SDLT based on an estimated market value. One month later, it is discovered that the market value was under-estimated. Beaky Ltd must amend the original return to show the correct value, within 14 days of discovering the error. See **8.17** for details of how to amend the return. Nine months after the original transaction, it is realised that Beaky Ltd and Mick Ltd are group companies. Beaky Ltd may, if it so wishes, further amend the return to claim group relief and seek repayment of the SDLT paid. However, amendment is not compulsory because it would lead to a decrease in the SDLT charge.

8.16 It is important to establish whether the required action is:

(1) submission of a new return for a new transaction, which may or may not be linked with the original transaction;

(2) submission of a further return for the original transaction, perhaps now modified in the light of subsequent events or facts; or

(3) amendment of the return originally submitted in respect of the original transaction.

In some cases, (1) will be necessary as well as either (2) or (3). As noted in **8.17**, there is no practical difference between (2) and (3). Even where amendment is not *required*, a purchaser may voluntarily amend a return within 12 months of the filing deadline for the original return (eg in order to claim a relief which was omitted from the original return, or to correct a calculation error which led to payment of the wrong amount of SDLT). If an error is discovered which led to an underpayment of SDLT, it is an offence to fail to amend the return which may give rise to a penalty (see **8.52**). A new return for a new transaction is generally made by completion of a new SDLT1 (whether paper or online), together with supplementary forms if necessary. If the new transaction is linked with a previous transaction, there is space on the return to note this fact. This linking may also lead to the need to amend the return, or to submit a further return, for the original transaction.

Example 8.4—Further return, later linked transaction

The facts are as in Example 4.21. Tanya submits an LTR (using form SDLT1) in respect of the first house purchase, on or before 24 January 2020. This shows tax chargeable of £5,500, being £125,000 at 3% plus £35,000 at 5%. When the second purchase completes, Tanya submits an LTR (another form SDLT1) in respect of the second purchase. In this return she claims multiple dwellings relief (see **5.57**) which results in tax chargeable on the second purchase of £17,714. She also makes a further return (by letter, not form SDLT1, see **8.17**) in respect of the original purchase, also claiming multiple dwellings relief and showing the tax now increased to £7,086. With this return, Tanya pays the additional tax of £1,586 now due on the first purchase. The new return for the second purchase, which has an 'effective date' (see **4.91** and **6.74**) of 15 June 2020 is due by 29 June 2020, as is the tax payable of £17,714 (*FA 2003, s 76(1)* as amended by *FA 2019, s 46(2)*). The further return for the first purchase and the payment of the additional tax due of £1,586 are due by 15 July 2020 (*FA 2003, s 81A(1)* prior to its amendment by *FA 2019, s 46(5)*). As noted below, the further return in respect of the first purchase is made by letter, not completion of form SDLT1.

How to submit further and amended returns

8.17 In principle, submission of a further return for the original transaction and amendment of the original return are different processes; the legislation specifies which is required in each situation. In practice, HMRC guidance states that each requirement is to be satisfied by the submission of a letter to the Stamp Office (see **Appendix A**) (www.hmrc.gov.uk/sdlt/return/amend.htm). The letter must quote the UTRN which appeared on the original return and set out details of the changes and/or further information, including any further payment required. The letter should refer to the appropriate numbered boxes on the original return, so it is important that a copy of that return be retained. Where the legislation specifies that a further return must be submitted but, in practice, HMRC require that a letter be sent, they are presumably relying on the fact that the regulations permit use of a form other than SDLT1 'in a form that has been approved by the Board' (see **8.7**). In the case of minor corrections not affecting the substance of the transaction (eg typographical errors, correction of vendor details, wrong title number, etc), HMRC are willing to accept amendment by telephone, but in the author's view it is always safer to write.

Correction of errors in returns

8.18 HMRC may also unilaterally correct minor errors and omissions, in which case notice must be given to the person(s) who submitted the return (*FA 2003, Sch 10, para 7(1)* and *(2)*). The person(s) to whom notice is given may reject the amendment (*FA 2003, Sch 10, para 7(4)*):

- by re-amending the return within the permitted 12 months, or
- if notice is received from HMRC later than nine months after the filing date, by giving notice that the amendment is rejected within three months of the date of issue of HMRC's notice.

This facility to correct obvious errors was well used in the early days of SDLT, but it is now much more likely that a return with errors which prevent processing will be rejected and will require re-submission after correction by the taxpayer. A major point in favour of online submission is that many errors are highlighted and must be corrected before the return can be submitted.

Practical completion of return forms

8.19 The return forms are input documents for an automated system, and the paper versions are designed to be machine read, which is why the regulations specify completion in black ink (*SI 2003/2837, reg 9*). The forms contain a series of numbered boxes and are very limited and limiting in terms of information which may be included. Some boxes are for matters such as names, addresses, dates and monetary amounts; beyond this, they are completed by inserting 'X' to show that a particular statement applies, or by inserting a letter or number to indicate which statement or item applies from a list.

8.20 Guidance on completion, including lists of the relevant codes, was previously contained in booklet SDLT6 'How to complete your Land Transaction Return', which was available as a paper booklet, a downloadable PDF file or an online interactive document. However, this was withdrawn on 2 July 2012 and replaced by separate guidance on the different forms. This is available at www.hmrc.gov.uk/sdlt/return/paper.htm. The guidance was last updated on 28 September 2018. Paper copies of the guidance are no longer available, although it is possible to print the online guidance. The guidance contains links to appropriate sections of the Stamp Duty Land Tax Manual and other HMRC pronouncements where it is thought these will be helpful. If the guidance is printed out for future use, it will still be safest also to check the current online version for recent changes.

SDLT Return forms were amended in April 2011 to require the input of information allowing HMRC to link together tax records of the purchaser (or lead purchaser if more than one). It is now necessary to disclose the National Insurance number of an individual or the UK or overseas tax reference number of a company or partnership. If the purchaser is VAT registered, the VAT number must also be shown on the principal SDLT1 form. If none of these identifiers is available, another unique identifier such as a passport or driving licence number is acceptable. If the purchaser has none of these numbers, it is necessary to contact the Stamp Taxes Helpline (see **Appendix A**) to obtain a reference number before submitting the return.

8.21 The LTR has two functions:

(1) to set out the information to establish the amount and timing of liability to SDLT; and

(2) to provide the government with statistical information (*FA 2003, Sch 10, para 1(4)*).

In relation to the purchase of properties leased to multiple tenants, prior to 1 March 2019 the purchaser was required to collate a lot of detail which may not be readily available. On or after 1 March 2019 the detail required has changed – see **8.24**. However, it will still be important to be aware of the requirements and to begin gathering information as early as possible to minimise the risk of submission of the return being delayed beyond the due date. This is particularly important given the reduction in the filing deadline from 30 days to 14 days. With the aim of making compliance with the revised 14-day time limit easier new forms SDLT3 and SDLT4 were introduced (*The Stamp Duty Land Tax (Administration) (Amendment) Regulations 2018, SI 2018/1319* which were laid before the House of Commons on 10 December 2018 and came into force on 1 March 2019). A number of questions have been removed from the SDLT4 form, and other questions have been changed to make them clearer, which should hopefully make it easier to comply with the new 14-day deadline.

8.22 In general, the manner of completion of the boxes is self-evident or adequately explained by the HMRC instructions, although careful close reading of the instructions is essential. This section of the book does not aim to replicate the HMRC guidance, and therefore provides comment only where something useful can be added. There is one important caveat: HMRC's instructions for completion of some of the forms have changed significantly over the last few years. The reader must take care to follow the latest instructions.

Form SDLT1

8.23

Box	Heading	Comment
1	Type of Property	Code '04' was added, with effect from 1 April 2016, and is to be used where the purchaser is an individual acquiring a residential property, and the individual owns more than one residential property at the end of the day which is the 'effective date' (see **4.91**). The use of code '04' means that the additional rate of SDLT applies to the transaction (see **4.39**). However, if the residential property being acquired is a replacement for the purchaser's main residence, which was sold in the three-year period prior to the 'effective date' of the transaction then code '04' should not be used and, instead, code '01' should be used. If the new residential property is a replacement for the purchaser's main residence which has not yet been sold, code '04' should still be used however the purchaser may be able to claim a refund of the additional rate of SDLT if the main residence is sold within three years of the purchase of the new main residence (see **4.56** et seq). Code '04' must also be used if the purchaser is a company or non-individual purchasing any residential property even if the property acquired is the only residential property owned. Code '01' should be used for the purchase of residential property where the additional rate of SDLT does not apply eg an individual purchaser replacing his main residence. Code '02' is used where the property being acquired is mixed use and code '03' where the property being acquired is non-residential.
2	Description of transaction	Care is needed because the meaning of terms used in the guidance notes differ slightly from normal legal meanings – a transfer of a leasehold interest, or a transfer of a freehold subject to a lease, is A (other, involving lease), not F (conveyance or transfer). Where L (the grant of a new lease or replacement lease) or A is entered here, it is very important to complete boxes 16 to 21 (in the case of A or L) and 22 to 25 (in the case of L) – see SDLTM62050 for further guidance.
3	Interest transferred or created	Code LG is labelled 'long leasehold', but in fact the length of the lease is irrelevant. Any lease at a ground or nominal rent with vacant possession is LG.
5	Restrictions etc	This requires judgement as to what is unusual; the entry in this box has no effect on whether the form will be processed, but omission of facts which could influence how HMRC view the transaction may make it more difficult to resist a discovery assessment later (see **8.47**). The examples of restrictions given by HMRC are: (a) the vendor has the right to buy the property back at less than market value; (b) the lease covenants restrict shop use; and (c) agricultural occupancy condition applies.

Box	Heading	Comment
9	Reliefs	'PFI relief' (see **5.17**) must be claimed as code 28 ('other relief'). The relief may reduce consideration to zero, but a return showing zero consideration may be rejected. If this applies, the normal approach seems to be to insert consideration of £1 and write a 'further information' letter to HMRC (see **8.47**) explaining that this has been done. Code 32 should be used for the first-time buyer's relief (see **5.47** et seq). New codes are introduced from time to time, so the guidance at www.hmrc.gov.uk/news/new-guide-sdlt.htm should be checked where necessary.
10	Consideration	It is a common error to put an entry here when a lease is granted at a premium. If a lease is granted, this box must be left blank – the premium and rent are reported later in boxes 22 and 23 (where zeroes are required if there is no premium/rent). However, for a lease it is still necessary to put a figure in Box 14 for the total amount of tax due. The total tax due for the lease will be the sum of the figures in boxes 24 (premium) and 25 (NPV of rent), each of which may be zero if, for example, relief is being claimed.
13	Linked transactions	The 'total consideration' box should show the aggregate capital consideration paid for linked transfers of freeholds and existing leases, plus any premiums paid on grant of new leases or amendment of existing leases where these are also linked. This should include amounts in respect of the transaction(s) reported on this SDLT1. However, it should not include any amount in respect of the NPV of rent on any leases. There is no place on the return to show the aggregate NPV of rents under linked leases. The aggregate NPV must be taken into account in calculating the entry in box 25 (Tax due in respect of NPV) – see **6.58** et seq for an illustration of the significance of this.
15	Total amount enclosed/ paid	If application has been made to defer payment of any of the tax (see **8.33**), HMRC will give instructions on completion of this box. If necessary, contact the Stamp Taxes Helpline (see **Appendix A**) for guidance. It is **not** possible to apply for deferral by entry on the return form – application must be made separately.
26	Number of properties	See **8.26** for use of schedules where 100 or more properties are involved.
28	Address	In paper returns, if the address does not fit in the space available, start writing it here and simply put on form SDLT3 the part which does not fit – do not write the whole address on the supplementary form, or you may receive an SDLT5 certificate with a jumbled address for the land, which the Land Registry may reject.

Box	**Heading**	**Comment**
29	Local Authority number	It is now compulsory to insert the Local Authority number, which can be obtained at SDLTM62320. Scottish Local Authority numbers ceased to be valid from 1 April 2015 as Land and Buildings Transaction Tax will apply to most land transactions in relation to land in Scotland (see **Chapter 2**) and use of these codes will lead to rejection of the return. Where a land transaction in relation to land in Scotland has an effective date on or after 1 April 2015, but remains liable to SDLT under the transitional rules (eg an SDLT lease that continues after a fixed term), an SDLT1 form must be filed in the normal way and code 9998, and not a Scottish local authority code, should be entered at box 29.
30, 31	Title number and NLPG UPRN	If this information is not readily available, these boxes can be left blank. This will have no effect on whether the form is processed successfully.
49–51	About the purchaser	See **8.20** for requirement if purchaser does not have an NI number or Unique Tax Reference number.
61	Agent authority	Accidentally leaving this blank is a major cause of agents failing to receive SDLT5 certificates or other communications from HMRC.

Form SDLT4

8.24

Part 2	About leases	Where a property is transferred while subject to more than one lease to tenants, the first lease is reported in questions 16 to 21 of form SDLT1. HMRC *originally* required details of all other leases to tenants to be reported on form SDLT4, or (where multiple leases were involved) as a schedule to SDLT4. This requirement caused confusion, because form SDLT4 is designed (and mainly used) for reporting details of leases which are themselves the subject of the transaction. HMRC have now clarified the matter: if the property transferred is subject to more than one lease to tenants, details of all except the first lease are to be reported on a schedule to form *SDLT1*, not on form SDLT4. From 1 March 2019 the schedule is only required to be filed whenever the transaction notified on the SDLT1 form relates to a non-residential or mixed-use property and is either the grant of a head lease or the sale of a freehold subject to a lease(s). This new schedule only requires the following details in relation to non-residential tenancies: (1) tenant name; (2) property address; (3) start date of the lease; and (4) end date of the lease. One schedule should be completed for each property notified on the SDLT1 form.

SPECIAL CASES

Linked transactions

8.25 Generally, separate transactions require separate returns, and it is normally acceptable to report the acquisition of separate properties on separate forms SDLT1, even if they are acquired under a single transaction or arrangement. Where two or more linked transactions (see **4.83**) have the same effective date, *FA 2003, s 108(2)* provides that the purchaser(s) may opt to make a single land transaction return as if all of the transactions formed a single notifiable transaction. If there are two or more purchasers, they must make the return jointly, which implies they have joint and several liability for payment of the SDLT and any interest and penalties which may arise from late submission/payment or errors. The statute indicates that the 'single return' approach is available for any such linked transactions. However, HMRC impose restrictions because a single LTR form can only cope with two or more transactions if they are sufficiently similar (see HMRC further guidance for question 13 of SDLT1 form – SDLTM62080). Therefore, it is only permitted to report two or more transactions on a single return if:

- the vendor(s) and purchaser(s) for each are identical and each transaction has the same 'effective date' (see **4.8**);
- the transactions all fall within the same category (ie one of the following: transfer of freehold; grant of lease; other transaction involving lease; other transaction); and
- either no relief is being claimed, or the same relief is claimed in respect of all transactions.

If this leads to a need to complete two or more returns when the legislation allows a single return and if the returns are late so that a penalty is chargeable under *FA 2003, Sch 10, para 3*, it is arguable that only a single penalty should be charged. However, it is likely that the matter will have to be argued with HMRC!

Multiple properties

8.26 Where linked acquisitions are reported on one form SDLT1, details of one of the properties must be included on form SDLT1, with the others on separate forms SDLT3 (and forms SDLT4 where the transaction includes the grant of leases). If many properties are acquired under a single transaction, it is possible to submit the SDLT3 and any SDLT4 information on schedules rather than on separate forms (SDLTM60215). This instruction originally applied to six or more properties, but now says it applies to 100 or more. It is probably worth asking in any case where the alternative is completion of an oppressively large number of forms SDLT3 and SDLT4. The schedule should include all of the details asked for on form SDLT3.

HMRC will provide guidance on acceptable formats for such schedules. The guidance notes suggest calling the SDLT helpline in the first instance but, in the author's experience, direct contact with the Stamp Office is best (see **Appendix A** for contact details). It is usually possible to construct a suitable spreadsheet; HMRC require an electronic copy, even if a paper copy is sent with a paper return, to allow them to copy and paste information into their systems. Most of the information entered on these schedules is for the purposes of government statistics rather than determining tax liability and, where information is not readily available, HMRC will often accept schedules with gaps – it is worth asking!

When to notify

8.27 For land transactions with an 'effective date' (see **4.91** and **6.74**) on or after 1 March 2019 the deadline for submission of a land transaction return is 14 days from the 'effective date' of the transaction (*FA 2003, s 76(1)* as amended by *FA 2019, s 46(2)*).

The 14-day time limit also applies to land transactions with an 'effective date' before 1 March 2019 which only become notifiable on or after 1 March 2019 (*FA 2003, s 76(1)* as amended by *FA 2019, s 46(2)* and *(10)(b)*).

If the 'effective date' (see **4.74** and **6.74**) of the transaction was before 1 March 2019, and the transaction became notifiable before 1 March 2019, then the LTR was due within 30 days from the 'effective date' of the transaction (*FA 2003, s 76(1)* prior to its amendment by *FA 2019, s 46(2)*).

If a further return is required as a result of an event occurring after the 'effective date', the further return is due within 30 days of the date of that event. In the case of a lease with uncertain or variable rent (see **6.37**), the latest date for submission of an amended return is 30 days after the end of the fifth year of the term of the lease, provided the grant of the lease has previously been notified (*FA 2003, Sch 17A, para 8(3A)* as introduced by *FA 2019, s 46(8)(c)* in relation to transactions with an 'effective date' on or after 1 March 2019, or transactions with an 'effective date' before 1 March 2019 but which only became notifiable after 1 March 2019). If the grant of the lease had not previously been notifiable, and it only became notifiable on or after 1 March 2019 as a result of the rent for the first five years being ascertained, then the land transaction return is required to be filed within 14 days of the rent for the first five years being ascertained (*FA 2003, Sch 17A, para 8(3)* as amended by *FA 2019, s 46(8)(c)*). Where the rent depends on the annual results of a business, the due date for filing the land transaction return may be before the rent for the fifth year has been finally determined. In that case, the return should be submitted using a reasonable estimate of the rent, and then amended as necessary once the rent is finally determined. As noted at **8.17**, if a return is submitted in respect of the original transaction, further and amended returns are to be submitted by way of a letter to the Stamp Office (see **Appendix A**), not by completion of further forms.

Penalties for late submission

8.28 If a return is submitted up to three months late, a penalty of £100 is chargeable, irrespective of whether SDLT is chargeable or whether the SDLT is paid on time. If the return is more than three months late, the penalty increases to £200. In addition, if a return is filed 12 months or more late, a tax-geared penalty may be charged. This penalty may be up to 100% of the tax chargeable on the relevant transaction (*FA 2003, Sch 10, paras 3–4*; SDLTM85905).

PAYMENT OF SDLT

Payment methods

8.29 Originally, payment of SDLT was linked to the submission of the return, so that the return was not regarded as duly submitted unless and until any SDLT had been paid. This link was broken by *FA 2007*, so that submission of the return and payment of the SDLT are now regarded as separate actions. The breaking of the link makes it very important to ensure that HMRC can identify sums received and attribute them to the correct return. To this end, the 11-digit UTRN of the related return must be quoted when SDLT is paid. SDLT may be paid by sterling cheque drawn on a UK bank, payable to 'HM Revenue & Customs Only', followed by the UTRN. If a single cheque is used to pay SDLT on several returns HMRC advise sending a schedule listing each UTRN against each amount. The cheque may be sent by post to the Stamp Office at the address shown in **Appendix A** or paid in at a bank or building society using the payslip(s) from the paper return(s). Alternatively (and, in the eyes of HMRC, preferably), payment may be made by means of 'Faster Payments', 'CHAPS' or 'Bacs'. Relevant bank account details for these purposes are at www.hmrc.gov.uk/payinghmrc/stamp-land.htm. If you are paying by CHAPS, and you are making a single payment to cover a number of transactions, you should first contact HMRC's Shipley Accounts Office (see **Appendix A**) for further information. Payments made by 'Faster Payments' generally reach HMRC on the same or next day, payments by CHAPS on the same working day if you pay within your bank's processing times and payments by Bacs usually take three working days.

Due date and deferral

8.30 For land transactions with an 'effective date' on or after 1 March 2019, or an 'effective date' before 1 March 2019 but where the transaction only became notifiable on or after 1 March 2019, SDLT is generally due 14 days from the 'effective date' of the transaction – usually the earlier of substantial performance of the agreement and legal completion of a transfer or execution of a lease (see **4.91**). See **8.27** for the general position in relation to the due date. There is no automatic right to defer payment where there are delays in paying consideration, occupying the property or determining the amount of consideration. If, for any reason, the amount of the consideration has not been finally determined when payment of SDLT falls due, payment must be based on a reasonable estimate. Further SDLT may then be due once the consideration is finally determined, and this must generally be paid within 30 days of that final determination. However, interest will be chargeable on this additional SDLT from the original due date of the main payment, unless deferral has been granted in respect of the additional tax.

8.31 If, at the effective date of a transaction:

- the SDLT cannot be finally determined because any amount of consideration is uncertain or contingent, and
- any part of that consideration falls or may fall to be paid more than six months after the effective date,

the taxpayer may apply to defer payment of SDLT on the consideration which falls to be paid later (*FA 2003, s 90*; *SI 2003/2837, Pt 4*, see SDLTM50900), potentially including any part which may fall to be paid within six months. However, it is not possible to defer payment on any element of the consideration which is certain or ascertainable at the 'effective date' (see **4.74** and **6.74**) or later date of application and either has already been paid or is known to become payable within six months of the 'effective date'. Deferral is only possible if uncertainty about the consideration arises from future events – if the amount of consideration depends on accounts drawn up to the 'effective date' but is not known at that date because the accounts have not yet been drawn up, it is not dependent on future events and deferral is not possible on these grounds. Deferral is not possible in respect of any SDLT which arises on rent under a lease, but deferral may be possible in respect of SDLT on a lease premium.

8.32 If deferral is granted, the notification of that fact will set out details of when further payments of SDLT must be made. If the specified payments are made by the specified dates, interest will not be charged (*FA 2003, s 87(3)(b)*). If payments are late, interest will be charged only from the dates on which they should have been made. The fact that deferral can be interest-free is the principal reason for going to the trouble of making an application. If deferral is not applied for (or refused), interest will be charged on any SDLT paid more than 14 days after the effective date (see **4.8**) of the transaction (*FA 2003, s 87(1)* and *(1A)* as introduced by *FA 2019, s 46(7)*), even though the amount of SDLT cannot be determined until some later date. It is important to consider applying for deferral in any case where further consideration may become payable at a later date, even if that further contingent consideration is expected to be negligible – retrospective application is not possible if the final amount is unexpectedly high!

Example 8.5—Deferral

On 1 January 2020, Elvis agrees to buy a freehold block of flats from Cliff for £10 million payable now and up to a further £5 million payable on 1 January 2021. The amount payable on 1 January 2021 will be determined in accordance with a formula where the only variable is the net rents received in the year to 30 June 2020. The agreement is completed without prior substantial performance on 31 March 2020. Cliff must pay SDLT on the £10 million consideration no later than 14 April 2020. He may apply to defer payment on the additional consideration because: (a) that consideration falls to be paid more than six months after the effective date of the purchase; and (b) the amount cannot be determined at the effective date (or later date of application) since it depends on rent receipts for a period ending after that date. However, if the contingent amount had depended on the net rents for the year to 31 March 2020, deferral would not have been possible. Although, at the effective date, that amount might not have been finally worked out, it would in principle be possible to know the amount at that date, so the amount is not 'uncertain' as defined by *FA 2003, s 51*. Equally, had the amount payable on 1 January 2021 been subject to a minimum, it would not be possible to defer payment of tax on that certain minimum amount because payment of it would not be contingent or uncertain. SDLT on that minimum would be due by 14 April 2020.

Applying for deferral

8.33 An application for deferral must be made no later than 30 days after the 'effective date' (see **4.91** and **6.74**) of the land transaction (*FA 2003, s 90*). For transactions with an 'effective date' before 1 March 2019, which became notifiable before 1 March 2019, the deadline for making the application was linked to the due date for filing the original return. Following the reduction in the period for filing the land transaction return to 14 days, for transactions with an 'effective date' on or after 1 March 2019, or transactions with an effective date before 1 March 2019 but which only became notifiable on or after 1 March 2019, this link no longer applies. It is understood that the 30-day deadline is rigidly enforced, and HMRC encourage early submission of applications, even before the transaction is finalised if possible. Application is made by letter to the Stamp Office (see **Appendix A**), marked 'SDLT Deferral Application' (SDLTM50900 et seq). The letter must set out:

- the identity of the purchaser;
- the location of the land involved;
- the nature of the contingency/uncertain payment;
- the amount of consideration for which deferral is sought (or a best estimate where it is uncertain);
- as full details of the times of expected payments as it is possible to give;
- a reasoned opinion as to when this part of the consideration will cease to be contingent or can be ascertained;
- a calculation of the SDLT payable on the total of the actual and the contingent/uncertain consideration (based on best estimates); and
- a calculation of the SDLT in respect of which the application to defer payment refers.

HMRC are entitled to ask for further information and are likely to do so if the transaction is unusual or if avoidance is suspected. If deferral is denied, it is possible to appeal (see **8.57** et seq), but in practice this will be worthwhile only where very large sums are at stake.

Interest on SDLT

8.34 As with other taxes, interest is charged on SDLT which is paid late (*FA 2003, s 87*), at the rates set by regulation under *FA 1989, s 178*. In general, the rate is the same as for income tax and NIC (see www.hmrc.gov.uk/rates/interest-late-pay.htm for details). The rate of interest on late paid SDLT is currently 2.60% per annum. From 29 September 2009 through to 22 August 2016 the rate of interest was 3% per annum but from 23 August 2016 it was reduced to 2.75% per annum. It was subsequently increased to 3% from 21 November 2017 and then further increased to 3.25% on 21 August 2018. The rate then fell to 2.75% from 30 March 2020 and then fell again to 2.60% from 7 April 2020.

In most cases, tax is late if it is paid after the due date, which is 30 days (however see paragraph below for circumstances in which a 14-day deadline applies) after the 'relevant date'. The relevant date in various situations is as follows:

(1) for an ordinary acquisition of a chargeable interest, whether by transfer or grant of a lease, the effective date;

(2) where certain events occurring after execution or earlier substantial performance of a lease are treated as the grant of a new lease (eg a

deemed surrender and regrant (see **6.32**), or transfer after a relief was claimed on grant (see **6.17**)), the date of the event which is treated as the grant of a new lease;

(3) where a relief is withdrawn as a result of a later event (eg group relief withdrawn because the purchaser leaves the group within three years), the date of the event giving rise to the withdrawal;

(4) where the tax arises on an earlier transaction as a result of a later linked transaction (eg because aggregation of the consideration increases the amount of the tax payable), the effective date of the later linked transaction;

(5) where tax arises on a 'growing' lease (see **6.12**), for periods commencing on or after 17 July 2013, the last day of the year or shorter period giving rise to the liability, For earlier periods, the day on which the lease becomes treated as being for a longer fixed term (ie the first day of the period giving rise to the liability); and

(6) where deferral has been granted as set out at **8.33**, the date on which the deferred SDLT payment is due.

Where the relevant date is determined by either (1), (4) or (5) above, and a land transaction return is required to be delivered within 14 days after that relevant date, then interest on overdue tax will run from the day after the end of that 14-day period until the tax is paid (*FA 2003, s 87(1A)* as introduced by *FA 2019, s 46(7)*). In any other circumstances interest will run from 30 days after the relevant date until the tax is paid (*FA 2003, s 87(1)*).

See SDLTM85930 for confirmation of these points.

Under the so called 'slab system' (which applied to residential property until 4 December 2014 and to non-residential and mixed use property until 16 March 2016: see **4.37**) if deferral was granted, interest would still arise where contingent consideration proved to be greater than expected and pushed the transaction into a higher SDLT rate. However, this should no longer be the case under the progressive tax structure which now applies to residential, mixed use and non-residential properties. This is because the tax paid on the initial consideration will not be changed when the final consideration is determined, as the total amount of the consideration chargeable does not affect the SDLT paid on the initial consideration, which remains the same, with any additional consideration being added to the initial consideration and taxed at the marginal rate(s).

When SDLT is repaid, interest is payable (*FA 2003, s 89*), again at the same rates as generally apply to direct taxes as set under *FA 1989, s 178*. Such interest is not income for tax purposes. The interest is payable for the period from receipt of the tax by HMRC to the date of repayment. At the date of writing (31 May 2020) the repayment interest rate is 0.5% and that has been the rate since 29 September 2009.

Example 8.6—Relevant date and interest charge

On 31 May 2020, David enters into a five-year lease of a commercial property at a provisional rent of £200,000 per year, but the amount is to be finally determined by reference to the performance of the business carried out in the property during the five-year term of the lease. On 13 June 2020, David pays SDLT on the basis of the £200,000 annual rent. On 14 June 2025, just after the end of the lease, the annual rent is finally determined to be £225,000. The SDLT liability is recomputed, and the additional SDLT is due 30 days (see **8.34**) after the date on which the rent is finally determined (*FA 2003, Sch 17A, para 8(3A)* as introduced by *FA 2019, s 46(8)(c)*). However, interest is charged on this further SDLT from 14 June 2020, being 14 days after the effective date (see **4.91**) of the lease (*FA 2003, s 87(1A)* as introduced by *FA 2019, s 46(7)*). It is not possible to apply to defer tax on rent, so the only way to escape this interest charge would be to over-pay SDLT on 13 June 2020 (*FA 2003, s 90(7)*).

Example 8.7—Deferral and interest charges

On 1 April 2020 Goliath buys a plot of bare land for consideration of £375,000 plus unascertainable consideration equal to 25% of the profit made on development and sale of the site. Goliath estimates that the unascertainable consideration will be £125,000. He successfully applies to defer SDLT on the unascertainable element of £125,000, and pays tax of £8,250, being the SDLT payable on the ascertainable consideration of £375,000 (£150,000 at 0%, £100,000 at 2% and £125,000 at 5%). When the development is sold on 31 March 2022, the contingent consideration proves to be £175,000. The SDLT payable on total consideration of £550,000 (£375,000 + £175,000) is £17,000 (£150,000 at 0%, £100,000 at 2% and £300,000 at 5%). Goliath pays tax of £8,750 (£17,000 – £8,250) on the £175,000 unascertainable amount by 30 April 2022 (ie 30 days after the 'effective date' of the transaction – see **8.34**) and no interest is charged (*FA 2003, s 87(1)* and *(3)(b)*).

Collection and enforcement

8.35 SDLT is due and payable, whether under a self-assessment (ie as a result of submission of a land transaction return), or under a determination or assessment by HMRC, unless deferral has been granted as outlined above or postponement has been agreed/granted (see below). HMRC are empowered to enforce payment of outstanding SDLT by distraint ('diligence' in Scotland) or by civil proceedings in magistrates' courts (for amounts not exceeding £2,000), county courts, the High Court or Scottish equivalents (*FA 2003, Sch 12*).

HMRC ENQUIRIES

8.36 The process for HMRC to enquire into an SDLT return is similar to that which applies to direct tax returns (*FA 2003, Sch 10, Pt 3*). It begins by HMRC giving notice of enquiry to the purchaser before the end of the enquiry period; it ends when HMRC give a 'closure notice'. This may be given because HMRC are satisfied that their enquiry is complete or because the Tax Tribunal gives a direction to that effect on application by the purchaser. The enquiry period is potentially relatively short, being nine months from:

- the filing date (which is itself 14 days after the effective date; see **4.91**) if the return was filed on time,
- the actual date of filing if the return was late, or
- the date of amendment if the return is amended by the purchaser.

8.37 However, if the notice of enquiry is given as a result of an amendment to the return, and the normal enquiry period for the original return has ended (or an enquiry into the original return has already been completed), the enquiry is limited to matters to which the amendment relates or are affected by the amendment (*FA 2003, Sch 10, para 13(2)*). Outside these time limits, HMRC may only pursue a potential underpayment of tax by making a 'discovery assessment' (see **8.46**).

Example 8.8—Time limits for enquiry into return

On 1 March 2020 (effective date and date of completion), Hattie Ltd buys a business from Eric Ltd. Payment takes the form of Hattie Ltd accepting responsibility for debts of the business amounting to £2 million plus an issue of shares in Hattie Ltd to Eric Ltd with a market value of £1 million. The business includes a commercial property provisionally valued at £1.5 million. On 12 March 2020, Hattie Ltd submits an LTR on the basis of this valuation, claiming relief under *FA 2003, Sch 7, para 8* (acquisition relief; see **5.27**). Hattie Ltd pays SDLT at 0.5% accordingly. On 1 February 2021, Hattie Ltd gives notice to amend the return, decreasing the value attributed to the property to £1.2 million. On 15 February 2021, HMRC give notice of enquiry into the return. The normal enquiry period for the original return ended on 15 December 2020 (nine months after the filing date), so the enquiry may only deal with matters affected by the amendment. In this case, it is considered that the enquiry may relate to the valuation of the property but not to the availability of acquisition relief.

8.38 As part of an enquiry, HMRC may demand to see documents and information, giving at least 30 days' notice (*FA 2003, Sch 10, para 14*). The purchaser may appeal against such a demand (see **8.58**). If no appeal is lodged, or after any appeal is settled, initial and daily penalties may be imposed for failure to produce the outstanding documents and information. In addition to a general right to demand documents and information from the purchaser, HMRC are given powers to seek information and documents from third parties, including tax accountants and other advisers. Exercise of these powers is subject to consent or review by the Tax Tribunal or, in some cases, a judge or sheriff. Situations in which these powers may be invoked are beyond the scope of this book. The relevant parties will normally require specialist advice in these cases.

8.39 While an enquiry is in progress, HMRC may amend the return if they conclude that additional tax is due and amendment is necessary to prevent a loss of the tax (*FA 2003, Sch 10, para 17*). Written notice of the amendment must be given to the purchaser. This power is normally only used where a prima facie underpayment has been established, but the taxpayer refuses to make an appropriate payment on account, suggesting there may be a risk of eventual default. The purchaser may appeal to the Tax Tribunal against the amendment and may apply to have collection of any additional tax postponed. Postponement may be agreed by HMRC, or the question may be determined by the Tax Tribunal if the taxpayer and HMRC cannot reach agreement.

8.40 The purchaser may also amend the return, if the normal 12-month period allowed for amendment (ie the 12-month period from the filing date) has not yet expired (*FA 2003, Sch 10, para 18*; see www.hmrc.gov.uk/sdlt/return/amend.htm). Voluntary amendment to correct any errors which have come to light may be taken into account in determining any penalty position (see **8.55**). HMRC may, however, reject the amendment if they do not agree with it.

8.41 HMRC and the purchaser may agree to refer matters to the Tax Tribunal during an enquiry (and, if they see fit, the First-tier Tribunal may pass the referral on to the Upper Tribunal). Subject to the normal rights of appeal through the courts, the decision of the Tribunal is binding on all parties.

8.42 Normally, enquiries are closed by HMRC giving notice of closure once they are satisfied no further amendments are required (*FA 2003, Sch 10, para 23*). The notice must make it clear whether any taxpayer amendments of the return are accepted. The purchaser may appeal to the Tax Tribunal against a closure notice (*FA 2003, Sch 10, para 35*). Alternatively, the purchaser may apply to the Tax Tribunal for a direction that the enquiry be closed (*FA 2003, Sch 10, para 24*). Details of the procedure are on the Tribunals Service website (see **8.59**).

FAILURE TO DELIVER A RETURN

8.43 If a purchaser fails to deliver a return, or if HMRC believe that a return should have been delivered, HMRC may issue a notice requiring delivery of a return (*FA 2003, Sch 10, paras 5, 25–27*). At least 30 days' notice must be given and the transaction in question must be specified. If the person to whom the notice is given fails to comply, HMRC may apply to the Tax Tribunal for the imposition of a daily penalty. There does not appear to be any provision for appeal against such a notice, for example on the grounds that the purported transaction to which it relates has not taken place, or is not notifiable, or that the person to whom notice was given is not the purchaser. Any penalty is in addition to those which apply automatically for late submission (see **8.28**). Alternatively or additionally, if no return is forthcoming, HMRC may make a determination of the SDLT which they believe to be unpaid, and this is then treated as a self-assessment (ie as if a return had been submitted) for the purposes of enforcement, including the charging of interest and penalties. A determination may not be made more than six years after the effective date (see **4.91**) of the transaction in question. If the taxpayer subsequently makes a self-assessment by delivering a return, provided this occurs not later than 12 months after notice of the determination is given or six years after the original due date for the return (whichever is later), the self-assessment displaces the determination. This, of course, then allows HMRC to launch an enquiry into the return. As an alternative, the taxpayer may appeal to the Tax Tribunal against the assessment, but only on the grounds that the transaction has not taken place or been substantially performed, or that it has but it is not notifiable. Logically, if such an appeal is successful, it should also displace any daily penalty awarded for failure to comply with HMRC's notice to deliver a return, but the legislation does not overtly say that this is so.

8.44 A further bizarre and potentially wholly unfair provision allows HMRC to treat a return (or any other document) as not having been delivered or made available if, whilst in their care, it has been destroyed or so damaged as to become illegible. The author is not aware of any case in which HMRC have in practice relied on this provision.

DISCOVERY ASSESSMENT

8.45 If a return has been made (or is deemed to have been made by virtue of a determination) and the enquiry period (see **8.36**) has not yet ended, any possible loss of tax will normally be investigated by launching an enquiry. Once an enquiry has commenced, if HMRC are concerned that recovery of additional tax is at risk, they may amend the return as described at **8.39**, thereby allowing action to be taken to collect the tax. Once the enquiry period has ended, or an enquiry has been completed, HMRC have no automatic right to reopen matters and seek further tax.

8.46 However, if no return has been made, or in certain circumstances where a return has been made but the time for launching an enquiry has passed, HMRC may assess any tax which they discover to have been underpaid (*FA 2003, Sch 10, Pt 5*). If a return has been made, a 'discovery' assessment may only be made to recover tax lost:

(1) as a result of fraud or negligence on the part of the purchaser or an agent or partner of the purchaser, or

(2) because, when the normal time for enquiry ended (or any previous enquiry was completed), HMRC could not, on the basis of information then available to them, have reasonably been expected to be aware of the loss of tax.

For the purposes of (2), information is available if it is contained in a land transaction return, has been furnished in the course of an enquiry, could reasonably be expected to be inferred from such information, or is notified to HMRC by the purchaser or a person acting on his behalf (*FA 2003, Sch 10, para 1(5)*).

8.47 In reliance on the last of these points, taxpayers and their agents often submit further information to HMRC at the time of submission of the LTR. HMRC guidance indicates that such further information should not be enclosed with paper returns, but rather should be sent to the Stamp Office (see **Appendix A**), quoting the UTRN(s) of the return(s) to which it relates.

8.48 The decision as to what further information, if any, to submit requires careful thought. Submission of further information may increase the likelihood of the transaction being selected for enquiry. If the treatment originally adopted in the return is clearly correct, any such enquiry will normally be fruitless, but will incur administrative costs. Alternatively, if there is genuine doubt over the treatment of the transaction, it will be important to ensure that the information submitted is sufficiently comprehensive. If HMRC cannot see the full facts and circumstances to enable them to make their own judgement of the treatment adopted, they are likely to consider that a discovery assessment is justified, should further information come to their attention later.

8.49 The general time limit for HMRC to make a discovery assessment is four years from the effective date of the transaction (*FA 2003, Sch 10, para 31(1)*). This period is extended to six years where the loss of tax is brought about carelessly by the purchaser or a 'related person' (*FA 2003, Sch 10, para 31(2)*). The period is further extended to 20 years where the loss of tax is:

(a) brought about deliberately by the purchaser or a 'related person'; or

(b) attributable to a person failing to deliver an LTR; or

(c) is attributable to an arrangement in respect of which a person has failed to give notification under the Disclosure of Tax Avoidance (DOTAS) legislation (see **9.26** et seq) (*FA 2003, Sch 10, para 31(2A)*).

If the purchaser has died, the period is shortened to four years from the date of death (or six years from the effective date of the transaction, if that is earlier) (*FA 2003, Sch 10, para 31(4)*). If the assessment is to recover an excessive repayment of SDLT, it may also be made at any time during an enquiry into the relevant return, or up to 12 months after the repayment is made, even if this is outside the normal time limit (*FA 2003, Sch 10, para 31(3)*).

8.50 The purchaser may appeal against a discovery assessment and may apply to have payment of any additional tax postponed (*FA 2003, Sch 10, para 35*). As in other cases, postponement may be agreed by HMRC, or the matter may be determined by the Tax Tribunal.

MISTAKE IN RETURN ETC

8.51 If a mistake is discovered in a return within the period allowed for amendment (usually up to one year after the normal submission deadline – *FA 2003, Sch 10, para 6(3)*), this should be dealt with by amending the return as set out at **8.40**. If this deadline is missed, it may be possible to make a claim for relief from excessive assessment arising from a mistake in a return. Claims made on or after 1 April 2011 may only be accepted if made within four years of the effective date of the transaction (*FA 2003, Sch 10, para 34* and *34B* as substituted by *F(No 3)A 2010, s 28* and *Sch 12*). There is no provision to extend this period where, for example, the return was made after the normal deadline. Prior to 1 April 2011, claims were permitted up to six years after the effective date, and most errors could be corrected. The amendments from 1 April 2011 place severe restrictions on the acceptable grounds for making a claim – for example, if there was a mistake in making or failing to make a claim or election, it is no longer possible to correct this by way of a claim under these provisions. Similarly, if the taxpayer knew or ought reasonably to have known the grounds for the claim before the normal period for making the claim had expired, relief under these provisions will be refused. See SDLTM5400 to SDLTM54120 for more details. If the claim is made on behalf of a partnership, all of the partners must nominate someone who was a partner at the time of the relevant transaction to make the claim. This provision may be to prevent a dissident partner seeking to change the treatment of an old transaction.

Making a claim under these provisions will also remove restrictions on HMRC's ability to make a discovery assessment. Therefore, careful analysis will be required before deciding to pursue such a claim.

A claim for relief may also be made where a person believes he has been assessed more than once in respect of the same transaction. There does not appear to be any time limit on such a claim (*FA 2003, Sch 10, para 33*).

PENALTIES, FINES AND OTHER SANCTIONS

Penalties

8.52 As noted at **8.34**, it is the view of HMRC that interest charged when SDLT is paid after the date on which it ought to have been paid does no more than compensate the government for loss of use of the money. As a separate matter, penalties are provided for various failures. SDLT is potentially within the new penalty regime in *FA 2009, Sch 55* but at the time of writing (May 2020) this had not yet been activated in respect of this tax. Meanwhile the current penalties are generally in *FA 2003, Sch 10* and *Sch 11, para 6*. Some are fixed amounts and apply automatically; others are for variable amounts up to a ceiling. They apply as follows:

(1) Late submission of return – up to three months after the due date, £100; three months or more after the due date, £200.

(2) Late submission of return – 12 months or more after the due date, an amount up to the amount of tax chargeable on the transaction. This is in addition to the penalty chargeable under (1).

(3) Failure to submit return after HMRC have given a formal notice to deliver – up to £60 per day of continuing failure. This requires a direction from the Tax Tribunal and is in addition to any penalty under (1) and (2).

(4) Careless or deliberate delivery of incorrect return, or failure to correct return after error has come to light – up to the amount of understated tax. This penalty was brought into the general *FA 2007* regime for penalties for incorrect returns (*FA 2007, Sch 24*) by *SI 2009/571*.

(5) Failure to keep and preserve records as required – up to £3,000.

(6) Failure to produce documents or information after formal notice has been given or obstructing an officer from HMRC in the course of an inspection – an initial amount of £300 and, for continued failure, a daily penalty of £60 and at the discretion of the Upper Tribunal a penalty based on the amount of the SDLT payable. However, these penalties cannot be imposed after the failure has been remedied, so they should be seen as encouragement to comply rather than punishment for not complying.

8.53 In principle, HMRC impose most penalties by making a formal determination (or, where indicated above, by seeking such a determination from the Tax Tribunal) and issuing a notice of the determination to the taxpayer (*FA 2003, Sch 14*). The taxpayer may then appeal against the determination, initially to the Tax Tribunal, subsequently to the courts (*FA 2003, Sch 14, para 5*). In the case of fraud, penalty proceedings may be brought in the High Court (or the Court of Session in Scotland) (*FA 2003, Sch 14, para 7*). The general time limit for determining a penalty or commencement of proceedings for a penalty is four years from the date on which the penalty was incurred (*FA 2003, Sch 14, para 8(1)*). However, where the penalty is payable in relation to a case involving a loss of tax brought about carelessly the time limit for determining the penalty is extended to six years (*FA 2003, Sch 14, para 8(4A)*). The period for determining the penalty is further extended to 20 years where the loss of tax is brought about:

(a) deliberately by the person; or

(b) by a person failing to deliver an LTR; or

(c) by an arrangement in respect of which a person has failed to give notification under the Disclosure of Tax Avoidance (DOTAS) legislation (see **9.26** et seq) (*FA 2003, Sch 14, para 8(4B)*).

For tax-geared penalties, the time limit for determining the penalty is extended to three years after determination of the tax (*FA 2003, Sch 14, para 8(3)*). A penalty for assisting in preparation of an incorrect return may be sought up to 20 years after the penalty was incurred (*FA 2003, Sch 14, para 8(5)*).

8.54 In practice, most fixed and daily penalties are paid without formal determination. These penalties will be waived only in the most exceptional circumstances – for example, if the taxpayer is able to show that the return was completed and posted in good time, but lost in the post, or if the taxpayer's agent suffered a serious illness at just the wrong time. Details are given in leaflet SD7 available from the HMRC publications and stationery service (see **Appendix A**) or online at www.hmrc.gov.uk/leaflets/sd7.pdf.

8.55 Most tax-geared penalties are included in a negotiated settlement, where it is rare for the maximum amount to be imposed. The amount of any such penalty will depend on matters such as size and gravity of adjustment and taxpayer cooperation; some guidance is given in a rather old Tax Bulletin, Issue 71, which may be found on the HMRC website at http://webarchive.nationalarchives.gov.uk/20101006151632/www.hmrc.gov.uk/bulletins/index.htm. Guidance on HMRC's general approach to tax geared penalties may be gleaned from their Compliance Handbook Manual at CH82000 et seq.

Fines and other sanctions

8.56 Any person who conceals, destroys or falsifies a document, the production of which has been requested or required, or permits or causes such concealment etc, if convicted, is liable to a fine and/or up to two years' imprisonment (*FA 2003, Sch 13, para 53*). A person who fails to comply with a court order to produce documents or information may be held to be in contempt of the relevant court and may be fined and/or imprisoned accordingly. As with other taxes, criminal prosecution is possible for the most serious cases involving fraud, potentially leading to fines and/or imprisonment. Dealing with such matters is not within the scope of this book.

APPEALS

8.57 There are various references in this chapter to appealing against HMRC decisions, determinations and assessments. The normal rules for appeals on direct tax matters apply equally to SDLT (*FA 2003, Sch 10, Pt 7*). These are set out at www.hmrc.gov.uk/complaints-appeals/how-to-appeal/direct-tax.htm on the HMRC website. Initially, appeals are made to HMRC. This may be done either by using the form usually supplied with the notice of decision etc, or by letter. A letter of appeal must set out the details necessary to allow HMRC to identify the tax return or transaction and decision involved (usually the HMRC reference) and the grounds of the appeal.

8.58 In general, the appeal must be made within 30 days of the decision, assessment etc. If the taxpayer and HMRC are unable to reach agreement on the disputed matter, HMRC may offer an 'independent review' (ie a review by one or more other HMRC officers). Within 30 days of such an offer, the taxpayer must decide whether to accept, or to refer the matter directly to the Tax Tribunal. If a review is accepted, it is still possible for the taxpayer to appeal to the Tax Tribunal if he does not accept the outcome of the review.

8.59 SDLT matters are dealt with by the First-tier Tribunal (Tax) of the Tribunals Service. Guidance on making an appeal or reference to the Tax Tribunal, and the necessary forms, are available on the Tribunals Service website at www.justice.gov.uk/guidance/courts-and-tribunals/tribunals/tax/index.htm, or may be obtained by writing to the Tribunal Service (see **Appendix A**).

RECORD KEEPING

8.60 Purchasers are required to keep and preserve whatever records may be required to enable the delivery of correct and complete returns (*FA 2003, Sch 10, Pt 2*). Such records include original contracts and transfer instruments, supporting maps, plans and other documents, and records of payments receipts and financial arrangements. The records must be kept for at least six years from the 'effective date' (see **4.91**) of the transaction. They must also be kept until any enquiry into the return is completed, and until HMRC no longer have the right to enquire into the return, if these dates are later than the six-year time limit. It is acceptable to keep the information from the documents (eg scanned copies) rather than the documents themselves. However, taxpayers may be concerned about the ability to demonstrate that such information is in accordance with the original document. So, in most cases, the original document is likely to be retained, albeit in a document storage facility, even if the information is also stored electronically.

8.61 The requirement to keep and preserve records applies where a return has to be made, but also where no return is required because the transaction is exempt (*FA 2003, Sch 11*) (see **8.3**). For most commercial transactions the requirement to keep records for six years is reasonable and in line with other record-keeping requirements. In the case of routine home purchases, where the property may well be re-sold within the six years, the requirement is not so clearly justified. Many homeowners, unaware of the requirement, are likely to dispose of records in a shorter period.

Chapter 9

SDLT Anti-Avoidance Rules

INTRODUCTION

9.1 Prior to the introduction of SDLT in 2003, it was relatively easy to minimise stamp duty costs on many property transactions. It had proven difficult to introduce effective anti-avoidance rules for this document-based tax. These were major factors in the decision to replace stamp duty with SDLT, a transaction-based tax not reliant on the manner in which the transaction is documented. The initial SDLT rules were not perfectly drafted and, inevitably, transactions were structured to take advantage of this and minimise tax. Initially, HMRC tackled this by introducing targeted anti-avoidance rules intended to prevent exploitation of specific reliefs and treatments. Eventually, it was concluded that these were having only limited success and, on 6 December 2006, a general anti-avoidance rule for SDLT was introduced in the form of *FA 2003, s 75A*. SDLT is also within the scope of the general anti-abuse rule (GAAR) introduced by *FA 2013, ss 206–215* (see **9.3**). Finally, SDLT is within the system for disclosure of tax avoidance schemes (DOTAS), but it has its own rules for determining what must be disclosed, and there are other differences from the system which applies to other taxes (see **9.26**). Disclosures under DOTAS have continued to lead to further targeted anti-avoidance provisions. Some changes have been made with retrospective effect, as promised by the Chancellor of the Exchequer in his 2012 Budget speech. An attempt to challenge these retrospective provisions by way of judicial review failed *(R (on the application of St Matthews (West) Ltd and others) v HMRC*, High Court, judgment 6 June 2014).

9.2 It is arguable that the introduction of the GAAR and *FA 2003, ss 75A–75C* has rendered some of the previous targeted anti-avoidance rules redundant, but they all remain in force. During the 2013 Finance Bill debates the government stated that, before relying on the GAAR, HMRC will first try to combat abuse by relying on existing specific anti-avoidance rules.

This chapter first looks briefly at the GAAR, then at *FA 2003, ss 75A–75C*. It then provides a list of specific targeted rules – these are dealt with more fully in the relevant chapters examining the transactions or reliefs to which they apply. Finally, it explores the SDLT version of DOTAS.

General anti-abuse rule

9.3 The general anti-abuse rule (GAAR) is set out in *FA 2013, ss 206–215* with procedural rules in *FA 2013, Sch 43.* HMRC guidance on the application of the GAAR can be found at www.hmrc.gov.uk/avoidance/gaar.htm. The rule applies to a wide range of taxes including SDLT and so is couched in fairly general terms. It applies to any arrangements, a main purpose of which is the obtaining of a tax advantage. 'Tax advantage' is not comprehensively defined but stated to include relief from or repayment of tax, reduction, avoidance or deferral of a tax liability, or avoidance of an obligation to deduct or account for tax. Where HMRC consider that the rule may apply, they will seek to make adjustments to counter the tax advantage. The taxpayer may then make a claim for 'consequential adjustments', effectively to relieve any multiple taxation caused by the initial adjustments. The making of adjustments is governed by the procedural rules in *FA 2013, Sch 43.* These require HMRC first to give written notice to the taxpayer, setting out what arrangements are considered to be abusive and why. The taxpayer has the opportunity to respond and refute HMRC's view. If HMRC are not satisfied with the response, they must refer the matter to the GAAR Advisory Panel for an opinion. After receiving representations from both the taxpayer and HMRC, the GAAR Advisory Panel must express an opinion on the matter. In the light of this, HMRC may then make adjustments, or instruct the taxpayer as to what adjustments must be made, to counter the tax advantage. Although the GAAR provisions do not specifically cover the matter, it appears to be assumed that adjustments made by way of assessment or refusal of a claim are potentially subject to appeal to the Tax Tribunals and beyond in the normal way.

SDLT differs from other taxes covered by the GAAR in that it is a transaction tax. It is perhaps less clear which arrangements have the saving of tax as a main objective when, in the absence of the transaction there would be no tax. Presumably HMRC would have sought to have applied the GAAR to combat the largely residential property sub-sale schemes which have been retrospectively attacked by specific legislation (see **5.16**).

FINANCE ACT 2003, SECTIONS 75A–75C

Introduction

9.4 These sections really form a general anti-abuse rule specifically aimed at SDLT and introduced more than six years before the GAAR. They potentially apply to all transactions other than those consisting of simple single steps, unless specifically excepted. They operate by comparing the total SDLT actually paid on all steps with the SDLT which would be payable on a 'notional transaction'. If the SDLT actually paid is less, any real land transactions are disregarded and, in their place, the notional transaction becomes chargeable. Credit is given for any SDLT paid on real transactions, and further SDLT is payable to bring the total up to that on the notional transaction.

9.5 *FA 2003, s 75A* was initially introduced by regulation; by the time it was confirmed by *FA 2007*, it had expanded to three sections, which now appear as *FA 2003, ss 75A–75C*. These sections demonstrate a hardening of attitudes to avoidance of SDLT, which was further illustrated by the June 2010 edition of 'Spotlight', HMRC's web publication about avoidance (see www.hmrc.gov.uk/avoidance/spotlights.htm), which made it clear that HMRC intended to attack schemes which sought to exploit 'sub-sale relief'. In any event the legislation governing 'sub-sale relief' has now been replaced by a relief in relation to pre-completion transactions which has been specifically designed to prevent avoidance (*FA 2003, Sch 2A* – see **5.8**). The final version of the *FA 2003, ss 75A–75C* provisions is in some ways more stringent than the original version but is still stated to apply with effect from 6 December 2006. During the parliamentary debates on the 2007 Finance Bill the government was eventually persuaded that this could amount to retrospective taxation, so a clause was introduced (*FA 2007, s 71(3)*) to state that, for transactions entered into before Royal Assent (19 July 2007), if the liability under the original version was less than that under the final version, the lesser liability would apply. This chapter deals with the final version of the rules. If, exceptionally, a transaction potentially within the scope of *FA 2003, s 75A* commenced prior to 19 July 2007 and is only now being dealt with, the transitional rules, which remain in *FA 2007*, should be checked.

9.6 As set out in the legislation, the test is completely objective – that is, there is no need to consider the motives of the parties. This means that a series of transactions which are not entered into with any intention of avoiding tax, but which happen to reduce the SDLT bill below that implied by the notional transaction, could still be caught. For this reason, it is not safe to ignore the rules merely because there is no avoidance motive; their application must be considered in all multi-step transactions.

9.7 HMRC guidance on the application of *FA 2003, ss 75A–75C* was updated on 15 January 2020 and can be found at SDLTM09060 to SDLTM09370. For the first time, as part of that updated guidance, HMRC have confirmed that they will provide non-statutory clearances on issues relating to *FA 2003, s 75A* via email at nonstatutoryclearanceteam.hmrc@hmrc.gov.uk. A non-statutory clearance is written confirmation from HMRC of their view of the application of tax law to a specific transaction which the taxpayer can rely on in most circumstances. Under HMRC's procedures a taxpayer can only request clearance if they:

- have fully read the relevant guidance (SDLTM09060 to SDLTM09370);
- have not been able to find the information they need; and

- are uncertain about HMRC's interpretation of tax legislation.

Any non-statutory clearance will need to be in line with the published guidance at www.gov.uk./guidance/non-statutory-clearance-service-guidance.

HMRC do however state that they will not provide clearances where, in their view, the transactions are undertaken for the purpose of avoiding tax, or where the clearance application only requests confirmation as to whether or not *FA 2003, s 75A* applies to the transaction. It is understood that areas where HMRC are likely to provide clearance would include the following:

- whether a transaction is a 'scheme transaction' for the purposes of *FA 2003, s 75A(1)(b)* (see **9.9** et seq),
- identifying who (P) and (V) are for the purposes of *FA 2003, s 75A(1)(a)* (see **9.8**);
- the amount of the chargeable consideration on the notional transaction for the purposes of *FA 2003, s 75A(5)* (see **9.11**); and
- whether a transaction is classed as an incidental transaction for the purposes of *FA 2003, s 75B* (see **9.16**).

Until the issue of the updated guidance in January 2020, HMRC generally refused to give any form of clearance in relation to *FA 2003, s 75A*. Therefore, whilst they will still not provide a clearance which merely requests confirmation that *FA 2003, s 75A* does not apply, they will now give clearance on the technical application of *FA 2003, s 75A* to specific transactions. This is to be welcomed and will help reduce some of the uncertainty around the application of *FA 2003, s 75A* to a transaction.

HMRC make it clear at SDLTM09090 that *FA 2003, s 75A* is different from other targeted anti-avoidance legislation in that it does not contain a tax avoidance 'main purpose' test and it will apply to transactions if they meet the conditions in the legislation, irrespective of the motives of the purchaser. This view is supported by a straightforward reading of the legislation and by the case law. The First-tier Tribunal decision in *Project Blue Limited v HMRC* [2013] UKFTT 378TC states: 'Whilst it is clear that the purpose of section 75A is to counteract the avoidance of SDLT, the provision contains no requirement that the taxpayer should have a tax avoidance motive or purpose as a precondition or defence to the application of the provision … Parliament obviously intended that the provision should apply regardless of motive'. In the decision of the Upper Tribunal ([2014] UKUT 0564 (TCC)), the presiding judge Mr Justice Morgan held that whilst there was no specific avoidance motive test in *FA 2003*, *s 75A*, a requirement that SDLT has been avoided is implicit as the section only applies if the tax saving test in *FA 2003, s 75A(1)(c)* is satisfied. However, this contention is open to debate as it is possible (and perhaps even common) for there to be a number of ways of structuring a transaction each of which may result in a different amount of SDLT being payable, and for a particular structure to be pursued, for wholly commercial reasons, but in circumstances where an SDLT saving is achieved. In such circumstances it is arguable that there is no SDLT avoidance, however *FA 2003, s 75A* could still apply. The decision of the Court of Appeal ([2016] EWCA Civ 485), given on 26 May 2016, also supports the view that *FA 2003, s 75A* can apply in the absence of an SDLT avoidance motive. Lord Justice Patten states at 39:

> 'The first is that Mr Thomas was wrong in my view in his submission that *s 75A* has no operation unless it can be shown that the object of the relevant scheme transactions was the avoidance of tax. Although, as the side-note to *s 75A* makes clear, the provisions were clearly introduced to combat the avoidance of SDLT, they operate according to their terms and nowhere in *s 75A* is there any reference to the purpose of the scheme transactions being tax avoidance or any requirement to establish the existence of such a purpose or objective as a pre-condition to the operation of the section. The UT [Upper Tribunal] was right in my view to reject Mr Thomas's construction of *s 75A* and to treat avoidance as spelt out by the conditions for the application of *s 75A* contained in *s 75A(1)*.'

Finally, this view was supported by the judgment of the Supreme Court ([2018] UKSC 30) given on 13 June 2018. In allowing HMRC's appeal Lord Hodge at 42 states:

> 'PBL's [Project Blue Limited] first argument, that section 75A could not apply because it had not been established that the parties entered into the transactions for the purpose of tax avoidance, failed before the FTT, the UTT and the Court of Appeal. In my view the tribunals and the Court of Appeal reached the correct conclusion. The heading of the section, "Anti-avoidance", is the only indication in the section which could support PBL's contention. The heading is relevant to assist an understanding as to the mischief which the provision addresses, but it says nothing as to the motives of the parties to the scheme transactions. There is nothing in the body of the section which expressly or inferentially refers to motivation. The provision was enacted to counter tax avoidance which resulted from the use of a number of transactions to effect the disposal and acquisition of a chargeable interest. It is sufficient for the operation of the section that tax avoidance, in the sense of a reduced liability or no liability to SDLT, resulted from the series of transactions which the parties put in place, whatever their motive for transacting in that manner. This is clear from subsection (1)(c) which compares the amount of SDLT payable in respect of the actual transactions against what would be payable under the notional land transaction in *section 75A(4)*, by which P acquired V's chargeable interest on its disposal by V.'

It is therefore clear that there is no requirement that an SDLT avoidance motive exist before *FA 2003, s 75A* can apply. If the actual liability to SDLT on a transaction is less than the liability which would arise under the notional transaction fiction of *FA 2003, s 75A* (see *FA 2003, s 75A(1)(c)*), then the anti-avoidance provision is in point, assuming that the other conditions in *FA 2003, s 75A(1)* are satisfied (see **9.8** et seq). This is subject to the proviso, which applies to all tax legislation, that *FA 2003, s 75A – 75C* must be read purposively and then applied to the facts of a particular case viewed realistically. The case law confirms that the purpose of *FA 2003, s 75A – 75C* is to counter SDLT avoidance schemes.

When do the rules apply?

9.8 They apply where one person (V) disposes of a chargeable interest, and another person (P) acquires it or a chargeable interest deriving from it. It does not matter that there may be various steps between the disposal and the acquisition, nor does it matter if the chargeable interest goes through various transformations between the disposal and the acquisition. The legislation was introduced to deal with schemes which involved precisely that kind of step and transformation. If the asset disposed of or acquired is not a chargeable interest, the rules do not apply.

In more complex transactions it may be difficult to determine the identity of V and P. At SDLTM09130, HMRC state that they do not have discretion when identifying V and P for the purposes of *FA 2003, s 75A*. Guidance on identifying P where there are multiple parties who could potentially be P is given at SDLTM09160. The guidance refers to the *Project Blue Limited v HMRC* [2018] UKSC 30 judgment and expresses the view that the court took a purposive approach to identifying P for the purposes of *FA 2003, s75A*. HMRC then state:

> 'Looking at the intention behind *section 75A*, the court identified the person who benefited from the adoption of the scheme transactions, and concluded that that person was P. Consequently, to identify P where there are multiple candidates, you must consider all of the scheme transactions and P will be the person who has obtained the tax benefit or who would have been liable to the tax had the scheme transactions not been pursued.'

HMRC are clearly referring to Lord Hodges's judgment in *Project Blue Limited v HMRC* [2018] UKSC 30 where he states at para 44:

> 'The task is to identify where the tax loss has occurred as a result of the adoption of the scheme transactions in relation to the disposal and acquisition of the relevant interest or interests in land. This in turn involves identifying the person on whom the tax charge would have fallen if there had not been the scheme transactions to which subsection (1)(b) refers

and which exploited a loophole in the statutory provisions' [emphasis added].

Arguably, therefore P should not only have obtained the tax benefit, which would not have been available had the scheme transactions not been undertaken, but P should also have exploited a loophole in the SDLT legislation. This approach aligns with the purpose of *FA 2003, ss 75A –75C*, which is to counter schemes designed to avoid the payment of SDLT.

Example 9.1—No transfer of a chargeable interest

X Ltd owns 100% of the shares of Y Ltd. Y Ltd owns a valuable property. X Ltd makes a loan to Y Ltd, allowing Y Ltd to pay a cash dividend to X Ltd, thus reducing the value of Y Ltd to £1. X Ltd then sells the shares of Y Ltd to unrelated party Z Ltd. Assuming there are no other steps, *s 75A* does not apply to the transaction, because there has been no disposal or acquisition of a chargeable interest. There may have been a saving of stamp duty on transfer of the shares, but stamp duty is not within the ambit of *FA 2003, s 75A*. Shares in a company are not 'chargeable interests', even if the company's only asset is property. However, this may change in future – from time to time, the government has threatened to introduce land-rich company rules, which may deem shares in such a company to be chargeable interests. It is also unlikely that this arrangement would fall foul of the GAAR in respect of stamp taxes, as stamp duty is not within the scope of that rule. However, such an arrangement may give rise to advantages in relation to other taxes and it would be important to consider the possible impact of the GAAR in this respect.

9.9 The rules only apply if there are 'a number of transactions' (which may include non-land transactions) involved in connection with the disposal and acquisition. To make sense of this provision, 'a number' must be taken to mean more than one. However, 'transaction' includes an agreement, offer or undertaking not to take a specified action, and any kind of arrangement, even if it would not normally be described as a transaction (*FA 2003, s 75A(2)*). In other words, apparently unilateral acts and failures to act may be regarded as transactions. It does not matter when the transactions occur – they merely have to occur 'in connection with' the disposal and acquisition. The transactions are referred to as 'scheme transactions' (*FA 2003, s 75A(1)(b)*). A transaction which occurs after the acquisition of the chargeable interest by P, may still be a scheme transaction.

Guidance is given at SDLTM09190 as to the meaning of 'involved in connection with' for the purposes of *FA 2003, s 75A(1)(b)*. For a transaction to be involved in connection with the acquisition and disposal of a chargeable transaction, so that it is a scheme transaction, it must be required to give effect to the transfer of the chargeable interest from V and P. The guidance states: 'If the outcome of a sequence of transactions could not be achieved without a particular transaction step, it is likely that it will meet the "involved in connection with" test and will therefore be a scheme transaction.'

9.10 The legislation (*FA 2003, s 75A(3)*) lists examples of 'scheme transactions' as follows, but makes it clear this is not an exhaustive list:

- acquisition of a lease derived from a freehold formerly owned by the vendor;
- sub-sale to a third party;
- grant of a lease to a third party subject to a right to terminate;
- exercise of a right to terminate a lease or take some other action;
- agreement not to exercise a right to terminate a lease or take some other action; and
- variation of a right to terminate a lease or take some other action.

It is clear from this list that transactions involving the grant and termination of leases were foremost in HMRC's collective mind when the rules were written. Although not exhaustive, this list is important when considering 'incidental transactions' (see **9.12**).

Example 9.2 (part 1)—Scheme caught by s 75A

Agnes owns a freehold residential property worth £2.1 million. She grants a lease to Bill to hold as nominee for herself. Bill is a friend but not otherwise connected with Agnes. The terms of the lease are as follows:

- yearly rent, one peppercorn, no premium; and
- term one month, but with an option (exercisable before the end of the month) to extend to 100 years in return for payment of £1.

There is no SDLT on the grant of the lease because it is treated as granted beneficially to the nominee (see **4.18**), and there is no reason to substitute the actual consideration with market value or any other figure. However, on the assumption that the option is likely to be exercised, the value of the freehold interest is now minimal. Agnes sells the freehold to Claire for £1. Again, there is no SDLT on this sale as there is no reason to substitute anything else for the actual consideration.

Agnes then undertakes to refrain from exercising the option to extend the lease if Claire pays her £2.15 million. There could possibly be an argument that this is a land transaction subject to SDLT, but in real, slightly more complicated arrangements based on this general structure, it was considered that this was not a land transaction. The overall result then is that Claire has spent £2.15 million to acquire a property but paid no SDLT.

There are a number of transactions, comprising the grant of the lease, sale of the freehold and undertaking not to exercise the option, so this series of transactions is potentially caught by *FA 2003, s 75A*.

The notional transaction

9.11 The rules only apply if the total SDLT paid on all transactions in the scheme is less than the amount which would be payable on a 'notional land transaction' (*FA 2003, s 75A(1)(c)*). This notional transaction is defined as a transaction effecting the transfer from V to P, for consideration (*FA 2003, s 75A(5)*) equal to the largest amount (aggregated if more than one):

- given by or on behalf of any one person: or
- received by or on behalf of V (or a person connected with V – *Corporation Taxes Act 2010, s 1122* applies in determining whether a person is connected with V),

by way of consideration for the scheme transactions. Reference to a notional land transaction sometimes causes confusion, because the legislation does not specify the nature of the transaction. However, this is unimportant. All that matters in this regard is that there is deemed to be a chargeable transaction for a specified amount of chargeable consideration, which determines the minimum SDLT charge.

For the purposes of *FA 2003, s 75A*, an amount of consideration also includes the money's worth value of any in kind consideration (*FA 2003, s 75C(9)*).

Incidental transactions and reliefs

9.12 In measuring the chargeable consideration for this notional land transaction, certain amounts must be left out of account. The amounts are:

- the consideration for any transaction which is merely incidental to the transfer of the chargeable interest (*FA 2003, s 75B(1)* – see **9.16**); and
- any consideration paid in respect of a transaction covered by any of the following reliefs (*FA 2003, s 75C(4)*):
  - *FA 2003, s 60* (compulsory purchase facilitating development);
  - *FA 2003, s 61* (compliance with planning obligations);

- *FA 2003, ss 63, 64* (demutualisation of insurance company or building society);
- *FA 2003, s 65* (incorporation of limited liability partnership);
- *FA 2003, s 66* (transfers involving public bodies);
- *FA 2003, s 67* (transfer in consequence of reorganisation of parliamentary constituencies);
- *FA 2003, s 69* (acquisition by bodies established for national purposes);
- *FA 2003, s 71* (acquisition by registered social landlord);
- *FA 2003, s 74* (collective enfranchisement by leaseholders);
- *FA 2003, s 75* (crofting community right to buy);
- *FA 2003, Sch 6A* (relief for acquisition by housing intermediaries etc); and
- *FA 2003, Sch 8* (charities relief).

These various reliefs are considered in more detail in **Chapter 5**. Without these exclusions, many of the reliefs would become relatively useless in real-life transactions which often involve multiple steps for entirely innocent reasons. Perhaps of more importance are the reliefs which are not listed above, the most important of which are the group, reconstruction and acquisition reliefs set out in *FA 2003, Sch 7*. HMRC are concerned that these reliefs may be exploited in ways which were not intended and are not keen to facilitate this (although this does beg the question of who is to judge the intention of reasonably plain legislation).

It should be noted that if a transaction is incidental, whilst the consideration for that transaction is ignored in determining the chargeable consideration for the notional transaction, the incidental transaction can still be a scheme transaction (see **9.9** et seq). If the transaction is only partially incidental to the transfer of the chargeable interest from V to P, the consideration should be apportioned on a just and reasonable basis between that part which is incidental and that part which is not incidental (SDLTM09240).

Example 9.2 (part 2)—SDLT payable under FA 2003, s 75A

The total SDLT paid on the basis of the scheme transactions is nil. The consideration for the notional transaction is £2.15 million (plus £1), being the aggregate amount given by Claire. Therefore, *FA 2003, s 75A* applies and the SDLT payable is calculated as follows (assuming that the additional rate of SDLT does not apply (see **4.39**)):

Chargeable consideration	Rate	SDLT
£	%	
125,000	0	Nil
125,000	2	2,500
675,000	5	33,750
575,000	10	57,500
650,001	12	78,000
2,150,001		171,750

This scheme is precisely the kind of arrangement that *FA 2003, s 75A* appears to be designed to block.

Effective date

9.13 The effective date of the notional transaction is the last date of completion of a scheme transaction or, if earlier, the last date of substantial performance of a scheme transaction (*FA 2003, s 75A(6)*). In the example above, this is likely to be the date on which Claire pays Agnes £2.15 million. If the transaction was a simple sale for £2.15 million, the effective date would typically be the date on which the consideration was paid, so this appears reasonable.

Exclusions from FA 2003, s 75A

9.14 The potential scope of *FA 2003, s 75A* is very wide. In particular, it could inhibit a legitimate arrangement of transactions in order to come within the terms of a relief or favourable treatment. To guard against this, there are two specific exclusions in *FA 2003, s 75A* itself, and some general restrictions on application set out in *FA 2003, ss 75B* and *75C*.

9.15 *FA 2003, s 75A* does not apply if the only reason for the reduced SDLT is that *FA 2003, ss 71A–73* (alternative property finance reliefs; see **5.37**) or *FA 2003, Sch 9* (right to buy etc reliefs; see **5.42**) apply (*FA 2003, s 75A(7)*). It is important to remember that the exclusion only applies if these reliefs are the *only* reason for the SDLT saving. A combination of steps which qualify for one of the reliefs with other steps risks losing the protection of the exclusion and bringing the whole transaction within the scope of *FA 2003, s 75A*.

FA 2003, s 75B – incidental transactions

9.16 Consideration for a real transaction in a series may be ignored in calculating the consideration for the notional transaction, if the real transaction is 'merely incidental' to the transfer of the chargeable interest from V to P. There is no comprehensive definition of 'merely incidental'. The legislation gives three examples of transactions which may be incidental (*FA 2003, s 75B(3)*), as follows, but the list does not claim to be exhaustive:

- a transaction undertaken for the purpose of constructing a building on the land;
- a transaction for the sale of anything other than land; and
- a loan or other provision of finance to enable someone to pay for part of the process by which the land transfer takes place.

Since the legislation only says these transactions 'may' be incidental, the list is of very limited use. It is further limited by the statement that transactions in the list at **9.10** are not incidental (*FA 2003, s 75B(4)*). A transaction cannot be regarded as incidental if it forms part of the process by which the transfer of the chargeable interest is effected, or if the transfer is conditional on completion of the transaction (*FA 2003, s 75B(2)*).

Certain transactions are specifically identified as not being incidental to the transfer of the chargeable interest from V to P (*FA 2003, s 75B(2)*):

- if the transaction, or a series of transactions of which it forms part, gives effect to the transfer of the chargeable interest;
- if the transfer of the chargeable interest is conditional upon completion of the transaction; or
- if the transaction is a scheme transaction specifically included in *FA 2003, s 75A(3)* (see **9.10**).

Example 9.3—Incidental transactions

The facts are as in Example 9.2 above, but Claire also pays Agnes £25,000 for the furniture and other chattels in the house. This is a payment for something other than land. Subject to confirmation that this represents a 'just and reasonable' allocation of the overall amounts paid, this will be regarded as an incidental transaction, and the amount paid will not be taken into account in determining the consideration for the notional land transaction.

Section 75C – other exclusions and conditions

9.17 A transfer of shares or securities is ignored for the purposes of *FA 2003, s 75A* if (but only if) it would otherwise be the first of a series of scheme transactions (*FA 2003, s 75C(1)*). This allows a degree of corporate reorganisation in order to permit a claim to relief on a subsequent land transaction.

If a transfer of shares or securities is ignored for the purposes of *FA 2003, s 75A*, that means that the consideration for the transfer of those shares or securities is not taken into account in determining the chargeable consideration for the notional transaction between V and P.

At SDLTM09280, HMRC confirm that:

> 'Pre-transfer administrative tasks relating solely to the transfer of shares or securities, for example shareholder approval for the transfer of shares to occur, will not usually be regarded as scheme transactions and can also be ignored when considering if the first scheme transaction would be a transfer of shares or securities.'

The exclusion applies only to a transfer of existing shares which means that any issue of new shares or securities will not be excluded from being a scheme transaction, even if it is the first of a series of transactions.

9.18 If a real transfer equivalent to the notional transaction would have been eligible for a relief, the relief applies to the notional transaction (*FA 2003, s 75C(2)*). The availability of a relief will be subject to the terms and conditions of that relief.

9.19 If the notional transaction is a transfer to a company which is connected with the vendor, *FA 2003, s 53* applies to deem the consideration to be the greater of:

(a) the market value of the chargeable interest transferred; and

(b) the actual consideration, including any VAT, given for the transfer.

(*FA 2003, s 75C(6)*) – see **4.29**)

When considering whether *FA 2003, s 53* applies you should also consider whether any of the exceptions in *FA 2003, s 54* are in point which, if they are, would result in the disapplication of *FA 2003, s 53*.

9.20 If the transfer of the chargeable interest from V to P constitutes an exchange (see **4.32** et seq), *FA 2003, Sch 4, para 5* applies to deem the consideration for that transfer to be equal to the greater of:

(a) the market value of the interest transferred under that notional transaction; and

(b) the market value of the property given by P in exchange together with any other consideration given.

(*FA 2003, s 75C(7)*)

Example 9.4—Exclusion of first step, transfer of shares

Henry owns all of the shares in two companies (Anne Ltd and Jane Ltd). Anne Ltd owns the freehold of a property which is let to Jane Ltd at a rent which is below the market rate. The lease held by Jane Ltd therefore has a capital value. Henry wants to put the value of the property into a single company, partly to extract cash and, later, to raise finance. Henry transfers the shares of Jane Ltd to Anne Ltd for payment in cash. He then arranges for Anne Ltd to transfer the freehold property to Jane Ltd as a contribution to capital (claiming group relief from SDLT), at which point the lease held by Jane Ltd collapses into the freehold by operation of law.

This is a series of transactions forming part of a single scheme. There is a transfer of property from Anne Ltd to Jane Ltd. This is for no consideration, but as a transfer to a connected company it is deemed to be for market value consideration. The notional transaction is the transfer from Anne Ltd to Jane Ltd, which is deemed to be for market value consideration by virtue of the application of *FA 2003, s 53* as noted above. The SDLT paid (nil) is less than would be payable on this notional consideration, so *FA 2003, s 75A* potentially applies. However:

(1) As the first step in the series, the transfer of shares of Jane Ltd to Anne Ltd is ignored. There is, therefore, only one step in the transaction (the transfer of the property to Jane Ltd), so *FA 2003, s 75A* does not apply.

(2) If there were other steps such that this was not enough to disapply *FA 2003, s 75A*, the notional transfer (being a transfer from Anne Ltd to Jane Ltd) should qualify for group relief just as the real transfer does. So, even if *FA 2003, s 75A* does apply, the SDLT charge could be removed by a claim to group relief.

9.21 It should be noted that the application of a relief to the notional transaction is subject to the normal conditions and restrictions which would apply in relation to that relief for a real transaction.

9.22 Other provisions which are applied to the notional transaction as they would apply to a real transaction are as follows:

- an interest in a property-investment partnership (see **7.29**) is treated as a chargeable interest (*FA 2003, s 75C(8)(a)*). This means that a transfer of an interest in a property-investment partnership that has 'relevant partnership property' (see **7.31** et seq), which includes a chargeable interest is within the scope of *FA 2003, s 75A*; and
- if any of the scheme transactions is entered into in connection with a transfer of an undertaking (such that *FA 2003, Sch 7, paras 7–8* apply), the notional transaction is also treated as entered into in connection with the same transfer (*FA 2003, s 75C(3)*).

9.23 Where V or P is a partnership, the normal partnership rules were originally applied in relation to a notional transaction which comprises a transfer of land to or from the partnership, from or to a partner or someone connected with a partner (see **7.13** and **7.19**). However, it was concluded that this might allow avoidance. *FA 2010, s 56* therefore amended *s 75C(8)* and inserted *s 75C(8A)* to ensure that the rules in *FA 2003, Sch 15, Pt 3* do not apply to any notional transaction which consists of a transfer to or from a partnership. As a result, any such notional transaction will be subject to SDLT as if it was a transfer between two ordinary persons. This may produce an unfair result where an actual transfer to a partnership involves more than one step, thus bringing *s 75A* into play.

Example 9.5—Potentially unjust result from application of *FA 2003, s 75A*

RST is a partnership of three otherwise unconnected individuals R, S and T, who share partnership profits equally. The partnership requires further premises. R's wife owns a suitable building which is currently vacant and in need of refurbishment. R's wife leases the building to R for ten years for no premium and a peppercorn rent. In turn, R sub-lets the building to the partnership for ten years at a market rent, but with the first year rent-free to reflect the cost of refurbishment which the partnership will incur.

If the transactions are regarded separately, no SDLT arises on the lease from R's wife to R, and SDLT will be chargeable on the partnership in respect of only 67% of the NPV of rents on the lease to the partnership: 33% of the NPV represents the interest effectively retained by R through his membership of the partnership (see **7.11** et seq for an explanation of this).

If the transactions are regarded as a series within *FA 2003, s 75A*, the notional transaction will be the grant of a lease at rent from R or R's wife (it does not matter which, for these purposes) to the partnership. The normal partnership rules will not apply, and the full NPV of rents under the lease to the partnership will be subject to SDLT. The SDLT cost will, therefore, be increased by the application of *FA 2003, s 75A*, even though there was no avoidance in the original series of transactions.

9.24 *FA 2003, s 75C(5)* and *(10)* makes it clear that any apportionment of amounts for the purpose of measuring consideration on the notional transaction must be on a just and reasonable basis, and that any SDLT paid in respect of an actual transaction which is ignored under *FA 2003, s 75A* is to be treated as paid in respect of the notional transaction. This, therefore, should avoid any element of double charge. However, it is possible that *FA 2003, s 75A* could apply to more than one group of steps in a complex series of transactions. This could lead to more than one charge under *FA 2003, s 75A*, even where a 'simple' transfer of the property from the original vendor to the ultimate purchaser would only have led to a single charge.

SPECIFIC ANTI-AVOIDANCE RULES

Introduction

9.25 Many of the conditions surrounding reliefs or treatments could be regarded as anti-avoidance rules. Their purpose is to ensure that the relief or treatment is only available in the circumstances envisaged by the government. Nonetheless, there are some specific rules which may be recognised as having been included to counter particular arrangements and may be properly regarded as anti-avoidance provisions. These specific rules are described at various points in this book, when dealing with the transactions or circumstances in which they may apply. For convenience, they are also listed below, with references. Some seek to attack specific structures which are considered to give rise to a tax advantage; others only apply if there is an avoidance motive. The rules apply whether or not the transaction is caught by *FA 2003 ss 75A–75C*; indeed, by denying a relief or treatment, the specific rules may ensure that the transaction is not within the terms of the general anti-avoidance rule.

Subject	**Description**	**Statute or other reference**	**Reference in this book**
Sub-sale relief	Alternative contracts No options Motive test	*FA 2003, ss 44A, 45A, Sch 2A, para 18*	**5.15** **5.16** **5.12**
Sale and leaseback relief	Not combined with other reliefs	*FA 2003, s 57A(3)(c), (d)*	**5.40**

Subject	**Description**	**Statute or other reference**	**Reference in this book**
Group, reconstruction and acquisition reliefs	Motive test	*FA 2003, Sch 7, paras 2(4A), 7(5), 8(5B)*	**5.28**
	Arrangements	*FA 2003, Sch 7, paras 2, 8(4)*	**5.25**
	Clawback on leaving group	*FA 2003, Sch 7, paras 3, 4A*	**5.30**
	Clawback on change of control	*FA 2003, Sch 7, paras 9, 11*	**5.33**
Alternative finance reliefs	Not combined with group or sub-sale relief	*FA 2003, s 73A* *FA 2003, s 45(3)*	**5.39** **5.16**
	Definition of financial institution and arrangements for change of control	*FA 2003, s 73AB, 73BA*	**5.38**
Charities relief	Change of use from charitable	*FA 2003, Sch 8, para 2*	**5.59**
Partnerships	Arrangements to transfer	*FA 2003, Sch 15, para 17*	**7.27**
	Withdrawal of value after land transfer	*FA 2003, Sch 15, para 17A*	**7.17**
Trusts	Grant of lease to bare trustee	*FA 2003, Sch 16, para 3(4)*	**4.18**
Leases	Assignment of lease after relief claimed on grant	*FA 2003, Sch 17A, para 11*	**6.17**
	Loan or deposit in conjunction with grant	*FA 2003, Sch 17A, para 18A*	**6.44**
Building contracts	Separation of building and land contracts	*Prudential Assurance v CIR* [1992] STC 863	Example 4.6

SDLT AND DISCLOSURE OF TAX AVOIDANCE SCHEMES (DOTAS)

Introduction

9.26 *FA 2004, Pt 7* introduced obligations for the notification of schemes for the avoidance of direct tax (potentially including SDLT). The legislation sets out the nature of the obligations in general terms and states on whom they fall. The detailed application is specified in regulations. SDLT was not initially in the list of taxes covered but was added in 2005. The rules governing the scope are now consolidated in the *Tax Avoidance Schemes (Information) Regulations 2012, SI 2012/1836* with effect from 1 September 2012. The nature of SDLT schemes brought within the rules was set out in the *SDLT Avoidance Schemes (Prescribed Descriptions of Arrangements) Regulations 2005, SI 2005/1868*. These regulations were amended by the *Stamp Duty Land Tax Avoidance Schemes (Prescribed Descriptions of Arrangements) (Amendment) Regulations 2012, SI 2012/2395*. As explained below, the rules for identifying notifiable SDLT schemes set out in these regulations are very different from the rules for other taxes.

FA 2014, Pt 4 provides for HMRC to demand accelerated payment of the tax which will arise if an avoidance scheme proves ineffective. On 15 July 2014 HMRC issued a list of reference numbers of 1,200 schemes notified under DOTAS, including schemes to mitigate SDLT, saying that demands for payment of tax in respect of these schemes would be made over the following 20 months. As at the time of writing (May 2020) the latest available list was for January 2020. The list is available at www.gov.uk/government/publications/tax-avoidance-schemes-on-which-accelerated-payments-may-be-charged-by-hmrc.

9.27 It is important not to be misled by the title – the regime is not restricted to complex avoidance schemes but may apply to the simplest modification to a transaction to reduce the tax cost. The parties to a transaction and anyone advising them may be required to make disclosure to HMRC in a very short time frame. There are penalties for failure to comply. For many advisers, the original penalties were insignificant, but the stigma of being identified as non-compliant was regarded as worse than any financial penalty. *FA 2010, Sch 17* increased the maximum potential penalty to £1 million, which is likely to be significant to all advisers. Many firms of advisers have instituted systems and procedures to ensure rapid identification of obligations. However, such systems are worthless unless the individuals providing advice are vigilant and recognise occasions when the rules apply.

It is important to remember that notification obligations fall on 'Promoters' and 'Scheme Users' automatically, without any prompting from HMRC. However, a person who only acts as an 'Introducer' is only required to give information to HMRC if HMRC specifically demand it.

Application to SDLT

9.28 SDLT was brought within the DOTAS regime from 1 August 2005. From that date, the rules applied to prescribed arrangements where the property in question was not purely residential and had a value of £5 million or more. Residential property with a value of at least £1 million was then brought within the rules from 1 April 2010 by *SI 2010/407*. Note that mixed residential/non-residential property was within the rules if the total value was £5 million or more and/or if the residential element was £1 million or more. However, the value thresholds were removed by *the Stamp Duty Land Tax Avoidance Schemes (Prescribed Descriptions of Arrangements) (Amendment) Regulations 2012, SI 2012 2395* for transactions with an effective date of 1 November 2012 or later.

Scheme reference numbers (SRNs)

9.29 As with other taxes, HMRC provide a scheme reference number (SRN) for each scheme disclosed (*FA 2004, s 311*). Prior to 1 April 2010, promoters of SDLT schemes were not obliged to notify users of the SRN, and users had no obligation to notify HMRC of the number of any scheme used. This was because HMRC's primary concern was to understand the nature of SDLT avoidance arrangements rather than to challenge specific schemes. From 1 April 2010, as is the case with other taxes, the SDLT SRN must be provided to users and reported by them to HMRC, along with other information (*FA 2004, ss 312–313*). HMRC have provided a new form for this purpose at www.hmrc.gov.uk/aiu/form-aag4sdlt.pdf (see **Appendix B**). It is evident that HMRC consider that the obligation for scheme users to report to HMRC applies only in respect of schemes first notified to them by promoters on or after 1 April 2010. The way in which regulations have been sequentially amended does not clearly support this. However, taxpayers should be able to rely on the clear statement in HMRC Guidance that the relevant date is 1 April 2010.

The absence of any requirement to report use of schemes first notified before 1 April 2010 (or perhaps 2009) is referred to in HMRC guidance as 'grandfathering'. It was decided that the grandfathering of certain politically sensitive schemes involving residential property and sub-sales is preventing HMRC from detecting their use. Regulations under *FA 2012, s 213* modified the rules to make users notify the use of those schemes (see **9.38**).

HMRC guidance

9.30 HMRC have provided general guidance on the application of the DOTAS rules. The latest version of this may be found online at www.hmrc.gov.uk/aiu/guidance.htm, or paper copies may be obtained from HMRC's publications department (see **Appendix A**). Some sections of this guidance do not apply to SDLT, and other sections apply only to SDLT. This guidance was last updated on 20 April 2018.

Notifiable arrangements and proposals

9.31 A notifiable arrangement is any arrangement which:

(1) falls within the description set out in the regulations (*SI 2005/1868*); and

(2) might be expected to enable any person to obtain an SDLT advantage as a main benefit from the arrangement (*FA 2004, s 306(1)*).

This is a two-pronged test. The mere obtaining of a tax advantage as a main benefit does not make the arrangement notifiable – it must also fall within the description set out in the regulations. Equally, an arrangement which happens to fall within the description set out in the regulations, but which does not have a tax advantage as a main benefit, is not notifiable. However, in the light of the severe penalties for failure to notify under these rules, most advisers 'play safe' and make a disclosure in all uncertain cases.

9.32 A notifiable proposal is a proposal for arrangements which would be notifiable if entered into (*FA 2004, s 306(2)*).

No hallmarks

9.33 In relation to income tax, corporation tax and capital gains tax, notifiable arrangements are those which have certain characteristics, referred to as 'hallmarks'. For those taxes, an arrangement is not notifiable unless it has one or more of the hallmarks. The 'hallmarks' have no application in relation to SDLT. Rather, the rules operate the other way round. *All* arrangements relating to the acquisition of chargeable interests, which might have a main benefit of enabling anyone to obtain a tax benefit in relation to SDLT, are notifiable, unless they fall within certain exclusions set out in *SI 2005/1868* as amended by subsequent regulations (see **9.28** and **9.38**), or are 'grandfathered' (see **9.37**). There is a useful flowchart in section 8 of the HMRC Guidance mentioned at **9.30**.

9.34 The exclusions are expressed in the form of six steps which the arrangement might involve, and two rules setting out which combinations of steps are acceptable. The order of the steps is not generally important. The steps are set out in the regulations as follows:

> **'Step A: Acquisition of a chargeable interest by special purpose vehicle**
>
> The acquisition of a chargeable interest in land by a company created for that purpose ("a special purpose vehicle").

Step B: Claims to relief

Making–

(a) a single claim to relief under any of the following provisions–

(i) *FA 2003*, section 57A (sale and leaseback arrangements);

(ii) *FA 2003*, section 58B (relief for new zero carbon homes);

(iii) *FA 2003*, section 58C (relief for new zero carbon homes: supplemental);

(iv) *FA 2003*, section 60 (compulsory purchase facilitating development);

(v) *FA 2003*, section 61 (compliance with planning obligation);

(vi) *FA 2003*, section 63 (demutualisation of insurance company);

(vii) *FA 2003*, section 64 (demutualisation of building society);

(viii) *FA 2003*, section 65 (incorporation of limited liability partnership);

(ix) *FA 2003*, section 66 (transfers involving public bodies);

(x) *FA 2003*, section 67 (transfer in consequence of reorganisation of parliamentary constituencies);

(xi) *FA 2003*, section 69 (acquisition by bodies established for national purposes);

(xii) *FA 2003*, section 71 (certain acquisitions by registered social landlords);

(xiii) *FA 2003*, section 74 (collective enfranchisement by leaseholders);

(xiv) *FA 2003*, section 75 (crofting community right to buy);

(xv) *FA 2003*, Schedule 6 (disadvantaged areas relief);

(xvi) *FA 2003*, Schedule 6A (relief for certain acquisitions of residential property);

(xvii) *FA 2003*, Schedule 6B (transfers involving multiple dwellings);

(xviii) *FA 2003*, Schedule 7 (group relief and reconstruction acquisition reliefs);

(xix) *FA 2003*, Schedule 8 (charities relief);

(xx) *FA 2003*, Schedule 9 (right to buy, shared ownership leases etc.);

(xxi) *FA 2003*, Schedule 61 to Finance Act 2009 (alternative finance investment bonds), or

(b) one or more claims to relief under any one of the following provisions–

(i) *FA 2003, section 71A* (alternative property finance: land sold to financial institution and leased to individual);

(ii) *FA 2003, section 72* (alternative property finance in Scotland: land sold to financial institution and leased to individual);

(iii) *FA 2003, section 72A* (alternative property finance in Scotland: land sold to financial institution and individual in common); or

(iv) *FA 2003, section 73* (alternative property finance: land sold to financial institution and resold to individual).

Step C: Sale of shares in special purpose vehicle

The sale of shares in a special purpose vehicle, which holds a chargeable interest in land, to a person with whom neither the special purpose vehicle, nor the vendor, is connected.

Step D: Not exercising election to waive exemption from VAT

No election is made to waive exemption from value added tax contained in paragraph 2 of Schedule 10 to the Value Added Tax Act 1994 (treatment of buildings and land for value added tax purposes).

Step E: Transfer of a business as a going concern

Arranging the transfer of a business, connected with the land which is the subject of the arrangements, in such a way that it is treated for the purposes of value added tax as the transfer of a going concern.

Step F: Undertaking a joint venture

The creation of a partnership (within the meaning of *FA 2003, Sch 1, para* 15) to which the property subject to a land transaction is to be transferred.'

9.35 The two rules setting out which combinations are acceptable are as follows:

'**Rule 1**

Arrangements involving any combination of Steps B, D, E and F, with or without a single instance of one of steps A, C and D, are excluded arrangements unless rule 2 applies. Note however that Step B is in two parts. It is HMRC's view that if there is more than one claim to any relief listed in part (a), or claims to reliefs in both part (a) and part (b), this combination is no longer within Step B and the arrangement is not excluded.

Rule 2

Arrangements are not excluded arrangements if they–

(a) include all, or at least two of, steps A, C and D; or

(b) involve more than one instance of step A, C or D.'

9.36 It is important to bear in mind that these rules merely make certain transactions exempt. Any multi-step transaction involving any steps other than steps A to F listed above, where the unlisted step(s) are essential to obtain the SDLT advantage, *cannot* be exempt from disclosure, no matter what combination of listed steps it involves.

Example 9.6—Step not in list, notification required

Notax LLP, a firm of tax advisers, develops a scheme for SDLT-free acquisition of leasehold commercial buildings. The scheme involves the client setting up an SPV (not a listed step), the SPV entering into a joint venture with the vendor (Step F), the SPV acquiring an interest in the property (Step A), and a claim to group relief (Step B). Under the rules set out above in **9.35**, this includes only one instance of a step listed in rule 2, so the scheme should be exempt from notification. However, the scheme also involves a step which is not listed but is essential to obtaining the tax advantage – setting up an SPV – so the scheme is not exempt from notification. In practice, it seems that few real schemes will be exempt from notification under these rules.

Arrangements which are 'substantially the same'

9.37 Separate, different schemes must be disclosed separately. However, once a scheme has been disclosed, no further disclosure is needed by the promoter if the same scheme is implemented again, whether for the same or different clients. This is subject to the exception mentioned in **9.38**. Equally, if subsequent implementation involves only minor differences such that the two schemes are substantially the same, no further disclosure is required (*FA 2004, s 308(5)*). HMRC have provided some guidance as to when schemes may or may not be regarded as substantially the same, as follows:

> 'In our view a scheme is no longer substantially the same if the effect of any change would be to make any previous disclosure misleading in relation to the second (or subsequent) client.
>
> In general provided the tax analysis is substantially the same we will regard schemes as "substantially the same" where the only change is a different client including a different company in the same group.

> We will not regard schemes as substantially the same where there are changes to deal with changes in the law or accounting treatment, changes in the tax attributes e.g. schemes creating income losses instead of capital losses or other legal and commercial issues.' (DOTAS guidance, last updated on 20 April 2018 para 14.2.3 at p 119)

9.38 From 1 April 2010, most arrangements are excluded from the need to disclose if they are the same, or substantially the same, as arrangements first made available for implementation before that date. This is generally referred to as 'grandfathering'. Where such arrangements related to non-residential property, they should have been disclosed under the rules then in force; however, this concession means that, in relation to residential property, only novel or significantly changed schemes need be disclosed. However *FA 2012, s 213* amended *FA 2004, s 308* to allow the Treasury to make further amendments to the rules by regulation. *The Stamp Duty Land Tax (Avoidance Schemes) (Specified Proposals or Arrangements) Regulations 2012, SI 2012/2396* came into force on 1 November 2012. These removed the grandfathering concession in respect of schemes which rely on sub-sale relief in combination with a distribution *in specie*, acquisition by a partnership or settlement, a gift or transfer at an undervalue, the grant of an option or an assignment or novation. Schemes relying on such combinations and used on or after 1 November 2012 have to be disclosed one more time. As a result, these schemes have been brought within the rules which require *users* of the schemes to disclose their use (see **9.53**). The retrospective revision of sub-sale relief in *FA 2013, s 194* (see **5.16**) and the new rules from 17 July 2013 (see **5.11**) were informed by disclosures under these provisions.

Example 9.7—Arrangements which are 'substantially the same'

Tax advisory firm Fiscality has developed an arrangement which allows a company to grant a lease to a fellow subsidiary at low SDLT cost, so there is no need to claim group relief and therefore no clawback if the lessee leaves the group. The arrangement requires the establishment of an orphan company registered overseas to hold an interest in the land as nominee. The arrangement was disclosed under the DOTAS rules before 1 April 2010, and was used by two separate clients of Fiscality. In December 2010, Fiscality concludes that using a nominee company established in a different overseas jurisdiction would make it easier to administer the arrangement without affecting the tax analysis. In the author's view, if the only change is to use a company established in a different jurisdiction purely for convenience, the new arrangement will be 'substantially the same' as the old arrangement and no new disclosure obligation will arise.

Shortly afterwards, Fiscality concludes that the tax analysis will be strengthened if the order of execution of two steps in the arrangement is reversed. This change will be sufficient to prevent the new arrangement from being 'substantially the same' as the old, and a new disclosure obligation will arise when the new version is 'made available for use' or, if earlier, when Fiscality first become aware of a transaction forming part of arrangements implementing the new version of the scheme (see **9.54**).

Promoters and introducers

9.39 *FA 2010, Sch 17* amended the provisions relating to identity and obligations of 'promoters' and introduced a new concept of 'introducers'. The amendments took effect from 1 January 2011 (*SI 2010/3019*).

9.40 From the beginning, the primary obligations have fallen on 'promoters'. A promoter is a person who, in the course of a tax advisory, banking or securities house business and in relation to a notifiable arrangement or proposal:

(1) is to any extent responsible for the design of the proposed arrangements, or

(2) makes a 'firm approach' to another person with a view to making the proposal available for implementation by that person or anyone else, or

(3) makes the proposal available for implementation by any person.

9.41 The second point was inserted by *FA 2010, Sch 17* to ensure the responsibility net is spread as widely as possible. A firm approach is made if, at a time when the arrangements have been 'substantially designed', information about them, including an explanation of the tax advantages, is communicated to anyone with a view to entering into transactions forming part of the proposal. Arrangements are substantially designed if, at that time, the nature of the transactions is sufficiently developed for it to be reasonable to believe that someone would enter into them (or into transactions not substantially different from them) in order to obtain the expected tax advantage.

9.42 Prior to *FA 2010*, the expression 'substantially designed' did not appear in the legislation, but HMRC relied on a similar concept to determine whether a scheme had been 'made available'. In the view of HMRC, a scheme is substantially designed at any time if, at that time, the nature of the transactions to form part of the scheme has been sufficiently developed for it to be reasonable to believe that a person who wishes to obtain the tax advantage communicated might enter into either:

- transactions of the nature developed at the time; or
- transactions not substantially different from those developed at the time.

(DOTAS Guidance last updated on 20 April 2018 para 3.6.2, see **9.30**). The rules are expressed in wide, all-inclusive terms, so that reporting obligations may arise at a very early stage.

9.43 The question of whether an arrangement is substantially designed or developed to such a stage etc is particularly unclear. In any case in which HMRC may allege that a promoter has failed to make timely disclosure, they may be expected to wish to see copies of emails, notes of telephone conversations and other similar evidence, to show the process by which the scheme was developed.

Example 9.8—Timing of obligations

Notax LLP is developing an arrangement which, they believe, will allow purchase of houses at a much reduced SDLT cost. On 1 February 2020, Mark, a partner in Notax, attends a conference with leading tax counsel at which counsel advises that their technical analysis is generally sound. Counsel highlights areas needing some further attention, such as the country of incorporation of a new company required to execute the arrangement. On 2 February 2020, Judith, another partner in Notax who has not been involved in developing the proposal, calls business contact Kim at the local branch of estate agent Houseller plc to tell him about the wonderful tax wheeze her firm has just developed, and to encourage Kim to talk to suitable house purchasers about it with a view to introducing her firm to them. There is an agreement in place between Notax and Houseller under which commissions are paid for successful introductions. Kim is not a tax person, so Judith does not give him any technical details, but she does outline the general steps required and explains that, if successful, the arrangement would reduce the SDLT cost of house purchase to less than one tenth of what it would otherwise be.

It is almost certain that Judith has fallen within paragraph (2) in **9.40** above and has triggered Notax LLP's disclosure obligations on 2 February 2020. It does not matter that Judith has given no technical details, nor that she personally was not involved in developing the arrangement. In the eyes of HMRC, Notax LLP as an entity is carrying on a tax advisory business and is the promoter.

9.44 A person is an introducer if he makes a marketing contact with another person in relation to a notifiable proposal. A marketing contact is made if the first person communicates information about the proposal to the second person, including an explanation of the expected tax advantage, with a view to anyone entering into the proposed arrangements. An introducer, provided he is not also a promoter, has no direct disclosure responsibilities, but may be required by HMRC to pass on to them such information as he has about the scheme.

Example 9.9—An 'introducer'

In Example 9.8, Kim immediately calls customer Irena who is negotiating to buy a UK house for about £2 million. He passes on the outline information received from Judith and asks Irena to think about talking to Notax LLP. Kim is not working for or as a tax adviser or a bank or securities house, so neither he nor Houseller can be a promoter. However, since Houseller stands to earn commission from the introduction, this is undoubtedly a 'marketing contact'. Therefore, Houseller is an introducer.

Example 9.10—No obligations

Following on from the previous example, Irena (who works for an advertising agency) mentions the Notax scheme to a colleague who is also about to buy an expensive house, passing on the contact details for Notax. Neither Irena nor her employer is carrying on a business as a tax adviser or a bank or securities house. Therefore, Irena cannot be acting as a promoter. This is a casual discussion with a colleague – Irena does not stand to make any financial gain from passing the information on to her colleague. Therefore, this is unlikely to be a marketing contact, and neither Irena nor her employer should be regarded as acting as an introducer.

Who is not a promoter?

9.45 A person who is only involved in the design of a scheme, and is not in any way involved in implementation or organising or managing implementation, is not a promoter if:

- his input is benign – that is, the advice he gives does not contribute to the tax-saving aspect of the scheme (eg advice as to whether a particular shareholding arrangement permitted a claim to group relief would be benign, but advice as to how to change the arrangement in order to qualify for group relief would not be benign), or
- he is not acting as a tax adviser – for example, an unrelated lawyer consulted only on the company law implications of a proposal would not be acting as a tax adviser, or
- he could not reasonably be expected to have sufficient information to know whether there is a disclosable scheme, or to be able to make that disclosure – for example, a newly appointed tax adviser might ask the outgoing tax adviser for an opinion on the implications of a proposed action (in the light of previous transactions) and the new adviser might use that advice in devising a notifiable proposal. However, if the outgoing

adviser is not given any details of the proposal, he probably could not reasonably be expected to have sufficient information to know whether there is a disclosable proposal or to make disclosure.

9.46 A person who acts purely as an intermediary or introducer, without being involved in design, implementation or management of implementation, is not a promoter (but HMRC may demand information from such a person following the activation of the changes in *FA 2010, Sch 17*; see **9.44**).

Co-promoters

9.47 If two or more persons are promoters in relation to the same (or substantially the same) proposal or arrangement, it is possible for only one disclosure to be made, and for this to be made by one of them, provided:

(1) the other promoter holds or is provided with the information disclosed to HMRC,

(2) the disclosing promoter provides HMRC with a note of the name and address of the other promoter, and

(3) (if the co-promoter becomes a co-promoter after initial disclosure has been made) the disclosing promoter provides the other promoter with a note of the SRN,

the co-promoter is exempt from making disclosure. Where the proposal or arrangement made by the co-promoter is not identical with that disclosed, it is for the co-promoter to decide whether it is sufficiently similar for the exemption to apply. Co-promoters are not exempt from other obligations, such as providing their client with SRNs.

Overseas promoters

9.48 In principle, the DOTAS rules apply to a promoter resident outside the UK. However, in practice it may be difficult for HMRC to enforce compliance, especially where the promoter is not carrying on business through a UK permanent establishment. If no promoter is resident in the UK, and the overseas promoter does not comply with DOTAS obligations, the obligations fall instead on any person (the 'client') who enters into any transaction forming part of the arrangements. Note that the obligations fall on 'any person who enters into any transaction …', which therefore includes the vendor, even though any tax advantage will normally accrue to the purchaser. A vendor who does not know about any arrangements which the purchaser may be implementing cannot be faulted for failing to disclose them. However, it is common for a vendor to know at least something of the purchaser's arrangements, so this is a matter over which vendors must take care.

These disclosure obligations are removed from the client(s) if a promoter complies with them (*FA 2004, s 309(2)*).

Arrangements with no promoter

9.49 If a person enters into a transaction forming part of notifiable arrangements in relation to which there is no promoter (eg a scheme which the taxpayer has developed himself), that person has responsibility for making an appropriate disclosure. This includes the situation where a scheme is devised by one company in a group and used by another in the same group. The group company devising the scheme is not regarded as a promoter but the company using the scheme must make disclosure.

Promoters with the benefit of legal privilege

9.50 In some circumstances, promoters who are lawyers may be able to resist providing some of the information required under DOTAS, on the grounds that the information is subject to legal privilege. If this happens, any user of the scheme is required to make the same disclosure as would be required if there was no promoter (see previous paragraph). However, as noted at **9.60**, the time limit for making disclosure is five days and not the 30 days which applies for 'in-house' schemes.

Duties of promoters

9.51 Promoters (or persons entering into a transaction if there is no promoter, or if there is no promoter in the UK and no overseas promoter complies with DOTAS):

- must provide HMRC with certain prescribed information (see **9.61** et seq), and
- must do this within the prescribed period after the relevant date (see **9.60**).

Promoters must make the disclosure by completing and submitting form AAG1 (see **Appendix B**), which may be downloaded for manual completion or completed and submitted online, as noted at **9.53**. In response to this, HMRC will normally provide a scheme reference number (SRN). The promoter must notify the SRN to any person to whom he is providing services in relation to the scheme, or any scheme which is substantially the same (see **9.37**). This notification must be made on form AAG6 which is downloadable from www.hmrc.gov.uk/aiu/aag6_sdlt.pdf. The number must be passed on within 30 days of the later of:

- the promoter first becoming aware of any transaction which forms part of the arrangements, and
- HMRC notifying the promoter of the SRN.

Promoters are also required to keep appropriate records and notify HMRC of details of clients implementing the schemes (see **9.64** below). *FA 2013, s 223* added a requirement that promoters must, if required by notice from HMRC, also supply prescribed details of any other persons whom the promoter might be expected to know may be a party to the arrangements. The details are prescribed in the *Tax Avoidance Schemes (Information) (Amendment, etc) Regulations 2013 (SI 2013/2592), reg 20*, which came into force on 4 November 2013 and comprises the name and address of any person, other than the client, who the promoter might be expected to know may be a party to the arrangements, but only those persons who may either sell the arrangements to another person or achieve the tax advantage themselves by implementing the arrangements, the tax reference numbers of such persons and sufficient information, to allow HMRC to understand the manner in which such a person is involved in the arrangements.

9.52 As noted above, the requirement to notify the SRN for SDLT schemes to the client was new from 1 April 2010. It appears that HMRC consider this only applies to schemes notified to HMRC from 1 April 2010, although the regulations appear to say that it applies to schemes notified from 1 April 2009.

Duties of scheme users

9.53 Also from 1 April 2010, obligations were imposed on users of SDLT schemes and others to whom an SRN is notified. Anyone who is notified of an SRN is now required to report their use of the scheme to HMRC, quoting the SRN. Some SDLT schemes operate by taking the transaction out of the charge so that, if the scheme works, there is no obligation to submit an SDLT return; in any case, the SDLT return has no space to report an SRN. To ensure relevant details are captured, HMRC have provided a new SDLT-specific version of form AAG4 (form AAG4 (SDLT) – see Appendix B) for scheme users to report details. The form can be downloaded from www.hmrc.gov.uk/aiu/form-aag4sdlt.pdf. Alternatively, the form may be completed and submitted online via a link at www.hmrc.gov.uk/aiu/forms-tax-schemes.htm. Use of this form is now compulsory in all cases. *FA 2013, s 223* added the requirement for the user to provide prescribed information to the promoter. The details are prescribed in the *Tax Avoidance Schemes (Information) (Amendment, etc) Regulations 2013*

(SI 2013/2592), reg 16, which came into force on 4 November 2013 and the information to be supplied to the promoter comprises the user's tax reference number and national insurance number or confirmation that the user does not have a tax reference number and/or a national insurance number.

9.54 Anyone to whom an SRN is provided is also required to notify it to anyone else they reasonably expect to be a party to, and to gain a tax advantage from, implementation of the scheme, using form AAG6, as noted at **9.51**. This must be done within 30 days of the later of:

- first becoming aware of any transaction which forms part of the arrangements, and
- receiving notification of the SRN.

Time for disclosure – promoters

9.55 The rules relating to timing of disclosure by promoters are the same as for other taxes. A scheme promoter is required to make disclosure within five days (excluding weekends and bank holidays) of the 'relevant date'. The relevant date is the earlier of the date on which the notifiable proposal is 'made available for use', and the date on which the promoter first becomes aware of any transaction forming part of arrangements implementing the proposal.

9.56 The legislation does not state when a proposal is regarded as 'made available for use'. The HMRC guidance draws a distinction between bespoke and marketed schemes. A marketed scheme – that is, one which is developed for possible use by a range or category of users – is made available when it:

- has been developed to such a stage that the promoter has a high degree of confidence in the tax analysis applying to it; and
- is communicated to the first potential user in sufficient detail that he could be expected to:
  - understand the expected tax advantages; and
  - decide whether or not to enter into it.

HMRC accept that, where a firm of advisers has an internal approval process, a proposal will not normally be regarded as made available before that approval has been given.

9.57 In contrast with this, a bespoke scheme – that is, one which is designed for a specific client's situation – is not generally regarded as being 'made available'. For such a scheme, the relevant date will therefore be the date on which the promoter first becomes aware of any transaction forming part of the arrangements. There is a danger here where more than one individual in a firm of advisers has contact with the client; if the first individual to learn that a transaction has been implemented does not understand the significance of this, the five-day deadline may easily be missed.

9.58 Occasionally, an adviser may outline a partially developed planning idea to a client, in such general terms that no proposal can yet be regarded as made available for use. The client may then do further development work and proceed to implement its own version of the arrangement without further reference to the adviser. It might be thought that, in this situation, the adviser has not made a notifiable proposal and has no disclosure obligations. However, even here the legislation seeks to impose obligations on the adviser. Having provided the basic idea, the adviser is likely to be regarded as 'to any extent responsible for the design of the proposed arrangements' and therefore a promoter. If no disclosure of the proposal has previously been made, the adviser is required to make disclosure within five days of first becoming aware of any transaction forming part of the notifiable arrangements. It is very difficult to be sure of capturing such information – good communications with clients and robust internal systems are essential!

Time for disclosure and other notification – scheme users

9.59 As noted at **9.29**, the general requirement for users to notify use of SDLT schemes was introduced in April 2010. The rules governing timing of this notification are *not* the same as for other taxes. The differences mirror the tight timetable for submission of SDLT returns, although that timetable has now become even tighter with the reduction in the filing/payment deadline from 30 days to 14 days. However, the 30-day deadline detailed below has not been changed. The deadlines are as set out below. Guidance on the nature and content of the various forms is also provided below.

Forms for disclosure and notification

9.60

Form	Responsible person	Reason	Deadline for receipt by HMRC or other party
AAG1	Promoter	Disclosing scheme	5 days from making available or becoming aware of first transaction in scheme
AAG2	User	Disclosing scheme from overseas promoter, no other disclosure made	5 days from entering into first transaction in scheme

Form	**Responsible person**	**Reason**	**Deadline for receipt by HMRC or other party**
AAG3	User	Disclosing scheme from lawyer claiming legal professional privilege	5 days from entering into first transaction in scheme
AAG3	User	Disclosing internally developed scheme, no external promoter	30 days from entering into first transaction in scheme
AAG4 (SDLT)	User	Notifying use of scheme with UK promoter (or overseas promoter who complies with disclosure requirement)	30 days from later of receipt of SRN and effective date of first transaction in scheme
AAG5	Anyone	Continuation sheet where information does not fit on another form	As related form
AAG6	Promoter and user	Informing other users of SRN	30 days from later of receiving SRN and becoming aware of first transaction in scheme

Content of disclosure

9.61 The forms noted above prescribe the information to be provided. Use of the appropriate forms (including the continuation sheet AAG5 where necessary) is compulsory. Notification given in any other way will not be regarded as sufficient. The forms are reproduced at **Appendix B**. PDF versions (for manual completion and posting) may be downloaded, or the forms may be completed and submitted online, via links at www.hmrc.gov.uk/aiu/forms-tax-schemes.htm. Most of the forms are the same as those used for disclosure of other direct tax schemes, but there is an SDLT-specific version of form AAG4. Most of the entries required on the forms are self-explanatory, and help on completion is available, if needed, in the HMRC guide mentioned at **9.30**.

9.62 The only sections of the forms which commonly cause difficulty are those in forms AAG1 to AAG3 relating to the description and explanation of the scheme. HMRC guidance (Guidance on DOTAS last updated on 20 April 2018 para 15.3.4) on this subject is as follows:

> 'Sufficient information is required to be provided such that an Officer of the Board of HMRC is able to understand how the expected tax advantage is intended to arise. The explanation should be in straightforward terms and should identify the steps involved and the relevant UK tax law. Common technical or legal terms and concepts need not be explained in depth.

If the scheme is complex then copies of any prospectus or scheme diagrams will help us understand what is proposed. But even where you send such documents you must still use form AAG 1, AAG 2 or AAG 3 as appropriate. Where such documents are supplied there is no objection to these documents excluding information that would identify a client.'

9.63 Each form has a separate section for identification of relevant statutory provisions, but in the author's view it is also likely to be necessary to refer to appropriate sections of legislation in the body of any description and explanation.

Requirement to notify HMRC of users

9.64 Under *FA 2004, s 313ZA*, inserted by *FA 2010, Sch 17*, a promoter who provides services to a client in connection with the arrangements is required to give information about the client to HMRC. The promoter must provide details of the name and address of each client to whom he has provided services in relation to a notifiable scheme (and to whom he would be required to provide the SRN: see **9.51**) together with the SRN of the scheme, details of the promoter's own name and address and the end date of the calendar quarter in which the services were provided. This information must be submitted within 30 days of the end of the relevant calendar quarter.

Example 9.11—Details to be disclosed

The following is an example of the level of detail which may be appropriate in describing/explaining a scheme. There is no suggestion that what follows is a description of a scheme which is currently or has previously been valid or effective – it is purely intended to illustrate the amount of detail which may be appropriate!

Title of arrangement: Partner retirement plan

Explanation:

(1) This arrangement permits a partner to withdraw from a property-investment partnership and a new partner to join the partnership at reduced SDLT cost.

(2) Statutory references are to Finance Act 2003.

(3) ABC is a property-investment partnership as defined in Schedule 15 para 14(8), established in [overseas territory]. The partners are A, B and C who are all individuals and otherwise unconnected and who share equally in the profits and capital of the partnership. Although

the majority of ABC's assets are chargeable interests (none of which was acquired from a partner or person connected with a partner), substantial other assets are held including property assets situated overseas.

(4) A wishes to retire and will withdraw value equal to his 33% share in the partnership capital; it is proposed to admit D, another individual who is not connected with A, B or C. D will contribute cash to secure a 33% share in the capital of the partnership.

(5) The partnership deed will be amended to specify that individual partners' shares entitle them to share in the economic value of specific assets. As a result, A's share will entitle him to share in the economic value of the overseas assets and a one-third share in just one chargeable asset; the shares of the other partners will entitle them to share in the economic value of the remaining chargeable assets plus a smaller share in the values of the non-chargeable assets. The values will be such that the overall partnership share of each partner will be unchanged. Appropriate legal advice has been obtained confirming that such subdivision is effective under the law of [overseas territory]. Copies of the current deed and draft amendment are available for inspection if required.

(6) The partnership will use a combination of cash already held and cash borrowed from a bank under an existing overdraft facility to pay A the value of his partnership share.

(7) D will contribute cash on admission to the partnership and will become entitled to the interests in assets relinquished by A.

Analysis:

(8) The division of assets into categories and subdivision of partnership interests will not affect any partner's partnership share as defined by Schedule 15 paragraph 34(2); therefore it will have no SDLT consequences.

(9) The withdrawal of A and admission of D will be a Category A Transfer of partnership interest as defined in Schedule 15 paragraph 14(3B). However the only relevant partnership property as defined in Schedule 15 paragraph 14(5) is the one UK property in which A has an economic interest. SDLT will be chargeable accordingly by reference to 33% of the market value of that property alone, in accordance with Schedule 15 paragraph 14(6) & (7).

Statutory provisions:

Finance Act 2003 Schedule 15 paragraphs 14(3B), (5)(c), (6), (7) and 34(2).

Information powers

9.65 If HMRC suspect that a scheme has not been disclosed, they are entitled to require anyone they suspect of being a promoter to formally state whether they consider a scheme to be disclosable and, if not, why not. The notice from HMRC will give a time by which a reply must be given – potentially, as short as ten days later – and penalties may be imposed for non-compliance. Beyond that, there are powers to require information to be given, but these generally require an order of the Tax Tribunal. These situations are beyond the scope of this book.

Penalties

9.66 The Tax Tribunal may impose penalties for failure to disclose a notifiable proposal or arrangement or for late disclosure, and for failure to comply with orders requiring disclosure or provision of information. The amount of the penalty may be up to £5,000, plus further amounts of up to £600 (or, in some cases, £5,000) for each day during which the failure continues. However, the Tax Tribunal is empowered to award penalties of up to £1 million in exceptional cases if the daily penalties are not considered sufficient to induce compliance. Any person in danger of suffering such penalties will doubtless require specialist advice beyond the scope of this book.

Chapter 10

Stamp Duty – General Rules

INTRODUCTION

10.1 The last comprehensive consolidation of stamp duty legislation was in the *Stamp Act 1891 (SA 1891)* and the *Stamp Duty Management Act 1891*. Unsurprisingly, the law has changed massively since then. The main changes have been to remove particular assets or transactions from the charge, so that *SA 1891, Sch 1*, which originally defined the scope of the tax, is now largely irrelevant. However, the principles set out in the body of *SA 1891* still apply, some sections of that Act having been amended by 21st-century *Finance Acts*.

Subsequent stamp duty legislation is scattered across more than a century of *Finance Acts*. Specific exemptions often appear in other legislation (eg an exemption for transfers in the privatisation of rail services; see *Railways Act 1993, s 112* and *Sch 9*). For this reason, when dealing with government-sponsored transactions, it is usually worth checking enabling legislation for exemptions. However, for most transactions the key legislation is found in *FA 1986, ss 66–85*, *FA 1999, Sch 13*, *FA 2003, ss 125* and *195*, and *FA 2019, ss 47* and *47A* (*FA 2019, s 47A* only applies from the date upon which *FA 2020* receives royal assent).

Some time ago the government embarked on a programme to remove redundant provisions from the statute book. *FA 2012, Sch 38* repealed several pages of stamp duty reliefs which have little or no current application, with effect from 6 April 2013. This small step of simplification was welcome. However, a better step might be to abolish stamp duty, bringing all UK share transactions into the SDRT net.

Indeed, on 10 July 2017 the Office of Tax Simplification (OTS) published its report on stamp duty on paper documents and recommended its reform, digitalisation and simplification. The recommendations made in the OTS's report, and the Chancellor of the Exchequer's letter dated 14 August 2017 responding to that report, are considered at **1.17**.

To date the only actions which have been taken are the introduction of a market value rule, for the purposes of both stamp duty and SDRT, on the transfer of listed and unlisted securities to a connected company (*FA 2019, ss 47, 47A, 48* and *48A* – see **10.12** and **12.9**), which was not a recommendation of the OTS. The market value rule in relation to unlisted securities only applies from the date upon which *FA 2020* receives royal assent.

This seems to be a case of HMRC introducing narrow pieces of legislation to counteract certain transactions which they view as tax avoidance rather than an implementation of the fundamental reform which is required.

10.2 Since 1 December 2003, stamp duty has been chargeable only on transactions in stock and marketable securities, and Transfers of interests in partnerships with stock or marketable securities amongst their assets. (In this book, the expression 'Transfer' is capitalised to make it clear that this is a reference to the potentially stampable document.) The restriction to stock and marketable securities is in *FA 2003, s 125*; however, the charge on Transfers of partnership interests is then reinstated by *FA 2003, Sch 15, paras 31–33*. The latter provision was something of a 'last minute' amendment, when it was realised that it might otherwise be possible to escape stamp duty on Transfers of securities by first contributing them to a partnership, then transferring the interests in the partnership. It is doubtful whether the charge on partnership interests has any significant practical effect. The application to partnerships is considered at **10.58**; the imposition of stamp duty on certain *issues* of securities is dealt with at **10.56**. The following paragraphs deal primarily with the application of stamp duty to Transfers of stock and marketable securities.

10.3 Although, in principle, stamp duty is chargeable on Transfers of a wide range of shares and securities, in practice the transfer of most debts is exempted by either the 'loan capital exemption' or the 'non-marketable debenture' exemption (see **10.17–10.18**). Transfers of units in unit trusts are outside the scope of stamp duty (*FA 1999, Sch 19, para 1*), but are instead subject to a special SDRT regime (see **12.31**).

10.4 There is no direct compulsion to pay stamp duty on Transfers – enforcement is indirect, arising from the fact that a stampable document cannot be used to register title or as evidence in a civil court unless duly stamped (*SA 1891, ss 14, 17*). It is sometimes asserted that a document which ought to be stamped but has not been stamped is not legally valid. This is not true. The problem is simply that the document cannot be used as evidence. So, in many cases, if sufficient evidence of the terms of a contract can be adduced without reference to any (stampable) document, it should be possible to enlist the help of the courts in enforcing the contract, even if no stamp duty has been paid. This principle was widely relied on when stamp duty applied to transfers of assets such as goodwill, when contracts were entered into on the basis of oral agreements and conduct (see **13.30**).

In most cases, the legislation does not specify who should pay stamp duty (the exception is an agreement for sale of an equitable interest – *FA 1999, Sch 13, para 7(1)*); but, in practice, the purchaser/transferee will normally pay or arrange stamping in order to cancel any SDRT charge (see **12.12**) and to be able to register ownership of the asset.

SCOPE – DOCUMENTS

Stamp duty on Transfers

10.5 A 'Transfer' is a document (the legislation used to refer to 'conveyance or transfer', but it seems to be thought that 'conveyance' should be reserved for land transactions, so references to that word were largely removed from the stamp duty legislation by *FA 2003*). The concept of a Transfer is bound up with the separation in English law between legal and beneficial ownership. Under English law, parties may agree to buy and sell an asset; they may take actions, such as payment of consideration and perhaps physically handing over the asset, to give effect to the agreement. However, for certain assets such as land and shares, this is not sufficient to complete the process. At this point, the purchaser may have some form of beneficial ownership of the asset, but he does not have legal title. He only gains legal title when all steps to perfect the transfer of title, as required by law, have been completed – and, in the case of UK shares held in certificated form, this includes execution of an appropriate Transfer document. (A different process applies to shares held in dematerialised form, such as quoted shares held in CREST – see **12.21** for further details.)

10.6 In the UK, the most common form of share Transfer is a stock transfer form. However, other documents may also function as Transfers. In particular, a document under which the registered owner of legal title acknowledges that he holds as trustee or nominee for someone else – a 'declaration of trust' – can function as a Transfer (see **10.14** and **Example 11.3**).

Restricted to Transfers on sale

10.7 Stamp duty is currently payable only if the Transfer is 'on sale' (*FA 1999, Sch 13, para 1*) – that is, there is valuable consideration which counts for stamp duty purposes. This general rule is subject to the exceptions introduced by *FA 2019, ss 47* and *47A* (*FA 2019, s 47A* only applies from the date upon which *FA 2020* receives royal assent) which impose a market value charge on the transfer of listed and unlisted securities to a company, in circumstances where the transferor is connected with the acquiring company, and certain other conditions are satisfied. This provision is discussed further in **10.12** below.

A Transfer for no consideration (eg a gift) used to be subject to a fixed £5 stamp duty charge, which could sometimes be escaped by completing a certificate on the form. But, in a welcome piece of administrative simplification, *FA 2008, Sch 32* abolished the fixed £5 charge for Transfers completed on or after 13 March 2008. From that date, a Transfer for no consideration is simply not liable (subject to the exception for transfers of listed and unlisted securities to a connected company – see **10.12**), there is no requirement to complete any certificate and the Transfer is deemed to be 'duly stamped' as soon as it is executed.

However, company registrars found it difficult to decide whether unstamped forms presented for registration of a change of ownership were genuinely exempt or had been left unstamped incorrectly. In April 2012, two new certificates were added to the back of the standard stock transfer form. Certificate 2 (see **10.8** et seq for the circumstances in which Certificate 1 on the reverse of the stock transfer form should be used) is to be completed when the transfer is exempt from stamp duty, for example, transfers in connection with divorce or the dissolution of a civil partnership or because, although there is consideration, there is no consideration which is chargeable stamp duty. The wording of the certificate is as follows:

> 'I/We certify that this instrument is otherwise exempt from ad valorem Stamp Duty without a claim for relief being made or that no chargeable consideration is given for the transfer for the purposes of Stamp Duty.
>
> I/We confirm that I/we have been authorised by the transferor to sign this certificate and that I/we am/are aware of all the facts of the transaction.'

The certificate should be signed either by the transferor(s) (in which case the second sentence should be omitted) or on their behalf.

An internet search should produce the stock transfer form as a downloadable PDF file.

Small transaction exemption

10.8 The main charging provision in *FA 1999, Sch 13, para 1* was amended by *FA 2008, s 98*, to remove the stamp duty charge where the consideration does not exceed £1,000 (*FA 1999, Sch 13, para 1(3A)*). Certificate 1 on the back of the stock transfer form should be used when this small transaction exemption applies. The wording of the certificate is as follows:

> 'I/We certify that the transaction effected by this instrument does not form part of a larger transaction or series of transactions in respect of which the

> amount or value, or aggregate amount or value, of the consideration exceeds £1,000.
>
> I/We confirm that I/we have been authorised by the transferor to sign this certificate and that I/we am/are aware of all the facts of the transaction.'

It is therefore only possible to certify if the *total* consideration for all relevant assets transferred in the same transaction or set of linked transactions does not exceed £1,000 (*FA 1999, Sch 13, para 6*).

10.9 In arriving at the total consideration, it is only necessary to take account of types of consideration which 'count' for stamp duty purposes (see **10.26**). It is also possible to leave out of account any consideration attributed on a just and reasonable basis to 'goods, wares or merchandise' (such as stock in trade of a retail business), intellectual property or goodwill, provided the Transfer itself does not also act to transfer those assets (*FA 1999, Sch 13, para 6(2)*). It would be unusual for a share Transfer to also transfer other assets, but this is a point where care may be needed in drafting documents.

However, amounts allocated to some other assets, especially debts and other financial assets, cannot be left out of account, even though no stamp duty will be chargeable in respect of them. Therefore, where there are such assets, a stock transfer form or other document transferring shares with a value below £1,000 may not qualify for certification, simply because the value of other relevant assets transferred under the same agreement take the total over £1,000.

10.10 As indicated above in **10.8**, when using the current version of the stock transfer form, Certificate 1 should be completed if the small transaction exemption applies. In relation to any other form of transfer document it is HMRC's view that:

(1) the certificate should be an integral part of the Transfer, not on a separate piece of paper (STSM011060) (it is not clear what should be done if there is simply no space on the transfer document to insert a certificate), and

(2) if the certificate is added after execution of the Transfer, it should be signed on behalf of all parties to the Transfer. Signature on behalf of the vendor is considered the more important and, in practice, such documents are not always signed by the purchaser.

10.11 Where a pre-printed certificate is not present, the following wording would be appropriate:

> 'The transaction effected by this instrument does not form part of a larger transaction or series of transactions in respect of which the amount or value, or aggregate amount or value, of the consideration exceeds £1,000.'

Example 10.1—Consideration below £1,000

Ian transfers to Joan the assets of his business trading under the name Tidy Gardens and comprising 100 shares in Tidy Gardens (Mudfield) Ltd (a company set up purely for name-protection purposes), various loose tools and garden supplies, and a memory stick containing technical information such as details of plants which do well in local areas plus customer and contacts lists. Joan pays consideration of £10,000 with an agreed (and just and reasonable) allocation of £5,500 to tools and garden supplies, £4,400 to the memory stick and £100 to the shares. The tools, garden supplies and memory stick should all be regarded as 'goods, wares and merchandise' and may be ignored in assessing consideration for the overall transaction, which is therefore £100. Provided the stock transfer form transferring the shares contains the certificate of value set out above, no stamp duty will be payable on it and there will be no need to submit it to the Stamp Office.

Part of the amount allocated to the memory stick may be for goodwill and intellectual property, but the provisions which abolished stamp duty on these assets also provided for them to be left out of account in determining the overall level of consideration (*FA 2000, Sch 34, para 4*; *FA 2002, Sch 37, para 3*). However, if the assets had included, say, £1,200 of customer debts, the allocated consideration for which was agreed at £901, this would not be left out of account, even though no stamp duty would be due on the transfer of the debts themselves. The total consideration would then be £1,001 (£901 + £100) and it would not be possible to add a certificate of value. Stamp duty of 0.5% of £100, rounded up to £5, would be due in respect of the consideration correctly allocated to the share Transfer.

Market value charge on transfer of listed and unlisted securities to a connected company

10.12 *FA 2019, s 47* provides that stamp duty will be chargeable on a Transfer (ie a document potentially chargeable to stamp duty) which conveys 'listed securities' to a company (or a company's nominee), if the person transferring the listed securities is 'connected' to the acquiring company (or is the nominee of a person 'connected' with the company), as follows:

(a) *Consideration in the form of money, stocks or securities or debt is given in return for the listed securities*

The consideration chargeable to stamp duty is the greater of: (a) the amount or value of the actual consideration given for the listed securities; and (b) the market value of the listed securities.

(b) No consideration in the form of money, stocks or securities or debt is given in return for the listed securities

The consideration chargeable to stamp duty is the value of the listed securities.

The value of the listed securities is the price which they might reasonably be expected to fetch on a sale in the open market at the date the Transfer is executed (*FA 2019, s 47(4)(b)*).

For the purposes of this provision 'connected' is as defined in *Corporation Tax Act 2010, s 1122* (*FA 2019, s 47(5)*).

'Listed securities' are stock or marketable securities which are regularly traded on: (a) a regulated market; (b) a multilateral trading facility; or (c) a recognised foreign exchange with (a), (b) and (c) having the same meaning as they have for *FA 1986, s 80B* (*FA 2019, s 47(2)*).

This market value rule had effect in relation to Transfers executed on or after 29 October 2018 (*FA 2019, s 47(10)*).

FA 2019, s 47A (inserted by *Finance Act 2020, s 77*) will apply if a Transfer (ie a document potentially chargeable to stamp duty) conveys 'unlisted securities' to a company (or a company's nominee) for consideration, and the person transferring the unlisted securities is 'connected' to the acquiring company, or is the nominee of a person 'connected' to the acquiring company, and some or all of the consideration consists of the issue of shares (*FA 2019, s 47A(1)*).

If the above conditions are met, *FA 2019, s 47A(3)* provides that the consideration chargeable to stamp duty is the greater of:

(a) the amount or value of the actual consideration given for the transfer of the unlisted securities; and

(b) the market value of the unlisted securities which are the subject of the Transfer.

The market value of the unlisted securities is the price which they might reasonably be expected to fetch on a sale in the open market at the date the Transfer is executed (*FA 2019, s 47A(5)*).

For the purposes of this provision 'connected' is as defined in *Corporation Tax Act 2010, s 1122* (*FA 2019, s 47A(6)*).

'Unlisted securities' are stock or marketable securities which are not regularly traded on:

(a) a regulated market;

(b) a multilateral trading facility; or

(c) a recognised foreign exchange,

with (a), (b) and (c) having the same meaning as they have for *FA 1986, s 80B* (*FA 2019, s 47A(2)*).

This market value rule has effect in relation to Transfers executed on or after the date on which *FA 2020* receives royal assent (*FA 2019, s 47A(8)*).

It is important to appreciate that the market value rule for listed securities applies irrespective of whether or not there is any actual consideration, and irrespective of the nature of any actual consideration. In contrast the market value rule for unlisted securities only applies if there is actual consideration for the transfer, and some or all of that consideration is in the form of the issue of shares.

Example 10.2—Market value rule on transfer of unlisted shares to a connected company in return for an issue of shares

Non-UK company Holdings SA ('Holdings') owns an unlisted UK company called Trading Co Ltd ('Trading Co') (current value £9 million) and a non-UK company called Investment Sarl (current value £1 million). Holdings has agreed to sell both companies to Acquisition Pty Ltd (a non-UK company) for £10 million. A direct transfer of Trading Co for £9 million would cost Acquisition Pty Ltd £45,000 of stamp duty. However, Holdings first transfers Trading Co to Investment Sarl in return for the issue of two shares by Investment Sarl. Investment Sarl already has 1,000 shares in issue, all held by Holdings. Further (and this is very important), under the company law and constitution governing Investment Sarl, all the shares are identical, giving shareholders identical rights in all respects. Holdings then transfers Investment Sarl to Acquisition Pty Ltd for £10 million.

Stamp tax analysis prior to FA 2020 receiving royal assent

For stamp duty purposes, the consideration given by Investment Sarl for Trading Co is simply the value of the two shares issued. This will be 2/1002ths of the £10 million value of Investment Sarl after the transfer of the Trading Co shares, being £19,960. Most of the value of Trading Co flows into the Investment Sarl shares already held by Holdings, but this value shift does not count as consideration for stamp duty purposes. The stamp duty on this transfer will be £100 (after rounding). The SDRT, on the other hand, would probably be £45,000 based on the increase in the value of Holdings' shares in Investment Sarl, ie £9 million. It is therefore essential that the Transfer of the Trading Co shares to Investment Sarl is submitted for stamping, in order to cancel the SDRT charge which otherwise arises. It is unlikely to be necessary to pay stamp duty on the Transfer of Investment Sarl to Acquisition Pty Ltd because the shares of Investment Sarl are not UK registered.

Stamp tax analysis once FA 2020 has received royal assent

The planning outlined above would no longer result in a stamp duty saving.

FA 2019, s 47A (inserted by *Finance Act 2020, 77*) will apply if a Transfer conveys 'unlisted securities' to a company, for consideration, the person transferring the unlisted securities is 'connected' to the acquiring company, and some or all of the consideration consists of the issue of shares (*FA 2019, s 47A(1)*). If *FA 2019, s 47A* applies then *FA 2019, s 47A(3)* provides that the consideration chargeable to stamp duty is the greater of:

(a) the amount or value of the actual consideration given for the unlisted securities; and

(b) the market value of the unlisted securities, which are the subject of the Transfer, as at the time of the Transfer.

In the case considered above, Holdings and Investment Sarl will be connected for the purposes of *Corporation Taxes Act 2010, s 1122*. In relation to the transfer of the shares of Trading Co by Holdings to Investment Sarl, the consideration will consist of the issue of two shares by Investment Sarl. *FA 2019, s 47A(3)* therefore provides that the consideration chargeable to stamp duty is the greater of:

(a) the amount or value of the actual consideration given for the Trading Co shares; and

(b) the market value of the Trading Co shares.

In this case, (a) will be £19,960 and (b) will be £9 million, and consequently the consideration chargeable to stamp duty will be £9 million, and stamp duty of £45,000 will therefore be payable.

Consequently, it can be seen that the introduction of the market value rule in relation to the transfer of unlisted shares to a company, by a connected party, in circumstances where all or part of the consideration given is the issue of shares, will defeat the type of planning outlined (stamp tax analysis prior to *FA 2020* receiving royal assent), as stamp duty will be payable on the market value of the unlisted shares transferred.

Sub-sales and successive transfers

10.13 Sometimes, perhaps most commonly in the course of a reorganisation, there is a need to transfer ownership of shares and securities several times in succession. In the interests of speed and efficiency, the parties may wish to rely on agreements for each transfer except the last, and then to execute a single Transfer of shares from the original owner to the final transferee. This is commonly referred to as a sub-sale. Provided the consideration paid by the final transferee is at least equal to the market value of the shares and securities, the Transfer will be liable to stamp duty only on that consideration. No stamp duty will be payable on the consideration paid by other parties under earlier agreements in the chain (*SA 1891, s 58(4)*).

However, if the shares and securities are within the charge to SDRT, any SDRT liability arising on those earlier agreements will remain chargeable, because no Transfer will be stamped in respect of those steps in order to cancel the SDRT (see **12.12** for further details). It will often be the case that the stamp duty charge on a transfer for some or all of the intermediate steps would be less than the SDRT charge, most commonly because a relief such as group relief (see **11.9**) could be claimed. Many reliefs apply only to stamp duty and not to SDRT. *In such a case, the sub-sale route should not be used.* Instead, a Transfer should be executed for each step in the series, and each Transfer should then be stamped.

10.14 Execution of a stock transfer form for each step may not be convenient, perhaps because it is considered that each such form should be stamped and registered before the next is executed. In that case, it may be simpler for the parties to execute a declaration of trust to act as the Transfer for each step, and to submit all of the declarations for stamping together. In this regard, see **Example 11.3**.

SCOPE – ASSETS

10.15 The legislative definitions of 'stock' and 'marketable security' are in *SA 1891, s 122.* They are not wholly enlightening, and the meaning of these terms is partly determined by judicial precedents, some of which are similarly ancient and difficult to interpret. The precise definition is not usually too important in practice, because most debt instruments which may fall within the definition are exempted under the 'loan capital' exemption (see **10.16**).

'Stock' includes shares (equity) of companies (UK and overseas) but also other 'instruments of a capital nature' issued by UK and overseas national and local government and by companies and societies. This includes many debentures and may include instruments issued by incorporated partnerships such as UK LLPs. In many cases, such stock will also be a security.

The term 'security' encompasses a wide range of instruments evidencing indebtedness. 'Marketable' is defined by statute as meaning capable of being sold on any stock market in the UK. This is considered to exclude securities issued by UK private companies, partnerships and individuals and many overseas entities, which are therefore automatically outside the scope of stamp duty unless they also fall within the definition of stock.

Exempt loan capital

10.16 Although many debt instruments issued by companies, governments and other organisations are within the definition of 'stock and marketable securities', they are mostly removed from the scope of stamp duty by the loan capital exemption in *FA 1986, ss 78–79*. For these purposes, loan capital includes:

- all government stock and marketable securities,
- debt instruments or any other borrowed capital of companies,
- capital raised as 'alternative finance investment bonds' within *FA 2005, s 48A*, and
- loan capital raised by certain international organisations.

The last of these is completely exempt from stamp duty on transfer (*FA 1986, s 79(3)*).

10.17 All other loan capital is exempt from stamp duty on transfer (*FA 1986, s 79(4)*) unless it has equity-like characteristics (*FA 1986, s 79(5)* and *(6)*), such as rights to:

(1) conversion into shares or other securities,

(2) receipt of further or other shares or securities,

(3) interest which is dependent on the results of a business or the value of other assets,

(4) interest at a rate greater than a reasonable commercial return, or

(5) repayment at a premium greater than that generally available on similar quoted securities.

Point (3) is disapplied in relation to wholly commercial 'capital market' loans (so-called 'ratchet loans'), where the interest rate increases if business results worsen or decreases if they improve, or where interest reduces if the borrower does not have funds to pay (*FA 1986, s 79(7A)*).

Points (3) and (5) are disapplied if the interest and/or amount repayable vary in accordance with the UK Retail Price Index or Consumer Price Index (*FA 1986, s 79(7)*).

Point (4) has in the past led to disputes with HMRC in relation to so-called 'junk bonds', which carry a high interest rate to reflect greater risk; but HMRC have generally accepted that these are at a commercial rate where comparable publicly issued bonds have been identified.

Point (4) is disapplied in relation to alternative finance investment bonds (often referred to as Islamic bonds), and point (5) is modified to require that the total amount repaid should not exceed the amount originally subscribed plus a reasonable commercial return (*FA 1986, s 79(8A)*).

The risk of loan securities failing to qualify as exempt loan capital is considered in more detail at **13.13**. Care is needed when dealing with debt instruments which are not plain vanilla loans at interest.

Other financial assets outside the scope

10.18 Some debt instruments may not be loan capital, perhaps because they are too short term to be regarded as capital, or perhaps because they arise other than through the borrowing of money. Such instruments are unlikely to be stock and, in many cases, they will not be marketable and so will automatically fall outside the scope of stamp duty. Any which are marketable will often be exempt by virtue of *FA 1999, Sch 13, para 25(a)* because they are debentures. Overall, it is highly unlikely that a straightforward debt instrument bearing a commercial rate of interest will be within the stamp duty charge.

10.19 Transfers to recognised investment exchanges, clearing houses etc, are exempt, if the exchange or clearing house has entered into an appropriate arrangement with HMRC. This exemption was introduced specifically to facilitate reforms to the securities markets, and is not considered further in this book.

10.20 *FA 2014, s 115* and *Sch 24, Pt 2* introduced a new exemption for shares traded on recognised growth markets but not listed on any market. The exemption removes all stamp duty charges in relation to the shares, apart from those applying to bearer securities (for which see **10.56**) for transactions entered into or transfers executed on or after 28 April 2014. For more information see **12.33**).

SCOPE – GEOGRAPHICAL

10.21 In principle there is no territorial limit to the application of the tax. However, the lack of direct enforcement provisions means that this can be ignored for completely non-UK transactions. However, in theory at least, any document with a sufficient connection with the UK can be subject to stamp duty. In this regard, the scope is effectively defined by *SA 1891, s 14* as covering any document executed in the UK, or any document transferring any property located in the UK, or any document of transfer relating to any matter or thing to be done in the UK. For these purposes, shares of UK incorporated companies and shares of foreign companies which are recorded on a share register located in the UK are regarded as located in the UK.

10.22 As a general principle, a document is executed where the last action occurs to make it legally valid/effective – usually addition of a signature but, in the case of documents signed in escrow, it may be satisfaction of the escrow conditions followed by dating and release on behalf of the signatory.

10.23 The idea of any matter or thing to be done in the UK is very wide, and might include the payment of sale proceeds out of a UK bank account, for example (see *Faber v IRC* [1936] 1 All ER 617; *IRC v Maple & Co (Paris) Ltd* [1908] AC 22). So, in theory, a document transferring German shares from a French person to a Dutch person can be subject to UK stamp duty if signed in the UK, or even possibly if signed in Italy but paid for out of a UK bank account. Given the lack of enforceability, in most such cases stamp duty can safely be ignored. However, the existence of a theoretical but unenforceable liability can be difficult to explain to clients, and administrative difficulty can arise in multinational transactions involving both UK and overseas share transfers. HMRC do not appear to understand the point clearly – for example, it has been known for the Stamp Office to reject a composite claim for group relief which included transfers of overseas shares because 'stamp duty is not payable on overseas shares'. This is, therefore, a piece of legislative nonsense well past its sensible abolition date. Its abolition has been recommended by the OTS – see **1.17**.

CALCULATING THE CHARGE

Rates

10.24 For Transfers of stock and marketable securities, the normal rate of stamp duty is 0.5% of the amount or value of the consideration for the Transfer (*FA 1999, Sch 13, para 3*). A higher rate of 1.5% applies to certain transactions (see **10.55**). If application of the rate does not produce a precise multiple of

£5, the charge is rounded up to the next £5 above (*FA 1999, s 112*). Restricting charges to multiples of £5 allows the stamping machines to be simpler than if they had to deal with lower denominations of duty; it also provides a small but useful increase in the tax take. The exemption for small transactions (consideration not exceeding £1,000) is mentioned at **10.8**, but apart from that, there is no 'zero rate band' and no variation in rate with consideration.

10.25 In principle, Transfers of interests in partnerships owning stock and marketable securities are subject to stamp duty at rates of up to 4%, depending on the amount of consideration. However, in practice, it is unlikely that such high rates would apply – see the explanation at **10.58**.

Consideration

10.26 In general, stamp duty is charged on the actual consideration given for a Transfer, irrespective of the value of the asset transferred (however see **10.12** in relation to the market value charge on the transfer of listed securities to a connected company, and on the transfer of unlisted securities to a connected company where some or all of the consideration is the issue of shares). This principle is modified in some cases where the transfer is in satisfaction of a debt (see **10.34**). Only cash, securities, debt and the assumption, satisfaction or release of a pecuniary liability count as consideration. This is HMRC's long-established interpretation of words now in *FA 1999, Sch 13, para 2*: 'the amount or value of the consideration for the sale'; see STM1.11 of the old Stamp Duty Manual for example. This contrasts with both SDRT and SDLT, where tax is chargeable by reference to any consideration 'in money or money's worth'. However, if relying on the restricted definition of consideration to escape or minimise stamp duty, care is needed in the wording of agreements, as shown in the examples below. The HMRC consultation document 'Stamp Taxes on Shares Consideration Rules' (7 November 2018) sought views on the alignment of the stamp duty and SDRT definitions of 'consideration' by adopting the SDRT 'money or money's worth' definition. However, respondents to the consultation were of the view that changes to the consideration rules in isolation were likely to add complexity, uncertainty and increased costs particularly on the insurance, pension, and fund industries creating a risk for the UK economy, and making the UK less attractive for investment. The government therefore decided at this stage not to proceed with the alignment of the stamp duty and SDRT definitions of 'consideration'.

Example 10.3—Consideration which does not count

Pauline agrees to transfer her shares in Big plc (a listed company), worth £1 million, to Robert in return for his collection of rare gemstones of similar value. The gemstones are not 'chargeable consideration' for stamp duty purposes. A stock transfer form may be completed showing 'nil' consideration. No stamp duty arises, certificate 2 (see **10.7**) on the reverse of the stock transfer form should be completed as there is consideration but it is not consideration chargeable to stamp duty, and there is no need for the document to be submitted to the Stamp Office for stamping. Note: Had the shares of Big plc been transferred to a company to which Pauline was 'connected' stamp duty would have been chargeable on the market value of the shares under *FA 2019, s 47* – see **10.12**.

Example 10.4—Satisfaction of a debt

Meanwhile, in an unrelated transaction, Pauline agrees to buy Sara's 100% shareholding in Tacky Ltd, an online jewellery retailer, for £1 on condition that Pauline also pays off Tacky's bank overdraft of £500,000 (thus releasing Sara from the guarantee she provided to the bank). The consideration for the Transfer of shares in Tacky is £500,001, and stamp duty at 0.5% rounded to the next £5 above is £2,505.

Example 10.5—Specified monetary value

The facts are as in Example 10.2 above, except that the agreement specifies that the consideration for the share transfer is £1 million, to be satisfied by transfer of the collection of gemstones. Although it may be subject to dispute, HMRC are likely to consider that stamp duty is payable on consideration of £1 million. This is on the grounds that the agreement creates a debt of £1 million (so the Transfer is for a debt) which is then satisfied by transfer of the gemstones.

When is a debt assumed?

10.27 The mere fact that a target company has outstanding debts does not mean that these debts are added to the consideration paid for the company. In Example 10.3 above, Pauline's agreement to pay off a debt counts as consideration. However, the debt is owed by Tacky Ltd, and Sara requires it to be paid off only because she needs to be released from her guarantee to the bank. Were it not for this, she might be happy to sell the shares leaving the debt in place, in which case the consideration would be £1 and it would be possible to certify the Transfer as a small transaction with no stamp duty liability.

10.28 Alternatively, if the debt must be paid off, it may be that a similar economic effect could be achieved without stamp duty cost. For example, Pauline could subscribe for further shares in Tacky Ltd, allowing Tacky Ltd itself to pay off the debt. No stamp duty should arise on the subscription. Other alternatives are less clear-cut – for example, Pauline might agree to ensure that Tacky Ltd pays off the debt. It may be open to dispute whether this amounts to the giving of consideration. Great care is needed in the wording of documents in such cases, and further specialist advice should be sought.

10.29 Shares are sometimes issued 'part paid' – that is, only part of the capital which the shares represent has been paid, and further amounts may become payable to the company at a later date. The liability to make such further payment falls on the shareholder who owns the shares when payment becomes due. When part-paid shares are transferred, provided payment of the further capital has not been called for (or if it has, it has been paid) at the date of the Transfer, stamp duty is chargeable only on the actual consideration given (STSM021210).

Distributions

10.30 In general, a distribution from a company to its shareholders is, by definition, for no consideration. The Stamp Office has occasionally claimed that a distribution of assets *in specie*, declared as a final dividend, should necessarily be re-characterised as the declaration of a dividend (creating a money debt) followed by the (stampable) transfer of the asset in satisfaction of the debt. It would doubtless be possible to create and satisfy a debt in this way. However, the idea that a distribution *in specie* should *necessarily* take this form appears to come from an over-enthusiastic application of an idea set out in STM4.404–4.408 of the old Stamp Duty Manual and is probably not correct; STSM021130 is a more accurate statement of the position. To minimise the risk of dispute, it is worthwhile ensuring, where possible, that distributions *in specie* from UK companies are declared as interim dividends, as these do not create a debt between company and shareholder. Distributions from non-UK companies will be subject to the law of the country in which the distributing company is established – it would be worth checking whether declaration of the *in specie* distribution creates a money debt due to the shareholder under the governing law of the company concerned.

Valuation of consideration

10.31 Consideration expressed in a foreign currency must be translated into sterling. If the Transfer specifies the exchange rate, that rate is to be used – although HMRC would seek to set aside an unrealistic exchange rate inserted to reduce the stamp duty. Otherwise, the translation is to be at the appropriate market rate on the day the Transfer is executed; and, for this purpose, HMRC normally seek to use the closing spot exchange rate as listed in the Financial Times (STSM021050).

Stock and securities as consideration

10.32 If consideration includes stock or marketable securities, these are to be valued at market value on the date of execution of the stampable document (which will not necessarily be the same as the date on which the securities given in consideration are transferred) (*SA 1891, s 55(1)*).

For quoted securities, HMRC adopt the capital gains tax basis of valuation (STSM021060) – that is, the lower of:

- midway between the highest and lowest price of bargains on the day, and
- the lower closing price for the day plus one quarter of the difference between the lower and higher closing prices.

If securities given in consideration are marketable but not quoted, HMRC's share valuation division is likely to become involved in agreeing the value.

10.33 Where the consideration includes securities which are not marketable, their value is taken to be 'the amount due on the day of the date thereof for principal and interest' (*SA 1891, s 55(2)*). This curious phrase is taken to mean the stated principal plus any interest due but unpaid at the date of execution of the stampable document.

Transfer in satisfaction of debt

10.34 Where assets are transferred to a person in satisfaction of a debt, the consideration is taken to be the amount outstanding on the debt, including any interest due but unpaid at the date of Transfer (*SA 1891, s 57*). However, provided the Transfer is to the creditor, if the amount of debt is greater than the value of the assets transferred, the consideration is restricted to the value of the assets transferred (*FA 1980, s 102*; STSM021080). To take advantage of this relief, the Transfer must be adjudicated by HMRC (see **10.48**).

Consideration payable later or in instalments

10.35 If consideration is payable after the Transfer is executed, or in instalments, stamp duty is chargeable on the total amount, with no discount or postponement to allow for delay in payment. However, where the instalments take the form of an annuity which may last longer than 12 years but ceases on a death, only the first 12 years' instalments are taken into account (*SA 1891, s 56(3)*).

In other cases where the instalments will or may continue for more than 20 years, only the first 20 years are taken into account (*SA 1891, s 56(2)*). The equivalent provision under SDLT only takes account of 12 years' instalments although, if these are variable, the highest 12 individual years are taken into account (see **4.28**).

VAT

10.36 Where consideration for a Transfer is subject to VAT, the VAT must be included in the amount on which stamp duty is chargeable (see *Glenrothes Development Corporation v IRC* [1994] STC 74). This will not normally be an issue in relation to Transfers of shares and securities, which do not normally give rise to VAT charges. It was widely regarded as unreasonable when stamp duty applied to Transfers of other assets, but the same principle has been carried into the SDLT regime (see **4.23**).

Unascertainable consideration

10.37 Stamp duty is only chargeable on consideration which is 'ascertainable' at the date of the Transfer. This principle is not overtly stated in the legislation, but see STSM021100 and 021110 for confirmation of the HMRC view. Consideration is ascertainable if it is possible to deduce, with certainty, one or more specific figures for it from documents or facts extant at the time of execution of the Transfer. It does not matter whether payment of that particular amount is certain or contingent on future events. If more than one figure can be deduced, the consideration is assumed to be the highest of these, in accordance with the 'contingency principle' explained below. Where any amount of consideration is genuinely unascertainable at that date, it will not be subject to stamp duty. Note that the test is whether the amount is capable of being ascertained, not whether it has been ascertained.

Example 10.6—Unascertainable consideration

On 1 January 2020, Conglomerate plc agrees to buy all of the shares in Dan Ltd (an unlisted company) from Daniel for cash consideration equal to twice the pre-tax profits of Dan Ltd for the year to 28 February 2020 (with no upper or lower limit). The share Transfer is executed on 1 February 2020. The consideration is entirely unascertainable at the date of the Transfer, because it is based on events which will happen after that date, so there is no consideration on which stamp duty may be charged. There is no requirement to submit the Transfer to HMRC for stamping.

Example 10.7—An ascertainable sum

The facts are as in Example 10.5, except that the consideration is specified to be at least £1 million. This is an ascertainable amount, and stamp duty will be chargeable on £1 million.

Example 10.8—An ascertainable sum, variable up or down

The facts are as in Example 10.5, except that the consideration is specified to be £1 million, plus twice the amount by which the profits for the year to 28 February 2020 exceed £500,000, or minus twice the amount by which they fall short of that figure. Stamp duty will again be charged on the £1 million, with no subsequent adjustment to the stamp duty if the consideration proves to be greater or less than £1 million.

Example 10.9—Ascertainable but not yet ascertained

The facts are as in Example 10.5, except that the share transfer is executed on 1 March 2020. The year has now ended, on the profits of which the consideration will be based. The profits are not yet likely to have been ascertained, but they are nonetheless ascertainable, because all events impacting on the profit figure have happened. Stamp duty will be chargeable on the actual consideration. Since it is unlikely this will be known when the deadline for payment of stamp duty arrives, Conglomerate plc may wish to apply for provisional stamping (see **10.47**).

10.38 The *LM Tenancies* case ([1996] STC 880) involved an attempt to render consideration unascertainable but limit the risk of change, by linking it to the value, a few days later, of a security with a very stable price. It was held that the consideration was not truly unascertainable and should be taken as the figure based on the value of the security at the date of the Transfer.

Contingency principle

10.39 The calculation of consideration is complicated by the application of the so-called 'contingency principle'. This principle, not explicit in the legislation, is based on case law, especially the *Underground Electric Railways* cases (STSM021120). The principle states that any sum stated to be payable by way of consideration on the happening of some contingency is subject to stamp duty as if certainly payable. The principle is subject to the question of whether the consideration is ascertainable, but generally means that the highest possible stamp duty is payable.

Example 10.10—Two or more ascertainable sums

The facts are as in Example 10.5, but the consideration is subject to a minimum of £500,000 and a maximum of £2 million. £500,000 and £2 million are both ascertainable sums, and the contingency principle requires the assumption that the higher amount of £2 million will be paid. Stamp duty is therefore chargeable on this sum, with no adjustment or refund if the actual consideration eventually proves to be less.

10.40 On occasion, when this principle has produced an unforeseen and manifestly unjust result, HMRC have been known to accept stamp duty based on actual consideration – but it would not be safe to rely on such largesse.

Different definitions of consideration for stamp duty and SDRT

10.41 The definition of consideration for SDRT purposes (see **12.4**) is wider than that for stamp duty purposes. As a result, the stamp duty on a Transfer may be less than the SDRT on the related agreement. In Example 10.5, SDRT would be chargeable on the actual consideration once finally ascertained. However, as explained at **12.11**, appropriate stamping of a Transfer within six years of the agreement to transfer the shares cancels the SDRT liability. Since, in that example, the stamp duty on a Transfer would be nil, it would clearly be a good idea to execute a Transfer (which, in this case, would immediately be deemed to be 'duly stamped'), in order to cancel the SDRT liability. This principle is widely relied on in order to mitigate stamp tax costs on share transactions (see Example 10.11 and **12.21**).

ADMINISTRATION

No need to stamp

10.42 If an exemption (as opposed to a relief – see **11.2**) applies (eg the loan capital exemption in *FA 1986, s 79(4)*) to eliminate any stamp duty charge, the Transfer is effectively deemed to be duly stamped, without any need to submit it to HMRC. As noted at **11.2**, it is possible for the availability of the exemption to be challenged, in which case the document may need to be submitted for adjudication, although in practice this rarely happens.

Routine stamping

10.43 Documents for routine stamping should be sent to the Stamp Office (see **Appendix A**) with payment of the duty and, if necessary, a brief note setting out the calculation of the duty. Most importantly, to guard against the stamped document going astray, an envelope should be included, addressed to the person to whom the stamped document must be returned. Long advocated by advisers, HMRC finally made this required practice in June 2014.

10.44 In accordance with *SA 1891, s 5*, all facts and circumstances affecting liability must be set out in the Transfer. In practice, important facts may be in a separate agreement rather than on the stock transfer form. Where relevant, a copy of any such agreement should be sent with the stampable document. In the past, when consideration for a transfer included issue of new shares, it was sometimes necessary to have the agreement itself stamped 'not liable to any duty' in order to satisfy *Companies Acts* requirements; those requirements have now changed, so that this is no longer necessary.

10.45 The deadline is 30 days after the date of execution of the transfer, and late submission or payment will lead to penalties and/or interest being charged (see **10.50**). Payment may be by cheque, or by bank transfer to the HMRC stamp duty account (see **Appendix A**). If bank transfer is used, an appropriate reference must be given to the destination bank and repeated in the papers sent to the Stamp Office – for example, the name of the transferee. Unless there is manifestly an error, the documents will normally be stamped on the basis requested.

10.46 In rare circumstances it may be important to have a transfer stamped on the day of execution, perhaps to enable registration of the transfer prior to a further transaction. Same-day stamping is possible, but it is essential that this be agreed with the Stamp Office in advance. If same-day stamping is required you should write to the Stamp Office ('same day' stamping service) giving as much detail as possible including: (a) a description of the transaction; (b) the number of instruments to be stamped; (c) the specific reason(s) for the request; and (d) the amount of the stamp duty payable. In exceptional circumstances a request for 'same day' stamping can be made by contacting the stamp taxes helpline on 0300 200 3510 (outside the UK: +441726209042). It will be necessary to convince the stamp office staff that same-day stamping is really necessary. HMRC make it clear that same-day stamping will only be available when there is a business critical requirement to have a document stamped and that the service cannot be used if the urgency could have been avoided by either party or their respective agents. Same-day stamping is not available if there is a requirement that the instrument be adjudicated (see **10.48**) either because a relief is being claimed (eg group relief) or for some other reason. HMRC expects the number of occasions on which same-day stamping will be required to be minimal.

Provisional stamping and 'wait and see'

10.47 Where the consideration for a transfer is ascertainable at the date of the Transfer, but not yet ascertained when the due date arrives (see Example 10.8), delay in submission of the Transfer for stamping will lead to interest and penalty charges. It will also prevent any change of shareholder from being registered (see **10.4**). Penalties may be avoided by lodging the Transfer with the Stamp Office, either for them to keep until the duty can be determined ('wait and see') or for provisional stamping. Interest will still be charged on late paid stamp duty, but this may be minimised by paying an estimated amount, to be adjusted later. If the taxpayer needs the stamped Transfer, or if the delay in finalising figures will be more than a few weeks, provisional stamping should be requested. The Stamp Office will require a formal undertaking *from the person submitting the document*, confirming that they will return it for adjustment of the duty once figures are finalised. For this reason, advisers may ask clients to submit the documents in such cases, so that the client may give the necessary undertaking.

Adjudication

10.48 Technically, routine stamping is always provisional – that is, if the document is then required for an official purpose such as evidence in court, it would be open to any party to challenge whether it was adequately stamped. In practice, most documents are stamped in this way and no problems arise. To obtain complete certainty, the document must be submitted for HMRC to express their formal opinion as to the amount of duty (and, where appropriate, penalties) due – normally referred to as adjudication. Once the amount of duty has been adjudicated (and assuming no appeal is lodged against this within 30 days), it is no longer open to challenge apart from, possibly, on grounds of fraud.

10.49 There are certain cases where adjudication is compulsory, particularly in relation to claiming reliefs. It is rare for parties to request adjudication when it is not compulsory, but it is possible for all documents. HMRC take adjudication seriously because of its finality. They will normally need to see all relevant documents and may seek further explanations; rarely, they may request assurances as to motives etc by way of formal statements (Statutory Declarations) from individuals involved in the transaction. Adjudication is evidenced by impressing an 'adjudicated' stamp on the document alongside the duty stamps. As noted at **10.4**, there is no general compulsion to pay stamp duty. However, once the duty on a document has been adjudicated, if it is not paid within 30 days, a further penalty may be added to the duty when eventually paid.

Interest and penalties

10.50 Although there is no general compulsion to pay stamp duty, payment later than 30 days after the date of execution of the Transfer will lead to the addition of interest to the amount of stamp duty (*SA 1891, s 15A*). Interest is rounded down to the nearest £5 and, if the total is less than £25, it is not charged. Apart from this, however, interest charges are never mitigated, and the document will not be stamped unless any interest is paid in addition to the stamp duty itself. As with other taxes, the rates are set by regulation in accordance with *FA 1989, s 178*. The interest rate at the time of writing (May 2020) is 2.60%. For the period 29 September 2009 through to 22 August 2016 the interest rate was 3.0%, however it fell to 2.75% from 23 August 2016 until 21 November 2017 when it was again increased to 3.0%, after which it was raised to 3.25% on 21 August 2018. From 30 March 2020 it was reduced to 2.75% after which it fell to 2.60% from 7 April 2020.

10.51 Penalties may be charged if a document is submitted for stamping after the deadline (*SA 1891, s 15B*). For a document executed in the UK, the deadline is the same as that for payment of duty: 30 days from execution. If the document is executed outside the UK, penalties do not arise unless it is submitted for stamping more than 30 days after first being brought into the UK. In practice, it will be rare for a Transfer of UK shares and securities to be executed and retained offshore, because of the SDRT implications (see **12.12**).

10.52 Provided the Transfer is submitted for stamping within one year of the deadline, the maximum penalty is 10% of the duty payable but capped at £300. If a Transfer is submitted for stamping more than one year but no more than two years after the deadline, the penalty becomes 20% of the duty payable, and for delays of more than two years the penalty is 30% of the duty payable. It follows that where a relief is successfully claimed, reducing the stamp duty to zero, no penalty will normally be charged. However, see **10.53** below.

10.53 Where the delay is more than one year the penalty may be higher if there is evidence that the failure to submit the document for stamping was deliberate. The more serious the reason for the delay, the greater the penalty is (STSM153020). A table showing the maximum and minimum penalty percentages, dependent upon the type of failure, is shown at STSM015020. It should be noted that if there is a reasonable excuse for the delay no penalty is payable (*SA 1891, s 15B(5)*). Examples of acceptable and unacceptable reasons for a delay in stamping a document are set out at STSM015040.

Repayment of stamp duty

10.54 Occasionally, it may be discovered that too much stamp duty has been paid. This may occur, for example, where assets are subsequently found to be exempt, where an available relief has not been claimed, where consideration was incorrectly allocated to chargeable assets, or where a Transfer was inadvertently duplicated and both were stamped. The Stamp Office is empowered to consider claims for repayment (*Stamp Duties Management Act 1891, s 10*). The original stamped document must be submitted to the Stamp Office (see **Appendix A**) with a letter claiming repayment and setting out an explanation of the circumstances. In most cases, the claim must be made within two years of the date of execution of the document in question. However, where the claim relates to repayment of duty overpaid in the course of provisional stamping (see **10.47**) the two-year time limit does not apply. Interest may be payable in accordance with regulations under *FA 1999, s 110* and *FA 1989, s 178* on stamp duty repaid and, at the time of writing (May 2020), the official interest rate for these purposes is 0.5%.

Higher rates on stock and marketable securities

10.55 Where stock or marketable securities are transferred to a clearance system or depository, any stamp duty charge is at the higher rate of 1.5% (*FA 1986, ss 67–72A*). In practice, such transfers are usually carried out electronically with no transfer document, so that the relevant tax is SDRT rather than stamp duty. The 1.5% higher rate charge to stamp duty does not apply to the issue of new shares into a clearance system or depository since stamp duty generally only applies to documents transferring existing shares. The relevant tax in relation to the issue of new shares into a clearance system or depository is SDRT (see **12.28**).

Bearer instruments

10.56 A 1.5% charge also arises on the *issue* of certain bearer instruments (*FA 1999, Sch 15, para 1(1)*), but subject to certain exemptions. In contrast with a registered security, a bearer instrument is a security or other financial asset which is transferable by delivery – that is, there is no need for a transfer document, but transfer is effected instead by giving the document which constitutes the asset to the transferee (*FA 1999, Sch 15, para 3*). Where stamp duty is due, it is charged on the market value of the security and is payable by the issuer (*FA 1999, Sch 15, paras 4* and *22*). This is the one situation in which disclosure and payment of the stamp duty liability are compulsory. It should however be noted that, with effect from 26 May 2015, a UK incorporated company has been prohibited from issuing new bearer shares. In addition, from 26 February 2016 all existing bearer shares issued by a UK incorporated company had to have been converted into registered shares or cancelled (the *Small Business, Employment and Enterprise Act 2015*). These changes are part of the UK Government's promotion of corporate transparency as the ownership of unregistered shares can be hard to determine.

10.57 If the stock, in registered form, would be exempt from stamp duty on transfer, no stamp duty is due on issue in bearer form (*FA 1999, Sch 15, para 14*). There are various other exemptions especially for stock expressed in a foreign currency (*FA 1999, Sch 15, para 13*). Issuers of bearer instruments will require specialist advice on compliance with stamp duty obligations. As far as holders of bearer instruments are concerned, a key point to note is that it is *possible* to transfer a bearer instrument by means of a transfer document rather than by delivery of the security itself, but if this is done, a stamp duty charge may arise if stamp duty was not charged on the issue of the bearer instrument (*FA 1999, Sch 15, para 2*).

Partnerships

10.58 With the introduction of SDLT, stamp duty charges were removed from most assets apart from stock and marketable securities. However, stamp duty remains chargeable on a Transfer of an interest in a partnership where the assets of the partnership include any stock or marketable securities (*FA 2003, Sch 15, paras 31–33*). The stamp duty charge is limited to the smaller of:

- the charge at 0.5% which would arise on a transfer of a proportion of the stock or marketable securities for market value consideration, however the consideration is reduced by the proportion of any loan secured solely on the stock or marketable securities; the proportion is the same as the fractional share in the partnership which is transferred; and
- the charge at rates of up to 4% on the consideration actually given for the transfer of the partnership share; for these purposes, the consideration is reduced by a proportion of the 'net market value' of any UK land and buildings held by the partnership, and that proportion is the same as the fractional share in the partnership which is transferred. The 'net market value' is the actual market value less any debt secured solely on the property. The logic of this is that SDLT will often be charged by reference to the value of the UK land and buildings (see **7.25**). (When this provision was first enacted, it was expected that SDLT would always be charged. The SDLT provisions have subsequently been amended so that no charge will arise on many transfers of interests in property-owning partnerships (see **7.29** et seq), but the stamp duty provisions have been left unchanged. This possibly indicates that HMRC understand the limited effect of the retention of stamp duty on such transfers.)

HMRC provide a couple of examples of calculation of stamp duty on partnership transfers at STSM091060 and SDLTM34610.

10.59 In practice, it appears unlikely that stamp duty will be paid on many transfers of partnership interests. Most partnerships do not have substantial holdings of securities liable to stamp duty; many transfers will be left unstamped because, unless there is a dispute between the parties, it seems unlikely that a stamped transfer document will be required; the net consideration given is often very low; where necessary, it may be possible to construct a transfer of a partnership interest without creating a Transfer document. Where a Transfer is created, it should be noted that any attempt by the partners to agree contractually that they will not challenge the validity of the Transfer on the grounds it is not stamped is ineffective because of *SA 1891, s 117* ('Conditions and agreements as to stamp duty void'). Where a stamped transfer document is required, it must be submitted for adjudication.

Stamp duty mitigation

10.60 There are three legitimate approaches to minimising the stamp duty cost when assets within the scope of the tax are transferred:

(1) Avoid creating a document which requires stamping. This approach was widely used when stamp duty applied to business assets such as goodwill, but is unlikely to be applicable in relation to transfers of UK stock and marketable securities because of the need to execute and stamp a document to cancel any SDRT charge (see **12.12**).

(2) Ensure the Transfer is within the terms of a relief or exemption and claim the relief where appropriate – see **Chapter 11**. Where a relief or exemption may be available, care is needed to ensure the transaction qualifies; reliefs and exemptions are often subject to precise and detailed conditions, and it is often too easy to accidentally fall outside these conditions.

(3) Minimise the amount which will be taken into account as consideration. Stamp duty is charged on the 'amount or value of the (actual) consideration'. There is no general requirement to substitute the market value of the assets transferred, even where the transaction is between connected persons and at an under-value. However, a market value rule applies to Transfers of 'listed securities' to a 'connected' company, and to Transfers of 'unlisted securities' to a 'connected' company where some or all of the consideration is an issue of shares (but only in relation to Transfers executed on or after *Finance Act 2020* receives royal assent) – see **10.12**.

Example 10.11—Actual consideration below market value

Mustard plc (M) is in the process of selling subsidiary Cress Ltd (C). C owns 50 shares in UK company Salad Ltd (S), an unlisted company, with an historic cost of £10,000 but a current market value of £1 million. M always intended to keep the shares in S, but the process to sell C has now advanced far enough to create genuine doubt over whether M still has beneficial ownership of C. Therefore, it is not certain that group relief (see **11.9**) will be available for the transfer of S shares to M at full value. However, if C is able to transfer the S shares to M for payment of historic cost only, the stamp duty will be limited to £10,000 at 0.5%, which is £50, instead of the £5,000 which would apply to a transfer at market value.

Example 10.12—Minimising consideration

Non-UK company Cabbage SA owns unlisted UK company Sprout Ltd (current value £12 million) and non-UK company Broccoli Sarl (current value £5 million). Cabbage has agreed to sell both companies to Kale Pty Ltd (a non-UK company) for £17 million. A direct transfer of Sprout to Kale for a consideration of £12 million would cost Kale £60,000 in stamp duty. However, Cabbage first contributes Sprout to Broccoli as a contribution to the capital of Broccoli (ie a gift), with no issue of shares or securities by Broccoli to Cabbage. Cabbage then transfers Broccoli to Kale for £17 million.

For stamp duty purposes, Broccoli has given no consideration for the transfer of Sprout as the shares were gifted to Broccoli by way of a capital contribution. The stock transfer form may therefore be completed showing 'nil' consideration. No stamp duty arises, as there is no consideration there is no requirement to complete any of the certificates on the reverse of the stock transfer form, and the Transfer is deemed to be 'duly stamped' as soon as it is executed (see **10.7**). There is therefore no need for the document to be submitted to the Stamp Office for stamping. No SDRT should arise on the agreement to transfer Sprout as no consideration is given in 'money or money's worth'. Even if the Transfer is executed, or the agreement entered into, on or after the date upon which *Finance Act 2020* receives royal assent, *FA 2019, ss 47A* and *48A* (market value rules for transfer of unlisted securities: see **10.12** and **12.9**) do not apply as there is no consideration comprising the issue of shares. It is unlikely to be necessary to pay stamp duty on the Transfer of Broccoli to Kale because the shares of Broccoli are not UK registered.

The direct tax and company law consequences of the transfer of Sprout, by Cabbage to Broccoli, by way of a contribution to capital, should be considered.

Chapter 11

Stamp Duty Reliefs

INTRODUCTION

11.1 Perhaps the best-known stamp duty relief is that for transfers between group companies, commonly referred to as '*section 42* relief' because it is governed by *FA 1930, s 42*. This is modified by *FA 1967, s 27* and subject to HMRC guidance given in SP 3/98. The other main legislation on stamp duty reliefs and exemptions is in *FA 1986, ss 75–85*, but there are also relevant provisions at various points in other *Finance Acts*. References are given in the text below. Guidance on reliefs may be found at STSM040000 et seq in the HMRC Stamp Taxes on Shares Manual, available at www.hmrc.gov.uk/so/manuals/stsmanual/index.htm. This interactive manual was published on 23 July 2014 replacing the old Stamp Duty Manual.

11.2 To be consistent with the chapters on SDLT and SDRT, this book uses the term 'exemption' to refer to a measure which applies automatically to remove or reduce a stamp duty charge, and 'relief' to refer to a measure which requires a claim to be made. This is, in some ways, a false distinction. Even where a Transfer is considered to be exempt from stamp duty, it is possible for someone to challenge this. (In this book, the expression 'Transfer' is capitalised to make it clear that this is a reference to the potentially stampable document.) The only way to prove that the exemption applies is to ask HMRC to adjudicate the liability, as explained at **10.48**; this effectively amounts to making a claim for the exemption. However, it is not common for an apparently exempt document to be challenged in this way; so, in practice, it is rarely necessary to have the availability of an exemption settled by adjudication.

In contrast, where a relief applies, the relevant document is usually specifically stated not to be properly stamped unless it has been subject to adjudication (eg *FA 1930, s 42(1)*). If the document is not properly stamped, any SDRT liability which has arisen on the underlying agreement is not cancelled (see **12.12**) – so proper stamping is essential.

11.3 There is generally no theoretical time limit on claiming a relief. However, if stamp duty is paid on a document and it is subsequently realised that a claim to relief could have been made, the claim must be lodged within two years of the date of execution of the document, or the stamp duty will not be repaid (*Stamp Duties Management Act 1891, ss 9–10*; STM7.3 et seq). Where an SDRT charge has arisen, the Transfer must be executed and duly stamped within six years of the effective date of the agreement which gave rise to the SDRT charge, if that charge is to be cancelled (see **12.12**).

This has sometimes been a problem when subsidiaries have been moved around within a group on an informal basis. A typical scenario is as follows:

- parent company decides that ownership of a company should be transferred within the group, and instructs the relevant subsidiaries to take the necessary actions;
- the subsidiaries pass the necessary board resolutions, perhaps with consideration for the transfer being left outstanding on inter-company account;
- the resolutions, taken together, amount to an agreement to transfer the shares, so an SDRT charge arises at that point;
- however, no formal share Transfer is ever processed.

After six years have passed, the SDRT charge cannot be cancelled. HMRC are aware of the issue, and have made it clear that, where such situations come to light, they will pursue the SDRT charge.

11.4 Reliefs and exemptions may also apply to Transfers of interests in partnerships, although the absence of any SDRT charge means that, sometimes, documents are left unstamped rather than incurring the administrative costs of making claims (see **10.4**). Most of the reliefs described here also applied to property transactions before the introduction of SDLT in 2003, and most of them have been carried forward to the SDLT legislation (but often with more stringent anti-avoidance rules).

Exemptions

11.5 Exemptions are wide in scope, and are not limited to certain types of transaction or participant. They are listed here, but described in greater detail in **Chapter 10**:

(1) transfers which are not 'on sale' (see **10.7**) – subject to the market value charge on the transfer of listed securities to a connected company, and on the transfer of unlisted securities to a connected company where some or all of the consideration is an issue of shares (see **10.12**);

(2) transfers for consideration not exceeding £1,000, if appropriately certified (see **10.8** et seq);

(3) transfers of exempt loan capital and other debt (see **10.16** et seq);

(4) transfers of units in a unit trust (see **12.3**);

(5) transfers to recognised investment exchanges, clearing houses etc, where an appropriate arrangement has been entered into between the exchange etc and HMRC; and

(6) transfers of securities traded on recognised growth markets but not listed on any market (*FA 2014, Sch 24, Pt 2*, see **12.33**).

It must be remembered that the mere fact that a security is registered overseas or issued by a non-UK entity does not make a Transfer of that security exempt from stamp duty. However, no SDRT liability will normally arise on an agreement to transfer such a security, so there would not normally be any practical need to stamp the Transfer (see **12.5** and **12.12**).

Share incentive plans etc

11.6 No stamp duty is chargeable on a Transfer of 'partnership shares' or 'dividend shares' by the trustees to an employee under a Schedule 2 share incentive plan (*FA 2001, s 95* as amended by *Finance Act 2019, s 50* which is treated as having effect from 6 April 2014).

GROUP, RECONSTRUCTION AND ACQUISITION RELIEFS

11.7 Group, reconstruction and acquisition reliefs apply only to Transfers between companies. 'Company' is defined in the legislation for group relief as meaning body corporate, and so potentially encompasses all UK incorporated entities such as private and public companies, statutory corporations and limited liability partnerships. It also includes overseas entities, provided they have the necessary characteristics. This aspect is not defined in the legislation governing the reconstruction and acquisition reliefs, probably because those reliefs originally applied only if the acquiring company was UK registered. However, it was realised that this could cause difficulties in relation to European law, and *FA 2006, s 169* removed the requirement for UK registration. Nevertheless, a body corporate can only function as a subsidiary in a group if it has ordinary share capital, and can only participate in the other reliefs if it has non-redeemable share capital (STSM042200 et seq).

11.8 HMRC have examined the characteristics of a range of foreign entities and have expressed their view as to whether they are regarded as bodies corporate for the purposes of stamp duty group relief. A fairly comprehensive list of foreign entities which HMRC will accept as being bodies corporate for the purposes of stamp duty group relief is at STSM042260. It is important to note however that this is only a list of those foreign entities which HMRC accept as being bodies corporate and no confirmation is given that the bodies have the equivalent of 'ordinary share capital' which is the other essential requirement if an entity is to be part of a stamp duty group (see **11.11**), unless it is the parent of that group. Consequently, even if a foreign entity is included on the list it will still be necessary, in many cases, to confirm that the entity has the equivalent of 'ordinary share capital'. If a foreign entity is not included at STSM042260, it is worth asking HMRC whether they have already considered it (see **Appendix A** for contact details). If they have not done so, they will usually require details of the law under which the entity is formed, and a legal opinion (in English, or translated) setting out why the entity should be regarded as a body corporate.

Group relief – general description

11.9 According to the legislation, this should be referred to as 'associated companies relief'; it is widely called '*section 42* relief', after *FA 1930, s 42* which sets out the basic rules. In this book, it is referred to as group relief. Group relief is available to remove the stamp duty charge on a Transfer which transfers a beneficial interest in an asset between two associated companies.

11.10 The reference to beneficial interest sometimes causes confusion, because it is often considered that the *beneficial* interest in an asset passes to the purchaser as a result of payment of the consideration under an agreement, while the Transfer does no more than transfer *legal title*. However, HMRC interpret the legislation as requiring only that the Transfer be a formal step in the process of transferring a beneficial interest. On this understanding, a stock transfer form or other document giving effect to an agreement to transfer an asset on sale is able to qualify for group relief. However, there is a related point which does cause difficulties. If a beneficial interest is to be transferred, the transferor must hold that beneficial interest at the start of the process and the transferee must hold it (even if only briefly) at the end. If the asset is ultimately to be transferred to a third party, care must be taken to ensure that the group companies do nothing in relation to that disposal which may lead to loss of beneficial ownership, until the intra-group Transfer has been completed. Beneficial ownership may be lost, for example, as soon as there is a binding commitment to sell the asset to the third party, even though no payment has been made. See STSM042230 for HMRC's comments on the point.

11.11 Companies are associated if one is the parent of the other, or a third company is the parent of both. A company is the parent of another if it:

(1) is beneficial owner of at least 75% of the ordinary share capital of the other,

(2) is beneficially entitled to at least 75% of any profits available for distribution to equity holders, and

(3) would be beneficially entitled to at least 75% of assets available for distribution in a winding up.

'Ordinary share capital' means all share capital apart from fixed-rate preference shares. The rules in *Corporation Tax Act 2010, Pt 5, chapter 6* (previously *ICTA 1988, Sch 18*) apply in considering (2) and (3), but omitting the paragraphs taking account of potential future changes in rights. Where ownership is indirect, the usual algebraic rule applies to determine the effective percentage ownership – see Example 5.3 (SDLT group relief) for an illustration. The requirement for *beneficial* ownership/entitlement is important. As noted below (**11.16**), an arrangement to break the group relationship by disposal of the transferor does not prevent group relief on a prior intra-group Transfer. However, if that arrangement has progressed too far, there may be a risk that the parent company has lost beneficial ownership of the transferor and that the group is therefore broken. Cases such as *Wood Preservation Ltd v Prior* ([1968] 2 All ER 849) provide guidance on this point. It is important that the necessary group relationship is intact at the time of execution of the Transfer – it is not enough for the companies to be associated only at the time of any agreement to transfer (see STSM042240).

Bodies corporate will not be associated if at the time the Transfer is executed arrangements exist under which at that time or some later time any person has or could obtain control, or any persons together have or could obtain control of the transferee but not of the transferor (*FA 1930, s 42(2)*). For these purposes 'control' is defined in *Corporation Tax Act 2010, s 1124* (*FA 1930, s 42(7)*) and means the power of a person to secure that the affairs of a company are conducted in accordance with that person's wishes through the holding of shares, possession of voting power or as a result of powers granted by the company's articles of association or other documentation regulating the company. The sort of circumstance at which this provision would seem to be aimed would be where a person has, for example, an option to subscribe for shares in the transferee and, if the option were exercised, that person would obtain 'control' of the transferee but not the transferor. In such circumstances it would seem that group relief would not be available, although arguably only if the option was capable of being exercised at the time the Transfer is executed.

There are exceptions to this rule for certain arrangements entered into by a joint venture company (*FA 1930, s 42A*) and certain arrangements involving a mortgage secured by way of shares or securities (*FA 1930, s 42B*).

Example 11.1—Group relief, associated companies

K LLP holds all of the shares in two UK companies, J Ltd and H Ltd. J Ltd also holds a portfolio of minority holdings of shares in key suppliers to K LLP. The partners of K LLP decide to transfer the shares of J Ltd into the ownership of H Ltd in return for an issue of H Ltd shares. They also decide J Ltd should transfer the shares of suppliers to H Ltd in settlement of an inter-company debt. K LLP, J Ltd and H Ltd are all associated companies for these purposes, so any Transfers between them are potentially eligible for relief. It should not matter whether the supplier shares are transferred before or after the Transfer of shares of J Ltd.

Group relief – partnerships within the structure

11.12 Because a UK LLP is a body corporate but has no share capital, it breaks the group relationship between companies above and below it in the structure even if, economically, the necessary 75%+ group relationship is there. As a result group relief cannot be claimed for transfers from (or to) a company above the LLP in the structure to (or from) the LLP itself or any company owned by the LLP. HMRC have previously been inconsistent in relation to this matter, sometimes allowing group relief, but the correct interpretation, as set out here, was confirmed in guidance published on 11 December 2014, see www.hmrc.gov.uk/so/group-rel-sdlt-sd.htm. This same guidance confirmed that English limited and general partnerships are regarded as transparent, so that the partners should be regarded as owning the partnership assets when determining whether the necessary group structure exists. In contrast Scottish limited and general partnerships have legal personality and it is HMRC's view that they cannot be 'looked through' in this way; however as they are not bodies corporate, they cannot be regarded as parents of groups either. This could have a major adverse impact as it means direct 'subsidiaries' of a Scottish partnership will not be grouped with each other, either. Again this is an issue which HMRC have not always treated in a consistent manner, often granting group relief when, on this interpretation, it is not due. The different treatment for English and Scottish partnerships contrasts with the normal tax position, under which if Scots law would produce a tax result which differs from that under English law, the English law result is applied both sides of the border. It is surprising that HMRC's treatment – doubtless technically correct – is politically acceptable.

Group relief – anti-avoidance

11.13 Anti-avoidance rules are set out in *FA 1967, s 27*. Relief is denied if the Transfer is made in connection with any arrangements under which:

(1) any part of the consideration is to be provided or received by anyone other than another group company,

(2) the transferor and transferee are to cease to be associated by the transferee leaving the group, or

(3) the asset being transferred was previously conveyed by anyone other than a group company.

These rules have the potential to deny relief in a wide range of relatively innocent transactions, so HMRC have issued guidance on how they apply them (SP 3/98). The key points of this are as follows:

(1) 'Arrangements' is a very wide term, covering informal understandings as well as formal contracts; there are arrangements if there is an expectation that the event or series of events will happen and no likelihood in practice that it will not.

(2) Nevertheless, relief may be denied if it is found that there are arrangements even if, in the event, those arrangements do not come to fruition.

(3) Relief is not denied merely because the transferee obtains third-party debt funding to buy the asset, but relief will be denied where the funding arrangement may lead to the transfer of the economic risk and reward of ownership of the asset out of the group – for example, if the transferee borrows at an economically unsustainable level, or the lender has shareholder-type rights which could allow it to take control of the asset.

(4) The rule relating to 'previous conveyance' was intended to prevent a specific type of avoidance device which relied on the stamp duty version of sub-sale relief. This is unlikely to be of interest in relation to Transfers of shares and securities, because of the application of SDRT (see **10.13**). Relief will not be denied if the asset was previously transferred into the group from a third party under a Transfer on which stamp duty was paid.

(5) In any case of doubt, HMRC reserve the right to see relevant documents and to require formal statements of the facts.

11.14 Until March 2000, HMRC routinely required group relief claims to be backed by a Statutory Declaration of the facts by an officer of the claimant company or its parent. It is now rare for this to be required, and claims are generally made by letter (see **11.17** et seq).

11.15 The most common point of doubt is whether there are offending arrangements, particularly where there is a possibility that the transferor and transferee companies will cease to be associated after the Transfer. It is generally accepted that mere uncommitted discussions with a third-party potential purchaser do not cause there to be arrangements, unless perhaps it is economically inevitable that the relevant company will be sold. However, signature of heads of terms for the sale, even though not legally obliging the vendor to proceed, is likely to bring arrangements into existence (STSM042270 and 042280; SP 3/98, para 6). To minimise risk, any intra-group Transfers should be done at the earliest possible stage, and certainly before any final decision is made as to whether the transferee company will leave the group.

11.16 The following matters often cause confusion:

(1) There is no question of stamp duty group relief being 'clawed back'. Clawback is a concept which applies only to SDLT. If stamp duty group relief is validly and successfully claimed on a Transfer, events thereafter have no impact on the claim. However, HMRC are entitled to have regard to subsequent events when considering claims, so it is wise to submit group relief claims quickly after the intra-group Transfer.

(2) Group relief will not usually be denied merely because there are plans for the asset itself to leave the group, provided that onward transfer of the asset is subject to stamp duty as normal – but, as noted above, care is needed in relation to timing of that onward disposal (see SP 3/98, para 9).

(3) No problem is caused by plans to dispose of the transferor, because the legislation specifically refers to the ownership of the transferee, provided those plans have not progressed too far (see **11.11**).

(4) A company may repurchase its own shares from a shareholder. This repurchase may qualify for group relief, provided the companies are in the necessary group relationship, subject to the usual anti-avoidance rules (STSM042250).

Example 11.2—Group relief

Jersey plc (J) owns 100% of Friesian Ltd (F), and Friesian Ltd in turn owns 100% of Galloway Ltd (G). It is decided to sell F but retain G. The group markets F, a preferred bidder is identified, and non-binding heads of terms are signed. Before there is any formal commitment to sell to that preferred bidder, G is transferred to J for cash. Assuming there are no other avoidance aspects, the Transfer of G should qualify for stamp duty group relief, even though there are certainly arrangements for F to leave the group. As noted at **11.10**, it is important that the group does not become committed to sell F before the group Transfer is finalised, or there may be a risk that J will have lost beneficial ownership of F, the companies thus ceasing to be associated for group relief purposes.

Example 11.3—Document essential for group relief

A multinational group headed by Dorian BV has a direct UK subsidiary Eve Ltd, which itself has a UK subsidiary Frank Ltd. It is decided that Frank Ltd should be sold. Eve Ltd agrees to transfer Frank Ltd to Dorian BV in satisfaction of a £10 million inter-company debt. In turn, Dorian BV agrees to sell Frank Ltd to a third-party purchaser. Dorian BV then instructs Eve Ltd to transfer the shares of Frank Ltd directly to the purchaser.

An SDRT liability of £50,000 (£10 million at 0.5%) arises on the agreement to transfer Frank Ltd to Dorian BV. A further SDRT liability arises on the agreement to sell Frank Ltd to the third-party purchaser. It is likely that a stock transfer form will be completed to transfer the shares from Eve Ltd to the third-party purchaser. The purchaser will normally pay stamp duty on this, which will cancel the SDRT liability on the second step. However, no document is executed to transfer the shares from Eve Ltd to Dorian BV, so the SDRT liability on that step remains payable. If, instead, a document had been executed to transfer the shares from Eve Ltd to Dorian BV, stamp duty group relief could have been claimed on this under *FA 1930, s 42*, and a successful claim would have cancelled the SDRT charge. A separate document would then have been required to transfer the shares from Dorian BV to the third-party purchaser.

A stock transfer form would not necessarily have been required for the transfer from Eve Ltd to Dorian BV; in appropriate circumstances, Eve could have executed a 'declaration of trust', declaring that it now held the shares of Frank Ltd on trust for the benefit of Dorian BV. This declaration of trust could have been submitted for stamping, without the need first to update the share register of Frank Ltd to show Dorian BV as the shareholder. In complex reorganisations, where shares of UK companies may be transferred several times in quick succession within a group, it is commonplace to effect Transfers by way of declarations of trust or similar documents, to avoid delays arising from the need to get documents stamped before share registers can be updated. As noted at **12.22**, where shares are held by a custodian, a 'letter of direction' fulfils a similar function. Appropriate legal advice should be taken where required, to establish what kind of documentation will be effective as a 'Transfer', which can then be submitted for stamping.

Group relief – claims process

11.17 Group relief is claimed by submission of documents to the Stamp Office (see **Appendix A**) for adjudication. The outside of the envelope should be clearly marked 'Stamp duty claim under FA 1930, s 42' to ensure it is sent directly to the correct section. The following documents must be sent (STSM042310):

(1) the original, executed Transfer(s) (typically, for shares, a stock transfer form);

(2) certified* copies of the Transfer(s);

(3) certified copies* of any agreements governing the Transfer;

(4) where the parties to the transaction are indirectly associated, a family tree*;

(5) a certified* copy of the register of members of all subsidiary and intermediate companies;

(6) where the consideration was payable in cash, a copy of the latest accounts of the transferee company to demonstrate that the company had sufficient cash to make the payment. A copy of any agreement with a third party about the provision of the consideration;

(7) copies of any other documents (eg board minutes, correspondence, agreements) which help explain the transaction and the reasons for it;

(8) a letter of claim; and

(9) a self-addressed envelope for return of the document. This reduces the risk that the stamped document might be returned to a registered office address as shown on the stock transfer form, for example.

* Items marked thus either are required to be 'certified', or may require certification, so it may be as well to have them certified at the outset. 'Certified' means either the normal certification by a solicitor or other appropriate lawyer that the document is a true copy of an original, or an equivalent statement signed by a director or the company secretary of the company in question. It is not clear why the copy of the Transfer needs to be certified, since HMRC will also have the original in front of them, but this is a long-standing requirement. If any of the companies is non-UK incorporated, it may also be necessary to provide a copy of its incorporation documents or other information, to satisfy HMRC that it is indeed a body corporate with issued ordinary share capital (see **11.11**). Again it is probably safest to have the copy incorporation documents certified.

11.18 The precise format of the letter of claim is not specified in the legislation, but HMRC do require it to make statements about particular matters. As a result, letters of claim tend to follow a fairly standard pattern. Guidance entitled 'The Mechanics of Making a Claim' can be found at STSM042310. The letter must explicitly state:

- that a claim under *FA 1930, s 42*, as amended, is made in respect of the documents (which must be listed at this point);
- details of the dates of all instruments on which relief is claimed;
- the authorised and issued share capitals of all companies in the group structure (or at least that part of it which includes the transferor, transferee and any intermediate companies up to a common parent) at the dates of all the documents. The reference to 'authorised' is probably redundant as UK companies are no longer required to have a specified level of authorised capital. The letter should also state whether any of the

shares carry a right to only a fixed dividend and no other share in profits. If a company has more than one class of share in issue the letter should provide details of the profit rights attached to each class of shares and set out the asset distribution rights attached to each class of shares in any winding up of the company;

- what shares are held by each shareholder in each subsidiary company;
- that it is intended that the existing shareholder relationships are to be maintained (or give details of any change envisaged);
- that the group relationship between the companies meets the requirements of *Corporation Tax Act 2010, s 151(4)(a), (b)* and *Pt 5, chapter 6* (previously *ICTA 1988, s 413(7), Sch 18*);
- that none of the bodies corporate is in liquidation (or give further details if they are);
- that the transferee body corporate intends to keep the beneficial ownership of the asset (or give details of any intended transfer onwards);
- the amount of the consideration and whether it was paid in cash, by issue of shares or securities, through an inter-company loan or from a third-party loan; and
- that none of the documents was executed in pursuance of, or in connection with, an arrangement as described in *FA 1967, s 27(3)* or *FA 1930, s 42(2)*, as appropriate.

11.19 Although some of these statements overlap and may seem unnecessary, HMRC do require them all to be made. The letter must be signed by an appropriate person with personal knowledge that the statements are correct: a director or other officer of the ultimate parent company, or of a company which is parent of a sub-group containing all of the other companies; a shareholder of the ultimate parent if that shareholder has a right to attend board meetings which discuss policy; a lawyer (in-house or external) acting for the parent company; or an administrator/receiver appointed to the parent company under insolvency law. For a long time, HMRC also readily accepted letters signed by other advisers (eg auditors and tax advisers) acting for the parent company, but they have been known to challenge whether these are based on personal knowledge, particularly of the intentions of the parties. It may, therefore, be safest for the letter to be signed by an appropriate officer of the parent company. However, HMRC state at STSM04310 that if a company's solicitor states in a letter of claim that 'I am informed and verily believe' then that should be acceptable.

Letters of claim qualified by phrases such as 'as far as I am aware' are not acceptable.

11.20 In major reorganisations, there may be numerous Transfers on which group relief is to be claimed, sometimes several transfers of the same shares. It is usually acceptable to combine all of the group relief claim letters into one, provided all relevant documents are made available for each Transfer. Where there are successive Transfers of the same shares, it is important that each step is completed by an appropriate Transfer document, in order to cancel any SDRT charge which would otherwise arise. However, there are possible company law difficulties in executing successive stock transfer forms before earlier forms have been stamped and the transfers registered. A solution may be for the original owner of the shares to execute a declaration of trust in respect of each successive transfer agreement, to confirm that it now holds the shares for the benefit of the new owner. Such a declaration acts as a Transfer and can be submitted for stamping.

11.21 Another potential issue, where there are successive transfers, concerns the question of beneficial ownership. If a company is committed to transfer shares onwards, even before it has acquired them, that company may never gain beneficial ownership; yet group relief is only available where beneficial ownership is transferred. Equally, if the transferor or transferee is itself to be transferred at a later stage in the reorganisation, there may be a risk that the necessary beneficial shareholding relationship does not exist when the earlier Transfer is made. Care should be taken in the timing of Transfers and the signature of agreements to minimise such risks. However, when dealing with purely internal group reorganisations, the author has not known HMRC to challenge the availability of group relief on these grounds. A challenge is perhaps more likely if the reorganisation is to be followed by disposal of some entities out of the group.

Reconstruction and acquisition reliefs – general description, common features

11.22 This section covers two reliefs (ie reconstruction relief, and relief for insertion of a new holding company) which remove the stamp duty charge for certain Transfers which do not involve any change in ultimate ownership but which may not qualify for group relief. There used to be a third relief (*FA 1986, s 76*), which could properly be described as acquisition relief and which limited the stamp duty rate to 0.5%, even where there was a change in economic ownership. Acquisition relief was useful when stamp duty applied to land and other assets but, because the normal stamp duty rate on transfers of stock and marketable securities is 0.5%, it became of very little practical use. The relief was abolished from 6 April 2013 (*FA 2012, Sch 38*). The equivalent relief in relation to SDLT, which remains in force, is described at **5.27**. The common feature of both remaining reliefs is that the consideration must include the issue of non-redeemable shares by the acquiring company, and either no other consideration, or only consideration from a very restricted list.

11.23 Reconstruction relief and relief for insertion of a new holding company are also subject to a general anti-avoidance condition, that the acquisition must be for bona fide commercial purposes and must not form part of a scheme or arrangement which has avoidance of stamp duty, income tax, corporation tax or capital gains tax as a main purpose. In many cases, taxpayers will seek advance clearance from HMRC that the transaction will qualify as a reconstruction for direct tax purposes. Where such clearance is given, HMRC should accept this as proving that this condition is satisfied. If no clearance is obtained, the relief may still be available, but it will be necessary to provide HMRC with further information to satisfy them on this point, as follows:

- a copy of the latest accounts of the 'target company' ('T' in the explanation below);
- full details of any scheme or arrangement of which this transaction forms part;
- confirmation that the 'acquiring company' ('A' in the explanation below) still holds the shares or undertaking of T, as appropriate; and
- a *detailed* (HMRC emphasis) note of the bona fide commercial reasons for the transaction.

Reconstruction relief

11.24 In the heading to the legislation (*FA 1986, s 75*), this is described as 'acquisition relief' but, because it applies only to schemes of reconstruction, it is widely known as 'reconstruction relief'. The relief reduces stamp duty to zero where, in pursuance of a scheme of reconstruction, a company (A) acquires all or part of the undertaking of another company (T). The consideration for the acquisition must consist of or include the issue of non-redeemable shares by A to all of the shareholders of T (*not* to T itself). The only other consideration permitted is that A assumes or discharges debts of T. The general anti-avoidance condition applies, as mentioned above.

11.25 The other stated condition is that, after the acquisition, the shareholders of A must be the same as those of T, and the proportion of shares in A held by each shareholder must be the same as the proportion of shares in T held by that shareholder. Minor variations in proportions, as a result of the inability to allot fractional shares, for example, are permitted. HMRC insist that the shares be properly issued for these purposes – that is, all formalities to record the shareholders in the statutory books of A must be completed – and shares in A may only be issued to a nominee if the equivalent shares in T were held by the same nominee for the benefit of the same beneficial owner. In determining these proportions, any shares held in treasury by T itself are ignored.

11.26 In view of the limited application of stamp duty, clearly the relief is only applicable where the undertaking of T consists of or includes stock or marketable securities, or interests in partnerships which hold stock or marketable securities. There is no statutory definition of 'undertaking', but tax case precedents indicate that the mere passive holding of assets, as investments for example, does not amount to an undertaking. Furthermore, for the undertaking of T to be 'transferred', A must carry it on in much the same form as did T. So, if T holds a portfolio of shares as an investment, or if, after transfer to A, the shares are held as investments, relief is not likely to be available; however, if T carries on a share dealing business and, after the transfer, A also carries on a share dealing business, the Transfer could qualify for relief. HMRC also accept that acting as the holding company of controlling interests in one or more trading companies may amount to an undertaking, providing the holding company does in practice act as a parent company, taking an appropriate interest in the running of the subsidiary/ies. So, if T holds a controlling interest in trading company Z, this may amount to an undertaking and the relief may apply on transfer to A. HMRC's comments on this matter are at STSM042380 in relation to stamp duty. Their comments in relation to SDLT are likely to be relevant here too (see SDLTM23201).

11.27 It is also the view of HMRC, again supported by precedent, that a transaction is not a reconstruction if there is any appreciable change in the ultimate ownership of the assets. The legislation does not explicitly require that the shares issued by A should be of the same class as each other or as the shares in T. However, if shares of different classes are issued and if these give the shareholders different economic rights, the transaction may not be a reconstruction and so may not qualify for relief. The following example is fairly complex, but illustrates many of the difficulties which can arise in relation to this relief.

Example 11.4—Reconstruction relief

Target Ltd (T) is the parent company of a trading group, holding all of the shares of trading companies Yak Ltd (Y) and Zebra Ltd (Z). The shareholders of T are two siblings, Rupert and Sandy, each holding 5,000 of the 10,000 £1 ordinary shares (all the same class) in issue. Rupert also holds 2,000 non-voting, non-cumulative 5% £1 redeemable preference shares, reflecting extra cash he put into the group many years ago. It is decided to separate Y and Z, with a view to the possibility that each sibling may wish to take a greater interest in a different company in future. It is proposed to liquidate T, transferring each of Y and Z under a new holding company (YH and ZH respectively) in return for an issue of shares to Rupert and Sandy. The following issues arise:

(1) The preference shares are a potential problem because they are redeemable, but all shares issued by YH and ZH must be non-redeemable. If YH and ZH issue non-redeemable preference shares to Rupert, their

economic value may not be the same as redeemable shares. A solution would be for the redeemable shares to be either redeemed or converted to non-redeemable shares before the reconstruction proceeds.

(2) The preference would be to give Rupert a greater interest in Y, and Sandy a greater interest in Z, taking care to ensure that each ended up with the same overall commercial value as at the outset. They consider the following possibilities:

(a) YH issues 20 £1 preference shares and 70 £1 ordinary shares to Rupert, and 30 £1 ordinary shares to Sandy in return for the shares of Y. ZH issues 70 £1 ordinary shares to Sandy and 30 £1 ordinary shares to Rupert in return for the shares in Z. Neither the transfer of shares in Y to YH nor the transfer of Z to ZH would qualify for *s 75* relief, because at the end of the process Rupert and Sandy would not hold the same proportion of shares in either YH or ZH as they initially held in T.

(b) YH issues 20 £1 preference shares and 50 £1 class A ordinary shares to Rupert, and 50 £1 class B ordinary shares to Sandy in return for the transfer of Y. ZH issues 20 £1 preference shares and 50 £1 class B shares to Rupert, and 50 £1 class A shares to Sandy in return for the transfer of Z. This could qualify for *s 75* relief, as the proportions of shares in each company held by each of Rupert and Sandy at the end are the same as the proportions initially held in T. However, if the relative economic values of the three classes of shares in each company differ from the relative economic values of the shares in T, it is likely that the transaction will not amount to a 'reconstruction' within the terms of the relief, and relief will be denied. To avoid this problem, the rights and entitlements arising from the class A and class B shares in each company must be the same. In short, the siblings cannot skew the relative interests in the two businesses, so that one has a greater share of Y and the other a greater share of Z. If they wish to change this relative ownership, that must be done as a separate matter at a later date. The preference shares remain a particular problem. As shares in T, they give Rupert a reserves-dependent entitlement to a dividend of £100 per year. To achieve the same with 40 £1 shares in YH and XH (20 in each), the coupon rate would have to be 250% – and even that assumes the shares in YH and ZH are of equal worth. It really would be easier to get rid of the preference shares before commencing the reconstruction.

Relief for insertion of new holding company

11.28 In the heading to the legislation (*FA 1986, s 77*), this is also described as relief for acquisitions, but the paragraph heading above is more accurate.

No stamp duty is chargeable on a Transfer of shares in one company (T) to another company (A) where the Transfer forms part of an arrangement for A to acquire all of the shares in T, provided other conditions are satisfied. Again, the general anti-avoidance condition applies (as mentioned in **11.23**), and the information listed there will have to be supplied if direct tax clearance has not been obtained for the transaction. The other conditions are that:

(1) the only consideration is the issue of shares in A to the shareholders of T;

(2) every shareholder of T immediately before the acquisition is a shareholder of A after the acquisition, and holds the same proportion of shares in A as previously held in T;

(3) if T has shares of different classes, the classes and relative proportions by number of each class are replicated in A;

(4) the proportion of shares of A of any particular class, in issue or held by any particular shareholder, is the same as the proportion of shares of that class in T, in issue or held by that shareholder, immediately before the acquisition; and

(5) at the time the instrument transferring the shares in T to A is executed there are no 'disqualifying arrangements' (as set out in *FA 1986, s 77A*) in existence (*FA 1986, s 77(3)(i)*). This additional condition only applied to instruments executed on or after 29 June 2016, however the 'disqualifying arrangement' could have been entered into at any time, including before 29 June 2016.

The reference to different share classes relates to the rights and characteristics of the shares, not particularly how they are labelled. So, if shares are labelled class A and class B purely to identify by which member of a consortium they are held and if they have identical rights etc, they will not be regarded as being of different classes. But shares which have different voting or dividend rights or different nominal values will be regarded as being of different classes.

The legislation specifically provides that the references to 'shares' and 'share capital' also include a reference to 'stock' (*FA 1986, s 77(4)*). For these purposes 'stock' takes its meaning from *SA 1891, s 122* by virtue of *FA 1986, s 114(4)*. The *SA 1891, s 122* definition of 'stock' refers not only to shares or share capital but also includes the *funded debt* of any county council, corporation, company, or society in the UK, or of any foreign or colonial corporation or society. Although not clear from this definition, HMRC Stamp Taxes takes the view that for these purposes 'funded debt':

> '… means "debt instruments" *issued* by the target company such as bonds and loan notes (irrespective of whether the note is exempt or chargeable to stamp tax if transferred independently) which can be traded separately in a manner akin to that of equities.'

They go on to state:

> 'We would not expect "funded debt" to include mortgages, bank loans, financing and overdrafts within the meaning because these are not normally issued and tradeable instruments with the characteristics of equity' (STSM042415).

Consequently, for an arrangement to qualify for relief under *FA 1986, s 77*, A must not only acquire all of the shares in T, it must also acquire any 'funded debt' issued by T, and A must then issue 'funded debt' which mirrors that issued by T. Therefore if T, for example, has issued loan notes to a shareholder or a third party, A must acquire those loan notes, along with all of the shares in T, and A must then itself issue identical loan notes to the shareholder or third party. However, mortgages, bank overdrafts, bank term loans, etc can be ignored.

11.29 Prior to 29 June 2016 there was no denial of the relief under *FA 1986, s 77* if the control of A changed shortly after the share for share exchange transaction took place. However, HMRC's view is that the purpose of the *FA 1986, s 77* relief is to ensure that there is no stamp duty charge where there is no real change of ownership of T following its acquisition by A. Consequently, a new condition was introduced in relation to instruments executed on or after 29 June 2016 which requires that, at the time the instrument transferring the shares in T to A is executed, there must be no 'disqualifying arrangements' in existence.

The term 'arrangement' is widely defined as including '… any agreement, understanding, or scheme (whether or not legally enforceable)' (*FA 1986, s 77A(6)*).

An arrangement will be a 'disqualifying arrangement' if it is reasonable to assume that the purpose, or one of the purposes, of the arrangement is to secure that (*FA 1986, s 77A(2)*):

- a particular person obtains control of A; or
- particular persons together obtain control of A.

For these purposes 'control' is defined in *Corporation Tax Act 2010, s 1124* and means the power of a person ('P') to secure by the means of holding shares or the possession of voting power in relation to A (or any other body corporate) so that the affairs of A are conducted in accordance with P's wishes. In addition 'control' can be exercised as a result of any powers conferred by the articles of association or other document regulating the affairs of A (or any other body corporate). Consequently, any arrangement under which a person or persons could acquire the majority of the shares in A, or the majority of the voting power in A, would be a 'disqualifying arrangement'. In the author's view, for such an arrangement to exist, the particular person or persons would have to have been identified at the time the relevant transfer is executed.

HMRC's view (STSM042460) is that "The fact that the arrangements are conditional or contingent does not prevent them from being disqualifying arrangements if it is reasonable to assume that the purpose or one of the purposes of the arrangements is for a particular person or particular persons together to obtain control of the acquiring company."

Example 11.5—*FA 1986, s 77A 'Disqualifying Arrangements'*

An Cala Ltd has five shareholders each holding 20% of the company's issued share capital. An Cala Ltd carries on a retail business and a wholesale distribution business. The shareholders cannot agree the future direction of the two businesses, and it is decided that three of the shareholders (Paul, Pamela and Caroline) should concentrate on the retail business and the other two shareholders (John and Ewan) should concentrate on the wholesale distribution business.

A new holding company ('Topco') is inserted above An Cala Ltd on a share for share exchange basis with Topco issuing shares to each of Paul, Pamela, Caroline, John and Ewan pro rata their existing shares in An Cala Ltd.

An Cala Ltd then distributes in specie its wholesale distribution business to Topco. Following which a demerger takes place pursuant to which Topco distributes its wholesale distribution business to Newco (a new company formed by John and Ewan) in return for Newco issuing shares to John and Ewan pro rata their respective shareholdings in Topco.

Following the demerger Paul, Pamela and Caroline will each have a 33.33% shareholding in Topco. As Paul, Pamela and Caroline acting together had control of Topco both before (60%), and after (100%), the demerger, it is considered that there should be no 'disqualifying arrangement' for the purposes of *FA 1986, s 77A*.

However, if the reorganisation had been structured so that John and Ewan were each to hold 50% of Topco then there would have been a 'disqualifying arrangement' for the purposes of *FA 1986, s 77A*, if it was reasonable to assume that John and Ewan were acting together to obtain control of Topco.

11.30 It is specifically provided that the following are not 'disqualifying arrangements' (*FA 1986, s 77A(3)* and *(4)*):

- any issue of shares by A as consideration for the acquisition of T within *FA 1986, s 77(3)*, and

- 'relevant merger arrangements' – such an arrangement will exist where the share for share exchange transaction between the shareholders of T and A is followed by a second share for share exchange between the shareholders in a second company (B) and A. The second share for share exchange transaction must meet the following conditions (*FA 1986, s77A(4)*):

  (1) the only consideration given by A for the acquisition of the whole of the share capital of B must be the issue of shares to the shareholders of B;

  (2) the acquisition of B must be for bona fide commercial reasons and must not form part of an arrangement with a main purpose of avoiding a liability to stamp duty, stamp duty reserve tax, income tax, corporation tax or capital gains tax;

  (3) after the acquisition of B has been made each person who was a shareholder of B must be a shareholder of A;

  (4) after the acquisition of B the shares in A must be of the same class as were the shares of B immediately prior to the acquisition and the relative proportions by number of each class of shares in B must be replicated in A; and

  (5) the proportion of shares of A of any particular class held by any particular shareholder, must be the same as the proportion of shares of that class in B held by that shareholder, immediately before the acquisition of B.

  In assessing whether conditions (4) and (5) above are satisfied the shares issued by A for the acquisition of T are ignored since, if this were not done, the conditions could never be satisfied. (*FA 1986, s 77A(4)(c)(i)*).

  As for *FA 1986, s 77*, the definition of 'shares' and 'share capital' within the meaning of 'relevant merger arrangements' includes 'funded debt' (see **11.28**). This means that A must not only acquire all of the share capital of B but must also acquire any 'funded debt' issued by B, and must then issue identical 'funded debt' to the persons who previously held the 'funded debt' in B (*FA 1986, s 77(4)*).

The exception of 'relevant merger arrangements' from 'disqualifying arrangements' means that *FA 1986, s 77* relief will still be available in relation to A's acquisition of T even if there is an 'arrangement' for A to acquire the whole of the share capital of another company (B), provided that under that 'arrangement' all of the shareholders of B are to become shareholders of A, the shareholdings (class and proportion of shares held) in A are a mirror image of the shareholdings in B immediately before the acquisition of B (ignoring the shares issued by A to acquire T), and the acquisition of B is for bona fide commercial reasons and not part of a scheme to avoid any of the taxes listed in point (2) above. See STSM042500 for HMRC's guidance on 'relevant merger arrangements'.

If the 'relevant merger arrangements' or the share for share exchange within *FA 1986, s 77(3)*, which are excluded from 'disqualifying arrangements', are part of a wider scheme or arrangement which has a purpose of securing that a particular person(s) obtains control of A (see **11.29** for the meaning of control), but those wider arrangements do not fall within *FA 1986, s 77A(3)*, then the 'relevant merger arrangements' or share for share exchange are treated as 'disqualifying arrangements' (*FA 1986, s 77A(5)*). See HMRC commentary on this point at STSM042470.

Finance Act 2020, s 79 amends *FA 1986, s 77A* ('Disqualifying arrangements') so that an arrangement for a change of control of the acquiring company will not be a 'disqualifying arrangement' provided certain conditions are satisfied. The amendments to *FA 1986, s 77A* apply to any Transfer executed on or after the date upon which *Finance Act 2020* receives royal assent.

The Explanatory Notes to the *Finance Bill 2019–21* indicate that the amendments to *FA 1986, s 77A* are aimed at 'partition demergers', which are a type of corporate reorganisation that can often involve a change of control of the acquiring company (referred to as 'A' above). In practice the corporate reorganisation would often include a 'capital reduction demerger', although the issue, at which the amendments to *FA 1986, s 77A* are aimed, could also arise on an 'exempt distribution demerger', if a new holding company is to be inserted as part of the reorganisation. The Explanatory Notes go on to state that if, as part of a 'partition demerger' which involves a change of control of A, *FA 1986, s 77* relief were not available on the insertion of a new holding company, this could result in a double charge to stamp duty, first on the insertion of the new holding company, and secondly on the demerger itself. *Finance Act 2020, s 79* is designed to prevent such a double charge to stamp duty provided certain conditions are satisfied.

The following is one example of a 'capital reduction demerger' which involves a change of control of the acquiring company, in this case TopCo.

Example 11.6—Capital Reduction Demerger – No 'Disqualifying Arrangement' for the purposes of *FA 1986, s 77A*

Target Co Ltd ('T Ltd') was established four years ago, and it has three shareholders who have owned their shares in T Ltd, since it was first established, in the following proportions:

(a) Ava, who holds 35% of the issued shares;

(b) Rory, who holds 30% of the issued shares; and

(c) Tamba, who holds 35% of the issued shares.

T Ltd carries on two autonomous businesses, being a recruitment agency business and a parcel distribution business. The shareholders cannot agree on the future plans for the two businesses and it is decided that Ava and Rory will concentrate on the recruitment agency business and Tamba on the parcel distribution business.

To achieve the desired corporate structure the following transactions are implemented:

(1) *A new holding company is inserted*

A new company ('Acquisition Co') is incorporated and it acquires all of the share capital of T Ltd on a share for share exchange basis. Acquisition Co issues shares to each of Ava, Rory and Tamba pro rata their existing shareholdings in T Ltd. Following this transaction Ava, Rory and Tamba respectively have 35%, 30% and 35% of the issued shares of Acquisition Co, and Acquisition Co holds all of the issued share capital of T Ltd.

(2) *T Ltd distributes its parcel distribution business to Acquisition Co*

T Ltd distributes in specie its parcel distribution business to Acquisition Co.

(3) *Acquisition Co reorganises its share capital*

Acquisition Co reorganises its issued share capital into 'R' shares (to be held by Ava and Rory) which give all of the rights to the recruitment agency business and 'P' shares (to be held by Tamba) which give all of the rights to the parcel distribution business.

(4) *Newco is formed by Ava and Rory*

A new company (Newco) is formed with Ava and Rory as the only shareholders.

(5) *Acquisition Co – Capital Reduction Demerger*

Acquisition Co reduces all of its issued 'R' shares (held by Ava and Rory) to nil and out of the distributable reserves created by that capital reduction it distributes in specie all of its shares in T Ltd to Newco. As consideration for the T Ltd shares Newco issues shares to Ava and Rory pro rata to their shareholdings in Acquisition Co.

Following implementation of the above transactions the revised corporate structure is as follows:

- Newco, which carries on the recruitment agency business through its wholly-owned subsidiary T Ltd, is owned 54% by Ava and 46% by Rory.
- Acquisition Co, which carries on the parcel distribution business, is owned 100% by Tamba.

Stamp tax implications

*Transfer conveying shares in T Ltd to Acquisition Co executed **before** Finance Act 2020 receives royal assent.*

A double charge to stamp duty would arise in these circumstances. First, on Acquisition Co's acquisition of T Ltd, as *FA 1986, s 77A* would apply to deny relief under *FA 1986, s 77*, as there would be a 'disqualifying arrangement' for the purposes of *FA 1986, s 77(3)(i)*. This is because an arrangement would exist for a particular person (ie Tamba) to obtain 'control' of Acquisition Co, for the purposes of *Corporation Tax Act 2010, s 1124*. After the reorganisation, Tamba clearly controls Acquisition Co as he holds 100% of Acquisition Co's share capital, whereas before the reorganisation Tamba did not control Acquisition Co, as he only held 35% of the share capital of Acquisition Co. A stamp duty charge would also arise on the distribution of T Ltd to Newco, with the consideration chargeable to stamp duty being the value of the shares issued by Newco as consideration for the shares in T Ltd. Relief would not be available under *FA 1986, s 75* (see **11.24** et seq) as the shareholdings in Newco do not mirror those in Acquisition Co after the reorganisation.

*Transfer conveying shares in T Ltd to Acquisition Co executed **on or after** Finance Act 2020 receives royal assent.*

As indicated above, *Finance Act 2020, s 78* is designed to avoid this double charge to stamp duty. It does this by amending *FA 1986, s 77A(2)* to state that a person who has held at least 25% of the issued share capital of the target company at all times during the 'relevant period' is not a person within *FA 1986, s 77A(2)(a) or (b)* ie is not a person seeking to obtain 'control' of the acquiring company. A new *FA 1986, s 77A(2A)* is inserted which states that the 'relevant period' is the period of three years ending immediately before the time at which the shares in the acquiring company are issued (or first issued) as consideration for the acquisition of the target company.

Consequently, as long as any shareholder who controls the acquiring company (A) after the 'partition demerger' has taken place held at least 25% of the target company throughout the period of three years ending with the issue of shares by A to acquire the target company, there should be no 'disqualifying arrangement' for the purposes of *FA 1986, s 77A*. This means that, provided all of the other conditions for relief under *FA 1986, s 77* are satisfied (see **11.28**), no stamp duty charge should arise on A's acquisition of the target company, as relief should be available under *FA 1986, s 77*.

In the corporate reorganisation outlined in Example 11.6 above, Tamba held more than 25% of the share capital of T Ltd for the four year period prior to T Ltd's acquisition by Acquisition Co, consequently the amendment to *FA 1986, s 77A(2)* will apply such that Tamba will not be treated as a person seeking to obtain control of Acquisition Co. As a consequence, *FA 1986, s 77(3)(i)* will not apply and, assuming all of the other conditions for relief under *FA 1986, s 77* are satisfied, no stamp duty should be chargeable on the Transfer of the T Ltd shares to Acquisition Co. A stamp duty charge would still arise on the distribution of T Ltd to Newco, with the consideration chargeable to stamp duty being the value of the shares issued by Newco as consideration for the shares in T Ltd. Relief would not be available under *FA 1986, s 75* (see **11.24** et seq) as the shareholdings in Newco do not mirror those in Acquisition Co after the reorganisation.

Potential issues with the amendment to *FA 1986, s 77A* are as follows:

- The requirement for a three year holding period prior to the reorganisation taking place may mean that the relief is not available. For example, if a group is looking to carry out a 'partition demerger' within three years of the target company being formed then the relief will not be available.

A target company may be owned by a number of shareholders, all of whom hold less than a 25% shareholding, and therefore it may not be possible to meet the threshold of holding at least 25% of the issued share capital of the target company.

11.31 The introduction of the additional condition that there must be no 'disqualifying arrangements' in existence at the time the instrument transferring T to A is executed will prevent the insertion of a new holding immediately prior to a sale to a third party (or the introduction of a new controlling shareholder). However, in these circumstances, it should still be possible to claim the relief provided the new holding company is inserted before any third-party purchaser (or new controlling shareholder) is identified, and therefore before any 'arrangement' to sell A to a particular person (or to introduce a new controlling shareholder into A) has come into existence. This is confirmed by HMRC at STSM042480 where it is stated:

> 'A reorganisation in advance of a potential future sale where no purchaser(s) has been identified will not be disqualifying arrangements for the purposes of FA86/s77A. For example, there may be a reorganisation of a group of companies to make the group better structured for sale in the future.'

It has been suggested by various commentators that *FA 1986, s 77A* was introduced to prevent the avoidance of stamp duty on the takeover of a UK company. This could be achieved by A, a non-UK incorporated company, being placed on top of T in such a way that no stamp duty was payable as relief was available under *FA 1986, s 77*, with a third-party purchaser then acquiring A free of UK stamp taxes, as no UK stamp tax is generally payable on the acquisition of shares in a non-UK incorporated company. However, in the author's view, it is unlikely that *FA 1986, s 77* relief would have been available in any event as *FA 1986, s 77(3)* provides that the relief is not available if the main purpose, or one of the main purposes, of A's acquisition of T is the avoidance of stamp duty.

At STSM042470 HMRC give their views on arrangements which would not constitute disqualifying arrangements for the purposes of *FA 1986, s 77A*. They make the point that for *s 77A* to apply 'there have to be arrangements where it is reasonable to assume that a purpose or one of the purposes of the arrangements is for a particular person or persons together to obtain control of the acquiring company'. They go on to say that 'In respect of "particular persons together" this is more than a numerical test. It must be reasonable to assume that the parties to the arrangements intend to act in such a way that particular persons together obtain control of the acquiring company'. This means that in Example 11.7 below there should not be a disqualifying arrangement for the purposes of *FA 1986, s 77A* provided the incoming shareholder is not acting together with one of the existing shareholders to control the new holding company.

Example 11.7

Cameron and Rory own 50% each of a trading company ('Tradeco'). Craig agrees to invest cash into Tradeco in return for a 10% shareholding. It is decided to create a new holding company ('Holdco') with a significant share capital to enable Craig to subscribe for shares in Holdco at par. Holdco is incorporated and acquires the existing shares in Tradeco in return for an issue of shares to Cameron and Rory. The shares issued to Cameron and Rory are of the same class as the shares they previously held in Tradeco and the shares are held in the same 50:50 proportion. Shortly after this reorganisation is completed Craig subscribes cash to Holdco in return for a 10% shareholding. It could be said that there is a change of control of Holdco in these circumstances as following the new investment Cameron (45%) and Craig (10%) could be said to control Holdco, as could Rory (45%) and Craig (10%). However, provided Craig is not acting together with either Cameron or Rory to control Holdco there should be no disqualifying arrangement for the purposes of *FA 1986, s 77A*.

11.32 The transaction must be part of the acquisition of all of the target company's share capital. If A already holds some shares in T (eg after stake building in a quoted company) or if any shares of T remain with another shareholder (eg a dissenting shareholder), the relief will not be available. In practice, therefore, the relief is only of use for insertion of a new holding company by a 100% shareholder or by agreement amongst a group of shareholders with 100% between them. This is most commonly done as a first step in a further reconstruction or reorganisation, or perhaps to put a 'clean' company at the top of a group prior to a stock market initial public offering. However, as discussed above, at the time that T is acquired by A there must be no disqualifying arrangement within the meaning of *FA 1986, s 77A*.

Example 11.8—Insertion of holding company

In Example 11.4, it is possible that the proposed reconstruction would be easier if, as a first step, a new holding company H Ltd was inserted between T and the shareholders, Rupert and Sandy. This might, for example, allow T to be liquidated first, thus removing any difficulty arising from an accumulated deficit on reserves. To this end, Rupert might establish H, taking one £1 ordinary share as founder subscriber. Rupert, Sandy and H would then agree that the shares in T be transferred to H in return for H issuing 2,000 £1 non-redeemable preference shares and 4,999 £1 ordinary shares to Rupert and 5,000 £1 ordinary shares to Sandy. Note the same comments apply as in the original example with regard to the redeemable preference shares. Note also that the key requirement is that numbers/proportions of shares held in H after the transaction are the same as those in T before. Since Rupert starts with one share in H, he must agree to be issued with one share less than expected, to ensure the final numbers are correct. In the original form of this relief, precise replication of proportions was vitally important, and real claims failed because the subscriber share was overlooked. However, an amendment inserted by *FA 2006* relaxed this requirement, and now proportional shareholding must be replicated 'as nearly as may be'. This relaxation was intended to allow for the inability to issue fractional shares, and still may not cover overlooking subscriber shares so, in order to be safe, they should be taken into account as suggested here.

Acquisition reliefs – claims process

11.33 Each of the reliefs just described is claimed by submission of documents to the Stamp Office (see **Appendix A**) for adjudication. The outside of the envelope should be clearly marked 'Stamp duty claim under FA 1986, s [75/77, as appropriate]' to ensure it is sent directly to the correct section. The following documents must be sent:

Item
The original, executed Transfer(s) (typically, for shares, a stock transfer form)
Certified* copies of the Transfer(s)
Certified copies* of any agreements governing the Transfer
Certified* copy of the register of members of the target company immediately before the Transfer
Certified* copy of the register of members of the acquiring company after the Transfer

Copies of any other documents (eg board minutes) which help explain the transaction and the reasons for it

A letter of claim

A self-addressed envelope for return of the stamped document**

* Items marked thus either are required to be 'certified', or may require certification, so it may be as well to have them certified at the outset. 'Certified' means either the normal certification by a solicitor or other appropriate lawyer that the document is a true copy of an original, or an equivalent statement signed by a director or the company secretary of the company in question.

** This became a requirement in June 2014 and reduces the risk that the stamped document might be returned to a registered office address, as shown on the stock transfer form, for example, rather than the postal address of the appropriate individual.

11.34 HMRC provide model letters of claim for these reliefs, originally reproduced in Stamp Taxes Bulletin 2/2013 but now available at STSM042430 (*s 77* claim letter) and STSM042440 (*s 75* claim letter), and there is also a checklist for *s 75* and *s 77* claims at STSM042450. The model letters are reproduced in **Appendix B**.

Charities relief

11.35 This is a simple relief – any Transfer to a charity or charitable trust is relieved from stamp duty (*FA 1982, s 129*) – and HMRC are keen to ensure that charities benefit from the relief where appropriate. Provided the Transfer is clearly to a registered charity, the transferee normally only needs to submit the Transfer to HMRC with a note of the charity's registration number and a request that the Transfer be adjudicated exempt under the charities exemption. If the charity is not registered, it may also be necessary to submit the deed or other document establishing the charity, and perhaps engage in correspondence to satisfy HMRC that the entity is indeed established for charitable purposes. It is, however, expected that HMRC will have regard to the definition of a charity for tax purposes in *FA 2010, s 30* and *Sch 6*. HMRC may challenge the availability of the relief where they do not believe the charity is managed by 'fit and proper' persons.

Relief for transfer to new LLP

11.36 No stamp duty is chargeable on a Transfer to a limited liability partnership within one year of formation of that LLP, provided the Transfer is, effectively, a step in the incorporation of some other form of partnership (such as an English or Scottish general or limited partnership) with no change in overall economic ownership (*Limited Liability Partnerships Act 2000, s 12*).

The partners in the LLP immediately after the Transfer must be the same as the partners in the old partnership immediately before, and the proportionate interest of each in the assets transferred must remain unchanged. The relief is available whether the assets were previously owned directly by the 'old' partnership or by a partner or other person holding as nominee for some or all of the partners. The Transfer must be submitted for adjudication for the relief to apply.

Recognised intermediary exemption etc

11.37 Any Transfer to a recognised intermediary (RI) is relieved from stamp duty (*FA 1986, s 80A*). An RI is a person who carries on a bona fide business of dealing in stock (or certain other financial instruments) and has been recognised for these purposes. Adjudication is required to take advantage of this relief, but a similar exemption (*FA 1986, s 88A*) also exempts such Transfers from SDRT and, in practice, most such Transfers are electronic and so only within the SDRT net; further details about this exemption are provided at **12.23**. Other reliefs are provided specifically to facilitate financial market activity in the form of repurchases and stock lending, where in practice recognised intermediaries are normally involved (*FA 1986, ss 80C–84*).

Demutualisation of insurance companies

11.38 A Transfer executed in connection with the demutualisation of a mutual insurance company is relieved from stamp duty. This allows the transfer of investments from the mutual insurer to the new company taking over the insurance business, without stamp duty cost, provided the Transfer is submitted for adjudication (*FA 1997, s 96*).

Mergers of unit trusts and related transactions

11.39 Transfers executed in connection with the merger of authorised unit trusts, conversion of an authorised unit trust into an open ended investment company (OEIC), or merger of an authorised unit trust into an OEIC, are relieved from stamp duty (*FA 1997, s 95*; *SI 1997/1156*).

Other reliefs

11.40 The *Stamp Duty and Stamp Duty Reserve Tax (Collective Investment Schemes) (Exemptions) Regulations 2013* provide an exemption from stamp duty in relation to contractual collective investment schemes – see **12.32**. This will be of interest only to professionals and those investing large sums.

Finance Act 2014 introduced provisions removing the charge to stamp duty on transfers of shares quoted on 'growth markets' such as the Alternative Investment Market of the London Stock Exchange (AIM) (*FA 2014, Sch 24, Pt 2*). From 28 April 2014, qualifying shares are removed from the scope of the principal charge to stamp duty and from other potential charges such as those on purchase of own shares and on transfer of shares to a clearance service or depositary. See **12.33** for details of which shares qualify.

There are numerous other reliefs from stamp duty, most of which are no longer relevant to real transactions since the scope of stamp duty was restricted to transfers of stock and marketable securities. In recognition of this, as mentioned at **10.1**, *FA 2012, Sch 38* abolished a number of redundant reliefs from 6 April 2013.

Chapter 12

Stamp Duty Reserve Tax (SDRT)

INTRODUCTION

12.1 SDRT was introduced by *FA 1986, ss 86–99*, in response to market developments under which the paperless transfer of beneficial ownership of shares became more common. Because no transfer document is produced, a paperless transfer does not give rise to stamp duty; SDRT is designed to collect the same amount of tax as stamp duty, even where there is no document. (In this book, the expression 'Transfer' is capitalised to make it clear that this is a reference to the potentially stampable document.) At that time, the London Stock Exchange was trying to develop an electronic trading platform ('Taurus'). The government of the day was eventually persuaded that charging stamp duty or SDRT would inhibit trading on this new platform, and *FA 1990, Pt III* was enacted to abolish both taxes on transfers of securities, from a date to be fixed by statutory instrument (the 'abolition day'). This date was intended to coincide with the launch of Taurus. Unfortunately, technical difficulties meant that Taurus was abandoned before completion. By the time the current electronic trading system was introduced in 1996, the government view had changed. *FA 1990, Pt III*, although still on the statute book, has not been activated, and both SDRT and stamp duty remain potentially chargeable on securities transactions.

12.2 SDRT is potentially within the rules for disclosure of tax avoidance schemes (DOTAS) but, at the time of writing (May 2020), regulations had not yet been made to activate this.

12.3 In practice, virtually all SDRT is paid on electronic stock market transactions (where it is collected automatically). The special SDRT regime, which used to apply to trustees and managers of UK unit trust schemes, was abolished from 30 March 2014. A general explanation of those arrangements is set out below, but detailed consideration of them is beyond the scope of this book. Outside these special areas of commerce, the main need is for taxpayers and advisers to understand how SDRT may arise on ordinary transactions in shares and securities, and how to ensure any such SDRT charge is appropriately dealt with. This chapter aims to provide that appreciation and understanding. In most cases, 'appropriately dealt with' means cancelled by execution of a Transfer document and ensuring it is 'duly stamped'. The interaction with stamp duty and the actions necessary to ensure cancellation of any SDRT charge are outlined below at **12.12**.

BASIC RULES

What gives rise to an SDRT charge?

12.4 SDRT arises when there is an unconditional agreement to transfer 'chargeable securities' for consideration in money or money's worth (*FA 1986, s 87*). The tax is chargeable whether the agreement is documented or not; in principle, it remains chargeable even if the transaction is subsequently abandoned, unless it can be argued that abandonment is evidence that the original agreement was not in reality unconditional. The normal rate is 0.5% of the consideration (*FA 1986, s 87(6)*), which is the same rate as stamp duty. As with stamp duty, a higher rate of 1.5% is chargeable in certain circumstances, but this is only likely to impact financial market transactions. However, the definition of consideration – anything which is money or money's worth – is far wider than for stamp duty (see **10.26**). As a result, an ordinary transaction may give rise to an SDRT liability which is greater than any stamp duty liability on the same transaction. It should also be noted that with effect from 29 October 2018 a market value charge arises on the transfer of 'listed securities' to a connected company – see **12.9** (*FA 2019, s 48*). In addition, from the date upon which the *Finance Act 2020* receives royal assent, a market value charge arises on the transfer of 'unlisted securities' to a connected company for consideration some or all of which comprises an issue of shares – see **12.9** (*FA 2019, s 48A* – inserted by *Finance Act 2020, s 78*).

Example 12.1—Contrast between SDRT and stamp duty

Abigale agrees to transfer 500 shares in UK company Brian Ltd to Carol, a professional decorator. In consideration, Carol agrees to redecorate Abigale's house (a job for which Carol would normally charge £6,000). The agreement gives rise to an SDRT liability of £30 (£6,000 × 0.5%), subject to possible debate over the 'value' of the decorating work. However, the 'consideration' simply does not count for stamp duty purposes, so no stamp duty is payable on any document transferring the shares. As noted below (**12.12**), if a document of transfer is executed and 'duly stamped' within the period allowed, this will cancel the SDRT charge.

Chargeable securities

12.5 Chargeable securities are defined in *FA 1986, s 99(3)–(12)*. These subsections begin with a blanket definition to include stocks, shares and loan capital, various interests in and options over such assets, and units in unit trust schemes. This definition is then restricted by excluding:

(1) securities which are neither UK registered nor paired with securities which are so registered. (It is uncommon for UK and non-UK securities to be paired. This particular provision was enacted to deal with the company formed to build the Channel Tunnel, which issued paired UK and French shares.);

(2) securities issued by an SE (a 'European company' formed under EC Council Regulation 2157/2001) unless its registered office is in the UK;

(3) units in a unit trust if all of the trustees are resident, and the registered office is maintained, outside the UK, or if it can only invest in assets which are themselves not within the charge to stamp duty, SDRT or SDLT;

(4) shares in an open ended investment company (OEIC) subject to equivalent requirements to those in (3);

(5) securities traded on a recognised growth market but not listed on that or any other market (see **12.33**);

(6) interests in depositary receipts; and

(7) stock or marketable securities, the transfer of which is exempt from all stamp duties.

In practice, the main categories which remain within the definition of chargeable securities are UK registered shares and UK registered corporate debt with equity-like characteristics (eg convertible debt). Most debt securities are not chargeable as a result of (7) above, because they are exempt from stamp duty on transfer in accordance with the exemption for 'loan capital' in *FA 1986, s 79* (see **10.16**). However, this exemption may not apply if the debt has equity-like characteristics such as convertibility, a return which depends on business results or asset values, the potential for repayment at a premium which is not reasonably comparable to the terms of debt listed on the London Stock Exchange, or a coupon which exceeds a reasonable commercial return. The last of these restrictions has caused many disputes in relation to so-called 'junk bonds', which carry a high interest rate in recognition of a high risk of default by the borrower. Where there is a transfer of a UK corporate debt, the terms of the debt should be checked carefully to ensure that they do not contain features which may disapply the *FA 1986, s 79(4)* exemption.

12.6 The scope of stamp duty was restricted in association with the introduction of SDLT in 2003. At that time, the rules excluding stock etc which is exempt from stamp duty were amended, presumably in an attempt to fit in with the new stamp duty rules. The result is a highly convoluted definition, written in such a way as to suggest that there may be securities which are, in practice, outside the stamp duty charge, but which may still be subject to SDRT. There are indeed such securities – units in a UK unit trust; it would have been simpler for the definition to say so.

12.7 Although not specifically excluding the securities from being 'chargeable securities', *FA 1986, s 90* lists a number of cases when no SDRT is chargeable, as follows:

- various agreements relating to unit trust schemes (see **12.31** for the special arrangements for unit trusts);
- agreement to transfer a non-UK bearer instrument, or many UK bearer instruments (but the exemption for UK instruments does not apply in certain cases, mainly where no stamp tax was payable on original issue of the instrument and it would be subject to stamp tax on transfer in registered form);
- agreement to transfer securities to a charity or charitable trust or to certain bodies established for national purposes; and
- agreement to transfer shares held in treasury by the company which issued them.

12.8 No SDRT liability arises on a conditional agreement until such time as it becomes unconditional *(FA 1986, s 87(3)(a))*.

Market value charge on transfer of listed and unlisted securities to a connected company

12.9 *FA 2019, s 48* provides that where a person who is connected with a company (or that person's nominee) agrees to transfer 'listed securities' to that company (or that company's nominee) (whether or not for consideration), or the person connected with the company (or that person's nominee) transfers listed securities to that company for consideration in money or money's worth, SDRT is charged as follows:

(a) *Consideration in the form of money or money's worth given in return for the listed securities*

The consideration chargeable to SDRT is the greater of: (a) the amount or value of the actual consideration given for the listed securities; and (b) the market value of the listed securities at the time the agreement is made.

(b) *No consideration in the form of money or money's worth given in return for the listed securities*

The consideration chargeable to SDRT is the value of the listed securities at the time the agreement is made.

The value of the listed securities at any time is the price which they might reasonably be expected to fetch on a sale in the open market at that time (*FA 2019, s 48(6)*).

For the purposes of this provision 'connected' is as defined in *Corporation Tax Act 2010, s 1122* (*FA 2019, s 48(7)*).

'Listed securities' are 'chargeable securities' (see **12.5**) which are regularly traded on: (a) a regulated market; (b) a multilateral trading facility; or (c) a recognised foreign exchange with (a), (b) and (c) having the same meaning as they have for *FA 1986, s 88B* (*FA 2019, s 48(2)*).

The market value rule also applies to the 1.5% SDRT charge where there is an agreement to transfer 'listed securities' to a depositary receipt issuer or clearance system (see **12.28**), and the person to whom the beneficial interest in the 'unlisted securities' (ie the person who is holding the 'unlisted securities' through the depositary receipt or the clearance system) is a company 'connected' to the transferor. If the amount or value of the consideration for any transfer of 'listed securities' to a depositary receipt issuer or clearance system is less than the value of those securities at the time they are transferred, the transfer is treated as taking place for an amount of consideration in money equal to that value (*FA 2019, s 48(4)* and *(5)*).

This market value rule has effect in relation to the SDRT charge under *FA 1986, s 87* (see **12.4**) where the agreement to transfer the listed securities is conditional and the conditionality is satisfied on or after 29 October 2018 or, where the agreement is unconditional, the agreement is made on or after 29 October 2018 (*FA 2019, s 48(12)*).

In relation to the 1.5% charge under FA 1986, *s 93* (Depositary receipts) and *s 95* (Clearance systems) (see **12.28**) the market value charge applies to any agreement to transfer listed securities on or after 29 October 2018.

FA 2019, s 48A, inserted by *Finance Act 2020, s 78*, applies where a person who is connected with a company (or that person's nominee) either (i) agrees to transfer 'unlisted securities' to that company (or that company's nominee) for consideration in money or money's worth, or (ii) the person connected with the company (or that person's nominee) transfers unlisted securities to that company for consideration in money or money's worth and, in either case, some or all of the consideration consists of the issue of shares (*FA 2019, s 48A(1)*).

Where *FA 2019, s 48A* applies, SDRT is chargeable on the greater of:

(a) the amount or value of the actual consideration given for the unlisted securities; and

(b) the market value of the unlisted securities at the time the agreement is made (*FA 2019, s 48A(3)*).

The value of the unlisted securities at any time is the price which they might reasonably be expected to fetch on a sale in the open market at that time (*FA 2019, s 48A(6)*).

For the purposes of this provision 'connected' is as defined in *Corporation Tax Act 2010, s 1122* (*FA 2019, s 48A(7)*).

'Unlisted securities' are 'chargeable securities' (see **12.5**) which are not regularly traded on:

(a) a regulated market;

(b) a multilateral trading facility; or

(c) a recognised foreign exchange

with (a), (b) and (c) having the same meaning as they have for *FA 1986, s 88B* (*FA 2019, s 48A(2)*).

The market value rule also applies to the 1.5% SDRT charge where there is an agreement to transfer 'unlisted securities' to a depositary receipt issuer or clearance system (see **12.28**), and the person to whom the beneficial interest in the 'unlisted securities' (ie the person who is holding the 'unlisted securities' through the depositary receipt or the clearance system) is a company 'connected' to the transferor. If the amount or value of the consideration for any transfer of 'unlisted securities' to a depositary receipt issuer or clearance system is less than the value of those securities at the time they are transferred, the transfer is treated as taking place for an amount of consideration in money equal to that value (*FA 2019, s 48A(4)* and *(5)*).

This market value rule has effect in relation to the SDRT charge under *FA 1986, s 87* (see **12.4**) where the agreement to transfer the unlisted securities is conditional and the conditionality is satisfied on or after the day on which *Finance Act 2020* receives royal assent or, where the agreement is unconditional, the agreement is made on or after the day on which *Finance Act 2020* receives royal assent (*FA 2019, s 48A(9)(a)*).

In relation to the 1.5% charge under *FA 1986, s 93* (Depositary receipts) and *s 95* (Clearance systems) (see **12.28**) the market value charge applies to any transfer on or after the day on which *Finance Act 2020* receives royal assent (*FA 2019, s 48A(9)(b)*).

It is important to appreciate that the market value rule for listed securities (*FA 2019, s 48)* applies irrespective of whether or not there is any actual consideration, and irrespective of the nature of any actual consideration. In contrast the market value rule for unlisted securities only applies if there is actual consideration for the transfer, and some or all of that consideration is in the form of the issue of shares (*FA 2019, s 48A*).

The SDRT market value rule covering agreements to transfer 'unlisted securities' to a connected company for consideration in 'money or money's worth', some or all of which comprises the issue of shares mirrors the equivalent stamp duty provision in *FA 2019, s 47A* – see **10.12**.

Administration and compliance

12.10 Liability to SDRT should be notified to HMRC and the tax paid by the 'accountable date' (*SDRT Regulations 1986, SI 1986/1711, regs 3, 4*). For financial market transactions, the accountable date is fixed by agreement between HMRC and the operators of the electronic transfer systems used on those markets; it is generally 14 days from the date of the transaction. In the rare cases where SDRT remains payable on non-financial market transactions, the accountable date is the seventh day of the calendar month following that in which the agreement is made or becomes unconditional. So, if an agreement to transfer shares is entered into on the last day of a month, SDRT obligations arise just seven days later.

12.11 Responsibility for notification and payment rests with the 'accountable person'. When a broker, or other market professional, acts in the transaction, that broker or other professional is the accountable person. When more than one such person is involved, the rules specify which one has the responsibility. The broker then normally adds the SDRT to the amount charged to the client; the client has no direct responsibility to HMRC, but is still liable for the tax, and this fact gives the market professional the right to recover the tax from the client.

In non-financial market transactions, the accountable person is normally the purchaser (*SI 1986/1711, reg 2*). No standard return form is specified; liability must be notified by sending appropriate information to the SDRT Unit at the Stamp Office (see **Appendix A**). The information required is a full description of the securities (including number/amount), amount of consideration, when the SDRT is due, and the fact that this is a private or off-market transaction. Payment may be made by any of the normal methods but, for any form of direct bank transfer, it will be important to check with HMRC to ensure the correct current destination bank account details are used. These are set out on the HMRC website at www.hmrc.gov.uk/payinghmrc/stamp-reserve.htm.

Interaction between SDRT and stamp duty

12.12 Chargeable securities are usually also 'stock or marketable securities'. Stamp duty is chargeable on Transfers of these types of asset, so clearly both stamp duty and SDRT can apply to the same transaction. To avoid a double charge, any SDRT charge is automatically cancelled (and any tax paid can be reclaimed) if a document giving effect to the transaction (usually a stock transfer form) is executed and 'duly stamped' within six years of the agreement (*FA 1986, s 92*). Private transactions in securities are almost invariably documented and any stamp duty paid. As noted at **12.15**, there are several reasons why it is often best to arrange to fall within the stamp duty regime.

12.13 In some circumstances, Transfers are automatically deemed to be 'duly stamped' (**10.42**), so that mere execution of the Transfer is sufficient to cancel the SDRT charge. In some other cases, especially where a relief is claimed, the Transfer is not duly stamped unless the liability has been adjudicated (see **10.48**). In yet other cases, adjudication is not required, and simple stamping with the correct duty is sufficient to render the Transfer duly stamped unless and until the adequacy of stamping is challenged. Thus, no SDRT is normally paid on such transactions; the main risk is that the parties fail to execute a suitable document and ensure it is 'duly stamped' before the six-year deadline. HMRC have made it clear that, where such cases come to light, they will pursue the outstanding SDRT.

12.14 Often, the execution and stamping of a Transfer will not happen until after the SDRT has technically become due and payable. In recognition of this, HMRC do not in practice seek to collect SDRT on private, non-financial market transactions, or pursue penalties for failure to notify liability, where it is expected that the liability will be cancelled within a few weeks. This delay effectively amounts to an interest-free deferral of payment of the tax. However, should the liability eventually prove payable, interest will be charged from the accountable date, and a penalty may be charged for failure to notify liability.

Issues in non-financial market transactions

12.15 In relation to non-financial market transactions, it is normally best to ensure that the stamp duty rules apply and that any SDRT liability is automatically cancelled for the following reasons:

- Stamp duty reliefs such as group transfer relief (*FA 1930, s 42*) and the reorganisation reliefs (*FA 1986, ss 75* and *77*) do not apply directly to SDRT. An appropriate document must be executed and submitted for stamping in order to claim the relief under the stamp duty rules and cancel any SDRT liability at the same time.

- The definition of 'consideration' for stamp duty purposes is more restricted than that for SDRT purposes. So, the tax bill is often less under stamp duty than under SDRT, but payment of the correct tax under the stamp duty rules is still sufficient to cancel a potentially larger SDRT liability.

12.16 Note that the document of transfer must transfer the securities to the person who was the original transferee under the agreement (or their nominee) – *FA 1986, s 92(1A)*. If A agrees to transfer to B, and B agrees to transfer to C, but there is a single stock transfer form from A to C, this does *not* cancel the SDRT charge on the A to B transfer agreement. In practice, this can be a particular problem where a relief is to be claimed on the A to B transfer. It is usually necessary to ensure that a transfer document is produced for each individual transfer step, to avoid incurring multiple SDRT charges (see Example 11.3).

12.17 In general, shares and securities issued by companies not registered in the UK are outside the scope of SDRT. The exception is where those shares are held on a share register in the UK. Some non-UK registered companies, especially those registered in the Channel Islands and the Isle of Man, maintain copies of their share registers in the UK – often for administrative convenience where, for example, the shareholders are in the UK. In these situations, care must be taken to ensure that the UK copy truly is no more than a copy of the main register kept in the country of registration. There is a risk that HMRC could allege that the UK 'copy' is in fact a main share register, bringing the shares within the UK SDRT net.

12.18 *FA 1986, s 88* specifies a few situations in which execution (and stamping, where necessary) of a Transfer does not cancel the SDRT charge. These are mostly anti-avoidance provisions to prevent exploitation of exemptions such as those for financial market operators. There are two cases of potential interest to ordinary investors – although, even here, a financial market professional will normally be involved and will deal with the SDRT obligations:

- units in a UK unit trust are exempt from stamp duty on transfer, but may still be liable to SDRT on agreement to transfer to anyone other than the managers of the scheme; execution of a Transfer does not cancel any SDRT charge; and
- when a company issues bonus shares or makes a rights issue, the right to receive the shares may be in 'renounceable letters of allotment' issued to the existing shareholders. Entitlement to the shares may be passed to others by transferring the renounceable letters. A Transfer is normally automatically exempt from stamp duty, but execution of a Transfer does not cancel any SDRT liability which may arise.

SDRT AND FINANCIAL MARKETS

12.19 The vast majority of quoted UK securities are held in electronic systems such as CREST (see below) and traded electronically, without production of any document of transfer. When a client buys quoted chargeable securities in this way, SDRT remains the final tax. The securities are usually purchased through market operators such as stockbrokers and banks; these are normally members of the relevant stock exchange (or 'qualified dealers'), and the SDRT regulations make them responsible for collecting and paying any SDRT which arises (*SI 1986/1711, reg 2*). When such an operator buys securities on behalf of a client, the SDRT is normally automatically added to the client bill by the electronic system and passed directly to HMRC. The client has no responsibility for notifying liability or making payment to HMRC.

12.20 Quoted securities are usually purchased for monetary consideration, and the liability under stamp duty would not be any less than under SDRT, so no disadvantage arises to the client from suffering SDRT. In fact, the SDRT liability is often slightly lower, because stamp duty is generally rounded to the next £5 above, whereas SDRT is only rounded to the nearest penny. The one exception is where the total consideration does not exceed £1,000, in which case stamp duty would be nil but SDRT is still charged.

CREST

12.21 Buying or selling securities generally involves two distinct stages: first, an agreement or contract; then a transfer in settlement of the contract. CREST ('Certificateless Registry for Electronic Share Transfer') is an electronic settlement system for quoted securities, originally established by a consortium of banks in the mid-1990s but since 2002 owned by the Euroclear Group. It formed a key part of the 1996 transition from paper-based transfers to electronic transfers on the London Stock Exchange. This transition was part of the general deregulation or freeing up of the market, colloquially referred to as 'Big Bang'. Stock market transactions are mostly processed within CREST without the need for paper documents. When the sale and purchase of securities within CREST is agreed, the brokers or other market operators acting on behalf of vendor and purchaser enter details of the transaction into the CREST system. Provided the details entered on behalf of vendor and purchaser agree, CREST matches them and processes the transfer. At the same time, CREST transfers the purchase/sale price between the accounts of the parties. Finally, CREST also collects (from the purchaser's broker's account) any SDRT due on the transaction and pays this to HMRC. As part of the compliance arrangement, each evening CREST sends details of that day's trades to HMRC.

Letters of direction

12.22 As explained above (at **12.15**), an SDRT charge may arise on certain agreements to transfer securities when no stamp duty would arise on a paper transfer, because the consideration for the transfer does not count for stamp duty purposes. In the financial sector, this commonly occurs in relation to large holdings of quoted securities in connection with mergers and consolidations – for example, certain mergers of pension funds. In theory, it would be possible to remove all of the quoted securities in question from CREST, carry out a paper transfer, then put them all back into CREST – but this would be an administrative nightmare, where hundreds of different securities might be involved. The securities are typically held on behalf of the pension fund or similar owner by custodians (often special purpose subsidiaries of banks). The transferor can effectively create a transfer document by issuing a letter of direction to the custodian, directing him to hold the shares for the benefit of the transferee. This is known as a letter of direction. It may be submitted for stamping if necessary and, once 'duly stamped', is sufficient to cancel any SDRT charge which would otherwise arise.

The 'recognised intermediary' exemption

12.23 The efficient operation of the securities market depends on the existence of traders who 'make a market' by offering to buy and sell securities from/to all comers. The profit on such trading, as a proportion of price, is often very small, and the imposition of SDRT would inhibit the market. An exemption is, therefore, available for the purchase of securities by appropriate market operators, generally referred to as 'recognised intermediaries' (RIs) (*FA 1986, s 88A*).

12.24 Initially, the exemption was restricted to persons (individuals, companies or other entities) which were members of the London Stock Exchange, although it was gradually expanded to include other exchanges. However, in order to comply with the requirements of the EU Markets in Financial Instruments Directive (MiFID), the scope of the exemption was considerably widened from November 2007 to include:

- 'trading platforms' which would not otherwise be regarded as fully functioning stock exchanges; and
- non-members of stock exchanges carrying on share trading who are authorised by a state in the European Economic Area to provide investment services or activities as set out in the Directive.

12.25 Note the use of the word 'recognised' – the relief does not apply unless the trader and/or trading platform has applied for and gained HMRC recognition for the purpose. HMRC may approve an exchange or platform for these purposes by making regulations under *FA 1991, ss 116, 117.* The exchange then takes on delegated responsibility for approving RIs in relation to transactions through that exchange. There is a steady stream of regulations granting approval of European exchanges or trading platforms – see for example *SI 2011/666.* In contrast, individual approval of authorised traders is obtained by direct application to HMRC.

12.26 An RI must not carry on any 'excluded business'. Excluded businesses encompass those which involve making or managing investments (eg insurance or running unit trusts) as well as the provision of services to related companies. In practice, financial services groups often also carry on excluded businesses, and so carry on their RI business through a separate company. However, a few have negotiated arrangements with HMRC under which they 'ring fence' their RI business within a single company and treat movements of stock between parts of the company as if they were sales and purchases.

Example 12.2—SDRT on market transactions

Harry instructs his broker, Irena Associates, to buy up to 10,000 shares in Jeremiah plc. Meanwhile, Karen instructs her bank Liam Corporation to sell her holding of 3,000 shares in Jeremiah plc. Irena Associates agrees to buy Karen's shares, initially on its own account. Because Irena Associates is a recognised intermediary, no SDRT arises on the purchase. Once Irena Associates has purchased a further 7,000 shares, it transfers all 10,000 to its client account, for the benefit of Harry. At the moment of transfer, CREST charges Irena Associates SDRT on the price which Harry is paying for the shares. As regards the 3,000 shares originally owned by Karen, one lot of SDRT is paid, just as if Karen had sold them directly to Harry (and the same is true in principle for the other 7,000 shares).

Contracts for differences (CFDs)

12.27 The relief is available to prevent double charges when a trader buys shares and sells them onwards to a customer. However, it applies to all purchases of chargeable securities by the intermediary and, in practice, one of the biggest uses is to allow traders to buy shares free of SDRT to hedge 'contracts for differences' (CFDs). Under a CFD, a customer gains the economic effect of having bought shares without actually buying them.

Example 12.3—Contracts for differences

Moira believes the shares of a quoted UK company Nick plc will increase in value over the next six weeks. Broker Olive Ltd agrees to write a CFD for

5,000 shares in Nick plc. Under the CFD, Moira immediately pays Olive Ltd an amount equal to the current price of 5,000 shares in Nick plc (plus a small commission). In return, Olive Ltd agrees that, in six weeks' time, it will pay Moira the value of 5,000 Nick plc shares at that time. Moira, therefore, is in the same economic position as if she had invested in 5,000 Nick plc shares for a fixed six-week period. However, writing the CFD does not involve any agreement to transfer securities, so no liability to SDRT arises for either party. Meanwhile, Olive Ltd does not wish to suffer the risk that Nick plc shares will rise in value, so it goes into the market and buys 5,000 Nick plc shares for its own account. Because Olive Ltd is a recognised intermediary, it does not pay SDRT on this purchase. In six weeks' time, it will sell the Nick plc shares and use the proceeds to pay Moira under the CFD.

A substantial proportion of all UK stock market transactions are thought to relate to the use of CFDs. HMRC do not generally seek to impose SDRT on such transactions, provided they are implemented with due care; there would probably be no point in trying to do so, as most such transactions would simply not happen if there was an SDRT cost. However CFDs have gained a negative reputation with the general public because many activities of traders which are thought to cause major fluctuations in prices of shares (and resulting economic instability) involve the purchase and sale of CFDs.

Depositories and clearing systems

12.28 Overseas investors often prefer to buy UK securities through a clearance system operating in their home country or in the form of depository receipts. The rate of SDRT is increased to 1.5% where there is an agreement to transfer securities to a depository receipt issuer or clearance system. The justification for this is that, while the securities remain within the clearance system or depository, subsequent transfers occur without imposition of SDRT.

The higher rate was previously also charged where new shares or securities were *issued* to a clearance system or depository receipt issuer, until this was found unlawful under EU law in two tax cases, both involving HSBC. The first, a 2009 European Court decision (*HSBC & Vidacos v HMRC*), considered the issue of shares to a European clearance system. The second, a UK 2012 First-tier Tax Tribunal decision (*HSBC & Bank of New York Mellon v HMRC*), decided that the EU Capital Duty Directive applies if the issuer of the securities is in the EU, irrespective of the location of the depositary receipt issuer. HMRC accepted this decision and invited claims for repayment of SDRT paid under the previous incorrect interpretation of the law, subject to the usual four-year time limit (see www.hmrc.gov.uk/so/sdrt-hsbc-holdings.pdf). However, in Stamp Taxes Bulletin 2/2012 (www.hmrc.gov.uk/so/bulletin02-2012.pdf), HMRC make clear their view that the decisions apply only to the specific capital instruments set out in the Capital Duty Directive. In practice the Directive covers all instruments by which companies commonly raise capital – shares, bonds, debentures, etc – but it appears that HMRC may be worried that unusual instruments may be devised to take advantage of the exemption in the course of tax avoidance.

The *European Union (Withdrawal) Act 2018* provides that existing EU law, including the EU Capital Duty Directive, will continue to apply in the UK until there is a change in the law. At the time of the November 2017 budget the government confirmed that there were no plans to change the law on this point when the UK leaves the EU. Therefore, the current law should continue and the 1.5% SDRT charge should not arise on the issue of shares, etc into a clearance system, or to a depository receipt issuer, as part of an arrangement to raise capital.

The 1.5% charge is sometimes referred to as a 'season ticket'. There is at least anecdotal evidence that, on average, such shares are transferred fewer than three times within the system before being transferred out of the clearance or depository system, so the 1.5% charge is probably punitive. Clearing systems can avoid the 1.5% charge by agreeing with HMRC to charge SDRT as normal on transfers (*FA 1986, s 97*).

The judgment in the *HSBC/Mellon* case includes comments which imply that the holder of a depositary receipt does not have beneficial ownership of the underlying security. HMRC have stated their view that these comments relate specifically to the position for this specific fact pattern under New York State law and have made it clear that they will continue to treat the holder of a depositary receipt as having beneficial ownership of the underlying security for direct tax purposes.

Public issues

12.29 When there is a public issue of shares, the underwriters typically take temporary ownership of any shares not immediately taken up, and then sell them in the market over the next few weeks. There is normally no SDRT or stamp duty on the issue of shares, but this process would give rise to an SDRT charge on the subsequent sale, which would add to the costs of the share issue. A relief (*FA 1986, s 89A*) therefore applies to stop this charge arising, provided the strict conditions are complied with.

Stocklending

12.30 In origin, stocklending was a process by which institutional investors 'lent' their investments to traders to allow them to sell shares they had not yet bought, all in the interests of maintaining market liquidity. However, this is not a true loan – rather, it is a sale and repurchase agreement which could have given rise to SDRT. So, to maintain liquidity, subject to stringent conditions, there is a relief (*FA 1986, s 89AA*). The process gained notoriety in 2008, as speculators borrowed huge numbers of bank shares, flooding the market with them, thus driving the share price down, in turn allowing them to buy back at a reduced price and return the loan – and all helped by an SDRT relief!

Unit trusts and open ended investment companies

12.31 In accordance with the *Stamp Duty and SDRT (Open Ended Investment Companies) Regulations 1997, SI 1997/1156*, references in these paragraphs to unit trusts should be regarded as including references to OEICs. Units in unit trusts are specifically exempted from stamp duty. If units in a UK unit trust are transferred directly between investors, the usual SDRT charge applies, and this cannot be cancelled by execution of a document of transfer. However, in practice, such units in publicly traded unit trusts are not usually transferred, they are surrendered to the manager (who then cancels them or reissues them to a new investor). No charge arises on the investor when this happens. Prior to 30 March 2014, under a special regime in *FA 1999, Sch 19*, the manager had to pay a composite SDRT charge which took account of numbers of surrenders and issues, and the composition of the unit trust investment portfolio. The manager recouped the SDRT cost through the margin between the prices at which they issued and repurchased units. There were some adjustments in 2011 to improve the fairness of the charge where one unit trust invested in another and some of the underlying investments were themselves exempt from SDRT. However this did nothing to alter the view of the industry that the regime was burdensome and unduly complex. The government accepted this view and the *Sch 19* charge was abolished for surrenders of units on or after 30 March 2014 by *FA 2014, s 114*. This provision led to lively debate in the passage of the Finance Bill through Parliament, the opposition labelling it as a gift to the rich.

Contractual collective investment schemes

12.32 Article 1.3 of Directive 2009/65/EC of the European Parliament and of the Council of 13 July 2009 requires Member States to make provision for the formation of undertakings for collective investment constituted in accordance with contract law. In the UK, the *Collective Investment in Transferable Securities (Contractual Scheme) Regulations 2013* (*SI 2013/1388*) modified the *Financial Services and Markets Act 2000* to allow such 'contractual schemes' to be set up and to be regulated by the Financial Conduct Authority. Contractual schemes are specifically excluded from the *FSMA 2000* definition of unit trusts. Broadly speaking, such schemes are intended to be mechanisms for groups of professional or wealthy investors to hold and manage investments in common. To this end, small retail investors are not permitted to participate directly.

The *Stamp Duty and Stamp Duty Reserve Tax (Collective Investment Schemes) (Exemptions) Regulations 2013* (*SI 2013/1401*) amend *FA 1986, s 90* and *FA 1999, Sch 13* to exempt from SDRT and stamp duty transfers of securities to a contractual scheme in return for units in the scheme, with effect from 28 June 2013. Transfers between entities holding the securities on behalf of the scheme are also exempted from both taxes.

Growth markets

12.33 In an attempt to encourage investment in smaller high-growth companies, *FA 2014, s 115* and *Sch 24* amended *FA 1986, Pt 4* to remove certain securities from the scope of both SDRT and stamp duty. From 28 April 2014, shares and other potentially chargeable securities are outside the charge to these taxes if they are admitted to trading on a recognised growth market but not listed on that or any other market. There is a detailed definition of 'recognised growth market', making it clear that the market must deal primarily with lower capitalisation companies with compound annual growth in revenue or employment of at least 20%. Markets must apply to HMRC for recognition to benefit from this change. There is a list of recognised growth markets at STSM041330 and at www.hmrc.gov.uk/fid/rse-recognised-exchanges.htm, which includes the Alternative Investment Market (AIM) in the UK. A company is 'listed' on a market if it is in the Official List maintained by the authority responsible for financial services in the country in question. In the UK, shares traded on the London Stock Exchange are generally 'listed', but those traded on AIM are not.

Chapter 13

Planning, Pitfalls and Legacy Liabilities

INTRODUCTION

13.1 The complexity and illogicality of stamp tax rules have often been exploited through contrived avoidance arrangements. However, increasing volumes of general and specific anti-avoidance legislation including, in the case of SDLT, the application of the general anti-abuse rule and the requirement to disclose novel planning arrangements, have dramatically reduced the scope for tax mitigation. Planning now is often as much a matter of avoiding unintended and unexpected additional liabilities as reducing the headline tax cost of a transaction.

This chapter draws together thoughts on planning, both to minimise costs and to avoid potential pitfalls arising from all three stamp taxes. It also considers situations in which current liabilities may arise or increase as a consequence of disturbing transactions carried out, or structures adopted, long ago.

References to particular arrangements or structures are included in this chapter purely for illustrative purposes. Their appearance should not be taken as advising that they succeed in reducing liabilities. Some of the arrangements described are believed to have been effective under previous legislation but have subsequently been blocked. It is essential that expert advice be taken before entering into any arrangement to mitigate tax, and no responsibility is accepted for the consequences of any persons acting or failing to act on the basis of the comments or examples in this book.

STAMP DUTY LAND TAX

Planning

13.2 SDLT mitigation has generally involved one or more of four general approaches:

(1) Arrange to have the benefit of a relief or exemption, or a combination of two or more reliefs or exemptions.

Example 13.1—Combining relief and exemption

Charles wishes to buy a house at a cost of £600,000 to give to his nephew Dylan. Charles contracts to buy the house, paying the usual deposit. He then agrees to sell it to Dylan for £1,000. The two purchases (by Charles and by Dylan) are substantially performed and completed at the same time. If the arrangement were effective, the purchase by Charles would be ignored and only the onward sale to Dylan would be subject to SDLT. The consideration for this is below the SDLT threshold, so no tax would be payable. Note that, even if this arrangement might once have worked, it is now blocked by the *FA 2013* changes to *FA 2003, s 45*, see **5.8** et seq.

(2) Avoid transferring land.

This may be achieved either by transferring something else (eg shares in a land-owning company) or by entering into a commercially different transaction.

Example 13.2—Transfer land-owning company

Dale Group plc owns a subsidiary company Hill Ltd which owns a number of valuable commercial properties. It is decided to sell one property. The other properties are transferred out of Hill Ltd to sister company Valley Ltd for cash, and surplus cash is paid out of Hill Ltd to Dale Group plc as a dividend/return of capital. The value of Hill Ltd is now the same as the value of the one remaining property which it holds. Hill Ltd is then sold. The purchaser has to pay stamp duty at 0.5% on the price paid for the shares, rather than SDLT at rates of up to 5% on a land purchase. Note that versions of this planning have been widely used in the past and, in principle, HMRC do not appear to have regarded it as objectionable. However, the specific circumstances of each transaction must be examined in detail to establish whether a version of the planning could be of use.

Example 13.3—Different transaction

Street Ltd owns land ripe for development. Street Ltd's first thought is to sell the land to a developer for onward sale after redevelopment, with a profit-sharing clause in the sale agreement to ensure Street Ltd shares in the benefits of the redevelopment. However, after careful thought, the directors of Street Ltd decide to retain the land for sale directly to the ultimate owner after contracting the development work to the developer. This is, of course, a commercially different transaction, potentially giving Street Ltd greater rewards but exposing the company to greater risks if the redeveloped property cannot be sold at the expected price. However, correctly structured, this could reduce the total SDLT cost by the amount which the developer would otherwise have paid. Care would be needed in structuring and documentation. An attempt to obtain the SDLT benefits of this alternative transaction whilst keeping the commercial effect of a straight sale to the developer is likely to fall foul of anti-avoidance rules.

---

(3) Reduce the value of the land transferred (with most of the consideration paid for something else) – see Example 9.2 for an explanation of a type of planning which may have been used until blocked by *FA 2003, s 75A*.

(4) Arrange to fall within a specific statutory treatment which gives rise to a low or zero SDLT charge.

Example 13.4—PFI relief

Litebuild plc is negotiating with Marsh Education Authority (MEA) to buy a disused school site for housing development. MEA intends to use the sale proceeds to pay part of the cost of rebuilding a college. It is agreed that MEA will grant to Litebuild a 30-year lease of the college site, and Litebuild will grant an underlease back to MEA for two days short of 30 years. Litebuild will rebuild the college, or procure its rebuilding, and will maintain the grounds and fabric of the building during the lease. In return, MEA will transfer the disused school site to Litebuild in part-payment for the rebuilding of the college, will make a one-off initial payment to cover the balance of the rebuilding cost, and will make yearly payments under the lease for the maintenance services. On the face of it, this arrangement could fall within the terms of *FA 2003, Sch 4, para 17* (PFI relief), so that no SDLT would be payable (see **5.17**). The facts outlined here appear readily to fall within the terms of this treatment. The treatment could be available for a transaction starting from a less favourable fact pattern, but it would be important to examine the precise circumstances of the parties and the proposed transactions before there could be any confidence that this would be the case.

13.3 Targeted anti-avoidance legislation and *FA 2003, ss 75A–75C* make it difficult to find 'off the shelf' combinations of these approaches which can be applied to a range of transactions to reduce the SDLT liability below the expected level. New versions of old ideas emerge from time to time, but the DOTAS rules allow HMRC to block them quickly with new legislation when necessary. HMRC now also have the benefit of the general anti-abuse rule in *FA 2013, ss 206–215* to deploy against any unacceptable arrangements which escape more specific anti-avoidance measures, see **9.3**.

13.4 The best approach is probably to have the fullest possible knowledge of the various statutory reliefs, exemptions and treatments which are available, so that these can be applied to each individual transaction in the most favourable way. In virtually every case, it remains essential to consider carefully whether the combination of steps required to complete the transaction bring it within the scope of *FA 2003, ss 75A–75C* (see **9.3** et seq) and whether any disclosure responsibility arises under the DOTAS rules (see **9.26**).

Pitfalls

13.5 At least as important is the need to be aware of the pitfalls waiting to trap the unwary. In relation to SDLT, these arise from current legislation and those listed here are mostly dealt with in more detail elsewhere, as indicated:

- clawback of relief previously claimed, where there is a change of control of a company (**5.29** et seq);
- transfer to a company which is connected with the transferor, but does not fulfil the precise and strict conditions to be treated as in a group with the transferor (**4.29**). Mere common ownership is not enough to qualify for group relief;
- informal arrangements for occupation of a property, which continue for long enough to give rise to a tenancy on which SDLT arises (**6.8** et seq);
- transfer of a lease, when relief was claimed on grant (**6.16**);
- transfer of property by operation of law, especially in non-UK mergers etc, which may still be treated as a transfer for consideration for SDLT purposes (**4.4**);
- withdrawal of cash or other value from a partnership after transfer of property to the partnership from a partner or connected person (**7.17**); and
- timing issues, being unaware of factors which can lead to SDLT becoming payable much earlier than commercial completion of a transaction or can lead to the expiry of time limits to claim relief or deferment of tax earlier than expected (**4.90** et seq; **8.33**).

13.6 In the context of transactions in land as well as other assets, there are also stamp duty pitfalls which arise from legacy structures – that is, structures and arrangements which were put in place in the course of previous tax planning, often many years ago. These may give rise to current liabilities if not dealt with in the correct manner. Examples are described at **13.26** et seq.

STAMP DUTY AND SDRT

13.7 There are no general anti-avoidance rules for stamp duty and SDRT equivalent to *FA 2003, ss 75A–75C* for SDLT. There are specific anti-avoidance rules relating to particular assets and transactions. SDRT is potentially within the DOTAS rules but, at the time of writing (May 2020), no regulations had been issued to activate this. Stamp duty is not within the DOTAS rules, presumably reflecting the fact that it is not strictly speaking a 'tax'.

SDRT planning

13.8 SDRT is only payable on an agreement to transfer chargeable securities. 'Planning' to minimise SDRT usually takes one of three forms, or a combination of them:

(1) minimising the amount of consideration which is subject to tax;

(2) transferring something which is not a chargeable security; or

(3) cancelling the SDRT charge by ensuring a Transfer document is executed and duly stamped (see **12.12**). (In this book, the expression 'Transfer' is capitalised to make it clear that this is a reference to the potentially stampable document.)

13.9 The first approach is mostly of interest for financial market transactions. It commonly involves the use of options and other financial instruments, detailed consideration of which is beyond the scope of this book. However, SDRT is only charged by reference to the value of consideration given in money or money's worth. Therefore, a transfer of valuable securities which is genuinely for zero or low consideration (eg between family members) will attract zero or low SDRT, the market value of the securities themselves being irrelevant. However, if listed securities are transferred to a company with which the transferor is connected a charge will arise based on the higher of: (a) the actual consideration given for the listed securities; and (b) the market value of the listed securities at the time the agreement to transfer is entered into – see **12.9**. Similarly, from the date upon which *Finance Act 2020* receives royal assent, an agreement to transfer unlisted securities to a company with which the transferor is connected, for consideration in 'money or money's worth' some or all of which comprises an issue of shares, is charged to SDRT based on the higher of:

(a) the actual consideration given for the unlisted securities; and

(b) the market value of the unlisted securities at the time the agreement to transfer is entered into – see **12.9**.

13.10 The second approach is also mainly of interest to financial and capital markets, although the risk of transferring securities which are *unintentionally* within the charge to SDRT is a pitfall described at **13.13**. Outside financial and capital markets, it may be possible to achieve SDRT-free transfer of chargeable securities by placing them in some kind of 'wrapper'.

Example 13.5—Chargeable securities in a wrapper

Serena owns 100% of the shares in a valuable UK incorporated company T Ltd (which is unlisted), which she intends to sell to Vera. Serena arranges to set up a Jersey-registered company U Ltd, and she subscribes £100 for 100 shares in the company. Once all formalities for formation of the company and issue of the shares have been completed, Serena sets up a Jersey-registered limited partnership, W LP, with herself and U Ltd as partners. Serena contributes the shares of T Ltd to W LP as partnership capital. This is a transfer for no consideration for stamp duty purposes, and execution of a stock transfer form by Serena is sufficient to cancel any SDRT charge which might otherwise arise. Serena then sells the shares of U Ltd and her interest in W LP to Vera for full value (the same as the value of T Ltd). Although this effectively transfers the shares of T Ltd to Vera, none of the assets actually transferred is within the charge to SDRT. Theoretically, the transfers may be subject to stamp duty but, as none of the assets is located in the UK, it is unlikely to be necessary to stamp the related documents. The benefit is shared with Serena through a price adjustment.

13.11 Alternatively, the nature of the security itself may be chosen to be outside the scope of SDRT.

Example 13.6—Securities outside the scope of SDRT

Yorrick intends to set up a company to manufacture better mousetraps. He anticipates that, within five years, he will be able to sell the successful company to a major manufacturer for a large sum. He therefore chooses to set up a company registered in the Isle of Man but managed and controlled in the UK. For most other tax purposes, this is treated in the same way as a UK incorporated company. But, provided Yorrick does not make the mistake of keeping the company's principal share register in the UK, its shares will remain outside the SDRT net when the time comes to sell.

13.12 In practice, for non-stock market transactions, the third approach (see **13.8**) is normally what automatically happens, and any planning is directed at minimising the stamp duty (see **13.17**).

Example 13.7—Rely on stamp duty definition of consideration

On 1 April 2020, Raj agrees to sell his minority holding of shares in unquoted UK company Courgette Ltd to Petra in exchange for Petra's collection of rare books, valued at £120,000. This agreement gives rise to an SDRT liability of

£600 which is technically payable by 7 May 2020. However, the consideration does not count for stamp duty purposes (see **10.24** et seq) so, provided a stock transfer form is completed no later than 31 March 2026, the SDRT charge will be cancelled. In these circumstances, where there is consideration but it is not consideration chargeable to stamp duty, the stock transfer form is deemed to be 'duly stamped' as soon as it is executed although the certificate on the reverse of the stock transfer form, stating that there is no chargeable consideration, should be completed (see **10.7**). If there is consideration of £1,000 or more which counts for stamp duty purposes such that a liability arises, the form would have to be executed and presented for stamping no later than 31 March 2026 in order to cancel the SDRT charge. It would generally be desirable to do this as soon as possible after 1 April 2020.

SDRT pitfalls

13.13 The main pitfall to be wary of is the risk of a security unintentionally being or becoming a 'chargeable security' and therefore within the SDRT net. The commonest category of chargeable security consists of shares in UK companies. Most loan capital and debt instruments, such as corporate bonds, as well as most shares of non-UK companies are outside the scope of SDRT (see **12.5**). However, bonds and other loan capital may be within the SDRT net if they have certain 'equity-like' characteristics. In particular, any of the four following factors may bring the security into the SDRT net:

(1) A high coupon/interest rate. If the interest rate exceeds 'a reasonable commercial return on the nominal amount of the capital', the security will not qualify for the loan capital exemption from stamp duty meaning that the security would be within the charge to SDRT (although it may still escape under other exemptions). This is often a problem in relation to so-called 'junk bonds', which have a high interest rate to reflect risk. It may be necessary to gather evidence that the interest rate is comparable to that on other publicly traded securities with a similar risk profile, to convince HMRC that the interest rate does not exceed a reasonable commercial return.

Example 13.8—High coupon bond

Ralph and Simon are brothers. Ralph owns all of the shares of travel agent Timeoff plc, a UK company. Timeoff needs additional funds, and Simon agrees to lend £2 million at an annual interest rate of 18%, reflecting perceived risk. The debt is formalised as a two-year bond. After six months, Ralph agrees to buy the bond from Simon for face value. The high interest rate means that the bond may not qualify for the loan capital exemption from stamp duty, and the agreement to transfer may therefore give rise to an SDRT charge of £10,000 (£2 million at 0.5%). The problem may be avoided if Ralph makes a new loan to Timeoff, allowing it to prepay the original bond to Simon – assuming the terms of the bond allow this.

---

(2) A variable interest rate, where the issuer of a debt security has the right to vary the interest rate, including the right to cancel or withhold a payment, or the interest varies in the light of business results or asset values. Note, however, that so-called 'ratchet loans', where the interest rate goes up to reflect increased risk when business results or asset values deteriorate (and/or goes down when values or results improve) may still qualify for exemption. Equally, no problem is caused by the fact that the interest or amount repayable on repayment may vary by reference to the UK Retail Price Index or a similar index.

Example 13.9—Variable interest rate bond

UK company Zebra plc borrows from a private equity firm P (which is also a shareholder) and issues a loan note which pays monthly interest at an annual rate of 3% above Bank of England base rate. The loan note provides that the interest rate will fall to base rate for the year following any year in which Zebra makes a loss but will increase to 6% above base rate for the year following any year in which Zebra makes a pre-tax profit of more than £1 million. No stamp tax consequences arise from the issue of the note. However, two years later, P agrees to sell the loan note to Q, a wealthy individual. The variable interest rate means the loan note will not qualify for the loan capital exemption from stamp duty and is a 'chargeable security' for the purposes of SDRT, so that the purchaser (Q) will be subject to SDRT on the sale price. Assuming it has no features which prevent it from being 'stock or marketable securities', a Transfer document will be subject to stamp duty on the sale price.

---

(3) Right of conversion into shares or other securities, or right to receive shares or securities, for example in lieu of interest. These are often called PIK notes, because interest is or may be 'paid in kind' – that is, paid by the issue of further debt instruments. It is understood however that whilst a right to receive securities in lieu of interest would technically preclude the loan capital exemption from applying to a transfer of the underlying securities (*FA 1986, s 79(5)*) HMRC Stamp Taxes take the view that provided the new securities issued in lieu of interest have identical terms to those of the underlying securities, and would themselves qualify for the loan capital exemption if they were transferred, then the loan capital exemption will apply to the transfer of the underlying securities. It should also be noted that if the security bears interest at an acceptable rate, but the *issuer* has a unilateral right to make interest payments in the form of further securities, and those further securities do not have identical terms of issue as the underlying security, the underlying security is not thereby

prevented from qualifying as loan capital until the issuer exercises that right and commits to making an interest payment in kind. This is because, until that time, the security does not carry a right, exercisable by the holder of the security, of conversion into another security.

Example 13.10—Right to further securities, PIK notes

Yak plc issues five-year loan notes to a consortium of investors. The loan notes provide for yearly payment of interest at 6%, which is considered to be a normal commercial rate, and repayment at par at the end of the term. However, they also give Yak plc the right to make up to two interest payments by issuing further loan notes with a face value equal to the amount of interest due, an interest rate of 10% per year and redeemable at par at the same time as the original notes (a PIK payment). Yak must give three months' notice of intention to make each PIK payment. The 10% notes, if issued, only provide for payment of interest in cash. In all other respects, both kinds of note qualify as exempt loan capital.

No SDRT arises on the issue of the notes. Unless and until Yak gives notice to make a PIK payment, the securities qualify for the loan capital exemption, and transfers in that period should not give rise to any SDRT. However, from the time Yak gives notice until after the PIK payment is actually made, the original securities cease to qualify for the loan capital exemption, and any transfers of those notes will be subject to SDRT. Once the PIK payment is made, the notes again qualify as exempt loan capital, unless or until notice of a further PIK payment is given.

Had the PIK notes been issued on identical terms to those of the original five-year loan notes (ie a 6% rate of interest, a right to make up to two interest payments by issuing further loan notes, etc) then, based on the views of HMRC Stamp Taxes, the loan capital exemption would have continued to be available even after Yak had given notice of the intention to make a PIK payment.

The notes issued in lieu of interest do not carry any PIK option, and so should qualify for the loan capital exemption on any transfers after they are issued, assuming the interest rate is not regarded as excessive.

---

(4) A high premium on repayment – for example, a bond with a face value of £100 is issued at a price of £100 but, at the end of its five-year life, the amount repayable is £160, being the face value plus a premium of £60. Remarkably, the same economic effect may be achieved without risk of falling within the SDRT net, by issuing the bond with a £160 face value but at a £60 discount, so that the amount paid at issue is £100. However, this may affect the treatment of the bond for other purposes.

Any of these characteristics may lead to denial of the loan capital exemption. This is a complex area, and specialist advice is likely to be needed to determine whether SDRT applies to any transfer if these characteristics are present.

13.14 The other main risk is that shares of a non-UK incorporated company, normally outside the SDRT net, will become chargeable securities if they are 'registered in a register kept in the UK' (*FA 1986, s 99(4)(a)*). As suggested at Example 13.6, non-UK incorporated companies (often incorporated in the Channel Islands or the Isle of Man) are widely and validly used by UK-based individuals and businesses. The share register of such a company is normally kept in the territory of incorporation, but a copy may be maintained in the UK for administrative convenience. Care must be taken to ensure that the UK document (or electronic record) is no more than a copy, and that the overseas register is the definitive document for determining the identity of the shareholders. HMRC have been known to examine this matter very closely, with a view to showing that the UK record is a definitive register so that the shares become chargeable securities.

Stamp duty planning

13.15 Stamp duty is currently chargeable only on documents effecting transfers of 'stock and marketable securities' and interests in partnerships owning stock and marketable securities.

13.16 In relation to transfers of partnership interests (in circumstances where the partnership holds stock and marketable securities), the simplest planning is to choose not to present any transfer document for stamping. This is effective provided the parties are satisfied that there is no need for a stamped document. A stamped document is normally only required if it is to be produced in evidence or used for other official purposes. Therefore, the most likely occasions on which a stamped document may be needed are in relation to a dispute between the parties or in order to prove to HMRC that the transfer has taken place. In practice, it appears to be rare for transfers of partnership interests to be stamped. An alternative approach is to structure the transaction so that there is no Transfer document which may require to be stamped. For example, an effective transfer of a partnership interest might be achieved by the outgoing partner withdrawing capital from the partnership, and the incoming partner introducing the same amount of capital. This may be regarded as a transfer for some purposes (including SDLT, where relevant – see **7.25** et seq). However, it should not be necessary to execute a Transfer and no stamp duty liability should arise.

13.17 It is usually only necessary to stamp a transfer document for stock and marketable securities, if they are chargeable securities, so that the SDRT charge is cancelled (see **12.12**) and any registration formalities may be completed.

The simplest form of planning is, therefore, to transfer securities which are not chargeable – for example, shares in a non-UK incorporated company – and then choose not to present the Transfer for stamping (but beware the risk of making them chargeable by keeping the register in the UK). Alternatively, it may be possible either to arrange to fall within the terms of a relief (see **Chapter 11**) or to minimise the consideration which is taken into account, as set out below.

13.18 See **10.26** et seq for discussion of the measurement of consideration for stamp duty purposes. Some planning has taken the form of attempting to make the consideration wholly unascertainable (see **10.37**), but there are risks. In particular, in the case of *L M Tenancies 1 plc v IRC* ([1996] STC 880), HMRC succeeded in arguing that linking consideration to the price of a publicly traded security, when that price was not likely to change much, did not make the consideration wholly unascertainable. It is safer to make the consideration ascertainable but low (see **10.58** et seq).

Stamp duty pitfalls

13.19 A major risk in relation to stamp duty is linked with the SDRT risk identified at **13.13**. Transfers of many shares and securities may theoretically be within the charge to stamp duty but, if the securities are outside the charge to SDRT, there is normally no imperative to stamp the Transfers. If shares or debt instruments unintentionally become chargeable securities, an SDRT charge will arise on an agreement to transfer for valuable consideration. This may be cancelled by stamping a Transfer, but that in itself will require payment of stamp duty unless the Transfer qualifies for a relief. In either case the transfer must be stamped within six years of the agreement to transfer, or it becomes impossible to cancel the SDRT charge (see **12.13**).

13.20 A related difficulty arises where different assets are transferred by means of the same Transfer. This is unlikely to be a problem where UK shares are transferred by means of a stock transfer form, because that form is normally only valid to transfer UK shares. However, where the Transfer takes the form of a declaration of trust (see Example 11.3), it would be possible for a single document to transfer UK and non-UK shares. This should generally be avoided!

Example 13.11—Mixed assets in a single Transfer

Reptile plc, a UK company, agrees to pay market value to buy the shares of two companies, Lizard Ltd and Gecko Ltd, both of which are unquoted, from Reptile's 51% shareholder, Zoo Inc. Lizard is a UK company worth £100,000, Gecko is a Cayman-registered company worth £1 million. The agreement gives rise to an SDRT liability of £500 (£100,000 at 0.5%). Reptile intends immediately to carry out a reorganisation which will involve further transfers of the shares of these companies, so it is agreed that Zoo Inc will execute a declaration of trust in favour of Reptile in relation to the shares. Zoo Inc will then eventually transfer the shares to the final shareholder within Reptile's group. Because Reptile is a UK company and makes payment out of a UK bank account, it is likely that any Transfer will relate to 'any matter or thing to be done' in the UK and so will be liable to stamp duty (see **10.17** et seq). If a single declaration of trust is executed, it will be necessary to pay stamp duty in relation to both the Lizard and the Gecko shares – a total of £5,500 (£1,100,000 at 0.5%) – before the Transfer can be regarded as 'duly stamped' thus cancelling the SDRT charge. To avoid the problem, separate declarations of trust should be completed for the two companies, allowing Reptile to stamp only the one relating to the Lizard shares. Alternatively, the SDRT could be paid on the Lizard shares and the declaration of trust could be left unstamped, but only if Reptile is happy it will never be necessary to produce the declaration of trust for any UK official purpose (see **10.3**).

13.21 Many other risk areas relate to specific reliefs (especially group and reconstruction reliefs), and these are described in relation to those reliefs in **Chapter 11**. It is important to note that the restrictions which may lead to denial of these reliefs only apply at the time of the transaction in respect of which relief is claimed. There is no question of stamp duty reliefs being clawed back as a result of subsequent events, although relief may be denied if there were arrangements for those subsequent events at the time of the original transaction. This is in contrast to the equivalent reliefs under SDLT, where a change in control too soon after the original transaction, even if unrelated to that original transaction, may lead to retrospective disallowance of the relief.

13.22 The other major pitfall in relation to stamp duty concerns the measurement of consideration and, more specifically, the impact of the contingency principle. As noted at **10.39**, under this principle any ascertainable consideration which may be payable on the happening of a particular contingency is regarded as payable and subject to stamp duty. In contrast with SDLT, there is no relief or adjustment if the consideration eventually proves not to be payable.

Example 13.12—Contingency principle

David buys the shares of a trading company from Goliath for consideration of £1 million payable now, plus further consideration equal to 20% of the company's trading profits for the next two years. The further payment is subject to a ceiling of £2 million. Meanwhile, Saul buys a similar company from Goliath for consideration of £1 million, plus 20% of the company's trading profits for the next two years with no ceiling specified. David will have to pay stamp duty of £15,000 (£1 million certain plus £2 million contingent, at 0.5%) but Saul will only have to pay £5,000 (£1 million at 0.5%), because the further consideration is wholly unascertainable.

Unfortunately, there is often a conflict between the desire to minimise stamp duty and the commercial need to limit the contingent consideration. As a result, David's fact pattern is perhaps seen more often than Saul's.

LEGACY LIABILITIES

13.23 When a company or other entity is bought, there is always a risk that the purchased entity has failed to comply with tax obligations and may harbour undisclosed liabilities, including stamp taxes. The purchaser will doubtless minimise the risk by a combination of due diligence investigation and warranties or indemnities. However, unexpected stamp tax liabilities may also arise on purchase of shares or assets, even though the vendor or purchased entity has fully complied with past obligations. This section seeks to highlight the liabilities that may arise.

SDLT

13.24 The acquisition of a company which has claimed group, reconstruction or acquisition reliefs from SDLT may lead to clawback of that group relief, as described at **5.29** et seq.

13.25 Apart from the normal SDLT charge, unexpected SDLT liabilities may also arise on the acquisition of existing leases. The acquisition of an existing lease may be treated as the grant of a new lease if certain reliefs were claimed on original grant of the lease – see **6.17** for details of this.

If the SDLT liability was not determined when a lease was granted (normally because the rent was variable or not finalised at that point), a new tenant taking on the lease may inherit ongoing obligations and liabilities – see **6.37** for details.

Stamp duty

13.26 In past years, stamp duty has been payable on Transfers of many different categories of assets, such as goodwill, intellectual property and, of course, land and buildings. Various structures and strategies were adopted to reduce or avoid this charge. These strategies and structures often merely defer the crystallisation of the charge, until such time as another event occurs.

Stamp duty has been abolished on Transfers of these categories of assets, but that abolition generally only applies to subsequent transactions. Normally, stamp duty remains potentially payable on documents relating to transactions entered into before the time of abolition. It is, therefore, important to understand the old transactions when dealing with the assets in question, in order to avoid having to pay the old stamp duty charges.

Documents executed and retained offshore

13.27 A Transfer of UK situs assets which are within the charge to stamp duty is liable to stamp duty, no matter where executed. However, if the document is executed and retained offshore, payment of any stamp duty may be deferred. This deferral is potentially permanent if the document is never brought to the UK. Alternatively, if it becomes necessary to stamp the document (eg in order to produce it in evidence in a civil court case), no late stamping penalty will be incurred, provided the document is presented for stamping within 30 days of first arrival in the UK. For documents executed before 1 October 1999, no late payment interest is incurred, provided the duty is paid within 30 days of the first arrival of the document in the UK.

For this reason, many transfers of certain types of asset (but not generally shares or registered land) have been executed and retained outside the UK (typically in the Channel Islands or the Isle of Man). Although stamp duty no longer applies to Transfers of such assets, those Transfers executed under the old rules remain subject to whatever stamp duty charge applied at the time of execution. To retain the benefit of not incurring interest and penalties should it eventually be necessary to stamp them, it is important that the documents are not brought to the UK in the meantime.

Shares and land

13.28 Offshore execution has not been widely used in relation to transfers of shares and securities. This is because a duly stamped Transfer is required: (a) for registration of the new owner in the company's books; and (b) since 1986, to cancel the related SDRT charge. For transfers of registered land prior to the introduction of SDLT, a duly stamped transfer was also required to change the owner at the Land Registry, so offshore execution was not appropriate. The alternative approach adopted for land transfers was generally known as 'resting on (or in) contract' or, less commonly, 'split title planning'. It was widely considered that this planning could not be used in Scotland because of differences in land law, although some lawyers maintained that these could be overcome. In an attempt to curtail the planning, any contracts for purchase of land for consideration exceeding £10 million executed after 24 July 2002 were treated as stampable Transfers.

Resting on contract

13.29 Bare legal title to the land was transferred to a nominee who held the land for the benefit of the beneficial owner (for reasons of land law, generally this would be two 'special purpose companies' or SPVs holding as joint trustees). With care, especially in relation to one anti-avoidance provision, such a transfer was liable only to a fixed stamp duty of £5 (50p prior to *FA 1999*). The vendor then entered into a contract to sell the land to the purchaser. The contract entitled the purchaser to call for a Transfer of the land. The purchaser paid the consideration (which gained him a beneficial interest in the land), and the vendor transferred the shares of the SPVs to the purchaser. The purchaser now had a beneficial interest in the land and control of the legal title through ownership of the SPVs which held title. This was generally accepted as equivalent to full legal and beneficial ownership. However, because no Transfer had been executed to transfer title to the purchaser, the purchase contract remained technically uncompleted and virtually no stamp duty had been paid.

If necessary, the purchaser could subsequently require the SPVs to transfer legal title to him. This Transfer would complete the purchase contract and so would crystallise the stamp duty charge on the original purchase. However, the charge would only crystallise at the date of the Transfer, so interest- and penalty-free deferral would have been achieved. In most cases, title was left in the hands of the SPVs, no Transfer was ever executed, and the stamp duty charge was not crystallised. When the time came for the purchaser to sell the land, the process could be repeated, leaving title in the hands of the same SPVs and transferring the shares in those companies. At that point, it became clear that the first sale and purchase would never be technically completed (because title to the land would never be transferred to the original purchaser), so the deferral of stamp duty on that original purchase would become permanent. This could be repeated many times on successive sales and purchases of the land. However, it would always be the case that the stamp duty on the latest sale and purchase in the sequence was merely deferred. That latest stamp duty charge would become payable if the latest purchase was completed by Transfer of legal title from the SPVs to the current beneficial owner.

Therein lies the danger. There may still be properties held in this 'split title' structure. If the structure is collapsed by transferring title from the SPVs to the beneficial owner, any deferred stamp duty on acquisition by the current beneficial owner will become payable. To avoid this problem, the structure must be maintained at least until the next time ownership of the land is transferred. The structure is not effective for saving SDLT, and so may as well be collapsed when a sale is entered into which is subject to SDLT, provided this can be done without also crystallising any old stamp duty charges. To achieve this, it is important that title is transferred directly from the SPVs to the purchaser under the contract which is subject to SDLT. Title must not first be transferred to the vendor under this latest contract.

Example 13.13—Completion of 'resting on contract' transaction

In 1971, Oldmoney Ltd purchased a prime city centre office building from Armateur Ltd for £2 million. The purchase was effected by the 'resting on contract' scheme – so the parties entered into a sale and purchase contract, Oldmoney paid the purchase price and Armateur transferred to Oldmoney the shares of two Jersey-registered SPVs (S1 and S2) which jointly held legal title to the land. No Transfer was completed in conformity with the contract and no stamp duty was paid. At the time, the rate of stamp duty was 2%, so duty of £40,000 was effectively deferred.

On 1 April 2020, Oldmoney contracts to sell the property to Newrich Ltd for £80 million. Newrich will pay SDLT of £3,989,500 (£150,000 at 0%, £100,000 at 2% and £79,750,000 at 5%) on the purchase. The contract provides that Oldmoney will convey the property to Newrich, and Newrich refuses to accept a conveyance from S1 and S2. The property is therefore first conveyed from S1 and S2 to Oldmoney. This crystallises the stamp duty charge deferred in 1971, and Oldmoney has to pay this before completing the onward conveyance to Newrich. Had Newrich accepted the conveyance direct from S1 and S2, the 1971 deferral of stamp duty would have become permanent and Oldmoney would have been spared the need to pay it. Under either scenario, beneficial and legal ownership of the property are reunited, whether in the hands of Oldmoney or directly in Newrich.

A potentially interesting subsidiary point arises. Stamp duty rates have increased since 1997 to a current maximum of 4% but, at each increase, the old rates have been retained for contracts already signed but uncompleted. So, there should be no risk of the increased rates applying on completion of Oldmoney's original purchase. For a brief period between 1 August 1972 and 30 April 1974, rates were reduced, and the reduction also applied to any contracts signed but uncompleted at the start of the period. This means that it should be possible to argue that if the original Oldmoney purchase is completed as noted above, the stamp duty payable should be reduced to £20,000 (£2 million at 1%, being the rate introduced from 1972). HMRC may not agree.

Avoiding a document; the memorandum rule

13.30 The practice of 'resting on contract' described above was really just a specific example of this general principle: because stamp duty is chargeable on certain documents, no stamp duty is payable if no Transfer document (or document which is deemed to be a Transfer) is created. It was the development of share transfers without a Transfer document which led to the introduction of SDRT. SDLT was introduced because avoidance of stamp duty on property transactions was widespread, much of it historically by resting on contract. It was also often possible to avoid a liability on transfers of other assets such as goodwill, intellectual property and interests in partnerships by avoiding creation of the wrong type of document. For such assets, there is generally no legal requirement for a Transfer document in a particular form; compliance with the terms of the contract itself (eg making payment) usually gives effect to the transfer. This means the contract itself was usually the document liable to stamp duty. To avoid stamp duty, it was necessary to avoid creating a written contract. The normal approach was for the vendor to make a written offer to sell to the purchaser. The purchaser accepted the offer by his action – paying the purchase price to the vendor's solicitors, for example – and not by anything in writing. In some cases, the purchaser accepted orally, the acceptance being video-recorded and given in front of reliable witnesses!

13.31 In relation to transactions of this kind, HMRC (relying on cases such as *Associated British Engineering Ltd v IRC* ([1941] 1 KB 15) considered that any document which recorded the agreement in such a way as to become a primary record of the contract was subject to stamp duty. On this basis, any memorandum which the purchaser prepared to record the terms could be subject to stamp duty, even if prepared purely for internal purposes and a long time after the original transaction. Of course, this was only relevant if there was a need to produce such documents for official purposes – but that included proving the terms of the contract to HMRC for other tax purposes!

As time passes, it becomes less likely that any such memoranda will be created or required for official purposes. However, taxpayers who were purchasers under such undocumented contracts should continue to think carefully before 'tidying up' old arrangements by creating written records for posterity.

Last word

13.32 The idea of countering 'tax avoidance' has great popular appeal. However, in relation to stamp taxes as other taxes, much 'planning' consists of trying to ensure complex rules do not give rise to commercially damaging liabilities. Stamp taxes are very different from taxes on income and profits and are often encountered only occasionally. As a result, the risk of accidental and unforeseen liabilities is high. It is hoped that this book may help reduce that risk.

Appendix A

Addresses, Contact Details, etc

SDLT RETURNS

If SDLT returns are not filed electronically, original paper returns and any accompanying cheques should be sent to HMRC at:

BT Stamp Duty Land Tax
HM Revenue and Customs
BX9 1LT
United Kingdom

Returns should not be folded and therefore require an A4 or larger size envelope. Only forms SDLT 1 to 4, plus plans if provided and cheques if that payment method is to be used, should be included – correspondence should be sent to the Stamp Duty Land Tax Office as noted below (see **8.8**).

In case of postal delay, the recommendation is that at least three working days are allowed for the return to reach HMRC. If you are paying SDLT by CHAPS, and you are making a single payment to cover a number of transactions, you should first contact HMRC's Shipley Accounts Office on 0843 504 0633. The address of the Shipley office is as follows:

HM Revenue and Customs
Shipley
BX5 5BD
United Kingdom

DOTAS FORMS

Paper copies of forms relating to DOTAS (see **9.26**) may be ordered from the Anti-Avoidance Group on 03000 588 993, but they may be more conveniently downloaded from www.gov.uk/guidance/forms-to-disclose-tax-avoidance-schemes, or completed online following links from that webpage. If not completed and submitted online, completed DOTAS forms must be sent to:

HM Revenue and Customs – Counter Avoidance
DOTAS Taskforce S0483
Newcastle upon Tyne
NE98 1ZZ
United Kingdom

OTHER FORMS AND LEAFLETS

Paper copies of other forms and explanatory leaflets may be ordered from the HMRC publications department. The postal address is PO Box 37, St Austell PL25 5YN, but HMRC strongly prefer requests to be made online using the form at www.hmrc.gov.uk/contactus/staustellform.htm or by phone to 0300 200 3511.

SCOTTISH TRANSACTIONS

As SDLT ceased to apply in relation to transactions over land situated in Scotland, with effect from 1 April 2015, an SDLT5 certificate will only be relevant for such a transaction with an effective date on or after that date if, unusually, the transaction remains liable to SDLT under the transitional provisions (see **2.19** et seq). If the SDLT return is filed online then it should be possible to print an SDLT5 straightaway. If a paper return has been filed then HMRC will send the SDLT5 by post. The SDLT5 should then be sent to the Registers of Scotland to register the transaction.

OTHER CORRESPONDENCE IN RELATION TO SDLT

All other correspondence for HMRC in relation to SDLT must be sent to the Stamp Duty Land Tax Office. The address is:

BT – Stamp Duty Land Tax
HM Revenue and Customs
[Reference]
BX9 1HD
United Kingdom

An appropriate reference or other description should be inserted in place of '[Reference]', as noted in the table below, to ensure that the correspondence is directed to the right section.

However payments of SDLT should not be sent to this office.

CORRESPONDENCE IN RELATION TO STAMP DUTY AND SDRT

Correspondence for HMRC in relation to stamp duty and SDRT should be sent to HMRC Birmingham Stamp Office at the following address:

HM Revenue and Customs – Birmingham Stamp Office
[Reference]
9th Floor, City Centre House
30 Union Street
Birmingham
B2 4AR
United Kingdom

Fax 03000 570 316

Telephone 0300 200 3510 (if outside the UK +44 1726 209 042)

An appropriate reference or other description should be inserted in place of '[Reference]', as noted in the table below, to ensure that the correspondence is directed to the right section:

Purpose of correspondence	**[Reference]**	**Paragraphs in this book; notes**
Submission of further information at same time as SDLT return is submitted*	SDLT (return, further information)	**8.47**
Amendment of SDLT return; submission of further return after ordinary return was submitted for original transaction*	SDLT amended/ further return	**8.17**
Advice on format of schedules listing multiple properties	Complex Transactions Unit	**8.26**
Application for deferment of SDLT	SDLT Deferment Application	**8.33**

Purpose of correspondence	**[Reference]**	**Paragraphs in this book; notes**
Claim for relief from excessive SDLT assessment, after normal period to amend return has expired*	SDLT Excessive Assessment claim	**8.51**
Submission of documents for routine stamping, including provisional stamping or 'wait and see' cases	Stamp Duty section	**10.42–10.45** If same-day stamping required, call 0300 200 3510 (outside the UK +44 1726 209 042) first
Submission of documents for adjudication, including claims to relief where adjudication is compulsory	Stamp Duty section (adjudication, *insert reference to the relief, eg Group Relief*)	**10.48**; **11.7**
Claim for repayment of stamp duty	Stamp Duty section (repayment claim)	**10.54**
Payment of bearer instrument duty	Stamp Duty Section (bearer instruments)	**10.56**
Enquiry as to status of foreign entity; enquiry/claim to be recognised as an Intermediary	Stamp Duty Section (Technical)	**11.8**; **11.37**; **12.23**
Notifying and paying SDRT (other than Financial Markets transactions)	SDRT	**12.10**

* UTRN of original return must be quoted in the heading to the letter; see **8.7**.

SAME-DAY STAMPING

In exceptional circumstances it may be essential to have documents relating to transfers of shares and securities stamped on the day of execution, or very rapidly afterwards (see **10.45**). HMRC may agree to arrange this but only if they are convinced it is absolutely necessary. It must be arranged in advance by writing to the Birmingham Stamp Office same-day stamping service or, in exceptional circumstances by calling 0300 200 3510.

THE STAMP TAX HELPLINE

HMRC assert that answers to most stamp tax questions can be found on their website, starting from www.hmrc.gov.uk/so. Although most information probably is on the website, it can be frustratingly difficult to find; where possible, this book gives addresses of appropriate pages. Furthermore, the website does not (and realistically cannot) deal with all technical nuances arising from real-life transactions. A telephone enquiry line is provided on 0300 200 3510 and the fax number is 03000 570 316. Unfortunately, like so many 'enquiry' numbers, this is answered by a recorded voice offering a limited range of menu options. If you do get through to a human being, he/she is not likely to be a technical expert and is unlikely to provide definitive answers to difficult questions. However, with persistence, it is possible to have questions referred to such experts who, in the author's experience, are generally helpful. If you obtain a name, it is possible to contact the person by email – HMRC email addresses are in the form firstname.lastname@hmrc.gov.uk.

TAX PAYMENTS

Cheques should be made payable to 'HM Revenue and Customs only' (*insert name of tax, eg SDLT*). For SDLT, the UTRN of the return to which the payment relates should be added to the payee line. However, for all three taxes, HMRC prefer electronic payment, either by Faster Payments, CHAPS, Bacs or by online debit or corporate credit card. HMRC maintain different bank accounts for the different taxes. Bank account details (including SWIFT codes and IBAN numbers for payments from outside the UK) may be found via links at www.hmrc.gov.uk/payinghmrc. The bank accounts have changed in recent years, so it is worth checking to ensure that current details are used (to avoid possibly being out of date, the details are deliberately not reproduced here). If payments are made electronically, it is important to quote an appropriate reference. For SDLT, this is the UTRN which appears on the paper return and payslip (see **8.7**) or on the electronic SDLT5 issued where returns are submitted online (see **8.11**). For stamp duty and SDRT, taxpayers may create their own reference numbers, but these should be quoted on the physical documents submitted for stamping or other correspondence, so that HMRC can easily link the payment to the document. HMRC suggest that taxpayers could use their name followed by the amount of the tax being paid with no spaces. For example: JBrown/250.00.

THE TRIBUNAL SERVICE

It is unlikely to be necessary to contact the Tribunal Service unless a matter is already in dispute with HMRC and under appeal – in which case, HMRC should provide appropriate contact details. The general address for correspondence, or to obtain a paper form for an appeal to the First-tier Tribunal is noted below. Forms and related information are available from the website.

First-tier Tribunal (Tax Chamber)
HM Courts & Tribunals Service
PO Box 16972
Birmingham
B16 6TZ

Telephone 0300 123 1024

Email: taxappeals@justice.gov.uk

Website: www.gov.uk/tax-tribunal

Appendix B

Sample Forms, etc

PART 1 – SDLT RETURN FORMS

HM Revenue & Customs

Land Transaction Return

For official use only

Your transaction return

How to fill in this return

The guidance notes that come with this return will help you to answer the questions.

- Write inside the boxes. Use black ink and capital letters.
- If you make a mistake, cross it out and write the correct information underneath.
- **Leave blank any boxes that don't apply to you** – please don't strike through anything irrelevant.
- Show amounts in whole pounds only, rounded down to the nearest pound. Ignore the pence.
- Fill out the payslip on page 7.
- Do not fold the return. Send it back to us unfolded in the envelope provided.
- **Photocopies are not acceptable.**

If you need help with any part of this return or with anything in the guidance notes, phone the Stamp Taxes Helpline on **0845 603 0135**, open 8.30am to 5.00pm Monday to Friday, except bank holidays. You can get further copies of this return and any supplementary returns from the orderline on **0845 302 1472**.

Online filing is quicker and easier. Find out more at **www.hmrc.gov.uk/sdlt**

Starting your return

ABOUT THE TRANSACTION

1 **Type of property**

Enter code from the guidance notes

If entering 02 or 03, make sure you complete form SDLT4 and box 72 of this form

2 **Description of transaction**

Enter code from the guidance notes

3 **Interest transferred or created**

Enter code from the guidance notes

4 **Effective date of transaction**

D D M M Y Y Y Y

5 **Any restrictions, covenants or conditions affecting the value of the interest transferred or granted?**
Put 'X' in one box

Yes No

If 'Yes' provide details

6 **Date of contract or conclusion of missives**

D D M M Y Y Y Y

7 **Is any land exchanged or part-exchanged?**
Put 'X' in one box

Yes No

If 'Yes' complete address of location

Postcode

House or building number

Rest of address, including building name

8 **Is the transaction pursuant to a previous option agreement?** Put 'X' in one box

Yes No

SDLT1 v2 PAGE 1 HMRC 01/11

ABOUT THE TAX CALCULATION

9 **Are you claiming relief?** Put 'X' in one box

☐ Yes ☐ No

If 'Yes' show the reason

☐☐ Enter code from the guidance notes

Enter the charity's registered number, if available, or the company's CIS number

For relief claimed on part of the property only, enter the amount remaining chargeable

£ . 0 0

10 **What is the total consideration in money or money's worth, including any VAT actually payable for the transaction notified?**

£ . 0 0

11 **If the total consideration for the transaction includes VAT, state the amount**

£ . 0 0

12 **What form does the consideration take?**
Enter the relevant code(s) from the guidance notes

13 **Is this transaction linked to any other(s)?**
Put 'X' in one box

☐ Yes ☐ No

Total consideration or value in money or money's worth, including VAT paid for all of the linked transactions

£ . 0 0

14 **Total amount of tax due for this transaction**

£ . 0 0

15 **Total amount paid or enclosed with this notification**

£ . 0 0

Does the amount paid include payment of any penalties and any interest due? Put 'X' in one box

☐ Yes ☐ No

ABOUT LEASES

If this doesn't apply, go straight to box 26 on page 3.

16 **Type of lease**

☐ Enter code from the guidance notes

17 **Start date as specified in lease**

D D M M Y Y Y Y

18 **End date as specified in lease**

D D M M Y Y Y Y

19 **Rent-free period**
Number of months

20 **Annual starting rent inclusive of VAT actually payable**

£ . 0 0

End date for starting rent

D D M M Y Y Y Y

Later rent known? Put 'X' in one box

☐ Yes ☐ No

21 **What is the amount of VAT, if any?**

£ . 0 0

22 **Total premium payable**

£ . 0 0

23 **Net present value upon which tax is calculated**

£ . 0 0

24 **Total amount of tax due - premium**

£ . 0 0

25 **Total amount of tax due - NPV**

£ . 0 0

Check the guidance notes to see if you will need to complete supplementary return SDLT4 *Additional details about the transaction, including leases.*

SDLT1 v2 PAGE 2

ABOUT THE LAND including buildings

Where more than one piece of land is being sold please complete the supplementary return SDLT3 or SDLT4 (for leases or assignments)

26 **Number of properties included**

27 **Where more than one property is involved, do you want a certificate for each property?** Put 'X' in one box

Yes No

28 **Address or situation of land**

Postcode

House or building number

Rest of address, including building name (continue on SDLT3)

Is the address continued on SDLT3? Put 'X' in one box

Yes No

29 **Local authority number**

30 **Title number, if any**

31 **NLPG UPRN**

32 **If agricultural or development land, what is the area (if known)?** Put 'X' in one box

Hectares Square metres

Area

33 **Is a plan attached?** Put 'X' in one box Note: the UTRN should be written on the plan

Yes No

ABOUT THE VENDOR including transferor, lessor

34 **Number of vendors included.** Note: if more than one vendor is involved complete boxes 45 to 48, and for three or more vendors complete SDLT2 for each one

35 **Title** Enter MR, MRS, MISS, MS or other title Note: only complete for an individual

36 **Vendor (1) surname or company name**

37 **Vendor (1) first name(s)** Note: only complete for an individual

38 **Vendor (1) address**

Postcode

House or building number

Rest of address, including building name

39 **Agent's name**

SDLT1 v2 PAGE 3

ABOUT THE VENDOR continued

40 **Agent's address**

Postcode

Building number

Rest of address, including building name

41 **Agent's DX number and exchange**

42 **Agent's email address**

43 **Agent's reference**

44 **Agent's phone number**

ADDITIONAL VENDOR

Details of other people involved (including transferor, lessor), other than vendor (1). If more than one additional vendor complete supplementary return SDLT2 *Land Transaction Return - Additional vendor/purchaser details.*

45 **Title** Enter MR, MRS, MISS, MS or other title

Note: only complete for an individual

46 **Vendor (2) surname or company name**

47 **Vendor (2) first name(s)**

Note: only complete for an individual

48 **Vendor (2) address**

Put 'X' if the same as box 38. If not, give address below

Postcode

House or building number

Rest of address, including building name

ABOUT THE PURCHASER including transferee, lessee

49 **National Insurance number of purchaser (1)**

If there is no National Insurance number you must complete boxes 50 or 51 of this form

Date of birth of purchaser (1)

D D M M Y Y Y Y

50 **If purchaser (1) is VAT registered, give their VAT Registration Number**

51 **If purchaser (1) is a UK company you must provide a UK company or partnership UTR number**

If purchaser (1) has no UK reference, give a tax reference from the country in which purchaser (1) is based

Enter the name of the country (see guidance notes)

SDLT1 v2 PAGE 4

ABOUT THE PURCHASER continued

52 **Number of purchasers included.** Note: if more than one purchaser is involved complete boxes 67 to 71, and for three or more purchasers complete an SDLT2 for each one

53 **Title** Enter MR, MRS, MISS, MS or other title
Note: only complete for an individual

54 **Purchaser (1) surname or company name**

55 **Purchaser (1) first name(s)**
Note: only complete for an individual

56 **Purchaser (1) address**

Put 'X' if the same as box 28. If not, give address below

Postcode

House or building number

Rest of address, including building name

57 **Is the purchaser acting as a trustee?** Put 'X' in one box

Yes No

58 **Give a daytime phone number** - this will help us if we need to contact you about your return

59 **Are the purchaser and vendor connected?**
Put 'X' in one box

Yes No

60 **To which address shall we send the certificate?**
Put 'X' in one box

Property (box 28) Purchaser's (box 56)

Agent's (box 63)

61 **I authorise my agent to handle correspondence on my behalf.** Put 'X' in one box

Yes No

62 **Agent's name**

63 **Agent's address**
Postcode

Building number

Rest of address, including building name

64 **Agent's DX number and exchange**

65 **Agent's reference**

66 **Agent's phone number**

SDLT1 v2 PAGE 5

ADDITIONAL PURCHASER

Details of other people involved (including transferee, lessee), other than purchaser (1). If more than one additional purchaser, complete supplementary return SDLT2 *Land Transaction Return - Additional vendor/purchaser details.*

67 **Title** Enter MR, MRS, MISS, MS or other title
Note: only complete for an individual

68 **Purchaser (2) surname or company name**

69 **Purchaser (2) first name(s)**
Note: only complete for an individual

70 **Purchaser (2) address**

Put 'X' if the same as box 56. If not, give address below

Postcode

House or building number

Rest of address, including house name, building name or flat number

71 **Is purchaser (2) acting as a trustee?** Put 'X' in one box

Yes No

ADDITIONAL SUPPLEMENTARY RETURNS

72 **How many supplementary returns have you enclosed with this return?**
Answer in respect of the SDLT2, SDLT3 and SDLT4 returns you have enclosed. If none, please put '0'

SDLT2 - Additional vendor/purchaser details

SDLT3 - Additional details about the land

SDLT4 - Additional details about purchaser (1) and the transaction, including leases

DECLARATION

73 **The purchaser(s) must sign this return.** Read the guidance notes in booklet SDLT6, in particular the section headed *'Who should complete and sign the Land Transaction Return?'*

If you give false information, you may face financial penalties and prosecution.
The information I have given on this return is correct and complete to the best of my knowledge and belief.

Signature of purchaser 1

Signature of purchaser 2

Please keep a copy of this return and a note of the unique transaction reference number, which is in the 'Reference' box on the payslip.

Finally, send your completed return to:
HMRC Stamp Taxes/SDLT, Comben House, Farriers Way, Netherton, Merseyside, Great Britain, L30 4RN,
or the DX address is: Rapid Data Capture Centre, DX725593, Bootle 9.

Please don't fold it - keep it flat and use the envelope provided. Fill out the payslip on the next page and pay in accordance with the 'Paying HMRC' instructions.

Paying HMRC

Secure and efficient ways to pay

Make sure you pay by the deadline.

Bank details for online or telephone banking, CHAPS, Bacs
You can make a transfer from your bank account by Faster Payments, CHAPS or Bacs. Use sort code 08-32-10, account number 12001020, account name 'HMRC Shipley' followed by the reference on the payslip.

By debit or credit card online
Go to www.gov.uk/pay-tax-debit-credit-card and follow the instructions.

At your bank or building society
Take your payslip to your branch and pay by cash or cheque.

Make cheques payable to 'HM Revenue and Customs only' followed by the reference on the payslip.

At the Post Office
Take your payslip to any participating Post Office and pay by debit card, cash or cheque made payable to 'Post Office Ltd'.

Payment questions?

For further payment information, go to www.gov.uk/dealing-with-hmrc/paying-hmrc

Other ways to pay

By cheque through the post
Make your cheque payable to 'HM Revenue and Customs only' followed by the reference on the payslip. Send your payslip and cheque to:
HM Revenue and Customs SDLT
NETHERTON
Merseyside
L30 4RN

Don't fold either the payslip or the cheque or fasten them together. A stamp for the correct postage is required.

By DX
As above, but send to:
HMRC SDLT
Rapid Data Capture Centre
DX725593
Bootle 9

5014538 HMRC 09/15

Please do not write or mark below this perforation

Santander Corporate & Commercial Bootle Merseyside L30 4UA | Trans cash | **Payslip** | HM Revenue & Customs | **bank giro credit** | **ABC**

159

24

Reference 311785749MG

Credit account number 225 0357

Amount due (no fee payable at PO counter) £

CHEQUE ACCEPTABLE

For official use

Name

Cashier's stamp and initials

Signature

Date

For official use

Barclays Bank Plc
Automated Bulk Credit Clearing
HM Revenue and Customs
Account number 63464695
11-47

CASH

CHEQUE

£

25-03-57

SDLT1/P HMRC 09/15

Please do not fold this payslip or write or mark below this line

311785749MG &7242250357 000000000 74 X

HM Revenue & Customs

Land Transaction Return

Additional vendor/purchaser details

When to fill in this return

You must fill in this return for each additional vendor and/or purchaser. The guidance notes will help you answer the questions.

If you need help with any part of this return or with anything in the guidance notes, please phone the Stamp Taxes enquiry line on **0300 200 3510**. For our opening hours go to **www.hmrc.gov.uk/contactus**
You can get further copies of this return from the Orderline on **0300 200 3511**.

Reference

Insert the reference number from the payslip on page 7 of the Land Transaction Return, SDLT1, here.

For official use only

Vendor or Purchaser

1 **Please indicate if this return is for an additional vendor or an additional purchaser.** Put 'X' in one box

Vendor Complete section below only

Purchaser Complete section below and the section over the page

Complete in all cases

2 **Title** Enter Mr, Mrs, Miss, Ms or other title
Note: only complete for an individual

3 **Surname or company name**

4 **First name(s)**
Note: only complete for an individual

5 **Address**
Postcode

House or building number

Rest of address, including house name, building name or flat number

Please turn over for additional purchaser details

Additional purchaser details

Only complete this section if this return is for an additional purchaser.

6 **Are the purchaser and vendor connected?**
Put 'X' in one box

Yes No

7 **Is the purchaser acting as a trustee?** Put 'X' in one box

Yes No

8 **Declaration**
The purchaser(s) must sign this return.
Read the notes in Section 1 of the guidance notes, 'SDLT6 Who should complete the Land Transaction Return'

If you give false information, you may face financial penalties and prosecution.

The information I have given on this form is correct and complete to the best of my knowledge and belief.

Signature of purchaser

SDLT2 v3 PG 2

HM Revenue & Customs

Land Transaction Return

Additional vendor/purchaser details

When to fill in this return

You must fill in this return for each additional vendor and/or purchaser. The guidance notes will help you answer the questions.

If you need help with any part of this return or with anything in the guidance notes, please phone the Stamp Taxes enquiry line on **0300 200 3510**. For our opening hours go to **www.hmrc.gov.uk/contactus**

You can get further copies of this return from the Orderline on **0300 200 3511**.

Reference

Insert the reference number from the payslip on page 7 of the Land Transaction Return, SDLT1, here.

For official use only

Vendor or Purchaser

1 **Please indicate if this return is for an additional vendor or an additional purchaser.** Put 'X' in one box

Vendor Complete section below only

Purchaser Complete section below and the section over the page

Complete in all cases

2 **Title** Enter Mr, Mrs, Miss, Ms or other title
Note: only complete for an individual

3 **Surname or company name**

4 **First name(s)**
Note: only complete for an individual

5 **Address**
Postcode

House or building number

Rest of address, including house name, building name or flat number

Please turn over for additional purchaser details

Additional purchaser details

Only complete this section if this return is for an additional purchaser.

6 **Are the purchaser and vendor connected?**
Put 'X' in one box

Yes No

7 Is **the purchaser acting as** a **trustee?** Put 'X' in one box

Yes No

8 **Declaration**
The purchaser(s) must sign this return.
Read the notes in Section 1 of the guidance notes, 'SDLT6 Who should complete the Land Transaction Return'

If you give false information, you may face financial penalties and prosecution.

The information I have given on this form is correct and complete to the best of my knowledge and belief.

Signature of purchaser

SDLT2 v3 PG 2

SCHEDULE 1

Regulation 2(7)

ADDITIONAL DETAILS ABOUT LAND

HM Revenue & Customs

Land Transaction Return

Additional details about the land

When to fill in this return

Fill in this return when you cannot fit all the details on the main Land Transaction Return, SDLT1. The guidance notes will help you to answer the questions.

If you need help with any part of this return or with anything in the guidance notes, please phone the Stamp Taxes Helpline on 0300 200 3510. For our opening hours go to www.gov.uk/hmrc/contact

You can get further copies of this return from the orderline on 0300 200 3511.

REFERENCE

Insert the reference number from the payslip on page 7 of the Land Transaction Return, SDLT1, here.

For official use only

ABOUT THE LAND

1 **Type of property**

Enter code from the guidance notes

2 **Local authority number**

3 **Title number, if any**

4 **NLPG UPRN**

5 **Address or situation of land**

Postcode

House or building number

Rest of address, including house name, building name, flat number or continuation from the SDLT1

Is this a continuation of the address in box 28 of the SDLT1 return

Yes No

6 **If agricultural or development land, what is the area (if known)?**

Hectares Square metres

Area

7 **Are there are any mineral or mineral rights reserved or excluded?**

Yes No

8 **Is a plan attached?** Put 'X' in one box
Note: the UTRN should be written on the plan

Yes No

9 **Interest transferred or created**

Enter code from the guidance notes

SDLT3 v4 PAGE 1 5014135 HMRC 09/18

THIS PAGE IS INTENTIONALLY BLANK

SDLT3 v4 PAGE 2

SCHEDULE 2

Regulation 2(8)

ADDITIONAL DETAILS ABOUT THE TRANSACTION, INCLUDING LEASES

HM Revenue & Customs

Land Transaction Return

Additional details about the transaction, including leases

When to fill in this return

You must fill in this return where additional information about the transaction and/or lease can be provided. The guidance notes will help you to answer the questions.

If you need help with any part of this return or with anything in the guidance notes, please phone the Stamp Taxes Helpline on 0300 200 3510. For our opening hours go to www.gov.uk/hmrc/contact

You can get further copies of this return from the orderline on 0300 200 3511.

REFERENCE

Insert the reference number from the payslip on page 7 of the Land Transaction Return, SDLT1, here.

For official use only

ABOUT THE TRANSACTION

1 **If this transaction is part of the sale of business, what does the sale include?**
Put 'X' in relevant boxes

Stock   Goodwill

Other   Chattels and moveables

What is the total amount of the consideration for the sale of the business apportioned to these items?

£ . 0 0

2 **If the property is for commercial use, what is it?**
Put 'X' in the appropriate box(es)

Office

Hotel

Shop

Warehouse

Factory

Other

Other industrial unit

3 **Have you applied for a ruling under CAP1 or non-statutory business clearance (NSBC) in relation to this transaction?**
Put 'X' in one box

Yes   No

If 'Yes' have you followed it when completing this return?
Put 'X' in one box

Yes   No   Ruling not received

4 **Is any part of the consideration contingent or dependent on uncertain future events?**

Yes   No

5 **Are you applying for deferment?**

Yes   No

6 **Are there any mineral or mineral rights reserved or excluded?**

Yes   No

7 **Give a description of the purchaser(s)**
Enter code from the guidance notes

SDLT4 v5   PAGE 1   5014146   HMRC 09/18

ABOUT LEASES

Complete if the transaction notified on SDLT1 is for the grant of more than one lease

8 **Type of property**

Enter code from the guidance notes

9 **Address or situation of land**

Put 'X' in this box if the same as box 28 on SDLT1

If not, give address below

Postcode

House or building number

Rest of address, including house name, building name, flat number or continuation from the SDLT1

10 **Local authority number**

11 **Title number, if any**

12 **NLPG UPRN**

13 **If the transaction is for land, what is the unit and area of measurement?** Put 'X' in one box

Hectares Square metres

Area

14 **Is a plan attached?** Put 'X' in one box

Note: the UTRN should be written on the plan

Yes No

15 **Interest transferred or created**

Enter code from the guidance notes

16 **Type of lease**

Enter code from the guidance notes

17 **Start date as specified in lease**

D D M M Y Y Y Y

18 **End date as specified in lease**

D D M M Y Y Y Y

19 **Rent-free period**

Number of months

20 **Annual starting rent inclusive of VAT actually payable**

£ . 0 0

End date for starting rent

D D M M Y Y Y Y

Later rent known? Put 'X' in one box

Yes No

21 **What is the amount of VAT, if any?**

£ . 0 0

22 **Total premium payable**

£ . 0 0

23 **Net present value upon which tax is calculated**

£ . 0 0

24 **Total amount of tax due – premium**

£ . 0 0

25 **Total amount of tax due – NPV**

£ . 0 0

SDLT4 v5 PAGE 2

PART 2 – DOTAS FORMS

HM Revenue & Customs Home Contact HMRC Help

Disclosure Of Avoidance Scheme - form AAG1

*indicates required information

Notification by scheme promoter

This form is for use by a scheme promoter notifying under 1 or both of:

- Section 308, Finance Act 2004
- Regulation 8 of the National Insurance Contributions (Application of Part 7 of the Finance Act 2004) Regulations 2012 (SI 2012/1868)

Guidance on making a disclosure is available in the Anti-Avoidance Group area: http://www.hmrc.gov.uk/aiu/index.htm

Scheme promoter's details

Name of promoter: *

Address line 1: *

Address line 2:

Address line 3:

Postcode:

Email address: *

Telephone number (including STD):

Internal reference number (if applicable):

If there is more than 1 promoter, please add their full name and address in the field below.

Co promoter's details:

Scheme details

Title, if any, of the proposal or arrangements:

Stamp Duty Land Tax schemes
Please tick the box below for Stamp Duty Land Tax (SDLT) avoidance - acquisition of chargeable interest (SI 2005 Number 1868).

☐ SDLT avoidance

Please tick 1 box below to indicate which type of property is the subject of the SDLT arrangement (optional).

☐ Residential property

☐ Non-residential property

☐ Use of property not known or mixed

Inheritance Tax schemes
Please select the hallmark or hallmarks which the disclosure is being made under from the list below. Please note that if you are making the disclosure under one of the two IHT hallmarks you must select which one. If the obligation to notify arose on or before 31 March 2018, you'll need to select 'Inheritance Tax 2011 (SI 2011/170)'. If the obligation to notify arose on or after 1 April 2018, you'll need to select 'Inheritance Tax 2017 (SI 2017/1172)'.

☐ Inheritance Tax 2011 (SI 2011/170)

☐ Inheritance Tax 2017 (SI 2017/1172)

☐ Confidentiality (SI 2006/1543)

☐ Premium Fee (SI 2006/1543)

Income Tax, CT, Capital Gains Tax and NIC schemes
Please tick the box below for the provision under which the disclosure is being made. If more than 1 provision applies, please tick all appropriate boxes.

The National Insurance Contributions (Application of Part 7 of the Finance Act 2004) Regulations 2012 (SI 2012/1868).

☐ National Insurance Contributions (NIC) Avoidance

Income Tax, Corporation Tax, Capital Gains Tax - The Tax Avoidance Schemes (Prescribed Descriptions of Arrangements) Regulations 2006 (SI 2006/1543).

☐ IT, CT, Capital Gains Tax Avoidance

The Annual Tax on Enveloped Dwellings (ATED) Avoidance Schemes (Prescribed Descriptions of Arrangements) Regulations 2013 (SI 2013/2571).

☐ Annual Tax on Enveloped Dwellings avoidance

For Income Tax (IT), Corporation Tax (CT), Capital Gains Tax (CGT) and National Insurance Contributions (NIC) avoidance, please tick the regulation below that applies. Where more than 1 regulation applies, please tick only the main applicable regulation.

☐ Regulation 6: Confidentiality (promoter)

- ▢ Regulation 8: Premium fee
- ▢ Regulation 9: Off market terms
- ▢ Regulation 10: Standardised tax products
- ▢ Regulation 12: Loss schemes
- ▢ Regulation 13: Leasing arrangements
- ▢ Regulation 18: Employment Schemes
- ▢ Regulation 19: Financial Product Schemes

Summary of proposal or arrangements

Summary: *

Summary - continuation:

Please enter an explanation of each element in the proposal or arrangements from which the expected tax and/or NIC advantage arises.

Explanation: *

Explanation - continuation:

Please enter the statutory provisions relevant to those elements of the proposal or arrangements from which the expected tax and/or NIC advantage arises.

Statutory provisions: *

Statutory provisions - continuation:

Declaration

I declare that the information I have given on this form is correct and complete to the best of my knowledge and belief, (please tick the box below).

☐ I agree with the above declaration*

Full name of individual completing* this form:

Capacity in which completed: *

After you click the 'Next' button you will see a preview page summarising the information you have provided. If this page is not displayed, please use the scroll bar to locate any missing or incorrect entries highlighted in red.

Back Next

HM Revenue & Customs Home Contact HMRC Help

Disclosure Of Avoidance Scheme - form AAG2

*indicates required information

Notification by scheme user where offshore promoter does not notify

This form is for use by the user of a scheme notifying under 1 or both of:

- Section 309, Finance Act 2004
- Regulation 10 of the National Insurance Contributions (Application of Part 7 of the Finance Act 2004) Regulations 2012 (SI 2012/1868)

Guidance on making a disclosure is available in the Anti-Avoidance Group area: http://www.hmrc.gov.uk/aiu/index.htm

Scheme user's details

Full name: *

Address line 1: *

Address line 2:

Address line 3:

Postcode:

Email address: *

Telephone number (including STD):

Internal reference number (if applicable):

Unique Taxpayer Reference * (UTR):

Promoter's details

Full name of promoter: *

Address line 1: *

Address line 2:

Address line 3:

Postcode:

Scheme details

Title, if any, of the arrangements:

Stamp Duty Land Tax schemes
Please tick the box below for Stamp Duty Land Tax (SDLT) avoidance - acquisition of chargeable interest (SI 2005 Number 1868).

- ☐ SDLT avoidance

Please tick 1 box below to indicate which type of property is the subject of the SDLT arrangement (optional).

- ☐ Residential property
- ☐ Non-residential property
- ☐ Use of property not known or mixed

Inheritance Tax schemes
Please tick the below box for Inheritance Tax (IHT) avoidance – transfers into trust (SI 2011 Number 170).

- ☐ IHT avoidance

Income Tax, CT, Capital Gains Tax and NIC schemes
Please tick the box below for the provision under which the disclosure is being made. If more than 1 provision applies, please tick all appropriate boxes.

The National Insurance Contributions (Application of Part 7 of the Finance Act 2004) Regulations 2012 (SI 2012/1868).

- ☐ National Insurance Contributions (NIC) Avoidance

Income Tax, Corporation Tax, Capital Gains Tax - The Tax Avoidance Schemes (Prescribed Descriptions of Arrangements) Regulations 2006 (SI 2006/1543).

- ☐ IT, CT, Capital Gains Tax Avoidance

The Annual Tax on Enveloped Dwellings (ATED) Avoidance Schemes (Prescribed Descriptions of Arrangements) Regulations 2013 (SI 2013/2571).

- ☐ Annual Tax on Enveloped Dwellings avoidance

For Income Tax (IT), Corporation Tax (CT), Capital Gains Tax (CGT) and National Insurance Contributions (NIC) avoidance, please tick the regulation below that applies. Where more than 1 regulation applies, please tick only the main applicable regulation.

- ▢ Regulation 6: Confidentiality (promoter)
- ▢ Regulation 8: Premium fee
- ▢ Regulation 9: Off market terms
- ▢ Regulation 10: Standardised tax products
- ▢ Regulation 12: Loss schemes
- ▢ Regulation 13: Leasing arrangements
- ▢ Regulation 18: Employment Schemes
- ▢ Regulation 19: Financial Product Schemes

Summary of proposal or arrangements

Summary: * [ ]

Summary - continuation: [ ]

Please enter an explanation of each element in the proposal or arrangements from which the expected tax and/or NIC advantage arises.

Explanation: * [ ]

Explanation - continuation: [ ]

Please enter the statutory provisions relevant to those elements of the proposal or arrangements from which the expected tax and/or NIC advantage arises.

Statutory provisions: *

Statutory provisions - continuation:

Declaration
I declare that the information I have given on this form is correct and complete to the best of my knowledge and belief, (please tick the box below).

☐ I agree with the above declaration*

Full name of individual completing* this form:

Capacity in which completed:

After you click the 'Next' button you will see a preview page summarising the information you have provided. If this page is not displayed, please use the scroll bar to locate any missing or incorrect entries highlighted in red.

Back Next

HM Revenue & Customs   Home   Contact HMRC   Help

Disclosure Of Avoidance Scheme - form AAG3

*indicates required information

Notification by scheme user where no promoter, or promoted by lawyer unable to make full notification

This form is for use by the scheme user notifying under 1 or both of:

- Section 310, Finance Act 2004
- Regulation 11 of the National Insurance Contributions (Application of Part 7 of the Finance Act 2004) Regulations 2012 (SI 2012/1868)

Guidance on making a disclosure is available in the Anti-Avoidance Group area:
http://www.hmrc.gov.uk/aiu/index.htm

Scheme user's details

Full name: *

Address line 1: *

Address line 2:

Address line 3:

Postcode:

Email address: *

Telephone number (including STD):

Internal reference number (if applicable):

Unique Taxpayer Reference * (UTR):

Scheme details

Stamp Duty Land Tax schemes

Title, if any, of the proposal or arrangements:

Please tick the box below for Stamp Duty Land Tax (SDLT) avoidance - acquisition of chargeable interest (SI 2005 Number 1868).

- ☐ SDLT avoidance

Please tick 1 box below to indicate which type of property is the subject of the SDLT arrangement (optional).

- ☐ Residential property
- ☐ Non-residential property
- ☐ Use of property not known or mixed

Inheritance Tax schemes
Please tick the below box for Inheritance Tax (IHT) avoidance – transfers into trust (SI 2011 Number 170).

- ☐ IHT avoidance

Income Tax, CT, Capital Gains Tax and NIC schemes
Please tick the box below for the provision under which the disclosure is being made. If more than 1 provision applies, please tick all appropriate boxes.

The National Insurance Contributions (Application of Part 7 of the Finance Act 2004) Regulations 2012 (SI 2012/1868).

- ☐ National Insurance Contributions (NIC) Avoidance

Income Tax, Corporation Tax, Capital Gains Tax - The Tax Avoidance Schemes (Prescribed Descriptions of Arrangements) Regulations 2006 (SI 2006/1543).

- ☐ IT, CT, Capital Gains Tax Avoidance

The Annual Tax on Enveloped Dwellings (ATED) Avoidance Schemes (Prescribed Descriptions of Arrangements) Regulations 2013 (SI 2013/2571).

- ☐ Annual Tax on Enveloped Dwellings avoidance

For Income Tax (IT), Corporation Tax (CT), Capital Gains Tax (CGT) and National Insurance Contributions (NIC) avoidance, please tick the regulation below that applies. Where more than 1 regulation applies, please tick only the main applicable regulation.

- ☐ Regulation 6: Confidentiality (promoter)
- ☐ Regulation 8: Premium fee
- ☐ Regulation 9: Off market terms
- ☐ Regulation 10: Standardised tax products
- ☐ Regulation 12: Loss schemes

☐ Regulation 13: Leasing arrangements

☐ Regulation 18: Employment Schemes

☐ Regulation 19: Financial Product Schemes

Summary of proposal or arrangements

Summary: *

Summary - continuation:

Please enter an explanation of each element in the proposal or arrangements from which the expected tax and/or NIC advantage arises.

Explanation: *

Explanation - continuation:

Please enter the statutory provisions relevant to those elements of the proposal or arrangements from which the expected tax and/or NIC advantage arises.

Statutory provisions: *

Statutory provisions - continuation:

Declaration

I declare that the information I have given on this form is correct and complete to the best of my knowledge and belief, (please tick the box below).

☐ I agree with the above declaration *

Full name of individual completing this form: *

[ ]

Capacity in which completed:

[ ]

After you click the 'Next' button you will see a preview page summarising the information you have provided. If this page is not displayed please use the scroll bar to locate any missing or incorrect entries highlighted in red.

Back Next

HM Revenue & Customs Home Contact HMRC Help

Disclosure of Stamp Duty Land Tax Avoidance Scheme - form AAG4 (SDLT)

*indicates required information

Notification of Scheme Reference Number by scheme user

Scheme user's details

Full name: *

Address line 1: *

Address line 2:

Address line 3:

Postcode:

Unique Transaction Reference Number if allocated:

Email address: *

Telephone number (including STD):

Scheme Reference Number:

Address of relevant property

Address line 1: *

Address line 2:

Address line 3:

Postcode:

Title number (if allocated):

Transaction details

Date of first land transaction: *

dd/mm/yyyy

Open market price: *

Declaration

I declare that the information I have given on this form is correct and complete to the best of my knowledge and belief.

☐ I agree with the above declaration

Full name of individual completing this form: *

Capacity in which completed: *

After you click the 'Next' button you will see a preview page summarising the information you have provided. If this page is not displayed please use the scroll bar to locate any missing or incorrect entries highlighted in red.

Back Next

HM Revenue & Customs

Disclosure of Tax Avoidance Schemes
Notification of Scheme Reference Number

You are involved in a Disclosed Tax Avoidance Scheme

Your scheme is NOT HM Revenue and Customs (HMRC) approved

You may not have been aware that you are involved in a Disclosed Tax Avoidance Scheme. However, you need to understand your responsibilities or you could face **significant penalties**. Being involved in tax avoidance means:

- HMRC may subject your tax affairs to close scrutiny and you may be marked out as a high risk taxpayer
- you may find yourself tied up in a dispute, which can last for years
- you may soon receive an Accelerated Payment Notice requiring you to pay any claimed tax saving
- you may end up in front of a tax tribunal with your tax affairs being made public
- you may have to **pay more in tax, interest and penalties** than the scheme claims to save you

Can you still withdraw?

If you are worried about what you have signed up to, want to withdraw from it, or discuss the implications with HMRC, phone **03000 588 993**.

For more detailed guidance, go to **www.gov.uk/government/publications/disclosure-of-tax-avoidance-schemes-guidance**

Failure to comply with any of the requirements below may lead to payment of significant penalties

Receipt of this notice means:

- you must report this Scheme Reference Number (SRN) to HMRC for all affected years on your tax returns or, in specific circumstances, on form AAG4, 'Disclosure of avoidance scheme' (or their IHT, SDLT or ATED equivalent forms, if applicable) - go to **www.gov.uk/forms-to-disclose-tax-avoidance-schemes** for information on how to do this and to download a copy if you are required to pass this form on
- when entering the SRN on a tax return, use **only** the boxes specified for that purpose - **don't enter the SRN in the white space** - the guidance notes for the tax return in question will specify where to put the SRN, which may be on special or additional pages
- you must pass a completed copy of this form to anyone you know may be a party to the scheme and who may obtain a tax or National Insurance contributions advantage - if you pass this form to another person enter the date (DD MM YYYY) below:

  [ ][ ] [ ][ ] [ ][ ][ ][ ]

- if you are an employer you must complete form AAG7, 'Disclosure of Tax Avoidance Schemes' and provide the SRN to each employee who is a party to the scheme

Important information on page 2.

Details to be provided by the promoter

1 **Promoter's full name**

2 **Promoter's full address**

Postcode

3 **Scheme Reference Number (SRN)**

4 **Brief description or name of the scheme**

5 **Date** DD MM YYYY

Things tax avoiders should consider

The vast majority of people in the UK don't try to avoid paying tax. They pay on time and without intervention from HM Revenue and Customs (HMRC). Some tax avoiders are not aware of the consequences.

Your scheme is not HMRC approved

Getting an avoidance Scheme Reference Number (SRN) doesn't mean HMRC has in any way approved or cleared the scheme. HMRC issues these numbers to identify and track you as a user of an avoidance scheme.

Most schemes don't work

You may be told that avoidance is legal but if the scheme doesn't work you'll have made an incorrect tax return which is not in accordance with the law. You are legally obliged to pay tax that is due and you may be charged interest and penalties if you try to avoid it.

It could cost you more than you bargained for

Avoidance schemes are complex. They can give rise to unintended additional tax consequences, and the fees you pay the promoter don't count as tax paid. So you could end up **paying much more than just the tax** you're trying to avoid.

You may have significant legal fees to pay

If the scheme is taken to litigation, you're likely to have large **legal fees to pay**. Your promoter may ask you to pay into a 'fighting fund' up front.

You could face criminal conviction

If you deliberately mislead or conceal information from HMRC, you could be prosecuted and convicted.

You could face negative publicity as a tax avoider

If you are named in court papers when a scheme is litigated, or your name is in a public register, you could be reported in the media as a tax dodger.

You'll have to pay the tax up front anyway

You won't get a cash flow advantage while HMRC investigates a scheme. New legislation means you'll have to **pay the disputed tax up front**.

Page 2

PART 3 – PRECEDENT LETTERS FOR STAMP DUTY CLAIMS UNDER FA 1986, SS 75 AND 77

These letters are based on model letters provided by HMRC at STSM042440 (s 75 claim letter) and STSM042430 (s 77 claim letter). Although the letters for the two reliefs are similar, there are sufficient differences to make it worthwhile to reproduce them separately. They are written on the assumption that all companies are UK registered, that certain details are set out in an agreement governing the transaction, and that the letter is submitted by an adviser acting for the claimant. They have been slightly adapted from HMRC's precedent letters to recognise changes in the UK Companies Acts, for example removing the concept of authorised share capital. They may require adapting further to accommodate characteristics of overseas companies or to reflect the precise form of the agreement. Where words may or may not be required, depending on circumstances, they are enclosed in square brackets. Information to be inserted is indicated in [square brackets] and in italics. In places the language used is quaint, but it is as well to use the approved wording so far as it fits the facts. It is also worth reviewing the draft agreement between the parties before execution, to ensure its provisions accord with the statements which must be made in the letter of claim.

In relation to claims for relief under FA 1986, s 77 the claim should also take into account the condition in FA 1986, s 77(3)(i) which requires that at the time the transfer is executed there are no 'disqualifying arrangements', within the meaning given by FA 1986, s 77A, in existence (see **9.29** et seq). *It should therefore be specifically stated in the letter claiming the relief that the condition in s 77(3)(i) is satisfied.*

There is a checklist for FA 1986, s 75 and s 77 claims at STSM042450.

(a) FA 1986, s 75 claim

Dear Sir

[name of claimant company]

1. We act for *[name of claimant company]* ("the Acquiring Company").

2. In connection with the transactions referred to below we hereby apply on behalf of the Acquiring Company for exemption from transfer duty under Section 75 Finance Act 1986.

3. The Acquiring Company, whose registered office is at *[address]* was incorporated in *[country]* on *[date]* under *[name of law]* with number *[registered number]*. A copy of the certificate of incorporation [and of certificate(s) of change of name] is enclosed marked "A".

4. *[Name of target company]*, ("the Target Company"), whose registered office is at *[address]* was incorporated in *[country]* on *[date]* under *[name of law]* with number *[registered number]*. A copy of the certificate of incorporation [and of certificate(s) of change of name] is enclosed marked "B". The register of members, or a list of all the members of the Target Company immediately prior to *[date of transaction]* certified by the [Registrars][Company Secretary] of the Target Company, is enclosed marked "C".

[Note – a computer print-out of the Register of Members may be used as "C" and need not be certified]

5. The Acquiring Company has acquired [the whole][part] of the undertaking of the Target Company in pursuance of a scheme for the reconstruction of the Target Company in order that *[set out brief reasons for explanation of the transaction]*.

6. By an agreement dated *[date]* and made between the Target Company and the Acquiring Company ("the Agreement"), it was provided (inter alia) that the Target Company should sell and the Acquiring Company should purchase [the whole][part] of the undertaking of the Target Company as described in *[refer to appropriate part of the Agreement]* ("the Business") in pursuance of a scheme for the reconstruction of the Target Company and that as consideration for such sale the Acquiring Company should allot credited as fully paid to all the shareholders of the Target Company the respective numbers of shares of the Acquiring Company as specified in *[refer to schedule or other part of the Agreement setting out the numbers and classes of shares to be allotted to each shareholder of the Target Company]* ("the Consideration Shares"). [In addition, the Acquiring Company [assumed] [discharged] certain liabilities of the Acquired Company as specified in Schedule ……… to the Agreement]. A copy of the Agreement is enclosed marked "D".

7. The said sale was duly completed on *[date]* when the Target Company transferred the business to the Acquiring Company.

8. At a meeting of [the Directors] *[or specify committee or similar]* of the Acquiring Company held on *[date]* the consideration shares were duly allotted to the shareholders of the Target Company pursuant to the provisions of the Agreement. We enclose marked "E" [and "F" respectively] a certified copy of the resolution of the Directors of the Acquiring Company passed on *[date]* [appointing the said committee and of the Resolution of the said Committee] making such allotment. We also enclose marked "G" a certificate under the hand of [the senior official of the Registrars][the company secretary] of the Acquiring Company, confirming that the names of the respective allottees of the Consideration Shares have been entered in the Register of Members of

the Acquiring Company in respect of the Consideration Shares, together with a list of all members of the Acquiring Company immediately following the allotment, certified by the [Registrars][company secretary] of the Acquiring Company and marked ["H"].

[Note – as in (4) above, a computer printout may be substituted and need not be certified]

9. It is confirmed that no part of the consideration for the acquisition consisted of the issue of redeemable shares in the Acquiring Company.

10. It is confirmed that, immediately after the acquisition:

    a. Each shareholder of the Target Company was also a shareholder of the Acquiring Company;

    b. Each shareholder of the Acquiring Company was also a shareholder of the Target Company;

    c. Each shareholder held the same proportion (or as nearly as may be the same proportion) of shares in the Target Company as that shareholder held in the Acquiring Company.

11. [No application for clearance under the relevant direct tax provisions] [An application for clearance under [section numbers]] was made by the Acquiring Company. [A copy of the application together with copies of the correspondence with HMRC is enclosed marked ["I"]].

[Note – if no clearance application was made, the information listed below must be supplied]

12. It is submitted that the acquisition was effected for bona fide commercial reasons and did not form part of a scheme or arrangement of which the main purpose or one of the main purposes is the avoidance of liability to stamp duty, income tax, corporation tax or capital gains tax and that the appropriate conditions of Section 75 of the Finance Act 1986 have been complied with, and accordingly exemption from ad valorem stamp duty under the head "Transfer on Sale" is claimed in respect of the Transfers executed pursuant thereto.

13. We enclose for adjudication [give adequate list or description of the documents enclosed] together with certified copies.

Further information to be provided if no clearance application was made as set out in (11) above:

1. A copy of the latest accounts of the Target Company;

2. Full details of any scheme, arrangement or overall transaction of which this transaction forms part;

3. Confirmation, if appropriate, that the shares in the Target Company are still held by the Acquiring Company and that there is no intention to dispose of them;

4. A detailed note of the bona fide commercial reasons for the acquisition.

(b) FA 1986, s 77 claim

Dear Sir

[name of claimant company]

Section 77, Finance Act 1986

We act for *[name of claimant company]* ("the Acquiring Company").

1. In connection with the transactions referred to below we hereby apply on behalf of the Acquiring Company for exemption from transfer duty under Section 77 Finance Act 1986.

2. The Acquiring Company, whose registered office is at *[address]* was incorporated in *[country]* on *[date]* under *[name of law]* with number *[registered number]* and immediately prior to *[date of transaction]* the issued share capital of the Acquiring Company was *[amount]* divided into *[give details of the classes, denominations and numbers of shares]* such shares being fully paid up *[or give details if shares were part paid]*. A copy of the certificate of incorporation [and of certificate(s) of change of name] is enclosed marked "A".

3. *[Name of target company]*, ("the Target Company"), whose registered office is at *[address]* was incorporated in *[country]* on *[date]* under *[name of law]* with number *[registered number]* and immediately prior to *[date of transaction]* the issued share capital of the Target Company was *[amount]* divided into *[give details of the classes, denominations and numbers of shares]* such shares being fully paid up *[or give details if shares were part paid]*. A copy of the certificate of incorporation [and of certificate(s) of change of name] is enclosed marked "B". The register of members, or a list of all the members of the Target Company immediately prior to *[date of transaction]* certified by the [Registrars] [Company Secretary] of the Target Company, is enclosed marked "C".

[Note – a computer print-out of the Register of Members may be used as "C" and need not be certified]

4. The transactions referred to below were carried out in order that [set out reasons for the transactions. If no direct tax advance clearance was

obtained, give a detailed explanation of the bona fide commercial reasons for the overall transaction].

5. By an agreement dated [date] and made between [names of shareholders of the Target company] ("the Shareholders"), the Target Company and the Acquiring Company ("the Agreement") it was provided (inter alia) that the Shareholders should sell and the Acquiring Company should purchase the respective numbers of shares of the Target Company as described in [refer to appropriate part of the Agreement] (such shares amounting in aggregate to the whole of the issued share capital of the Target Company and that as consideration for such sale the Acquiring Company should allot credited as fully paid to the Shareholders (being all the shareholders of the Target Company) the respective numbers of shares of the Acquiring Company as specified in [refer to schedule or other part of the Agreement setting out the numbers and classes of shares to be allotted to each shareholder of the Target Company] ("the Consideration Shares"). A copy of the Agreement is enclosed marked "D".

6. The said sale was duly completed on [date] when the Shareholders delivered to and in favour of the Acquiring Company duly executed transfers of the whole of the issued shares, together with relevant Share Certificates, of the Target Company. [Immediately following such delivery one Ordinary Share of the Target Company was transferred to [name] as nominee of the Acquiring Company.]

7. At a meeting of [the Directors] [or specify committee or similar] of the Acquiring Company held on [date] the consideration shares were duly allotted to the shareholders of the Target Company pursuant to the provisions of the Agreement. We enclose marked "E" [and "F" respectively] a certified copy of the resolution of the Directors of the Acquiring Company passed on [date] [appointing the said committee and of the Resolution of the said Committee] making such allotment. We also enclose marked "G" a certificate under the hand of [the senior official of the Registrars][the company secretary] of the Acquiring Company, confirming that the names of the respective allottees of the Consideration Shares have been entered in the Register of Members of the Acquiring Company in respect of the Consideration Shares, together with a copy of the register of members, or a list of all members, of the Acquiring Company immediately following the allotment, certified by the [Registrars][company secretary] of the Acquiring Company and marked ["H"].

[Note – as in (4) above, a computer printout may be substituted and need not be certified]

8. Immediately after the acquisition the issued share capital of the Acquiring Company was *[give details of classes, denominations and numbers of shares]* such shares being fully paid up *[or give details if not]*.

9. It is confirmed that immediately after the acquisition the classes of shares in the Acquiring Company were in the same proportions (or as nearly as may be the same proportions) as they had been in the Target Company.

10. It is confirmed that, immediately after the acquisition the proportion of shares of any particular class in the Acquiring Company held by each respective shareholder was the same (or as nearly as may be the same) as the proportion of shares of that class in the Target Company held by that shareholder immediately before the acquisition was made.

11. [No application for clearance under the relevant direct tax provisions] [An application for clearance under *[section numbers]*] was made by the Acquiring Company. [A copy of the application together with copies of the correspondence with HMRC is enclosed marked ["I"].

[Note – if no clearance application was made, the information listed below must be supplied]

12. It is submitted that the acquisition was effected for bona fide commercial reasons and did not form part of a scheme or arrangement of which the main purpose or one of the main purposes is the avoidance of liability to stamp duty, income tax, corporation tax or capital gains tax and that the appropriate conditions of Section 77 of the Finance Act 1986 have been complied with, and accordingly exemption from ad valorem stamp duty under the head "Transfer on Sale" is claimed in respect of the Transfers executed pursuant thereto.

13. I/We confirm that at the time of execution of the acquisition of the Target Company's share capital there are no further related or subsequent transactions which together may be regarded as 'disqualifying arrangements' under Section 77A of the Finance Act 1986.

14. We enclose for adjudication *[give adequate list or description of the documents enclosed]* together with certified copies.

Further information to be provided if no clearance application was made as set out in (11) above:

1. A copy of the latest accounts of the Target Company;

2. Full details of any scheme, arrangement or overall transaction of which this transaction forms part;

3. Confirmation, if appropriate, that the Acquiring Company still holds the shares of the Target Company and that there is no intention to dispose of them (or give details if disposal will occur in the course of a greater overall transaction);

4. A <u>detailed</u> note of the bona fide commercial reasons for the acquisition.

Appendix C

Stamp Taxes – HMRC Revised Procedures as a Result of Covid-19 (Coronavirus)

SDLT

There have been few changes to HMRC's procedures regarding SDLT as a result of Covid-19.

All correspondence must still be sent by post, which may lead to delays given the current postal issues being experienced as a result of the pandemic (May 2020).

The following points should however be noted:

(1) Under current law a person has a period of 3 years from the 'effective date' of the purchase of their new main residence to sell their previous main residence and claim a refund of the higher rate of SDLT (see **4.74**). However, a new *s 76* amending *FA 2003, Sch 4ZA* was introduced at the Report Stage of the *Finance Act 2020* to extend the three-year time period where there are 'exceptional circumstances that could not reasonably have been foreseen' which prevented the sale of the previous main residence within the prescribed three-year period. In such circumstances the three-year period is extended to such longer period as HMRC may allow in response to an application made in accordance with new *FA 2003, Sch 4ZA, para 3(7B)*. The Covid-19 pandemic will be 'exceptional circumstances that could not reasonably have been foreseen' for these purposes. The extension of the three-year time limit will only apply if the new main residence was purchased on or after 1 January 2017, so that the three-year period ended on or after 1 January 2020. On 3 June 2020, SDLTM09807 was introduced, which outlines HMRC's views as to what will constitute 'exceptional circumstances

that could not reasonably have been foreseen' and it is specifically stated that such circumstances might include:

- being prevented from selling the property owing to government guidance during the Covid-19 pandemic. For example, the Ministry of Housing, Communities and Local Government issued guidance in response to the Covid-19 pandemic advising against the marketing of properties in most cases from 26 March to 13 May 2020; or
- other action taken by a public authority preventing the sale of the property.

See **4.74** for more details regarding the extension of the three-year period to claim a repayment of the higher rate of SDLT and **4.84** as regards the process for claiming a repayment of the higher rate of SDLT.

(2) Taxpayers will have an extra three months to appeal any HMRC decision that is dated February 2020 or later, however appeals should be submitted as soon as possible.

(3) If, as a result of Covid-19, a taxpayer fails to meet their SDLT obligations (filing of a land transaction return and payment of the tax) within the prescribed 14- or 30-day period, such a failure will be accepted as a reasonable excuse, provided they remedy the failure as soon as they are able to do so.

(4) If, as a result of COVID-19, a taxpayer is having difficulties paying an SDLT liability it may be possible to defer payment by speaking to the HMRC team dealing with SDLT debt enquires. The SDLT debt enquiries helpline number is 0300 200 3844.

STAMP DUTY

As a result of measures put in place to stop the spread of Covid-19, HMRC has temporarily changed the way it deals with stamp duty.

The following points should be noted:

(1) Payment of stamp duty

Payment must be made electronically by Faster Payment, Bacs or CHAPS and not by any other means. If you cannot make an electronic payment you should email stampdutymailbox@hmrc.gov.uk. When making an electronic payment a reference should be provided so that HMRC can identify your payment. HMRC suggest using your name followed by the payment amount, with no spaces eg JBrown/300.00. If you are a solicitor or adviser making a payment on behalf of a client, you can use your client's reference or matter number as the payment reference. HMRC warn that a payment could be delayed if the wrong reference is used.

Payments from UK bank accounts

The following details should be used to make a payment from a UK bank account:

Sort code: 08 32 10

Account number: 12001098

Account name: HMRC Birmingham Stamp Office

Payments from overseas bank accounts

The following details should be used to make a payment from an overseas bank account:

Account number (IBAN): GB02BARC20114773618595

Bank Identifier Code (BIC): BARCGB22

Account name: HMRC Birmingham Stamp Office

HMRC's banking address is as follows:

Barclays Bank Plc
1 Churchill Place
London
United Kingdom
E14 5HP

(2) Providing details of the transaction by email

As a result of the temporary measures put in place to stop the spread of Covid-19, you cannot post details of the transaction to HMRC. Once any stamp duty liability has been paid, as discussed above, you must email details to HMRC at stampdutymailbox@hmrc.gov.uk. The email should include the following information:

- the payment reference (see (1) above);
- the payment amount;
- the date of payment;
- an electronic copy (for example, a scanned PDF) of either the:
  - signed and dated stock transfer form; or
  - instrument of transfer (other than a stock transfer form); or
  - form SH03 for a return of a purchase of own shares.

A power of attorney can be used if necessary.

HMRC will accept electronic signatures whilst the temporary Covid-19 measures are in place.

If your stock transfer form or other instrument of transfer does not include the following information, details of the following should also be given:

- name of the company whose shares are being transferred,
- details of the shares being transferred including the date of transfer,
- the name of the parties to the transaction, and
- the amount of the consideration.

HMRC will contact you by email if they have any questions. If they have no questions, and are able to process the transaction, they will send you a letter by email confirming the following:

- receipt of the payment of the stamp duty;
- details of the transaction(s) to which the confirmation relates and the reference code; and
- assurance that HMRC will not pursue a penalty against the company registrar for registering the change in ownership of the shares based on the documents supplied to HMRC. This confirmation from HMRC should be sent to the company registrar (together with the stock transfer form and share certificate) to enable the registrar to update the register of members.

No stock transfer forms are currently being stamped.

(3) Claims for relief from stamp duty

Claims for relief from stamp duty should be emailed to HMRC at stampdutymailbox@hmrc.gov.uk indicating the type of relief being claimed (including group relief and the reconstruction reliefs). Electronic versions of the documents and the relevant claim letter (see **11.17** and **Appendix B**) should be attached to the email (for example, a scanned PDF) and HMRC will accept electronic signatures. To reduce file sizes HMRC will only require a list of shareholders and details of the shares they hold for each company, rather than a full copy of the register of members. If HMRC are satisfied that the relief is due it will send an email, with a letter, covering the following:

- details of the transaction(s) to which the confirmation relates and the reference code,
- assurance that HMRC will not pursue a penalty against the company registrar for registering the change in ownership of the

shares. This confirmation should be sent to the company registrar for registering the change in ownership of the shares (www.gov.uk/guidance/stamp-duty-reliefs-and-exemptions-on-paper-shares).

(4) Request an opinion from HMRC

If you request an informal or formal opinion from HMRC regarding stamp duty the request should be emailed to HMRC at stampdutymailbox@hmrc.gov.uk together with the requisite information to enable HMRC to provide the opinion and an electronic copy of any relevant documents (www.gov.uk/guidance-stamp-duty-getting-an-opinion-about-a-payment-or-penalty).

(5) Stamp Duty on pre-2003 land transactions (see 13.26 et seq)

HMRC have put in place temporary procedures covering these transactions due to Covid-19. Where HMRC would usually accept only hard copy posted documents, they are now accepting signed and dated documents by email instead. Currently they can only accept electronic payments and they will provide a confirmation letter in place of a stamped document to allow the transaction to be registered. HM Land Registry have agreed to accept the confirmation letter in place of the stamped document. Further information can be found at www.gov.uk/guidance/stamp-duty-land-transfers-before-december-2003.

(6) Free stamping of replacement instruments under s 12A of SDMA 1891

It may be necessary to ask HMRC for replacement documentation to be stamped, for example because documents have been lost in the postal system or through some other means or have been accidentally spoiled in some way.

In line with the changes made to straightforward stamping processes, whilst the temporary Covid-19 measures are in place HMRC will not be physically stamping replacement instruments of transfer where the original stamped instrument has been lost or spoiled.

Instead, the application for free stamping should be emailed to the stamp duty mailbox (stampdutymailbox@hmrc.gov.uk) enclosing an electronic version (scanned/pdf) copy of the replacement instrument and the required undertaking. If the application is approved by HMRC, a confirmation letter referencing that the original instrument has been lost will be issued.

(7) Repayment of stamp duty

The main requests for stamp duty refunds under the temporary process will be when:

There is an overpayment when a transaction is first notified to HMRC

In these cases, HMRC will either determine the overpayment when the email notification is reviewed, or the overpayment will be brought to HMRC's attention in the transaction notification email. In these circumstances HMRC will provide a letter confirming the transaction and deal with the repayment separately.

The overpayment of stamp duty is discovered after the transaction has been notified to HMRC

An email should be sent to stampdutymailbox@hmrc.gov.uk, with an electronic copy of the Transfer attached. The email should include the names of the parties involved and the reason for the repayment claim. The words 'repayment' or 'refund' should be included in the email subject so that HMRC can easily identify the claim.

Repayments

HMRC will only be able to process repayments electronically – they cannot issue a cheque. For safety and security reasons, once the repayment amount has been checked HMRC will ask the claimant to use Dropbox to provide their bank account details.

Bank account details must not be emailed to HMRC – HMRC cannot process any repayments where the bank account details are provided in an email.

Dropbox

Dropbox is a safe and secure tool that has been approved by HMRC's Data Security team.

Claimants that agree to use Dropbox will be sent a secure weblink by email so that they can upload their bank account details. The link will only be valid for 48 hours. If it expires before the details are uploaded, then HMRC will need to provide a new secure link. Only the claimant and designated HMRC Officers will be able to access the Dropbox link. The claimant will not need to download any additional software or computer programs to use this tool.

Bank account details should be provided in a PDF document. Once HMRC have valid bank account details, they will be able to process the repayment. In the majority of cases the repayment will be by Faster Payment and HMRC will email the claimant once the repayment has been authorised so that they know when they will receive the payment.

Stamping documents

For any repayment cases dealt with by HMRC under the temporary process, they request that the Transfer is physically resubmitted to them once they are able to stamp documents again. This will allow any Transfer to be stamped in accordance with the repayment given.

If a repayment claim has previously been posted to the Birmingham Stamp Office but was not processed before the temporary procedures were put in place then the claim can be resubmitted to HMRC electronically. If the claim is not resubmitted electronically, the repayment will not be processed until the temporary measures end.

(8) Physical stamping of documents once temporary measures cease

Once the temporary measures cease to apply, and documents are again being physically stamped, it will be possible to represent original documents for physical stamping where those documents were previously dealt with electronically under the temporary measures. The confirmation letter that HMRC have sent in place of stamping the document must be sent to HMRC, alongside the original document for stamping, to ensure that no late notification penalties are charged.

SDRT

As a result of measures put in place to stop the spread of Covid-19, HMRC has temporarily changed the way it deals with stamp duty reserve tax (SDRT).

Payment must be made electronically by Faster Payment, Bacs or CHAPS and not by any other means.

SDRT is paid on agreements to transfer shares and securities through the CREST system (see **12.21**) or in a non-financial market transaction outside of CREST (see **12.10**). The payment deadlines, payment reference numbers and HMRC bank account details are different in each case.

Shares and securities transferred through the CREST system

CREST automatically deducts SDRT from chargeable trades and pays the tax over to HMRC. Therefore, no manual payment or notice is required.

Shares and securities transferred outside of the CREST system

If shares and securities are transferred in a non-financial market transaction outside of CREST, the purchaser must send HMRC a written notice providing the following information:

- details of the buyer and seller;
- a description of the securities transferred including the number transferred;
- any relief or exemption, or both, claimed;

- details of the consideration given in money or money's worth for the securities; and
- a reference number, chosen by you, so HMRC can identify the payment.

If the payment could have been made through CREST but was not, the deadline for both the payment and the written notice is 14 days from the date of the trade. If the payment could not have been made through CREST, the deadline for both the payment and the written notice is the 7th of the month after the calendar month in which the agreement was made.

SDRT-related documentation that would usually be sent by post should be emailed to the SDRT mailbox at mailbox.sdrt@hmrc.gov.uk.

Payments from UK bank accounts

The following details should be used to make a payment from a UK bank account:

Sort code: 08 32 10

Account number: 12237210

Account name: HMRC Stamp Office Shares Unit

Payments from overseas bank accounts

The following details should be used to make a payment from an overseas bank account:

Account number (IBAN): GB89BARC20114733702596

Bank Identifier Code (BIC): BARCGB22

Account name: HMRC SDRT

HMRC's banking address is as follows:

Barclays Bank Plc
1 Churchill Place
London
United Kingdom
E14 5HP

Index

[*References are to paragraph number and appendices*]

E